Nepal

THE ROUGH GUIDE

D1549312

ROUGH GUIDE CREDITS

Text editor:	Kate Berens
Series editor:	Mark Ellingham
Editorial:	Martin Dunford, John Fisher, Jack Holland, Jonathan Buckley, Greg Ward, Jules Brown, Graham Parker
Production:	Susanne Hillen, Andy Hilliard, Gail Jammy, Vivien Antwi, Melissa Flack, Alan Spicer
Publicity:	Richard Trillo
Finance:	Celia Crowley

This book is dedicated to Krysia, who was with me when I first set foot in Nepal, and has never wavered since.

Special thanks for help in this edition must go first to Dadi Ram Sapkota, translator, researcher, fact-checker and friend. Other people who provided invaluable insights and assistance are: Heather Alexander, for numerous and enthusiastic contributions; Amoghachitta, who greatly assisted with the Buddhism section; Bijaya at NETWAC; Hikmat Bisht, for loyal correspondence from Mahendranagar; Jo Chittenden, one of the visionary founders of KEEP; Bev Craig, for notes on Kakarbitta; Matt Damon and Jennie Tollenaere, for dispatches from the far west; Alan Deverell, for information on Sundarijal; Sadhu Ram Dhakal, for excellent Newari food; Keith Dowman, for Boudha tips; Sallie Fisher of Nepal Traveller; Sally Fryer, for instant flight answers; James Giambrone of Indigo Gallery; Prof. Mangal Raj Joshi; Roopendra .(Roopie) Joshi of Caravan International and the Third World Café, for his impulsive hospitality; Gopal Sunder Lal Kakshapati; Peter Knowles (Slime), for information on all whitewater matters; Wendy Brewer Lama, for trekking updates; Alan Lawson and Gauri Pradhan (CWIN), for information on street children; Rakesh Manandhar; Julia Preece, for hints on driving and camping; Rachel Reilly of UNHCR, who provided background on the Bhutanese refugees; Dave Richards of Nepalwatch UK, a dedicated campaigner; Bhogendra Sharma of CVICT; Dilip Sharma; Shankha Shrestha; Gopal Siwakodi; Andy Swartzman; Dennis Tuma; and Marc-Alain Widowson, for the facts on rabies.

Thanks too to all at Rough Guides who helped produce this book, especially Kate Berens, who edited it; Andy Hilliard and Alan Spicer for typesetting; Susanne Hillen and Vivien Antwi for handling the production; Ellen Sarewitz for proofing; Micromap Ltd for revised maps; and Jack Holland for all his help on the first edition.

The publishers and authors have done their best to ensure the accuracy and currency of all the information in *The Rough Guide to Nepal*; however, they can accept no responsibility for any loss, injury or inconvenience sustained by any traveller as a result of information or advice contained in the guide.

This second edition published October 1993 by Rough Guides Ltd, 1 Mercer Street, London WC2H 9QJ. Reprinted December 1993.

Distributed by the Penguin Group:

Penguin Books Ltd, 27 Wrights Lane, London W8 5TZ
Penguin Books USA Inc, 375 Hudson Street, New York 10014, USA
Penguin Books Australia Ltd, 487 Maroondah Highway, PO Box 257, Ringwood, Victoria 3134, Australia
Penguin Books Canada Ltd, 10 Alcorn Avenue, Toronto, Ontario, Canada M4V 1E4
Penguin Books (NZ) Ltd, 182–190 Wairau Road, Auckland 10, New Zealand

Originally published in the UK by Harrap Columbus.
Previous edition published in the United States and Canada as *The Real Guide Nepal*.

Typeset in Linotron Univers and Century Old Style to an original design by Andrew Oliver.
Printed in the UK by Cox & Wyman, Reading, Berks.

Illustrations in the Guide by Hal Aqua; Incidental illustrations in Part One and Part Three by Edward Briant. Illustration on p.1 by Tommy Yamaha; Illustration on p.335 by Sally Davies.

416pp
includes index

British Library Cataloguing in Publication Data
A catalogue record for this book is available from the British Library

ISBN 1-85828-046-X

Nepal

THE ROUGH GUIDE

Written and researched by
David Reed

Contributors
Andy Balestracci, Charles Leech, Anna Robinson,
Carol Tingey, Kesang Tseten and Gopal Yonjan

THE ROUGH GUIDES

HELP US UPDATE

We've gone to a lot of effort to ensure that this second edition of *The Rough Guide to Nepal* is completely up-to-date and accurate. However, things do change – places get "discovered", transport connections change, restaurants and guest houses get renamed – and any suggestions, comments or corrections would be much appreciated. We're particularly keen to hear of accounts of travels to remote and untried destinations.

We'll credit all contributions, and send a copy of the next edition (or any other Rough Guide if you prefer) for the best letters. Please mark letters "Rough Guide Nepal Update" and send to:

Rough Guides, 1 Mercer Street, London WC2H 9QJ
or Rough Guides, 375 Hudson Street, 4th Floor, New York NY 10014.

THANKS

Special thanks to the following readers for their letters: Karen and Richard Berry; Anne and Stephen Blackburn; Diana Emerson; Julia Gooding; Karen Howard; Barrie Jenkins; William Main; Paul Martin; Andrew Olson; Carolyn Owens; Matt Padwick; Heinz Scheifinger; and Robert M. Wyburn.

CONTENTS

INTRODUCTION

Nepal forms the very watershed of Asia. Landlocked between India and Tibet, it spans terrain from subtropical jungle to the icy Himalaya, and contains eight of the world's ten highest mountains. Its cultural landscape is every bit as diverse: a dozen major **ethnic groups**, speaking as many as fifty dialects, coexist in this narrow, jumbled buffer state, while two of the world's great **religions**, Hinduism and Buddhism, overlap and mingle with older tribal traditions – yet it's a testimony to the Nepalis' tolerance and good humour that there is no tradition of ethnic or religious strife. Unlike India, Nepal was never colonized, a fact which comes through in fierce national pride and other, more idiosyncratic ways. Founded on trans-Himalayan trade, its dense, medieval **cities** display a unique pagoda-style architecture, not to mention an astounding flair for festivals and pageantry. But above all, Nepal is a nation of unaffected **villages** and terraced hillsides – more than eighty percent of the population lives off the land – and whether you're trekking, biking or bouncing around in packed buses, sampling this simple lifestyle is perhaps the greatest pleasure of all.

But it would be misleading to portray Nepal as a fabled Shangri-la. One of the world's poorest countries (if you go by per capita income), it suffers from many of the pangs and uncertainties of the Third World, including overpopulation and deforestation; **development** is coming in fits and starts, and not all of it is being shared equitably. Heavily reliant on its big-brother neighbours, Nepal was, until 1990, run by one of the last remaining absolute monarchies, a regime that combined China's repressiveness and India's bureaucracy in equal measure. The **people's movement** (*jana andolan*) of 1990 ushered in democracy and tapped a vast reservoir of idealism; yet a change of government has changed little for the average struggling Nepali family.

All this means that travelling in Nepal isn't a straightforward or predictable activity. **Getting around** is tough and time-consuming, and facilities in most places are rudimentary – Nepalis are well used to shrugging off inconvenience with the all-purpose phrase, *Ke garne?* ("What to do?"). Nepal is also a more fragile country than most – culturally as well as environmentally – so it's necessary to be especially sensitive as a traveller; tips for minimizing your impact are given in *Basics*.

Topography is obviously a key consideration when travelling in Nepal; generally speaking, the country divides into three altitude zones running from west to east. The northernmost of these is, of course, the **Himalayan chain**, broken into a series of *himal* (massifs) and inhabited, at least part of the year, as high as 5000m. The largest part of the country consists of a wide belt of middle-elevation **foothills** and **valleys**, Nepal's traditional heartland; two ranges, the Mahabharat Lekh and the lower, southernmost Chure (or Siwalik) Hills, stand out. Finally, the **Tarai**, a thin strip of flat, lowland jungle and farmland along the southern border, has more in common with India than with the rest of Nepal.

Where to go

Given the country's primitive transport network, most travellers stick to a well-worn circuit, with the result that certain sights and trekking routes have become rather commercialized. Don't be put off: the beaten track is remarkably thin and easy to escape in Nepal – and this guide is intended, first and foremost, to give you the confidence to do just that. It's the out-of-the-way places, the ones not written up in any book, that you'll remember most fondly on your return.

Everyone touches down in **Kathmandu** at some point, but for all its exotic bustle, the capital is rather rough going these days – logistically it makes a good base, but you won't necessarily want to spend lots of time there. Hindu temples, Buddhist stupas, rolling countryside and huddled brick villages provide incentives for day trips in the prosperous **Kathmandu Valley**, as do the historically independent city-states of **Patan** and **Bhaktapur**. The surrounding central hills are surprisingly undeveloped, apart from a couple of mountain view points, yet a few lesser routes, such as the road to the **Tibet border** (which is, if anything, falling into disuse) and especially the **Tribhuwan Rajpath**, make for adventurous travel – and even better mountain-biking.

The views get more dramatic, or at least more accessible, in the **western hills**. **Pokhara**, set beside a lake under a looming wall of peaks, is the closest thing you'll find to a resort in Nepal; other hill towns – notably **Gorkha** and its impressive fortress – offer scenery with history to boot.

It's in the teeming jungle and ethnic villages of the **Tarai** that Nepal's diversity really becomes apparent. Most travellers venture no further than **Chitwan National Park**, where endangered Asian one-horned rhinos are easily viewable, but three other parks and wildlife reserves are out there for the more adventurous. **Lumbini**, Buddha's birthplace in the western Tarai, is stunningly peaceful and unwesternized, as is **Janakpur**, a Hindu holy city in the east. Rolling tea plantations, weekly markets and a rich cultural mix figure prominently in the spectacular and little-visited **eastern hills**, most easily reached from the Tarai.

The **Himalaya** are covered separately in the last chapter of the guide, along with all hill areas that fall within the government's prescribed **trekking regions**. Special rules apply in this roadless half of Nepal: distances are reckoned in days of walking, and trailside inns provide only basic shelter. The terrain can vary from infernal valley bottoms and cultivated foothills to lush rhododendron forests and glacial deserts. You'll encounter people everywhere you walk, and the cultural interactions are often, in retrospect, the most rewarding part of a trek.

Climate and when to go

It's hard to generalize about the climate of a country ranging in elevation from near sea level to Mount Everest. About the only thing that can be said is that all but a few parts of Nepal are governed by the same monsoonal pattern (see box overleaf), with temperatures varying according to elevation (see chart). Five **seasons** prevail in Nepal, but these are not mere meteorological divisions: whenever you choose to go, you'll have to weigh weather against other factors, both positive (mountain visibility, festivals, wildlife) and negative (crowds, disease).

Probably half of all tourists visit Nepal in the **autumn** (October to November), and for good reasons. The weather is clear and dry, and temperatures aren't too cold in the high country nor too hot in the Tarai. With the air washed clean by the monsoon rains, the mountains are at their most visible, making this the most popular time for trekking. Two major festivals also fall during this season. The downside, however, is that the tourist quarters are heaving and hustley, it's hard to find a decent room, you'll wait ages for food and for trekking permits, and people are short on ready smiles and chat.

In **winter** (December and January), the snow line descends to 2000–3000m, and though it never snows in Kathmandu, the "mists of Indra" make the capital feel cold and clammy (especially in unheated budget lodgings). Most travellers head down into India, leaving the trekking routes and guest houses fairly quiet – too quiet, sometimes, as many restaurants pare down their menus for the season.

Spring (February to mid-April) brings warmer temperatures, longer days, weddings and more festivals. The rhododendrons are in bloom in the hills towards the end of this period, and in the Tarai the thatch has been cut, making this the best time for viewing wildlife. All of which creates another tourist crush, albeit not quite as bad as in the autumn. The one factor that keeps people away is a disappointing haze that obscures the mountains from lower elevations, though it's usually possible to trek above it.

The **pre-monsoon** (mid-April to early June) is stifling at lower elevations, and dusty wind squalls are common. People get a little edgy with the heat; this is the time for popular unrest, but also for the Kathmandu Valley's great rain-making festival. Trek high, where the temperatures are more tolerable.

Nepalis welcome the **monsoon** (June to September), which breaks the enervating monotony of the previous months, and makes the fields come alive with rushing water and green shoots. The rains rinse and renew the land. This can be

---

THE MONSOON

*Listen to these humming downpours in the night
and the doors to godly pleasures will unfold themselves.*

Lekhnath Poudyal (1885–1966), "Thoughts on the Rainy Monsoon"

Nepal's climate is governed by the **monsoon**, one of the world's great weather phenomena. A seasonal wind (the word derives from the Arabic for "season"; the Nepali word for monsoon is *barkhaa*), the monsoon is driven by extreme temperature fluctuations in Central Asia. As air over the Asian land mass warms in late spring and early summer, it rises, sucking air in from the ocean periphery to take its place. The air drawn from the south, passing over the Indian Ocean, is laden with moisture; as soon as it's forced aloft and cooled (whether by updrafts over hot land, or by a barrier, such as the hills and mountains of Nepal), it reaches its saturation point and drops its moisture. With the arrival of autumn, the flow reverses: cooling over the continent blows dry air outwards, bringing clear, stable conditions.

That's the theory, though in practice this huge, complex system is affected by countless variables such as land temperatures, jet-stream patterns, topography and late-season typhoons. The further inland you are, the harder it is to predict the outcome. Nepal is at the end of the line of the eastern arm of the South Asian monsoon sweeping up from the Bay of Bengal, which means it gets a month or so of **pre-monsoon** – a period of false storms and dry lightning – before the moist air arrives.

In Nepal, the **rains** generally advance from east to west in early to mid-June, and drop more precipitation overall in the east than in the west. They build slowly, reaching a peak in July and early August, then taper off again until clear weather returns by early October. Even at the monsoon's height, however, it doesn't bring continuous torrential rain – more usually it's intermittent showers and longer overnight soaks. Local terrain and other factors can affect rainfall considerably: areas lying in the "rain shadow" north of the Himalaya see very little monsoon moisture, while south-facing slopes may receive precipitation long before the plains to the south do. The latter effect is most dramatic where monsoon winds slam into high ranges with few intervening foothills, as they do around Pokhara. The **winter monsoon** also brings a few days of rain in late January, again most pronounced around Pokhara.

AVERAGE TEMPERATURE AND RAINFALL																	
	FEB			APR			JUN			AUG			OCT			DEC	
	°C Min Max	rain cm		°C Min Max	rain cm		°C Min Max	rain cm		°C Min Max	rain cm		°C Min Max	rain cm		°C Min Max	rain cm
Ilam (1200m)	10 18	0		16 25	6		18 25	32		19 25	28		16 25	8		8 18	0
Janakpur (70m)	9 24	1		16 35	4		24 36	23		25 34	24		20 29	5		10 24	0
Jumla (2420m)	-3 13	4		3 22	3		13 24	7		15 24	17		6 24	4		-5 15	0
Kathmandu (1300m)	4 20	3		11 27	6		19 29	29		20 28	36		13 26	6		2 20	0
Namche (3450m)	-6 6	2		1 12	3		6 15	14		8 16	24		2 12	8		-6 7	4
Pokhara (800m)	8 21	3		15 30	9		20 29	57		21 29	71		17 26	22		7 20	0
Sunauli (90m)	10 26	1		18 37	6		24 38	28		26 35	41		21 30	8		10 25	0

a fascinating time to visit, when Nepal is at its most Nepali, but there are many drawbacks: mountain views are rare, leeches come out in force along the mid-elevation trekking routes, roads wash out, flights get cancelled, and disease runs rampant as the rising water table brings the entire contents of Kathmandu's sewers to the surface.

What to bring
As a rule, travel light. You can buy or rent most things in Kathmandu. This section goes over the essentials that are worth bringing from home or picking up specially in Nepal. If you think you might go trekking, see Chapter Seven for an additional list of recommended items.

An internal-frame **backpack** is probably best for heaving your things around on buses and rikshas, especially if you're also travelling in other parts of Asia. A travel pack, with shoulder straps that can be zipped out of sight, will help dispel lingering "hippy" prejudices when dealing with officialdom; best of all is one in which all compartments can be secured with a single padlock. A lightweight daypack also comes in handy for short excursions.

The **clothes** you bring will depend very much on the time of year, and where you expect to be going. For warm weather you'll want lightweight cotton garments – loose-fitting but modest, and covering enough to ward off sun and bugs. Shorts and a swimsuit are worth bringing (especially for rafting), but heed the advice given in "Cultural Hints", p.42. A waterproof shell or poncho is advisable at any time of year. For cooler seasons, try to dress in layers: a T-shirt, long-sleeved shirt, sweater or polyester pile jacket and shell will set you up for almost any weather. Running shoes or any sort of durable, lightweight **footwear** will be adequate for most conditions in Nepal, even on a trek, though higher up you'll need something waterproof. You'll also need a backup pair in case those get wet; flipflops, available locally, will do in warm weather. Sport sandals are perfect for the monsoon or rafting.

For the sun, bring **sunscreen**, **lip balm**, **sunglasses** and a brimmed **hat**; an umbrella (available locally) acts as an effective parasol at low elevations, and is indispensible during the monsoon. If you're heading to the Tarai, especially between April and October, bring **mosquito repellent**; you can buy coils locally. **Toiletries** are pretty easy to come by in Kathmandu, but bring tampons, plus anything out of the ordinary. Medicines are covered in the health section and the trekking chapter, but obviously bring any prescribed **medications**. If you wear **glasses** or contact lenses, make sure to pack a spare pair.

Carry valuables in a **money belt** or neck purse; a small **padlock** (available locally) is an effective deterrent to would-be thieves. **Earplugs** are a must for shutting out the sound of barking dogs at night. In cheap lodgings, a **sleeping sheet** is an insurance policy against bedbugs and the like. A **musical instrument** or portable **game** will help break the ice and while away some dead hours.

And finally, some odd essentials: a **torch (flashlight)**, **small towel**, **sewing kit**, a length of **cord** for drying clothes, and sealable **plastic bags** for keeping things separate in your pack.

Some words of warning

The 1990s have already brought great upheaval to Nepal, and there's probably more still to come. As this book goes to press, Nepal stands at a critical juncture: the political system, economic development, the established social order, and the country's mercurial relationship with India all seem to be in a worrying state of flux. Another popular uprising can't be discounted.

But while political instability is unlikely to have much of a direct effect on your plans, other changes inevitably will. No guidebook can reliably predict quite how things will be by the time you get to Nepal, but the following recent trends give an idea of what's in store:

• New **road-building** is moving trailheads further into the hinterland, making some treks shorter and the transport to them longer. Many existing roads are deteriorating, meanwhile, forcing most traffic onto a few main highways.

• **Tourist bus** services are proliferating, making travel to certain places easier, but also turning those places into tourist traps.

• **Rural electrification** is proceeding steadily, bringing not only lights but also videos, satellite TV and a whole lot more contact with the outside world.

• The growth of **budget tourist ghettos** has been a major theme of the past decade. However, as word gets out that these quarters are ugly and overbuilt, we may begin to see a tourist backlash against them.

• **Ripoffs and hustle** are on the rise, owing to an influx of Indian (especially Kashmiri) immigrants and high unemployment.

• Nepal is getting more and more **packaged**: for no good reason other than heavy marketing, guided tours, organized treks and safaris have become common, even for budget travellers.

• **Prices** have historically risen faster than average in the tourist areas, though oversupply may reverse this trend; off the beaten track, prices if anything tend to decline in real terms.

PART ONE

THE

BASICS

GETTING THERE BY AIR

If Nepal is your only destination, flying direct to Kathmandu is the logical option. However, only a few airlines serve this route: flights in the spring and (especially) autumn high seasons get booked up months ahead, while during slack times carriers sometimes refuse to confirm reservations until they've decided whether it's worth their while to fly.

You'll get the best deals through "consolidators" or discount agents, who sell off excess seats for the airlines at rock-bottom rates. Try the agents listed on the following pages, or check out the ads in the Sunday newspaper travel sections. If you're not on a fixed schedule, or if you're planning to move on to other countries within Asia, consider buying a one-way ticket to Kathmandu – return or onward tickets are often cheaper there than they are at home, although of course they may be hard to come by in the high season.

FROM THE UK AND IRELAND

The cheapest flights **from London** hover between £430 and £600 return, depending on the season. The fastest flights, stopping off in Frankfurt and Dubai, take around sixteen hours. *Royal Nepal Airlines Corporation* (*RNAC*), *Lufthansa*, *Biman Bangladesh* and *PIA*, which all discount their fares through consolidating agents, tend to offer the best deals. Handily, *Biman's* low-season fares apply during part of Nepal's high season, although you have to stop over in Dhaka. *RNAC* and *Lufthansa* flights stop in Frankfurt and Dubai, *PIA* flights in Karachi. For really no-frills service at a rock-bottom price, try *Aeroflot*, which goes via Moscow.

You're unlikely to save money by flying **via Delhi**, but the seat availability might be better,

 DISCOUNT AGENTS IN THE UK AND IRELAND

Campus Travel, 52 Grosvenor Gardens, London SW1 (☎071/730 8111); 541 Bristol Rd, Selly Oak, Birmingham (☎021/414 1848); 39 Queen's Rd, Clifton, Bristol (☎0272/292494); 3 Emmanuel St, Cambridge (☎0223/324283); 53 Forest Rd, Edinburgh (☎031/225 6111); 13 High St, Oxford (☎0865/242067); also in YHA shops and on university campuses all over Britain.

Council Travel, 28a Poland St, London W1 (☎071/437 7767). General student discount agent.

Royal Nepal Airlines Corporation (RNAC), 114 Tottenham Court Rd, London W1P 9HL (☎071/387 1541).

STA Travel, 74–86 Old Brompton Rd, London SW7 (☎071/937 9962); 25 Queen's Rd, Bristol; 38 Sidney St, Cambridge; 88 Vicar Lane, Leeds; 75

Deansgate, Manchester; 36–38 George St, Oxford; and offices at the universities of Birmingham, Kent, London (all colleges) and Loughborough.

Trailfinders, 42–48 Earls Court Rd, London W8 (☎071/938 3366); 194 Kensington High St, London W8 (☎071/938 3939); 58 Deansgate, Manchester (☎061/839 6969).

Travel Cuts, 295a Regent St, London W1 (☎071/255 2082).

United Air Travel, 5–6 Coventry St, London W1V 7FL (☎071/734 6668) – agent for *Biman Bangladesh, Aeroflot* and others.

USIT, Aston Quay, O'Connell Bridge, Dublin 2 (☎01/778117); 13b College St, Belfast BT1 (☎0232/324073). Ireland's main outlet for discounted, youth and student fares.

especially during the high season. About a dozen airlines fly this route, typically charging £420–500 return – a specialist agent can recommend the cheapest current deals – with connecting flights to Kathmandu adding about £100 each way.

From other cities in Britain and Ireland, an agent should be able to route you through London or Frankfurt, where you can pick up an *RNAC* flight. Fares can sometimes work out about the same as for flights from London – though from Ireland it may be worthwhile getting a cheap flight or ferry to England and then booking to Kathmandu from there.

FROM THE USA AND CANADA

At least four airlines – *PIA, Thai, Singapore* and *Lufthansa* – fly direct to Kathmandu from the US, although none operates a nonstop service. Plenty of other airlines fly to Delhi, Bangkok and other Asian cities, where you can catch a connecting flight to Kathmandu, so when seat availability is tight it's well worth asking about alternative routings.

From the West Coast, standard round-trip economy fares cost $1600 and up, but you can do better than this by shopping around – discount fares hover around $1300 in high season, and may be even cheaper at other times. At the time of writing, *Thai* was doing the heaviest discounting. Many airlines can take you as far as Hong Kong, Bangkok or Singapore, where you'll typically have to switch to *Royal Nepal Airlines Corporation* (*RNAC*) or *Thai*. Ticketing through on two different carriers tends to be no cheaper than going direct, though, and may entail an overnight at your own expense.

The story is similar if you're flying **from the East Coast** via Europe or the Middle East, and fares are comparable. The cheapest direct flights going this way are often with *PIA*, stopping in Karachi. You may wind up crossing the Atlantic with one airline and then switching to another – there are any number of permutations, but it's common to change at London, Frankfurt or Delhi to connect with the twice-weekly *RNAC* flight. In terms of price, it might not make much difference to fly west instead of east, in case you've got a Far Eastern stopover in mind.

Internal connecting flights from central US cities will add around $250 to the above fares.

FROM CANADA

As with flights from the States, direct flights **from Canada** are all routed through hubs in Europe or the Far East. Discount fares from Toronto and Vancouver can be had for as little as CDN$1350 – standard fares may be as much as double that.

FROM AUSTRALIA AND NEW ZEALAND

From Sydney or **Auckland**, one-way fares to Kathmandu start at about A$1200, but chances are you'll be stopping elsewhere en route: *Thai, Qantas, Lauda* and *British Airways* fly from Sydney to Bangkok for A$700 each way (reckon on about $1000 more from Perth); fares to Delhi are about the same as to Kathmandu. One of the best agents is *STA Travel*, with branches throughout Australia and New Zealand. Head offices are at 224 Faraday St, Carlton, Melbourne 3053 (☎03/347 4711), and 10 High St, PO Box 4156, Auckland (☎09/309 9723). Incidentally, *STA* discounts fares for under-26s.

DISCOUNT AGENTS IN NORTH AMERICA

Air Brokers International, 323 Geary St, Suite 411, San Francisco, CA 94102(☎1-800/883-3273).

Council Travel, 205 East 42nd St, New York, NY 10017 (☎212/661-1450); 312 Sutter St, San Francisco, CA 94108 (☎415/421-3473); and many other regional outlets.

Himalayan Treasure and Travel, 3201 Carlson Blvd, El Cerrito, CA 94530 (☎510/526-2005 or 1-800/223-1813).

STA Travel, 48 East 11th St, New York, NY 10003 (☎212/477-7166 or 1-800/777-0112); 106 Geary St, San Francisco, CA 94108 (☎415/391-8407); and several other offices on the east and west coasts.

Third Eye Travel, 33220 Sandpiper Place, Fremont, CA 94555 (☎510/487-9010 or 1-800/456-3393).

Travel Cuts, 187 College St, Toronto, ON. M5T 1P7 (☎416/979-2406); and outlets on most Canadian university campuses.

Travel International, Ives Building, 114 Forrest Ave, Suite 205, Narbeth, PA 19072 (☎1-800/334-9294). Discount travel club, membership $45.

ASIAN CONNECTIONS

One-way fares between the following Asian cities and Kathmandu don't vary that much, although it's still always worth shopping around. Note that *Royal Nepal Airlines Corporation* (*RNAC*) and *Indian Airlines* (*IA*) give 25 percent off to under-30s on the Calcutta, Delhi and Varanasi flights, although the latter carrier has a bad reputation for overbooking flights.

Bangkok ($190–220) – *Thai, RNAC*
Bombay ($250) – *RNAC*
Calcutta ($96) – *IA, RNAC*
Delhi ($142) – *IA, RNAC*
Dhaka ($86–101) – *Biman Bangladesh, RNAC*

Hong Kong ($320–344) – *RNAC, Thai*
Karachi ($170) – *PIA*
Singapore ($294–320) – *Singapore, RNAC*
Varanasi ($71) – *IA*

PACKAGES

Package trips exist only in a specialized sense in Nepal, being based around trekking, rafting, cycling or wildlife-viewing itineraries. These can cost as much as ten times what you'd spend by doing things independently (around £50–100/ $75–150 per day, not taking into account the cost of the flight), but may be worth considering if you're on a tight schedule. A sampling of companies and addresses is given over the page. "Outdoor Pursuits" has more to say about these activities.

OVERLAND ROUTES TO NEPAL

The classic Asia overland trip is still alive and kicking, despite periodic political reroutings. Leaving Europe behind at Istanbul, the usual route traverses Turkey, angles down through Iran, crosses Pakistan and enters India at Amritsar; Iran is off-limits to US passport holders, however, who have to fly from Istanbul to Karachi. Several overland expedition operators in the UK (see box overleaf) run 6- to 18-week trips in specially designed vehicles all the way through to Kathmandu. Expect to pay between £700 and £1500 for the one-way trip from London, depending on the level of luxury.

FROM INDIA

Transport connections between **India** and Nepal are well developed, with travel agents in Delhi, Darjeeling and other major train junctions in the north selling **bus** packages to Kathmandu. However, these are often ripoffs, and in any case it's an easy matter to ride to the border and make your own way from there – you'll almost certainly end up on the same Nepali bus, anyway.

Three **border crossings** are of principal interest to travellers: Sunauli, the most popular entry point, reachable from Delhi, Varanasi and most of north India (via Gorakhpur); Birganj, accessible from Bodh Gaya and Calcutta (via Patna); and Kakarbitta, serving Darjeeling and Calcutta (via Siliguri). These crossings are described fully in the relevant sections of Chapters Five and Six. At the time of writing, three others (Nepalganj, Dhangadhi and Mahendranagar) were also open to tourists, and others near Janakpur and Biratnagar sometimes seemed to let foreigners through; but public transport to these points is patchy, and given Nepal's fickle relationship with India, you can't be sure ahead of time that you'll be let through. Enter the country via one of the conventional crossings to avoid a wasted journey, and if you're up for adventure on the way out, check with Central Immigration in Kathmandu before setting off to find out what else is open.

BY PRIVATE VEHICLE

Nepal used to be *the* place to sell **vehicles** – particularly vans – but an official crackdown on the trade has removed the financial incentive to drive in Nepal (reportedly, however, there are still ways round this). Needless to say, bringing a vehicle into Nepal is a hell of a commitment, and requires nerves of steel to cope with precarious

TREKKING, OVERLAND AND SPECIALIST OPERATORS

NORTH AMERICA

Above the Clouds Trekking, PO Box 398, Worcester, MA 01602 (☎1-800/233-4499 or 508/799-4499 in MA). Trekking, rafting, mountain-biking.

Himalayan Travel, 112 Prospect St, Stamford, CT 06901 (☎1-800/225-2380 or 203/359-3711). Trekking, rafting, wildlife, mountain-biking.

Himalayan Trekking & Wilderness Expeditions, 1900 Eighth St, Berkeley, CA 94710 (☎1-800/777-TREK or 510/540-8040 in CA). Trekking, rafting, wildlife.

InnerAsia, 2627 Lombard St, San Francisco, CA 94123 (☎1-800/ 777-8183 or 415/922-0448 in CA). Trekking, wildlife.

Journeys, 4011 Jackson Rd, Ann Arbor, MI 48103

Mountain Travel-Sobek, 6420 Fairmount Ave, El Cerrito, CA 94530 (☎1-800/227-2384 or 510/527-8100 in CA). Trekking, rafting, wildlife.

Overseas Adventure Travel, 349 Broadway, Cambridge, MA 02139 (☎1-800/221-0814 or 617/876-0533 in MA). Trekking, rafting, wildlife.

Wilderness Travel, 801 Allston Way, Berkeley, CA 94710 (☎1-800/368-2794 or 510/548-0420 in CA). Trekking, wildlife.

Womantrek, PO Box 20643, Seattle, WA 98102 (☎206/325-4772). Trekking.

Worldwide Adventures,36 Finch Ave W, North York, ON. M2N 2G9 (☎1-800/387-1483 or 416/221-3000 in ON). Trekking, rafting, wildlife, mountain-biking.

UK

Classic Nepal, 33 Metro Ave, Newton, Derbyshire DE55 5UF (☎0773/873497). Trekking, rafting, wildlife.

Detours, 80 Stuart Rd, Wimbledon Park, London SW19 8DH (☎081/946 6295). Unique operator of culturally sensitive tours; also trekking.

Encounter Overland, 267 Old Brompton Rd, London SW5 9JA (☎071/370 6951). Overland, trekking, rafting, wildlife.

Exodus Expeditions, 9 Weir Rd, London SW12 0LT (☎081/675 5550). Overland, trekking, rafting, wildlife.

Explore Worldwide, 1 Frederick St, Aldershot, Hants GU11 1LQ (☎0252/319448). Trekking, rafting, wildlife.

High Places, 15 Spring Hill, Sheffield S10 1ET (☎0742/682553). Trekking, rafting, wildlife.

Himalayan Kingdoms, 20 The Mall, Clifton, Bristol BS8 4DR (☎0272/237163). Trekking, rafting, wildlife.

Himalayan Quest, 12 Euston Place, Leamington Spa, Warks CV32 4LR (☎0926/450835). Trekking, rafting, cycling, wildlife.

Sherpa Expeditions, 131a Heston Rd, Hounslow, Middx TW5 0RD (☎081/577 2717). Trekking, rafting, wildlife.

Top Deck Travel, 131–135 Earls Court Rd, London SW5 9RH (☎071/370 4555). Overland.

roads, drunk drivers, slow-moving vehicles, nonexistent law enforcement, horrendous city traffic, parking nightmares, sacred cows and fatalistic pedestrians. The tradeoff is that you don't have to deal with Nepali buses, and you get to go at your own pace, bring lots more gear and have your own personal space.

To import a car or other four-wheeled vehicle into Nepal you'll have to show a **carnet de passage**, a document intended to ensure you don't illegally sell the vehicle in the country. A *carnet* is available from the *AA* or similar motoring organization in your home country or the country where you purchased the vehicle. You'd also do well to come equipped with an **international driving licence**.

You can enter Nepal via any official border crossing (see above), though Birganj is the easiest to deal with. If you've made it this far with a vehicle, Nepal border formalities will seem a breeze – customs might spend an hour or two over your *carnet*, but you shouldn't have to pay any money. For tips on driving in Nepal, see p.19.

BY BICYCLE

Entering Nepal by **bicycle** involves no special paperwork. The main approaches are summarized in the "Mountain biking routes in Nepal" box on p.186, and "Outdoor Pursuits" later in this chapter tells you what you need to know if you're planning on bringing a bike to Nepal.

FROM TIBET

Any advice to do with travelling in **Tibet** is liable to be out of date by the time it's in print, so seek current information before going to Tibet in anticipation of being able to cross into Nepal. However, at the time of writing, China was allowing individual travellers to exit Tibet at Khasa (Kodari on the Nepal side) on the Lhasa–Kathmandu highway, but was only allowing groups to go in the other direction. Charter buses ply a standard three-day quasi-sightseeing route

from Lhasa via Shigatze, Gyantse and Tingri to the border, where you'll have to walk a bit (or, if the road is washed out, a lot) and then spend another full day on a Nepali bus to Kathmandu.

If you've managed to **cycle** all the way to Lhasa, you ought to be fit and acclimatized enough to make it the rest of the way to Nepal – but needless to say, this is an extremely arduous journey along an unpaved road, crossing two passes of at least 5000m, and should only be attempted in good weather.

RED TAPE AND VISAS

All foreign nationals (except Indians) need a visa to enter Nepal. Thirty-day tourist visas are issued on arrival with a minimum of fuss at Kathmandu airport and at official overland entry points. Fees change often and without warning, but single-entry visas currently cost $20 (or equivalent), $40 for double and $80 for multiple entry. Have a passport-size photo at the ready, and if possible bring cash for the visa fee.

Getting a visa from an overseas **Nepalese embassy or consulate** will cut down on paperwork on arrival, but it's really only worth doing if you happen to be in the neighbourhood or if you're one of those people who has to have everything sorted out before you go. The fees are supposed to be the same as those given above, but there are some anomalies – the London embassy charges £20 for UK passport-holders. See box for addresses.

Tourist visas can be **extended**, up to thirty days at a time, for a maximum of three months. Extensions are granted only at the Kathmandu or Pokhara **Central Immigration** offices – a simple procedure, although high-season queues can run to two hours or more, especially just before and after the week-long festival of *Dasain* in October. The cost is $5 per week for the first thirty days' extension, $10 per week thereafter. You must also show official receipts proving that you have changed **$20 a day** (or the equivalent in any foreign currency) to cover the period of your extension – if you wanted to stay another month, for instance, you'd have had to change $600. Note that exchange receipts are issued not only by banks but also by all hotels, trekking/rafting companies and travel agencies that require payment in foreign currency.

Visa regulations have been getting steadily tighter in recent years. Central Immigration's current position is that they'll allow tourists a **maximum** of four months in Nepal in any calendar year, and no more than three months at a time. If you stay a full three months, you'll have to leave the country for a month before being allowed to re-enter. Given extenuating circumstances, Central Immigration may grant a fourth consecutive month. The fine for overstaying is double the amount that you would have paid had you properly extended your visa.

TREKKING PERMITS

A tourist visa is technically valid only in the fraction of Nepal served by roads. To visit anywhere more than a day's walk off a main road you need to get a **trekking permit** from Central

Immigration – even if you don't intend to trek. For most trekking areas, the per-week fee is the same as for a visa extension. Central Immigration offices will process simultaneous applications for visa extensions and trekking permits, but you still have to pay both fees.

A trekking permit isn't required for any of the places described in this book *except* the areas covered in Chapter Seven, *The Himalayan Trekking Regions*, where you'll find a more detailed discussion of trekking permits.

NEPALESE EMBASSIES AND CONSULATES

Australia: 377 Sussex St, Sydney 2000 (☎02/264 7197); 18-20 Bank Pl, Melbourne 3000 (☎03/602 1271); 195 Adelaide Tce, Perth 6000 (☎09/221 1207).

Bangladesh: Road No. 2, Baridhara Diplomatic Enclave, Baridhara, Dhaka (☎2/601790).

Belgium: 149 Lamorinierstraat, B-2018 Antwerp (☎03/230 8800).

Canada: 3/0 Duport St, Toronto, ON M5 RIV9 (☎416/968-7252).

Denmark: 13 Teglgardsstr, DK-1452, Copenhagen (☎01/143175).

France: 45 rue de Acacias, 75017 Paris (☎46.22.48.67).

Germany: Im Hag 15, D-5300 Bonn 2 (☎0228/343097).

India: Barakhamba Rd, New Delhi 110001 (☎11/332 9969); 19 Woodlands, Sterndale Rd, Alipore, Calcutta 700027 (☎33/452024).

Italy: Piazzale Medaglie d'Oro 20, 00136 Rome (☎06/345 1642).

Netherlands: Prinsengracht 687-1017-Jv, Amsterdam (☎031/20 241530).

Norway: Haakon Viis Gt. - 5, PO Box 1384 Vika, 0116 Oslo (☎02/414743).

Pakistan: 506 Street No. 84, Attaturk Ave, Ramna G-6/4 Islamabad (☎5/823 642).

Sweden: Eriksbergsgatania, S-114 30, Stockholm (☎08/200353).

Switzerland: Schanzengasse 22, PO Box CH-8024, Zurich (☎01/47 59 93).

Thailand: 189 Soi 71, Sukhamvit Rd, Bangkok 10110 (☎2/391 7240).

UK: 12a Kensington Palace Gdns, London W8 4QU (☎071/229 1594).

USA: 2131 Leroy Pl NW, Washington DC 20008 (☎202/667-4550); 1500 Lake Shore Dr, Chicago, IL 60610; 473 Jackson St, San Francisco, CA 94111 (☎415/434-1111); Suite 110, 16250 Dallas Pkwy, Dallas, TX 75248 (☎214/931-1212); 212 15th St NE, Atlanta, GA 30309 (☎404/892-8152).

COSTS, MONEY AND BANKS

Your money goes a long way in Nepal. Off the tourist routes, it can actually be hard to spend US$5/£3 a day, however willing you might be to pay more. On the other hand, Kathmandu and some of the other tourist traps can burn a hole in your pocket rather faster than you might have expected in the Third World. While even in the capital it's still possible to keep to $5/£3 a day, the figure can effortlessly balloon to $20/£13 or more simply by trading up to slightly nicer hotels and restaurants. The cost of seeing Nepal, then, depends in large part on the proportion of time you spend on and off the beaten track.

The price of **accommodation** varies considerably, depending on where you stay and when. Really basic rooms can almost always be found for $1.50/£1 or less. Prices aren't automatically higher in tourist areas, but most travellers take up the option of paying more for a few creature comforts: figure on $4–10/£2.50–6.50 for a double room in the high season. Off-season rates can plummet by fifty percent or more, but it's up to you to bargain. Prices for single rooms are usually lower, and dorm beds are often available, but you generally save money by doubling up.

Food, cheap as it is, tends to be the biggest daily expense for budget travellers. Normally, a tourist Nepali or Tibetan dinner will run to $1–2/60p–£1.30, rising to $8/£5 or more in a really posh place. Western meals typically come to $2/£1.30 or more. However, *daal bhaat*, the all-you-can-eat national meal of rice, lentils and curried vegetables, costs about 50¢/30p just about anywhere, and you can fill up on road snacks for just pennies.

As long as you stick to buses, the cost of **transport** is trifling. Most bus journeys cost $2/£1.30 or less, and they're so uncomfortable that you probably won't want to move around very often anyway. However, the stakes go up dramatically if you fly (one-way fares are generally in the region of $50–150/£33–100).

No matter how tight your budget, it would be foolish not to **splurge** now and then on some of the things that make Nepal unique: trekking on your own is quite cheap, but you might prefer to hire a porter for $4/£2.50 a day, or even pay upwards of $20/£13 a day for a fully catered trek; rafting and wildlife trips also work out to be relatively expensive, but well worth it; and few will be able to resist buying at least something from Nepal's rich range of handicrafts.

THE ALMIGHTY DOLLAR

Nepal's inflation rate now seems to be moderating, but in recent years it has run at 20–30 percent annually. Rupee prices quoted in this book should therefore be adjusted accordingly. However, prices in US dollars – still the most coveted foreign currency in Nepal – tend to remain fairly constant from one year to the next, since the exchange rate compensates for inflation. Hotels and travel operators are wise to this, and quote their prices in dollars – and in fact most tourist businesses tend to express prices over Rs1000 or so in dollars.

A final point: some independent travellers make a wild show of pinching pennies, which Nepalis find pathetic – they know how much an air ticket to Kathmandu costs. Others throw money around too freely, which only proves they deserve to be parted from it. Bargain where appropriate, but don't begrudge a few rupees to someone who's worked hard for them, and try to spend your money where it will do the most good.

MONEY

Nepal's unit of currency is the **rupee**, which is divided into 100 paisa. The rupee is now fully convertible, meaning that the government allows the **exchange rate** to be set by the open market – at the time of writing, the rate was Rs46.5 to the US$ (£1=Rs72), and 150 Nepalese rupees to 100 Indian rupees (where confusion might arise, it's common practice to refer to the two currencies as NC and IC respectively).

Almost all Nepali money is paper: notes come in denominations of Rs1, 2, 5 10, 20, 50, 100, 500 and 1000. Coins, used mainly for almsgiving, are 5, 10, 25 and 50 paisa and 1 rupee; 50 paisa is sometimes called a *mohar*. One minor annoyance of travelling in Nepal is **getting change**. In tourist areas it's no problem, but trying to pass a Rs100 (or larger) note to a village merchant or a riksha driver is sure to invite delays, since few Nepalis can afford to keep much spare change lying around. It gets to be a game of bluff between buyer and seller, both hoarding a wad of small notes for occasions when exact change is vital.

If at all possible, **carry US dollars**, which are more widely accepted. Other hard currencies can be exchanged at major banks and luxury hotels. **US dollar travellers' cheques** aren't quite as liquid as cash, but they're obviously more secure, and they bring a slightly higher official exchange rate. A **credit card** is a handy backup – in tourist areas you can draw funds against *Amex*, *Visa* or *Access/Mastercard* (although the last two charge hefty commissions) – and an increasing number of businesses now accept plastic.

BANKS

Using banks in Nepal is, by Asian standards, surprisingly hassle-free. Two national banks (*Rastriya Banijya Bank* and *Nepal Bank*) and several private ones maintain tourist branches at the airport, at various strategic locations in

Kathmandu and Pokhara, and at all the overland border crossings, as well as somewhat less efficient offices in every town of any consequence. The government banks give a slightly better rate and/or charge less commission than the private ones. Banking **hours** vary: the Kathmandu airport branch operates around the clock, and other tourist branches keep generous hours – specific timings are given where they're notable – but the lesser branches generally change money only Mon–Thurs & Sun 10am–2pm, Fri 10am–noon.

Hold onto all **exchange receipts**. You'll need them not only when applying for visa extensions, but also to **change money back** when you leave. You're allowed to change back up to fifteen percent of what you've got receipts for. This can only be done at the airport or one of the official border crossings, however, where you're likely to be told that they're out of the currency you want and you'll have to take yen, zlotys or whatever; if entering India, it's easier just to change your NC into IC unofficially at the border.

Wiring money to Nepal takes two to three working days. Have funds transferred to *Nepal Grindlays Bank*, Thamel and Naya Baneswar (☎977-1-212683; telex 2531 GRINDLY NP); *Nepal Indosuez Bank*, Durbar Marg (☎977-1-228229; telex 2435 INDOSU NP); *Nepal Arab Bank*, Kantipath (☎977-1-220089; telex 2385 NABIL NP); *Nepal Bank*, New Road (☎977-1-225904; telex 2220 LUXMI NP). Needless to say, verify bank details before having money sent.

THE BLACK MARKET

As we were going to press, the government's move to make the rupee fully convertible seemed certain to put an end to Nepal's currency **black market**. This section is included here just in case things don't go as planned.

Dollars changed unofficially in Nepal fuel the grey market in electronics goods, purchased in Hong Kong and Singapore and sold at a profit in Nepal. They may also be sent to Hong Kong to buy gold ingots, which are then smuggled back through Nepal to India where they're used to redeem gold-backed mortgages and dowry loans. By participating, you're theoretically thwarting a poor country's attempt to defend its currency and undermining its development efforts. In practice, though, the black-market differential is exploited even by the government, and a de facto two-tiered system probably works out best for all concerned. At any rate, there's no vast profit to be made on the black market, so why sweat it either way?

Changing on the black market involves no danger of arrest and very little of rip-off. You can expect to get 10 to 20 percent over the bank rate in Kathmandu, somewhat less in Pokhara (there's no black-market premium anywhere else). Big bills – $100 or $50 – fetch the best rate, while small denominations, travellers' cheques and other currencies may not even be worth the effort. Let a tout take you to his boss the first time, and you can conduct future transactions direct with the dealer to cut out the middleman (when in doubt, try a carpet shop). The market fluctuates from day to day, and it goes without saying that moneychangers will always try to give less than the going rate. Shop around, bluff, and walk out of the door until you find the limit. Inspect all notes very carefully.

HEALTH AND INSURANCE

Health is not one of Nepal's strong points. Sanitation is a problem, and a lot of bugs make the rounds, especially during the monsoon and immediately after it. But don't panic – by coming prepared and looking after yourself while you're in the country, you're unlikely to come down with anything worse than the local version of Delhi belly.

This section deals with health matters mainly in the context of Western-style medicine; traditional ayurvedic and Tibetan practices are discussed later in the "Spiritual pursuits" section.

BEFORE YOU GO

No **inoculations** are required for Nepal, but hepatitis A, typhoid and meningitis jabs are recommended, and it's worth ensuring that you're up to date with tetanus, polio, mumps and measles boosters. All of these can be obtained in Kathmandu, often more cheaply than at home, but obviously it's better to get nasty things like injections out of the way before starting your trip.

If you have any medical conditions or concerns about your health, don't set off to a place like Nepal without first seeing a **doctor**. Also, consider seeing a **dentist** before you go – you don't want to have dental work done in Nepal if you can help it.

RECOMMENDED INOCULATIONS

Hepatitis A isn't the worst disease you can catch in Nepal, but the frequency with which it strikes travellers makes a strong case for immunization. Transmitted through contaminated food and water, it can lay a victim low for several months with exhaustion, fever and diarrhoea – and may cause liver damage if mixed with alcohol. A new (1992) vaccine has been shown to be extremely effective – it's still rather expensive, but lasts for life. The protection given by gamma globulin, the traditional serum of hepatitis antibodies, wears off quickly and the injection should therefore be had as late as possible before departure. The standard dosage is 2ml for one month, up to 5ml for four months.

Typhoid is endemic in Nepal and is also spread through contaminated food and water, but outside of the monsoon it's fairly rare. It produces a persistent very high fever, which is treatable. Vaccination can be by injection (two shots are required if you haven't been inoculated before) or orally – the tablets are somewhat more expensive, but a lot easier on the arm.

The risk-benefit decision on the **meningitis** jab is more debateable. Spread by airborne bacteria, this is indeed a very unpleasant disease that attacks the lining of the brain, and can be fatal. However, the last epidemic was in 1983, and some authorities believe a recurrence is unlikely thanks to control measures. The injection causes few side effects, and lasts for three years.

You should have a **tetanus** booster every ten years, whether you travel or not. Assuming you were vaccinated for **polio** in childhood, only one (oral) booster is necessary during your adult life. Immunizations against **mumps** and **measles** are recommended for anyone who wasn't vaccinated as a child and hasn't already had these diseases.

OPTIONAL MEASURES

Malaria hasn't been eradicated in Nepal – as is sometimes claimed – and the effectiveness of mosquito-control measures (using DDT) appears to be waning. Malaria doesn't occur above 1000m – Kathmandu and most hill areas are higher than this. However, you need to guard against it if you're planning to travel in the Tarai, especially between April and October. The best prevention is mosquito netting or repellent (see below). There is no vaccination against malaria, but taking regular doses of "prophylactic" tablets will provide a fair degree of immunity. Recommended courses vary from country to country, but doctors in Nepal, who should know, prescribe 500mg of Chloroquine once a week, starting one week *before* entering the malarial area and continuing until three weeks *after* leaving it. Some also prescribe a daily dose of proguanil or mefloquine against chloroquine-resistant malaria. And just in case, bring along three tablets of Pyralfin (aka Fansidar), to be taken as a one-time dose in the event of contracting malaria out of reach of medical help. Incidentally, all these medicines are much cheaper and more readily available in Kathmandu than in Europe or North America.

Although **rabies** is a problem in Nepal, the best advice is just to give dogs and monkeys a wide berth. Vaccination against it is expensive and time-consuming, and probably only worth it if you expect to be spending an unusual amount of time around animals. The pre-exposure ("human diploid cell") vaccine involves a series of three injections over a four-week period, which produces a protective antibody level for three years; if you get bitten, you'll still have to get two more shots, but that's better than the six you'd have to get without the pre-exposure course.

Like malaria, **Japanese B encephalitis** is carried by mosquitoes. While it's a potentially fatal disease, it's confined to very remote portions of the Tarai where few foreigners are likely to go. The inoculation is in the form of two injections, one to two weeks apart.

Don't bother with the **cholera** inoculation – few authorities now believe it's worthwhile.

PRECAUTIONS

The lack of sanitation in Nepal is sometimes overhyped – it's not worth getting too uptight about it or you'll never enjoy anything, and run the risk of rebuffing Nepalese hospitality.

A few common-sense precautions are in order, though, starting with the **water**: stick to tea or bottled drinks, or purify water with iodine (for more on this, see the trekking chapter). Many guest houses provide water in drip-filter units, but make sure it's been boiled.

When it comes to **food**, usually it's flashy tourist restaurants and "Western" dishes that bring the most grief: more people get sick in Kathmandu than anywhere else. Be particularly

> For advice on **altitude sickness** and other trekking hazards, plus a **first-aid checklist**, see p.303.

wary of prepared dishes that have to be reheated – the lasagne may look fantastic, but just ask yourself how long it's been on display there in the heat and the flies. Nepali food is usually fine and you can probably trust anything that's been boiled or fried in your presence, although meat can sometimes be dodgy. Raw, unpeeled fruit and vegetables should always be viewed with suspicion, and you should always verify that salads in tourist restaurants have been soaked in an iodine or potassium permanganate solution.

You need to be particularly vigilant about **personal hygiene** while travelling in Nepal. That means, above all, washing your hands often. Keep any cuts clean, and treat them with iodine to prevent infection. If you're staying in cheap guest houses, bring a sleeping sheet to keep fleas and lice at bay. Wear shoes at all times, since scabies and hookworm can be picked up through bare feet. Take the usual precautions to avoid sunburn and dehydration.

When travelling in the Tarai, minimize your exposure to malaria by depriving **mosquitoes** of the opportunity to bite you. They're hungriest from dusk to dawn: during these times, wear repellent and/or long-sleeved clothes (watch out especially for ankles), and sleep under netting or burn mosquito coils. Remember, though, that very few mosquitoes carry malaria, so you don't need to worry over every bite.

AIDS is not, as yet, a significant health problem in Nepal, although a small number of Nepali prostitutes returning from India have been identified as HIV positive. Prostitution is not common in Nepal itself, but young Nepali women are frequently lured (or kidnapped) from their homes to Indian brothels, where they are in great demand (see p.366). Your main sexual threat, however, is apt to be other foreigners – use the same precautions that you would at home.

SELF-HELP

Chances are, at some point during your travels in Nepal you'll feel ill. In the vast majority of cases, it won't be something you need to see a doctor about, and sod's law says it will happen somewhere remote and inconvenient anyway. The following information should help with **self-diagnosis**, although it is *not* presented as a substitute for professional medical advice.

Antibiotics definitely shouldn't be taken lightly: they can increase susceptibility to other problems by killing off "good" as well as "bad" organisms in your gut, and some may cause allergic reactions or other unpleasant side-effects. Also, the more a particular antibiotic is used, the sooner organisms build up a resistance to it. It's not a bad idea to travel with a course of one or more of the drugs mentioned here, but make sure you have the dosage explained to you. In the case of serious or persistent intestinal problems, you're strongly urged to have a **stool test** done at a clinic (see below), where the doctor can make an authoritative diagnosis and prescription.

INTESTINAL TROUBLES

Diarrhoea is the most common bane of travellers. If it's mild and not accompanied by other major symptoms, it probably won't require any treatment and should pass of its own accord within a few days. In the meantime, however, it's essential to replace the fluids and salts you're losing down the drain – Jeevan Jal, sold in packets everywhere, is a cheap and effective rehydration formula. Some people recommend starving the bug, which will at least slow the flow, but the best advice is simply to follow your appetite. Diarrhoea tablets such as Lomotil and Immodium will at least plug you up if you have to travel, although this undermines the body's efforts to rid itself of the infection.

If the diarrhoea comes on suddenly and is accompanied by bad **cramps** and **vomiting**, there's a good chance it's food poisoning, which is brought on by toxins secreted by foreign bacteria. There's nothing you can do for food poisoning other than keep replacing fluids, but it should run its course within 24 to 48 hours. If it doesn't, a course of antibiotic such as ciprofloxacin, norfloxacin, or trimoxazole may be necessary (note that resistence to the latter has reduced its effectiveness in Nepal).

If the diarrhoea is more severe, or if you see **blood** or **mucus** in your stool, the cause may be amoebic dysentery or giardiasis. These also frequently produce a **temperature** alternating with **chills**. Occasionally, dysentery can even produce **constipation**, while giardiasis is often recognizable by **rotten-egg belches** and **farts**. Giardiasis is more commonly contracted while trekking, and involves one to two weeks' incubation time, which may help you rule it out if you haven't been in the country that long. Both giardiasis and dysentery are treatable with tinidazole, an antiprotazoal. Again, be sure to keep rehydrating.

FEVER

Flu-like symptoms – fever, headache, catarrh, aching muscles – may mean nothing more serious than the latest virus floating around on Kathmandu's bad air. Respiratory infections are also easy to catch in smoky trailside inns on less developed trekking routes. Rest and aspirin/paracetamol should do the trick. However, strep throat or a bronchial infection will require an antibiotic course such as erythromycin or amoxycillin. Flu symptoms and **jaundice** (yellowing of the eyes) point to hepatitis, which is treated with rest and a plane ticket home.

A **serious fever** or delirium is cause for real concern. Diagnosis is tricky, but safe to say the sufferer needs to be got to a doctor as quickly as possible. To begin with, try bringing the fever down with aspirin or paracetamol. If the fever rises and falls dramatically every few hours, it may be malaria, which, in the absence of medical help, can be zapped with three tablets of Fansidar. If the fever is consistently high for four or more days, it may be typhoid – again, only if no doctor is available, treat with ciprofloxacin/norfloxacin or chloramphenicol.

MINOR SYMPTOMS

Minor **muscle cramps**, experienced after heavy exercise or sweating, may indicate you're low on salt – a teaspoon of salt will bring rapid relief. Likewise, a simple **headache** may just mean you're dehydrated. (However, a severe headache, accompanied by eye pain, neck stiffness and a temperature, could mean meningitis – in which case get to a doctor pronto.)

Itchy skin is often traced to insect bites – not only obvious ones like mosquitoes, but also fleas, lice or scabies picked up from dirty bedclothes. The latter, a burrowing mite, goes for the webbed spaces between fingers and toes. Shampoos and lotions are available locally. Air out your bedding and wash your clothes thoroughly.

ANIMAL BITES

For **animal bites** or scratches, *immediately* wash the wound with soap and water for as long as half an hour, depending on severity, then treat it with iodine, 40–70 percent alcohol or 0.1 percent quaternary ammonium compound (brand name Cetrimide), then hightail it to one of the Kathmandu clinics for a series of five very expensive injections over the course of a month. The disease's incubation period is between ten and ninety days. If feasible, you're supposed to capture the animal alive for observation.

GETTING MEDICAL HELP

In a non-emergency situation, make for one of the traveller-oriented **clinics** in Kathmandu. Run to Western standards, these can diagnose most common ailments, write prescriptions, and also give inoculations. A veritable cornucopia of Indian-manufactured medicines is available without prescription from **pharmas** (pharmacies) in all major towns.

Almost all qualified **doctors** and specialists are based in Kathmandu – in the event of a serious injury or illness, contact your embassy there (see "Listings" at the end of Chapter One) for a list of recommended physicians. **Hospitals** are listed in the Kathmandu and Pokhara sections of the guide; other hospitals are located in Patan, Tansen and the bigger Tarai cities, though they're often poorly equipped.

INSURANCE

In the light of all this, **travel insurance** is too important to ignore. Besides covering medical expenses and emergency flights, it also insures your money and belongings against loss or theft – however, check the fine print to make sure the per-article limit will cover your most valuable possession (a camera, for instance).

Most travel agents and banks offer short- and long-term policies, covering possessions and travel and health provisions. In general, **premiums** for middle-of-the-road policies cost about $60/£40 per month, cheaper by the year. If you plan to go **trekking or rafting**, don't buy a policy that specifically excludes such "dangerous activities". You might have to pay extra for this coverage, but without it you could be left footing the bill for an expensive helicopter rescue – worse, the chopper might not even be sent if it looks like you won't have the funds to pay for it.

Don't forget that flights paid for with a major **credit card** or charge card offer some automatic cover (but usually only while you're actually travelling to and from your destination). Also, if you're a **student** you may be able to get coverage under a college medical plan, and likewise a **homeowners' policy** may cover loss or theft of possessions while on holiday.

You'll need to keep **receipts** for any medicines you have to buy, or treatment you pay for, to claim from your insurance company once you're home. Similarly, should you have anything stolen, report the theft to the police (see "Police and Trouble") as soon as possible, and keep a copy of your statement.

INFORMATION, MAPS AND GUIDES

Nepal's Tourism Department runs on a shoe-string budget, letting the free market fill the gap with a confusing welter of advertising.

There are no tourist offices outside the country, and those few in Nepal are chronically starved of printed materials and completely bereft of maps. They can, however, sometimes come up with information on festival dates, local bus schedules and the like.

You'll always get the most useful information from other travellers. Check the informal **noticeboards** in restaurants around the tourist quarters for news of upcoming events or to find travelling or trekking companions. In Kathmandu, the adjacent offices of the **Kathmandu Environmental Education Project** and the **Himalayan Rescue Association** can help out with information on trekking routes and conditions. Despite its unabashed advertorialism, **Nepal Traveller**, a free monthly magazine distributed to the big hotels and travel agencies, is the best of several sources of what's-on information.

A NOTE ON PLACE NAMES

Even though Devanaagari (the script of Nepali and Hindi) spellings are phonetic, transliterating them into the Roman alphabet is an inexact science. Some places will never shake off the erroneous spellings bestowed on them by early British colonialists – for instance Durbar Square, which according to widely accepted phonetic rules (see p.383) should be spelled "Darbaar". Where place names are Sanskrit- or Hindi-based, the Nepali pronunciation sometimes differs from the accepted spelling – the names Vishnu (a Hindu god) and Vajra (a tantric symbol) sound like "Bishnu" and "Bajra" in Nepali. This book follows local pronunciations as consistently as possible, except in cases where this would be out of step with every map in print. Having said that, it's often hard to get a consensus on pronunciation – some people say Hetauda, others Itaura; some say Trisuli, others Tirsuli – so keep an open mind while map-reading.

MAPS

The best **country map** you'll find in the tourist bookshops is one produced by *Mandala* on a scale of 1:800,000, which is reasonably reliable for roads and towns but not at all helpful for trails. A larger (1:500,000) three-sheet version of the same is available through *Maps of Nepal* in Baneswar in Kathmandu (near the *Everest Hotel*). They also sell a series of five 1:250,000 maps put out by the Suspension Bridge Division which, though of no use to trekkers, is highly recommended for mountain-bikers venturing beyond the Kathmandu Valley (a 1:125,000 set is also available, but only in Devanaagari). The prettiest map of the country, published by *Nelles*, is appallingly inaccurate – much of it is pure fiction.

Inexpensive **city maps** of Kathmandu and Pokhara are sold everywhere, but maps of other cities simply don't exist. The *Geo-Buch* (or *Schneider*, named after its cartographer) "Kathmandu Valley" is getting out of date, but still indispensable if you plan to do any serious exploring of that area. Free brochures containing sketch maps of **national parks** and wildlife reserves are available from the Department of National Parks and Wildlife Conservation, Thapathali, Kathmandu, although the office is not used to dealing with tourist queries. *Tiger Tops'* Kathmandu office sells a useful map of Chitwan National Park. Other than in Chitwan, maps simply don't exist in the parks themselves. **Trekking maps** are detailed in Chapter Seven.

All of the above maps are available in the bigger Kathmandu bookshops, although you'll save a little money by buying maps published outside of Nepal before you go.

GUIDES

Hiring a **guide** is a great way to get under the skin of Nepal: you'll have instant introductions everywhere you go, and will probably be invited home to meet the family, which will give a perspective on Nepalis' lives that you couldn't possibly gain on your own. You'll also learn all sorts of things you won't get from a book (Nepali swear words, for instance).

Most people only think of hiring a guide for a **trek** (more on this in Chapter Seven), but a guide is even more essential when tracking **wildlife** in the Tarai parks. A growing number of travellers are discovering that they can escape the crowds of Chitwan by hiring a guide there and then moving on to remoter parks, which are otherwise accessible only on an expensive package. A guide can also save you money and protect you from ripoffs when **shopping**.

Would-be guides often position themselves strategically at temples and palaces, but these "pay me what you will" characters often end up blackmailing you for more than they're worth. Better to go through an innkeeper, travel agent or someone you've already done business with.

An inexperienced guide hired informally may accept as little as Rs200 a day; someone with better English will demand up to Rs500 a day, and an agency will charge even more for a licensed guide. Generally, you get what you pay for.

GETTING AROUND

Travel in Nepal expands to fill the time allotted to it: no matter where you're going, it always seems to take all day to get there. Distances aren't great, but in a mountainous country there's no such thing as a straight line; paved roads are few, narrow and poorly maintained.

The usual way to get anywhere is by bus (apart from one short line around Janakpur, Nepal has no rail network), although the odd internal flight, if you can afford it, can save a good deal of time and discomfort. But the best way to experience Nepal is to walk or cycle — which often doesn't take much longer than going by bus.

BUSES

Buses ply every paved road in Nepal, as well as quite a few of the unpaved ones. The bus network is completely and chaotically privatized – there seem to be as many bus companies as there are buses, and as many ticket sellers as tickets – but there is some method to the madness. Except for the tourist services, all route prices are fixed. These depend less on distance than on the state of the road and the time it takes to make the journey; for day buses it works out to about Rs8–10 per hour, somewhat higher for night buses (see box).

Timetables are nonexistent and departure times are only approximate: always get a third opinion. You'll find details of the major bus routes listed at the end of each chapter.

Few travellers are ever quite prepared for the sheer **slowness** of bus travel in Nepal. Allowing for bad roads, overloaded buses, tea stops, meal stops, police checks, constant picking up and letting off of passengers, and the occasional flat tyre or worse, the average speed in the hills is barely 25km per hour; in the Tarai you might touch 50kph.

TOURIST BUSES

Regularly scheduled **tourist buses** connect Kathmandu with Pokhara, Tadi Bazaar (the access point for Chitwan National Park) and Nagarkot. Additional services may start up in time.

The vehicles are usually in good condition and the drivers know what they're doing, making for a much **safer** ride than in a regular bus. Tourist buses aren't supposed to take any more passengers than there are seats (they usually pick up a few anyway), so the journey should also be more comfortable and somewhat faster. Those billed as minibuses are slightly faster still. **Luggage** stored under the tarpaulin on the roof should be okay, but lock it just to be sure, and keep valuables with you inside.

Tickets (which cost roughly double the ordinary fare) are widely touted in Kathmandu and Pokhara, and buses depart from the tourist quarters of those cities, which saves you the trouble of hoofing down to the bus station (or the expense of taking a taxi).

SAJHA BUSES

Quasi-government *Sajha* buses run a limited day service between the major cities in central Nepal. Donated by Japan, these converted city buses are roomier, faster and also safer than regular buses (they're supposed to have good brakes). Because *Sajha* buses don't have roof racks, **luggage** must be stowed inside.

Tickets are only bookable the day before departure, usually through a special booth at or near the main bus station (see below). Departures are from the station.

EXPRESS AND NIGHT BUSES

Express buses hardly live up to their name, but after a ride in a local bus (see below) you'll know that there's at least some relative truth to it. Besides calling at all major towns en route, an express bus will stop as often as necessary on the way out of town until it's full, and will also let passengers off right and left as it approaches its final destination. That means there'll be a lot of humanity clogging up the aisles and competing for seats that are already too narrow for the average Western frame. Still, given a window seat, a sound vehicle and a sober driver (not always assured), it should be a tolerable trip.

Nepali **night buses** aren't as luxurious as those in other Asian countries, but for a few rupees more they do provide reclining seats and adequate legroom. Departures are in the late afternoon or early evening, to arrive the following morning – on relatively short routes, this means taking long meal breaks at horrible waysides in the middle of the night. Don't expect to get any sleep.

Express and night buses usually have a special hold where you can stow your **baggage** upon payment of a fee (up to fifty percent of the seat price). This is a very worthwhile insurance policy against theft, especially on night buses. You'll have to make the arrangements at the company's head office at the time of departure; make sure you get a receipt for your bag, and have any valuables noted on the receipt.

LOCAL BUSES

Local buses are ancient, battered contraptions with seats designed for midgets. Lack of safety is a real concern in these buses, which are often overworked, overloaded and poorly maintained. When you read a newspaper story about a bus plunging into a river, drowning some infeasibly large number of people, chances are it was a local.

With local buses, the idea is to cram as many passengers in the aisle as possible – indeed, a bus isn't making money until it's nearly full to bursting, and it can get awfully suffocating inside. This can lead to infuriating false starts, as the driver inches forward and the conductor runs around trying to round up customers, since no bus can leave the station with empty seats. Once on

the road, the bus will stop anytime it's flagged down. On shorter routes, buses have no fixed departure times and simply leave whenever they fill up. Long-distance buses tend to set off in the morning in order to arrive at their destination before dark.

Unless your **bag** is small, it will have to go on the roof; during daylight hours it should be safe there so long as it's locked, but again, keep all valuables on your person. **Riding on the roof** can actually be quite pleasant in good weather, but it's illegal and you'll only be allowed to do it in remote areas between checkposts – also bear in mind that in an accident it's the passengers on the roof who get mashed first.

STATIONS AND TICKETS

Open-air **bus stations** (*bas park* or *bas istand* in Nepali) are typically the smelliest, dustiest and muddiest parts of town. Each service will have a ticket booth or desk somewhere in the vicinity, though they're rarely marked in English – you just have to ask around, if you're not approached first. In Kathmandu and Pokhara you may find it easier to make arrangements through a ticket agent (but heed the warnings given in the "On from Kathmandu" section of Chapter One), while in other cities with inconveniently located bus stations you can ask your hotel to send someone to buy a ticket for you.

Tickets for longer journeys should be booked at least a day in advance – several days ahead during the big autumn festivals, when buses are packed with people heading back to their villages – or you could end up in one of the torture seats over the rear wheels. Always check the seating chart, if there is one, to see what's available. Normally seats can be reserved only at the bus's point of origin; getting on midway is seldom a problem, but you'll probably have to stand, or ride on the roof. Tickets for shorter journeys are purchased on board.

SAMPLE BUS FARES					
These fares were compiled when the exchange rate was Rs46=$1. Use them for relative purposes only. **Kathmandu to**:					
Bharabise	Rs70	Jiri	Rs80	Sunauli	Rs86
Birganj	Rs75	Kakarbitta	Rs200	Tadi Bazaar	Rs53
Gorkha	Rs43	Nepalganj	Rs210	Tansen	Rs100
Janakpur	Rs106	Pokhara	Rs70	Trisuli	Rs60

TRUCKS

If no buses are going your way, you can always flag down a **truck**. Mostly they're ungainly Indian-built Tatas, ferrying fuel to Kathmandu or building materials to hill boomtowns; many in the Tarai are "Public Carriers" – gaily decorated hauliers-for-hire from India. Almost all do a side-line in hauling passengers, and charge set fares comparable to what you'd pay on a bus. Fully laden, they go even slower than buses. The ride is comfortable enough if you get a seat in the cab, and certainly scenic if you have to sit or stand in the back – either way, the trip is bound to be eventful.

However, trucks aren't licensed as passenger vehicles, and so take little interest in passenger **safety**: watch your luggage. Women journeying by truck will probably prefer to join up with a companion.

If you're really stuck, you could try **hitching**. There aren't many private vehicles in Nepal, though, and anyone you manage to flag down will expect money.

PLANES

Internal flights aren't such a bargain now that tourists are charged inflated dollar prices on all routes. Even so, there may be times when $75 seems a small price to pay to avoid spending 24 hours on a bus, or a week retracing your steps along a trail.

Given Nepal's mountainous terrain, aircraft play a vital role in the country's transport network, especially in the west, where planes are often used to carry in food during the winter. Of the forty towns and villages with **airstrips**, almost half are two or more days' walk from a road. Most flights begin or end in Kathmandu, but two other **airports** in the Tarai – Nepalganj in the west, Biratnagar in the east – serve as secondary hubs. Popular destinations, such as Lukla in the Everest region, get up to six flights a day, while obscure airstrips may receive only one flight a week. Some operate only seasonally. For frequencies and flight times, see "Travel Details" at the end of each chapter.

In 1992, three new **airlines** – *Nepal Airways*, *Everest Air* and *Necon Air* – joined *RNAC* in providing services within Nepal. No one knows exactly how this privatization bid will play out. So far the consumer appears to be the winner, as competition has brought about better service and cut down on delays, but whether Nepal's tiny market can really support four airlines seems doubtful. Some observers foresee one or two going to the wall; others predict the newcomers will corner the profitable tourist routes, leaving *RNAC* with the remote subsidized services.

Book **tickets** through a travel agent, who will have a handle on who's flying where, and when. At off-peak times or away from the trekking routes – in the Tarai, for instance – you shouldn't have any trouble getting a seat. However, during

INTERNAL FLIGHTS

- All-weather airports
- Seasonal airstrips

TIBET

INDIA

0   100 km

Simikot
Darchula
Baitadi
Bajhang
Bajura
Dipayal
Jumla
Sanfebagar
Mahendranagar
Dhangadhi
Birendranagar
Dolpa
Jomosom
Chaurjhari
Tikapur
Manang
Rolpa
Baglung
Nepalganj
Dang
Pokhara
Bharatpur
KATHMANDU
Bhairawa
Meghauli
Lukla
Phaplu
Taplejung
Ramechhap
Rumjatar
Tumlingtar
Simara
Lamidanda
Bhojpur
Janakpur
Biratnagar

SAMPLE INTERNAL AIR FARES

The following are one-way fares on *RNAC* – other carriers' prices may vary slightly, and they're all bound to go up.

Kathmandu to:		Jumla	$127	Pokhara	$61
Bharatpur	$50	Lukla	$83	Taplejung	$110
Biratnagar	$77	Mahendranagar	$160	Tumlingtar	$44
Dhangadhi	$149	Meghauli	$72	**Pokhara to:**	
Janakpur	$55	Nepalganj	$99	Jomosom	$50

the trekking season, most flights out of airstrips along the popular trails are booked up months, even years, in advance by trekking agencies. If you're finding you can't get a seat, all is not lost. Agencies often **overbook**, releasing their unused tickets on the day of departure, so you may be able to buy a returned ticket from the airline that morning. If that's cutting it too fine, try offering the big agencies $10–20 over face value for one of their spares. Another strategy is to **go against the flow**: taking advantage of optimum weather, agencies all tend to fly their groups into the popular airstrips (Lukla, for instance) at the same peak times – so at those times you can often get a seat going in the *other* direction.

Buying a ticket is only half the battle, however, since any number of things can delay or cancel a flight, **weather** being the most common. Pilots will not fly if they can't see the ground (sensibly enough, considering some of the places they're expected to land). When planes are grounded, or commandeered by VIPs, **delays** multiply throughout the system. Since clouds usually increase as the day wears on, delays often turn into **cancellations**. If your flight is cancelled, rather than getting on the next available flight, you may be placed at the bottom of a waiting list; in busy times or during extended periods of bad weather, the wait can be several days. Pad your schedule accordingly.

DRIVING

Rented cars generally come with a driver in Nepal. Arranged through a travel agent in Kathmandu or Pokhara, a chauffeur-driven car will run to about $50–75 a day. It makes more sense to rent a taxi (see below). In any case, you're better off not having to grapple with Nepal's treacherous roads and daunting traffic laws: killing a cow carries the same penalty as killing a person, up to twenty years in prison.

But if you've brought your own vehicle into the country, here are some **driving tips**. First, drive defensively: Nepalis, normally so good-natured, become impatient maniacs behind the wheel (it has to do with status). Fortunately, it's only in Kathmandu that things get really hairy. Observance of traffic signals is fairly lax, and at some four-way junctions you may find the signal only controls traffic coming from two directions. On roundabouts, the biggest and boldest have priority. Drivers use their turning indicators only haphazardly; tempos and minibuses will often pull over without warning, so you have to learn to second-guess them. Finally, take special care around pedestrians, who, even in cosmopolitan Kathmandu, often behave as if they've just walked out of the forest.

Filling stations can be found on main roads at the outskirts af all major towns, so it's generally no problem getting fuel. At the time of writing, the cost of petrol was Rs29 per litre.

MOTORCYCLES

You won't exactly be helping Nepal's smog problem by renting a **motorcycle**, but you may well decide that if you can't beat 'em, join 'em – and there's no denying that motorcycling is a tremendously liberating way of getting around. It's just about the fastest way to travel moderate distances, allowing you to explore more country in less time than on a bicycle, and giving you much more flexibility about where and when to stop than on public transport. However, note that almost all rentals are 100cc models – that's enough power to take two riders up and down most Nepali roads, but you won't want to be travelling hundreds of kilometres on one.

Motorcycles can be rented in Kathmandu and Pokhara for about Rs400 a day; petrol is extra. You're supposed to produce a driving licence from your home country or an international driving licence (though they rarely ask to see it), and you'll be expected to leave an air ticket or a large sum of money as a deposit. Motorcycling carries some risk, and a serious drawback is that rented bikes carry no insurance – if you break anything, you pay for it. Stick to back roads (they're more pleasant anyway), and beware of wet dirt roads, which can be extremely slick.

BICYCLES

Renting a **bicycle** (*saikal*) spares you having to deal with any of the above. One-speeders (usually Indian-made *Hero* models) are good enough for most around-town cycling: they're incredibly heavy, but sturdy, and have built-in locks.

For a few rupees more, a **mountain bike** will get you there in greater comfort, and is essential for longer distances or anything steep. However, you don't always get what you pay for, and no rental is going to be up to any serious or remote use – for that you'll need to bring your own. Mountain bikes made in India are tinny and utterly unreliable; Taiwanese and Hong Kong models are poor cousins to the ones exported to the West, and they don't have a lot of staying power, but the better ones will see you through. (More tips on mountain biking are given in "Outdoor Pursuits", below, and on p.186.)

Cycles are rentable all over Kathmandu and Pokhara. Elsewhere, rental shops are rare, but you may be able to strike a deal with a lodge owner or cycle repairman. Check brakes, spokes, tyres and chain carefully before setting off – the last thing you want is for something to break on a remote mountain road. Repair shops are everywhere, but they won't have mountain bike parts.

A bell is pretty well essential if you plan to do any city pedalling. Theft is a concern, especially with a flashier bike – be sure to bring it inside your guest house compound at night.

CITY TRANSPORT

Few cities in Nepal are so large that you're dependent on public transport. Where available, **city buses** and minibuses are usually too crowded, slow or infrequent to be worthwhile. Three-wheeled, pedal-powered **rikshas**, common in Kathmandu and the Tarai, are slow and bumpy, but handy for short runs when you've got bags or aren't sure where you're going. Be sure to establish the fare before setting off (Rs5–20 per kilometre, depending on how touristy the place is).

Taxis, identified by black number plates and yellow tops, are confined mainly to Kathmandu and Pokhara, and you'll find details on their idiosyncrasies in the relevant sections; a metered ride should cost about Rs8–10 per kilometre, but on popular tourist routes, fixed fares work out to be around twice that. You can hire a taxi by the day for $15–50, depending on distance – worth considering to get to certain trekking trailheads with your wits intact.

Tempos (motor rikshas) – three-wheeled, passenger-carrying scooters – are nasty little beasts, putting out noxious fumes and jamming Kathmandu's streets, but they're a force to be reckoned with. They come in two forms. The ones with meters have room for two passengers and are more common than taxis, though only slightly cheaper. Others, operating on set routes, fit six (barely), set off when they're full, and usually charge only a few rupees per head.

ACCOMMODATION

Finding a place to sleep is hardly ever a problem in Nepal, although only the established tourist centres offer much of a choice.

GUEST HOUSES

Kathmandu and Pokhara have their own tourist quarters where fierce competition among **budget guest houses** (often called lodges) ensures great value for money. In these enclaves, even the cheapest places (Rs75 or less for a double) provide hot running water, flush toilets, foam mattresses and clean sheets. They're never heated – they can be very cold in winter – but most offer a garden or roof terrace, a supply of (supposedly) boiled and filtered water and a phone. Innkeepers speak excellent English, and can arrange anything for you from laundry to trekking-porter hire. Nepal has only a couple of **youth hostels**, in Patan and Pokhara.

Upmarket guest houses (for lack of a better term) are becoming increasingly popular. These tend to be more spacious, private buildings with carpeting and furniture in the rooms, toilet paper in the bathrooms, and maybe a lobby of sorts; the better ones will provide an electric heater in winter. Most are registered with the government, which means they quote their prices in dollars (about $5–12 for a double with attached shower) and add ten percent tax on top. Many of them even accept payment by credit card.

Off the beaten track, however, you may have to settle for something less salubrious: stark concrete floors (painted red to hide the betel stains), cold-water showers and smelly squat toilets are the rule, and often not much English is spoken. Sheets and cotton quilts are usually provided, but it's a good idea to bring your own sleeping sheet (a sleeping bag is seldom necessary). Noise is always a problem – bring earplugs. In the Tarai, mosquito netting (or mosquito coils) and a ceiling fan that works are crucial. Sometimes, though, the most primitive lodges – the ones with no electricity, where you sit on the mud floor by a smoky fire and eat with your hosts – can be the most rewarding of all.

Trekking inns are another matter altogether, and are described in Chapter Seven.

The cheeriest and most efficiently run guest houses are highlighted throughout the guide, but remember that recommendations are often self-defeating and can result in instant price hikes. Also, watch out for name-changes, a common ploy to evade taxes (or a bad reputation).

HOTELS AND JUNGLE LODGES

It's hard to generalize about the more **expensive hotels**. Most – usually the bigger ones – are overpriced and insulate guests from the Nepal they came to see, but there are a few admirable exceptions which, in their own way, offer unique experiences of the country. After a trek or a long spell of roughing it, a night or two in one of these hotels can be just what the doctor ordered. A government rating system awards hotels from one to five stars, but this is a vaguer guide to quality than price. Rated hotels add ten to fifteen percent tax, according to their number of stars.

Jungle lodges and tented camps inside the Tarai wildlife parks are the most expensive hotels of all; a stay in one is indeed the experience of a lifetime, but if $100–200 a night is beyond your reach there are plenty of more affordable outfits just outside Chitwan National Park.

CAMPING

Perhaps surprisingly, **camping** doesn't come high on the agenda in Nepal. Much of the country is well settled, every flat patch of ground is farmed, and rooms are so cheap that camping offers little savings. The only developed campsites are in Kathmandu and Pokhara.

It's a different story, of course, if you're rafting or trekking, and camping is (theoretically) permitted in the Tarai wildlife parks. Long-distance cyclists might also find it useful to bring

---

ROOM PRICE SCALES

All guest houses and hotels in this book have been price-graded according to the scale outlined below. The rates quoted represent the cheapest available double room in high season – at other times, you should be able to secure a room at a rate of one or even two grades below that given. You should also be able to negotiate a better rate for longer stays. In the lowest categories, the cheapest rooms will generally be those with a "common" (shared) bathroom. Where all rooms come with their own attached bath, this is denoted by a B prefix to the code. Where both common and attached baths are available, two codes are given – for example, ①/B②.

Single travellers can usually expect a discount of 20 to 40 percent off the price of a double.

① Less than Rs75 ($1.50 if quoted in US dollars)			
② Rs75–150 ($1.50–3)	③ Rs150–250 ($3–5)	④ $5–8	⑤ $8–12
⑥ $12–20	⑦ $20–40	⑧ $40–70	⑨ Over $70

a **tent** along, to avoid spending nights in roadside flea-pits en route to more interesting places. Between October and May many terraces are left fallow, and farmers won't expect you to ask permission to camp so long as you're respectful.

Set up well away from villages, unless you want to be the locals' entertainment for the evening. Don't burn wood. An unattended tent will probably be safe if zipped shut, but anything left outside is liable to be pinched.

EATING AND DRINKING

Nepal — specifically Kathmandu — is renowned as the budget eating capital of Asia. Sadly, its reputation is based not on Nepali food, but on the skilful aping of Continental and other cuisines: pizza, chips (fries), "buff" (buffalo) steaks and apple pie are the staples of tourist restaurants. Outside the popular areas, travellers' chief complaint is the blandness of the diet.

Yet Nepal lies at the intersection of two great culinary traditions, Indian and Chinese, and if you know what to look for you'll find good, native renditions of everthing from tandoori to stir-fried dishes. The simple cooking of the hills — Nepal's heartland — is essentially a regional variation of north Indian, comprising rice, lentils, curried vegetables and meats, and chutneys. In the Tarai, *roti* (bread) and the vast range of Indian snacks and sweets comes into play, while in the mountains the diet is essentially Tibetan, consisting of soups, pastas, potatoes and breads.

WHERE TO EAT

Enterprising budget **tourist restaurants** in Kathmandu and Pokhara show an uncanny knack for sensing exactly what travellers want and simulating it with the most basic ingredients. Some specialize in Italian, "Continental", Chinese, Tibetan, Indian, Mexican or even Japanese food, but the majority attempt to do a little of everything; display cases full of extravagant cakes and pies are a standard come-on. There's no denying that the food is tasty — especially after a trek — but the scene has grown progressively more gross and surreal over the years, and quite a few travellers end up getting sick from the food in such places (see "Health").

Tourist restaurants are notoriously hard to recommend, as chefs are forever jumping ship and taking their menus with them. And don't assume that a crowded place must have good food: tourists tend to judge restaurants by their ambience, and in any case the more diners there are, the slower the service will be. That said, a popular restaurant's high turnover should ensure fresher ingredients.

Local **Nepali restaurants** (*bhojanalaya*) are traditionally humble affairs, offering a limited choice of dishes (or no choice at all). Menus don't exist, but the food will normally be on display or cooking in full view, so all you have to do is point. Utensils should be available on request, but if not, try doing as Nepalis do and eat with your hand — the right one only (see "Cultural Hints" for more on social taboos relating to eating). In towns and cities, eateries tend to be dark, almost conspiratorial places, unmarked and hidden behind curtains. On the highways they're bustlingly public and spill outdoors in an effort to win business. Tarai cities always have a fancy (by Nepali standards) restaurant or two, patronized by businessmen and Indian tourists. Confusingly, restaurants are often called "hotels"; hotels are called "lodges".

It might take some time before you start appreciating the fine differences between *bhojanalaya* and other traditional establishments. **Teahouses** (*chiya pasal*) really only sell tea and basic snacks, while the simple **taverns** (*bhatti*) of the Kathmandu Valley and the western hills serve alcoholic drinks and basic Nepali meals.

Trailside, both *chiya pasal* and *bhatti* are typically modest operations run out of family kitchens. **Sweet shops** (*mitho pasal*), found in bigger towns and identified by their display cases of sweets, also do tea and perhaps yoghurt (usually called curd; *dahi* in Nepali) and beaten rice.

Street vendors sell fruit, nuts, roasted corn, fried bread and, in the Tarai, various fried specialities. But when you're travelling, as often as not the food will come to you — at every bus stop, vendors will clamber aboard or hawk their dishes through the window.

Vegetarians will feel at home in Nepal, since meat is considered a luxury. Imaginative preparations are rare, though: rice, lentils, vegetable curry and noodles are the standard offerings everywhere. As a rule, vegetarian dishes get more interesting and varied the closer you get to India, with some orthodox Hindu restaurants near the border billing themselves as vegetarian-only. Tourist menus invariably include meatless items, which are often excellent.

Nepalis generally start the day with nothing more than a cup of tea, eat a full meal around mid-morning, then carry on until the second big meal of the day at dinnertime. The Western concept of **breakfast** doesn't tie in very well. Again, tourist restaurants have this covered — many do excellent set breakfast deals, with eggs, porridge, muesli and the like — but out in the sticks you'll have to adjust your eating schedule, or make do with a greasy omelette or packet noodles.

NEPALI AND NEWARI FOOD

Daal bhaat tarkaari (lentil soup, white rice and curried vegetables) isn't just the most popular meal in Nepal — for many Nepalis it's the *only* meal they ever eat, twice a day, every day of their lives; indeed, in much of hill Nepal, *bhaat* is a synonym for food. It's a potentially boring dish, admittedly, and if you spend much time trekking or travelling off the beaten track you'll probably quickly tire of it. That said, a good **achhaar** (chutney) — made with tomato, radish, wild plum or whatever grows locally — can liven up a *daal bhaat* tremendously. The food will invariably be served on a *thali*, a gleaming steel platter divided into compartments; one price covers unlimited refills, except in a few establishments that adhere to the "plate system". Add the *daal* and other condiments to the rice in the main compartment, a little at a time, knead the resulting

mixture into mouth-sized balls with the right hand, then push it off the fingers into your mouth with the thumb.

You'll often be able to supplement a plate of *daal bhaat* with small side dishes of **maasu** (meat), marinated in yoghurt and spices and fried in *ghiu* (clarified butter) or oil. In Indian-influenced Tarai towns you can often get *taareko daal*, fried with ghee and spices to produce a tastier variation, and *roti* (bread) instead of rice. **Soups** (*surwa*) are sometimes available: *tama surwa*, made with bamboo shoots, is popular. You could make a meal out of rice and **sekuwa** (kebabs of spicy marinated meat chunks) or **taareko maachhaa** (fried fish), both common in the Tarai. Nepali **desserts** include *khir* (rice pudding) and *sikarni* (thick, whipped yoghurt with cinnamon, raisins and nuts). Other traditional Nepali dishes are more localized, or reserved for special occasions, but well worth the effort of tracking them down.

The **Newars** of the Kathmandu Valley have many specialities of their own, most of them based around two mainstays, buffalo and radish. The Newars use every part of the buffalo: **choyala** (buff cubes fried with spices and greens), **kachila** (a paté of minced raw buff, mixed with ginger and mustard oil) and **momocha** (meat-filled steamed dumplings) are the more accessible dishes; others are made from tongue, stomach, blood, brain, bone marrow and so on. Beans play a role in several other preparations, notably **kwati** (a soup made with several varieties of sprouted beans) and **woh** (black lentil flour pancakes). Various vegetable mixtures are available seasonally, and radish turns up in myriad forms of *achhaar*. Order two or three of these dishes per person, together with *bhaat* or *chiura* (beaten rice, a common dry substitute for cooked rice), and share them around.

INDIAN FOOD

A full description of Indian dishes isn't possible here. The ones you're most likely to encounter in Kathmandu are from **northern India**, such as **Mughlai** curries (thick, creamy and mildly spiced) and **tandoori** meats (baked in a clay oven, called a *tandoor*, with special spices). *Roti* (bread) is the accompaniment to north Indian cuisine: *chapati* (round, flat pieces of unleavened bread) are always available in Indian restaurants, *naan* (bigger, chewier and puffier versions of the same), *paratha* (fried bread) and *papad* (pappa-

A GLOSSARY OF FOOD TERMS

The following list should give an idea of what to ask for in restaurants, although tourist places will usually have an English menu.

Basics

Bread	*Roti*	Innkeeper (male)	*Sahuji*	Rice (uncooked)	*Chaamal*
The bill	*Bil*	(female)	*Sahuni*	Rice (beaten)	*Chiura*
Butter	*Makhan*	Knife	*Chakku*	Salt	*Nun*
Chutney, Pickle	*Achhaar*	Milk	*Dudh*	Spoon	*Chamchaa*
Egg	*Phul*	Oil	*Tel*	Sugar	*Chini*
Food	*Khaanaa*	Pepper (ground)	*Marich*	Sweets, Candy	*Mithaai*
Fork	*Kaata*	Plate	*Plet*	Water	*Paani*
Glass	*Gilaas*	Rice (cooked)	*Bhaat*	Yoghurt, Curd	*Dahi*

Common Nepali Dishes

Daal bhaat tarkaari	Lentil soup, white rice and curried vegetables.	*Samosa*	Pyramids of pastry filled with curried vegetables.
Dahi chiura	Curd with beaten rice.		
Pakauda	Vegetables dipped in chickpea-flour batter, deep fried.	*Sekuwa*	Spicy, marinated meat kebab.
		Taareko maachhaa	Fried fish.

Common Tibetan Dishes

Momo	Pasta shells filled with meat, vegetables and ginger, steamed.	*Thukpa*	Soup containing pasta, meat and vegetables.
Kothe	The same, fried.	*Tsampa*	Toasted barley flour.

Vegetables (*Saabji* or *Tarkaari*)

Aubergine	*Bhanta*	Coriander	*Dhaniyaa*	Peas	*Kerau, Matar*
Beans	*Simi*	(Cilantro)		Potato	*Alu*
Cabbage	*Banda Kobi*	Corn	*Makai*	Pumpkin	*Pharsi*
Carrot	*Gaajar*	Garlic	*Lasun*	Radish	*Mulaa*
Cauliflower	*Kaauli*	Lentils	*Daal*	Spinach, Greens	*Palungo,*
Chickpeas	*Chaana*	Mushroom	*Chyaau*		*Saag*
Chili pepper	*Khursaani*	Onion	*Pyaaj*	Tomato	*Golbheda*

Meat (*Maasu*)

Beef	*Gaiko maasu* (rare: taboo for most Nepalis)	Chicken	*Kukhuraako maasu*
		Mutton	*Khasiko maasu*
Buffalo ("Buff")	*Raangaako maasu*	Pork	*Bungurko maasu*

Fruit (*Phalphul*) and Nuts

Apple	*Syaau*	Lemon	*Kagati*	Peanut	*Badaam* (*Mampale*
Banana	*Keraa*	Lime	*Nibuwaa*		near India)
Cashew	*Kaaju*	Mango	*Aaph*	Pineapple	*Bhuikatahar*
Coconut	*Nariwal*	Orange,	*Suntalaa*	Pistachio	*Pista*
Date	*Chhokada*	Mandarin		Raisin	*Kismis*
Guava	*Ambaa*	Papaya	*Mewaa*	Sugar cane	*Ukhu*

Spices (*Masaala*)

Aniseed	*Sop*	Chili	*Khursaani*	Ginger	*Aduwaa*
Cardamom	*Sukumel,*	Cinnamon	*Daalchini*	Saffron	*Kkesari*
	Elaaichi	Clove	*Lwang*	Turmeric	*Besaar*

Some common terms			
A little	Alikati	Delicious	Mitho
A lot	Dherai	Hot	Taato
Another	Aarko	Spicy	Piro
Boiled (water)	Umaaleko (paani)	Stir-fried	Bhuteko
Cooked	Paakeko	Sweet	Guliyo
Cold	Chiso	Vegetarian	Sahakaari
Deep-fried	Taareko	I don't eat meat	Ma maasu khaanna

dums – crispy fried starters made from chickpea flour) usually so. In the Tarai the best bets are **masaala** (meaning spicy, although it isn't really) curries, and you generally can't go wrong with **kofta**, spiced vegetable dumplings in curry.

In Kathmandu you'll also run across **south Indian** canteens, which serve a completely different and predominantly vegetarian cuisine. The staple dish here is the **dosa**, a rice-flour pancake rolled around curried potatoes and vegetables, served with **sambar** (a savoury tamarind sauce) and coconut chutney. You can also get *idli* (mashed rice, usually accompanied with *sambar*), *dahi vada* (lentil-flour dumplings in curd) and various vegetable curries.

And as for the incredible array of Indian **sweets**, well, that could fill a book in itself. A selection: *laddu*, yellow and orange speckled chewy balls; *jelebi*, deep-fried pretzels of sweetened batter; *barphi*, fudgy squares made from reduced milk, often decorated with edible silver leaf; *koloni*, a softer version of the same; *lal mohan*, brown spongy balls in sweet syrup; and *ras malai*, sweet spongy cakes in cream. Really good sweets are only found in the bigger Tarai towns – Nepali attempts just don't cut it.

TIBETAN FOOD

Strictly speaking, "Tibetan" refers to nationals of Tibet, but the people of the Nepal Himalaya, collectively known as Bhotiyas, together with the people of several other highland ethnic groups, all eat what could be called Tibetan food.

Momo, arguably the most famous and popular of Tibetan dishes, are available throughout hill Nepal. Distant cousins to ravioli, the half-moon-shaped pasta shells are filled with meat, vegetables and ginger, steamed, and served with hot tomato *achhaar* and a bowl of broth. Fried *momo* are called *kothe*. Put the same stuffing ingredients inside a flour pastry shell and fry it and you get *shyaphagle*, a sort of Tibetan meat pie.

Tibetan cuisine is also justly celebrated for its excellent hearty soups, collectively called **thukpa**, consisting of homemade pasta strips or noodles, meat and vegetables in broth.

For a special blow-out, try **gyakok**, a huge meal for two that includes chicken, pork, prawns, fish, tofu, eggs and vegetables, and which gets its name from the brass container it's served in; *gyakok* is only found in tourist restaurants and has to be ordered several hours ahead. In trekking lodges you'll encounter frisbee-shaped items called **Tibetan bread** which, though unappealing on their own, are made more interesting by the addition of honey or peanut butter.

The average Tibetan seldom eats any of the above: the most common standbys in the high country are **potatoes**, boiled or made into pancakes (*riki kur*), and **tsampa** – toasted barley flour, mixed with milk or tea to make a sort of gruel, or eaten plain.

ROAD FOOD AND SNACKS

Road food is a genre in itself – there's certainly no need to go hungry when you're travelling. If you've time to sit down, ask for a plate of **pakauda**, fried, bready nuggets of battered vegetables, served with hot sauce, or **tarkaari ra roti**, vegetable (usually bean) curry served with a few pieces of fried bread that in India would be called puris. Another refreshing possibility is **dahi chiura**, a mixture of yoghurt and beaten rice that isn't so different from the "muesli curd" served in tourist restaurants. If you're in more of a hurry, you can always grab a handful of **samosa**, fried pyramids of pastry filled with curried vegetables, or carry away *daal paara* (fried lentil patties), *chap* (potato and garlic, battered and fried), *taareko phul* (boiled egg, battered and fried) or other titbits on a leaf plate.

If nothing else, there will always be packet **noodles** (usually referred to by brand name: *Rara, Maggi, Waiwai* or *Yum Yum*), which can

TOBACCO AND *PAAN*

Nepalis love their **cigarettes** (*churot*). Even if you don't smoke, consider carrying a pack – cigarettes are much appreciated as tips. Factories in Janakpur and Birganj manufacture dozens of cheap brands, most of them from a mixture of Nepali and Indian tobacco. The most popular filtered brands are *Shikhar*, *Yak* and *Khukuri*; cheap non-filters such as *Bijuli* and *Deurali* are big with porters. Cheapest of all are **bidi**, rolled single leaves of the poorest tobacco, tied together in bundles of twenty (ask for *ek muthaa*). After the evening meal, old men will often be seen smoking tobacco in a **hookah** (hubble-bubble), or occasionally passing around a *chillum* (clay pipe).

Many Nepali men make quite a show of preparing **snuff** (*surti*), slapping and rubbing it in the palm of their hand and mixing it with lime before placing a pinch behind the lower lip. *Surti* comes in little foil packets hung outside *kiraana pasal*, village stalls that sell cigarettes, matches, biscuits and the like.

At least as popular, particularly near India, is **paan**, the tobacco-like indulgence that Westerners often wrongly call **betel**. *Paan* sellers sit like priests in their little booths, and ordering *paan* is a hallowed ritual. The *paan* wallah starts with a betel leaf, upon which he spreads five basic ingredients: *katha* (a special paste that produces *paan*'s characteristic red colour), *chuna* (a spice), *supaari* (a nut), *mitha masaala* (a mixture of sweet spices) and lime paste (to leach the other ingredients). After that, the possibilities are endless, although in general most *paan* will be either of the *jharda* (tobacco) or *mitha* (sweet) variety. For those who haven't got time for the whole performance, *paan* wallahs also sell foil packets of *paan parag*, a simple, ready-made *jharda* mix. Other than nicotine in the tobacco, there's nothing narcotic about *paan*.

either be boiled as a soup or stir-fried as **chow mein**. Roadside vendors peddle **chatpate** (a mixture of peas or soybeans, radish, chilli, salt and lemon, all whisked together and served on a leaf), roasted peanuts, coconut slivers, corn on the cob, *sel roti* (doughnuts), and whatever **fruit** is in season – in winter, have a chomp on a length of sugar cane.

Imported **chocolates** are sold in Kathmandu and Pokhara, and waxy Indian substitutes can be found in most towns. **Biscuits** and cheap boiled sweets are sold at roadside stalls everywhere. *Kwality* **ice cream**, available throughout the Kathmandu Valley and Pokhara, is safe. **Cheese**, a relatively recent innovation produced from buffalo and yak milk, comes in several styles and is sold in tourist areas and "factories" along trekking routes. (In the hills you might also come across *churpi*, a native version of cheese made from dried buttermilk or yoghurt – it's inedibly hard, and is normally softened by being added to soup.)

DRINKS

Tea (*chiya*), something of a national beverage in Nepal, comes with milk (*dudh*) and heaps of sugar (*chini*) unless you insist otherwise. Tibetans and Bhotiyas take it with salt and yak butter, which is definitely an acquired taste. Tourist establishments also produce lemon tea and "hot lemon". **Coffee** (*kaphi*) is instant and undistinguished – "espresso" is a big buzzword on tourist menus these days, but aside from a few notable exceptions it's made with Nescafé.

Water (*paani*) is automatically served with food in Nepali restaurants – unless you really know what you're doing, stick to the bottled stuff (*Bisleri* and *Star*). Inexpensive **soft drinks** are safe and sold in "cold stores" just about everywhere, but prices rise steadily as you move into roadless areas; *Coke*, *7-Up* and most other international brands are available. Fresh lemon soda, made with lemon (or lime) juice and soda water, makes a good alternative if you want to cut out sugar. Tourist restaurants serve freshly squeezed **fruit juices** – orange, apple, mango, guava and papaya, according to season – but the mark-up on these is enormous, and roadside juice shacks have turned it into a real racket. Tinned juice and fruit drinks in cartons are widely available. A **lassi**, a blend of yoghurt, water or ice (beware), sugar and fruit (or salt), always goes down nicely, and helps take the heat out of a curry.

Beer (*biyar*) makes another fine accompaniment to Nepali and Indian food. *Tuborg* and *San Miguel*, brewed locally with foreign assistance, are serviceable lagers and have taken over the market in short order. Of the local brands, *Iceberg* is full-bodied but heavy, while *Star*, the cheapest, is on the rough side. All of these come in 650ml bottles, occasionally in (non-recyclable) aluminium cans.

An amazing and amusing selection of ersatz **spirits** is bottled in Nepal, ranging from *Ruslan* vodka to *Ye Grand Earl* whisky ("Glasgow – London – Kathmandu"). They're cheap and on the whole nasty, but tolerable if disguised by liberal quantities of soft drinks. *Khukuri 'XXX'* rum is actually quite palatable with Coke. Imported spirits and wine are exorbitant. Look out for regional specialities like the apricot and apple brandies of Marpha, north of Pokhara, and the aniseed-based *dudhiya* (so called because it goes milky when added to water) of the eastern Tarai. Unless you're desperate, give so-called "country liquors" such as *Urvashi* a miss. Shops sell spirits in convenient quarter-litre bottles, restaurants by the "peg" (measure). You can even get improvised **cocktails** in Kathmandu's tourist bars.

Nepalis are avid home brewers and distillers. ***Chhang*** is the generic term for any beer made from rice or other grains, typically fermented in cast-off mountaineering expedition barrels; cloudy (sometimes almost porridgy) unfiltered *chhang* is called *jaand*. **Raksi**, the most popular alcoholic drink in Nepal, is a distilled version of the same and bears a heady resemblance to tequila. Harder to find, but perhaps the most pleasant drink of all, is a brew-it-yourself Sherpa concoction called **tongba**. The ingredients are a jug of fermented millet, a straw and a flask of hot water: you pour the water in, let it steep, and suck the mildly alcoholic brew through the straw until you reach the bottom; repeat four or five times. Two *tongba* can easily lubricate an entire evening.

COMMUNICATIONS: POST, PHONES AND THE MEDIA

Due to Nepal's isolation, it's not hard to fall out of touch with the rest of the world while you're there. International telephoning is surprisingly easy – though expensive – but post is usually slow and patchy, and English-language newspapers and magazines are only available in two major cities.

POST

Mail takes at least ten days, sometimes a lot longer, to get to or from Nepal. Nepal's main **Poste Restante** service, in Kathmandu, is reasonably efficient, the one in Pokhara less so. Mail should be addressed: Poste Restante, GPO,

Kathmandu, Nepal. Letters are filed alphabetically in self-serve trays. To reduce the risk of misfiling, your name should be printed clearly with the surname underlined or capitalized; it's still always a good idea to check under your first initial, too. Oversized envelopes are filed on separate shelves. Parcels can be received, but they may not arrive intact, so anything of value should be sent registered. Mail is held for about two months, and can be redirected on request.

American Express handles mail only in Kathmandu (see "Listings" at the end of Chapter One). You need to be carrying *Amex* cheques or a card to use the service. US citizens can receive mail c/o the Consular Section of the **American Embassy** in Kathmandu.

Send letters or cards from Kathmandu, where they've got a higher probability of reaching their destination. If you must send them from another town, take them to the post office and have the stamps franked before your eyes. Never use a letterbox: the stamps will be removed and resold, and your correspondence will be used to wrap peanuts. Some guest houses and shops will take mail to the post office for you, but make sure they're reliable. **Post offices** in the major cities sell stamps and aerogrammes for overseas posting – opening hours are given in the guide.

Sending **parcels** is a whole other story. The cheapest method, but thoroughly exasperating, is to take it yourself to the Foreign Post Section, around the corner from the Kathmandu GPO (Mon–Fri & Sun 10.15am–1.30pm). Bring the parcel packed, but open for inspection. You begin by filling out a yellow customs form and paying a small tax on the value of the item (no prizes for being truthful). Then a wizened old man stitches the parcel up in cheesecloth (about Rs100) and you have it officially sealed with wax, and finally the parcel is weighed (surface rates are Rs500–800 for the first kg and Rs150–200 for each additional kg, depending on destination). The whole business takes an hour and a half even if there's no queue, and you're wise to set aside the whole morning.

Shipping agents in Kathmandu will do all this work for you (and provide packing materials), but their tariffs are somewhat higher than the post office's. Be sure you're dealing with a reputable company (a few are recommended at the end of the Kathmandu chapter). **Air freight services** are competitive with the post office's air mail, and more reliable. Don't entrust shipping to a handicrafts shop unless it's tied to a major hotel.

PHONES

Public **phones** in Nepal are rare indeed, and usually broken. Tourist lodges will let you make **local calls** for a few rupees, trunk calls for about Rs30 per minute. Phone numbers change frequently: **directory enquiries** (☎197) might be able to help.

Making **international calls** is easy from Kathmandu and Pokhara, where even lowly guest houses have direct-dialling facilities. In recent years, entrepreneurs have set up tourist telephone services on every corner – all they need to get started is a phone, a table, a chair and a stopwatch. These businesses advertise themselves with the acronyms **ISD/STD/IDD** (international subscriber dialling/standard trunk dialling/international direct dialling). Rates are Rs150–200 per minute, depending on the country (minimum 3min). You can save 20–25 percent if you're willing to brave the queues at a telegraph office in one of the bigger cities or a local telephone office in one of the growing number of smaller towns with satellite link-ups. At the time of writing it was only possible to **call collect** from Nepal to the UK, Canada and Japan, but most guest houses will let you have your party call you back (ISD places charge a fee for this).

Many of the international dialling joints and luxury hotels have **fax** services. **Telegrams** can be sent from the Central Telegraph Office in Kathmandu, but a twenty-word message will cost you more than a three-minute phone call. Incoming telegrams can be collected at Poste Restante.

THE MEDIA

Despite only 40-percent literacy, Nepal boasts an astonishing 460 **newspapers** – an outgrowth of two noble Brahmanic traditions, punditry and gossip. Of the handful printed in English, only the *Rising Nepal* is widely circulated, and outside Kathmandu it's always a day or more out of date. It's pretty much a government mouthpiece, but still manages in spite of itself to shed light on current events in Nepal. The weekly *Independent* (published Wednesdays, available only in the capital) covers issues with greater candour and depth, but it's aimed at political insiders. **Foreign publications** such as the *International Herald Tribune*, *USA Today*, *Asian Wall Street Journal*, *Time* and *Newsweek* are sold in Kathmandu and Pokhara, but nowhere else. For British newspapers, try the British Council in Kathmandu.

The government-run **Radio Nepal** is by far the most influential of the nation's media, catering to the illiterate majority of Nepalis and reaching villages well beyond the reach of any newspaper. With a daily format of traditional and pop music, news bulletins, English language lessons, dramas and development messages, it has been a powerful force for cultural and linguistic unity, though demands by various ethnic groups for programming in their native tongues has recently become a hot political topic. The station carries English-language news bulletins daily at 8am and 8pm, and relays the **BBC World Service** in Kathmandu from 11pm to 12.15am. If you're travelling with a short-wave radio, you can pick up the World Service at 15.31, 11.75 and 9.74 MHz.

Nepal-TV, with transmitters in Kathmandu, Pokhara and Biratnagar, broadcasts Nepali and Indian shows mainly in the early morning and evening, with the news in English at 9.40pm – check the daily schedule in the *Rising Nepal*. **STAR satellite TV**, out of Hong Kong, beams MTV, BBC World Service TV and various American reruns.

OPENING HOURS AND HOLIDAYS

Shops in Nepal keep long hours, and in tourist areas usually stay open seven days a week. But when dealing with officialdom remember that Saturday, not Sunday, is the day of rest – and bureaucrats like to knock off early on Friday, too.

In theory, **government offices**, **post offices** and **museums** are open Mon–Thurs & Sun 10am–5pm, Fri 10am–3pm; in winter (mid-Feb to mid-Nov), closing time is 4pm Mon–Thurs & Sun. These schedules often get truncated at either end, though.

Banks in tourist areas are generous with their hours (see the "Listings" sections in the guide), but elsewhere you'll have to do your transactions between 10am and 2pm Mon–Thurs & Sun, 10am–noon on Fri. **Travel agents** tend to work a five-day week, 9am or 10am–6pm, Mon–Fri; airline offices are the same but they take a lunch break at 1–2pm. **Embassy** and consulate hours are all over the place: see the Kathmandu chapter for a rundown.

Complicating matters is Nepal's hectic calendar of **festivals** and **holidays**, which can shut down offices for up to a week at a time. Dates vary from year to year – Nepal has its own calendar, beginning in mid-April and consisting of twelve months that are completely out of step with the Western ones. (The Vikram Sambat calendar began in 57 BC. Thus the Nepali year beginning in April 1994 is 2051 VS.) Religious festivals, meanwhile, are calculated according to the *lunar* calendar (see the next section). Tibetan festivals follow yet a different calendar.

NATIONAL HOLIDAYS

Prithvi Narayan Shah's Birthday – January 10 or 11.

Basanta Panchami – late January or early February.

Shiva Raatri – late February or early March.

Democracy Day – February 18 or 19.

Nawa Barsa (Nepali New Year) – April 13 or 14.

Janai Purnima – late July or early August.

Dasain – a full week off in October.

Tihaar – three days off in late October or early November.

Queen's Birthday – November 7 or 8.

Constitution Day – December 15 or 16.

King's Birthday – December 28 or 29.

Guru Purnima – late June or early July.

FESTIVALS AND ENTERTAINMENT

Stumbling, perhaps accidentally, onto a village festival may prove to be the highlight of your travels in Nepal (and given the sheer number of them, you'd be hard pressed not to). Though most are religious in nature, merrymaking, not solemnity, is the order of the day, and onlookers are always welcome. However, some celebrations, while public, are also personal: don't photograph worshippers without asking permission.

Music and dance are also integral parts of the culture – so much so that they can only be briefly introduced here; for more detailed coverage, see *Contexts*.

FESTIVALS

Festivals are a sophisticated brand of performance art in Nepal, as exotic as the religions that underlie them, which may be Hindu, Buddhist, animist or a hybrid of all three (see *Contexts*). **Hindu events** can take the form of huge pilgrimages and fairs (*mela*), or more introspective gatherings such as ritual bathings at sacred confluences (*tribeni*) or special acts of worship (*puja*) at temples. Many involve animal sacrifices and jolly family feasts afterwards, with priests and musicians usually on hand. Parades and processions (*jaatra*) are common, especially in the Kathmandu Valley, where idols are periodically ferried around on great, swaying chariots. **Buddhist festivals** are no less colourful, typically bringing together maroon-robed clergy and lay pilgrims to walk and prostrate around stupas (dome-shaped monuments, usually repainted specially for the occasion), chant from sacred texts and make splendid, otherworldly music.

Festival **dates** vary from year to year, as most are governed by the lunar calendar, and determining them more than a year in advance is a highly complicated business best left to astrologers. Each lunar cycle is divided into "bright" (waning)

and "dark" (waxing) halves, which are in turn divided into fourteen lunar "days". Each of these days has a name – *purnima* is the full moon, *astami* the eighth day, *aunsi* the new moon, and so on. Thus lunar festivals are always observed on a given day of either the bright or dark half of a given Nepali month. Confused? The easiest strategy is just to consult a current Nepali calendar (sold in tourist bookshops) or, less reliably, a tourist information office.

Similarly jubilant (and public), Nepali **weddings** are always scheduled on astrologically auspicious days, which fall in the greatest numbers during the months of Faagun, Magh, Chaitra and Baisakh (see festival box). The approach of a wedding party is often heralded by the sound of a hired brass band – one of colonialism's stranger legacies, sounding like a Dixieland sextet playing in a pentatonic scale – and open-air feasts go on until the early hours. The bride usually wears red – an auspicious colour – and for the rest of her married life she will colour the parting of her hair with red *sindur*.

Funeral processions are understandably sombre and should be left in peace. The body is normally carried to the cremation site within hours of death by white-shrouded relatives; white

---

NEPAL'S MAJOR FESTIVALS

Nepal doesn't have any truly national festivals, but the following are the most widely observed events, plus a few notable local ones worth trying to coincide with. Many other local festivals are listed at the end of each chapter.

MAGH (Jan–Feb)

Magh Sankranti – Looking forward to warmer weather and lengthening days, the first day of Magh (Jan 14 or 15) is an occasion for ritual bathing at all sacred river confluences. More bathing takes place on the new-moon day after Magh Sankranti, especially at Devghat.

Basanta Panchami – A one-day spring festival celebrated on the fifth day after the new moon in most Hindu hill areas. School playgrounds are decorated with streamers and children have their books and pens blessed.

FAAGUN (Feb–March)

Losar – Tibetan New Year falls on the new moon of February and is celebrated with three days of drinking, dancing and feasting. This is the highlight of the calendar in Buddhist highland areas, as well as in Boudha and other Tibetan settlements near Kathmandu and Pokhara.

Shiva Raatri – Falling on the new moon of Faagun, "Shiva's Night" is marked by bonfires and evening vigils in all Hindu areas, but most spectacularly at Pashupatinath, where tens of thousands of pilgrims and sadhus (holy men) gather for Nepal's best-known *mela* (religious fair). Children collect firewood money by holding pieces of string across the road to block passersby – foreigners are considered easy prey. Nepalis say the festival is usually followed by a final few days of winter weather, which is Shiva's way of encouraging the Indian sadhus to go home.

Faagun Purnima (Holi near India) – Nepal's version of the spring water festival, common to many Asian countries, is an impish affair lasting about a week. During this period, anyone – bus passengers included – is a fair target for water balloons and coloured powder (usually red, the colour of rejoicing), and it culminates in a general free-for-all on the full-moon day of Faagun.

CHAITRA (March–April)
Seto Machhendranth Jaatra – Four-day chariot procession through Kathmandu, similar to the Machhendranath Raath festival in Patan.

BAISAKH (April–May)
Nawa Barsa – Nepali New Year, which always falls on the first day of Baisakh (April 13 or 14), is observed with local parades and the like. Bhaktapur's celebration, known as Bisket Jaatra, is the most colourful, combining religious processions with a rowdy tug-of-war.

Machhendranath Raath Jaatra – Arguably Nepal's most spectacular festival: thousands gather to watch as the image of Machhendranath, the Kathmandu Valley's rain-bringing deity, is pulled around the streets of Patan in a swaying, sixty-foot-high chariot. It moves only on astrologically auspicious days, taking four weeks or more to complete its journey.

Buddha Jayanti – Anniversary of the Buddha's birth, enlightenment and death, celebrated at Swayambhu on the full-moon day of Baisakh.

SAAUN (July–Aug)
Janai Purnima – The annual changing of the sacred thread (*janai*) worn by high-caste Hindu men takes place at various sacred bathing sites throughout the country on the full-moon day of Saaun. Mass observances are held at Gosainkund, a holy lake high in the mountains north of Kathmandu, and Patan, where it's an occasion for serious splashing.

Gaai Jaatra – A Kathmandu festival in honour of cows (*gaai*), who are said to guide dead souls to the underworld with their tails. On the day after Janai Purnima, young boys are dressed up in fanciful cow costumes and followed by family and friends through the streets of the old city.

BHADAU (Aug–Sept)
Tij – On the third day after the new moon of Bhadau, Hindu women fast and ritually bathe to wash away their sins and make offerings to their husbands. The most popular bathing site is Pashupatinath, near Kathmandu.

Indra Jaatra – A wild week of chariot processions and masked-dance performances in Kathmandu. On the last day, the king receives a special *tika* (an auspicious mark on the forehead) from the "living goddess" and beer flows from the mouth of an idol in Durbar Square.

Yartung – A swashbuckling fair held at Muktinath, in the Annapurna trekking area, featuring horse-racing, dancing, drinking and gambling.

ASHOJ (Sept–Oct)
Dasain (known as **Dashera** near India) – Although Hindu in origin, Nepal's greatest festival is enthusiastically embraced by members of almost all religious and ethnic groups. It stretches over ten days leading up to the full moon of Ashoj, but the liveliest action, as far as outside observers are concerned, takes place on Durga Puja, the ninth day, when animals are sacrificed to the goddess Durga in honour of her victory over demons. On Bijaya Dasami (the "Victorious Tenth Day"), elders bestow *tika*, which on this day consist of a red paste mixed with rice. Dasain is a time for families to gather (buses can get very crowded with homeward-bound passengers), and you'll see swings and miniature ferris wheels set up to entertain the kids.

KARTIK (Oct–Nov)
Tihaar (**Diwali** near India) – The "Festival of Lights" lasts for five days, starting two days before the new moon of Kartik. On the first, crows are honoured as the messengers of death, while on the next three days dogs, cows and bulls are garlanded. More significantly, houses throughout the hills and Tarai are trimmed with hundreds of candles and oil lamps on the third night, called Lakshmi Puja, in the hope of attracting Lakshmi, the goddess of wealth. Trusting in her, many Nepalis gamble on street corners and student groups make the rounds singing "*Diusire*", a form of musical fundraising, during this festival. On the fifth day, Bhaai Tika, sisters give their younger brothers *tika* and sweets. Firecrackers have become a big part of the fun for kids (and a source of stress for everyone else) for weeks around Tihaar time.

MANGSIR (Nov–Dec)
Biwaha Panchami – As many as 100,000 pilgrims converge on Janakpur for this five-day gathering, five days after the new moon of Mangsir. The highlight is the re-enactment of the wedding of Ram and Sita, the divine, star-crossed lovers of the *Ramayan*, one of the great Hindu epics.

Mani Rimdu – Held at Tengboche in the Everest trekking region around the full moon of the ninth Tibetan month (usually Nov), this colourful Sherpa masked dance dramatizes Buddhism's victory over the ancient Bon religion in eighth-century Tibet. A similar event is held in May or June at Thami.

is the colour of mourning for Hindus, and the eldest son is expected to shave his head and wear white for a year following the death of a parent. Many of the hill tribes conduct special shamanic rites to guide the deceased's soul to the land of the dead.

MUSIC AND DANCE

Music is as common as conversation in Nepal. In the hills, travelling minstrels (*gaaine*) make their living singing ballads and accompanying themselves on the *sarangi*, a hand-carved, four-stringed fiddle. Teenagers traditionally attract the attention of the opposite sex by exchanging teasing verses. After-dinner singalongs are popular, even in sophisticated Kathmandu, and of course music is indispensable in all festivals.

Traditional Nepali music is getting swamped by a rising flood of Indian film music, with its surging strings and hysterically shrill vocals. Yet Nepali folk music still gets a good airing; in contrast, it sounds mercifully calm and villagey. Tapes are widely sold on street stalls. In tourist restaurants, you're more likely to hear dinosaur rock, reggae or new-age muzak.

Nepali music is almost inseparable from **dance**, especially at festivals. Nepali dance is an unaffected folk art – neither wildly athletic nor subtle, it depicts everyday activities like work and courtship. Each region and ethnic group has its own distinct traditions, and during your travels you should get a chance to join a local hoedown or two, if not a full-blown festival extravaganza. Look out, too, for the muscular stick dance of the lowland Tharus, performed regularly at lodges

outside Chitwan National Park. Staged **culture shows** in Kathmandu and Pokhara are a long way from the real thing, but they do provide a sampling of folk and religious dances, and hint at the incredible cultural diversity contained in such a small country. Most troupes perform such standards as the dance of the *jhankri* (shaman-exorcists still consulted by many, if not most, hill Nepalis); the sleeve-twirling dance of the Sherpas; the flirting dance of the hill-dwelling Tamangs; the Tharus' fanciful peacock dance; perhaps a formal priestly dance, to the accompaniment of a clasical *raga* (musical piece); and at least one of the dances of the Kathmandu Valley's holiday-loving Newars.

CINEMA AND THEATRE

Nepal's love-hate relationship with India is perhaps best illustrated by its **cinema**: Nepalis might grouse about India's cultural imperialism, but that doesn't stop them rushing to see the latest schmaltz and pyrotechnics from Bombay. Nepali and Hindi are similar enough that movies aren't usually dubbed. Nepali films are still the exception, and are less slick than Indian productions, but much more popular when they're on. **Video** parlours and rental shops are now commonplace in Kathmandu, where kung-fu epics from Hong Kong are almost as popular as Indian imports.

Theatre is poorly developed in Nepal. Occasional (and unpublicized) plays are performed at the National Theatre and, even less frequently, at the Royal Nepal Academy, both in Kathmandu.

SHOPPING

Nepal's handicrafts scene is as rich and varied as its culture, having been influenced by hundreds of years of trade and religious exchange with Tibet and India. In addition, the influx of Tibetan artisans since 1959 has enriched the marketplace immeasurably, while tourist demand, ironically, has helped fuel something of an artistic renaissance. You can pick up distinctive gifts, souvenirs and clothes for a song, or if your budget runs to it, spend a fortune on carpets and *objets d'art*.

WHERE TO SHOP

Ninety-nine percent of crafts outlets are concentrated in the Kathmandu Valley and Pokhara: that's where the buyers are, and just about all of the mass-produced stuff is actually made there. Competition is intense. You can't stroll the tourist strips without being importuned by **curio sellers** cradling "priceless" goods in white cloths, or be beckoned from the sidelines by operators of makeshift stalls; their overheads are low and so, at least in theory, should be their prices. More reputable **shops**, galleries, "emporia" and boutiques have better selections and aren't so hard-driving (many have fixed prices). A number of excellent **non-profit outlets** exist in the Kathmandu Valley, and in Patan – Nepal's handicrafts capital – you'll also find **"factory" showrooms**, where you can watch the wares being made.

Quite a few items sold in tourist areas are made elsewhere, though, and needless to say it's more fun (and cheaper) to pick them up at their source. Best buys are noted in the relevant sections of the guide, along with a few local specialities that can't be found anywhere else.

Except where prices are clearly marked as fixed (and sometimes even then), you'll be expected to **bargain**. Bargaining is very much a matter of personal style, but in Nepal it's always lighthearted, never acrimonious. There's no firm guide as to what to expect to have knocked off, although prices are always softer on the street. The initial asking price can be anywhere from 10 to 200 percent over the going rate, depending, to a certain extent, on how gullible you look. All the old chestnuts (never show the least sign of interest, let alone enthusiasm; walking away will always cut the price dramatically) still hold true; but most important is to know what you want, its approximate value, and how much you're prepared to pay. Never start to haggle for something you definitely don't intend to buy – it'll end in bad feelings on both sides. Sellers always speak English in tourist areas, but everywhere else you'll need some rudimentary Nepali to bargain properly.

If you're contemplating making a big purchase, hiring a knowledgeable **guide** will save you money many times over what you spend on the guide's fee – but make absolutely sure you're getting independent counsel, and not just being taken on a tour of brother-in-laws' shops.

No matter what the seller says, very few items are older than last week. Genuine **antiques** – anything over 100 years old, or anything customs officials might think is that old – have to be cleared for export by the Department of Archeology, Ram Shah Path, Kathmandu. Get the dealer to take care of the paperwork.

METALWARE AND JEWELLERY

Artisans of the Kathmandu Valley have been casting bronze, brass and copper **statues** of Buddhist and Hindu deities for at least 1300 years – an unbroken artistic tradition with few parallels worldwide. The images are produced by the lost-wax process, in which a model is carved out of wax, surrounded by clay and then fired, melting the wax and leaving a terracotta mould; small pieces can be cast from a single mould, but larger ones have to be assembled from up to a dozen pieces, the joins concealed by ornate embellishments.

Statues are cast mainly in the style of Tibet (Nepal's main customer for centuries), depicting a tremendous variety of Buddhas, *bodhisattva* and defenders of the *dharma*, each characterized by a certain posture, weapon or other identifying feature. Patan is the traditional casting centre. Prices depend on size, metal and workmanship, but are never cheap – at least Rs5000 for a 20cm-tall image. The best-quality images will have carefully detailed fingers and eyes, and the metal will be without pits or spots.

Many brass **pots** and **vessels** are wonderful pieces of design. The large water jugs that Nepali women cradle against one hip may be too big to tote home, but small incense holders, *raksi* pourers, *puja* trays, oil lamps and *jal* urns are all attractive and relatively cheap.

Every hill bazaar has its metalsmiths who sell **gold** and **silver** at the going rate and, for a modest charge, will tap it into an earring, nose ring, necklace clasp, bracelet or any other form in which a woman wants to display the family wealth. Common to almost all hill women are *pote*, a necklace consisting strands of glass beads drawn together with a cylindrical gold ornament. Shops in Kathmandu sell **jewellery** made of silver, white metal and semiprecious stones, which, though designed entirely for the tourist market, are nonetheless attractive.

Gem sellers in Kathmandu deal in a wide range of cut and uncut stones at reasonable prices (though they're cheaper in Agra in India). Garnet, tourmaline, ruby, aquamarine, citrine ("golden topaz") and cat's eye come from mines in Nepal's Ganesh Himal and eastern hills; turquoise, amethyst and sapphire come from Tibet, coral from India and lapis lazuli from Afghanistan. Most stones are cut and polished in India. Take care when buying, as gem quality and cut can make a vast difference to value. Turquoise is often fake (bite it to see if the colour comes off).

WOOD, PAPIER MÂCHÉ AND PAPER

Nepali **woodcarving** reaches its apex in Bhaktapur, where you'll find everything from modest Buddha busts and Ganesh figures to exquisite, full-size window frames. Miniature replicas of Bhaktapur's famed Peacock Window are ubiquitous, and artisans are increasingly turning out non-traditional items such as animals, cassette boxes and chess sets. Pieces are carved with mallet and chisel out of one of several types of wood, most of them from the Tarai. The most common are *sal*, a hard, heavy, chocolate-coloured wood like teak; *sisu*, similar but with more grain to it; *chaab*, a cheaper, softer, honey-coloured wood; and *korma*, also light in colour but harder than *chaab*. Prices depend not only on size but also the type of wood and the quality of carving: Rs1000 should get you a finely detailed 20cm figure.

Wooden masks are used by Tibetans and highland Nepalis in religious dances and shamanic rituals. The genuine articles are rarely sold, but replicas are widely available in tourist areas; in the never-ending battle for tourists' attention, craftsmen are now souping up their masks with overlain metal designs.

Thimi is famous for its **papier mâché masks**, copies of those used in the masked dances of the Kathmandu Valley in which dancers take on the persona of the deity represented. The Nawa Durga (Nine Durgas) and their attendant deities Ganesh, Shiva and Bhairab are the ones most commonly recreated for tourist consumption, ranging from full size down to bite size. The Nawa Durga also take the form of **puppets** with clay or papier mâché heads and multiple wooden arms.

Lokta, an indigenous form of **handmade paper**, makes a fine purchase. In winter, when there's little else going on, hill people gather the bark of the *daphne* bush, boil it, beat it to a pulp, mix it with water, pour the mixture into floating frames, and finally sun-dry it on fallow terraces. The result is a rough but richly textured parchment which is then block-printed to produce calendars, stationery and greeting cards.

CARPETS

Tibetan-style hand-woven **carpets** have come a long way from their folk roots. What started out, thirty years ago, as a modest income-generator for Tibetan refugees has become far and away

Nepal's biggest export item – and a multi-ethnic creative collaboration. The traditional Tibetan form has been reinvented, with a unique look and lustrous, hard-wearing texture brought about by the use of synthetic dyes, blended Tibetan and New Zealand wool, standardized manufacture and modern chemical washing processes. In recent years the field has been enlivened by an explosion of contemporary colour schemes and designs.

Many foreigners prefer carpets in earthy, pastel **colours**, assuming them to be traditional and presumably coloured with vegetable dyes. Actually, traditional Tibetan carpets come in bright, almost gaudy hues – the earth tones are in vogue because of foreign demand. Synthetic dyes can produce any colour or shade, whether muted or bright, whereas vegetable dyes have a more limited range. Carpets made of all-Tibetan wool and/or vegetable dyes are rare, and more expensive.

Traditional Tibetan **designs** are bold and simple – angular dragons, flowers, clouds or various auspicious symbols, usually against a plain field and contained within a geometric border. Most carpets being produced these days are further simplified, using large, open fields, and combining traditional motifs with abstract patterns.

Carpets are woven throughout the Kathmandu and Pokhara valleys. Compared to Middle Eastern makes, Tibetan-style carpets have deeper, more luxuriant pile, but lower knot densities and coarser patterns. The best **shopping** is in the Jaulakhel area of Patan, and you'll find more information about their manufacture in that section. The choice is vast, so take your time: compare carpets in different price ranges for subtlety of colour and design, quality of finish and embossing, and knot count (usually 40 to 80 per square inch). Make sure the ratio of vertical to horizontal knots isn't less than 2 : 3.

Prices are dependent on all these factors, plus of course **size**. To give a relative idea of price, figure on paying Rs400 apiece for *khakama* (50cm squares), which make fine seat covers, or Rs5000 for a standard *khaden* (1m x 2m).

Chain-stitch tapestries are a recent Indian introduction to the Kathmandu handicraft scene, brought by traders fleeing the tourist meltdown in Kashmir. Some are now being made in Nepal, but most are imported.

TEXTILES AND CLOTHING

Nepali designers are also applying their creative talents to **textiles** and, as with carpets, adapting indigenous designs in stylish new ways. Most of these items are produced by tiny cottage-industry outfits and have yet to find their way overseas, but the fleeting success of "Tibetan" caps shows there's a receptive market.

Dhaka, a brightly patterned cotton weave made on hand looms in the eastern and western hills, has long been used to make *topi* (men's caps), *cholo* (women's half-length blouses) and shawls. Palpali *dhaka*, the preferred make for *topi*, comes from Tansen (aka Palpa), and you'll find more about it in that section. Women's cooperatives are now producing *dhaka* in colour schemes and patterns aimed squarely at Western tastes, and turning it into scarves, ties, placemats, jackets, handbags – you name it. One group also markets *allo*, a wool-like material woven from the pounded bark of nettle stems.

Other cotton weaves, including **khadi** (traditional homespun) and many forms of sari material, are produced locally all over. These, too, turn up in innovative incarnations – block-printed, quilted and hand-stitched – from pot holders and tea cosies to cushion covers and bedspreads. Less impressive are the cheap cotton dresses and drawstring pants sold in all the tourist areas.

Pashminā, a cashmere-like wool gleaned from the softest hair of goats, is made into shawls which are worn by many Kathmandu Valley residents in winter. These are good purchases, but be sure you're not buying acrylic. Sweaters, socks and other **woollens**, knitted in Tibetan settlements everywhere, are amazingly cheap, but often suffer from quality-control problems – many will quickly fall apart at the seams. Ask which grade of wool the garment is made from. For more durability and better styling, it's worth paying more at one of the pricier boutiques in Kathmandu or Patan. Tibetan-style black **felt** with rainbow trim is another budget-wear staple, finding its way into not only caps but also jackets, bags and the like.

Tibetan wrap-around dresses, called *chuba*, can be bought off the peg or custom-made by shops in Kathmandu and Boudha. Intricate (and expensive) **Bhutanese embroidery** also turns up in specialist shops in Kathmandu and Boudha.

Silk is a new industry in Nepal, with just a few manufacturers in the Kathmandu Valley producing thread and raw material. Others weave Indian thread into *dupian*, which looks like raw silk but is softer, shinier and more expensive, and fine *crepe de Chine*.

Nepal's burgeoning garment industry has been quick to experiment with all these materials and more, producing cheap designer **ready-made** Punjabis and the like – the sort of clothes you wouldn't feel silly about wearing again back home. High **fashion** has hit Nepal, too, and is patronized not only by foreigners but also by a growing clientele of wealthy Nepalis. Boutiques in Kathmandu and Patan display some stunning original pieces melding Western and local influences; in global fashion terms, these are quite cheap, and all the more exciting for their obscurity.

PAINTINGS

Like so many things in Nepal, *thangka* – Tibetan scroll paintings – are now cranked out for the tourist market, yet the best ones remain undiminished by commercialization, and even the cheapest can't hide the dense Buddhist symbolism inherent in the form. The production process and subject matter of these vibrant, intricate paintings is discussed on p.96.

Thangka are produced not only by Tibetans but also by Tamangs and, increasingly, by artisans of other Nepali ethnic groups. In addition, *paubha* – scroll paintings in the style of the Kathmandu Valley's Newars – are undergoing a modest revival after near-extinction earlier this century. *Paubha* are created in much the same way as *thangka*, but they tend to contain less background detail, focusing instead on a central deity, who may just as easily be Hindu as Buddhist.

Before **buying** a *thangka* or *paubha*, first watch a painter at work in Kathmandu, Patan or Bhaktapur – the main production centres – to get an appreciation for how painstaking the art is, and try to get someone to explain the imagery and the meanings behind it. When you see one you like, examine the detail of the eyes, facial expression and fingers of the main figure; background figures should also stand up to scrutiny. Many paintings aimed at tourists make a great show of their "gold" paint: real gold won't come away when a moist finger is pressed against it. Most "old" *thangka* have been aged with wood smoke. A halfway decent small (15cm x 30cm) *thangka* will **cost** at least Rs1000, though poor ones will go for much less than that. A large (90cm x 120cm) one, using microscopic brush-strokes and genuine gold paint, will cost hundreds or thousands of dollars.

So-called **Mithila art** has caught on in the past few years. These brightly coloured folk paintings, which keep alive age-old religious and fertility symbols, are created by women in the villages surrounding Janakpur in the eastern Tarai; you can read more about them in that section. However, they're most easily bought in the non-profit shops of Kathmandu or Patan, where Mithila motifs are reproduced not only on paper but also pottery and papier mâché.

Batiks, depicting typical Nepali scenes, are an inexpensive artform introduced in the past two decades as an income-generator for disabled people in the Kathmandu and Pokhara valleys.

MISCELLANEOUS CRAFTS & POTTERY

Khukuri, the deadly knives of Nepal's feared Gurkha soldiers, are Nepal's most ubiquitous souvenirs. Bhojpur, in the eastern hills, is the traditional forging centre, but knives are heavily peddled in Kathmandu. An authentic one will have a moon-shaped notch at the base of the blade to channel the blood away, and its sheath will contain two small tools for sharpening and honing. Prices start at Rs250, but a city-slicker model with a buffalo-horn handle will cost several times that.

The Kathmandu Valley and Pokhara are awash with Tibetan knicknacks, though the vast majority of these are manufactured in Nepal or India. The range of items is formidable: **prayer wheels**, amulets, charm boxes, bracelets (usually inscribed with the mantra, *Om mani padme hum*), prayer-flag printing blocks, *chhang* pots, masks, turquoise and coral jewellery, musical instruments and many other bizarre artefacts. Much of it has been artificially aged, and the turquoise is often fake. A couple of shops in Kathmandu sell nothing but **musical instruments**, including *sarangi* (Nepal's version of a fiddle) and *jhankri* (shaman) drums.

Simple, unglazed **pottery** is produced by *kumal* (potters) throughout the hills. Very little of it rises above the level of mundane implements, but the potters of Bhaktapur and Thimi turn out a few ornamental items – candlesticks, elephant-shaped plant pots and so on. Some of the non-profit shops are beginning to sell non-traditional, glazed pieces. Ceramics don't travel well, though, so you'll have to wrap them carefully.

OTHER ITEMS

Attractive caddies of Nepali **tea** make great presents or souvenirs. They're sold mainly in the Kathmandu Valley, but the tea itself is cultivated in the eastern hills around Ilam (just over the border from Darjeeling), and you'll find an account of processing and grading in that section. Two principal varieties are grown for export: Ilam, which has a full flavour much like Darjeeling, and Kanyam, smokier but considered superior by many. If you're not bothered about presentation, loose tea is much cheaper than the boxed stuff and can be sealed in plastic for travelling.

Incense can also bring back fond memories of Nepal after your return. Sweet-smelling Indian sticks are available in every bazaar. Tibetan mixtures, made in Nepal and sold mainly in Tibetan neighbourhoods such as Boudha and Swayambhu, are redolent of juniper.

There's no need to lug a library along when travelling in Nepal: Kathmandu and Pokhara each have dozens of **bookshops** devoted to travel, fiction and classics, new and used, in English and other European languages, Western imports and cheaper Indian imprints. Kathmandu, especially, seems to have more booksellers per capita than anywhere in the English-speaking world. Most will buy books or trade as well. The bigger tourist outlets also stock compilation **cassettes** of Nepali and other regional music which, though relatively expensive, give an overview of musical styles with English titles (see "Music and Dance" in *Contexts*). Cheaper tapes produced for the home market are available in local shops and stalls.

OUTDOOR PURSUITS

It hardly needs to be said that Nepal is ideal for outdoor enthusiasts. Most come to trek, but rafting, cycling and wildlife- and bird-watching are also well developed. None requires any previous experience.

All of these activities are covered in more detail later in the guide – this section goes over what you need to know before leaving home.

TREKKING AND HIKING

Even if you're not the outdoor type, **trekking** is a rare pleasure that shouldn't be passed up: it's the only way to get *into* the Himalaya, as opposed to looking at them from a distance, and is by far the best way to experience Nepal's constantly changing landscape and people-scape. Though the trails are sometimes steep, most people won't find trekking too demanding (and if it isn't hard enough for you, there's always the Everest Marathon). A trek normally lasts at least a week, but you'll get more out of it if you can set aside two or more weeks. Most people don't trek with a group, and wait until they get to Kathmandu before making any arrangements, but those with lots of money and little time may want to book through a trekking agency in their home country. Note that travel insurance is all the more essential if you plan to trek.

Equipment can be rented cheaply in Nepal, and it's no problem to store unneeded stuff while you're on the trail. For an **equipment checklist**, plus a full rundown on trekking **preparations and routes**, see Chapter Seven, *The Himalayan Trekking Regions*. A list of **overseas trekking agencies** appears in the "Getting There" section at the beginning of the book.

Day hikes – which offer many of the rewards of trekking with none of the red tape – are described throughout the guide.

RAFTING

Compared to treks, **rafting** trips tend to be shorter, more expensive (per day), less work, not as cold nor as hot, more exciting at times, and culturally less interactive. Nepal's whitewater is fine for first-timers, and from the river you can get fresh angles on villages and religious gatherings at sacred confluences. Most rafting compa-

nies offer a standard three-day trip, and provide all camping gear; some organize longer trips and raft-trek packages. **Bring** clothes and shoes you don't mind getting wet, a swimsuit, towel, sunglasses, suntan lotion and insect repellent. Birdwatchers will find binoculars invaluable.

The same rivers that attract so many rafting parties are even better for **kayaking**. Some rafting companies can also arrange kayak trips. Those experienced enough to organize their own trip will want to weigh the benefits of bringing kayaks from home versus renting them in Kathmandu (about Rs750/day) – but note that the supply is limited in high season.

Information on **rivers, costs and equipment** is given on p.195, and a listing of **rafting companies** is given on p.102.

MOUNTAIN BIKING

A **mountain bike** is the most appropriate technology of all for Nepal's rugged roads. Bikes can be rented at many outlets in Kathmandu and Pokhara, and a growing number of companies run organized tours. Bring your own mountain bike (*not* a touring bike), if possible, to save money and avoid technical difficulties – it'll be superior to anything you can rent in Nepal. Airlines will accept a bicycle as baggage at no extra charge, so long as it doesn't put you over the weight limit. No special container is needed, but you'll be expected to deflate the tyres and swivel the handlebars to be parallel with the frame. Serious gear wallahs will want to time their trip to Nepal to coincide with the annual Himalayan Mountain Bike Festival in late November/early December.

Accessories are scarce in Nepal, so if you're planning any kind of a substantial independent tour, bring the following items from home: panniers (a light rucksack might suffice if you anticipate a lot of bike-carrying); helmet; water bottle; pump; all relevant tools, patch kit, extra tubes and spare parts; security cable; breathable waterproof clothing (eg, Gore-Tex); cycling gloves and shorts; shock cords (spiders); and a bell.

General tips on **bicycle rental** are given in "Getting Around", earlier in *Basics*. **Cycle-tour operators** are listed in the Kathmandu chapter on p.103. For more on **routes, equipment and techniques**, see p.186.

WILDLIFE VIEWING

Viewing **wildlife** in the Tarai is safariing with a distinctly Asian flavour: the animals most commonly seen include rhinos, monkeys, several kinds of deer and the occasional bear – tigers are spotted only rarely – and the most fun way to see them is atop an elephant. For an overview of Nepal's wildlife, see "Natural History" in *Contexts*. **Bring** lightweight clothes (neutral colours best), a sun hat, swimsuit, sunscreen, insect repellent, shoes you don't mind getting wet, and binoculars if you have them. From November to February you'll also need warm clothes and a jacket.

Chitwan National Park (p.233) is the easiest game reserve to get to, and the only one geared for budget travellers, although it's heavily used: **Bardia National Park** (p.261) and **Sukla Phanta Wildlife Reserve** (p.265) are untouristed alternatives. Bird-watchers can notch up hundreds of species around Phulchowki at the southern edge of the Kathmandu Valley, or explore seldom-visited **Koshi Tappu Wildlife Reserve** (p.280). Mammals aren't as easy to see in the hills, though you might catch a glimpse of tahr while trekking.

SPORTS

It's often said that Nepalis are a martial race; certainly military parade grounds are more common than playing fields, and the **martial arts** are big among urban youth. Team sports aren't common, though city and club **football (soccer)** teams often square off at the National Stadium in Kathmandu, and basketball is beginning to catch on in schools.

The big tourist hotels in Kathmandu have **swimming** pools and **tennis** courts, and some of them allow outsiders to use their facilities for a fee (usually steep). There's also a health club in Kathmandu, as well as two **golf** courses in the Kathmandu Valley and a third in Dharan.

SPIRITUAL PURSUITS

Nepal is a great place to go to challenge your Western assumptions, study other systems of thought and open yourself to other ways of experiencing life. The tolerant atmosphere encourages experimentation and provides several traditional disciplines to delve into.

Moreover, Nepal is turning into quite a spiritual supermarket. The past few years have seen an explosion of outfits teaching yoga and meditation in the Kathmandu Valley, and centres in the other tourist watering holes can't be far behind. The allied health fields of ayurvedic and Tibetan medicine are also attracting a growing interest among travellers in Nepal. Many programmes are designed for those who are just starting out and don't require a lengthy commitment, although some do. Note that it's advisable to book any residential courses well in advance – fax numbers/addresses are given where possible.

This section provides a quick introduction to a few major practices. For general background on Hinduism and Buddhism, which provide their philosophical bases, be sure to see the section on religion in *Contexts*.

YOGA

Contrary to what's often put about in Western manuals, **yoga** is not just exercises – it's a system of spiritual, mental and physical self-discipline, designed to bring about mastery of the self and true awareness of the self's oneness with the universe. There are several classical schools of yoga, but the ones that fit most easily into Western lifestyles come under the category of *raja yoga* and share eight "limbs" or steps (*astanga*), which represent an ascending path to self-control. The first two are the moral limbs, divided into dos and don'ts; after that come the three external limbs, *asana* (correct posture), *pranayama* (correct breathing) and *pratyahana* (control of the senses); followed finally by the three internal limbs, *dharana* (concentration), *dhyana* (meditation) and *samadhi* (superconsciousness).

Yoga's reputation for headstands and the like comes from **hatha yoga**, which places special emphasis on the three external methods to purify the body as an aid to developing the self. The term comes from the syllables *ha* and *tha*, representing inhalation and exhalation, since breath-control techniques, along with various postures, form such an important part of this practice. Another popular variant, **kundalini yoga**, stresses meditation. The individual visualizes the process of enlightenment as a serpent, coiled near the base of the spine, rising through six psychic centres (*chakra*) in an ascending progression of consciousness, finally reaching the seventh, highest level.

Several **yoga centres** are located in and around Kathmandu, and are rounded up in the Kathmandu chapter on p.99.

BUDDHIST MEDITATION AND STUDY

Meditation is closely related to yoga, and the two often overlap: much of yoga (*kundalini*, for example) involves meditation, and Buddhist meditation draws on many Hindu yogic practices. However, meditation centres in Nepal generally follow the Buddhist – particularly Tibetan Buddhist – tradition.

Buddhist meditation is a science of mind. To Buddhists, mind is the cause of confusion and ego, and the aim of meditation is to transcend these. **Vipassana** ("insight") is the kernel of all forms of Buddhist meditation; related to *hatha yoga*, it emphasizes the minute observation of physical sensations and mental processes to achieve a cool, clear understanding of mind. Another basic practice common to most schools of Buddhism, **shamatha** ("calm abiding" – coopted by New Agers as "be here now") attunes and sharpens the mind by means of coming back again and again to a meditative discipline (breathing, visualization, etc). Theravada Buddhists consider *vipassana* to be sufficient for the attaining of enlightenment. At least two centres in the Kathmandu Valley run rigorous residential courses in this practice – see the *Kathmandu* chapter for details on one that caters to foreigners.

Tibetan Buddhist centres start students out with *vipassana* and *shamatha*, which form the foundation for a huge armoury of elaborate meditation practices. An adept will cultivate Buddha-like qualities through visualization techniques – meditating on the deity that manifests a particular quality, while chanting the *mantra* and performing the *mudra* (hand gesture) associated with that deity. The Tibetan Buddhist path also involves numerous rituals, such as prayer, offerings, circumambulation and other meritorious

acts, and committed followers will also take vows. Kathmandu has several centres offering introductory courses.

A big part of Tibetan Buddhism is the teacher–disciple relationship; more advanced students of the *dharma* will want to **study** under one of the lamas at Boudha (see p.119), some of whom give discourses in English.

AYURVED

Ayurved is the world's oldest form of medicine still being practised. Dating back five thousand years, the "knowledge of life" is a holistic medical system that assumes the fundamental sameness of self and nature. Unlike the allopathic medicine of the West, which is all about finding out what's ailing you and then killing it, *ayurved* looks at the whole patient: disease is regarded as a symptom of imbalance, so it's the imbalance that's treated, not the disease.

Ayurvedic theory holds that the body is controlled by **three forces** (*tridosha*), which are a reflection of the forces within the self: *pitta*, the force of the sun, which is hot and rules the digestive processes and metabolism; *kapha*, likened to the moon, the creator of tides and rhythms, which has a cooling effect and governs the body's organs, fluids and lubricants; and *vata*, wind, which relates to movement and the nervous system. The healthy body is one that has the three forces in balance. To **diagnose** an imbalance, the ayurvedic doctor goes not only by the physical complaint but also family background, daily habits and emotional traits.

Treatment of an imbalance is typically with **herbal remedies** designed to alter whichever of the three forces is out of whack. Made according to traditional formulas using indigenous plants, ayurvedic medicines are cheaper than imports, which is why the Nepali government is encouraging their production. In addition, the doctor may prescribe various forms of **yogic cleansing** to rid the body of waste substances. To the uninitiated, these techniques will sound rather offputting – for instance, swallowing a long strip of cloth, a short section at a time, and then pulling it back up again to remove mucus from the stomach.

You'll find **ayurvedic doctors** and clinics throughout the Hindu parts of Nepal, but those who are able to deal with foreigners are confined mainly to Kathmandu.

TIBETAN MEDICINE

Medicine is one of the traditional branches of study for Tibetan Buddhist monks, and **Tibetan medicine** is based on the same philosophical and magical principles as Tibetan Buddhism.

Like *ayurved*, from which it derives, Tibetan medicine promotes health by maintaining the correct balance of **three humours**: *beken*, inert matter or phlegm, which when out of balance is responsible for disorders of the upper body; *tiba*, heat or bile, which is associated with intestinal diseases; and *lung*, meaning wind, which may produce nervousness or depression.

Tibetan medicine is as much a spiritual discipline as a physical one. Part of a Tibetan doctor's regular practice is to meditate on the "medicine Buddha", a manifestation of the Buddha's compassion, wisdom and healing power. The physician **diagnoses** the patient's imbalance by examining the tongue, pulse and urine, and by determining the patient's psychological state through questioning. He'll then prescribe a **treatment** to counteract the imbalance, which initially may only be a change of diet or behaviour (for instance, "cold" disorders – those to do with wind – are treated with "hot" foods and activities). For quicker relief, he'll prescribe one of a range of herbal-mineral tablets, which have been empowered by special rites.

Recommended **clinics** specializing in Tibetan medicine are listed in the Kathmandu and Boudha sections.

PHOTOGRAPHY

Everyone's a National Geographic photographer in Nepal – ethnic peoples, mountains, wildlife, temples and festivals all make winning subjects. But beware of experiencing your trip through a lens. The camera can provide great memories, but don't hesitate to put it away when it's getting in the way of the real thing.

EQUIPMENT

The first rule of packing photo gear is to keep it to what you can realistically carry. For many, if not most, people, this will mean sticking to a pocket-sized 35mm **point-and-shoot** model with a built-in flash. These cameras are unobtrusive, lightweight and easy to use; the fancier ones with automatic zooms can do just about everything. The drawback is a lack of versatility, since you can't usually override the automatic functions.

Bringing an **SLR camera** involves a tradeoff between higher performance versus extra bulk and security precautions. To get the most out of your SLR you'll want to bring a decent selection of accessories. Zoom **lenses** lighten your load, minimize lens changes and give you a whole range of focal distances to choose from. Two or three should do it: something in the 35–80mm range, an 80–200mm, and a wide angle (24mm works well). On longer lenses, the lower the f-stop available, the more flexibility you'll have.

You'd also do well to bring polarizing or split-density **filters** to cut down on glare, plus UV filters to protect lenses. A **flash** is useful for filling in shadows, and a **tripod** for long exposures indoors. And if you're carrying all that booty, you'll want to make sure it's protected in some sort of **bag** – either over the shoulder, strapped to the chest or around the waist – which you shouldn't let out of your sight.

If you think you might go rafting, a **waterproof camera** could save you some grief; a regular camera will have to be kept stowed away in a storage box most of the time while on the river.

Most major brands of **film** (prints and slides) are easily obtainable in Kathmandu for slightly more than what they cost back home; in other tourist areas the selection is pretty thin and often out of date, while off the beaten track you'll be lucky to find any film at all. Have a selection of both fast (ASA/ISO 200–400) and slow (100, 64 or even 25) film on hand to deal with different conditions. If you're bringing film into the country, pack it in a lead bag (available in camera shops) or carry it as hand baggage and have it hand-checked – the dosage of checked-luggage X-ray machines may damage film. Labs in Kathmandu and Pokhara **process** most types of film (but not Kodachrome), many offering one-hour service.

Bring any other camera hardware you think you might need, especially spare **batteries** (which go flat quickly in cold temperatures).

All the comments about bulk and security for still cameras apply even more so to **video cameras**. Note that Nepal's electricity is 220V/50 cycles, which means North Americans won't be able to recharge battery packs without a transformer.

TECHNIQUE

People always make good photos, but be sensitive. Always ask first, and if they say no, don't press it. Try to make photography a fun, two-way process: let people take pictures of their friends, or of you with their friends; it also helps if you can show pictures of your own family or home. Take time to establish intimacy, rather than just barging in and "taking" pictures. Unless you've got a Polaroid, don't mislead people into thinking they'll get an instant portrait of themselves. Never offer money, and if someone demands *bakshish* for a photo, just put the camera away – this is a form of begging (see below) and should be discouraged. Never photograph masked festival dancers, who are believed to embody the deities they represent.

Postcard-perfect shots of **scenery** with clear blue skies aren't always the ones that stand out when you get home. Clouds, fog and rain often add more drama. Look for unusual images, things you've never seen before. Rather than trying to make big, sweeping statements with your photos, try zooming in on **details** that capture something essential about the scene or culture. Go for action shots that will serve as a springboard for a story.

Light levels and contrast can be very high on sunny days in Nepal – especially at high elevations. To get around this, plan on doing most of your shooting in the early morning or late afternoon. Tones are especially mellow at these times, producing the best results, and in any case some of the most interesting scenes occur just after dawn. If you can't avoid midday conditions, use a flash to fill in shadows on faces, especially if the subject is relatively dark against a bright background. To get the correct exposure without a flash, walk up close or zoom in, so the subject fills the frame, before reading the meter. For snow shots, meter off something of a neutral shade, like your hand or the darkest part of the sky.

CULTURAL HINTS

Customs and traditions run deep in Nepal. Few Nepalis get the chance to travel abroad, or even to see foreign films or media, so their only exposure to the outside world is through travellers. This puts a great responsibility on visitors to be sensitive to Nepali ways and values, and to project a favourable image of foreigners.

Many different ethnic groups coexist in Nepal, all with their own complex customs. In the Kathmandu Valley, where they mix the most, there's a necessarily high degree of tolerance of different clothes and lifestyles – a fact that travellers sense, and often abuse. Away from the tourist areas, however, these groups are quite parochial, and foreign ways may cause offence.

The dos and don'ts listed here aren't as inflexible as they might sound. You'll make gaffes all the time and Nepalis will rarely say anything. The list is hardly exhaustive, either: when in doubt, do as you see Nepalis doing. The important thing is to show a willingness to adapt and learn.

EATING

Probably the greatest number of Nepali taboos – to an outsider's way of thinking – have to do with **food**. One underlying principle is that once you've touched something to your lips it's polluted (*jutho*) for everyone else. If you take a sip from someone else's canteen, try not to let it touch your lips (and the same applies if it's your own canteen – you're expected to share). Don't eat off someone else's plate or offer anyone food you've taken a bite out of (with one exception: a wife may eat her husband's leftovers), and don't touch cooked food until you've bought it.

Another all-important point of etiquette is **eat with your right hand only**. In Nepal, as in most Asian countries, the left hand is reserved for washing after defecating; you can use it to hold a glass or utensil, but don't eat, wipe your mouth, pass food or point at someone with it. It's considered good manners to give and receive everything with the right hand – or, to convey respect, with both hands. Also remember that the family hearth is sacred, so don't throw rubbish or scraps into it.

THE ECOTOURISM TRAVELLERS' CODE

These tips come courtesy of the Nepal Tourist Watch Centre, an organization established to preserve Nepal's heritage and environment through responsible tourism. You can visit their office near the Big Bell Café in Kathmandu's Durbar Square (daily 2–6pm; ☎216248).

1. Travel in a spirit of humility and with a genuine desire to meet and talk with the local people.
2. Be aware of the feelings of other people, thus preventing what might be seen as offensive behaviour. Remember this especially with photography.
3. Get acquainted with local customs; respect them; people will be happy to help you.

4. Remember that you are one of thousands of visiting tourists. Do not expect special privileges.
5. Make no promises to local people unless you are certain you can fulfill them.
6. Cultivate the habit of asking questions instead of knowing all the answers.
7. If you really want a home away from home, why travel?

HOUSES AND TEMPLES

Other rules have to do with **caste**. In a Hindu society, foreigners, however much they might be courted for their money, are technically casteless. In most places this isn't a big deal – and at higher elevations, people are mostly Buddhist and couldn't care less about caste – but in Hindu areas not geared up for tourists, especially in the far west, your presence will be polluting to orthodox Hindus; don't expect to eat or sleep in a Hindu house.

Major Hindu **temples** or their inner sanctums are usually off-limits to non-believers, who are technically outcastes. Respect this: what seems like elitism is just Hindus' way of keeping a part of their culture sacred in a country where nearly everything is open to inspection by outsiders. In most cases, you can see everything from outside anyway. Where you are allowed in, be respectful, take your shoes off before entering, don't take photos unless you've been given permission, and leave a few rupees in the donation box. The same goes for Buddhist monasteries. If you're granted an audience with a lama, it's traditional to present him with a *kata* (a ceremonial white scarf, usually sold nearby). Walk around Buddhist stupas and monuments clockwise – that is, keep the monument on your right.

CLOTHING AND THE BODY

Nepalis are innately conservative in their attitudes to **clothing**. Not a few are still shell-shocked from the hang-loose styles of the hippy era, and wary of all budget travellers as a result. A woman is expected to dress modestly, with legs and shoulders covered, especially in temples and monasteries: a dress or skirt that hangs to mid-

calf level is best; trousers are acceptable, but shorts or a short skirt are offensive to many. A man should always wear a shirt in public, and long trousers if possible (men who wear shorts are assumed to be of a low caste). It's equally important to look clean and well groomed – travellers are rich, Nepalis reckon, and ought to look the part. You can flout these traditions, but you'll only shut yourself off from the happy encounters with locals that make travelling in Nepal so pleasant.

Nudity is a sensitive issue. Only women with babies or small children in tow bare their breasts. When Nepali men bathe in public, they do it in their underwear, and women bathe fully clothed. Foreigners are expected to do likewise. Nepal has some idyllic hot springs, but most are heavily used as bathing areas; don't scare the locals off by stripping. Paradoxically, it's deemed okay to shit in the open, as in many villages there are no covered toilets – but out of sight of others, in the early morning or after dark. Men may pee in public away from buildings – discreetly – but women have to find a sheltered spot.

Still other conventions pertain to **the body**. In Nepal, the forehead is regarded as the most sacred part of the body and the feet the most unclean. It's impolite to touch an adult Nepali's head, and it's an insult to kick someone. Take your shoes off when entering a private home, or follow the example of your host. When sitting, try not to point the soles of your feet at anyone. On a related note, it's bad manners to step over the legs of someone seated: in a crowded place, Nepalis will wait for you to draw in your feet so they can pass.

Nepali views about **displays of affection** are the opposite of what most of us are used to. It's considered acceptable for friends of the same sex to hold hands or put their arms around each other in public, but not for lovers of the opposite sex. Couples shouldn't cuddle or kiss in public, nor in front of a Nepali host.

OTHER THINGS

Try to convey an accurate impression of your home country – both its good and bad points – and play down materialistic standards of success. Don't rub Nepalis' noses in technology and fashions they can't afford. Nepali society is rich in the traditions of family and community that are so often mislaid in the West, but like traditional societies worldwide it is under attack, and we are only now beginning to see that tourism is a major corrupting agent.

Finally, **be patient**. Nepal is a developing country and things don't always work or start on time. It's unrealistic to expect things to be like they are at home, even if the menu or brochure makes them sound like they will be. If a restaurant is slow in filling your order, you have to remember they've probably only got one stove. Getting angry or impatient will only confuse Nepalis and won't resolve the problem. The Nepali way of dealing with setbacks isn't to complain, or even to keep a stiff upper lip, but to laugh. It's a delightful, infectious response.

To get by with a minimum of disappointment in Nepal, the best strategy is to scale back your expectations, always double- and triple-check important arrangements, take all assurances with a pinch of salt (Nepalis will sometimes tell you what they think will make you happy rather than the truth), and find something fun to do while you're waiting.

BEGGARS AND TOUTS

Dealing with beggars is part of travelling in Nepal, as in most developing countries. The pathos might initially get to you, as well it should, but most people adjust fairly quickly. A thornier dilemma, which will plague you as long as you're in Nepal, is how to cope with panhandling kids and pushy touts.

A small number of bona fide **beggars** make an honest living from *bakshish* (alms). Hindus and Buddhists alike have a long and honourable tradition of giving to lepers and the disabled, as well as sadhus and monks. Destitute women make up another large contingent of the begging population: it's terrifyingly easy for a Nepali woman to find herself alone in the world, either widowed or divorced – perhaps for failing to bear a son or because of a dowry dispute. There are no unemployment or social security benefits in Nepal; anyone who can't work and has no family for support generally turns to begging. Few would choose to do so if they had an alternative.

Giving is, of course, a personal decision. You might resolve only to give to the most needy-looking, or the most persistent, or the most dignified. You might conclude that almsgiving only treats the symptoms of poverty, and decide to support a charity trying to address the causes instead. On the other hand, you could argue that direct giving gets one hundred percent of the money to the target, with no administration, red tape or corruption. At any rate, it's important to give the matter some thought (see also "Development Dilemmas" in *Contexts*).

In the hills, ailing locals will occasionally approach foreigners for **medicine**, knowing that they usually carry first-aid kits. It's probably best not to make any prescriptions unless you're qualified to diagnose the illness. However, before leaving the country you can donate unused medicines to the dispensary at Kathmandu's Bir Hospital, which distributes them to the destitute, or to the Himalayan Yogic Institute, which gives them to Buddhist monks.

CHILDREN

Throughout Nepal – but principally along the tourist trails – **children** will hound you for money, candy and worthy-sounding objects like pens. Sometimes they're cute, usually they're a pain in the arse. They're not orphans or beggars, they're just ordinary Nepali schoolkids having a go. Unless they're collecting money for a festival – which is a legitimate tradition – **don't give them anything**. It will only encourage obnoxious behaviour, take away their dignity and start them on a life of toadying to tourists. Don't even try to rationalize it by thinking you'll give only to well-behaved kids: that's how monsters are created.

It's natural and noble to want to share your wealth with less well-off people, but dispensing rupees and pens only leads Nepalis to expect something for nothing and saps the country's traditional self-reliance.

Saying no isn't easy. Kids will sometimes tag along for hours, giving you the Chinese water-torture treatment. In groups they can be unbearable. Remember that for them it's a game – they're just out for entertainment. The best defence is a sense of humour. If you can speak a little Nepali, try teasing them back. They're either going to laugh *at* you or *with* you, and you might as well make it the latter.

Kathamandu's **street children** are another matter. They're begging for real, but you should still think twice before giving to them – see p.78.

TOUTS AND OTHER MIDDLEMEN

Indian-style hustle is on the rise in Nepal. You'll get a major dose of it at the airport or any major bus station, where packs of **touts** lie in wait to accost arriving tourists with guest-house cards. They also cruise the tourist strips of Kathmandu,

offering black-market rupees or dope. However, Nepali touts for the most part aren't as parasitic as their Indian brethren, and if you're entering Nepal from north India, where aggressive touts have to be dealt with firmly, adjust your attitude: they'll usually leave you alone if asked nicely, whereas they'll take a rude brush-off personally. That said, many touts in Nepal these days are in fact Indian, and may require more drastic measures.

Kathmandu and Pokhara are full of other lone entrepreneurs and middlemen – touts by any other name. **Ticket agents** (see the "On from Kathmandu" section in Chapter One), riksha wallahs, innkeepers and guides are ever anxious to broker services and information. Naturally they take a cut, but as with touts, they usually get their commission from the seller; your price is bumped up correspondingly. Is it a ripoff? Ripoff is a relative term. If you don't know where to spend the night or change money, a tout's services are certainly worth a few rupees. In general, though, cutting out the middleman gives you more control over the transaction.

POLICE AND TROUBLE

Nepal is one of the safest countries in the world, which is all the more remarkable when you consider the gulf between rich and poor. However, reports of theft seem to be on the rise, and political uncertainty may be bringing a general rise in lawlessness.

The only real concern still is **petty theft**, and then chiefly from fellow travellers. Common

sense suggests a few precautions. Carry valuables in a money belt or pouch around your neck at all times. Bring along a padlock for securing your room and baggage; it doesn't have to be big – deterrence is the main thing. In a dormitory, keep your kit locked up and your camera gear with you. A bag stowed on the roof of a bus is probably safe if it's lashed under the luggage tarpaulin (see "Getting Around"), but have all your valuables with you inside.

If you're robbed, report it as soon as possible to the police headquarters for the district in which the robbery occurred. They're apt to be friendly and consoling, if not much help. For insurance purposes, go to the Interpol Section of the police headquarters in Durbar Square or Naksal, Kathmandu, to fill in a report, a copy of which you'll need to keep for claiming from your insurer once you're back home. Bring a photocopy of the pages in your passport containing your photo and your Nepalese visa, together with two passport photos. Dress smartly and expect an uphill battle – they're jaded by stolen-travellers'-cheque scams.

Violent crime is extremely rare. Women probably shouldn't walk alone after dark, but the danger of getting raped or assaulted in a populated area is statistically insignificant. The countryside is equally safe, except for one or two stretches along the Tibetan border where the government still hasn't quite introduced law and order. In the light of a few isolated trekking incidents, it's advisable not to walk alone in remote parts (see Chapter Seven).

There are several ways to get on the wrong side of the law, none of them worth it. **Smuggling** is the usual cause of serious trouble – drugs and gold are the big no-nos, and if you get caught with commercial quantities of either you'll be looking at a more or less automatic five to twenty years in prison (see "The Jails" in Chapter One for a description of that edifying experience).

Give a wide berth to anyone in Hong Kong or Singapore offering "courier" jobs to Kathmandu: smuggling illicit electronics into Nepal, or antiques out, could also land you behind bars.

While it would be incredibly stupid to go through immigration control with drugs, discreet **possession** inside the country carries virtually no risk; flash dope around, though, and you could conceivably get shopped by an innkeeper.

In Nepal, where government servants are poorly paid, a little **bakshish** sometimes greases the wheels. Nepalese police don't make busts simply in order to get bribes, but if you're accused of something it might not hurt to make an offer, in an extremely careful, euphemistic and deniable way. This shouldn't be necessary if you're the victim of a crime, although you may feel like offering a reward.

WOMEN'S NEPAL

Nepal is a relatively easy place for a woman to travel. In most parts of the country you'll be of interest mainly as a foreigner rather than as a woman, and, as such, the atmosphere is tolerant and inquisitive rather than threatening or dangerous.

DEALING WITH MEN

Nepali society is on the whole chaste, almost prudish; **men** are almost universally respectful, and perhaps a little in awe, of foreign women. **Sexual harassment** is on the whole low-key,

and need rarely upset your travels. Staring and catcalling are on the increase in Kathmandu – mostly by groups of young lads who seem to have acquired the stereotype, gleaned from imported videos, of all Western women as sexually available – but it's nowhere near as bad as in India, or indeed most of Asia, and it rarely goes any further than words.

A woman travelling or trekking **alone** won't be hassled so much as pitied. Going alone (*eklai*) is most un-Nepali behaviour. Locals (of both sexes) will ask if you haven't got a husband – the question is usually asked out of genuine concern, not as a come-on. Teaming up with another female stops the comments as effectively as being with a man. Again, you'll ensure a better reception if you wear a long skirt and a modest top – shorts and skimpy clothes are considered offensive.

On **public buses**, you can request a seat in the front compartment, which is generally set aside for women and children. About the only form of discrimination you'll encounter is during toilet stops, when you'll have to hunt around for a sheltered place while men are free to pee by the side of the road (yet another reason to wear a long skirt).

Tarai cities and border towns are another matter, unfortunately: some men here, as in northern India, have some real misconceptions about Western women, and may try for a surreptitious grope or even expose themselves. Travelling with a man automatically shields you from this sort of behaviour. If that isn't possible, or if you resent having to do so, don't be afraid to make a public scene in the event of an untoward advance – that's what a Nepali woman would do. Though he'll pretend it wasn't him, all eyes will be upon him and he'll never try it again.

Of course, you may find you want to strike up a **relationship** with a Nepali man. If so, you should have no trouble finding eligible candidates in the bars of Kathmandu's Thamel quarter, but be aware that these gentlemen are not without their own agendas: exotic romance, conquest, perhaps even a ticket out of poverty-stricken Nepal. If you suspect ulterior motives, let him down gently but firmly and he'll usually retreat gracefully. Quite a few women travellers fall for trekking or rafting guides – the men of highland ethnic groups, such as Sherpas, have very similar views to ours on sexual equality – and Kathmandu has a small but growing community of women who have married and settled there.

MEETING WOMEN

A frustrating aspect of travelling in Nepal is the difficulty of making contact with **Nepali women**. The tourism industry is controlled by men. Women, who are expected to spend most of their time in the home and are given fewer educational opportunities, have little contact with foreigners and speak much less English. If you're lucky enough to be invited to a Nepali home for a meal, chances are the women of the house will remain in the kitchen while you eat, only emerging to clear the plates and eat the leftovers. Upper-class women are free of these restrictions and are often well educated, but of course they don't have to work so they, too, have few dealings with travellers.

The sexual politics are different among highland ethnic groups, which is as good a reason as any for going **trekking**. Along trekking routes, many women run teahouses single-handedly while their husbands are off guiding or portering. Proud, enterprising and flamboyant, these *didis* are some of the most wonderful women you're likely to meet anywhere. Language may be a problem off the popular trails, but that doesn't rule out all communication. On buses, women will be much more approachable in the front compartment. And anywhere you go, having a child with you will always open doors.

For more on **women's issues** in Nepal, see "Development Dilemmas" in *Contexts*. The Rough Guide Special, *Women Travel: Adventures, Advice and Experience*, gives one Western woman's account of living and working in the country.

STAYING ON

Volunteering, studying or working while in Nepal can add a satisfying focus to your trip, and deepen your understanding of another way of life.

Unfortunately, the government is making it a lot harder to stay on legitimately these days, the main obstacle being that you can't stay longer than three months at a time on a tourist visa, or four months in any twelve-month period. To stay longer than this, you generally have to get a non-tourist visa through a recognized work or study programme before entering the country.

ON A TOURIST VISA

If you feel you've received a lot from Nepal, **volunteering** is a good way to give something back. Mother Teresa's Sisters of Charity run an old people's hospice in Pashupatinath and welcome walk-in help on a day-to-day basis. Tulsi Meher Ashram, a training centre for destitute women located out beyond the international airport, can use people with design experience or creative handicraft ideas – contact them through *Mahaguthi* outlets in Kathmandu or Patan. The *Kathmandu Environmental Education Project* and *Himalayan Rescue Association* offices in Kathmandu need volunteers during the trekking season. Tashi Palkhel, one of the former Tibetan refugee camps near Pokhara, welcomes help, and no doubt many other aid organizations wouldn't say no to a willing dogsbody.

People with **medical qualifications** are always needed. The *Himalayan Rescue Association* accepts four doctors each autumn and spring to staff its high-altitude aid posts; the waiting list is two or three years long, but it can't hurt to write to Dr David Shlim, Director, Himalayan Rescue Association, GPO Box 495, Kathmandu, Nepal.

Numerous language schools in Kathmandu offer intensive **courses** in Nepali, Newari or Tibetan – see "Listings" at the end of the Kathmandu chapter. Opportunities to study yoga and Tibetan Buddhism are summarized in the "Spiritual Pursuits" section.

It's against the rules to work on a tourist visa, but plenty of people do anyway – notably as **trekking and rafting guides**. However, you'd have to have made several trips to Nepal, or already be experienced and well connected in the adventure-travel business, to find work as a guide. Guides are usually hired on a freelance basis, so the work is only seasonal, and immigration restrictions now make it hard for non-Nepalis to stay in the country for more than two treks in a row. Qualified **masseurs** and **yoga/meditation instructors** may be able to find work in Kathmandu – try contacting the places listed towards the end of that chapter.

If you haven't got any particular skills and just want an open-ended arrangement for a few weeks or so, **teaching English** is a good way to become a temporary local. Language schools in Kathmandu and Pokhara take people on with no previous experience, although the pay is negligible. The *American Language Centre* in Dhobichaur, Kathmandu, pays for teachers with ESL/EFL experience or degree.

STAYING LONGER

Postings with the **Peace Corps**, **VSO** and other national voluntary agencies abound, providing you've got the relevant skills and the determination to stay two or more years. People with experience in education, health, nutrition, agriculture, forestry and other areas are needed. Such organizations don't instigate their own projects, but place volunteers in existing projects where technical help is needed. Many other **aid agencies** (such as Action Aid, Save the Children, CARE and Oxfam) operate in Nepal and occasionally take on specialists. See "Development Dilemmas" in *Contexts* for an idea of what to expect.

Several American universities run **study programmes** in Nepal. The University of Wisconsin-Madison's School of South Asian Studies (750 University Ave, Madison, WI 53706) places students in Nepal for a full year. The Experiment in International Living (Kipling Rd, Brattleboro, VT 05301) has its own campus in Naksal, Kathmandu (☎414516). The Naropa Institute (2130 Arapahoe Ave, Boulder, CO 80302) runs a thirteen-week course on Tibetan Buddhism each autumn at Boudha.

The only known way to get a non-tourist visa after you've already arrived in Nepal is to study at Tribhuwan University's *Campus of International Languages* in Kathmandu. One-year courses in Nepali, Tibetan, Sanskrit and Newari begin in July, which isn't climatically convenient, although they're considering offering a six-month Nepali course starting in February. Classes run for two hours a day, five days a week, and a year's tuition costs $525. Apply no later than June with a letter of recommendation from your embassy or university to: Campus Chief, Campus of International Languages, Exhibition Road, Bhrikuti Mandap, Kathmandu, Nepal (☎226713). The university will sort out your visa.

DIRECTORY

Addresses don't exist in Nepal: few streets even have names, and houses are never numbered. In cities, though, intersections or neighbourhoods (*tol*) usually have names and these are gradually lending themselves to the major streets nearby.

Children Travelling with children can be both challenging and rewarding – kids always help break the ice with strangers, and among Nepalis they unleash even more than the usual hospitality (although the lack of privacy may prove to be a problem). Poor sanitation, dogs, traffic and steep slopes are hazards parents have to watch out for. Special *doko* (wicker baskets) are available for carrying young ones, but disposable nappies/diapers and baby foods aren't. Older children might turn up their noses at some of the food.

Contraceptives Condoms and birth-control pills are available in pharmacies everywhere. Consult one of the clinics in Kathmandu for other contraceptive advice.

Customs Officers are fairly lax on entry, but they might note fancy video gear in your passport so you can't sell it in Nepal. They check more thoroughly on departure, mainly to make sure you're not smuggling antiques out.

Disabled travellers Nepal's steep slopes and uneven pavements make for a hard time; stairs and steps are a fact of life throughout the hills. However, a safari in one of the Tarai wildlife parks is perfectly feasible, and even a trek, catered to your needs by an agency, might not be

out of the question. Try *Himalayan Holidays*, PO Box 5513, Kathmandu (☎01/228933; fax 272866). For general information on disabled travel abroad, get in touch with the *Royal Association for Disability and Rehabilitation*, 25 Mortimer St, London W1 (☎071/637 5400); the *Society for the Advancement of Travel for the Handicapped*, 26 Court St, Brooklyn, NY 11242 (☎718/858-5483); or *Mobility International USA*, PO Box 3551, Eugene, OR 97403 (☎503/343-1248).

Drugs Cannabis grows wild throughout hill Nepal, and old folks sometimes smoke it as an evening tonic. Touts in Kathmandu – shady characters, but not informants – mostly peddle local hash, and also whisper offers of opium and heroin from the Golden Triangle. See the section on "Police and Trouble" for legalities.

Electricity is 220 volts/50 cycles per second, where you can get it. The bigger hill towns and most of the Tarai are electrified, as are an increasing number of villages. Virtually all power is generated by hydroelectric projects, so power cuts ("load shedding") are common in spring when water levels get low.

Embassies and consulates are all in Kathmandu: see "Listings" at the end of Chapter One.

Emergencies Where there's a phone, dial ☎100 for the police or ☎102 for an ambulance – but it's better to get a Nepali-speaker to do the talking. Registering with your embassy can expedite things in the event of an emergency.

Gay Nepal Nepalis will tell you gay sex doesn't happen, or it's "something that Indians do". There are no gay bars or meeting places or any support network whatsoever, even in the capital. Yet in a society where the sexes are kept well apart before marriage, and men routinely hold hands and sleep together, it obviously goes on. Gay couples will certainly feel a certain freedom in being able to be close in public – but obviously not *too* close. The only approach a gay traveller is likely to get is from touts who might offer, at the end of a long inventory of drugs, "nice Nepali girls", and if that doesn't work, boys. But it's nothing like the scene in, say, Thailand.

Laundry Tourist guest houses generally take laundry, although the turn-around time depends on the weather. Rates are reasonable. If you're doing your own, detergent is sold in inexpensive packets in Kathmandu, although a concentrated liquid is less messy.

Left luggage Guest houses will always store bags for you, an invaluable service if you go trekking or anytime you just want to travel light. The usual charge is a few rupees per item per day, but some places waive this if you take a room when you return.

Time Nepal is 15 minutes ahead of India – just to be contrary, one suspects. That makes it 5 hours 45 minutes ahead of London, 12 hours 45 minutes ahead of New York, 15 hours 45 minutes ahead of Los Angeles, and 21 hours 45 minutes ahead of Sydney.

Tipping Not expected, except in the classier restaurants where service is often added to the bill anyway (figure ten percent), but a few rupees on a dinner at a budget tourist place is appreciated. Don't tip taxi drivers.

Toilets Where they exist, these range from "Western" (sit-down) flush jobs to two planks projected over a stream. In lodges – tourist ones aside – the norm is a squat toilet, usually pretty stinky and flyblown. A public toilet will often be nothing but a designated field; when in doubt, you should ask *Chaarpi kahaa chha?* (Where is the toilet?). Don't throw paper down squat toilets: put it in the basket provided. Toilet paper is only provided in pricier hotels. Nepalis use a jug of water and the left hand (try it yourself – you might form a subtle bond with the culture).

PART TWO

THE

GUIDE

TIBET

THE HIMALAYAN
TREKKING REGIONS

THE
KATHMANDU
VALLEY

THE WESTERN
HILLS

THE WESTERN
TARAI

THE
CENTRAL
HILLS

THE HIMALAYAN
TREKKING REGIONS

KATHMANDU

THE EASTERN TARAI
AND HILLS

0   100 km

INDIA

CHAPTER ONE

KATHMANDU

F looded with foreign aid, beset by tourism and Indian profiteering, **Kathmandu** couldn't have been expected to remain untouched, yet it's surpassing itself in its headlong haste to join the global village. Only a few years ago, you could just about dismiss its tourist quarters and fitful modernity as aberrations in an otherwise medieval city of breathtaking architecture, dark alleys and sacred cows. Now, the picture is more confused. Not that Nepal's capital has entirely abandoned its traditional identity, but the laissez-faire melding of new influences with old eccentricities has produced a stressful, often overwhelming, urban environment.

There are, in fact, a thousand Kathmandus, layered and dovetailed and piled on top of one another in an extravagant morass of misery, chaos and dignity. With a population of 700,000 people – it's doubled in a decade – Kathmandu is Nepal's biggest and most cosmopolitan city: a meeting place of a dozen ethnic groups, and the hometown of the Newars, Nepal's master craftsmen and traders extraordinaire (see p.68). Trade, indeed, created Kathmandu – for at least a thousand years it controlled the most important caravan route between Tibet and India – and trade has always funded its Newar artisans. Little wonder, perhaps, that Kathmandu has so deftly embraced the tourist business.

The Kathmandu most travellers know, **Thamel**, is like a thumping, Third World theme park, all hotels and hoardings and promises, promises, with touts flogging carpets and hashish to holiday hippies, while the words "Cake and Pie" blaze from restaurant windows like a mantra. The shrinking **old city**, though squeezed by traffic and commercial pressures, is still studded with ageless temples and shrines. Its narrow lanes seethe with an incredible crush of humanity, echoing with the din of bicycle bells, religious music, construction and car horns, reeking of incense, spices, sewage and exhaust. There are, too, the outcaste shantytowns down by the river, the decrepit, urine-scented ministry buildings, the swanky five-star shopping streets, the sequestered suburbs, the burgeoning bazaars. But above all, the predominant images of contemporary Kathmandu are those of growth, in all its familiar and dispiriting forms: traffic jams and clouds of choking fumes; coolies stacking bricks and shovelling sand against screens for mortar; a jostling skyline of rooftop water storage tanks, TV antennas, satellite dishes; legions of shiny aid agency Land Cruisers; mobs of tourists; gangs of *goondas*, angry young men reinventing themselves with leather jackets and long hair; suburban sprawl, student demonstrations, riot police, power cuts, families on motorbikes, advertisements for kitchen appliances. In other words, Kathmandu is coming to resemble any other Asian metropolis.

Nevertheless, Kathmandu is likely to be your first port of call in Nepal – all international flights land in the capital, and most roads lead to it – and you probably won't be able to avoid spending at least a couple of days here. It's the obvious place to sort out your affairs: it has all the **embassies** and airline offices, Nepal's main **poste restante**, and a welter of **trekking and travel agencies** for arranging treks, rafting and cycle trips. At least as important, in the minds of long-haul travellers anyway, are the capital's **restaurants** and the easy social scene that surrounds them, all of which makes Kathmandu the natural place to get your initial bearings in Nepal.

All things considered, though, you'd be well advised to get your business here over with as soon as possible. If you're intending to do any sightseeing around the valley, you'd be better off basing yourself in the healthier surroundings of Boudha, Patan or Bhaktapur (see Chapter Two), or even further out in Nagarkot or Dhulikhel (see Chapter Three). These days, the smart money is on staying outside Kathmandu and making day trips in, not vice versa.

A little history

People must have occupied what is now Kathmandu for thousands of years, but chroniclers attribute the city's founding to Gunakama Deva, who reigned in the early eighth century – by which time sophisticated urban centres had already been established by the **Lichhavi** kings at Pashupatinath and other sites in the surrounding valley. Kathmandu was originally known as Kantipur, but it later took its present name from the Kasthamandap ("Pavilion of Wood") that was constructed as a rest house along the main Tibet–India trade route in the late twelfth century, and which still stands in the city centre.

The city rose to prominence under the **Malla** kings, who took control of the valley in the thirteenth century and ushered in a golden age of art and architecture that lasted more than five hundred years. All of Kathmandu's finest buildings and monuments, including those of its spectacular Durbar Square, date from this period. At the start of the Malla era, Kathmandu ranked as a sovereign state alongside the valley's other two major cities, Bhaktapur and Patan, but soon fell under the rule of Bhaktapur. The cities were again divided in the fifteenth century, and a long period of intrigue and rivalry followed.

Malla rule ended abruptly in 1769, when Prithvi Narayan Shah of Gorkha, a previously undistinguished hill state to the west, captured the valley as the first conquest in his historic unification of Nepal. Kathmandu actually did rather well out of the new order, being made capital of the new nation and seat of the new **Shah** dynasty. The Shahs rule to this day, although from 1846 to 1951 they were politically outmanoeuvred by the powerful **Rana** family, who ruled as hereditary prime ministers and left Kathmandu with a legacy of enormous white (now mouldy grey) Neoclassical palaces. The capital remains the focus of all national political power – the 1990 democracy movement led, inevitably, to the palace gate – while its industrial and financial activities continue to fuel a round-the-clock building boom.

ARRIVAL AND ACCOMMODATION

Despite chaotic first appearances, Kathmandu is surprisingly easy to get to grips with; the touts, like everything else, become much more manageable once you've dumped your bags. The following, along with the map overleaf, should help with **orientation**.

Tradition has it that old Kathmandu was laid out in the shape of a *khukuri* knife. Positioned at what would be the hilt of the knife is **Durbar Square** – a non-stop carnival set amidst temples, monuments and the former royal palace – while the city's oldest neighbourhoods stretch northeast and (to a lesser extent) south-west. **New Road**, the city's best-known shopping street, runs east from the square. Kathmandu's budget hotels are concentrated in two areas: **Thamel**, north of Durbar Square in a new part of town, and Jhochhen, better known as **Freak Street**, immediately south of the square.

Suburban Kathmandu sprawls mainly east of **Kantipath**, the main north–south thoroughfare, and is dominated by two landmarks, the **Royal Palace** and the **Tudikhel** (parade ground). Most of the expensive hotels, restaurants and airline offices huddle along **Durbar Marg**, the broad boulevard running south from the palace gate. West of the Bishnumati River is not, strictly speaking, part of Kathmandu, but the hilltop temple of **Swayambhu** is close enough to be reached easily on foot.

The **maps** provided in this chapter should suffice for most purposes, but for more detail you'll want to pick up a tourist map (sold everywhere, and handed out free at the airport) or, better still, HMG Survey Department's "Central Kathmandu" (for map outlets, see "Listings" at the end of this chapter).

Arriving by air

Arriving by air at **Tribhuwan International Airport**'s shiny new terminal, 5km east of the city centre, you'll first have to deal with **immigration**. If you haven't already got a visa, fill out a visa application form and join the queue; you'll need

KATHMANDU

Nagarjun Ban & Trisuli

Budhanilkantha

BALAJU

RING ROAD

Bishnumati River

NAYA BAZAAR

Main Bus Park

US Embassy

PANIPOKHRI

LAZIMPATH

Hotel Shangrila

Community Craft Centre

Bluebird Supermarket

VSO

Hotel Manaslu

Peace Corps

Hotel Shanker

BALUWATAR

CIWEC Clinic

BHATBHATENI

Australian Embassy

HADIGAUN

Boudha & Pashupatinath

Police

Bangladesh Embassy

NAKSAL

Nag Pokhri

Kamal

Indian Embassy

British Embassy

LAINCHAUR

Hotel Ambassador

Thayabhu

Royal Palace

KANTIPATH

Nepal International Clinic

Hotel Yak & Yeti

ARG

PAKNAJOL

LEKHNATH MARG

Hotel Malla

Kesar

Central Library

Immigration

TRIDEVI MARG

THAMEL

British Council

Hotel de l

Kathmandu Peace Guest House

Kathmandu Guest House

KALDHARA

DHALKO

Dikey Guest House

Dhaulagiri Guest House

CHHETRAPATI

Shoba Bhagwati Mandir

Bijeshwari Bahal

Swayambhu

Hotel Vajra

N

0   500 m

one passport-size photo and $20 or hard-currency equivalent in cash – and worn notes aren't accepted. An exchange window in the immigration hall cashes travellers' cheques. Having a visa already will save a few minutes on the immigration process. Baggage claim is downstairs, where if you're quick you might be able to snag a free trolley. The **bank**, to the right as you exit customs, offers somewhat unfavourable rates, so change only what you need to get started – bear in mind that all guest houses change money. A nearby **tourist information** desk hands out free city maps and the odd brochure.

The guest house **touts** at the airport can be awful. Brace yourself before leaving customs, and have a plan. One strategy is to fix on a particular guest house and immediately hire a taxi to take you there; phone ahead using a white courtesy phone (if it's working), or just name a place where you know there'll be other fallbacks nearby if it's full. Alternatively, entertain offers from touts, choose one, and see what kind of room you end up with (you can always change the next day). Either way, as soon as you've made a decisive action the other touts will back off. **Taxi** fares into town are quasi-fixed at Rs100 (supplement charged for extra passengers) – buy a coupon from the cooperative association desk and present it to one of the member drivers. If you're in a group of three or more, the *NATA Limousine/Transfer Service* might actually work out to be less expensive. At the time of writing, the **blue (Sajha) bus** was out of commission, but when and if it's running it offers a cheap but slow alternative; once in town it heads north along Kantipath, and drops passengers off within a few minutes' walk of most guest houses and hotels. Touts usually offer a "free" ride if you stay in their lodge, but of course the fare just gets added on to the room price.

Arriving by bus

By the time you read this, Kathmandu's huge and light-years-more-hygienic new long-distance **bus park** should be operational. Just off the Ring Road in Gongabu, about 3km north of the city centre, it's supposed to handle all **public day buses**, including all services from the Indian border. Again, the same strategies for dealing with touts at the airport will apply here, as they did at the old bus park (which by now should be accommodating valley bus services). Taxis and tempos are supposed to use their meters into town from here, and the daytime fare shouldn't be more than Rs50 (see "Getting around", below).

There's a possibility that **Sajha** and **night buses** might also begin operating out of the new bus park, but more probably these services will continue dropping passengers off near the GPO at Bhimsen Tower, from where it's a five-minute walk to Freak Street or a ten-minute riksha ride to Thamel. **Tourist buses** deposit passengers either in Thamel or at Bhimsen Tower.

Getting around

Getting around is easiest on **foot** in the old city, by **bicycle** everywhere else. One-speed bikes can be rented literally everywhere in Thamel and Freak Street (Rs25–40 a day), and many guest houses have their own cycles for rent. **Mountain bikes** are almost as common, but often of disappointing quality. They range from about Rs50 a day for a useless one-speed Indian model to Rs150–200 for a Taiwanese 18-speed that's probably ready for retirement – but shop around early (or even the night before) and you might find a gem. Several operators in Thamel and Freak Street rent out 100cc **motorcycles** for about Rs400 a day.

The telephone code for Kathmandu and the Kathmandu Valley is ☎01.

You'll need to leave a plane ticket or some travellers' cheques as security, and you're supposed to show a driving licence. Bargain for a long-term discount on any of these.

Vehicles with more than two wheels make slow progress through the old part of town, but have their place for longer journeys. Pedal **rikshas** cruise for customers nearly everywhere; needless to say, establish terms before setting off. **Taxis** and **tempos** (motor rikshas) are metered, but usually the meters are out of date, so find out ahead of time what percentage they're adding. Drivers will usually try to bargain, and outside the hours of 9am to 8pm (approximately) they add another fifty percent to the fare. They tend to hang out at the main Thamel intersection, along Durbar Marg, at the top of Freak Street and at the bus station, but they get scarce after dark – try the night taxi service (☎224374). Fixed-route tempos shuttle on various routes, generally starting from near the *Air India* office on Kantipath, where they create the most almighty jams. Cheapest (no more than Rs5), but slowest and most crowded, are the **public buses** and minibuses, which run along regular but unnumbered routes; details are given where relevant in this chapter and the next. They're easiest to cope with if you can get on at the starting point and stay on till the end.

Information

For nuts-and-bolts practical information, bypass the official tourist offices and make for the **Kathmandu Environmental Education Project (KEEP)**, which shares an upstairs office on Tridevi Marg with the **Himalayan Rescue Association (HRA)**. These nonprofit organizations specialize mainly in trekking tips, but staff may be able to help with other matters, and the notice board in the hall outside is useful for finding trekking partners, selling or buying equipment, or hearing about events. Similar notice boards can be found outside the *Kathmandu Guest House* and in other guest houses and restaurants.

The airport **tourist information office** is really only good for free city maps. The staff at the Ministry of Tourism (Mon–Thurs & Sun 9am–6pm in summer, 9am–5pm in winter, Fri 9am–4pm), behind the National Stadium, are indifferent and unhelpful, but they hand out free colour posters and mediocre country maps, subject to availability. A third tourist information office on Ganga Path (the western portion of New Road) is handicapped by an almost complete lack of literature.

Accommodation

Kathmandu is well stocked with all kinds of **accommodation**. At the budget end of the spectrum, it's just a matter of hitting the guest houses: they're all cheek by jowl, so if one's full you can just try the next. In the autumn high season the prominent Thamel lodges fill up early, yet there'll always be vacancies at smaller places nearby.

You might want to consider staying outside Kathmandu – for possibilities, see the sections on Boudha (p.116), Patan (p.128) and Bhaktapur (p.150).

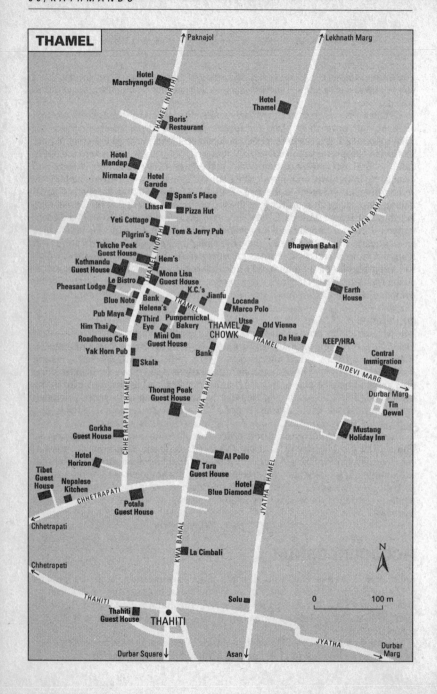

THAMEL

↑ Paknajol
↑ Lekhnath Marg

THAMEL (NORTH)

Hotel Marshyangdi

Hotel Thamel

Boris' Restaurant

Hotel Mandap

Nirmala

Hotel Garuda

■ Spam's Place

Lhasa ■ Pizza Hut

BHAGWAN BAHAL

Yeti Cottage ■

Pilgrim's ■ Tom & Jerry Pub

Tukche Peak Guest House

Kathmandu Guest House

Le Bistro ■

Pheasant Lodge ■

Hem's

Mona Lisa Guest House

Bhagwan Bahal

THAMEL (NORTH)

Blue Note ■ Bank

Helena's

Pub Maya ■ Third

Him Thai ■ Eye

Roadhouse Café ■

Yak Horn Pub ■

■ Skala

K.C.'s

Jianfu

Pumpernickel Bakery

Mini Om Guest House

Bank

THAMEL

THAMEL CHOWK

Locanda Marco Polo

Utse

Old Vienna

Da Hua

THAMEL

Earth House

KEEP/HRA

Central Immigration

TRIDEVI MARG

Durbar Marg →

Tin Dewal

CHHETRAPATI THAMEL

Thorung Peak Guest House

KWA BAHAL

Mustang Holiday Inn

Gorkha Guest House

Hotel Horizon

Al Pollo

Tara Guest House

Hotel Blue Diamond

Tibet Guest House

Nepalese Kitchen

CHHETRAPATI

Potala Guest House

JYATHA THAMEL

← Chhetrapati

KWA BAHAL

← Chhetrapati

■ La Cimbali

N

THAHITI

Solu ■

0   100 m

Thahiti Guest House

THAHITI

JYATHA

Durbar Marg

↓ Durbar Square

Asan ↓

Budget places

Budget tourism in Nepal was born on **Freak Street** (Jhochhen Tol) in the late 1960s, and, being the least modern area nowadays, its prices are the lowest (rooms start at less than Rs50). In the 1980s, **Thamel** emerged as a smarter, more respectable alternative both for basic guest houses (rooms from Rs75) and more upmarket establishments (rooms usually $8–20, plus tax). More latterly, with land prices in Thamel going through the roof, guest houses have started springing up in unlikely **off-the-beaten-track** locales, and these may well be your best bet for avoiding the tourist treadmill.

Prices are influenced by supply and demand, and thus fairly fluid. Rates given here are for high season, but in slow times expect discounts of up to fifty percent. You should also be able to negotiate a better rate for longer stays. Take all recommendations with a pinch of salt, because maintenance in the budget category is pretty much nonexistent and so anywhere that's clean and good value one year probably won't be the next.

As a rule, Kathmandu innkeepers are tremendously helpful and good-humoured people. During the winter, when Kathmandu can be cold and clammy, they'll provide kapok quilts, but only the most upmarket guest houses have heaters. Finally, try to get a room that doesn't overlook the street: Kathmandu's barking dogs, banging pots and clattering shutters are enough to wake the dead.

Freak Street

Little remains to remind you of **Freak Street**'s hippy heyday. Bona fide hippies have been an endangered species in Nepal ever since 1974, when the present king, then new to the throne, passed a series of immigration and drug laws that made life more difficult for them. Yet Freak Street certainly comes out better these days in a comparison with Thamel – it's quieter, less polluted and crowded, and it generally retains more traditional buildings and ways. And while it trails in the tourist restaurant department, it's within easy walking distance of New Road's many excellent Indian eateries. Some have rightly pointed out that the traditional buildings here would be more dangerous in the event of an earthquake, but then if you've observed modern Nepali construction methods you wouldn't necessarily have much faith in the city's new buildings, either.

For locations, see the South of Durbar Square map.

ROOM PRICE SCALES

All guest houses and hotels have been price-graded according to the scale outlined below, which represents the cheapest available double room in high season; codes prefixed by B denote the cost of a room with attached bathroom. See *Basics*, p.21, for a fuller explanation of the system.

① Less than Rs75	⑤ $8–12
($1.50 if quoted in US$)	⑥ $12–20
② Rs75–150 ($1.50–3)	⑦ $20–40
③ Rs150–250 ($3–5)	⑧ $40–70
④ $5–8	⑨ Over $70

Annapurna Lodge (☎213684). The biggest of the old Freak Street pack, with a choice of two in-house restaurants. ②/B③.

Buddha Guest House (no phone). Stark, but small and friendly. B③.

Century Lodge (☎214241). The building, though dilapidated, features some fine traditional carved windows. ②/B②.

G.C. Lodge (☎214609). A real dive, mentioned here only for its knock-down prices. ①.

Kantipur Guest House. Friendly, unpretentious place in a less touristed street, although rooms in this old building are chilly in winter. ②.

Kumari Lodge (☎222498). Right on Durbar Square, it's as grotty as they come but it might be worth it for one of the triple rooms with a view in the front; don't bother with the cheaper rooms at the back. ②.

Welcome Friendly Home. Kathmandu's oldest surviving guest house, and invariably packed in high season. A nice place to be for Christmas, when the owners throw a party on the roof. ②.

Thamel and around

Thamel used to be a restful, if unreal, haven – a place you could look forward to getting to after some hard travelling or trekking. Now, at least in the high season, it's just something to be endured, and the much-touted restaurants are little compensation. The lanes are lethal cocktails of pollution and traffic (Thamel Chowk, where the taxis attempt to turn around, should be renamed Thamel Choke), everything is in a permanent state of flux, and a bitter taste of Indian hustle hangs in the air. Sooner or later the authorities will have to ban traffic on at least some streets – but there's no relief yet in sight.

That said, if you've just arrived and your brain is still six time zones out to sea, Thamel can help ease you into things until you feel ready to sally forth. It's painting by numbers here, with every imaginable convenience at your fingertips, though bear in mind it's a rather long, jostling walk to the sights of Kathmandu.

CHEAP GUEST HOUSES

Gorkha Guest House, Chhetrapati Thamel (☎221434). Run-of-the-mill rooms compensated for by loads of patio and roof seating. ③/B④.

Mini Om Guest House, Thamel (☎229288). Basic, but cheap and admirably tucked away, considering its central location. ③.

Mona Lisa Guest House, Thamel (☎411388). Right in the trendy heart of Thamel, cheap but noisy. ③/B④.

Pheasant Lodge, Thamel (☎417415). One of several cheap and cheerful outfits tucked away in a quiet yet central cul-de-sac. ②.

Tara Guest House, Kwa Bahal (☎220634). Small but pleasant garden, and basic rooms. ③/B④.

Tukche Peak Guest House, Thamel (☎414803). Reasonably quiet for such a central location; has the advantage of a pleasant outdoor restaurant. ③/B④.

Yeti Cottage, north Thamel (☎412818). A funky old building shaped like a grand piano with a good restaurant and plenty of greenery; a favourite with overland groups. ④.

UPMARKET GUEST HOUSES

Earth House, Bhagwan Bahal (☎418436). New place with a nice roof terrace, located near Bhagwan Bahal on an interesting (but rapidly modernizing) street. ④/B⑤.

Hotel Garuda, north Thamel (☎416776). A smart place with friendly staff. B⑥.

Hotel Horizon, Chhetrapati Thamel (☎220904). Very secluded down a quiet side lane, with decent rooms and plenty of rooftop seating. ④/B④.

Kathmandu Guest House, Thamel (☎413632). Thamel's original guest house is still the best, set well back from the noisy street, with efficient management and a gorgeous garden. It's a huge and social place: exciting or pretentious, depending on your outlook. Rooms are always in demand, and booked up well ahead during the high season. Old wing ③/B⑥; new wing B⑦.

Mustang Holiday Inn, Jyatha Thamel (☎226794). This longstanding favourite has gone way upmarket of late – the lobby has a TV now, and all rooms have phones. Other places along this lane are somewhat cheaper, though still relatively expensive – try *Imperial Guest House* (☎229339), or *Hotel White Lotus* (☎226342). B⑤.

Potala Guest House, Chhetrapati (☎226566). Central, with a garden. B⑤.

Thorung Peak Guest House, Kwa Bahal (☎224656). Friendly, efficient and quiet, with well-appointed rooms (all with phones) and a great roof terrace. ⑥/B⑥.

Tibet Guest House, Chhetrapati (☎214383). Friendly, and with a really lovely roof garden. ⑤/B⑥.

Off the beaten track

The touts and carpet-sellers of the tourist strips pale very quickly, as Kathmandu veterans well know. Here are a few out-of-the-way guest houses to help you steer clear of the scene. If you've just arrived, see if any of these names rings a bell with the touts at the airport or bus station (they're often employed by places tourists wouldn't easily find on their own), and if so, you'll save yourself some grief getting settled in.

CHEAP GUEST HOUSES

Diyalo Guest House, Mahabaudha – see North of Durbar Square map (☎270528). Very bare-bones establishment, and not too hot on spoken English, but the area is lively and well placed for old Kathmandu, Thamel and New Road. ②.

Hotel Shrestha, Tahachal – off the main Kathmandu map, west of *Peace Guest House* (☎270528). Quiet and out of the way, this might be a good choice if you've got kids with you. ②/B④.

Peace Guest House, Tahachal – see main Kathmandu map (☎271093). This place outfreaks Freak Street – it attracts a real skinflint crowd, but it's friendly, clean and has generous rooms and a big roof terrace. Short but fairly wretched walk to Durbar Square. Some rooms have baths. ①/B③.

Thahiti Guest House, Thahiti – see Thamel map (☎270528). Clean rooms, laid-back management, high rooftop terrace, good central location on an as-yet-uncommercialized street with several good *bhojanalaya*; the guest house has a quirky tourist restaurant of its own. B⑤.

UPMARKET GUEST HOUSES

Dhaulagiri Guest House, Dhalko – see main Kathmandu map (☎213393). Reasonably clean, sequestered from the humdrum neighbourhood it's in. ⑤/B⑥.

Dikey Guest House, Dhalko – see main Kathmandu map (☎215996). Friendly, helpful, clean. ④/B⑥.

Hotel Sayapatri, Bhote Bahal – see South of Durbar Square map (☎223398). Ten minutes' walk from Freak Street, reasonably secluded and festooned with flowers. There are several cheaper possibilities in this neighbourhood, though less English is spoken. B⑥.

Kathmandu Peace Guest House, Paknajol – see main Kathmandu map (☎414623). Secluded, with good views north and west from rooftop, though the rooms are ordinary and it's a hike to old Kathmandu. ⑤/B⑥.

Tibet Peace Guest House (☎415026), on the same lane, is a relative newcomer with better facilities and similar prices, but poorer views. ⑤/B⑥.

Camping

Motorists beware – central Kathmandu is a nightmare for driving. Do not attempt to enter with a camper or other large vehicle: the streets are too narrow and crowded, and you'll be constantly defeated by the one-way system.

For **camping**, your only developed option is *Tourist Camp*, thoughtfully located just off the Ring Road near Swayambhu, where the overnight charge is about Rs50 per vehicle and showers are available. To find it, go north along the Ring Road to Swayambhu, turn east on the road that runs south of the hill, and look for a metal gate about 200m on the right (it may not be marked). You could also try Rani Ban (see p.127), which has zero facilities but a wonderful jungly setting (Rs50–100 per vehicle). Or drive up to Changu Narayan (Chapter Two), Nagarkot, Dhulikhel or Kakani (Chapter Three), all within an hour or so of Kathmandu and much less nerve-wracking than other urban options.

Hotels

Kathmandu's listed **hotels** are more spread out, so it's advisable to have a particular place in mind before setting off. Most are members of the *Nepal Hotel Association*, which operates a reservation desk at the airport. Tax of twelve to fifteen percent (rising with the number of stars) isn't included in the prices given below. Payment has to be made in foreign currency. Except where indicated, refer to the main Kathmandu map for locations.

Moderate

Hotel Ambassador, Lazimpath (☎410432). All mod cons at a reasonable price. Two stars. B⑦.

Hotel Blue Diamond, Jyatha Thamel – see Thamel map (☎226392). No great shakes, but the cheapest air conditioning in Nepal. Two stars. B⑦.

Hotel Manaslu, Lazimpath (☎410071). Pleasant oasis with a nice front lawn, popular with aid workers and their visitors. Two stars. B⑦.

Hotel Mandap, north Thamel – see Thamel map (☎413321). Comfortable retreat in a popular part of Thamel, which for some people might represent the best of both worlds. Two stars. B⑦.

Hotel Vajra, Bijeshwari (☎272719). Unquestionably the best in its class: beautifully appointed, with a library, theatre and art gallery, and tremendous views of Swayambhu from the roof terrace. Definitely worth a splurge. Two stars. ⑥/B⑦.

Expensive

Everest Hotel, Baneswar (Airport Road; ☎220567). Pool, tennis, gym, disco. Five stars. B⑨.

Hotel de l'Annapurna, Durbar Marg (☎221711). Pool, sauna, the works. Five stars. B⑨.

Hotel Malla, Lekhnath Marg (☎410320). Small, with an excellent Chinese restaurant. Four stars. B⑨.

Hotel Marshyangdi, north Thamel – see Thamel map (☎414105). Swanky hotel that sits strangely amidst the budget fracas of Thamel. Three stars. B⑧.

Hotel Shangrila, Lazimpath (☎412999). Tucked away in embassyland. Four stars. B⑨.

Hotel Shanker, Lazimpath (☎410151). Converted Rana palace with an entrance that has to be seen to be believed. Three stars. B⑨.

Hotel Yak & Yeti, Durbar Marg (☎222635). Kathmandu's finest: pool, tennis, opulent restaurants. Five stars. B⑨.

Hotel Yellow Pagoda, Kantipath (☎220337). Central. Breakfast included. Three stars. B⑧.

THE CITY

The scene on Thamel avenue today: a very pretty pale-brown cow standing on the sidewalk, between a cigarette stand and an umbrella repairman, her head lifted straight up, perpendicular with the ground, while a ten-year-old boy heading home from school stood there, reaching up and scratching the animal's neck. Meanwhile all the tourists pointing to the fruit-bats hanging in the trees. The smell of bat shit and garbage and day-old murk, literally Another Shitty Day in Paradise. Shangri-la's getting wasted, but you can still stand on the street corner in Kathmandu and scratch her heavy velvet throat.

Jeff Greenwald, *Mister Raja's Neighborhood*

The Kathmandu most travellers come to see is the old city, a tight tangle of narrow alleys and numerous temples immediately north and south of the central **Durbar Square**. It's a bustling, intensely urban quarter where tall, extended-family dwellings – built of traditional brick and wood or, increasingly, concrete – block out the sun, while dark, open-fronted shops crowd the lanes, and vegetable sellers clot the intersections. Though the city goes to bed early, from before dawn to around 10pm there's always something happening somewhere. Early morning is the best time to watch people going about their daily religious rites (*puja*), adorning idols with red paste (*sindur*) and marigold petals. If you walk around after dinner, especially in the neighbourhoods of Indrachowk, Asan and Chhetrapati, you'll frequently run across mesmerizing devotional hymn-sings (*bhajan*).

This is only one side of Kathmandu, though, and not necessarily representative of the rest. Across the Bishnumati River, just **west** of town, is a more newly settled and rapidly developing area; the famous Swayambhu stupa, magnificently set on a conical hill here, has attracted a large community of expatriate Tibetans, whose culture is a world apart from that of Kathmandu's indigenous Newars.

Most commerce these days is conducted **east** of the old quarter: the boulevards around the Royal Palace are wide and businesslike, lined with airline offices and five-star hotels, while tinny, congested bazaars sprawl further to the south and east. The northeast is given over to quiet, tree-lined suburbs.

Durbar Square

Teeming, touristy **Durbar Square** is the natural place to begin sightseeing. The old royal palace (*durbar*), running along the eastern edge of the square, takes up more space than all the other monuments here combined. Kumari Chowk, home of Kathmandu's "living goddess", overlooks the square from the south. The square itself is squeezed by the palace into two parts: at the southern end is the Kasthamandap, the ancient building that probably gave Kathmandu its name, while the northern part is taken up by a varied procession of statues and temples.

Hanuman Dhoka

The rambling **old royal palace** (Mon–Thurs & Sun 10.30am–4.15pm, 10.30am–3.15pm in winter, Fri 10.30am–2.15pm; Rs10) – usually called **Hanuman Dhoka**, after its main entrance – was built over the course of almost four centuries. Its oldest, eastern wings date from the mid-sixteenth century, but in all likelihood

KATHMANDU
DURBAR SQUARE

0   50 m

N

MAKHAN

GANGA PATH

Taleju Mandir

Pancha Mukhi
Hanuman

MUL
CHOWK

LOHAN
CHOWK

Bank

Basantapur
Tower

Jagannath
Mandir

Palace
Entrance

Hanuman Dhoka
(Royal Palace)

NASSAL
CHOWK

Freak Street →

DURBAR
SQUARE

Kalo
Bhairab

Pratap
Malla

Seto
Bhairab

Tribhuwan
Museum

BASANTAPUR
SQUARE

Drums

Vamsagopala

Taleju
Bell

Shiva
Parvati

Gaddi
Baithak

Kumari
Chowk

KOT

District
Police HQ

PYAPHAL

Maju
Dewal

DURBAR
SQUARE

Trailokya
Mohan

Kabindrapur

Maru
Ganesh

MARU

Simha
Sattal

Kasthamandap

there was a palace on this spot before then. Malla kings built most of the rest by the late seventeenth century, and after capturing Kathmandu in 1768, Prithvi Narayan Shah added (in characteristically martial fashion) four lookout towers at the southeastern corner. Finally, the Ranas left their mark with the garish Neoclassical facade along the southwestern flank. Nepal's royal family last lived here in 1896, before moving to the northern end of town, retaining the complex for ceremonial and administrative purposes.

Only a fraction of the five-acre palace and grounds is open to the public; entrance is through **Hanuman Dhoka** (Hanuman Gate), a brightly decorated doorway at the east side of the northern part of Durbar Square. The gate is named after the popular monkey god Hanuman, whose statue stands outside – you won't recognize him, smothered under a layer of *sindur* paste, but that's the way Nepalis like him. Ram's right-hand man in the Hindu *Ramayan* epic, Hanuman has always been revered by Nepalese kings, who, like Ram, are held to be incarnations of the god Vishnu. On the left as you enter stands a masterful sculpture of another Vishnu incarnation, the man-lion Narasimha, tearing apart a demon, followed by a series of portraits of Shah kings, beginning with Prithvi Narayan Shah.

The entrance opens to **Nassal Chowk**, the large central courtyard that provided the setting for King Birendra's coronation in 1975, and which is still used for important royal functions. The brick wings that form its southern and eastern flanks date from the sixteenth century and boast painstakingly carved wooden doorways, windows and struts – check out the door jambs beaded with tiny skulls. At the northeast corner of the square, the five-tiered pagoda-like turret, notable for its round roofs, is the **Pancha Mukhi Hanuman Mandir**. Mul Chowk and Lohan Chowk, the equally ornate courtyards just visible through doorways to the east, are closed to the public.

The Tribhuwan Museum and Basantapur Tower

Your only chance to get a peep at the palace interior, the **Tribhuwan Museum** (same hours as Hanuman Dhoka) features a typically indulgent display of memorabilia from the reign of the present king's grandfather, Tribhuwan, who restored the monarchy in 1951 and opened up Nepal to the outside world. Genuinely interesting, however, is the exhibit of jewel-studded coronation ornaments, including elephant dressings, howdahs (elephant platforms) and a throne. There's also a small numismatic wing, displaying coins dating back to the Buddha's time from the kingdom of Kapilvastu.

The museum leads to the massive eight-storey **Basantapur Tower**, the biggest of the four raised by Prithvi Narayan Shah in honour of the four main cities of the Kathmandu Valley (Basantapur – "Place of Spring" – refers to Kathmandu). You can ascend to a kind of crow's nest enclosed by pitched wooden screens to get fine views in four directions, while the sound of flute sellers drifts up from the square below. The highest mountains visible are those of the Langtang Himal, just peeking up above the Gosainkund Lekh. To take pictures from the tower, enter through a separate doorway at the south end of Nassal Chowk, since cameras aren't allowed in the museum.

The palace exterior

Two sights along the outer walls of the palace are worth mentioning. Just to the north of the entrance is a **stone inscription** in fifteen languages, carved in 1664 by King Pratap Malla, the prime architect of Durbar Square's temples, who also

KATHMANDU CULTURE: THE NEWARS

Although only a minor ethnic group in national terms, the **Newars** account for three-quarters of Kathmandu's population and exert a cultural influence in Nepal far beyond their numbers. Some scholars make the Newars out to be descendants of the Kiratas, who ruled the Kathmandu Valley between the seventh century BC and the second century AD, while others say they go back even further than that; in any case, the Newar community has had to absorb successive waves of immigrants, refugees, traders and usurpers ever since, resulting in a complex cultural matrix.

Centuries of domination by foreign rulers have, if anything, only accentuated the uniqueness of Newar culture. For 1500 years the Newars have sustained an almost continuous artistic flowering: under the Lichhavis they produced acclaimed stone carvings, and under the Mallas and Shahs they've excelled in wood, metal and brick. They're believed to have invented the **pagoda**, and it was a Newar architect, Arniko, who led a Nepali delegation in the thirteenth century to introduce the technique to the Chinese. The pagoda style of stacked, angled roofs finds unique expression in Nepali (read Newar) temples, and if you look closely you'll see that it's echoed in the overhanging eaves of Newar houses, too.

The shape of Newar settlements goes right to the roots of Newar civilization: farming and trade. As farmers, Newars build their **villages** in compact, urban nuclei to conserve the fertile farmland of the valley. As traders, they construct their houses with removable wooden shutters, so that the ground floor can double as a shop. Scattered, in part, by the shortage of land in the valley, Newar traders have colonized lucrative crossroads throughout Nepal, recreating bustling **bazaars** wherever they go.

But above all, Newars are consummate city-builders. The fundamental building-block of old Newar **cities** is the **bahal** – a set of buildings joined at right angles around a central courtyard. Kathmandu is honeycombed with *bahal*, many of which were originally built as Buddhist monasteries but have reverted to residential use during two centuries of state-sponsored Hinduism. (*Bahal* architecture was applied to palaces as well, as a look at a map of Durbar Square will readily demonstrate.) Another uniquely Newar invention is the **guthi**, a benevolent community trust based on caste or kinship links that handles the upkeep of temples (*mandir*) and fountains (*hiti*), organizes festivals, arranges cremations and, indirectly, ensures the transmission of Newar culture from one generation to the next. Kathmandu's *guthi* have been on the decline since the 1960s, however, when land reform deprived them of much of their income from holdings around the valley, and with young Newars losing interest in traditional ways they are gradually being marginalized into social clubs.

Newars are easily recognizable: one dead giveaway is that they carry heavy loads in baskets suspended at either end of a **shoulder pole** (*nol*), whereas other Nepali hill people carry things on their backs, supported by a tumpline from the forehead. As for **clothing**, you can usually tell a Newar man by his waistcoat, and a woman by her shawl (it used to be the fashion for Newar women to wear their saris in complicated pleats, requiring upwards of twenty-five metres of material, but these days most follow the Indian style). Newars still speak among themselves in **Newari**, a Tibeto-Burman language with many borrowings from Nepali (see "Language" in *Contexts*), and several Newari newspapers are published in Kathmandu; but with the lure of good government jobs strong, many young Newars are neglecting their native tongue for Nepali. For a detailed description of Newar **religion**, see *Contexts*.

fancied himself something of a linguist. The inscription is supposed to be a poem to the goddess Kali, and the story goes that if anyone can read the whole thing, milk will gush from the tap. Look for the two words in French and one in English.

Stuck onto the palace's southwestern end like a barnacle is the **Gaddi Baithak**, a ponderous addition from 1908 that pretty much sums up Rana-era architecture. If you didn't know Nepalese history you might say it had a whiff of the Raj about it, and in a way you'd be right: while India was under British rule, Nepal was labouring under its own home-grown colonialists, the Rana line of isolationist prime ministers. Purists bemoan the building's distorting effect on Durbar Square's proportions, but while it's admittedly out of step with traditional Nepali architecture, it certainly peps up the square with a dash of mock bravado.

Kumari Chowk

Immediately south of the Gaddi Baithak stands **Kumari Chowk**, the gilded cage of the Raj Kumari, Kathmandu's "living goddess". In case there was any doubt, Kumari Chowk proves Kathmandu is no stuffy, dead museum: no other temple better illustrates the living, breathing and endlessly adaptable nature of Nepalese religion, and its freewheeling blend of Hindu, Buddhist and downright bizarre elements.

The cult of **the Kumari** – a prepubescent girl worshipped as a living incarnation of Durga, the demon-slaying Hindu mother goddess – probably goes back to the early Middle Ages. Jaya Prakash, the last Malla king of Kathmandu, institutionalized the practice when he built the Kumari Chowk in 1757. According to legend, the king either committed some sexual indiscretion against a Kumari, or disbelieved a girl who claimed to be the goddess – in any case Jaya Prakash, who is remembered as a particularly paranoid and weak king, was so consumed by guilt that he erected the building as an act of atonement. He also established the tradition – continued to this day – that each September during the Indra Jaatra festival, the Kumari should bestow a *tika* (auspicious mark) on the forehead of the king who was to reign for the coming year. In 1768, the hapless Jaya Prakash was driven into exile on the eve of Indra Jaatra, and the conquering Prithvi Narayan Shah slipped in and took the *tika*. Kathmandu's Raj Kumari is the pre-eminent of eleven in the valley.

Although the Kumari is supposed to be a Hindu goddess, she is chosen from the Buddhist Shakya clan of goldsmiths, according to a **selection process** reminiscent of the Tibetan Buddhist method of finding reincarnated lamas. Elders interview hundreds of Shakya girls, aged three to five, short-listing those who exhibit 32 auspicious signs: a neck like a conch shell, a body like a banyan tree, eyelashes like a cow's and so on. Finalists are placed in a dark room surrounded by freshly severed buffalo heads, while men in demon masks parade around making scary noises. The girl who shows no fear and can correctly identify belongings of previous Kumaris, and whose horoscope doesn't clash with the king's, becomes the next Kumari. She lives a cloistered life inside the Kumari Chowk – her feet are never allowed to touch the ground – and is only carried outside on her throne at Indra Jaatra and four or five other festivals each year. Durga's spirit leaves her when she menstruates or otherwise bleeds, whereupon she's retired with a modest state pension. The transition to life as an ordinary mortal can be hard, and she may have difficulty finding a husband, since tradition has it that the man who marries an ex-Kumari will die young. The present

> For background information on the various gods, their symbols and styles of worship, see "Religion" in *Contexts*. Definitions of various Nepali religious terms are also given in the glossary at the end of *Contexts*.

Kumari was installed in 1986, when she was four years old, so she's likely to reign well into the 1990s. The Kumari Chowk's exterior has recently been restored to expose its original brickwork, long buried under Rana plaster. Non-Hindus aren't allowed past the **interior courtyard**, which is decorated with exquisitely carved (if weathered) windows, pillars and doorways. When she feels like it, the Kumari, decked out in exaggerated eye makeup and jewellery, shows herself at one of the first-floor windows, at which time one of her handlers generally whips round for donations. She's believed to answer her visitors' unspoken questions with the look on her face. Cameras are okay inside the courtyard, but photographing the Kumari is strictly forbidden.

Temples and monuments

Dozens of freestanding temples (*mandir*), stepped platforms (*dewal*) and statues litter Durbar Square; the following stand out as highlights.

The Kasthamandap

If legend is to be believed, the **Kasthamandap**, standing at the southwestern end of the square, is Kathmandu's oldest building, and one of the oldest wooden buildings in the world. It's said to have been constructed from the wood of a single tree in the late twelfth century (Simha Sattal, the smaller version to the south, was made from the leftovers), but what you see is mostly the result of several renovations since 1630. An open, pagoda-roofed pavilion (*mandap*), it served for several centuries as a rest house (*sattal*) along the Tibet trade route, and probably formed the nucleus of early Kathmandu. This corner of the square, called Maru Tol, still has the look of a crossroads, with sellers hawking fruit and veg off bicycles, and the city's indigents still sleep in the Kasthamandap at nights.

The Shah kings converted the Kasthamandap into a temple to their protector deity*, **Gorakhnath**, whose statue stands in the middle of the pavilion. A Brahman priest usually sets up shop here to dispense instruction and conduct rituals. In four niches set around are shrines to Ganesh, the elephant-headed god of good fortune, which supposedly represent the celebrated Ganesh temples of the Kathmandu Valley (at Chabahil, Bhaktapur, Chobar and Bungamati), thus enabling Kathmandu residents to pay tribute to all four at once. The building to the southeast of the Kasthamandap is **Kabindrapur**, a Shiva temple mostly patronized by musicians and dancers.

---

*A word about the confusing matter of royal deities. Gorakhnath, a mythologized Indian guru, is revered as a kind of guardian angel by all the Shah kings. Taleju Bhawani, to whom many temples and bells are dedicated in the Kathmandu, Patan and Bhaktapur Durbar Squares, played a similar role for the Malla kings. The Kumari has been worshipped by the kings of both dynasties, but mainly as a public gesture to secure her *tika*, which lends credibility to their divine right to rule. Finally, the present king, Birendra, exercising the prerogative of all Hindus, has taken as his own family deity Dakshin Kali, whose shrine is at the southern edge of the Kathmandu Valley.

The rest of the southern square

Immediately north of the Kasthamandap stands yet another Ganesh shrine, the unassuming but ever-popular **Maru Ganesh**. A ring on Ganesh's bell is usually the first stage in any *puja*, and the shrine is the first stop for people intending to worship at the other temples of Durbar Square, royalty included. Ganesh's trusty "vehicle", a rat, is perched on a plinth of the Kasthamandap, across the way.

The three-roofed temple between the Kasthamandap and the Kumari Chowk is the seventeenth-century **Trailokya Mohan**, dedicated to Vishnu. The *das avatar* dance takes place here during the October Dasain festival, in which masked dancers portray the ten incarnations of Vishnu. A much-photographed statue of the angelic **Garud**, Vishnu's man-bird vehicle, kneels in his customary palms-together *namaste* position in front of the temple. The broad, bricked area east of here is **Basantapur Square**, once the site of royal elephant stables, where souvenir sellers now spread their wares.

Moving north, the huge seventeenth-century **Maju Dewal** sits high atop a pyramid of nine stepped levels. Climb to the top for a sweeping, god's-eye view of the square and all its hubbub, but don't expect to escape the roving bangle-sellers and students anxious to practise their English. From this height you can look straight across at the rectangular **Shiva Parvati Mandir**, erected in the eighteenth century by one of the early Shah kings. Painted figures of Shiva and his consort Parvati lean out of the first-floor window, looking like they're about to toss the bouquet and dash off to the honeymoon suite.

Seto Bhairab and Kalo Bhairab

North of the Shiva Parvati temple, the square narrows and then opens out to another temple-clogged area. Ranged along the left (western) side are the **Taleju Bell**, the octagonal **Vamsagopala**, and a pair of ceremonial **drums** from the eighteenth century. To the right, set against the palace wall but not very visible behind a wooden screen, is the snarling ten-foot-high gilded head of **Seto Bhairab** (White Bhairab), a terrifying, blood-swilling aspect of Shiva. One day a year, during Indra Jaatra in September, the screen comes down and men jostle to drink rice beer flowing out of a pipe in Bhairab's mouth. The column nearby supports a gilded statue of **King Pratap Malla** and family, a self-congratulatory artform that was all the rage among the Malla kings of the late seventeenth century.

North of this, on the other side of the small Degu Taleju Mandir, the massive, roly-poly image of **Kalo Bhairab** (Black Bhairab) dances on the corpse of a demon. Carved from a single twelve-foot slab of stone, it was found in a field north of Kathmandu during the reign of Pratap Malla, but probably dates to Lichhavi times. It used to be said that anyone who told a lie in front of it would vomit blood and die; one story has it that when the chief justice's office stood across the way, so many witnesses died while testifying that a temple had to be erected to shield the court from Kalo Bhairab's wide-eyed stare.

A Newar and his *nol*

The Jagannath and Taleju temples

Between Pratap Malla's column and his multilingual inscription on the palace wall stands the sixteenth-century pagoda-style **Jagannath Mandir**, dedicated to the god whose runaway-chariot festival in India gave us the word "juggernaut". The struts supporting the lower roof of this temple contain Kathmandu's most tittered-about **erotic carvings**, although such carvings are actually quite common in Nepali temples: once you know where to look, you start noticing them everywhere. Scholars can't seem to agree on the significance of these little vignettes, which often feature outrageous athletics, threesomes and bestiality. Some suggest that sex in this context is being offered as a tantric path to enlightenment, and as evidence they note that such scenes generally appear on the lower portions of struts, separated from the gods and goddesses above by lotuses (symbolic of transcendence). A more popular belief is that the goddess of lightning is a chaste virgin who wouldn't dare strike a temple so decorated. In any case, Hanuman, who guards the nearby palace entrance, is spared the sight by the globs of *sindur* over his eyes.

Set atop a twelve-tiered plinth and rising 40m above the northeast end of the square, the **Taleju Mandir** was erected in the mid-sixteenth century by King Mahendra Malla, who built it to outdo the Taleju temples of his rivals in Patan and Bhaktapur, and decreed that no building should exceed it in height – a ban that remained in force until the middle part of this century. Kathmandu's biggest temple, it looks down on you with haughty grandeur. It's open only on the ninth day of Dasain, and then only to Nepalis, who make sacrifices to Durga in the courtyard. Taleju Bhawani, a south Indian goddess imported in the fourteenth century by the Mallas, is considered by Hindus to be a form of the mother goddess Durga, while Buddhist Newars count her as one of the Taras, tantric female deities.

Other, minor temples dotting the northern square belong mainly to Shiva. Inside each, the god is worshipped as a *linga*, a stone phallus that to a Shaiva (follower of Shiva) is as potent a symbol as the cross is to a Christian. The infamous **Kot Courtyard**, which once lay northwest of the square, is now taken up by a walled police compound. It was here that the Machiavellian general Jang Bahadur Rana engineered a grisly massacre of 55 of the king's top brass in 1846, thereby clearing the way to proclaim himself prime minister and establish the hereditary line that was to rule Nepal until 1951.

North of Durbar Square

Kathmandu's oldest, liveliest streets lie north and northeast of Durbar Square. You could make a more or less circular swing through the area (as this section does), but you'll almost certainly be diverted somewhere along the way. At any rate, the sights described here are only a backdrop for the old city's fascinating street life.

Indrachowk and Kel Tol

The old trade route to Tibet passes through Durbar Square and becomes a narrow lane where it rounds the Taleju Mandir. Passing through **Makhan Tol** – the name harks back to a time when butter (*makhan*) was sold here – it runs a gauntlet of *thangka* (Buddhist scroll painting) sellers and then takes a northeast-

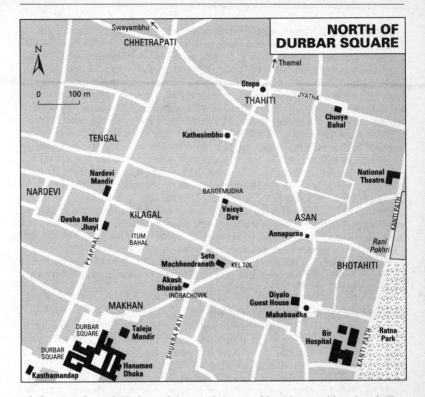

erly bearing through Kathmandu's now defunct goldsmiths' neighbourhood. The first big intersection you reach is **Indrachowk**, named in honour of the original Hindu king of the gods. A sort of Asian Zeus, complete with thunderbolt, Indra fell from grace in India centuries ago, but in the Kathmandu Valley he's still revered as a rainmaker and rates his own festival (Indra Jaatra). The gaudy house-like temple on the west side of the crossroads – its front decorated with European ceramic tiles, a common practice earlier this century – is that of **Akash Bhairab** (Sky, or Blue, Bhairab), who in the best anything-goes spirit of Hinduism sometimes trades places with Indra. The upstairs temple is out-of-bounds to non-Hindus, but you can see the scary black mask of Bhairab paraded around Kathmandu during Indra Jaatra.

Shopping is good around Indrachowk. *Pashmina* shawls are sold from the steps of shrines in the intersection, and colourful bead necklaces (*pote*) and tassels (*dhaago*) hang in curtains from the stalls of the **Pote Pasal**, a small market area to the southeast. *Pote*, worn by virtually all married women in hill Nepal, typically consist of numerous strands of glass beads, all of the same colour, drawn together with a cylindrical gold ornament known as a *tilhari*; the beads are strung with deft speed, each strand anchored with a big toe or a nail. Many married women also weave *dhaago* into their hair – these are always red, a colour that indicates married status. The stalls here are owned mainly by Muslims, descendants of Kashmiri traders who migrated to the valley three centuries ago.

The tumultuous street heading north from Indrachowk is the direct route to Thamel, but the old Tibet road continues diagonally to the small square of **Kel Tol** and the seventeenth-century temple of **Seto Machhendranath** (White Machhendranath), one of two main shrines to the protector god of the Kathmandu Valley (the other is in Patan). Newars universally call this god Karunamaya, but the Nepali/Indian name prevails generally. Machhendranath's white mask, which you can see from the threshhold of the temple, is wheeled around the city on a chariot in late March or April. The well-concealed building features some beautiful gold and brass work on the outside, but an iron grille, installed to thwart temple thieves, robs it of its aesthetic appeal. This kind of precaution is still unusual in Nepal, a country whose artistic riches are all the more remarkable for being so public, but theft, driven by demand from Western collectors, has become an increasingly common occurrence in the past decade or so. The entrance is a gate at the west side of the square.

Beyond Kel Tol, the street is known mainly for its brass, copper and stainless steel wares: you'll see a bewildering array of incense holders, *thaal* (trays), water jugs, and vessels designed to hold water or cow's urine for *puja*. On the left, **Tilang Ghar**, a former Rana general's residence, is decorated with a stucco frieze of marching soldiers. The three-tiered octagonal **Krishna Mandir** just beyond is no longer active, and has been half obscured by the encroachments of surrounding buildings.

Asan, Mahabaudha and Bangemudha

The last and most exuberant intersection along this route is **Asan Tol**, north Kathmandu's principal fruit and vegetable market and the main gathering point and hiring centre for labourers (*kuli* in Nepali and Hindi – hence "coolie"). Spices, homemade balls of soap, candles, oil, incense and other household wares are sold here, as are flowers during festivals. The brass-roofed pagoda at the south side of the square is the temple of **Annapurna**, the goddess of grain and abundance, and a manifestation of Lakshmi, the popular goddess of wealth. A lavish little affair, the pagoda bristles with icons and imagery, and its roof is strung with electric bulbs like a Christmas tree. Annapurna is represented by a silver *kalash*, or vessel.

From Asan, the trade route angles up to Kantipath and the modern city, and an alley heading south leads to **Mahabaudha**. This plain white stupa, stuck in a rather unattractive square, takes its name from the big, harlequin-painted statue of the Buddha in an adjacent shelter. Just east of Mahabaudha, Kathmandu's removal men wait for work: you see them all over town, pushing loads around on rubber-wheeled flatbed carts, almost always in bare feet and shorts – like porters, they are usually of the Tamang tribe (see p.178).

Walk westwards from Asan and you'll return to the main Indrachowk–Thamel lane at **Bangemudha**. Just south of this square is the odd shrine to **Vaisya Dev**, the Newar toothache god. Commonly billed as the "Toothache Tree", it's actually the butt end of a log, embedded in the side of a building, and locals believe you can cure toothache by nailing a coin to the log. (Bangemudha – "Crooked Stick" – refers to the legendary tree from which the log was cut.) Vaisya Dev's curative powers are now stronger than ever, thanks to the help of several nearby dentists. Fans of ancient sculpture might appreciate the tiny fifth-century figure of the Buddha at the north end of Bangemudha, though its tacky tiled niche does it no favours.

Kathesimbhu, Thahiti and Thamel

Kathesimbhu, central Kathmandu's biggest stupa, stands in a square off to the left about 200m north of Bangemudha. The temple is only a modest replica of the more impressive Swayambhu stupa (its name is a contraction of "Kathmandu Swayambhu"), but for those too old or infirm to climb to Swayambhu, rites performed here earn the same merit. According to legend it was built from the earth left over after Swayambhu's construction; Lichhavi-era sculptures rounda-bout attest to the antiquity of the site, but the stupa itself probably dates to the seventeenth century. The square doubles as the playground for a local school and is best avoided during playtime.

Traffic circulates around another stupa at **Thahiti**, the next square north on the way to Thamel. Because they're continually replastered, stupas never look very old and are hard to date, but this one probably goes back to the fifteenth century. One of Kathmandu's finest old *bahal*, the seventeenth-century **Chusya Bahal** stands about two blocks east of Thahiti. You'll recognize it by the two stone lions out in front and a meticulously carved wooden *torana* (decorative

---

KATHMANDU BABYLON

There is a prevalent, if unacknowledged, belief among Thamel's budget travellers that they can dress and behave any way they like because they're in Nepal. Mistaking Nepalis' tolerance for amorality, they show their contempt (or at best ignorance) for local ways. They get away with it only because Thamel *isn't* Nepal, but a weird Nepali Disneyland, a projection of the collective longings of budget travellers. Travellers have recreated Nepal in their own image, and Nepalis, seeing an easy opportunity, have happily obliged. They know they can make more money selling bad lasagne than good *daal bhaat*, and they can draw more customers by playing Pink Floyd than Narayan Gopal.

A kind of apartheid prevails in Thamel, an enclave where Nepalis are in the minority, and always in a subservient role. Sometimes it has the appearance of a colonial club where natives and dogs aren't allowed, and it almost seems as if the whole setup has been designed to make travellers feel good in some perverse, racist way. To be waited on, to have such leisure and choice for so little money, to be sought after, even to be hassled – the subtext is always, you're richer and more important here than in your home country, you're a big cheese here, you're in control because you've got the bucks and everyone wants to be your friend.

For too many travellers, Thamel is a budget base camp for fleeting assaults on Nepal – a space module from which to explore the surface of an alien planet. Sequestered in their bunker, surrounded by other foreigners and eating only Western food, they get just as superficial and distorted a view of the country as those who stay in the Oberoi. "The rich are different," Fitzgerald once said, to which Hemingway is supposed to have replied, "Yes, they have more money." In Kathmandu, that's often the only difference between "travellers" and "tourists".

Thamel is a living manifestation of what's wrong with budget travel. It's travel narrowing the mind; travellers foisting their own culture on their hosts, rather than learning, with an open mind and all due humility, from another society; travellers always taking, rather than seeing travel as a two-way exchange; travellers dashing from one budget bolthole to the next and closing their eyes to the reality in between.

You might say that tourists get the destinations they deserve. In the case of Thamel, we have no one but ourselves to blame for how it's turned out. We are always looking for that cheap paradise – well it doesn't exist, or it can't remain paradise for long.

Playing a *maadal*

shield) above the doorway, both standard features of a *bahal*. The building is now privately owned, but you can get a look at the courtyard from the threshhold.

In the tourist zone north of Thahiti, old buildings are few and about the only sights are the goodies in the restaurant windows. To find a monument in the vicinity of **Thamel**, you could visit **Bhagwan Bahal**, a little-used pagoda that lends its name to an area north of Thamel (a sign in front calls it "Bikrama Sila Mahabihar"). A feature of this temple is the collection of kitchen pans and utensils nailed to the front wall, placed there as offerings to the deity.

Chhetrapati south to Durbar Square

At the southwestern fringe of Thamel lies boisterous **Chhetrapati**, an intersection of almost perpetual motion. Though the neighbourhood lacks any ancient monuments, it supports a central *pati* resembling an Edwardian bandstand around which religious processions and impromptu musical jamborees are almost daily occurrences. During Shiva Raatri, sadhus build fires on the platform and light up their chillum, and during Tihaar the iron railings are decorated with oil lamps.

From Chhetrapati it's a straight run south to the Kasthamandap; this street is favoured as an assembly point for protest marches, since the police can't easily secure it. The **Nardevi** area, to the west of the temple of the same name, has acquired quite a reputation as an important centre of ayurvedic medicine, with a college, hospital and many doctors' practices and pharmas. To the east, **Kilagal** is the domain of fruit and vegetable sellers, and a few potters who sell their wares from the steps of a squat Mahadev temple erected in memory of King Tribhuwan. Kilagal is sometimes still called Bhedasingh (Sheep Horn), a reminder of the days when livestock was traded here. Just to the south of Kilagal, the large flag-stoned piazza of **Itum Bahal** is still used for grain-drying during the harvest, but the old buildings that surround it are steadily being replaced and the traditional *bahal* ambience is ebbing.

Continuing south towards Durbar Square you get back into atmospheric eighteenth-century neighbourhoods, with several large *bahal* dating back as far as the fourteenth century tucked away down dark alleys. Keep an eye out on the east side of the street for the **Desha Maru Jhayl** – literally, the "Country Nowhere Window" – a window grille of staggering complexity which, even in a country abounding in outstanding woodwork, is considered unique. Carved from a single block of wood, it predates the house in which it's now set.

South of Durbar Square

South Kathmandu – the old part, at least – is a smaller area, less medieval, less bustling, and much poorer. Except for the area from Freak Street across to the GPO, it's completely untouristed and a fair representation of reality in modern, urban Nepal.

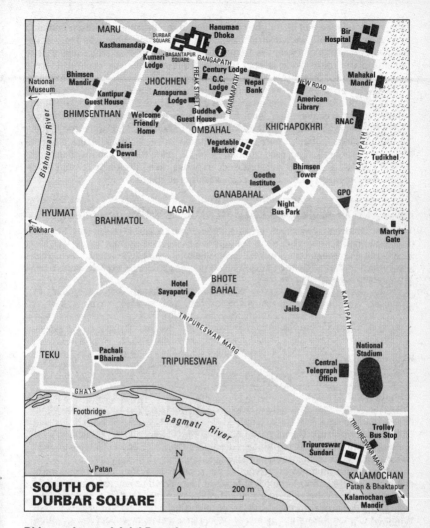

Bhimsenthan and Jaisi Dewal

A small square southwest of the Kasthamandap, down a lane leading to the
Bishnumati River, **Bhimsenthan** is named after one of Nepal's favourite gods.
Bhimsen was one of the famous five brothers of the Hindu *Mahabharat*, a mortal
hero who has been adopted as the patron saint of Newar merchants: you'll see
pictures of him in shops everywhere. According to legend, Bhimsen came to
Kathmandu as the manservant of a bride from eastern Nepal, who was married
off to a farmer who lived on the west bank of the Bishnumati. Unaware of his new
servant's identity, the farmer put Bhimsen to work in the fields; Bhimsen
proceeded to work miracles with the rice, and the farmer, finally recognizing the

god, granted him a plot of land he could reach in three strides. Bhimsen bounded across the river and settled at Bhimsenthan. The temple here was built in the early eighteenth century, but is frequently renovated to look much newer. The shrine on the upper floor is open only to Hindus, while the ground floor is, fittingly, occupied by shops.

Jaisi Dewal, a seventeenth-century Shiva temple, stands in a square several blocks south of the Kasthamandap down a different road. A three-tiered pagoda without much ornamentation, its size alone is impressive. *Linga*-spotters can ogle the eight-foot-high monster at the foot of the temple, which has to be the biggest in the kingdom (although only a raw, uncarved stone, it's nonetheless authentically proportioned). The road continues south, past Takan Bahal's fourteenth-century stupa – mossy and cracked, it looks like a mouldy orange – to **Tripureswar Marg**, an important east–west thoroughfare.

SURVIVORS: KATHMANDU'S STREET CHILDREN

Street children, like so many urban problems, are a relatively recent phenomenon in Kathmandu. Ground down by rural poverty, abetted by new roads and bus services, a growing number of children are running away to the capital in search of a better life. Some are lured away by men promising high-paying jobs in tourism. These promises often prove false.

The charity Child Workers in Nepal (CWIN) estimates that more than five hundred children – some as young as five, and invariably male – live on Kathmandu's streets, and their number is rising daily. They call themselves *khate*, a word that may be translated as "survivor". Most are lone runaways or orphans, though some live with their squatter families. The young **beggars** who roam Thamel and Durbar Marg, barefoot and clutching dirty cloths for warmth, are perhaps the more "acceptable" face of homelessness. Living relatively well off tourist handouts, however, they spurn training programmes and education, and grow up illiterate, unskilled and unemployable – your alms will do more good if given to a charity working with beggars, rather than to the beggars themselves. The majority of street children scrounge a meagre existence as **rubbish pickers**, selling what salvageable materials they can find. Some wangle work as casual labourers or *kanchha* (errand boys), but in such a vulnerable position they run a high risk of exploitation. Some pick pockets, or drift into drugs or prostitution. The best a *khate* can hope for is to find steady work as a labourer, bus conductor or perhaps a riksha wallah.

In a country where sixty percent of the population is living below the poverty line, it's easy to overlook the plight of street kids. Yet the conditions Kathmandu's *khate* endure are far more debilitating than mere rural poverty. **Homeless**, they sleep in doorways, *pati* (open shelters) or unfinished buildings. **Hungry**, they often subsist on food thrown out by tourist restaurants, and many suffer from malnutrition. Weakened by toxic chemicals in the rubbish piles, pollution and contaminated water, few are without **disease** (CWIN reports that twenty percent have tuberculosis). They're regularly **beaten** by the police, who regard them as bad for tourism, and during visits by foreign delegations they may be thrown in prison or loaded into buses bound for India. And perhaps most damaging of all, they are deprived of the traditionally supportive environment of family and community, and instead must deal with daily rejection.

CWIN, one of several organizations working with Nepali street children, operates a "common room" near its office off Tripureswar Marg to provide food, education, health care and play for children. Volunteers and donations are needed. For more information, contact CWIN at PO Box 4374, Kathmandu (☎271658).

Pachali Bhairab and the ghats

The most interesting part of south Kathmandu begins with **Pachali Bhairab**, an open-air shrine marooned in a light industrial area south of Tripureswar Marg (follow the path opposite the *Hotel Valley View*). The tiny gilded idol of Bhairab stands in a peaceful courtyard, dwarfed by a huge pipal tree and a brass, life-sized human figure laid out like a pharaoh's casket. This is a *betal*, Bhairab's vehicle and a likeness of death which, in Nepali Hinduism, is believed to protect against death (the old principle of fighting fire with fire); *betal* normally take the form of miniature skulls or skeletons at temple entrances, and this one is unusual for being so large. An esoteric parade involving Bhairab and other gods converges here on the fifth day of Dasain.

Things get weirder as you follow the path from Pachali Bhairab down to the **Bagmati River**. Derelict, languid but strangely mesmerizing, the **ghats** (platforms by the river's edge, used for Hindu cremation and worship) here stretch as far as the eye can see in either direction. Statues, temples and all manner of neglected artefacts are jumbled along the shore – especially at the point where the Bishnumati joins the Bagmati – and you could easily spend several hours picking around among them. Cremations are often held at Teku *masan*, the cremation ground near the confluence, and kites wheel overhead in large numbers. The buffalo you see along the riverbanks today will be your sizzling steak or *momo* tomorrow – they're slaughtered here in the early mornings. A footbridge crosses the river to an as yet unmodernized section of Patan.

The biggest riverside temples are more than 1km to the east of the bridge, but to get to them you're faced with two equally unappealing prospects. One is to join the buzzing, sputtering stream of crosstown traffic along Tripureswar Marg, Kathmandu's strongest entry in the Bangkok lookalike sweepstakes. The other is to follow a trail along the riverbank, where you'll see scenes of utter deprivation. Kathmandu's very poorest – rubbish-pickers, butchers, sweepers – live here in makeshift shanties amid piles of trash and channels of raw sewage.

Lurking inside a crumbling courtyard near the junction of Tripureswar Marg and Kantipath, the massive pagoda of **Tripureswar Sundari** has been squatted by a collective of low-caste families; it was erected in the early nineteenth century in memory of an assassinated king by his widow. Further south, the marvellously hideous **Kalamochan Mandir** is a study in Rana excess and faded glory. Resembling a grotesque white wedding cake, it was completed in 1852 by the first of the Rana prime ministers, the homicidal Jang Bahadur, who is said to have buried the ashes of those killed in the Kot massacre in its foundation, mafia-style; the brass gargoyles snarling at its four corners are fitting testaments to his ambition. The way in is through the entrance marked "Nepal Association for the Welfare of the Blind".

New Road, Freak Street and Bhimsen Tower

Rebuilt after the disastrous 1934 earthquake, **New Road** (Juddha Sadak) cuts a swathe of modernity through the old city. Wealthy Nepalis and Indian tourists regard it as a magical duty-free bazaar and swarm its shops for perfume, rice warmers and myriad other grey-market goods imported from Hong Kong. Nepali peasants visiting the capital stand transfixed at the sight of holiday snaps rolling off automatic photo-processing machines. It's all heady stuff for Nepal – the "supermarket" here even boasts an escalator. The statue at the west end of New Road commemorates Prime Minister Juddha Shamsher Rana, who is credited with rebuilding the road (and much of Kathmandu) after the earthquake. **Pipal Bot**, a venerable old tree about midway along the road's south side, provides a natural canopy for newspaper vendors and is a favourite gathering place for Kathmandu's intelligentsia and gossip mongers.

Freak Street (Jhochhen Tol), like Thamel, isn't prime sightseeing territory, although nowadays tour groups come in search of the hippies that gave Freak Street its name – you still get the occasional sighting – or just to take a trip down memory lane. On a cultural note, the pair of *chaitya* in front of the *Paradise Restaurant* illustrate the unique synthesis of Hindu and Buddhist imagery that's so common in the Kathmandu Valley: the Buddha would probably be appalled, but his images are carved around suggestively phallic *linga*, and set atop bases that symbolize the female genitalia (*yoni*).

The lane heading east from here leads to Kathmandu's main **vegetable market**, located in an unpaved compound: fish and other smelly items are sold in the street in front. Further east, **Bhimsen Tower** ("Dharahara" in Nepali), the tall minaret-like tower overlooking the GPO, is of no earthly use to anyone except

---

THE JAILS

One of the more thought-provoking, not to mention worthy, things you can do while in Kathmandu is to visit Westerners held in the capital's four **jails**. Since families are expected to provide for most of the prisoners' needs, foreigners are particularly badly off. Most are held in one of the jails south of the GPO (Central, Badragol or Women's); a fourth facility is located in Dilli Bazaar.

At any given time, as many as half a dozen **Westerners** may be imprisoned or awaiting trial in Kathmandu, mainly on charges of smuggling gold or drugs. Five years is a typical sentence, with no time off for good behaviour: a favourable appeal verdict usually doesn't result in freedom, only a shortened sentence, and every prisoner can tell a sorry tale or two about shady lawyers and indifferent embassy officials. **Nepalis** receive the same rough justice, plus they are liable to be imprisoned for political reasons. A 1992 Amnesty International report on Nepal found no prisoners of conscience since the restoration of democracy; however, Nepali organizations say that the present government detains its political opponents almost as diligently as its predecessor, the only difference being that the detainees are now officially served with charges.

Conditions are grim. For food, inmates receive a half-kilo of "black" (fermented) rice and *daal* each day, plus a few rupees with which to buy vegetables at the prison shop. They sleep on the floor, with up to fifty to a room. No clothes or bedding are provided. Still, the prisoners here can consider themselves lucky they aren't locked away in provincial jails, beyond the normal range of human-rights organizations, where beatings and **torture** are still said to be used in interrogation. Torture is deeply ingrained in Nepal's police force, and while the 1990 constitution guarantees compensation to victims of torture, the national assembly has yet to enact any legislation to make this possible.

Daily **visiting hours** are 7am–5pm (but check: times may vary). You must ask for prisoners by name – check posters around Thamel and Freak Street to find out who's being held where. Inmates appear at the barred doorway of what looks like an animal stable, while visitors stand behind a chain, so conversations are far from private. Most prisoners will be grateful just for a chat, but don't go without bringing something tangible: food, vitamins, toiletries, books, clothes, blankets and cash are all appreciated.

land surveyors. It was built in 1832 by the prime minister, Bhimsen Thapa, possibly in imitation of Calcutta's Ochterlony Monument, which had been erected only four years earlier. A story is told that Bhimsen Thapa, sitting astride his horse, leapt off the tower, creating the nearby **Sun Dhara** (Golden Water Tap) where he landed. Three of Kathmandu's four **jails** are located south of here, down a side street off Kantipath – turn right just after the Ministry of Finance.

Swayambhu and around

Even if temple-touring makes your eyes glaze over, don't miss **Swayambhu** (or Swayambhunath), perched on a hill 2km west of Thamel. To begin with, it's a great place to get your bearings, geographically and culturally, in your first few days in Nepal: the hill commands a sweeping view of the Kathmandu Valley, and the temple complex, overrun with pilgrims and monkeys, is a real eye-opener.

But there's much more if you dig for it. The two-thousand-year-old stupa is the most profound expression of Buddhist symbolism in Nepal (all *bahal* in the valley contain a replica of it), and the source and central location of the valley's creation myth. There's evidence to believe the hill was used for animist rites even before Buddhism arrived in the valley two thousand years ago. Tantric Buddhists consider it the chief "power point" of the Kathmandu Valley, and one chronicle states that an act of worship here carries thirteen billion times more merit than anywhere else.

Since the Chinese invasion of Tibet in 1959, the area surrounding Swayambhu has become home to hundreds of Tibetans in exile. You'll see them and many other Buddhist pilgrims making a full circuit around the hill, queueing up to spin gigantic fixed prayer wheels and frequently twirling their own hand-held ones. The place is so steeped in lore and pregnant with detail that you'll never absorb it all in a single visit. Try going early in the morning at *puja* time, or at night when the red-robed monks pad softly around the dome, murmuring mantras and spinning the prayer wheels. Make a final visit on your last day in Nepal and see how your perceptions of it differ from your initial trip.

Swayambhu's main **festivals** are Buddha Jayanti (April or May) and Losar (in February or March), when pilgrims throng around the stupa and monks splash arcs of saffron paint over it in a lotus-flower pattern. Many also flock here each morning during the month of Gunla (August or September) to mark the "rain's retreat" with music and offerings to the monks.

Getting there

The main entrance is at the eastern foot of the hill and **getting there** is a simple matter on foot or cycle. From Thamel the easiest way is via Chhetrapati, where a small road heads straight towards Swayambhu, passing the *Hotel Vajra* en route. From Freak Street or Durbar Square, take the rustic lane running northwestwards from the Kasthamandap. Either way, it should take about twenty minutes to walk it. If you're cycling, the local kids will expect you to cough up a few rupees' protection money for your bike – failure to comply invites a flat tyre. A city bus also runs at irregular intervals between Ratna Park (north of the Tudikhel) and the eastern entrance, and taxis drive up to a small car park near the top, just west of the stupa.

SWAYAMBHU

A paved road circles the base of the hill. For **food**, follow the road around to the south, near the turning for the car park, where you'll find the *Iko* and *Tourist Corner* cafés, sedate descendants of the hippy hangouts that once thrived here. Other budget eateries have sprung up along the Ring Road, which passes just west of the hill. Although there are several other ways up the hill, the steep main path from the **eastern entrance**, with its 365 centuries-smoothed steps, is the most dramatic. The **Buddha statues** near the bottom are seventeenth-century, while a second group further up was donated in the early part of this century. The slates heaped up along the path are *mani* stones, inscribed, in Tibetan script, *Om mani padme hum* ("Hail to the jewel in the lotus"), the ubiquitous Buddhist mantra.

The stupa

According to Buddhist scriptures, the Kathmandu Valley was once a snake-infested lake (geologists agree about the lake: see "Natural History" in *Contexts*). Long ago – 91 eons ago, to be exact – a perfect, radiant lotus flower appeared on the surface of the lake, which the gods proclaimed to be Swayambhu ("Self-created"), the abstract essence of Buddhahood. Manjushri, the *bodhisattva* of knowledge, drew his sword and cut a gorge at Chobar, south of Kathmandu, to drain the lake and allow humans to worship Swayambhu. As the water receded, the lotus settled on top of a hill and Manjushri established a shrine to it, before turning his attention to ridding the valley of snakes* and establishing its first civili-

---

*The Kathmandu Valley harbours a powerful and abiding *nag* (snake spirit) cult. During the summer festival of Nag Panchami, emblems are placed above each door-way to appease the *nag*, who are able to release or withhold the life-giving monsoon rains. They're also considered the rightful owners of everything under the earth, which explains why the authorities are loath to allow archeological excavations. Upset a *nag* and you could bring on an earthquake.

zation. Another legend tells how, when Manjushri cut his hair at Swayambhu, the hairs that fell on the ground grew into trees, and the lice turned into monkeys.

The apparently simple structure of **the stupa** belies an immensely complex physical representation of Buddhist cosmology, and the purpose of walking round it – always in a clockwise direction – is to meditate on this. The solid, whitewashed dome symbolizes the womb or creation. Set in niches at the cardinal points, statues of **dhyani (meditating) Buddhas** correspond to the four elements (earth, air, fire and water) and a fifth, placed at an angle, to the sky or space. Like the rainbow colours produced by the refraction of pure white light, each represents a different aspect of Buddhahood: the hand positions, colours and "vehicles" (the animal statues below) of each are significant. The *dhyani* Buddhas are the same characters who appear on virtually every *chaitya* around the Kathmandu Valley. At each of the sub-cardinal points sit **female counterparts**, who according to the Buddhist tantric view of things represent the wisdom aspect that must be sexually united with the compassionate male force to achieve enlightenment.

The gilded cube surmounting the stupa surrounds a thick wooden pillar, which may be considered the phallic foil to the female dome. The **eyes** painted on it are those of the all-seeing Adi-Buddha (primordial Buddha), staring in all four directions; what looks like a nose is actually the Nepali figure "one", conveying the unity of all things. A **spire** of thirteen gold disks stacked above the pillar represents the thirteen steps to enlightenment. The *torana*, or gold plaques above the painted eyes, also show the five *dhyani* Buddhas, known collectively as the *panchabuddha*. Finally, the umbrella at the top symbolizes the attainment of enlightenment: some say it contains a bowl filled with precious gems.

Shrines around the stupa

The stupa is surrounded by an incredible array of shrines and votive whatnots, most of which have been donated over the past four centuries by merit-seeking kings and lamas. The bronze sceptre-like object at the top of the steps is a vastly oversized **vajra**, a tantric symbol of power and indestructibility; its pedestal is carved with the twelve animals of the Tibetan zodiac. The twin bullet-shaped *shikra* on either side of this, known as **Pratappur** and **Anantapur**, were installed by King Pratap Malla during a seventeenth-century dispute with Tibet, on the advice of an Indian guru. The story of the king's gift, and his subsequent victory over the Tibetans, is engraved on the twin bells in front of the *shikra*.

Moving around clockwise, as is the custom at all stupas, the brick hut to the south of Anantapur is **Vasundhara Mandir**, dedicated to the earth goddess Vasundhara, who's more or less synonymous with Annapurna and Lakshmi, the goddesses of grain and wealth respectively. Further on – past the priests' quarters and a number of *chaitya* – is a small marble-faced shrine

A *chaitya*

to **Vayu**, the Vedic god of wind and storms. The **museum** (daily except Sat 10am–5pm; donation), behind, contains a formidable range of bas-relief statues of gods, Hindu as well as Buddhist, which, though beautiful to look at, are so tersely identified that they'll leave you hopelessly confused by the Nepali pantheon. Next door and up a flight of steps, the **Deva Dharma Mahavihar** is a small, uneventful monastery that's open to the public, and in front of this, close to the stupa behind protective caging, stand two acclaimed bronze statues of the **White and Green Taras**, princess wives of an eighth-century Tibetan king.

At the far side of the stupa squats a gilt-roofed temple built to appease **Harati**, the smallpox goddess, whom Newars worship as a form of **Ajima**, or Grandmother, a more general protectress of children. A legend relates how Harati was originally an abductor of children: when the people complained to the Buddha, he stole one of Harati's own children, forcing her to realize the pain she caused humans and repent of her ways. Harati/Ajima's shrine is extremely popular, and you'll see queues of mothers with kids in tow, waiting to make offerings. The nineteenth-century idol was carved to replace an earlier one smashed by King Rana Bahadur Shah after his wife died of smallpox. Following rites observed throughout hill Nepal, petitioners toss handfuls of flower petals and rice at the image, sprinkle a bit of consecrated water (*jal*) onto the image and themselves, and finally receive a *tika* from the resident priest.

The **International Buddhist Library**, housed upstairs in a former *bahal* behind the Harati Mandir, always seems to be closed, but the roof above is good for an overview of the stupa area. (Looking in the other direction, the huge mansion on a hill to the west belongs to Jogmer Shrestha, a former *panchaayat* wallah – the new political climate doesn't seem to be doing him any harm.)

Agnipur, an insignificant-looking lump on the pavement in the extreme north-west corner of the complex, marked by two tiny lions in front, is a seldom-visited shrine to the Vedic fire god Agni, the relayer of burnt offerings to heaven. **Nagpur**, a bathtub-sized tank at the north point of the stupa, propitiates the valley's snake (*nag*) spirits, and when it's not filled with water you can see the idol (looking more like a draught excluder than a snake) at the bottom. Finally, the **Shree Karma Raj Mahavihar**, an active monastery at the northeast corner of the compound, contains a big Buddha and numerous butter candles, which Tibetan Buddhists light in much the same way Catholics do; you can catch the sonorous chanting of the monks at around 3 or 4pm everyday.

Shantipur

A 1500-year-old mystery surrounds **Shantipur**, the otherwise plain, box-like building northwest of the stupa. Shanti Shri, a fifth-century holy man, is supposed to have sealed himself in a vault beneath the temple to meditate, vowing not to emerge until the valley needed him. Commentators write that he subsequently attained a mystic state of immortality, and according to devout believers he's still in there.

King Pratap Malla, who entered the chamber in 1658 to seek magical help in ending a drought, experienced adventures worthy of Indiana Jones. According to scholar Keith Dowman, the king recounted how he entered alone and descended to the second subterranean level. In the first room "bats as large as kites or hawks came to kill the light", while in the second room "ghosts, flesh-eating spirits and hungry ghosts came to beg", clutching at anyone who failed to pacify them. Of the third room he said, "if you cannot pacify the snakes by pouring out milk, they chase and bind you. Having pacified them you can walk on their bodies". Finally, Pratap Malla found the saint in an almost skeletal form, and was rewarded with a *nag* rain-making emblem. Faded frescoes on the walls of the outer sanctum show scenes from the *Swayambhu Purana*, a recent (seventeenth-century) scripture that recounts the story of Manjushri's sword act and other creation myths. Shantipur, also known as Akashpur ("Sky-place"), completes a cycle of shrines to the five elemental spirits: earth, air, fire, water (snakes) and sky.

Other sights around the hilltop

The **Manjushri Shrine**, located on a western spur of the hilltop, comes second only to the main stupa in antiquity – the canopied *chaitya* is reckoned to be 1500 years old. Manjushri, the Buddhist god of wisdom and founder of civilization in the valley, is traditionally depicted by an empty niche in the *chaitya*, but an image of Saraswati, the Hindu goddess of learning, was placed in the niche three hundred years ago, and so the shrine is now on the pilgrimage circuit for Hindus as well. Schoolchildren make a special trip here on *Basanta Panchami*, in late January or early February, to have their books and pencils blessed.

The rest of the hilltop is littered with other obscure monuments. In addition, several **Tibetan monasteries**, which as a rule welcome visitors, have been built in the area since 1959, and more seem to be going up all the time. Many Westerners study Tibetan Buddhism here (see "The Dharma Scene", p.119).

The morbidly amusing **Natural History Museum** (daily except Sat 10am–4pm; Rs5) also lurks nearby, at the southern base of Swayambhu hill. Its jumbled collection of stuffed birds and shrivelled animals in old-fashioned display cases looks like it was cobbled together from the trophy rooms of hoary old Rana hunters. The weirdness is fun for its own sake, though, and the specimens might give you an idea of what to look for when you get to the mountains or jungle. (See also "Natural History" in *Contexts*.)

East of Swayambhu: Bijeshwari

Bijeshwari, along the west bank of the Bishnumati on the way to Swayambhu, used to be Kathmandu's execution ground; Henry Ambrose Oldfield, one of the few Europeans allowed to tour Nepal in the last century, attended a beheading here and pronounced the place "a regular Golgotha". While Tibetan immigrants have broken the taboo against settling near the cursed ground, a fear of ghosts still endures, as do two important but little-visited temples.

Bijeshwari Bahal, perched at the top of a flight of steps above the river, is the centre of worship of an esoteric Buddhist goddess, Bijeshwari (Lord of Victory), who is also known as Akash (Sky) Jogini and sometimes counted as the fifth of the valley's Bajra Joginis, the wrathful aspects of the tantric Tara goddesses. The inner courtyard is thick with *chaitya* and stone figures, and doors around the perimeter are painted with probing pairs of eyes – a reminder to worshippers that the Buddha is watching, and an injunction to look inward.

Just upstream stands a new cremation pavilion, and beyond that, the Hindu **Shobha Bhagwati Mandir**. Bhagwati is a common Nepali name for the mother goddess, and this idol of her is considered to be among of the most powerful in the valley: early in the morning you might see political candidates, students preparing for exams, or anyone requiring quiet strength, coming here to do *puja* to her.

South of Swayambhu: the National Museum

The museum concept is somewhat redundant in Nepal, given the wealth of heritage displayed out in the open. But theft and modernization are forcing a belated move to safeguard national treasures, many of which can be seen in the **National Museum**, based in an old Rana armoury 1km south of Swayambhu (daily except Tues 10.30am–4.30pm summer, 3.30pm winter, Fri closes 2.30pm; Rs5, Rs10 extra for camera). It's no curatorial coup, and shouldn't be considered a substitute for the valley's countless living exhibits, but you'll come away with a better appreciation of the intertwining of religion, art, myth and history in Nepal. And on a clear day, the view from the roof of the art building is easily worth the admission price.

Count on spending most of your time in the **art building**, the white plaster one on your left as you enter. Two rooms of stone sculptures showcase an amazing artistic consistency spanning almost two thousand years, from the Lichhavi period through the tantric-influenced Malla dynasties – though motifs and styles change, the common element is a wild diversity of gods and themes inspired by the vast and imaginative canon of Hindu mythology. Two more rooms of metalwork pay tribute to a later artform which blossomed under patronage from Tibet. A trio of absolutely stunning fourteenth-century bronzes of the tantric deity Samvara and his consort form the centrepieces of this exhibit – such passion, such fire! To Western eyes, the tantric *yab yum* (sexual intercourse) motif and its gory attendant imagery (skull cups, daggers, blood) may seem pretty peculiar, yet on some intuitive level it's a powerful celebration of life in all its creativity and weirdness and danger. A final room displays a couple of dozen rare *paubha* (Nepali scroll paintings) from the sixteenth century on, and a later series of miniatures exhibiting a marked Rajasthani influence.

The **history building**, a Rana-style mansion across the compound, is hardly worth the walk. It's almost as if the downstairs was meant to be a joke: the natural history section includes a mugger crocodile mislabelled as a gharial, the bones of a blue whale (why?) and an assortment of shrivelled mammals and birds, while another room features an international doll collection (check out the embarrassing specimens donated by your country!) and a moon rock. Upstairs, endless displays of weaponry do little to dispel the stereotype of the Nepalis as a "martial" race (although a pair of leather cannon, captured during a skirmish with Tibet in 1856, is a genuine rarity). More interesting than what's included, perhaps, is what's left out. This is Nepalese history as rewritten by the Shahs and Ranas, who've ruled Nepal for the past two centuries; the country's lower classes and ethnic groups, and any history prior to the Shah conquest, are not given a mention.

Eastern neighbourhoods

For travellers, the area east of Kantipath is mainly of interest for airline offices and restaurants, not sightseeing. But while you're in the neighbourhood it's worth stopping to take a closer look at a few odds and ends.

The Kesar Library, Royal Palace and Durbar Marg

The **Kesar** (Kaiser) **Library** (Mon–Thurs & Sun 10am–5pm, Fri 10am–3pm; free), located in the compound marked "Ministry of Education and Culture", east of Thamel, is your best shot at seeing the inside of a former Rana palace. The library of Field Marshal Kesar Shamsher Rana (1891–1964) looks like a featured spread in the Nepali edition of *Better Homes and Gardens*: long shelves of European books, a suit of armour, a stuffed tiger and portraits of all the famous people the field marshal ever shook hands with shed intriguing light on a member of Nepal's pre-1951 ruling elite. Another sort of colonial landmark, **Fora Durbar**, the swish R&R compound for American expats, hides behind high brick walls just north of the British Council.

An architectural travesty from the 1960s, the creepy new **Royal Palace** looks like something out of Buck Rogers, with echoes of the Mormon Tabernacle. Built on the site of an earlier palace dating from the turn of the century, it was inaugurated in 1970 for King (then Crown Prince) Birendra's wedding; its Newari name, Narayanhiti Durbar, refers to a water tap (*hiti*) east of the main entrance. Guarded by soldiers, the palace is open to the public only on the tenth day of Dasain, when Nepalis queue up to receive *tika* from the king and queen. The things that resemble black handbags dangling from the trees out front are bats; at dusk, they and about a million crows wheel overhead, creating an almighty racket.

Running south from the palace, **Durbar Marg** is the capital's premier address: one *ropani* of land (a plot 23m square) here sells for the staggering sum of up to $500,000.

Rani Pokhri and around the Tudikhel

Rani Pokhri (Queen's Pool), the large square tank east of Asan, is older than it looks. It was built in the seventeenth century by King Pratap Malla to console his queen after the death of their favourite son; the shrine in the middle, which is opened one day a year during the Diwali festival, is more recent.

West of the pool stands the mouldering edifice of **Durbar High School**, established in the late nineteenth century to educate the children of the Rana aristocracy and their hangers-on for jobs in a nascent bureaucracy. To the east rise the Rana-era **clocktower** (like Bhimsen Tower, a landmark only in the functional sense) and Kathmandu's two **mosques**. Muslims first settled in Kathmandu as traders five centuries ago, and now represent only a tiny fraction of Nepal's half-million "Musalmans". Nearby Trichandra College, whose students have a reputation for militancy, was a flashpoint of anti-government riots in 1990, when its walls were painted with such slogans as "Do or Die for Democracy".

Kathmandu's **Tudikhel** is the biggest military parade ground in Nepal; Percival Landon, an early twentieth-century traveller, proclaimed it "level as Lord's", and indeed the expanse seems quixotically flat in so mountainous a country. An institution rooted in Nepal's warring past, the *tudikhel* is a feature of every town of consequence throughout the hills. The king turns out to review occasional displays of pomp and circumstance here (notably during Ghoda Jaatra in March or April), and bronze statues at each corner of the parade ground depict past Rana prime ministers on horseback striking suitably swashbuckling poses.

On the Kantipath side of Tudikhel stands the **Mahakal Mandir**, whose modern surroundings have in no way diminished the reverence of its worshippers: passing pedestrians and motorists almost always touch a hand to the forehead. Mahakal – to Hindus a form of Bhairab, to Buddhists a defender of *dharma* – is depicted here trampling a corpse (signifying ignorance), holding a skull-cup of blood and wearing what look like glacier goggles. The **Bhadrakali Mandir**, at the southeast corner of Tudikhel, has been turned into a traffic roundabout but remains a popular wedding venue. The nearby **Martyrs' Gate** commemorates the four ringleaders of a failed 1940 attempt to overthrow the Rana regime.

Singha Durbar

Undoubtedly the most impressive structure ever raised by the Ranas, **Singha Durbar** dominates the governmental quarter in the southeastern part of the city. Once the biggest building in Asia, the prime ministers' palace of 1700 rooms was built in 1901 by Chandra Shamsher Rana, who employed workers round the clock for a year to complete the pile and fill it with such European extravagances as Carrera marble floors, crystal chandeliers and gilt mirrors, all for the then unconscionable sum of Rs2.5 million. Up to 1500 servants were required to maintain the prime minister and his household in the style to which they were accustomed.

The complex was mostly destroyed by fire in 1973, but has since been partially rebuilt. You can go right past the guards at the sweeping front gate to have a look at the luxurious gardens and the gleaming white colonnaded main wing. Numerous governmental ministries and departments are housed here and in crumbling old mansions nearby.

Dilli Bazaar, Baluwatar and Maharajganj

Kathmandu's eastern and northeastern neighbourhoods have absorbed the lion's share of recent city growth, and while these areas don't have much of scenic interest, they certainly provide insights into suburban Nepal.

Crowded **Dilli Bazaar** and **Bag Bazaar** pretty much sum up one end of the spectrum, with their typing institutes, lawyers' cubbyholes and shops selling office furniture and "suitings and shirtings". ("Fine Art", incidentally, means sign-painting – there's always work for sign-painters in ever-changing Kathmandu.) The other extreme is found further north in the shady lanes of **Baluwatar** and **Maharajganj**, where old money, new money and foreign money hide in walled compounds, and caretakers water the flowers for highly paid absentee development consultants.

Between the two lie the hopeful settlements of a burgeoning middle class, who build their houses one floor at a time, as funds allow, and send their children off in uniforms to "English boarding schools" with names like "Bright Future" and "Little Flower". An "English" education is almost universally viewed as the key to success in the capital: whether these children are being educated to think for themselves is debatable, but they may well help Nepal escape its cycle of poverty.

Hadigaun

Another world away, **Hadigaun**, on the edge of the northeastern suburbs, is the nearest place to Thamel to find typical Newar village life in action. You'll see better as you go further out into the valley, but Hadigaun's old brick houses, dirt streets and farm animals are remarkably well insulated from the hurlyburly of the city. Indeed, the settlement is probably as old as Kathmandu.

Evidence of Hadigaun's age comes from the overgrown shrine of **Dhum Barahi**, a further 1km northeastwards (head north out of Hadigaun, and when in doubt always take the right fork). Inside the small brick shelter, which is completely engulfed in the roots of an enormous pipal tree, a whimsical fifth-century image illustrates the tale of Barahi (Vishnu in his incarnation as a boar) rescuing the earth goddess Prithvi from the bottom of the sea. Scholars rave about this sculpture because it dates from a time when there were no established rules for depicting Vishnu as a boar, nor for how a boar should look while fishing the earth from the sea. Locals say the shrine was built at the same time as the nearby Boudha stupa to appease Vishnu, who out of jealousy had caused the stupa's spire to collapse while under construction.

KATHMANDU PRACTICALITIES

There's no comparison between Kathmandu and other cities in Nepal. The capital has all the best restaurants, the only bars, the majority of entertainment, the broadest (though not the cheapest) selection of handicrafts, and a whole roster of practitioners in yoga, meditation and alternative therapies – not to mention all the embassies and airline offices.

Eating

Now secure in its reputation as a gastronomic oasis, Kathmandu continues to refine its technique. Scores of **restaurants** and **cafés** line the lanes of the tourist areas, and more spring up after each monsoon. Quite a few carry on in a funky, student-coffee-house style – they're like time capsules from the early 1970s – but a growing number are emulating French bistros, American diners and even English pubs. While **Tibetan**, **Chinese** and **Indian** food have long been taken for granted in Kathmandu, **European** specialities predominate these days; American-style **pies and cakes**, though overrated, are ever-popular; and even **Japanese**, **Thai** and **Mexican** dishes are available. Sometimes the food is ingeniously authentic, sometimes you have to use your imagination. The best news of all is that fine **Nepali** and **Newari** food – traditionally only served in private homes – is increasingly available not only in tourist restaurants but also in reasonably sanitary local eateries, and is slowly taking its place among the other distinguished regional Indian cuisines.

As with lodgings, **Thamel** has all the newest, trendiest and most credible budget restaurants – though some are getting so stylish they're pricing themselves out of the budget category. **Freak Street** is noticeably cheaper for eating, but it's got a smaller and less interesting selection of establishments. Kathmandu's best and most expensive restaurants are generally found near, or sometimes inside, the deluxe hotels around **Durbar Marg**. You'll find restaurants marked on the Thamel map, but those in other areas unfortunately couldn't be squeezed onto the maps.

Even at the top end, **prices** are reasonable. As a guide, places decribed here as cheap will charge Rs75 or less per person for a full dinner; inexpensive restaurants will run to about Rs150, maybe as high as Rs200 with beer; moderately priced ones will charge more like Rs200–300, and expensive ones Rs300–600. Phone numbers are given for restaurants where it's advisable to book ahead for dinner.

It's all too easy to overemphasize food in Kathmandu – it can also be the greatest peril of staying here. More travellers get **sick** in the capital than anywhere else, and eating in "reputable" restaurants is no guarantee of hygiene. Indeed, Nepali restaurants are arguably safer, since chefs know what they're doing when they prepare Nepali food. Heed the words of caution given in "Health and Insurance" in *Basics*, and don't be taken in by an apparently clean dining room or shiny cutlery.

Nepali and Newari

The Nepali and Newari places listed below are geared for tourists and tend to be on the expensive side, but well worth it. At the other extreme are Kathmandu's many dirt-cheap *bhojanalaya*, which advertise themselves with a curtain (usually green) hung over the entrance and are impossible to recommend by name. Most are merely the Nepali equivalents of a greasy spoon – the better ones are tucked down a couple of alleys just north of Asan in the direction of Thahiti, and along the lane from Asan to Chhetrapati. Don't waste your money on the "special Nepali meals" touted by budget tourist restaurants, which usually turn out to be overpriced *daal bhaat*. See "Eating" in *Basics* for a rundown of Nepali and Newari dishes.

Bhanchha Ghar, Kamaladi (east of the Clocktower; ☎225172). Nepali nouvelle cuisine, featuring such delicacies as wild boar, wild mushroom curry and buckwheat chapatis – truly wonderful. Expensive.

Naachghar, in the *Yak & Yeti Hotel* off Durbar Marg (☎413999). Top-flight Nepali, Indian and Western cooking; set dinner in a palatial setting with nightly culture shows in season. Expensive.

Nepalese Kitchen, Chhetrapati. A serviceable budget version of the others listed here, demonstrating that there's more to Nepali cuisine than *daal bhaat*. Live music some evenings. Moderately priced.

Thayabhu, Lazimpath, immediately south of the *Hotel Shanker* (☎411570). Introductory Newari menu, tour-group atmosphere – they really push the set menu, which isn't much of a deal. Moderate.

Tibetan, Chinese and Thai

Tibetan restaurants offer some of the cheapest tourist food in Kathmandu; cheaper still are the many *momo* kitchens throughout the old city, notably around Mahabaudha. Again, see *Basics* for descriptions of popular Tibetan dishes. Chinese food can be reasonably priced, although the best restaurants are found in deluxe hotels like the *Malla*.

Da Hua, Bhagwan Bahal. Good all-round Chinese. Inexpensive to moderate.

Him Thai, Chhetrapati Thamel. The food won't astound anyone who's just flown in from Bangkok, but it's tasty and there's copious seating in this once-grand (now scruffy) Rana mansion – outdoor candlelit seating is romantic on a warm night. Moderate.

Jianfu, Thamel. Basic Mandarin and Szechuan fare, clean, good service, central location. Inexpensive to moderate.

Lhasa, north Thamel. Excellent Tibetan soups, fiery *momo* and – best of all – *tongba* (do-it-yourself millet beer). Cheap.

Mountain City, in the *Hotel Malla* on Lekhnath Marg. Delicious Chinese food; Szechuan a speciality. Moderate.

Nanglo, Durbar Marg (☎223498). Reliable Chinese food in an unfortunately lounge-like setting. Expensive.

New Mandarin, Freak Street. Good for both Chinese and Tibetan dishes. Cheap.

Solu, Jyatha Thamel. A locals' hole-in-the-wall that does *tongba*. Very cheap.

Utse, Thamel. Cheap Tibetan and Chinese food in a fun atmosphere.

Indian

Perhaps the best measure of the Indian population in Kathmandu is the number of Indian restaurants – they're popping up everywhere. The more expensive ones serve food every bit as good as you'll find in India, and even the cheapies (mostly around New Road) do some fine pure vegetarian dishes. Indian cuisine is also summarized in *Basics*.

Bangalore Coffee House, corner of Jamal and Durbar Marg, near *American Express*. Great south Indian vegetarian food in an efficient upstairs canteen – authentic, right down to the toilets. Very cheap.

Ghar-e-Kebab, Durbar Marg (☎221711). Superlative north Indian food, live music, strange nightclub interior. Expensive.

Gupta Bhojanalaya, off New Road north of the American Library. Hole in the wall serving vegetarian south Indian dishes. Cheap.

Moti Mahal, Durbar Marg. Tandoori food rivalling that of *Ghar-e-Kebab*, though the decor isn't as swanky. Moderate.

New Kebab Corner, in the *Hotel Gautam* just off Kantipath. Expats swear by this place. Moderate.

Shere Punjab, on a back street running parallel to New Road, east of Pipal Bot. Basic in-and-out Punjabi canteen. Cheap.

Shiva's Sky, New Road. Vegetarian and non-veg dishes in a sociable atmosphere. Moderate.

Tansen, Durbar Marg (☎224707). Top-notch tandoori and other Indian dishes served on burnished copper in minimalist surroundings. Expensive.

Tripti, off New Road north of Pipal Bot. Lively little pure vegetarian place serving south Indian fare. Cheap.

European

Keep telling yourself: this is not what I came to Nepal for . . . Still, there are times when you feel like you've eaten a lifetime's worth of lentils and you could just murder a pizza.

G's Terrace, Thamel. High-cholesterol Bavarian specialities (would you believe *zwiebelrostbraten?*). Moderately priced.

La Cimbali, Kwa Bahal, Thamel. A small café with a nice atmosphere and fair pizza. Cheap.

La Dolce Vita, Thamel. Kathmandu's most upscale Italian restaurant. Inexpensive, except for the wine.

Locanda Marco Polo, Thamel. Though variable in quality, the Italian food is reasonably authentic for the price. Cheap.

Mike's Breakfast, off Durbar Marg – enter via the *Yak & Yeti* driveway. Terrific pizza (Monday nights only). Moderate.

Old Vienna, Thamel. Schnitzel and crêpes, tasty but marred by Muzak. Moderate.

Pizza Hut, north Thamel. Small dining room, good atmosphere and really rather good thin-crust pizza. Inexpensive.

Japanese

Sushi is out of the question, but Nepali-style sukiyaki comes fairly close to the mark. Try miso soup if your stomach's acting up.

Fuji, Kantipath. Good food, beautiful decor. Expensive.

Koto, Durbar Marg (☎226095). Probably the best value for money on the Japanese front. Inexpensive to moderate.

Kushi Fuji, Durbar Marg (☎220545). More authentic, but more expensive.

Vegetarian

There are only a few all-vegetarian tourist restaurants worthy of recommendation, but every restaurant serves at least a few meatless dishes; even Tibetan places will usually do vegetable *momo*. See also Indian restaurants.

Boris', north Thamel. This Rajneesh establishment now serves some meat, but vegetarian dishes are prepared in a separate kitchen; it's run by the son of Boris Lissanevitch, Kathmandu's legendary Russian restaurateur. Menu selections are highly imaginative, and served in either a traditional Nepali room, a Boris theme room or an enclosed outdoor patio. Moderately priced.

Nirmala, north Thamel. Tasty meals from a short but varied menu. Inexpensive.

Paradise, Freak Street. Not desperately creative, but soups, pasta and cheesy dishes will fill your boots. Cheap.

All-rounders

The overwhelming majority of budget places fall into this catch-all category: jacks of all trades and usually masters of none. The old standbys are "buff" (water buffalo: cows are sacred, remember) steaks, pastas, cakes and pies.

Al Pollo, Kwa Bahal. A cosy atmosphere makes this place popular, despite unremarkable offerings. Inexpensive.

Café de la Cabine, Thahiti, in the *Thahiti Guest House*. Snug wood-and-rattan decor, mellow music, little-of-everything menu; the offbeat location is a plus. Inexpensive.

Cosmopolitan, Freak Street. The best pasta and steaks south of Durbar Square; salad with every dish, if you dare. Inexpensive.

Helena's, Thamel. The cake display window here is Thamel's most popular tourist sight; the usual menu, but a gloomy decor. Inexpensive.

K.C.'s, Thamel. A perennial favourite: cosy surroundings, reliable menu, generous portions; big on "sizzling" dishes and killer desserts. Moderately priced.

Oasis, Freak Street. The only patio dining on Freak Street. Inexpensive.

Rainbow, at the *Yeti Cottage* in north Thamel. Good, stodgy food and plenty of it; mellow garden seating. Inexpensive.

Breakfast and lunch places

You can't beat Kathmandu's cafés for breakfast or lunch on a warm day, though they're not so accommodating in winter. Besides the places listed below, many all-rounders offer set breakfasts, which often represent great value for money (especially if you like eggs).

For a picnic lunch, try *Pumpernickel Bakery* for bread and *Nepal Dairy* on Kwa Bahal for cheese. "Cold stores" in tourist areas sell biscuits, beer, chocolate and the like, while a couple of speciality shops on Dharmapath (near Freak Street) carry imported items you won't find anywhere else. Supermarkets in Thamel (on the corner of Bhagwan Bahal), Lazimpath and Tripureswar Marg also stock a wide range of goodies. For fruit and vegetables, hit the open-air markets around Asan and south of New Road.

Big Bell Café, Durbar Square. Seating is on the roof of an unfinished building, but so close to the temples you can practically touch them. Cheap.

Le Bistro, Thamel. A fully fledged restaurant, but its strong suit is café seating – it's popular, so get there early. Try also the neighbouring *Eclipse*, a perfect people-watching vantage point. Inexpensive.

The Gourmet, Thamel (inside *Old Vienna*). Spotless German deli, looking eerily out of place here, serving authentic wursts and pâté. Inexpensive.

Hem's, Thamel. The rooftop terrace is ideal for sipping tea and writing postcards, although the food isn't much to write home about. Inexpensive.

The Lunch Box, just off Freak Street. Ever popular, but better for breakfast than lunch. Cheap.

Kay Kay's, Freak Street. Another favourite for good-value breakfasts. Cheap.

Mike's Breakfast, Durbar Marg. Absolute bliss for breakfast – garden tables, classical music and spot-on food – Americans' eyes will mist over at the corn muffins, waffles and fresh coffee. Stiff competition for tables, though. Relatively expensive.

Pumpernickel Bakery, Thamel. A sort of Mecca for skinflints. Immensely popular for croissant sandwiches and sticky buns, with seating in a pleasant garden out back. Cheap.

Skala, Chhetrapati Thamel. Limited menu, but the courtyard is nicely secluded from the hubbub. Inexpensive.

Desserts

K.C.'s, *Helena's* and many other restaurants listed above produce spectacular confections, some of which actually taste as good as they look. If none of those hits the spot, try one of the following.

Angan, corner of New Road and Shukra Path. Fantastic Bengali sweets (buy them by the piece), also ice cream. Inexpensive.

Nirula's, Durbar Marg and New Road. American ice cream parlour meets Indian bureaucracy. The ice cream's pretty good, though. Inexpensive.

The Snowman, just off Freak Street. Classic subterranean hippy hangout, a real time warp – in fact, the atmosphere's better than the cakes and pies. Cheap.

Nightlife and entertainment

For a capital, Kathmandu is pretty sleepy: most restaurants start putting up their chairs around 9.30pm, and drinking is supposed to stop at 10pm. **Bars** are still a speciality item, found only in Thamel and the big hotels. Attending a **culture show** is probably a more enlightening alternative – or better yet, catch an evening music session at Kel Tol or Chhetrapati – but perhaps the best idea of all is to retire early and rise early the next morning, when the city is at its best.

Bars

Thamel's **bar** scene is still small, but growing. The area around the *Kathmandu Guest House* is mutating into quite a little throbbing scene in the evenings, with duelling sound systems blaring across the alleyways, noisy bands of revellers looking for action, and the cops and the riksha wallahs waiting outside for closing time.

A handful of nightspots serve up beer, improvised cocktails and music; as with restaurants, they're more like a Nepali's imagination of what a bar must be like than the real thing, but on the whole they're fine for meeting, mixing and prolonging an otherwise short evening. Unlike Thamel restaurants, which are frequented almost exclusively by travellers, the bars here attract a fair share of well-off Nepali lads, who aren't very representative of Nepalis in general. They'll latch onto any unescorted foreign female, but usually only to flirt. In the high season, bars often keep serving until the wee hours behind drawn curtains and locked doors. Don't forget to warn your innkeeper if you think you're going to stay out late, or you could get locked out. Reputations rise and fall from season to season, but the establishments listed below appear to be in for the duration.

In addition, all the expensive hotels feature sedate **cocktail lounges**, usually open to non-residents. And though it's hardly likely you came to Nepal to gamble, the *Soaltee Oberoi* lays on free buses from the other major hotels to its foreigners-only **casino** (admission free; show your air ticket within one week of arrival and you'll be given free tokens).

Blue Note, Chhetrapati Thamel. A canny concept: eclectic jazz and blues, beatnik ambience, though perhaps too well lit.

Pub Maya, Chhetrapati Thamel. Very popular meeting place, loud music, happy hour.

Road House Café, Chhetrapati Thamel. More like a restaurant than a bar, but okay for an after-dinner drink.

Rum Doodle Restaurant's "40,000 1/2-Foot Bar", north Thamel, on the side street behind *Yeti Cottage*. Kathmandu's oldest nightspot (but recently relocated), cultivating a cluttered *après trek* atmosphere.

Spam's Place, north Thamel. A home-away-from-home for Aussies and Poms – the atmosphere is that of a make-do pub in a far-flung colony.

Third Eye, Chhetrapati Thamel. An atmosphere worthy of a 1970s encounter session – kick off your shoes, cross your legs and groove on the touchy-feely vibes.

Tom and Jerry Pub, north Thamel. An established and surprisingly bar-like bar; free popcorn during happy hour.

Yak Horn Pub, Chhetrapati Thamel. Dark, primitive and loud.

Culture shows

Music and dance are essential parts of Nepali culture, and perhaps nowhere more so than in Kathmandu, where neighbourhood festivals and parades (not to mention weddings) are an almost daily occurrence. Touring other regions of the country, you'll encounter other, markedly different styles of music and dance (see *Contexts*), and while it's more fun to see these performances in their native context, it's worth checking out a **culture show** before you leave the capital to get a taste of Nepal's folk and performing arts.

The *Hotel Vajra* (☎271545) puts on the most authentic and varied programmes. In the high season, its resident Kalamandapa ensemble and other visiting troupes account for about three music and/or dance performances a week; in addition, the *Vajra*'s own Studio 7 company presents occasional dramatic productions. Shows at the big tourist hotels tend to be geared more for tour groups. The New Himalchuli Cultural Group does a fairly conventional performance in an auditorium beside the *Hotel Shanker* (☎410151), north of the Royal Palace; ditto the show at the *Hotel de l'Annapurna* (☎221711) on Durbar Marg. Tickets for all the above should cost around Rs100–150; phone for times.

Dinner shows at the deluxe hotels are expensive and pretty stagey, but you can at least count on good eating: try the *Yak & Yeti*'s *Naachghar Restaurant* (☎413999) or the *Sherpa Grill* at the *Hotel Sherpa* (☎227000), both in the Durbar Marg vicinity.

Ghazal

An Indian style of music, **ghazal** has recently started catching on in Nepal, or at least in the capital. You won't often find *ghazal* performed in tourist spots – troupes tend to work the more upscale Indian restaurants, where they provide dinnertime accompaniment from a platform over to the side somewhere. A typical ensemble consists of amplified tabla, harmonium and guitar; the singer, who gets top billing, croons in a plaintive, nasal voice. Love is the theme, and the sentimental lyrics – typically in Urdu, but increasingly in Nepali – draw from a long tradition going back to the great Persian poets.

The most consistent *ghazal* **venues** are the *Amber* and *Ghar-e-Kebab* restaurants on Durbar Marg, the *Mughal Mahal* on Tripureswar Marg (just up from the *Bluebird Supermarket*) and, down in Patan, the *Patan Gate Restaurant*. Some Thamel restaurants also host shows in the off-season to bring in business – *Kathmandu Restaurant and Pizza Hut*, on Chhetrapati, does them fairly regularly.

Theatre and cinema

Outside the tourist arena, scheduled performances of the arts are rare, but that's hardly surprising considering how much goes on all the time in public. Groups allegedly rent out the **National Theatre** on Kantipath for dance, drama and musical events, although the box office seems to be perpetually shut.

Despite stiff competition from video parlours, Kathmandu's several **cinemas**, showing the latest Indian blockbusters in Hindi, are still popular. The easiest ones to get to are the *Jai Nepal Chitra Ghar*, one block east of the Royal Palace entrance, and the *Bishwa Jyoti* on Jamal. Showtime is generally noon, 3pm and 6pm daily and tickets cost just pennies. Some Thamel restaurants show videos – thrill to such greats as "Basic Instant" and "City Silkers".

Shopping

Kathmandu is the obvious place to do some serious **shopping**, especially if it's your last stop before leaving the country. For an overview of handicrafts available in Nepal, see *Basics*; just about all of them are sold in or around Kathmandu. Usually items will be cheaper where they're actually made, but keen competition keeps prices low in the capital. The majority of wool, metal and wood items are made in the valley anyway, and many "Tibetan" items are imported from India.

Souvenirs and curios

If you're in the market for a **khukuri** knife, you won't have to go far: street vendors and shops sell them wherever there are tourists. Brass sets of **bagh chal**, Nepal's own "tigers and goats" game, are almost as common. Stalls and shops between Indrachowk and Asan sell all manner of household **brassware**, and *Chainpur Brass* at the palace end of Durbar Square does a line in high-quality pieces crafted in the eastern hills. A couple of small shops in Thamel are devoted to Nepalese **musical instruments**, while hack minstrels around Thamel play bad renditions of *Frère Jacques* on *sarangi* (traditional fiddles) and peddle cheap bamboo flutes in Durbar Square.

Vendors in Basantapur Square and Thamel flog vast arrays of **Tibetan curios**, though most items are Tamang, not Tibetan. It's all attractive stuff, but much of what is claimed to be silver, turquoise, coral or ivory is fake, and virtually none of it is antique. The same goes for **jewellery** sold in tourist shops. **Gem** sellers are grouped mainly at the east end of New Road. The *pote pasal* near Indrachowk is the place to go for traditional **glass beads**. For gift boxes of **tea**, try shops along Ganga Path (the western end of New Road) and opposite Central Immigration.

Countless boutiques sell identical ranges of **Indian handicrafts**, predominantly chain-stitch tapestries, papier mâché and sandalwood boxes. These guys are particularly adept at fleecing unwary tourists. They also sell **furs** – fox, jungle cat, "snow" cat and the like, most hunted in the wild in India and all technically legal, though snow leopard, clouded leopard and other endangered species are also said to be obtainable, despite being protected under international conventions. The trade persists because of lax regulation, but it could be stopped, or at least slowed, if enough travellers raise hell.

Certain handicrafts, though widely sold in Kathmandu, are better bought elsewhere in the valley: **metal statuettes** are a Patan speciality, **wood carvings** are best in Bhaktapur, and **papier mâché masks**, **puppets** and **pottery** are all better represented in Thimi and Bhaktapur. Kathmandu **carpet**-sellers offer some good deals, but don't buy until you've had a chance to see carpets being made in one of the many factories in the Kathmandu Valley or around Pokhara (see p.140 for background on the carpet industry). The best selection is in Patan's Jaulakhel district.

THANGKA

A good **thangka** is the product of hundreds or even thousands of hours of painstaking work. A cotton canvas is first stretched across a frame, gessoed and burnished to a smooth surface that will take the finest detail. The desired design is next drawn or traced in pencil using a grid system and precise proportions; there is little room for deviation from accepted styles, for a *thangka* is an expression of religious truths, not an opportunity for artistic licence. Large areas of colour are then blocked in, often by an apprentice, and finally the master painter will take over, breathing life into the figure with lining, stippling, facial features, shading and, finally, the eyes of the main figure. Mineral- and vegetable-based paints are still used for the best paintings, but most nowadays are acrylic.

For discussion purposes, *thangka* can be grouped into four genres. The **Wheel of Life**, perhaps the most common, places life and all its delusions inside a circle held firmly in the clutches of red-faced Yama, god of death. The wheel's "rim" depicts the twelve causes of misery, while its "spokes" show the six sensual realms, where dwell the damned, ghosts, animals, humans, demigods and gods; all are caught in Yama's grip – even the gods – and only the Buddha exists outside the wheel. A second standard image is the **Buddha's life story**, tracing the major events of his life starting in the upper right and proceeding clockwise, dominated by an enlightened Buddha in the centre. Many *thangka* feature tantric **deities**, either benign or menacing; Avalokiteshwara, the Lord of Compassion, is a favourite. Such an image serves as a meditation tool in visualization techniques, in which the subject identifies with the deity's godly attributes or recognizes its demonic ones in him or herself. **Mandala**, too, are used in meditation. Symbolically, the subject moves through the three rings of the outer circle (representing the three parts of human nature that must be controlled), through the inner hexagram, towards the figure of the Buddha at the centre.

Thangka and other fine art

It's hard to say where to look for bargains on **thangka** and **paubha**, since there are so many standard depictions and levels of quality that any comparison of prices is often an apples-and-oranges exercise. The biggest grouping of dealers is in Makhan Tol, north of Durbar Square, but there are many others along Tridevi Marg and elsewhere in Thamel. As with carpets, don't commit yourself to a *thangka* until you've shopped around and seen them being painted in Patan or Bhaktapur. To get a grounding in styles and prices with less pressure, visit one of the handicrafts emporia on New Road and Jamal, or *Indigo*, below.

The non-profit shops listed in the next section sell mass-produced **Mithila paintings**, though nothing special.

Indigo Gallery, Kwa Bahal (daily except Wed 11am–7pm). Top-of-the-line *thangka* and *paubha*.

Nepal Association of Fine Arts (NAFA) Gallery, Naksal (daily except Sat 11am–5pm). Contemporary works by Nepali painters and sculptors.

October Gallery, inside the *Hotel Vajra*, Bijeshwari (daily except Sat 9–11am & 5–8pm). Nepali paintings.

Non-profit shops and contemporary crafts

One of the most encouraging developments in recent years has been the rise of **non-profit shops** in Kathmandu and Patan. By providing outlets for women, disadvantaged people and workers' cooperatives in some of Nepal's remotest hill areas, they increase employment and channel money where it's most needed. They also appear to avoid the pitfalls of other development projects in the hills, where lavish foreign aid has often led Nepalis to expect something for nothing.

These projects tend to specialize in non-traditional, contemporary crafts. Weavers in the eastern and western hills produce unusual forms of *dhaka* and other **textiles**, adapted for foreign tastes; a UNICEF project in Bhaktapur makes beautiful greeting cards of **handmade paper; leather** goods and **batiks** are made by local lepers, while other groups produce **toys, ready-made clothes**, and ingenious articles out of bamboo and even pine needles.

Although these crafts are beginning to be widely imitated, many can still be found only in non-profit outlets. The majority of these are found in Patan, but the following have branches in Kathmandu.

Community Craft Centre, Lazimpath (Mon–Fri & Sun 9.30am–6pm, Sat 10am–5pm). Woollens, *dhaka* and other textiles, also ceramics and paper.

Mahaguthi II, Durbar Marg, just north of *Hotel de l'Annapurna* (daily except Sat 10am–6pm). Aided by Oxfam, it supports a home for destitute women; mainly textiles, some jewellery and other gift ideas.

Nepal Women's Organization Shop, Lazimpath (Mon–Thurs & Sun 10am–5pm, Fri 10am–3pm). Specializes in block-printed cottons, with some quilted cotton items, woollens, toys and paper.

Clothing and fashion

Thamel and Freak Street are full of shops selling **wool sweaters**, jackets, mittens and socks, which are among Nepal's best bargains – just steer clear of the cheap garments, which fall apart at the seams. Similarly inescapable around here are **kit bags**, **caps** and other fashion items made from black felt with Tibetan rainbow fringes. Hardly fashionable, though many people lap them up, are **T-shirts** and **ready-made clothes**; watch out when you wash them because the cheap fabrics shrink and the colours run. **Tailors**, usually found inside the same clothing shops, are skilled at machine-embroidering designs on clothing.

Shawls and scarfs made of **pashmina**, a fine goat's wool only a cut below cashmere, are cheapest at Indrachowk. **Topi**, the caps that Nepali men wear in much the same way Westerners wear ties, are sold around Asan Tol. You'll find **sari material** in shops north of Indrachowk, although for discriminating textile buyers, Patan and Bhaktapur (see Chapter Two) are the places to go. Other traditional textiles are sold in the non-profit shops (see above).

Bagh Bazaar has several outlets marketing Indian- and Nepali-style **fashions**. For really attractive Western clothes with a Nepali flavour – especially silks – hit the boutiques along Durbar Marg. The following can be recommended.

Everest Handloom Silk, Tridevi Marg, opposite *KEEP*. Nepali raw silk by the metre, plus silk readymades under the "Namaste" brand.

Mandala Art & Boutique, Durbar Marg, near *Nirula's*. Chinese silk garments, hand-painted in Nepal in striking colours; also silver jewellery, Indian-made leather items.

Rage, Durbar Marg, north of the Clocktower. Designer fashions for women and men.

Silk Palace, Durbar Marg, opposite the *Hotel Woodland*. Factory showroom with Kathmandu's widest selection of Nepali-woven, Indian-grown silk material, Western designs (dresses, men's shirts, ties, etc) and saris.

Books

Kathmandu has a great collection of English-language **bookshops**, and browsing them is one of the city's main forms of nightlife – many stay open till 10pm. Most are nameless holes-in-the-wall. Don't forget that they'll buy back books at half price. *Pilgrim's* is still the best of the serious shops.

Educational Booksellers, next to the Mahakal Mandir. Mostly textbooks, but there's also a good range of Penguin Classics.

Pilgrim's Book House, Thamel, north of the *Kathmandu Guest House*. Extensive reference sections on all things Nepali: religion, mysticism, health, travel, language, development; also postcards, paper, cassettes, incense, supplies. A second outlet 100m to the south specializes in antiquarian rarities.

Ratna Book Distributors, Bagh Bazaar, near the *French Cultural Centre*. General range of reference and fiction.

Meditation, yoga and astrology

Not surprisingly, Kathmandu is an important centre for spiritual pursuits. This section sketches out the general possibilities, concentrating on established outfits that cater specifically for Westerners; a scan through the posters in the popular lodges and restaurants will no doubt turn up others. See also the organizations listed in the next section on alternative therapies, as there's a lot of overlap between all these disciplines. You'll find brief introductions to meditation and yoga in "Spiritual Pursuits" in *Basics*, and for more on astrology see "A Visit to the Astrologer" on p.350.

Meditation

The Mahayana Buddhist **Himalayan Yogic Institute** (☎413094; PO Box 817, Kathmandu), located in Baluwatar, conducts weekly teachings on *dharma*, hosts a revolving schedule of day-long workshops and courses on Tibetan Buddhist meditation and related Tibetan arts (Rs250), and has a library and meditation room (daily 9am–6pm). HYI is affiliated with Kopan Monastery, north of Boudha, where it offers seven- to ten-day meditation courses during the autumn and spring (about Rs350 per day, including food and lodging).

Nepal Vipassana Centre (☎225237; PO Box 133, Kathmandu) runs ten-day courses on *vipassana*. These aren't for the frivolous: daily meditation begins at 4.30am, and silence is kept for the full ten days. To register or pick up a pamphlet on the course, visit the centre's Kathmandu office (Mon–Fri 10am–5.30pm), well hidden in an unmarked building off a courtyard behind *Nabil Bank* on Kantipath. All courses are funded by donations.

The **Kathmandu Buddhist Centre** (PO Box 5336, Kathmandu) holds introductory talks on Western Buddhism a few times a week during the tourist seasons – check around on notice boards for the location. They also conduct one-day courses in Buddhism and two-day meditation workshops (both Rs350 per day) at their premises next door to *Hotel Ganesh Himal*, to the southwest of Chhetrapati Chowk, and five-day residential courses ($60, all-in) in a restored *bahal* in Patan.

Opportunities also exist for individual study under Tibetan lamas – see the "Boudha" section in Chapter Two.

If you're of the Rajneesh persuasion, you'll be pleased to learn that Kathmandu supports a thriving Osho industry which includes a travel agency, a bimonthly magazine and three meditation centres. The **Asheesh Osho Meditation Centre** (☎271385) in Tahachal and a second site in Lazimpath conduct one-hour dynamic meditation sessions every morning; these are open to all and the fee is a dona-tion. The third venue, **Osho Tapoban Forest Retreat Centre** (☎271385; PO Box 278, Kathmandu), located in a beautiful setting north of Nagarjun Ban, puts on three- and eight-day scheduled retreats as well as daily meditations and discourses, charging about Rs100–200 per night for basic accommodation and good vegetarian food. If you can't get through to the centres themselves, contact *Osho World Travel* on Tridevi Marg (☎225392).

Yoga

Patanjali Yoga Centre (☎272321; fax 229459), located east of the National Museum in Chhauni, offers classes and residential courses in pure *astanga yoga*, a balance of the eight traditional systems of yoga. The director, Yogacharya Sushil Bhattacharya, is highly respected in yoga circles. Daily early-morning and afternoon meditation/*hatha yoga* sessions are open to all (Rs100). Residential study in *hatha yoga*, yoga philosophy, diet and health costs Rs500 per day. Four-week yoga/trekking programmes and one-month yoga teacher-training courses are also offered.

Ananda Yoga Centre, a retreat facility in a lovely setting in the valley 12km west of Kathmandu, caters for both beginning and advanced students of yoga. The teacher is Shri Vikashananda, who brings an eclectic approach to *hatha yoga*, *pranayama*, meditation, yogic cleansing, diet and naturopathy. You can set your own itinerary and the cost is Rs250 a day, including room and board. For informa-tion contact *Shangrila Prints* (☎410693) on Tridevi Marg or *Anu Prints* (☎411957) in Thamel.

Yoga House (☎417900), run by English expat Chrissie Gregory, offers morn-ing and evening *hatha yoga* classes on a drop-in basis (Rs200 for 90min). It's in Tangal, about a ten-minute bike ride east of Thamel: follow the road north of the Royal Palace eastwards until it becomes dirt, and where it passes a pond on the left look for a house with coloured umbrellas on the roof.

The **Himalayan Yogic Institute** (see "Meditation" above) also does one-day beginners' workshops on *hatha yoga* (Rs250).

Astrology

It's best not to mention **astrologers** in the Kathmandu area by name, partly because few of them speak English, but mostly because they all have their own flocks to look after and it wouldn't be fair to rain hordes of foreign horoscope-seekers down on them. Try offering your innkeeper or a guide a commission to take you to his astrologer and to translate for you – you'll get a fascinating glimpse into an extremely important but behind-the-scenes aspect of Newar life.

To have a **horoscope** prepared you'll need to make an appointment first, and when you go you'll be expected to provide the exact time and place of birth (if you don't know the time, the astrologer may be able to improvise by reading your palm). It'll take the astrologer up to a week to produce an annual chart, even longer for a full span-of-life chart. You'll need to schedule a separate session for him to interpret it for you and answer any questions you may have; the fee for the entire service may run to Rs500 or more. Whatever you may think of astrology or your particular reading, at the least you'll come away with a beautiful and unique work of art.

Alternative therapies

Many of what we in the West call alternative therapies are, of course, established practice in Nepal. The full range of remedies is actually quite a bit greater than what you see in this section, which, like the previous one, focuses on what's accessible to the average visitor. Again, refer to "Spiritual Pursuits" in *Basics* for a bit of background on these practices.

Ayurved

Nepal's oldest ayurvedic clinic, **Arogya Ashram** (☎470776), run by Dr Kashi Raj Upadhya, is also well known for its herbal steam baths and yogic massages. It's located out in Gaushala – to find it, head east from Kamal Pokhri towards Pashupatinath, and the ashram will be on your right just before you get to the Ring Road.

For a private consultation, try **Dr Mana Bajra Bajracharya** (☎223960), who operates a small clinic and dispensary in Mahabaudha. He also sells books on ayurvedic medicine. To find his practice, head north of the Mahabaudha stupa towards Asan and take the first left, then look for the sign on the left. **Dr Ram Narayan Shah** at the Ayurvedic Hospital in Nardevi, about 200m west of the Nardevi Mandir on the left, will also treat foreigners.

To fill ayurvedic prescriptions, visit the **Gorkha Ayurved Company** (☎228625) south of Chhetrapati Chowk, or if your Nepali is up to standard, try any of the ayurvedic pharmas lining the lane running west from the Nardevi Mandir.

Tibetan medicine

Kunphen Tibetan Medical Centre (☎213820) has two locations in Kathmandu: the main clinic, due north of Chhetrapati Chowk, keeps daytime hours, while a branch clinic in the *Hotel Star*, next door to the *Kathmandu Guest House*, treats patients in the evenings. Both are basically front offices for a Tibetan medicine company, whose products they sell, but their services come highly recommended.

There's also a Tibetan medicine clinic out in Boudha – see the Boudha section in Chapter Two for details.

Massage

First the bad news. Many of the numerous signs around Thamel advertising **"massage"** have been put there by complete charlatans attracted by the princely sums tourists will pay to have their bodies rubbed. Spurred by demand from foreigners (mostly Indians), a growing number offer "erotic massage" as performed by a "female assistant" (read wife).

That said, there are some professional masseurs around, though they come and go; ask to see their credentials, which should be from a certified yoga school. The price of an hour's massage, after bargaining, should settle somewhere around Rs200–300. Two centres that can be recommended are **Arogya Ashram**, which offers yogic massage, and **Yoga House**, which holds courses in Thai-style massage (phone numbers and locations given above). **Michael Keller** (☎410252), an American expat in Kathmandu, specializes in "structural body work".

On from Kathmandu: travel practicalities

Life in Kathmandu is easy – too easy. Get out before you start gathering moss; later, you'll wonder why you stayed so long. What follows is a full rundown on buying tickets, arranging transport and trips, and getting visas. If you can't find what you're looking for here, try the "Listings" and "Travel Details" sections at the end of the chapter.

Travel within Nepal

For better or worse, most people make Kathmandu their base for travels within Nepal. The country is so centralized, with Kathmandu its transport hub, that a grand tour easily becomes a series of trips out from the capital and back again. This, admittedly, has its advantages: you can make good use of the tourist bus services, which all begin or end in Kathmandu, and can choose from the most reputable trekking, rafting and cycle-touring companies. It's also easy to leave luggage in Kathmandu, allowing you to travel lightly around the country.

Ticket agents

With their funfair signs advertising "Bus and Train to India" and "Exciting Jungle Safari", **ticket agents** are the used-car salesmen of Nepal, preying on travellers' faith in the apparently limitless possibilities of Kathmandu. Though they make themselves out to be budget travel agencies, they're not registered with the government and they offer very limited services. Many are inept, and some are downright dishonest. Even the honest ones too often make promises they're in no position to fulfil. Naturally, they all mark up the price of the tickets they sell.

For seats on local buses, a ticket agent can save you the trouble of making an extra trip to the bus station, and his commission may be money well spent. However, for tickets to Pokhara or India, it's advisable to deal directly with the ticket-issuing company (see sections below) – using a middleman only increases the chances of something going wrong.

Go to a registered travel agent (see below) to arrange air tickets, car rental or anything involving telexes and the like.

Tourist bus operators

Several companies operate regular **tourist bus** services. Tickets cost about double the regular bus fare; book as far in advance as possible during the busy seasons. The buses depart from near Central Immigration on Tridevi Marg.

TO POKHARA
At the time of writing, bus companies plying the **Kathmandu–Pokhara** route were:

Memoire Tours & Travels, Thamel (☎414270).
Osho World Travel, Tridevi Marg (☎224258).
Pagoda Travel & Tours, Basantapur Square (☎216871).
Pancha Buddha Tours & Travels, Thamel (☎223156).
Student Travels & Tours, Chhetrapati (☎220334).
Swiss Travels & Tours, Khichapokhri (☎222318).

TICKET AGENT LINGO

Make sure you and your ticket agent are speaking the same language. The following is a list of some terms ripe for misunderstanding.

Tourist bus – Theoretically, one that stops only for food and viewpoints, and admits only as many passengers as there are seats.

Minibus – Usually a 24- or 32-seater, capable of making somewhat better time than a full-size bus.

Swiss bus – A meaningless misnomer: they're all Indian!

2x2 – Two seats on either side of the aisle: that means more room per person that the usual 2x3 or 3x3.

Folding seats – Sometimes these really work, but were you to recline one you'd crush the person behind you.

Reporting time – The time the tea sellers want you to be there.

Departure time – Reporting time.

TO TADI BAZAAR (CHITWAN)
Companies operating tourist buses **to Tadi Bazaar** (for Chitwan National Park):
Baba Travels & Tours, Thamel (☎418894).
Paradise Tours & Travels, Jyatha Thamel (☎225898).

Domestic airlines

Refer to the "Getting Around" section of *Basics* for tips on making the most of **domestic flights**. The domestic airlines also offer what they call a "mountain flight", a one-hour scenic loop towards Everest costing $99, but book through a travel agent for the best seat allocation. Note that *RNAC*'s services to Pokhara, Lukla, Meghauli and Bharatpur, plus the mountain flight, are handled by its international office (see box below).

Everest, Durbar Marg (☎224188).
Necon, Kamal Pokhari (☎417986).
Nepal Airways, Kamal Pokhari (☎412388).
RNAC, New Road, located down the first alley west of *RNAC*'s main international building (☎214862).

Rafting operators

Unless you *really* know what you're doing, you'll have to join a group to go **rafting** in Nepal. Most rafting operators are based in Kathmandu; there are a few inexpensive outfits in Pokhara, but their trips are run on a more sedate stretch of river. Smaller Kathmandu companies tend to offer only three-day trips on the Trisuli River for around $15–20 a day, but for reasons explained in the rafting section (p.195), companies in this price bracket are hard to recommend. The ones listed here are more reputable, hence more expensive.

Equator Rafting, at *Tukche Peak Guest House,* Thamel (☎416717; fax 417190; Box 5282, Kathmandu). Experienced guides, good equipment, communal cooking. Trips on the Trisuli, Sun Kosi and Karnali for $35–60 a day. Kayaks available.

Great Himalayan Rivers, Lazimpath (☎410937). Established company offering Trisuli trips for $35 a day and Sun Kosi trips for $55 a day.

Everything to do with **trekking** is covered in Chapter Seven.

Himalayan Encounters, in the forecourt of the *Kathmandu Guest House* (☎417426). Trips encourage group participation and appeal to gung-ho types. Three-day Trisuli trip costs $99, ten days on the Sun Kosi $450.

Himalayan River Exploration, Naksal (☎414073; fax 414075; PO Box 170, Kathmandu). Reliable rafting operator handling mainly overseas bookings. Trisuli trips start at $100, Sun Kosi $500.

Ultimate Descents, at *Yeti Cottage*, north Thamel (☎412818; fax 411833). Specializing in longer expeditions, such as the Sun Kosi, Karnali and Tamur, generally priced at $45 per day.

White Magic, Jyatha Thamel (☎226885; fax 227372; PO Box 2118, Kathmandu). Regularly rafts the Trisuli and Sun Kosi, and occasionally the Seti, Karnali and Kali Gandaki. Around $40 a day.

Mountain-bike tours

At least three companies in Kathmandu offer mountain-bike tours, and this number is bound to grow. Tips for touring on your own are given on p.186, and rental information is given in the "Getting around" section near the beginning of this chapter.

Equator Mountain Biking, at *Tukche Peak Guest House*, Thamel (☎416717; fax 417190; Box 5282, Kathmandu). Day trips in the valley from $20, overnights to Nagarkot $70. Can arrange customized trips.

Himalayan Mountain Bikes, Gairi Dhara, but soon to move to a Thamel location (☎225875; fax 416870; PO Box 2236, Kathmandu). Nepal's original cycle outfitter, running tours ranging from one to thirteen days. Two- to four-day trips ($80–160) are frequent, but book ahead for longer ones (which cost up to $1385). Also offers cycling, rafting and trekking combos.

Surendra's Trekking, Jyatha Thamel (☎228033; fax 222026; PO Box 2078, Kathmandu). Day tours ($25) and ad hoc excursions from two to eight days ($90–450), plus some scheduled cycling, rafting and trekking trips in the two-week range (from $900).

Wildlife package tours

Although most of the **budget lodges** near Chitwan National Park have booking offices in Kathmandu, their packages are poor value. See the Chitwan section in Chapter Five for full details on doing it yourself.

For **luxury jungle lodges and tented camps**, you do need to book ahead. See the relevant listings for Chitwan National Park (p.233), Bardia National Park (p.261) and Sukla Phanta Wildlife Reserve (p.265).

Leaving Nepal

Overland connections between Nepal and India are well developed, not to say comfortable; Kathmandu is the usual setting-off point, since it's the only place in Nepal to get an Indian visa. For all other countries you'll almost certainly fly: see the box overleaf for details on international airline offices and recommended travel agents. It's worth shopping around, as even supposedly standard airfares may vary from one agent to the next.

If you're **flying** out of Nepal, remember that there's an astronomical Rs600 airport tax – and it may well go higher. Also, don't forget to reconfirm your return flight – see the box for addresses and phone numbers – at least 72 hours prior to departure or you'll lose your seat (just to be sure, ask for a computer printout for verification).

RECOMMENDED TRAVEL AGENTS

Everest Travel Service, with branches on Kantipath (☎221392) and Ganga Path, just off Durbar Square (☎222217).
Kathmandu Travels & Tours, Ganga Path, just off Durbar Square (☎222511).
Marco Polo Travels, in the forecourt of the *Kathmandu Guest House* (☎414192).

Natraj Tours & Travels, Durbar Marg (☎222014); also a branch in the *Kathmandu Guest House* forecourt (☎418755).
Student Travels & Tours, Chhetrapati (☎220334).
Yeti Travels, Durbar Marg (☎211234).

INTERNATIONAL AIRLINES

See the "Getting There by Air" section in *Basics* for sample air fares between Kathmandu and other Asian cities.

Aeroflot, Kantipath (☎212397).
Air Canada, Durbar Marg (☎222838).
Air India, Kantipath (☎223815). Flights from Kathmandu are handled by *Indian Airlines* (see below).
Biman Bangladesh, Durbar Marg (☎222544).
British Airways, Durbar Marg (☎222266).
Dragon Air, Durbar Marg (☎223162).
Indian Airlines, Durbar Marg (☎223053). India's domestic airline, but

it also operates flights from Kathmandu.
KLM, Durbar Marg (☎224895).
Lufthansa, Durbar Marg (☎221900).
Northwest, Lekhnath Marg (☎410089).
PIA, Durbar Marg (☎223102).
Qantas, Durbar Marg (☎220245).
RNAC, corner of Kantipath and New Road (☎220757).
Singapore, Durbar Marg (☎220759).
Thai, Durbar Marg (☎223565).

Overland to India

Many travellers get burned by scams involving **tickets to India**. Given that a typical bus–train package involves three different tickets and as many as six companies or agents, the chances of something going wrong are high. Ticket sellers in Kathmandu know that few travellers will come back to complain.

All **bus–train packages** to India involve travelling by public bus to the border at Sunauli, and then by Indian bus to Gorakhpur, the nearest broad-gauge train station to Kathmandu. It's probably worth paying double in Kathmandu to have a confirmed sleeper out of Gorakhpur, since tickets are hard to obtain there, but Kathmandu ticket sellers require at least a week to arrange train tickets and they demand money up front. When you return to pick up your ticket, you may be told that it's being held at the border – and when you get to the border, you may be told it's in Gorakhpur. If the ticket isn't ready when it was promised, demand your money back and take your chances with the ticket scalpers in Gorakhpur. Be particularly careful when booking first-class sleepers, as there's a racket in replacing them with second-class sleepers or first-class seats. Never surrender your receipt to anyone – without it, you've got no proof of what you paid for.

Bus-only deals to Darjeeling, Delhi and a few other Indian cities are less chancey. On the other hand, there's less reason to book an Indian bus so far in advance; if you want to save money, take any bus to the border and book your seat on the Indian bus there. At least one company (*Pagoda*) runs a regular direct **bus** to Delhi; other outfits lay on occasional direct services to Goa and such places, but they're overpriced and must be horrendously long journeys. Note that a Darjeeling permit is no longer necessary to exit Nepal at Kakarbitta on the eastern border.

Not quite full yet

Just a handful of companies package tickets to India from Nepal, and all other agents deal through them. Of these, the most reliable appear to be:

Pagoda Travels & Tours, Basantapur Square (☎216871).
Shikhar Nepal Tours & Travels, Chhetrapati (☎228163).
Shiva Travels, Chhetrapati (☎215650).
Student Travels & Tours, Chhetrapati (☎220334).

The Indian visa two-step

Those geniuses at the Indian embassy (☎410900), off Lazimpath in Lainchaur, have come up with a new and improved **visa** application process – allow *one week* to work your way through it.

Application hours are 9.30 to 11am, Monday to Friday. The time-consuming part of the procedure is obtaining "clearance" from Delhi, which is needed before your visa application can even be considered. Queue up at Counter B, where they'll take a fee off you (Rs300 at last count) and send a fax with your details to Delhi. Wait five to seven days for the reply. Then come back, collect your clearance document and report to Counter A (why B first, then A? you'll understand when you get to India), where you actually apply for your visa. Visas cost Rs250 per month and you'll need to supply a couple of passport photos. Note that a multiple-entry visa costs no more than a single-entry one. Your visa should be ready for collection later the same day.

Attention British, French, German, Dutch, Austrian, Spanish and Italian passport holders! Still more adventures await you. *Before* going through the above process, you must first get a "recommendation letter" from your embassy.

Travelling to Tibet

At the time of writing, the Nepal–**Tibet** border was open only to **individual travellers** exiting Tibet, not vice versa, and Chinese visas were being issued only to tour groups in Kathmandu. This is likely to change, but individuals intending to enter Tibet overland will probably still have to get their Chinese visa in Hong Kong. Otherwise, consider booking a one-way flight to Lhasa through *China Southwest Airlines*, who will arrange your visa for about $50.

A few Kathmandu travel agents arrange **group tours** (minimum size three people), but these are strictly chaperoned by official guides and there's little chance of being allowed to leave the group to travel independently. They're also expensive at $600 and up for five days. Allow at least a week for a visa to be issued, and try the following agencies.

Arniko Travels & Tours, Kamalpokhari (☎414594).
China Southwest Airlines, Kamaladi (☎419770).

Nepal Travel, Ramshah Path (☎412899).
Tibet Travels & Tours, Tridevi Marg (☎410303).

Visas for other Asian countries

If you're moving on to other parts of Asia, the following embassies and consulates in Kathmandu issue **visas**. Formalities often change, so it's worth calling ahead.
Bangladesh, Naksal (☎414943). Apply Mon–Fri 9am–noon; visa ready in 24 hours.
Burma (Myanmar), Chakpat, Patan (☎521788). Visas issued only through travel agents.
China, Baluwatar (☎411740). Visas issued only through travel agents.
Pakistan, Panipokhri (☎410565). Apply Mon–Thurs & Sun 2–3pm; visa ready in one or two days.
Thailand, Thapathali (☎213910). Apply Mon–Fri 9am–noon; visa ready in 24 hours.

Listings

American Express c/o *Yeti Travels Pvt Ltd*, Hotel Mayalu, Ground Floor, Jamal (daily except Sat 10am–1pm & 2–5pm; ☎13596). As usual, you can receive mail at the office if you can produce an *Amex* card or travellers' cheques.

Banks *Nepal Bank's* main exchange counter is on New Road (daily 7.30am–7.30pm). *Nepal Grindlays Bank* in Thamel (daily except Sat 10am–5pm) is handy, but it gets crowded. Other branches of *Nepal Bank, Rastriya Banijya Bank, Nepal Grindlays* and *Nabil* can be found on Freak Street, Kantipath and Lazimpath and inside the Central Immigration office (daily except Sat 10am–4pm). See "Costs, Money and Banks" in *Basics* for details on having funds wired to Nepal.

Black market Kathmandu is really the only place in Nepal where changing money on the black market is worthwhile. The most common fronts are carpet shops and shipping agents in Thamel and Freak Street; touts prowl incessantly during opening hours. Rates fluctuate, but large-denomination dollar notes should fetch 15–20 percent over the official rate. Lodge owners and shopkeepers will usually be eager to accept hard currency, but at slightly less than the black market rate.

Car rental Exorbitantly expensive: a Toyota Corolla with driver costs $50–75 a day. Better to hire a taxi (about $20 a day, but very negotiable; fuel may be extra).

Central Immigration Tridevi Marg, just east of Thamel. For general information on trekking permits and visa extensions, see "Red Tape and Visas" in *Basics*. Application hours are Mon–Thurs & Sun 10.30am–1pm (12.30pm in winter), Fri 10.30am–noon. The queues can be distressingly long in the busy seasons – the wait tends to be shorter later in the day. You can retrieve your passport later the same day. Beware Dasain in October, when the bureaucrats knock off for at least a couple of days. Nearby studios do instant passport photos for Rs100–150 (24-hr places on New Road are cheaper).

Credit cards *Amex, Visa* and *Mastercard* are accepted at major hotels and many boutiques. You can draw **cash** against *Visa* or *Mastercard* at *Grindlays* in Thamel and other banks on Kantipath and Durbar Marg – look for the signs.

Drugs All kinds are sold by the same sallow touts who change money. Foreign buyers are invariably overcharged, but the price is still low by any standard.

Embassies and consulates *Australia*, Sanepa (Mon–Thurs 10am–12.30pm; ☎527224); *Canada*, Lazimpath (Mon–Fri 9am–noon; ☎415193); *Denmark*, Baluwatar (Mon–Fri 10am–noon; ☎413010); *France*, Lazimpath (Mon–Fri 9am–12.30pm; ☎412332); *Germany*, Gyaneswar (Mon–Fri 9am–noon; ☎416832); *Israel*, Lazimpath (Mon–Fri 8.30am–3.30pm; ☎411811); *Netherlands*, Kumaripati, Patan (Mon–Fri 10am–noon; ☎522915); *Sweden*, Khichapokhri (Mon–Fri 8.30–11am; ☎220939); *UK*, Lainchaur (Mon–Fri 8.30am–12.30pm; ☎414588); *US*, Panipokhari (Mon, Wed & Fri 9–11am & 2–4pm; ☎411179). For visas for other Asian countries, see above.

Emergencies Police ☎226998 or 226999; Ambulance ☎211959; Red Cross ☎228094.

Fitness *Kathmandu Fitness Centre*, Lazimpath (☎412473), offers aerobics classes and weight-training sessions.

Hospitals, clinics and pharmas For emergencies, *Bir Hospital* (☎221988) on Kantipath is the most central; *Teaching Hospital* (☎412303) in Mahrajganj and *Patan Hospital* (☎522266) in Lagankhel, Patan, are further afield but very professional. For inoculations, stool tests and other diagnostics, make for the *CIWEC Clinic* in Baluwatar (☎410983; 24-hr line; consulting hours Mon–Fri 9am–noon & 1–3.30pm), or *Nepal International Clinic*, a block east of the Royal Palace entrance (24hr; consulting hours daily except Sat 9.30am–5pm; ☎412842). Both offer Western-standard facilities, but are expensive. *CIWEC* also sells some excellent information sheets on health matters. *Kalimati Clinic* (Mon & Fri 10–11.30am & 12.30–2.30pm, Wed 11am–2pm;☎271873) in southwest Kathmandu is cheaper for inoculations, and your fee helps subsidize a local immunization programme. Pharmas are in every neighbourhood; *Sajha Swastha Sewa*, opposite the Mahakal temple on Kantipath, is open 24hr.

Language courses *Namaste Language School* (☎215660) in Chhetrapati is highly recommended. The Peace Corps (☎410019) or Experiment in International Living (☎414516) might be able to suggest other outfits. For longer-term study opportunities, see "Staying On" in *Basics*.

Laundry Cleaners are everywhere around Thamel, and most lodges will send laundry out – in by 9am, back by 6pm.

Libraries The *British Council* on Kantipath has an admirable little collection, where you can pore over recent UK papers and magazines (summer Mon–Fri 10.30am–6pm; winter Mon–Fri 10am–5pm). On New Road, the *American Cultural Center*'s library is smaller, but features Kathmandu's only copies of the *New Yorker* (Mon–Fri 11am–6pm).

Maps All the usual city and trekking maps are sold by street vendors and bookshops; *Pilgrim's Book House* in Thamel arguably has the most comprehensive selection. For avid cartographers, *Maps of Nepal*, 300m west of the *Everest Hotel* on the road to Bhaktapur, carries an intriguing range of political and resource maps.

Newspapers and magazines The *Rising Nepal* and other local publications sell out early at *Pilgrim's* and at Pipal Bot on New Road. The *International Herald Tribune, USA Today, Time, Newsweek* are available at most bookshops.

Photography Print and slide film is widely available at only slightly higher than Western prices; shops along New Road are competitive. High-quality processing labs in Thamel and on New Road offer same-day service on print and E6 transparency films – *Lotus Colour* is recommended.

Police Report thefts to the district police headquarters, which in Kathmandu is in Durbar Square; ask for the Interpol section. The national police HQ and Interpol office is in Naksal.

Post The GPO sells stamps, aerogrammes and such Mon–Thurs & Sun 9am–7pm, Fri 9am–3pm, and for Poste Restante Mon–Thurs & Sun 10.15am–4pm, winter 10.15am–3pm, Fri 10.15am–2pm. Many lodges will run letters down to the GPO. *Pilgrim's* sells stamps for a 10-percent fee. Cheap postcards and other writing materials are sold outside the GPO gate. Send parcels from the Foreign Post Section, around the corner from the GPO on Kantipath (daily except Sat 10.15am–1pm) – see *Basics* for the procedure – or use a shipping agent (below).

Radio and TV *Radio Nepal* reads English-language news bulletins at 8am and 8pm. *Nepal TV* broadcasts the news in English at 9.15pm and also carries BBC World Service and CNN feeds. *STAR* satellite TV provides continuous MTV, BBC news and recycled English-language dross.

Shipping agents *Sharmasons Movers*, Kantipath (☎222709); *Mountain Packers & Movers*, Thamel (☎416697); *Atlas Cargo Service*, Thamel (☎412335). For air freight, try *Atlas Packers & Movers*, Durbar Marg (☎224254).

Sports The *National Stadium*, at the southern end of Kantipath, hosts frequent **football (soccer)** matches, and is also the headquarters for various martial arts clubs. The *Soaltee Oberoi, Everest Hotel* and *Yak & Yeti* all have **tennis** courts, open to non-residents for a fee. For **golf**, make for the *Royal Nepal Golf Club*, near the airport (greens fees Rs200), or *Gokarna Safari Resort* (see Chapter Two).

Swimming pools Kathmandu's public pool, behind the National Stadium, is open daily (except winter) for morning and afternoon sessions (Sun women only), and admission is only Rs15 for women, Rs20 for men. *Hotel de l'Annapurna* charges non-guests Rs350 to use its pool and Rs300 for the sauna, while use of the *Yak & Yeti*'s pool costs Rs250. *Hotel Woodlands*' facilities are less appealing (Rs175). If you can afford to wait three weeks for security processing, you can swim at Phora Durbar on an ICS membership (see "Tours" below).

Telephones Wherever two or three tourists are gathered together, ISD/STD/IDD outfits (see *Basics*) will be also – they're generally open 8am–10pm and accept credit cards. Most lodges charge similar rates for overseas and trunk calls, and will let you make local calls for a few rupees. To save 20–25 percent on overseas dialling or to make a late-night call, head for the *Central Telegraph Office* opposite the National Stadium, which is open 24 hours a day, seven days a week; the queue can range from a few minutes to over an hour.

Tours Various travel agencies run day tours – you'll see their brochures everywhere – but the most interesting ones are put together by *ICS* (International Community Services; Mon–Fri noon–3pm; ☎225044), a non-profit organization located in the British Council compound on Kantipath. You have to take out an annual membership, but it's only Rs150.

Trekking equipment Almost anything can be rented in Thamel or Freak Street, including climbing gear. Figure on about Rs25 per day for a good sleeping bag, pack or parka. Bring small items like water bottles and sunglasses from home, where they're cheaper, and don't bother renting boots since it's no good trying to break them in on the trail. As for woollens, you might as well buy.

festivals

Your chances of coinciding with a festival while in Kathmandu are good, since the capital spends about a month out of every year partying. Those listed here are just the main events; neighbourhood festivals happen all the time. Dates are determined according to the lunar and Nepalese calendars, and vary from year to year – enquire at the tourist office for dates, or consult a Nepalese calendar, available in tourist bookshops.

MAGH (Jan–Feb)

Basanta Panchami The spring festival is marked by a VIP ceremony in Durbar Square, while children celebrate Saraswati Puja on the same day at Swayambhu.

FAAGUN (Feb–March)

Losar Tibetan New Year, observed at Swayambhu but more significantly at Boudha, described in Chapter Two.

Shiva Raatri "Shiva's Night" is celebrated with bonfires in Kathmandu, but the most interesting observances are at Pashupatinath, described in Chapter Two.

Faagun Purnima (Holi) Popular week-long water-splashing festival, reaching a climax on the full moon.

CHAITRA (March–April)

Seto Machhendranath Jaatra A flamboyant four-day procession in which the white mask of Machhendranath is placed in a towering chariot and pulled from Jamal to an area south of Freak Street.

Ghora Jaatra Equestrian displays at the Tudikhel.

BAISAKH (April–May)

Nawa Barsa Nepali New Year (April 13 or 14): Kathmandu holds parades, but Bhaktapur's festivities are more exciting (see Chapter Two).

Buddha Jayanti The anniversary of the Buddha's birth, enlightenment and death, celebrated at Swayambhu.

SAAUN (July–Aug)

Ghanta Karna Demon effigies are burned on street corners throughout the city.

Nag Panchami A day set aside for the propitiation of snake spirits with offerings and worship.

Gaai Jaatra The Cow Festival, marked by processions led by garlanded boys costumed as cows.

BHADAU (Aug–Sept)

Indra Jaatra A week of chariot processions and masked-dance performances; on the last day, the king receives a special *tika* from Kathmandu's "living goddess" and beer flows from the mouth of Seto Bhairab in Durbar Square.

ASHOJ (Sept–Oct)

Dasain A mammoth ten-day festival celebrated in most parts of Nepal; in Kathmandu, mass sacrifices are held at the Kot courtyard near Durbar Square on the ninth day, Durga Puja, and the king bestows *tika* on all and sundry at the Royal Palace on the last day.

KARTIK (Oct–Nov)

Tihaar The Festival of Lights, celebrated here (as in most places) with masses of oil lamps throughout the city and five days of special observances.

travel details

BUSES

For bus and minibus services **within the Kathmandu Valley**, see "Travel Details" in Chapter Two. As for long-distance buses, you've four kinds to choose from:

Tourist buses leave from Tridevi Marg to Pokhara (2–7 daily, depending on season; 6–7hr) and Tadi Bazaar (for Sauraha/Chitwan; 0–2 daily; 6hr). Consider using one of these services if your destination is somewhere en route.

At the time of writing it wasn't clear whether **Sajha buses** would continue departing from Bhimsen Tower or move out to the new bus park. They go to Bhairawa (1 daily; 9hr); Birganj (2 daily; 10hr – stops at Tadi Bazaar for Chitwan after 6hr); Gorkha (2 daily; 6hr); Hetauda (1 daily; 8hr – via Rajpath) and Janakpur (1 daily; 10hr); Tansen (1 daily; 12hr) and Trisuli (1 daily; 4hr). Tickets go on sale the day before at a booth east of Bhimsen Tower.

Express and local buses depart from the main bus station, on the Ring Road north of Kathmandu. Buying tickets is confusing, since several companies operate out of a score of booths, and seats sometimes sell out the day before – if you can buy a ticket through an agent, go for it. Services to Banepa (frequent; 1hr 30min); Bhairawa/Sunauli (8 daily; 9–10hr); Bharabise (3 daily; 7hr); Birganj (4 daily; 10hr); Butwal (4 daily; 12hr); Dhulikhel (frequent; 2hr); Dhunche (2 daily; 8hr); Gorkha (4 daily; 6hr); Jiri (2 daily; at least 12hr); Pokhara (8 daily; 8–9hr); Tadi Bazaar (3 daily; 6hr); Tansen (3 daily; at least 12hr) and Trisuli (4 daily; 4hr).

Most **night buses** were at the time of writing still departing from Bhimsen Tower, but be on the alert in case the launchpad switches to the new bus park. Services to Bhairawa (2 nightly; 11hr); Biratnagar (7 nightly; 18hr); Birganj (2 nightly; 10–12hr); Dharan (6 nightly; 18hr); Hetauda (4 nightly; 9hr – via Rajpath); Janakpur (6 nightly; 12hr); Kakarbitta (3 nightly; at least 18hr); Nepalganj (2 nightly; at least 15hr); Pokhara (8 nightly; 10hr); Sunauli (4 nightly; at least 10hr) and Tansen (1 nightly; 14hr).

PLANES

Flight schedules are seasonal and, with the introduction of private domestic carriers, highly volatile. Consult a travel agent for the latest information. The following list gives a rough idea of services to the most notable of the thirty-odd airstrips that can be reached directly from Kathmandu (others require plane changes, usually in Pokhara, Nepalganj or Biratnagar).

From Tribhuwan Airport to Bharatpur (1–3 daily; 25min); Biratnagar (1–3 daily; 1hr); Dhangadhi (1–2 weekly; 2hr); Janakpur (2–3 weekly; 35min); Jomosom (0–3 weekly; 45min); Jumla (1–3 weekly; 1hr 20min); Lamidanda (1–2 weekly; 35min); Lukla (0–6 daily; 40min); Mahendranagar (0–1 weekly; 2hr 15min); Meghauli (1–3 daily; 35min); Nepalganj (1–2 daily; 1hr 30min); Phaplu (0–3 weekly; 35min); Pokhara (3–7 daily; 35min); Taplejung (1 weekly; 1hr 15min) and Tumlingtar (2–5 weekly; 1hr).

CHAPTER TWO

THE KATHMANDU VALLEY

Few places on earth can rival the **Kathmandu Valley**'s combination of natural and man-made beauty. Despite suburbanization and industrialization, the fertile, terraced valley maintains its traditional ways in a hundred huddled brick villages, most of which rarely see foreigners; much of the valley floor still shimmers in an undulating patchwork of paddy fields – brown, golden or brilliant green, depending on the season – crisscrossed by rutted paths and country lanes. But above all it's the valley's incredible wealth of art and architecture that overwhelms visitors, just as it did the early explorers. "The valley consists of as many temples as there are houses, and as many idols as there are men," gushed William Kirkpatrick, the first Englishman to reach Kathmandu, and generations of travellers since have accurately (if patronizingly) described it

as a "living museum". If most of this chapter is devoted to temples and holy sites
– there are no forts, you'll notice – it's because religion is the best and most fascinating window on Nepali culture.

Until two hundred years ago, this protected bowl *was* Nepal (and for many hill
people outside the valley, it still is). At that time, Kathmandu was only one of
three major city-states constantly battling for dominance: **Patan**, just across the
Bagmati River, controlled the southern part of the valley, while **Bhaktapur** ruled
the east. These historical divisions are profoundly ingrained in valley society, and
they live on in religious practices, festivals and even dress. This chapter divides
the valley into three sections, as much for practical reasons as historical ones,
since roads and transport have developed out of the old patterns of settlement.

The sheer density of sights in the valley is phenomenal. Roads radiate out to
dozens of towns and villages, and you won't go wrong with any of them. Hindu
holy places abound: the great pilgrimage complex of **Pashupatinath**, the sleeping Vishnu of **Budhanilkantha**, the sacrificial pit of **Dakshin Kali** and the hilltop temple of **Changu Narayan** are the most outstanding. If Buddhism is your
main interest, head for the great stupa of **Boudha**, the centre of Tibetan
Buddhist worship and study in Nepal, or the *bahal* of **Patan**, the valley's most
Buddhist city. For medieval scenes, try **Kirtipur**, **Bungamati** or, best of all,
Bhaktapur. For views, you're spoilt for choice – the protected areas of **Shivpuri**,
Rani Ban and **Godavari** stand out, but almost any hill will do.

Getting around the valley is generally easiest by **bike** (see p.186 for tips on
mountain-bike touring) or **motorcycle**. In the sections that follow, bus routes are
mentioned where they exist (fares are usually just a few rupees), but unless it's
stated otherwise, take it as given that the quickest way to get there is with your
own wheels. **Walking**, on the other hand, is often more rewarding: distances are
small, trails are everywhere, and people will usually be happy to give directions.
The *Schneider* colour **map** of the valley is by far the best for serious walking,
although *Mandala*'s much cheaper dyeline job will probably suffice.

NORTH OF KATHMANDU

Chapter One covers Kathmandu within the Ring Road; this section deals with the
remainder of the northern valley. Most people will treat the sights described here
as **day trips** from Kathmandu – some places are theoretically within walking
distance of town – but if you're interested in Buddhism, or you're just getting fed
up with Kathmandu, an **overnight stay** in Boudha would be a smart move.

Pashupatinath

Often likened to Varanasi in India, **PASHUPATINATH** (pronounced Posh-*potty-*
not) is Nepal's holiest Hindu pilgrimage site: a time-warp enclave of exotic
temples, cremation ghats, ritual bathers and half-naked sadhus. The sacred
complex lies just beyond the Ring Road, 4km east of Kathmandu – incongruously
close to the modern airport, but fortunately sheltered from it in a wooded ravine.
Pashupatinath, together with the associated temples of Gorakhnath and
Ghujeshwari, is a heady cocktail of Hindu – and to a lesser extent Buddhist –
proceedings, spiked with some of the most bizarre mythology in the world.

Buses from Kathmandu's Ratna Park drop you off southwest of the temple area at Gaushala, a busy, modern intersection on the Ring Road; the lane angling downhill from the northeast corner of the intersection leads to the western side of the temple area. If you're **cycling**, follow Tridevi Marg east past the Royal Palace, take the first right after Durbar Marg, then a left on the first main road (Kamal Pokhari), and follow that road over the Dhobi Khola and all the way to Gaushala. You'll probably have to pay a few rupees to have your bike "watched".

The site's layout favours an anticlockwise circuit on foot, first around Pashupatinath's temples and ghats, then up to Gorakhnath, on to Ghujeshwari and back. Instead of returning to Pashupatinath, however, you might want to continue on to Boudha, which is only a kilometre or so further northeast along a rough track.

The Pashupatinath complex

The **temples of Pashupatinath** straddle the Bagmati River, which is thought by Hindus to be the holiest in the Kathmandu Valley, and this specific stretch the most sacred of all. To die and be cremated here is to be released from the cycle of rebirths, according to tradition. Wives used to commit *sati* on their husbands' funeral pyres here, and although the practice was outlawed early this century, it's still widely believed that husbands and wives who bathe here together will be remarried in the next life. **Bathing** is considered especially meritorious on full-moon days, on Magh Sankranti (usually Jan 14) and Bala Chaturdashi (late Nov or early Dec), and, for women, during the festival of Tij (late Aug or early Sept). The entire complex overflows with pilgrims from all over the subcontinent during the **festival** of Shiva Raatri (held on the new moon of late Feb or early March). Devout locals also come for special services on full moon days and on the eleventh lunar day (*ekadashi*) after each full and new moon.

Foreigners are free to observe most of these rituals, but it's essential to respect the privacy of bathers and worshippers. Be especially sensitive about photographing people and cremation pyres: you wouldn't want tourists snapping away at your mother's funeral, would you?

Shiva is the principal deity here, in one of his more benign forms: **Pashupati, Lord of the Animals**, in whose name the king of Nepal ends all his public addresses, and to whom praises are sung on Radio Nepal at the start of each broadcasting day. Several tales are told of how Shiva came by this title. Nepali schoolchildren are taught that Shiva, to escape his heavenly obligations, assumed the guise of a one-horned stag and fled to the forest here. The other gods pursued him and, laying hold of him, broke off his horn, which was transformed into the powerful Pashupati *linga*. The *linga* was later lost, only to be rediscovered at its present site by a cow who magically began watering the spot with her milk.

PASHUPATI MANDIR

Approaching from the west through the hamlet of Pashupathinath, a lane leads past trinket stalls and sweet shops to the main gate of the **Pashupati Mandir** – the holy of holies for Nepali Shaivas, followers of Shiva. Like many orthodox Hindu temples, it's only open to Hindus (in Nepal, Buddhists, Sikhs and Jains are included as Hindus). From the outside, though, you can glimpse the two symbols that are found in front of almost every Shiva temple, their gargantuan proportions here a measure of the temple's sanctity: a two-storey-high *trisul* (trident), and the enormous brass (and anatomically authentic) backside of Nandi, Shiva's faithful bull, who is yet another reminder of the god's procreative power. The best view of the whole compound can be had from a terrace high above the opposite (east) bank of the river.

Hidden inside, the famous **Pashupati linga** is supposed to display four carved faces of Shiva, plus a fifth, invisible one on the top; Buddhists claim one of the faces is that of the Buddha. Hindus associate this *linga* with yet another Shiva myth, in which the god transformed his phallus into an infinite pillar of light and challenged Brahma and Vishnu – the other members of the Hindu trinity – to find the ends of it. Brahma flew heavenward, while Vishnu plumbed the depths of hell; both were forced to abandon the search, but Brahma falsely boasted of success, only to be caught out by Shiva. Shaivas claim that this is why Brahma is seldom worshipped, Vishnu gets his fair share, and Shiva is revered over all.

The gold-clad pagoda dates from the early seventeenth century, but inscriptions indicate that a temple has stood here since at least the fifth century, and

SADHUS, YOGINS AND GANJA

Sadhus, those dreadlocked, ashen waifs usually seen lurking around Hindu temples, are essentially an Indian phenomenon. However, Nepal, being the setting for many of the amorous and ascetic exploits of Shiva (the most popular deity among sadhus), is a favourite sadhu stomping ground – and nowhere more so than Pashupatinath, which is rated as one of the four most important Shaiva pilgrimage sites. During the festival of Shiva Raatri, Pashupatinath hosts a full-scale sadhu convention, which draws pilgrims from all over the subcontinent. The government lays on free firewood for the festival.

Shaiva sadhus follow Shiva in one of his best-loved and most enigmatic guises – the wild, dishevelled **yogin**, the master of yoga, who sits motionless atop a Himalayan peak for eons at a time and whose hair is the source of the mighty Ganga (Ganges) River. Sadhus live solitary lives, always on the move, subsisting on alms and owning nothing but what they carry. They bear Shiva's emblems: the *trisul* (trident), *damaru* (two-sided drum), a necklace of furrowed *rudraksha* seeds, and perhaps a conch shell for blowing haunting calls across the cosmic ocean; some smear themselves with ashes, symbolizing Shiva's role as the destroyer, who reduces all things to ash so that creation can begin anew; and on their foreheads is usually painted a trident-shaped *tika*. (In addition to the

A *sadhu*

trident, sadhus employ scores of other *tika* patterns, each with its own cult affiliation and symbolism.)

Given Shiva as a role model, Shaiva sadhu theology – insofar as it exists – is a bloody-minded business. As befits followers of a mountaintop ascetic who is also the god of the phallus, sadhus practice celibacy, performing diverse contortions and mortifications of the flesh to free themselves from sensual passions, yet radiate a smouldering sexuality. Of one famous sadhu it was said that he had so completely marshalled his sexual energies that he bled semen; and until recently a popular sadhu at Pashupatinath publicly performed feats of hoisting large stones with a string tied to his penis. Similarly, sadhus refrain from alcohol, but blithely get stoned out of their heads on **ganja**, whose transcendental powers were supposedly discovered by Shiva. Marijuana, which grows wild thoughout hill Nepal, is smoked by sadhus in a *chillam*, and with each toke on the vertical clay pipe they intone "*Bam Shankar*" – "I am Shiva".

some historians suspect it goes back to the third century BC, when the ancient village of Deopatan, which once occupied the rise just to the west, is said to have been founded. The temple apparently emerged as a hotbed of tantric practices in the eleventh century and remained so for four hundred years, until the Malla kings reined things in by importing conventional Brahman **priests** from south India – an arrangement that continues to this day. Wearing the ceremonial orange robes of the Pashupata sect, the priests array the *linga* in brocade silk and bathe it with curd, ghee, honey, sugar and milk.

Hindu pilgrims are expected to distribute offerings to the priests and then make a circuit of the temple and a dozen other secondary shrines and images scattered about the precinct.

ALONG THE WEST BANK

Many of the buildings around the main temple, including the tall, whitewashed ones overlooking the Bagmati's west bank, are *dharmsala* (pilgrims' rest houses), here set aside for devout Hindus approaching death. In their final hour, the dying will be laid out on a sloped stone slab with their feet in the Bagmati and given a last drink of the holy river water. Cremations are held continuously on two **burning ghats** along the embankment: Arya Ghat, north of the footbridges, is reserved for the royal family and VIPs, while Ram Ghat, to the south, is used by other members of the higher castes. The cremations are carried out by the families of the deceased.

The small pagoda between the two footbridges is the **Bachhaleshwari Mandir**, dedicated to Shiva's consort Parvati in one of her mother-goddess roles. Next to it stands a newish ten-foot terracotta frieze of Narayan (alias Vishnu) and other sculptures of Ganesh and Gauri (Parvati). Running south along the west bank is another string of metal-roofed *dharmsala*, which you can explore in a limited way. Sticking out of the embankment in front of the next-to-last is a small but priceless seventh-century **Buddha statue**, looking rather out of place in this Hindu Lourdes, and, ensconced in a round brick battlement just to the south, a neglected bumper-sized *linga*. The southernmost building shelters two temples in its courtyard, the oval **Raj Rajeshwari** and the gilded pagoda of **Nawa Durga**.

Behind the *dharmsala* broods the gothic bulk of **Pancha Dewal**, whose five Mughal-style cupolas are visible from high up on the opposite bank. This now serves as an old people's home, operated by **Mother Theresa's Missionaries of Charity**, and though emphatically not a tourist site, it is an excellent place to experience a different side of Nepal as a volunteer. The sisters need help each morning changing and cleaning sheets, helping residents wash, clipping nails, scrubbing pots and so on – real humble work, but that's the whole idea of it. The entrance to the compound is on the north side; look for the sisters (who speak English) in their trademark white saris with blue trim.

THE EAST BANK

Crossing over to the east bank along the southernmost bridge, the first thing you'll reach is a pockmarked slope: a **burial ground**, where plots are reserved for sadhus, infants and people too poor to afford wood for a funeral pyre.

Moving northwards and uphill, you'll enter a wide, paved enclosure which during Shiva Raatri is chock-a-block with sadhus doing mysterious and sometimes gruesome penances. Two small temples are found here: the one with a statue of Garud in front is called **Lakshmi Narayan**, in honour of Vishnu (aka Narayan) and his wealth-bringing wife Lakshmi; the other is the **Ram Janaki**, containing statues of Ram – Vishnu's incarnation as a mortal in the *Ramayan* epic – and his whole family, including Hanuman the monkey king, who helped rescue Ram's wife Sita from the clutches of a Sri Lankan demon. Sita is popular among Nepali Hindus, since she was born in Janakpur in the eastern Tarai (see p.275). These temples, along with the **Ram Mandir** in the next compound, are disappointingly recent and un-Nepali. Temples at Pashupatinath are built and rebuilt often, renovations being the standard way of winning favour with gods and men, and wealthy Indian patrons are among the principal contributors to the development fund. Further north along the river, the eleven great **shivalaya** (boxy *linga* shelters) were erected in honour of women who committed *sati* on the pyres opposite.

Gorakhnath

The main stairway up the east bank carries on up through Mrigasthali Ban, the forest where Shiva is supposed to have cavorted as a stag, to the mellow **Gorakhnath Mandir** at the top of the hill. Visiting this compound, after the sensory overload below, is like entering a soundproofed room. The temple itself, a medium-sized *shikra* structure dedicated to the patron deity of the Shah kings, isn't interesting – what will amaze you is the sight of hundreds of **shivalaya** arranged in crumbling rows in the forest, mottled by shade and shafts of sunlight. The place has the romantic, ruined feel of an overgrown cemetery, with broken statuary lying undisturbed and stone inscriptions recording long-forgotten decrees. You could easily mistake the *shivalaya* for tombs, but their iconography – the *trisul*, statues of Nandi and Shiva (always with an erection), the *linga* atop the *yoni* – proclaims them to be Shiva shrines. It's a fine spot for a picnic, though you have to watch out for the thieving monkeys.

The onion dome rising above the trees to the southeast of Gorakhnath is the **Bishwarup Mandir** (entrance only to Hindus), dedicated to Vishnu in his many-limbed "universal form". Dominating the sanctum, however, is a six-metre-tall statue of Shiva and Parvati in the state of *yab-yum* (sexual union).

Ghujeshwari and back

The **Ghujeshwari** (or Guhyeshwari) **Mandir** sits at the bottom of the path that continues downhill from Gorakhnath. Here, too, non-Hindus can only peek from outside, but the legend behind this temple is one of the all-time masterpieces of Hindu surrealism. The story goes that Shiva's first wife, Sati, offended by some insult, threw herself onto a fire (giving rise to the term *sati*, or *suttee*); Shiva retrieved her corpse and, blinded by grief, flew to and fro across the subcontinent, scattering parts of the body in 51 sacred places. Ghujeshwari is where Sati's vagina (some say her anus) fell. As a consequence, the temple here represents the female counterpart to Pashupatinath and is held to be every bit as sacred, its chief focus being a well into which worshippers throw offerings. Buddhists consider Ghujeshwari to be one of the valley's four mystic Bajra Joginis – powerful tantric goddesses – and the site to be the seed from which the Swayambhu lotus grew.

From Ghujeshwari a lane follows the river back around to Pashupatinath, passing **Gauri Ghat**, a peaceful spot where the river enters the Pashupatinath ravine and monkeys leap from branches and cliffs into the water. The road crosses the river here and circles around to the village of Pashupatinath, while a trail past the river crossing takes a more direct route up and over **Kailash Hill**. This grassy knoll, named after the Tibetan mountain where Shiva does his meditating, gives good views of the mountains as well as the Pashupatinath area.

Boudha (Boudhanath)

To ancient travellers along the Kathmandu–Tibet trade route, the ten-kilometre corridor from Pashupatinath to Sankhu was known as the zone of *siddhi* (super-natural powers), where guardian deities dwelt and all wishes were granted. The biggest, most auspicious landmark along this route was – and still is – the great stupa at **BOUDHA** (or **BOUDHANATH**), about 5km east of downtown Kathmandu.

One of the world's largest stupas, Boudha is generally acknowledged to be the most important Tibetan Buddhist monument outside Tibet – Tibetans simply call it Chorten Chempo, "Great Stupa" – and since 1959 it has become the Mecca of **Tibetan exiles** in Nepal. Tibetans now run most of the businesses along the main road and around the stupa, while the construction of monasteries has created a regular suburban sprawl to the north: despite the coach parties and souvenir sellers, Boudha gives you a thorough dunking in Tibetan culture, both its proud past and anxious present. Dusk is the best time to be here, after the day-trippers have gone, when the resonant chanting of monks and the other-worldly cacophony of their music drifts from the upper rooms of the houses that ring the stupa, and pilgrims perform *kora*, shuffling and prostrating their way around the dome.

If you want an extra helping, go during the **festival** of Losar in February, when Boudha hosts the biggest celebration of the Tibetan New Year in Nepal. Another busy time is the full moon in March, when hill Tamangs (see p.178) – the original guardians of the stupa – converge here to arrange marriages, and hundreds of eligible brides are sat around the stupa for inspection. Full moon and new moon days in general attract more pilgrims, since acts of worship earn more merit on these days.

The site

Assigning a reliable age to Boudha is impossible, and historians are left at the mercy of legends, which seem to fix its origins around the fifth century AD.

A **Tibetan text** relates how a daughter of Indra stole flowers from heaven and was reassigned to earth as a lowly poultryman's daughter, yet prospered and shamed the valley's wealthy folk by building a gigantic stupa to honour the Buddha of the Previous Age. Tibetans attach great importance to this tale because it's attributed to Guru Padma Sambhava, Tibet's first and best-loved evangelist. Interestingly, in the same manuscript the guru warns of an invasion by a giant enemy, which would scatter the Tibetan people south into Nepal and India.

The **Newar legend** has a firmer historical grounding, involving a drought that struck Kathmandu during the reign of the early Lichhavi king, Vikramajit. When court astrologers advised that only the sacrifice of a virtuous man would bring rain, Vikramajit commanded his son Manadeva to go to the royal well on a moonless night and decapitate the shrouded body he would find there. Manadeva obeyed, only to find that he had sacrificed his own father, and so to expiate his guilt he erected the Boudha stupa.

Around the stupa

While less embellished than Swayambhu, Boudha is in its own way more interactive: you can climb up onto **the stupa**'s base, and during the windy autumn months kids fly kites from it. The dome is elevated on three *mandala*-shaped plinths of decreasing size, which reinforce the notion of the stupa as a meditation tool. As usual, the primordial Buddha's searching blue eyes are painted on the four sides of the central spire, and above them rise the thirteen golden steps to *nirvana*. Instead of five *dhyani* Buddhas, however, 108 (an auspicious number) much smaller images are set in niches around the dome.

The small **Ajima shrine** at the far side of the stupa shelters the image of a nasty goddess dining on a hapless victim. Ghoulish though she may look, Newars worship Ajima as a grandmother-protectress of children; she is also known as Harati, goddess of smallpox. Next door is a room-sized prayer wheel – all are welcome to spin it – and on the other side of the shrine you'll see the tanks where whitewash is mixed during festivals.

Boudha's **pilgrims** are arguably its greatest attraction, as the stupa is famed throughout the Himalayan region for its wish-fulfilling properties. Prayer wheels, heavy silver jewellery and rainbow-striped aprons are good general indicators of Tibetan origins. The men of Kham, in eastern Tibet, wear red tassels in their long hair, as do the Dolpa-pa of northwest Nepal, many of whom winter here. Nomads from the central Tibetan plateau wear sheepskin *chuba* (coats) with extra-long sleeves. Bhutanese men and women keep their hair cropped short and wear distinctive embroidered robes. Ladakhi women are distinguished by their velvet dresses, and high-crowned silk hats with small wings on either side. In addition, Nepali Bhotiyas (p.313) and Tamangs visit Boudha in force, although the stupa has no special attraction for Buddhist Newars.

THE DHARMA SCENE

Boudha's Western community is well established, but to become a part of it you need either an introduction or a lot of time, since serious Western students of *dharma* tend to regard tourists as spiritual interference. If you're ready, however, you'll find a teacher here. Many Westerners rate Boudha as the best place in the world to **study** Tibetan Buddhism, for although Dharmsala in India is better known because the Dalai Lama is based there, the presence of the Tibetan government-in-exile creates a politically charged atmosphere that can distract from serious study. Moreover, Dharmsala is heavily dominated by the Dalai Lama's Gelug-pa order, whereas at Boudha all four sects are well represented, making it easier to sample the different traditions.

The Chinese occupation of Tibet killed or drove away an entire generation of teachers, and Boudha's line-up of **lamas**, though formidable, reflects this: most are either very old or rather young. By far the most popular among the *dharma* set is **Chokyi Nyima**, abbot of Ka Nying Shedrupling Monastery, who speaks excellent English and holds open teachings most Saturday mornings. He also runs meditation courses during the tourist season (for more on Chokyi Nyima, see "Tibetan Exiles in Nepal" in *Contexts*). His younger brother, **Tsokney Rinpoche**, who's abbot of a monastery near Swayambhu, is also accessible and frequently gives teachings at Ka Nying Shedrupling. The death in 1992 of **Dingo Khyentse** of Shechen Tenyi Dargyeling Monastery has left a large gap, but this may in time be filled by his grandson, **Rabjam Rinpoche**, and **Trangu Rinpoche** of the Trangu Tashi Chökorling Monastery, who teaches a course each December–January. Kopan Monastery (north of Boudha, off the map), whose **Yeshe Lama** passed away in 1986, remains as busy as ever with a full schedule of Gelug activities; curiously, a young Spanish boy is being groomed as Yeshe's *tulku* (reincarnation). Other teachers include **Choge Trichen**, who runs Jyamchen Monastery and is also abbot of the Tibetan *gompa* at Lumbini, and **Kenpo Tsultrim Gyamtso** of the Marpa Institute on Mahakal Road (the road that forks left west of the *Tara Gaon* and leads to Kopan).

Western monks wear the same maroon robes and have taken the same monastic vows as Tibetan monks but, partly because of visa restrictions, aren't expected to make the same commitment to a monastery. While Tibetan monks live at their monastery, maintaining the building and making visits to the local community, Westerners are free to come and go. Given a three-month visa, most cram as much personal instruction as possible into their time, and then try to maintain a long-distance teacher–disciple relationship from home. Some follow their lama on speaking tours overseas, which are conveniently scheduled during the soggy monsoon months. In any case, a lifestyle with one foot in the West and the other in the East requires either sponsorship or independent means. A separate wing of the *dharma* crowd consists of Westerners living in Boudha for a season of **individual study**. Some are just trying Buddhism on for size, others are earnestly shopping around for a lama. Most lamas and teachers at Boudha give occasional open talks – with or without English translation – and normally agree to one-on-one meetings with anyone who shows a keen interest. If you go to a teaching, present the lama with a **kata**, a ceremonial white scarf, which he will then return to you. Pick up a cheap rayon *kata* in any shop that deals in Tibetan clothing, and they'll show you how to fold it.

To find out about upcoming teachings, check out the notice board at the *Bir Restaurant*, or try asking some of the regulars there. But if you've had no prior experience with Buddhism, you'd probably want to test the waters first by enrolling in a **meditation course**. The retreats run by the *Himalayan Yogic Institute* and the *Kathmandu Buddhist Centre* are the usual place to start; Kopan Monastery (affiliated with *HYI*) also holds a month-long course each November (see p.98).

The monasteries and back lanes

The past decade has seen an unsettling spate of monastery-building at Boudha, and at last count there were 37 *gompa* (monasteries) scattered around the neighbourhood. All four of the major Tibetan Buddhist sects (see "Religion" in *Contexts*) are represented at least twice – for a partial listing of names and sects, refer to the Boudha map.

The older **monasteries** around the stupa keep their doors open most of the time, and welcome spectators during their morning and dusk *puja*. Furnishings and icons are broadly similar in each. The gilded statues at the front of the assembly hall (*lhakang*) will usually represent the Buddha, various *bodhisattva*, or the founder of the monastery's sect. Spread out in front of these are likely to be oil lamps, which monks and pilgrims continually replenish; heaps of rice piled onto three-tiered silver stands, which are objects of meditation; conical dough-cakes (*torma*) symbolizing deities; and offerings of fruit, coins, flowers and incense. Frescoes on the walls depict fearsome guardians of the faith, symbolic deities and historical figures, or, like *thangka*, express the complex cosmology of Tibetan Buddhism (see p.96).

If you follow either of the two lanes heading **north of the stupa**, the romance evaporates in short order: this is Boudha the boomtown, an unplanned quagmire of garbage-strewn lanes, unlovely new buildings, schools and carpet factories. Indeed, the area from Boudha to Gokarneswar accounts for the largest share of the valley's carpet manufacture, a dubious distinction that contributes to serious water pollution as well as pretty awful congestion out on the main road in front of the stupa. It's a disturbing picture of the bittersweet present – and forseeable future – of the Tibetan diaspora. The monasteries here, secluded behind high

Painting of a *dharmapala* (protector of the faith) in a Buddhist monastery

walls and iron gates, have been deliberately named after *gompa* in Tibet that were destroyed by the Chinese, and it's hoped that, besides keeping the flame of Tibetan Buddhism alight and preserving traditional art forms, they'll help bring about the resurrection of their namesakes. Money is pouring into Boudha from all over the world (particularly from the Far East) to build them, but looking at the results you might wonder whether the Tibetans are being driven down the infamous road of good intentions.

Further afield

Boomtown aside, Boudha makes a good springboard for several walks and bike rides in this part of the valley. **Kopan Monastery**, occupying a beautifully leafy ridge about 3km due north of the stupa, is an easy target. Further along this ridge to the east lies **Pulahari Monastery** (also accessible from Gokarneswar – see below), where a stupa containing the remains of the recently deceased abbot, Jamyung Kongtrol Rinpoche, has the makings of an important pilgrimage stop. From either of these points, it's a delightful three-hour hike north along the ridge to **Nagi Gompa**, and another hour's descent to Budhanilkantha.

In the opposite direction, Pashupatinath is only about a half-hour's walk south of Boudha. The path – revoltingly smelly at first – sets off from the main road almost opposite the entrance to the stupa. Sankhu, Gokarneswar and Sundarijal, described in the next section, all make fine excursions on a bike.

Practicalities

The coach-party crush is at its worst between mid-morning and late afternoon – Boudha is much pleasanter after hours. There's also a good range of budget and moderately priced accommodation, so it's well worth staying overnight. If you haven't come by bicycle, crowded **minibuses** and buses leave frequently from Ratna Park near the *Air India* office.

Accommodation
All of Boudha's hotels are off the map, some of them so far-flung you practically need to take a taxi to get to the stupa. The budget accommodation is closer to the heart of things.

BUDGET PLACES
Bir Restaurant, on the main road just west of the stupa entrance (☎470790). Good location and camaraderie, but often filled with long-term *dharma* types. ③.
Hotel Tashi Delek, across the street from the *Bir* (☎471380). The south-facing rooms have balconies that overlook paddy fields, but they're perilously close to the public latrines. ③.
Lotus Guest House, down a lane north and east of the stupa. Operated by the next-door monastery, this clean but spartan guest house offers Boudha's best value and location. ④/B④.
Snowlion Lodge, on the main road about 400m east of the stupa entrance, off the map (☎4470341). Comparable to the *Tashi Delek*, but further from the stupa. ②/B③.

HOTELS
Maya Guest House, east of the *Snowlion* (☎470866). Gorgeous garden; price includes breakfast and transport from Kathmandu. B⑥.
Stupa Hotel, east of the *Maya* (☎470400). Large and efficient, but on the sterile side. B⑦.
Tara Gaon Resort Hotel, off the main road nearly 1km west of the stupa (☎470409). A strange government-run affair, reportedly not long for this world – a fancy new *Hyatt* is supposed to take its place. B⑦.

Eating
Although Western **food** is readily available in the places listed here, you'd be foolish to miss trying Tibetan specialities such as the ravioli-like *kothe* and *momo*, chunky *thukpa* soup, and *tongba* (hot millet grog) – check out the many cheap and cheerful local eateries along the main road or northeast of the stupa.

Bir Restaurant, west of the stupa on the main road. Still the main meeting place for long-term Westerners in Boudha, with a cosy atmosphere and inexpensive (though unremarkable) food.
Dergey Restaurant, adjoining the stupa. A rather gloomy place with a limited Chinese/Tibetan menu.
Double Dorjee Restaurant, on the main road (south side), 300m east of the stupa. A funky little place with unpredictable food.
Stupa View Restaurant, overlooking the stupa on the north side. Boudha's premier restaurant, with prices to match. All-vegetarian and fairly imaginative dishes (good pasta and tofu), plus there's a full bar and a roof terrace.
Tibet Restaurant, northeast of the stupa. One of several holes-in-the-wall serving Tibetan basics in this neighbourhood.

Other practicalities

Run-of-the-mill souvenirs at Boudha are notoriously overpriced, but this is the place to come if you're seeking genuinely obscure or **antique** items. Keep an eye out for Tibetan musical instruments, jewellery, flasks, butter-tea churns and prayer-flag printing blocks.

For **books** on Buddhism, try the *Tibet Book Centre*, on the south side of the main road 300m west of the stupa entrance, or *Dharma Books*, overlooking the stupa. Cassette **tapes**, not only of music but also teachings by local lamas, are sold at a couple of places around the stupa. Near the entrance you can buy **film**, and there are even travel agents and international telephone offices.

For **Tibetan medicine** (see *Basics*), visit doctors S. Chusang Rinpoche and Sangye Tsultrim (☎411995), who run a clinic north of the stupa, at the intersection just west of the Ka Nying Shedrupling Monastery.

The Sankhu road

The paved road past Boudha – the old trade route to Tibet – begins at Chabahil on the Ring Road and rolls eastwards as far as Sankhu. It's a gentle ride on a bicycle, the only hazard being the sheaves of rice and wheat that farmers spread out during harvest time, and can be combined with visits to Nagarkot or Changu Narayan. From Ratna Park, an erratic **minibus** service plies the whole way to Sankhu; four buses a day go as far as Gokarna Ban; and dozens cover the stretch to Chabahil and Boudha.

Chabahil

Just off the Ring Road, **CHABAHIL** is part Kathmandu suburb and part Boudha Tibetan spillover, a cluster of shops and concrete buildings without much character, though it's one of the valley's older settlements.

Tibetans have been drawn to Chabahil's **stupa** (known locally as Dhando Chaitya), which despite its newish appearance dates to Lichhavi times. An ancient chronicle states it was constructed by Dharmadeva, a fifth-century king, although legend attributes it to Charumati, who settled here and married a local prince after accompanying her father Ashoka on his apocryphal pilgrimage to the Kathmandu Valley in the third century BC. The prince, Devapala, is credited with founding Deopatan, one of the valley's ancient capitals, which stood just south of here near Pashupatinath. In a brick shelter at the south end of the compound stands a sixth-century statue of Padmapani Lokeshwar, carved in black stone.

Chabahil's Nepalis rally round the **Chandra Binayak**, one of the valley's four principal Ganesh temples, located west of the main Chabahil intersection.

Gokarna Ban

Gokarna Ban, 3km east of Boudha, looks and feels more like an English country estate than a **royal game reserve** (April–Sept daily 7am–6pm; Oct–March daily 8am–5.30pm; Rs50). The "game" in this onetime royal hunting preserve consists mainly of tame deer, monkeys, plenty of birds and a few tigers safely penned up in a three-acre enclosure, so promises of "safari adventure" are fairly hyperbolic. On Saturdays the park is mobbed with picnicking locals. *Gokarna Safari Resort* (☎410063) manages all activities – which include golf, elephant rides and horse rides – and also operates a **hotel** (⑦).

Opposite the park entrance is the headquarters of the *Nepal Disabled Association*, which runs a roadside sales shack specializing in wicker items. Five kilometres beyond here, a trail to the south crosses the Manohara River on a temporary bridge (dry season only) and ascends the ridge to Changu Narayan.

Sankhu

An important trade and spiritual centre in ancient times, **SANKHU**, 20km east of Kathmandu, now drifts on as a Newar backwater in a far corner of the valley. You could easily pedal out here on a one-speeder, but Sankhu is best seen as a stopover along the back route down from Nagarkot, which is only possible on a mountain bike. A few shops sell cold soft drinks, but food is scarce.

Sankhu's abiding claim to fame is its temple to **Bajra Jogini**, whose gilded roof glints from a grove of trees on the otherwise barren hillside above town. To make the two-kilometre hike, follow the dirt road northwards out of town and then bear left on a stony path that heads straight for the temple. Sankhu Bajra Jogini is the most senior of a ferocious foursome of tantric goddesses specially venerated in the Kathmandu Valley. To Buddhist Newars, her main devotees, she represents the wrathful, corpse-trampling, female aspect of Buddhahood; her implicitly sexual role in a supernatural union of opposites earns her the esoteric "tantric" label.

The slightly dilapidated **temple** dates from the seventeenth century, but inscriptions elsewhere record that a shrine stood here a thousand years earlier. Next to the temple is a small shrine containing a replica of the Swayambhu stupa. The compound is pleasantly shaded, but overrun by monkeys – the place literally stinks of them. Animal sacrifices performed in front of a triangular stone representing Bhairab, just below the temple, sadly don't include monkeys.

The Sundarijal road

Branching off from the Sankhu road at Jorpati, 1km east of Boudha, a second road rumbles along even more rurally as far as Sundarijal in the extreme north-eastern corner of the valley. The paved surface soon gives out, but it's still delightful cycling country, with handsome three-storey brick houses, feathery bamboo forests and a steady stream of pedestrians along the route. Four **buses** a day leave from Ratna Park for Sundarijal.

Gokarneswar

Located 4km up the Sundarijal road, **GOKARNESWAR** overlooks the Bagmati River where it cuts through a low ridge (Gokarna Ban game reserve is just across the river, but there's no access from here). A tranquil spot, it has been an important cremation and pilgrimage site since ancient times, and is marked by the imposing **Gokarna Mahadev**, dedicated to Shiva. Despite UNESCO conservation efforts, the fourteenth-century temple appears slightly worse for wear. Its most unusual feature is an outdoor gallery of stone **sculptures** representing an unorthodox cross-section of the Nepalese pantheon – you'll see a bearded Brahma, a skeletal Chamunda (a form of Kali) and a snake-hooded Buddha, among others. Inside the temple stands a beefy *linga*, while the smaller temple nearby contains a beautiful eighth-century statue of Parvati, Shiva's consort. The highlight of the **festival** calendar here is Gokarna Aunsi, Nepali "Father's Day", held in late August or early September.

From Gokarneswar you can **hike** up to Pulahari Monastery on the long ridge to the west, and from there northwards to Nagi Gompa or westwards to Kopan.

Sundarijal

The scenery wanes somewhat beyond Gokarneswar. Although **SUNDARIJAL**, 15km from Kathmandu, isn't a brilliant destination in itself, it's the most accessible trailhead for treks in the Helambu region. The steep climb up alongside the cascading Bagmati River – no more than a stream here – would be much prettier without the hulking iron pipe that crisscrosses the trail: much of Kathmandu's water supply comes from the upper Bagmati.

Sundarijal is the home of the **Himalayan Rescue Dog Training Centre**, located at the west end of the village. Founded in 1989 by Dutchman Ingo Schnabel, the centre provides the only search and rescue service in Nepal. It is also a good source of up-to-date **trail information**, can arrange **guides**, and supplies basic **room and board** (①). The centre relies on donations.

Budhanilkantha and Shivpuri

A paved road leads 8km north from Kathmandu to **BUDHANILKANTHA**, site of the Jalasaya Narayan (Sleeping Vishnu), one of the valley's most impressive reminders of its semi-mythic early history. There's a small village with basic teahouses nearby, but the Vishnu statue, set in a walled compound, is the only attraction of the place. Try to make it here in time for the morning *puja* (9–10am), when things are most interesting.

Buses to Budhanilkantha leave from Rani Pokhri every half-hour or so. **Cycling**, you'll want a mountain bike for the last steep bit (and for any longer rides – see below). From Budhanilkantha you can walk to the summit of Shivpuri, the second-highest point of the valley rim.

The Sleeping Vishnu (Jalasaya Narayan)

The five-metre **Sleeping Vishnu (Jalasaya Narayan)** reclines in a recessed water tank like an oversized astronaut in suspended animation. The figure's origins are obscure: local people say it was unearthed by a farmer two thousand years ago, having been carved and dragged here at some remote point in time, but most art historians believe its style pinpoints it to the seventh or eighth century AD. In the fields to the east, piles of bricks and a lone statue provide further evidence that this must have been a substantial settlement in ancient times.

Budhanilkantha's name has been a source of endless confusion and not a little religious rivalry. No one claims it has anything to do with the Buddha (*budha* here means "old"), though that doesn't stop Buddhist Newars from worshipping the image as Lokeshwar, the *bodhisattva* of compassion. The real puzzler is why Budhanilkantha (literally "Old Blue-Throat"), a title which unquestionably refers to Shiva, has been attached here to Vishnu. The myth of **Shiva's blue throat**, a favourite in Nepal, relates how the gods churned the ocean of existence and inadvertently unleashed a poison that threatened to destroy the world. They begged Shiva to save them from their blunder and he obliged by drinking the poison. His throat burning, the great god flew up to the range north of Kathmandu, struck

Jalasaya Narayan

the mountainside with his trident to create a lake, Gosainkund, and quenched his thirst – suffering no lasting ill effect except for a blue patch on his throat. Shaivas claim a reclining image of Shiva can be seen under the waters of Gosainkund during the annual Shiva festival there in August, which perhaps explains the association with the waterborne figure of Budhanilkantha.

Nonetheless, the Budhanilkantha sculpture bears all the hallmarks of Vishnu or, as he's often called in Nepal, **Narayan** (pronounced Nuh-*rai*-n): "having waters for his abode". It depicts Vishnu at his most cosmic, floating in the ocean of existence upon the snake Sesh (or Ananta, which in Sanskrit means "never-ending"); from his navel will grow Brahma and the rest of creation. Each year the god is said to "awaken" from his summer slumber during the Haribondhini Ekadashi **festival** in late October or early November, an event that draws thousands of worshippers.

One person who never puts in an appearance, as a matter of policy, is the king of Nepal. Some say the boycott goes back to the seventeenth-century king Pratap Malla, who was visited by Vishnu in a dream and warned that he and his successors would die if they ever visited Budhanilkantha; others say it's because the king, who is half-heartedly held to be a reincarnation of Vishnu, must never gaze upon his own image.

Up to Shivpuri

At 2732m, **Shivpuri** (or Sheopuri) offers excellent views of the Himalaya off to the west, from Jugal and Ganesh Himal out to Himalchuli. The summit can be reached in about four hours by one of two trails (at least). You'll need to pack a lunch and sufficient water, and the vertical gain, nearly 1300m, shouldn't be taken lightly. You can **camp** on the flat, grassy summit to catch the best views first thing in the morning; clouds often move in by lunchtime.

From Budhanilkantha, follow the paved road straight uphill until it veers to the right and crosses a stream, where the more **direct trail** to the summit leaves the road and continues up the west side of the stream before entering the walled Shivpuri Watershed. After passing through a doorway, it climbs steadily, crosses a dirt road, enters a forest and meets the ridge; from here, a less-used trail branches off from the main one and follows the ridge eastwards for another two hours to the top. The **other route** sticks to the paved road until the main Shivpuri Watershed gate, and from there follows the dirt road to the right, contouring around and up the ridge to the east. Where the road finally rounds this ridge, take a trail up to **Nagi Gompa**, a former Tamang monastery now run by Sikkimese nuns, and continue along the ridge to Shivpuri. Another trail leads back down from Nagi Gompa, following the ridge south to Boudha or Gokarneswar.

The Shivpuri Watershed contains some superb, and still largely untested, **mountain biking** possibilities. From the main entrance, the dirt road to the left snakes generally eastwards for at least 15km, from which point the hill resort of Kakani (see Chapter Three) is about 2km further east along the ridge by trail. For a shorter day ride, descend from the Tokha Hospital (marked "Sanitorium" on the *Schneider* map) along a steep, sandy road that brings you back to Budhanilkantha.

AGRICULTURE IN THE VALLEY

Agriculture employs two out of three residents of the Kathmandu Valley, the **farmers** a mixture of Newars, Brahmans, Chhetris and Tamangs (see Chapters One and Three for background on these ethnic groups). Newar farmers, called Jyapus, dig their fields with a two-handed spade called a *kodaalo* (*ku* in Newari) – it's back-breaking work – and live in close, brick settlements on the valley floor, while the other groups tend to use bullock ploughs and build detached, mud-walled houses around the fringes. Many are tenant farmers and are expected to pay half their harvest as rent.

Low enough to support two or even three main crops a year, and endowed with a fertile, black clay – *kalimati*, a by-product of sediment from the prehistoric lake – the valley floor has been intensely cultivated and irrigated for centuries. **Rice** is seeded in special beds shortly before the first monsoon rains in June, and seedlings are transplanted into flooded terraces no later than the end of July – normally women do this job, using their toes to bed each shoot in the mud. The stalks grow green and bushy during the summer, turning a golden brown and producing mature grain by October.

Harvest time is lazily anarchic: sheaves are spread out on paved roads for cars to loosen the kernels, and then run through portable hand-cranked threshers or bashed against rocks. The grain is gathered in bamboo trays (*nanglo*) and tossed in the wind to winnow away the chaff, or, if there's no wind, *nanglo* can be used to fan away the chaff. Some sheaves are left in stacks to ferment for up to two weeks, producing a sort of baby food called *hakuja*, or "black" rice. The rice dealt with, terraces are then planted with **winter wheat**, which is harvested in a similar fashion in April or May. A third crop of pulses or maize can often be squeezed in after the wheat harvest, and vegetables are raised year-round at the edges of plots. The important thing is never to let any land go to waste: valley farmers will sooner make bricks from the clay soil than let a field lie fallow.

The lot of valley farmers has improved in recent years. **Land reform** in the 1950s and 1960s, which didn't work too well in most parts of the country, was more rigorously implemented near the capital, helping to get landlords and moneylenders off the backs of small farmers. However, Kathmandu's **prosperity** is bringing problems. In the past decade, while the valley's population has nearly doubled to one million, housing (and the brick "factories" that make it possible) has been chewing up farmland at an alarming rate – a trend that threatens to accelerate, as ever more hill people flock to the valley for a piece of the action. At the same time, skyrocketing land prices and the declining quality of life in the capital are only adding to the pressure on farmland. Those who can are fleeing the inner city, just as they have every other city in the world, and are rapidly creating a **suburban**, commuter culture. In the absence of any greenbelt regulations, valley farmers and *guthi* (temple trusts) are steadily selling out, as their valuable farmland becomes even more valuable as real estate.

Balaju and Rani Ban

The road to Trisuli (see Chapter Three) passes a couple of worthy sights before it climbs out of the valley. **Tempos** (departing from the north side of Rani Pokhri) follow a fixed route to Balaju and almost as far as the Rani Ban gate, but both of these destinations are within easy **cycling** distance of Kathmandu – and a mountain bike will stand you in good stead once you get to Rani Ban.

Balaju

If **BALAJU**'s "Water Garden" isn't as ravishing as its name suggests, neither is the Balaju Industrial Estate as awful as it sounds. The water garden is where Kathmandu comes to picnic and paddle on Saturdays, and for the jaded traveller it can provide some welcome relief from the commotion of the city. The park is only 2km northwest of Thamel along the road to Trisuli, behind a municipal-looking fence at the foot of a wooded hill. Admission is Rs1.50 plus a few rupees to park your bike.

In the northeast corner of the grounds lies a **Sleeping Vishnu**, a smaller version that scholars now believe to be contemporaneous with the one at Budhanilkantha. An earlier theory held that it was only a copy, commissioned in the seventeenth century by King Pratap Malla when he was barred from visiting the original, leading to its nickname Balanilkantha ("Young Blue-Throat"). Balaju's other claim to fame – for Nepalis, at least – is **Baaisdhaara**, a bathing tank fed by twenty-two (*baais*) stone spouts (*dhaara*), which really rocks with bathing worshippers on the day of the full moon in April.

Simple **food** – snacks, *momo* and *daal bhat* – is available from diners out on the main road. At the other end of the spectrum is *K.C.'s Consequence*, hidden up an obscure lane striking off from the southwestern edge of the industrial estate. The brainchild of the owner of *K.C.'s* in Thamel, it serves imaginative dishes combining Western and indigenous elements in surprising ways – but it's way overpriced and difficult to find.

Rani Ban

Once in Balaju, you might as well continue on up the road another 3km to the entrance of **Rani Ban** (or **Nagarjun Ban**), a large and surprisingly wild royal forest preserve (daily, hours vary with season but generally closes at dusk; pedestrians and cyclists Rs5, motorcyclists Rs15, cars Rs50). An unpaved road winds to the summit of 2096-metre **Jamacho**, but you can hike more directly up the ridge along a five-kilometre trail starting at the entrance. The north side of this ridge is riddled with limestone **caves**, including one where the famous second-century Buddhist saint Nagarjuna meditated and died, or so it's said. At the summit, a **stupa** decorated with fluttering prayer flags and penetrating eyes marks the spot where the Buddha sat during an apocryphal visit to the Kathmandu Valley, and a small **lookout tower** commands a panoramic view of the valley and the Himalaya, notably Ganesh Himal.

Several **alternative routes** return to the valley below. If you can find it, the most interesting one is an obscure trail that starts from the road southeast of the lookout tower and descends in a southeasterly direction through thick forest and past several limestone caves, one of which contains a large image of the Buddha. The trail eventually meets the Jamacho road, which you can either follow back to the entrance (3km), or part of the way to a military post (1km), from where you can leave the forest reserve for the village of Rani Ban and muddle back down to Balaju or Swayambhu. Another trail from Jamacho makes for the slightly higher summit 1km to the west, then curves south down to the rather seedy temple of **Ichangu Narayan**, from which a rough road leads east to the Ring Road behind Swayambhu.

PATAN AND THE SOUTHERN VALLEY

The southern valley is as well endowed with sights as the north, and no less accessible. Once you cross the Bagmati River you're in **Patan** – even the cows commute. Good roads fan out from Kathmandu and Patan to the hilltop outpost of **Kirtipur**, the holy places of **Chobar** and **Dakshin Kali**, and the wilds of **Godavari**, while rougher roads strike out towards a dozen other rural settlements.

Although everything is within day-tripping range of Kathmandu by bus or bike, **staying in Patan** will give you a head start. The valley's second city – a world apart from Kathmandu – deserves more than just an afternoon's visit, and is increasingly geared up for overnight guests. Except for one luxury operation in the hills south of Patan, however, accommodation isn't available anywhere else in the southern valley.

Patan (Lalitpur)

PATAN (*Paa*-tun) likes to recall its old name **LALITPUR** ("City of Beauty"), and although now largely absorbed by greater Kathmandu, this once-powerful independent kingdom still maintains a defiantly distinct identity. Compared to Kathmandu it's quieter, less frenetic and more Buddhist (there may be a correlation). Above all, it remains a proud city of **artisans**: Patan produces nearly all Nepal's fine metalwork (the sounds of tapping and filing ring out from workshops all over town), and its craftspeople have created some of the most extraordinarily lavish temples, *hiti* and *bahal* in the country. *Bahal* – their doorways always guarded by cuddly stone lions with unscary overbites – are a particular feature of Patan, and a few still function as active monasteries. In the past two decades, Patan has also emerged as the de facto **foreign aid** capital of Nepal: the UN delegation and diverse smaller organizations are scattered around the western suburbs, as are the residences of many expats who commute to the big USAID headquarters just across the river.

In legend and fact, Patan is the oldest city in the valley. **Manjushri**, the great lake-drainer, is supposed to have founded Manjupatan, the forerunner of Patan, right after he enshrined Swayambhu, while the so-called Ashokan stupas, earthen mounds standing at four cardinal points around Patan, seem to support the legend that the Indian emperor **Ashoka** visited the valley in the third century BC (historians are sceptical). More reliable legend ascribes Patan's founding to **King Arideva** in 299 AD. By the seventh century Patan had emerged as the cultural and artistic capital of Nepal, if not the entire Himalayan region. It maintained strong links with the Buddhist centres of learning in Bengal and Bihar – thereby playing a role in the transmission of Buddhism to Tibet – and when these fell to the Muslims in the twelfth century, many scholars and artists fled to Patan, setting the stage for a renaissance under the later **Malla kings**. Patan existed as part of a unified valley kingdom until the late fifteenth century, then enjoyed equal status with Kathmandu and Bhaktapur as a sovereign state until 1769, when Prithvi Narayan Shah and his Gorkhali band conquered the valley and chose Kathmandu for their capital. One of Patan's charms is that its historic core is frozen much as it was at the time of defeat.

Arrival and orientation

Frequent **minibuses** shuttle from Ratna Park and Martyrs' Gate in Kathmandu to Lagankhel, Patan's main bus park, or you could **cycle** from Kathmandu in a few minutes (in Patan bikes can be rented around Pulchowk, in front of the *Hotel Narayani*). Patan itself has few rikshas, but within the old part of town you can easily get around on foot.

Old Patan developed along two intersecting axes, which extended out to the four **Ashokan stupas**. The northern route, now pedestrianized, takes in Patan's **Durbar Square** and also the famed **Golden** and **Kumbeshwar temples**. Patan's western axis (known as **Mangal Bazaar** where it meets Durbar Square) serves as the main way into town from Kathmandu. The busy southern road runs past the **Machhendranath Mandir** and the **Lagankhel bus park**, while the eastern road skirts the temple of **Mahabuddha**. The Tibetan crafts centre of **Jaulakhel** is located at the southwestern edge of the city.

Coming over the main bridge from Kathmandu, you can enter the city via the Western Stupa or more directly via **Patan Dhoka** (Patan Gate) – the latter route is confusing, though. An alternative route crosses the Bagmati via a footbridge from the Teku area of Kathmandu, entering Patan through its northwestern suburbs.

Durbar Square

Patan's **Durbar Square**, while smaller and less monumental than Kathmandu's, comes across as more refined, not to mention less touristy. Maybe it's because the city of artisans has a better eye for architectural harmony; or because Patan, which hasn't been a capital since the eighteenth century, has escaped the continuous meddling of monument-building kings. That said, the formula is similar to that in Kathmandu, with a solemn royal palace looming along one side and assorted temples grouped in the remaining public areas of the square.

The Royal Palace

Patan's richly decorated **Royal Palace** was largely constructed during the second half of the seventeenth century, but substantially rebuilt after the Gorkhali invasion of 1769 and the 1934 earthquake. It consists of three main courtyards, each with its own entrance.

The small, southernmost courtyard, **Sundari Chowk**, contains what must surely be one of the grandest bathtubs in the world. **Tusha Hiti**, the seventeenth-century sunken royal bath, is done up like a hall of fame of Hindu gods and goddesses. Its brass spout, the only bit of metal here, is decorated with Shiva and Parvati, while the bath itself is shaped like a *yoni*, the symbol of female sexuality, and ringed with *nag* (serpents). At one end of the bath stands the obligatory statue of Hanuman the monkey god, plus a "holy stone" on which the kings of Patan performed *puja* after bathing, and at the other end a replica of the Krishna Mandir, one of the temples outside. The courtyard is covered in ornate woodwork, including many fabulous carved doorways, windows, *torana*, and images of deities individually set into niches like icons.

Mul Chowk, the next courtyard to the north, served as the actual royal family residence. A sadly deteriorated gilt door in the right-hand wall, leading to the private Taleju Mandir, is flanked by statues of the Indian river goddesses **Ganga** and **Jamuna**, the latter riding a *makana* – a mythical cross between a crocodile

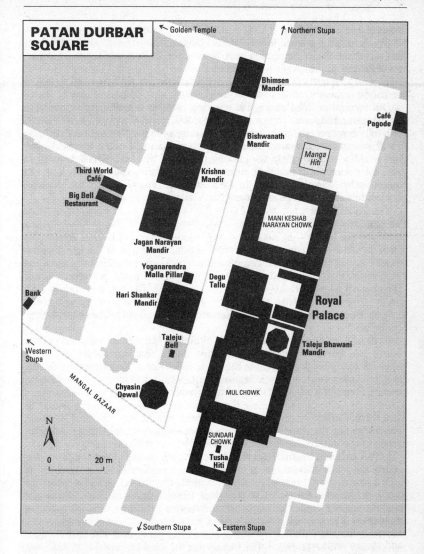

PATAN DURBAR SQUARE

← Golden Temple   ↑ Northern Stupa

Bhimsen Mandir

Café Pagode

Bishwanath Mandir

Manga Hiti

Third World Café

Big Bell Restaurant

Krishna Mandir

MANI KESHAB NARAYAN CHOWK

Jagan Narayan Mandir

Yoganarendra Malla Pillar

Degu Talle

Bank

Hari Shankar Mandir

Royal Palace

Taleju Bhawani Mandir

← Western Stupa

Taleju Bell

MANGAL BAZAAR

Chyasin Dewal

MUL CHOWK

N

0   20 m

SUNDARI CHOWK

Tusha Hiti

↓ Southern Stupa   ↘ Eastern Stupa

and an elephant, whose curling snout decorates almost every public water spout in Nepal. Behind and to the left of Mul Chowk rises the octagonal, three-tiered **Taleju Bhawani Mandir**.

Yet another Taleju temple, the monolithic **Degu Talle** towers just north of Mul Chowk. Seven storeys high and the tallest building on the block, the temple was erected in 1640 by Siddhi Narsingh Malla, during whose reign much of the palace and square were built. It had to be completely rebuilt after being razed in the 1934 earthquake. The tower is permanently locked except during the autumn Tihar festival, when a priest is supposed to refill a pipe with ganja for the departed king. Behind it, just off a small *chowk* once used for courtly performances, you'll find a small branch of the non-profit *Mahaguthi* handicrafts shop. This *chowk* retains its connection with dance since it also contains the headquarters of Patan's autumn festival committee.

The northernmost courtyard, **Mani Keshab Narayan Chowk**, once served as the palace of another noted seventeenth-century king, Yoganarendra Malla. It, too, suffered in the 1934 quake, and was only clumsily rebuilt; it's now undergoing extensive renovations, which are supposed to be completed sometime in 1994. When reopened, the building will once again house the **National Bronze Art Museum**, an impressive exhibit of idols, *torana* and other temple decorations – although it's widely acknowledged that all the best Nepali bronzes (a generic term for works cast from copper, brass and various alloys) were long ago bought up by foreign collectors. In the meantime, you can admire the stunning gold window above the entrance, depicting Vishnu and a heavenly host.

The square

Starting at the newer – eighteenth-century – southern end of Durbar Square, the octagonal stone **Chyasin Dewal** in front of Sundari Chowk is the lesser of the square's two Krishna temples. Some say the temple was raised in memory of the eight wives that committed sati on a king's funeral pyre, but others say it spontaneously appeared the day after the cremation. The cast-iron **Taleju Bell** was the first to be erected in the valley, in 1736; keen civic rivalry among the three valley capitals prompted Bhaktapur and Kathmandu to follow suit with their own bells.

North of here, the finely carved **Hari Shankar Mandir** is dedicated both to Vishnu (sometimes called Hari) and Shiva (alias Shankar), while the statue mounted on a pillar and praying to the Degu Talle depicts **Yoganarendra Malla**. An angry cobra rears up like a halo behind the king, and atop the cobra's head perches a gilded bird. Like all god-fearing rulers of the valley, Yoganarendra would have made sure to appease the *nag*, animist snake spirits who deliver or withhold the valley's rains; and as for the bird, chroniclers state that the king, upon abdicating the throne to become a wandering ascetic, told his subjects that as long as the bird remained they would know he was still alive.

If the two-tiered **Jagan Narayan**, built in 1565, is the oldest temple in the square, the most unusual one is the seventeenth-century **Krishna Mandir**. Its central structure, a Mughal-style *shikra*, is girdled by three levels of stone verandas, with detailed scenes from the great Hindu epics, the *Mahabharat* and *Ramayan*, carved along the lintels. An incarnation of Vishnu, Krishna is one of the best-loved characters of the *Mahabharat*: superhuman baby, mischievous lad, seducer of milkmaids and heroic slayer of the evil king Kamsa. The upstairs sanctum (closed to non-Hindus) displays images of the whole cast of the *Mahabharat*. *Bhajan* is sung here most nights, and devotees gather at the temple on Krishna's birthday in August or early September.

The **Bishwanath Mandir** contains a copy of the Shiva *linga* of the same name in Varanasi, India. The temple collapsed in 1990, but has been seamlessly restored. Last but not least, the seventeenth-century **Bhimsen Mandir** is dedicated to the ever-popular god of Nepalese traders, who pitch coins into the windows of the gilded first floor. Across the way, one of the valley's best-preserved bathing tanks, **Manga Hiti**, has been flowing since the sixth century.

North and west of Durbar Square

Some of Patan's most interesting sights – the Golden and Kumbeshwar temples and the ghats – lie north of Durbar Square, but there's also plenty of serendipitous exploring to be done among the back alleys west of the square.

Hiranyavarna Mahavihara ("Golden Temple")

Dark and masonic (if it weren't for the sign, you'd never think of entering), the **Hiranyavarna Mahavihara** – commonly dubbed the **"Golden Temple"** – is the most opulent little temple in Nepal. The three-tiered pagoda occupies one side of the cramped courtyard of Kwa Bahal, a still-active twelfth-century Buddhist Newar monastery and the spiritual hub of old Patan. During early-morning *puja*, the *bahal* is a fascinating theatre of Nepali religion in all its perplexing glory. A donation is expected, and note that you're not allowed to bring anything made of leather inside.

The temple's brass-clad facade, embossed with images of Buddhas and Taras, is regarded as the pre-eminent example of large-scale repoussé **metalwork** in Nepal, while in the middle of the courtyard a small, lavishly ornamented shrine contains a priceless silver and gold *chaitya*. Both the shrine and the main temple are draped with what look like long brass neckties; these *pataka* are supposed to provide a slide for the gods when they descend to answer the prayers of their worshippers. Buddha is the main image in the temple, and various Buddhas and *bodhisattva* are represented in alcoves around the courtyard. Mounted on the wall to your left as you enter, a chalkboard lists the astrological year and festivals in Newari.

One block to the east, the three-tiered **Radha Krishna Mandir** has recently been restored by the Kathmandu Valley Preservation Trust, an organization which hopes to tackle several other derelict temples and residences in this area. The lovers Krishna and Radha, to whom this temple is dedicated, are a favourite subject for sandalwood carvers.

Kumbeshwar Mahadev

The **Kumbeshwar Mahadev**, Patan's oldest temple and one of only two freestanding five-tiered pagodas in Nepal (the other is in Bhaktapur), was built as a two-roofed structure in 1392, and despite the addition of three more levels it remains well proportioned and to all appearances sturdy. Shiva is the honoured deity here: inside you can see a stone *linga* and a brass one with four faces; Nandi, Shiva's patient mount, waits outside. The temple apparently owes its name to an episode in which a pilgrim at Gosainkund, the sacred lake high in the mountains north of Kathmandu, dropped a pot (*kumbha*) into the water there. Much later, the same pot appeared in the water tank here, giving rise to the belief that the tank is fed by an underground channel from Gosainkund, and adding to Shiva's roll of titles that of Kumbeshwar – Lord of the Pots.

Shiva

Thanks to this connection, Kumbeshwar's water tank is regarded as an alternative venue during Gosainkund's great annual **festival**, Janai Purnima. Falling on the full moon day of late July or early August, Janai Purnima is the ceremony in which Brahmans and Chhetris formally change the sacred thread (*janai*) that distinguishes them as members of the "twice-born" castes. At Kumbeshwar, thousands come to pay respect to a *linga* erected in the middle of the tank, and a big part of the festivities is for bathers to see how much water they can splash at spectators.

Elsewhere in the temple courtyard stands the shrine of **Bangalamukhi**, an obscure goddess whose tiny idol is encased in an ornate silver frieze.

The Northern Stupa . . . and on to the ghats

Just northeast of the Kumbeshwar Mahadev, the **Northern Stupa** is the smallest and most central of the Ashokan mounds, and the only one that's been sealed over with plaster. Although it doesn't look wildly interesting for a 2200-year-old monument, you can let your imagination dwell on what treasures or relics Ashoka might have buried here – the contents are unlikely ever to see the light of day, since archeological digs are prohibited in the valley.

The stupa stands at the abrupt edge of the city. From here the road south plunges back between brick tenements and neglected temples to Durbar Square; northwards, it wends through farmland towards Patan's **Sankhamul Ghat**, a kilometre-long embankment near the junction of the Manohara and Bagmati rivers (confluences are regarded as auspicious locations). Though a holy place, it's also rather sombre: funeral processions arrive bearing bodies to the cremation platforms, and across the river – under the shadow of the *Everest Hotel* – are some of Kathmandu's most destitute dwellings. Atop the bank behind the ghats stands the brick *shikra* of **Jagat Narayan**, named after its builder, the nineteenth-century prime minister Jagat Shamsher.

West of Durbar Square

From **Mangal Bazaar**, which these days sells mainly cloth and tourist odds and ends, central Patan's main drag heads out towards the Western Stupa. One of Patan's less touristed former monasteries, **Hakhu Bahal**, rises on the left after 300m. Its courtyard crowded with lotus pedestals, indicative of divinity, the *bahal* is the home of Patan's Kumari.

Though little more than a grassy mound beside a busy intersection, the **Western Stupa** comes alive on one day a year when it serves as the starting point of the great chariot procession of Rato Machhendranath (see below). A nearby shelter displays retired *ghama* – long, upward-curving chariot yokes – from past festivals.

The northwestern quarter of old Patan is a jumble of *bahal*, none particularly worth singling out; the lane leading from the Golden Temple west to Patan Dhoka takes you past quite a few. The next lane further south, which parallels the main road to the Western Stupa, is the site of Patan's small fruit and vegetable **market** and eventually opens out into Pim Bahal, a large and less than glamorous square that contains what some hold to be a **fifth Ashokan stupa**, although no records mention it before the fourteenth century.

A small bazaar area surrounding an unremarkable city gate, **Patan Dhoka** had its finest hour during the 1990 *jana andolan* (people's movement), when it stood on the front line of an all-out revolution. Nearly a month before the government's final capitulation Patan was declared "liberated", with ditches dug across every road into the city, and defiant residents vowing to kill any opponent of the *andolan* who dared enter. Several police cars and buses met their end at narrow Patan Dhoka – and throughout the uprising the banned Nepali Congress Party flag flew from the gate.

South and east of the square

South of Durbar Square you essentially have two choices. The southbound street passes the Machhendranath temple and other sights en route to the Lagankhel bus park, while the continuation of Mangal Bazaar leads southeastwards to Mahabuddha. The area directly east of Durbar Square, though short on specific sights, is an active artisans' quarter.

Bishwakarma Mandir and Ibaha Bahal

One of Patan's most charming streets runs parallel to Mangal Bazaar, a block to the south. This is an area of metalsmiths and sellers, which perhaps accounts for the **Bishwakarma Mandir**'s facade of hammered brass and froggy copper lions standing guard, Bishwakarma being the god of artisans.

Patan's second-oldest monastery, **Ibaha Bahal**, stands one block further to the south. Founded in 1427, the *bahal* was latterly converted into a school and finally fell into disrepair. In 1990 the Nippon Institute of Technology began restoring it, and by the time you read this it should be up and running again as a fully functional Buddhist centre and school.

Machhendranath Mandir

Outwardly, Patan's **Machhendranath Mandir** resembles many others: a huge seventeenth-century pagoda adorned with beautifully carved struts, elegant *torana* and an ill-advised layer of modern tiles. It stands in an extra-large grassy compound called Ta Bahal, about 300m south of Durbar Square, reached by following a flagstoned path west from the main street.

Scene during the Machhendranath Rath festival

What makes this temple so extraordinary, however, is its idol, **Rato Machhendranath** (Red Machhendranath), a painted shingle of sandalwood which, for several weeks beginning in late April, is the object of the most spectacular festival in Nepal. Older than his white counterpart in Kathmandu, Rato Machhendranath is a god of many guises. To Buddhists he's Avalokiteshwara or Lokeshwar, the *bodhisattva* of compassion. To Newars he's Karunamaya or Bunga Deo, the androgynous god of agricultural prosperity. As Machhendranath, the progenitor of the *nath* (lord) cult, he's the spirit of a seventh-century Hindu guru who once taught the Shah kings' beloved saint, Gorakhnath. Legend has it that Gorakhnath once visited the valley and, offended that he wasn't accorded a full reception, caused a drought by rounding up all the rain-bringing snakes. The locals sent a posse to fetch Machhendranath from Assam, who came to their rescue in the form of a bee. Wishing to pay tribute to his guru, Gorakhnath had to release the snakes, whereupon the rains returned and Machhendranath came to be revered as a rain-maker.

Machhendranath's **festival** is an electric event in which the god's image is pulled through Patan in a tremendously unwieldy chariot crowned by a twenty-metre-high swaying tower of poles and vegetation; special blessings are promised to anyone whose house gets bashed by the wayward spire. Lurching along in stages, the chariot takes four or more weeks to travel from the Western Stupa to Jaulakhel. On the final day, at a time ordained by the astrologers, the god's magical jewelled vest is displayed to the crowd. Since the procession culminates just before the monsoon, Machhendranath always obliges with rain: bring an umbrella.

Minnath and on to the Southern Stupa

Set behind a *hiti* (sunken bathing tank) across the street, the smaller sixteenth-century **Minnath Mandir** is dedicated to yet another mythologized Indian saint. Historically supposed to have been Machhendranath's guru, Minnath has been transmuted by popular tradition into his brother, son or even daughter, and follows Machhendranath in a smaller chariot of his own during the procession.

The main road continues south from here past the chaotic minibus park at **Lagankhel**, then jogs left; straight ahead lies an army base and a pair of overgrown water tanks that feed Patan's many *hiti*. It's not really worth travelling another kilometre south to visit the grassy **Southern Stupa** – the biggest of the four – although anyone bound for the Patan Industrial Estate (see "Shopping") will pass right by it.

Mahabuddha

Nicknamed "Temple of a Thousand Buddhas", **Mahabuddha** is not your average Nepali temple. Constructed entirely of terracotta tiles – each one bearing the Buddha's image – this remarkable rococo structure mimics the famous Mahabodhi Temple of Bodhgaya in India, where its builder, an enthusiastic seventeenth-century Patan architect, had previously meditated for several years. Although the likeness is only approximate, the temple introduced to Nepal the Indian *shikra* form, which to this day remains prevalent around Patan. Reduced to rubble during the 1934 earthquake, it was put back together rather like Humpty Dumpty; the smaller temple beside it was built from the spare parts.

Mahabuddha stands just off a brick-paved street about 500m southeast of Durbar Square, with a narrow passage on the right providing an entrance; so tightly is it hemmed in by residences, the temple is like a casket that's been upended to fit in a hole. For the best view, follow a sign to the top floor of one of the surrounding buildings, which – surprise, surprise – is a metal handicrafts studio.

Other eastern sights

Uku Bahal lies just south of Mahabuddha, behind an arch guarded by large, curly-maned lions. The now-defunct Buddhist monastery, though it's undergone a recent renovation, is believed to be Patan's oldest – the wooden struts on the north side of the courtyard date from the thirteenth century. Its ornate principal temple, known as **Rudravarna Mahavihara**, is surrounded by a small menagerie of bronze animals and mythological beasts.

North and east of Mahabuddha, **Dupat** is a poor and not altogether welcoming neighbourhood whose close, dark alleys are nevertheless crawling with atmosphere. The **Eastern Stupa** is way out in the sticks, beyond the Ring Road.

Jaulakhel and the zoo

Patan's Tibetan ghetto, **Jaulakhel** (often transliterated as Jawalakhel) is arguably the best place in the valley to watch carpets being made, although as a cultural experience it doesn't compare with Boudha or even Swayambhu. Tour groups tend to spoil the atmosphere. Everything revolves around the recently modernized weaving and sales centre, 1km south of the Western Stupa (weaving daily except Sat 8am–noon & 1–8pm; sales office closes at 5pm).

Tibetans started pouring into the Kathmandu Valley immediately after the Chinese annexation of Tibet and the flight of the Dalai Lama in 1959. By 1960 their plight prompted the International Red Cross to set up a transit camp at Jaulakhel, later assigned to the Swiss Red Cross, which in turn formed the Swiss Association for Technical Assistance (offices just north of here) to help Tibetans on a long-term basis. SATA encouraged carpet-making and other cottage industries, and by 1964 the Jaulakhel "transit camp" was a registered company, whose increasing sales have brought wealth and a degree of autonomy to the Tibetan community here. No one calls Tibetans "refugees" anymore. A generation on, those with enough money have left the centre to establish businesses and live closer to the Buddhist holy places, while the thousand Tibetans remaining here are, sadly, the ones who can't afford to leave.

Jaulakhel is not a jolly place, and the shoddy brick residences seem to be the work of people only reluctantly putting down roots. There's a small **gompa** with a big prayer wheel just opposite the sales centre, but that's about it on the sightseeing front. For cheap Tibetan **food**, investigate the eateries up the hill towards town from the sales centre – *Michael Jackson's Restaurant* gets raves. For a fancier meal, head down the hill to *Bakena Batika* (see "Eating", below).

The zoo

Nepal's only **zoo** (daily 10am–5pm, closes 4pm in winter; Rs10) – often rendered "jew" by Nepali-speakers – lies en route to Jaulakhel, just past the big Jaulakhel Chowk roundabout. Conditions for the animals leave much to be desired (if only the admission fee went to pay for animal feed!), but a visit might be in order for close-up views of species that can otherwise only be glimpsed in the mountains or the Tarai. Highlights include almost-tame rhinos, far-from-tame tigers, graceful blackbuck antelope, ungainly nilgai, beautiful clouded leopards, and a bevy of birds (for an account of Nepal's wildlife, see "Natural History" in *Contexts*). For Rs40 you can take a spin around the grounds on an elephant, and women in red saris in front of the entrance will tell your fortune.

Practicalities

Patan is not Kathmandu (thank the gods). It has tourist sights, but not, as yet, tourist quarters. This means that facilities are comparatively limited, but you won't lack for anything – and if you do, Kathmandu is just a short ride away.

Patan has at least two **banks** with foreign-exchange facilities: *Rastriya Banijya*, at the southwest corner of Durbar Square, and *Nepal Grindlays*, just off Jaulakhel Chowk. The **post office** is at Patan Dhoka (Mon–Thurs & Sun 10am–5pm, Fri 10am–3pm), but you'd be better off using the one in Kathmandu.

Accommodation

While Patan welcomes day-trippers, it seems less keen on visitors staying overnight. There's a distinct lack of high-quality budget **accommodation**, and such as there is in the budget category is generally priced higher than its Kathmandu equivalent. This situation is changing quickly, however, as more and more Thamel refugees find their way here. Arrive early and you should have no trouble finding a room. The picture is better for hotels in the middle and high range, most of which are located comfortably close to the aid offices northwest of town.

BUDGET PLACES

Café de Patan, Mangal Bazaar (☎525499). Well-maintained rooms above a highly regarded restaurant. Central location. ③.

Golden Temple de Corner, southeast of the Golden Temple. At the time of writing, this restaurant was hoping to open a few guest house rooms "in a few months".

Laxmi Guest House, east of Jaulakhel Chowk (☎523968). A very stark option, only worth considering if you're desperate. B③.

Losa Guest House, Mangal Bazaar (☎526374). A grungier, cheaper, but still friendly alternative to *Café de Patan*, next door. Good rooftop views. ③.

Mahendra Youth Hostel, just north of Jaulakhel Chowk (☎521003). Lonely but quiet dorms. ① (10 percent off for IYHF members – whoopee).

Patan Gate Guest House, Patan Dhoka. Gloomy and depressing – again, treat as a last resort. ②.

MODERATE AND EXPENSIVE HOTELS

As well as the places listed below, another possibility at the top end of the range is the *Hatiban Pine Ridge Resort*, located above the Dakshin Kali road 10km southwest of Patan (☎415652;B⑨).

Aloha Inn, Jaulakhel Chowk (☎522796). Small and functional. Two stars. B⑦.

Bakena Batika, just north of the Ring Road, Jaulakhel (☎523998). A small, rusticated place with stylish nouveau Nepali decor and a good in-house restaurant. One star. B⑦, including breakfast.

Hotel Greenwich Village, Kopundol (☎521780). Idiosyncratic, with a good view. Two stars. B⑧.

Hotel Himalaya, Kopundol (☎523900). Really posh, with a swimming pool. Four stars. B⑨.

Hotel Oasis, Pulchowk (☎522746). Dumpy, but with tennis courts and use of the pool at the affiliated *Hotel Narayani*. Two stars. B ⑦.

Summit Hotel, Kopundol (☎521894). Beautiful Nepalese architecture, terrific view, swimming pool. Two stars. B⑨ (discounts in low season).

Eating

When it comes to **eating**, the choice in Patan is definitely smaller than in Kathmandu. This can be a problem at lunchtime, when places around Durbar Square get packed by day-trippers, but at night you'll feel like you've got the place to yourself. Sitting at a table overlooking the square on a balmy evening, with the temples lit from within, it can be magical.

CAFÉS AND LUNCH PLACES

Bakery Café, Jaulakhel Chowk. Nepali yuppie hangout, serving pizza, *momo*, ice cream, etc.

Big Bell Restaurant, west side of Durbar Square. Small, basic eatery with a better range of Nepali and Indian dishes than Western fare.

Café de Patan, Mangal Bazaar. Consistently good (tourist) food, phenomenal lassis, courtyard and roof terrace seating, Nepali and New Age music (cassettes for sale).

Café Pagode, northeast corner of Durbar Square. The usual overpriced Durbar Square overlook: the sunny rooftop terrace is literally a tourist trap, but understandably so.

Golden Temple de Corner Restaurant, southeast of the Golden Temple. Well placed for views of the Golden Temple and Durbar Square. Average food, though cheap.

Patan View Restaurant, Mangal Bazaar (east). Modest rooftop seating, passable Western/ Nepali food (very good *momo*).

Third World Restaurant, west side of Durbar Square. A designer Nepali restaurant serving superb food and offering the best views of Durbar Square. Somewhat pricey, but worth it.

Woody's Pumpernickel Bakery, Jaulakhel Chowk. Passable sandwiches, croissants and cakes.

OTHER TOURIST RESTAURANTS

Bakena Batika, Jaulakhel, 100m south of the carpet weaving sales centre. Lovely garden restaurant specializing in Westernized Nepali dishes. Expensive, by Patan standards.

Patan Gate Restaurant, Patan Dhoka. Good Indian food with nightly *ghazal* entertainment.

Mahanagari Restaurant, Kopundol. Basic Indian food, sahib service, reasonable prices.

Samurai Restaurant, Kopundol. Rather poor attempt at a Japanese restaurant (most items are Chinese, anyway), but inexpensive.

BHOJANALAYA

Patan's most famous **bhojanalaya**, *Woh Naacha* is renowned for its *woh*, a sort of fritter made from soaked and pounded black lentils which accompanies various Newari dishes. The place doesn't have a sign, of course, but it's just off Durbar Square, behind the *Third World Restaurant*.

For a night out, Patan residents head for one of several (relatively) fancy *bhojanalaya* around Patan Dhoka or Jaulakhel Chowk – in the latter area you'll also find Nepali-style snack bars that do espresso coffee, sweets, and that odd local speciality, roast chicken. Places around Lagankhel are pretty dingy, but will suffice if you're waiting for a bus.

Shopping

Even if you're not in the market to buy anything, Patan is the best place in Nepal to watch **handicrafts** actually being made. The Patan Industrial Estate does a little of everything, Jaulakhel mainly produces carpets, while Patan's many non-profit shops, supported by the earnest local aid community, stock some excellent contemporary crafts made by disadvantaged workers.

Film is sold near Durbar Square and Lagankhel, and there's a quick photo-processing place north of Lagankhel.

TRADITIONAL HANDICRAFTS AND CARPETS

Despite its forbidding name, the **Patan Industrial Estate** is industrious in the nicest possible way. Located just beyond the Southern Stupa, the laid-back "estate" consists of a dozen or so factory showrooms, mainly pitched at coach parties, which means that independent travellers are generally left to mosey round the work areas without any pressure. The fixed prices are rarely undercut anywhere else (a prayer wheel will be as little as half what it costs at Jaulakhel), but then the money isn't going to a good cause.

Perhaps the most fascinating workshops are those of the **metalsmiths**, who mass-produce statuettes by the lost-wax process, and repoussé and filigree work with a hammer and punch. You can also watch craftspeople painting **thangka** and chiselling **wood** statuettes, doors and windows. This is also a good place to shop for **gems**: the outlets here are reputable, and should be happy to go over the subtleties of stone quality and cuts.

For **carpets**, the obvious place to start is the Jaulakhel Tibetan centre, where you can observe the actual weaving process. The sales centre's fixed prices are useful for gauging the market, but you'll probably get away with paying less in one of the many private shops along the road leading back up to Patan, where they'll do deals.

CONTEMPORARY CRAFTS AND FASHION

The main drag from Kathmandu, where it passes through the Kopundol area, is known to English-speakers as "Fashion Row". Most of Patan's many non-profit outlets are clustered along here, as are several boutiques specializing in contemporary fashions.

Dhaka Weaves Ltd, Kopundol, up a dirt lane north of the *Hotel Himalaya* (daily except Sat 10am–5pm). Factory showroom with a full range of locally produced *dhaka* shawls, cushion covers and other accessories.

THE CARPET INDUSTRY

If you've read the section on shopping in *Basics*, you'll know that there's not much Tibetan about so-called Tibetan carpets. Nonetheless, they do have their origin high up on the Tibetan plateau, where sheep are bred for their unusually long, high-tensile **wool**. Brought into Nepal by yak and mule train over passes in the far west, the Tibetan wool is blended with processed New Zealand wool and then carded and spun into yarn. Although **carding** machines are increasingly being used, **spinning** is still done exclusively by hand to produce a distinctive, slightly irregular look. The yarn is then taken to a **dyeing** plant, where it's dipped in vats of boiling dye (mostly chemical dyes are used) and sun-dried before being rolled into 200-gram balls, coded for colour and batch, and stored in warehouses. Weavers can then order up their colours by number, as instructed by a pattern or their carpet master.

As throughout Asia, weavers sit on benches in front of tall looms – but that's as far as the similarity goes. Tibetan-style carpets are produced by the **cut-loop method**, which bears little relation to the process employed by Middle Eastern and Chinese artisans. Rather than tying thousands of individual knots, the weaver loops the yarn in and out of the vertical warp threads and around a horizontally placed rod; when the row is finished, the weaver draws a knife across the loops, freeing the rod, and the loops, cut in half, form the pile. This method enables relatively speedy production – one person can produce a 1m x 2m carpet in about seven working days – but it results in a rather low density of 40–80 "knots" (loops) per square inch. Rather than **beating** each row down with an iron mallet, which in Middle Eastern carpets helps to create a tight weave, Tibetan-style weavers deliberately use wooden mallets for a looser, blanket-like feel.

The weaving done, carpets are taken off the looms and **trimmed** with shears to give an even finish. **Embossing**, an optional stage, subtly separates the colours to

Dhankuta Sisters, Kopundol (Mon–Thurs & Sun 10am–5.30pm). Small non-profit outlet for village women in the eastern hills, selling *dhaka* clothes and place settings, plus some *allo*, wicker work and Mithila paintings.

Dhukuti, Kopundol (Mon–Fri 9am–7pm, Sat & Sun 11am–7pm). Run by a village and low-income project marketing association, Patan's biggest non-profit shop stocks a wide variety of cotton and quilted-cotton crafts, wool sweaters, dolls, copper vessels, basketry and leather.

Dzambala Boutique, Kopundol, north of the *Hotel Himalaya* (Mon–Thurs & Sun 10am–8pm). Hand-painted silk garments, silver jewellery, leather bags and garments.

Hastakala, Kopundol, opposite the *Hotel Himalaya* (Mon–Fri & Sun 9.30am–6pm, Sat 10am–5pm). Good selection and display of woollens, *dhaka*, quilted cottons, ceramics, paper, Mithila art and general gift items.

Himalayan Leather Crafts, east of Jaulakhel Chowk (daily except Sat 9am–6pm). Run by the Nepal Leprosy Trust, this outlet sells leather goods (handbags and wallets, mostly), ceramics, batiks and pine-needle place mats.

Manushi, Kopundol (daily except Sat 10am–7pm). Small place selling the tie dyes, block prints and woodwork made by the Centre for Women and Development.

Mahaguthi, Kopundol, with a smaller branch inside the Royal Palace, behind the Degu Talle (daily 10am–6.30pm). Aided by Oxfam, this supports a home for destitute women with a good selection of textiles, plus pine-needle crafts, toys and other items.

Women's Skills Development Project, Pulchowk, just west of the UN Complex (Mon–Thurs & Sun 10am–5pm, Fri 10am–3pm). The sales outlet for the Nepal Women's Organization (offices behind) specializes in block-printed cottons, with some quilted cotton items, woollens, toys and paper. You can watch women at work behind the shop.

---

highlight the design. Finally, carpets must be **washed** to remove dirt and excess dye, an industrial process which, in the absence of effective controls, pollutes local streams with chemicals that have been linked with birth defects.

Marketing is more sophisticated than it might at first appear. The carpets so haphazardly displayed in tourist shops represent only a tiny tip of the iceberg – most are in fact made to order for the export market and air-freighted to wholesalers in Frankfurt and London. A handful of export traders, led by the Carpet Trading Company, founded in 1966 with help from the Swiss Association for Technical Assistance (SATA), handle international distribution.

In thirty years, Nepal's carpet industry has grown into a more than $100 million industry, accounting for two-thirds of the country's exports and **employing** (directly and indirectly) 300,000 people. Having long ago outstripped the Tibetan exile labour pool, it now provides work for members of every ethnic group, especially the poor and landless who might otherwise be forced into bonded labour or prostitution. It's an economist's dream – but some observers fear it may be a nightmare in the making.

The industry appears to be responsible for an alarming rise in **child labour** in Nepal, even as other carpet-producing countries are enacting laws to stop exploitation. There's also concern about the tens of thousands of workers who would find themselves instantly unemployed should Tibetan carpets fall out of favour. But what no one disputes is that the carpet industry is far too concentrated in the Kathmandu Valley, which lacks the infrastructure to cope with such an influx of workers, resulting in air and water **pollution**, traffic, social dislocation and land speculation. The government has talked of trying to move the industry to Hetauda, near Chitwan National Park: aside from the fact that this would only shift the problem, it's hard to imagine what inducements could be offered to dislodge manufacturers from the valley, although a mooted second international airport near Hetauda might do the trick.

Kirtipur

Once-proud **KIRTIPUR** ("City of Glory") occupies a long, low battleship of a ridge 5km southwest of Kathmandu. An historic stronghold commanding a panoramic view of the valley, the town is ideal for wandering, yet seldom visited – outsiders tend to get stared at. Poor Kirtipur is still shunned and pitied in the Kathmandu Valley, more than two centuries after its spirit was broken by an act of spectacular cruelty and humiliation.

Established as a western outpost of Patan in the twelfth century, Kirtipur had gained nominal independence by the time Prithvi Narayan Shah began his final conquest of the Kathmandu Valley in 1767. The Gorkha king, who had himself been born and raised in a hilltop fortress, considered Kirtipur the strategic lynch-pin of the valley and made its capture his first priority. After two separate attacks and a six-month siege, with no help forthcoming from Patan, Kirtipur surrendered on the understanding it would receive a total amnesty – instead, in an **atrocity** intended to demoralize the remaining opposition in the valley, Prithvi Shah ordered his troops to cut off the noses and lips of every man and boy in Kirtipur. "This order was carried out in the most exact way," wrote the early twentieth-century traveller Percival Landon, "and it adds rather than detracts from the savagery of the conqueror that the only persons spared were men who were

KIRTIPUR

skilled in playing wind instruments. The grim statistic is added that the weight of the noses and lips that were brought to Prithvi Narayan in proof that his order had been obeyed amounted to no less than eighty pounds." The rest of the valley fell within a year.

Kirtipur's hilltop position, once a strategic asset, has become a serious handicap to development, for although a road was belatedly pushed up to the neglected upper town, almost all of Kirtipur's commerce has shifted to **Naya Bazaar** (New Market) at the southern base of the hill. Considering its nearness to Kathmandu, the town remains shockingly backward (and none too sanitary); the population of 10,000 is served by only one part-time doctor. Many residents are Jyapus (members of the Newar farming subcaste), who work the fields below the town and in spring and autumn haul their sheaves up and thresh the grain in the narrow streets. Others, whose land was appropriated for the building of **Tribhuwan University**, just to the east, now commute to jobs in Kathmandu or produce handicrafts behind closed doors. The university (Nepal's largest, with 5000 students) was the scene of student hunger strikes and clashes with police in late 1992, when the government privatized the cafeteria and doubled the price of a meal to Rs8 – illustrating the teething troubles Nepal faces in trying to introduce a market-based economy to live more within its slender means.

Frequent **minibuses** run from Ratna Park to the Tribhuwan University gate, from where it's a fifteen-minute walk up to the village. If you're **cycling**, follow the Dakshin Kali road about 1km beyond the Ring Road, turn right at the red-brick university gate, and take the left fork another 1km later – there's a steep, uphill slog at the end. Other footpaths lead to Kirtipur from the Prithvi (Kathmandu–Pokhara) Highway and Chobar. For **food**, you can't expect much more than an omelette or a plateful of chow mein in Naya Bazaar.

Bagh Bhairab Mandir

The road from the university ascends to the saddle of Kirtipur's twin-humped ridge and deposits you in a weedy square outside the prodigious **Bagh Bhairab Mandir**, which serves double duty as a war memorial and a cathedral to Bhairab in his tiger (*bagh*) form. Mounted on the outside is a collection of rusty weapons captured during the siege of Kirtipur – either by the Gorkhalis or the defenders, depending on whom you ask. Local musicians perform *bhajan* early in the morning and around dinnertime near the shrine just left of the main door, and on Tuesdays and Saturdays people sacrifice animals to it. Also kept in this courtyard is an image of Indriani, the Cinderella of the Hindu pantheon, who was bossed around by the other goddesses until she miraculously turned a pumpkin into gold. Kirtipur's biggest **festival** is in early December, when Indriani and Ganesh are paraded through town on palanquins.

Uma-Maheshwar Mandir and Chilandeo Stupa

A pleasantly confusing maze of stony alleys, Kirtipur is great for wandering, and navigating isn't hard so long as you stick to the ridgeline. The northwestern end of town is predominantly Hindu, the southeastern Buddhist.

At the top of the northern, Hindu hump stands the elephant-guarded **Uma-Maheshwar Mandir**, mainly of interest for its sweeping view of Kathmandu, Swayambhu and the distant whitecaps of the Jugal Himal. Kathmandu's quaint **aerial ropeway** runs just north of here; built in 1925, before any roads connected the valley to the outside world, it's since been upgraded and is still used for ferrying heavy freight. The atmospheric **Chilandeo Stupa** crowns the southern hill, its exposed brickwork lending a hoary antiquity generally lacking in better-maintained stupas. Chilandeo (also known as Chilancho Bahal) is commonly believed to have been erected by Ashoka – though if Ashoka really built every stupa attributed to him he would have had little time for anything else. The ridge that rears up so impressively to the southwest is Champadevi (see below), one of the high points along the valley rim.

Naya Bazaar and beyond

Naya Bazaar's only attraction sits below the road where it rounds the southeast flank of the Kirtipur ridge. A Thai-style Theravada temple, the **Nagara Mandapa Kirti Vihara** was completed in 1989 with money donated by the Thai king and an array of the great and good of Thailand. (*Thai Airways* has shamelessly put up a hoarding on a separate image hall on the strength of a measly Rs10,000 contribution.) In the minimalist Theravada tradition, the main sanctuary is unadorned except for an altar groaning with assorted gilded Buddhas and *bodhisattva*. A statue outside honours Pragyananda Mahastho Viraya, the elderly patriarch of all Nepali Theravada Buddhists, who lives in Patan.

You can walk to the crest of **Champadevi** in three to four hours by following the dirt road southwest from Naya Bazaar and then west to Machhegaun ("Fishville"), from where a trail switchbacks up to a saddle on the ridge just north of the highest of several summits (2502m); the views of the high Himalaya from this knoll are excellent. To return you could follow the ridge eastwards, up and over a lower summit and down to the Dakshin Kali road at several points (see below); however, flagging down full-to-bursting buses along this road isn't great fun and the full circuit is more easily done in reverse.

The Dakshin Kali road

The longest and most varied of the valley's roads begins in Kathmandu and ends at the famous sacrificial shrine of Dakshin Kali, a distance of 18km. En route it passes several temples, some beautiful stretches of forest, pleasant rest stops and fine views as it rises more than 300m above the valley floor.

Ganesh III (7132 m)   Ganesh I (7406 m)   Shisha Pangma (8046 m)   Gangchenpo (6297 m)

Ganesh II (7150 m)

THE HIMALAYA AS SEEN FROM KATHMANDU VALLEY

Appallingly crowded **minibuses** depart for Dakshin Kali from Martyrs' Gate in Kathmandu roughly every hour, more often (and even more crowded) on Saturdays. Kathmandu travel agents offer guided **tours** on Tuesday and Saturday mornings (about Rs200), or you could hire your own **taxi** (about Rs500 round-trip to Dakshin Kali with stops). For real independence, though, go by **mountain bike**, which takes about an hour and a half.

Chobar Gorge

When Manjushri drained the Kathmandu Valley of its legendary lake, **Chobar Gorge** was one of the places he smote with his sword to release the waters, and as the Bagmati River slices through a wrinkle in the valley floor here it really does look like the work of a neat sword stroke. A path along the west bank scrambles up to two caves housing Shiva mementoes – only for those who like dark, confined spaces.

Jal Binayak, a seventeenth-century Ganesh temple, stands where the Bagmati, swollen with the accumulated gunge and sewage of the valley, emerges from the gorge. Built on a rocky outcrop, the tip of which is worshipped as Ganesh, it's full of the usual bells and bell-ringing. High above the river, an iron **footbridge**, custom-cast by a Glasgow foundry and assembled here in 1907, gives a good view of the chasm and Jal Binayak; the vista would be better if it weren't for the unfortunate siting of the Himal Cement Factory (the source of much of the valley's modern concrete construction and pollution) just downstream from the temple.

Chobar

Various paths lead from the main road up to **CHOBAR**, a former outpost of Patan at the top of the deceptively tall hill west of the gorge. The walk begins unpromisingly – the lower slopes look like they're being carried away by earth-movers – but higher up the northern valley spreads out handsomely.

Chobar huddles around its idiosyncratic **Adinath Mandir**, the front of which is completely decorated with pots, pans and jugs. Various explanations are cited for the practice of offering kitchen utensils to Lokeshwar, the temple's deity: newlyweds will say it ensures a happy union, others claim it's a necessary rite to send a recently departed loved one off to a prosperous next life. Like so many traditions,

Dome Blanc (6830 m)   Dorjelakpa (6990 m)   Lengpogang (7083 m)   Phurbi Chhyachu (6637 m)

the act has become independent of its origins, and may hark back to a time when metal implements were new technology and decorating a temple with them was a way to keep it looking spiffy and up-to-date – just as other temples are often graced by mirrors, photographs and European tiles. Lokeshwar is worshipped here in the form of a red mask, which bears a close resemblance to Patan's Rato Machhendranath.

Taudaha and hikes to Champadevi

Beyond the cement plant, the road begins climbing through attractive country-side and after 2km passes **Taudaha**, the Kathmandu Valley's only lake of note. According to legend, when Manjushri drained the valley he left Taudaha as a home for the snakes, and the belief persists that the serpent king Karkatoka still lives at the bottom, coiled around a heap of treasure. Jang Bahadur Rana, prime minister in the middle of the last century, is said to have tried to dredge the lake for booty but gave up because of its depth. Nowadays Taudaha is considered sacred and is off-limits to hunters and fishermen. *Hatiban Pine Ridge Resort*, the first of what promises to be a new breed of swanky hotel hideaways in the Kathmandu Valley, sits above the road southwest of here.

The road ascends steadily for another 6km to its highest point, a little beyond Pikhel. The villages of Khokana and Bungamati rest in tight whorls on the plateau across the river. Trails to **Champadevi**, the ridge to the west, start from near Taudaha, Pikhel and Pharping (see below). A hike up one and down another will take four to six hours, not including time spent at the top. The first trail begins where the road makes an abrupt bend beyond Taudaha, climbing steeply southwestwards to gain the ridge and then more gradually along it to the nearest, stupa-marked summit (2278m). From Pikhel, a trail heads north to the ridge, passing through a splendid pine forest, then tracks northwest to join the first trail. The Pharping route (best taken going down if you intend to get a seat on the bus) follows a dirt road up a valley south of the ridge as far as a duck pond, where it veers northwards straight up to the ridge. You can continue westwards along the ridge to the highest summit (2502m), and from a saddle beyond here down to Kirtipur.

Sesh Narayan (Yanglesho)

Cool, quiet and shady, **SESH NARAYAN** crouches under a wooded hillside 2km beyond Pikhel and is regarded as a holy spot by both Hindus and Buddhists. Hindus worship Vishnu here as the mighty creator, who formed the universe out of the cosmic ocean; the snake Sesh (or Ananta), the "remainder" of the cosmic waters after Vishnu's creation, is symbolized by the four tranquil **pools** beside the road.

Steps from there lead to Narayan's **temple** at the base of a limestone overhang, whose serpentine rocks and roots no doubt inspired Vaishnavas to make the Sesh connection. Buddhists, meanwhile, call this grotto **Yanglesho** and hold it to be the place where Guru Padma Sambhava, the eighth-century founder of the Nyingma-pa sect of Tibetan Buddhism, wrestled with a horde of *nag* and turned them to stone. This episode marked a turning-point in Padma Sambhava's career – allegorically, it probably refers to the saint's struggle to introduce his brand of tantric Buddhism from India – which accounts for the presence of a **gompa** next to the Sesh Narayan temple.

Pharping

PHARPING is located a few hundred metres beyond Sesh Narayan, straight ahead up a side road where the main road swerves left. Unexpectedly large and lively for this distant corner of the valley, the town is only just beginning to register the changes of electricity and concrete construction. Ironically, Nepal's first hydroelectric plant was built here, in 1911, but the power generated all went to light Singha Durbar. A fifteen-minute walk uphill brings you to the golden-roofed **Pharping Bajra Jogini**, one of the valley's four tantric temples dedicated to the angry female aspect of Buddhahood. You can go upstairs – a rare privilege – and view the two prancing images of Bajra Jogini, each holding a skull cup and knife.

A short path leads further up the hill to a monastery sometimes used as a retreat by Buddhist Westerners. Introduce yourself and the monks will show you the **Padma Sambhava Cave** in the courtyard; the irrepressible guru, whose image stands among butter candles, apparently meditated in this grotto as well as at Yanglesho. Buddhists say the handprint to the left of the cave entrance and the "footprints" in the centre of the couryard are those of Padma Sambhava (Hindus claim they were left by Gorakhnath). The site has grown to be a major pilgrimage stop for Tibetan Buddhists, and has spawned several other nearby *gompa* of Padma Sambhava's Nyingma-pa sect.

Dakshin Kali

The best and worst aspect of **DAKSHIN KALI** is that everything happens out in the open. The famous sacrificial pit of Southern Kali – the last stop for hundreds of chickens, goats and pigs every week – lies at the bottom of a steep, forested ravine, affording an intimate view of Nepali religious rituals; unfortunately, the public bloodbath also attracts busloads of camera-toting tourists. For the full show in all its Technicolor gore, go on a Saturday or Tuesday morning, but if you're squeamish or wish to avoid the crush, try visiting in the afternoon or on another day. Whenever you go, respect the privacy of worshippers, especially if you're taking pictures.

The road from Pharping switchbacks down into the ravine, ending at a small bazaar of stalls selling food, drinks and sacrificial accessories. The **shrine** is directly below, positioned at the auspicious confluence of two streams. Tiled like an abattoir (for easy hosing down) and covered with a brass canopy, the sacred

---

A NOTE ON HINDU SACRIFICE

Hindu animal **sacrifice** is superficially similar to what the Old Testament patriarchs did, but Hindus don't kill animals to prove their loyalty to a deity so much as to propitiate it. Kali, the usual recipient, doesn't care about the personal sacrifice her worshipper has made in order to get an animal, all she wants is the blood. Nepalis lead their offerings to the slaughter tenderly, often whispering prayers in the animal's ear and sprinkling its head with water to encourage it to shrug in assent; they believe that the death of this "unfortunate brother" will give it the chance to be reborn as a higher life form. Only uncastrated males, preferably dark in colour, are used. At Dakshin Kali, men of a special caste slit the animals' throats and let the blood spray over the idols. Brahman priests (referred to as *bahun, pandit* or *pujari*) oversee the butchering and instruct worshippers in all the complex rituals that follow – the priests like to make things obscure to keep themselves in demand. However, you don't need to speak Nepali to get the gist of the explanations.

area consists of little more than a row of short statuettes, Kali being the heavily decorated one on the right. You can get a good view of the whole area from a secondary shrine on a promontory high above the far side of the ravine.

Dakshin Kali is as much a picnic area as a holy spot. The sacrifice done, families make for the pavilions that surround the shrine and merrily barbecue the remains of their offerings.

The Bungamati and Chapagaun roads

Two minor roads south of Patan make for some easy, off-the-beaten-track cycling through rustic villages and countryside. The first, mostly unpaved road leads directly to delightful Bungamati, summer home of Rato Machhendranath; the second is paved as far as Chapagaun and its nearby forest temple. You can pedal to either town on a one-speeder, but with a mountain bike you'll be able to make a circuit of both as well as roam all over the southern end of the valley. Buses also run along both roads.

Bungamati and Khokana

From a distance, you could almost mistake **BUNGAMATI** for a well-preserved Tuscan village: scrunched together on a hillock, its tall, block-like brick houses, with their tiled roofs sloping in different directions, look distinctly Romanesque. Irregular **buses** from Patan's Jaulakhel drop you off along the road a short walk northeast of the town.

Close up, Bungamati is quintessentially Newar, and what at first looks like a tiny village quickly envelops you in its self-contained world. All alleys eventually lead to the broad, teeming central plaza and the great white *shikra* of **Machhendranath**, whose more ancient name is Bunga Deo ("God of Bunga"). According to legend, Bungamati marks the spot where Machhendranath, having arrived in the valley in the form of a bee to save it from drought, was "born" as the valley's protector-rainmaker. Each summer at the end of Patan's Rato Machhendranath festival, the god's red mask is brought to the Bungamati temple for a six-month residency, while every twelfth year Machhendranath's lumbering chariot is pulled all the way to Bungamati.

One kilometre to the north, **KHOKANA** resembles Bungamati in many ways, but somehow lacks the character and magnetism of its neighbour. Its pagoda-style **Shekali Mai Mandir**, a massive three-tiered job, honours a local nature goddess. Midway between Khokana and Bungamati stands the poorly maintained **Karya Binayak**, another of the valley's four Ganesh temples. Marijuana grows in profusion around here.

Thecho and Chapagaun

THECHO, 8km south of Patan, is the largest town in this rural, undulating end of the valley, while **CHAPAGAUN**, 1km further south, is a smaller but similarly brick-built settlement. Thecho has a touch more atmosphere, Chapagaun more to eat. Hourly minibuses from Patan's Lagankhel serve both towns. Strangely, Chapagaun boasts a bicycle rental shop.

More attractive than either town, the seventeenth-century **Bajra Barahi Mandir** is secreted in a small wood 500m east along a track from Chapagaun. Despite Shiva imagery, the temple is dedicated to a tantric goddess; like the Bajra

Joginis, Bajra Barahis represent the female, creative power of divinity. This goddess gets her share of worship and sacrifice on Saturdays, but most visitors come to picnic in the park.

From Chapagaun, you've several options for **cycling on**. The Bajra Barahi track continues eastwards and eventually meets the Godavari road (see below), while a trail heading west from Chapagaun crosses the pretty Nakhu Khola and bends north to join the Bungamati road. The main Chapagaun road carries on to the mildly interesting Lele Valley.

The Godavari road

The greenest, most pristine part of the valley is its southeastern edge, where you'll find something now all too rare in Nepal, or at least around the Kathmandu Valley: virgin forest, once the dominant feature of the middle hills, which has come under increasing pressure in recent years from an exploding population desperate for fuel and farmland (see "Development Dilemmas" in *Contexts*). One way to take in the greenery is by visiting the Royal Botanical Garden; another is to hike or ride up Phulchoki, the highest point on the valley rim. The starting point for both is **Godavari** (pronounced Go-*daa*-vari), 10km southeast of Patan near the end of a straight paved road.

Hourly **minibuses** from Patan's Lagankhel bus park go as far as the Jesuits' St Xavier School in Godavari; since the road gains more than 200m along the way, **cyclists** will need a machine with gears.

The Royal Botanical Garden
To reach the **Royal Botanical Garden** (daily 10am–5pm; Rs2), follow the main road to the left of the St Xavier School for 1km, then turn left again down to the car park and main gate. Despite their modest size, the grounds contain some idyllic paths, streams and picnic areas; highlights are the orchid house and fern shed. If you're expecting well-labelled plants and trees you'll be disappointed, but the Department of Medicinal Plants publishes a map (Rs2 at the ticket booth) and guide booklet in English (Rs10) that are of some help in identifying species. The garden receives fairly enthusiastic support from the government – not surprising, perhaps, in a country where flowers play a major part in worship and medicine is largely based on plants.

Another pleasant spot nearby is the spring-fed water tank of **Godavari Kunda**, 300m past the botanical garden turning on the Godavari road, which hosts a big *mela* every twelve years during July and August (last held in 1991). Alternatively, you can leave the garden via a back way on the western side, and keep following it for a long walk around the small valley to the north. The three- or four-hour circuit takes you past **Bishanku Narayan**, a Vaishnava pilgrimage cave high up in a notch at the far end of the valley. Kathmandu seems incredibly far away.

Phulchoki
The road bearing straight ahead to the right of the St Xavier School switchbacks and spirals right to the top of **Phulchoki** – a 1200-metre ascent on mostly loose gravel, making it very hard going for mountain-bikers. The trail to the summit starts behind the shrine to **Phulchoki Mai**, the mother goddess of these parts, 500m up the road and just opposite the entrance to an unsightly marble quarry.

This hike takes about three hours, and crosses the road a few times; the trail can be very slippery. Set off as early as possible to beat the afternoon clouds.

Phulchoki means **"Place of Flowers"**, which is entirely apt. If you know what to look for, you'll see orchids, morning glories, corydalis and, of course, rhododendrons; March and April are best for catching them in bloom. The whole mountain is covered by tall, luxuriant **forest**, and as you climb from its subtropical base to its temperate summit you pass through mixed stands of oak, chestnut, walnut, bamboo, laurel and rhododendron. It's a great place for **birdwatching** – a trained eye is supposed to be able to spot a hundred or more species in a day – and even better for **butterflies**, which are apparently attracted to the flowers during spring.

If the **summit** (2762m) isn't wreathed in clouds, you'll have a magnificent view of a wide swathe of the Himalaya (notably Gauri Shankar) and practically the entire Kathmandu Valley. The effect is only slightly marred by the presence of a microwave relay station, erected with Canadian assistance, which is the summit road's *raison d'être*.

BHAKTAPUR AND THE EASTERN VALLEY

The valley's eastern arm maintains a discreet cultural, as well as geographical, distance from Kathmandu. Perhaps because it lay off the main India–Tibet trade route all those years, its Hinduism has scarcely been diluted by Buddhism. Creeping Westernization has been slower to take root here, too, and concrete has made few inroads against native brick. Fashions at this end of the valley remain conservative, especially among Jyapu women: most still wear the traditional black and red-trimmed *pataasi*, wrapped around the waist in tiers, giving the effect of a flamenco skirt; hitched up in back, these often reveal tattoos above the ankles, believed to be necessary for a woman to enter heaven.

Everywhere is within day-tripping range of Kathmandu, but for more detailed exploration a stay in the medieval time capsule of **Bhaktapur** is a must. Trails radiate in all directions from here, the temple complex of **Changu Narayan** making an immensely rewarding excursion, particularly for fans of Nepali sculpture. Bhaktapur is also a staging post for Nagarkot, and can serve as a springboard for trips up the Arniko Highway to Dhulikhel and beyond (see Chapter Three). For some reason, the "bye-bye one rupees" mobs at this end of the valley are particularly insufferable – your best defence is a dogged sense of humour.

Bhaktapur (Bhadgaun)

In the soft, dusty light of evening the old city of Bhaktapur, with its pagoda roofs and its harmonious blend of wood, mud-brick and copper, looked extraordinarily beautiful. It was as though a faded medieval tapestry were tacked on to the pale tea-rose sky. In the foreground a farmhouse was on fire, and orange flames licked like liquescent dragon's tongues across the thatched roof. One thought of Chaucer's England and Rabelais's France; of a world of intense, violent passions and brilliant colour, where sin was plentiful but so were grace and forgiveness ...

Charlie Pye-Smith, *Travels in Nepal*

BHAKTAPUR

0   200 m

To Kathmandu

To Changu Narayan
(by foot)

To Nagarkot &
Changu Narayan

To Minibus Stop

To Kathmandu

To Kathmandu

To Trolley Bus Stop
& Surya Binayak

To
Nala

Mahakali

Navpokhu
Pokhri

Lamuga
Pokhri

Kwathandau
Pokhri

Nawa Durga
Dhyochhen

Ganesh
Pokhri

Bhimsen

Neg Pokhri

Café de Peacock

Dattatreya

Pujari
Math

Wakupati
Narayan

TACHAPAL

Maheshwari

TACHO

GOLMADHI

Tadhunchen
Bahal

Nyatapola

Bhairabnath

Ti Mahadev
Narayan

PASIKHEL

CHUPING
GHAT

TAUMADHI

Royal
Palace

DURBAR SQUARE

POTERS
SQUARE

RAM
GHAT

Jotrilingeshwar
Mahadev

Jaya Barahi

MANGEL GHAT

Hanumante River

HANUMAN GHAT

Kathmandu's field of gravity weakens somewhere east of the airport; beyond, you fall inexorably into the rich, heady atmosphere of **BHAKTAPUR** (also known as **BHADGAUN**). A medieval world unto itself ("remote – willingly remote – from her neighbours, and one of the most picturesque towns in the East," wrote Percival Landon), Bhaktapur is Nepal's most perfectly preserved city. Bricks everywhere, streets paved with bricks in herringbone and parquet patterns, houses built of bricks and carved wood: brick and wood, the essential media of Newar city-builders. Well clear of the Ring Road, with no industrial zone, no diplomatic enclave and few suburbs, Bhaktapur feels more like a big village than a small city. Its streets and alleys are all the more suited for wandering, thanks to the fifteen-year restoration and sanitation programme of the German-funded Bhaktapur Development Project – there are some "medieval" features, like open sewers, that everyone can do without.

The "City of Devotees" was probably founded in the ninth century, and by 1200 it was ruling Nepal. In that year Bhaktapur witnessed the launch of the Malla era when, according to the Nepalese chronicles, King Arideva, upon being called out of a wrestling bout to hear of the birth of a son, bestowed on the prince the hereditary title Malla ("wrestler") – to this day, beefy carved wrestlers are the city's trademark temple guardians. Bhaktapur ruled the valley until 1482, when Yaksha Malla divided the kingdom among his three sons, setting in train three centuries of continuous squabbling. It was a Bhaktapur king who helped to bring the Malla era to a close in 1766 by inviting Prithvi Narayan Shah, the Gorkha leader, to aid him in a quarrel against Kathmandu. Seizing on this pretext, Prithvi Narayan conquered the valley within three years, Bhaktapur being the last of the three capitals to surrender.

Bhaktapur drapes across an east–west fold in the valley, its southern fringe sliding down towards the sluggish Hanumante River. Owing to a long-term westward drift, the city has two centres (residents of the two halves stage a boisterous tug-of-war during the city's annual Bisket festival) and three main squares. In the west, **Durbar Square** and **Taumadhi Tol** dominate the post-fifteenth-century city, while **Tachapal Tol** presides over the older east end.

You'll arrive by one of two routes. The handy **trolley bus**, departing from the National Stadium south of Kathmandu's GPO every fifteen minutes or so, drops you on the main road about ten minutes' walk south of town, as do buses coming down from Dhulikhel and points east. Arriving by **minibus** from the main Kathmandu bus park, you'll be deposited near Sidha Pokhri, about five minutes west of Durbar Square; buses to Nagarkot leave from here. Bhaktapur has no rikshas and just a few resident taxis, but it's compact enough to be explored on foot. **Bikes** can be rented near the west end of Durbar Square.

Durbar Square

Bhaktapur's **Durbar Square** hasn't got quite the same gusto as its namesakes in Kathmandu and Patan. Isolated near the city's edge, it's neither a commercial nor a social focal point, and consequently the only locals you see here are either preying on tourists or cutting across the square to somewhere else. The 1934 earthquake, which knocked the stuffing out of Bhaktapur, claimed a number of the square's temples and left a great void in its middle. Despite all that, it boasts one of Nepal's proudest artistic achievements – the Golden Gate – plus the National Art Gallery.

DURBAR SQUARE AND TAUMADHI TOL

To Dattatreya Square

25 m

0

Sundari Chowk

Royal Palace

Water Tank

National Art Gallery

DURBAR SQUARE

Palace of 55 Windows

TALEJU CHOWK

Golden Gate

Taleju Bell

Bupathindra Malla Pillar

Pashupati Mandir

Chyasilin Mandap

Batsala Durga

Shiva Guest House

Bhaktapur Gate Restaurant

Tadhunchen Bahal

Golden Gate Guest House

Marco Polo Restaurant

Nyatapola Guest House

Nyatapola

Traditional Guest House

Bank

TAUMADHI TOL

Bhairabnath

Café Nyatapola

Til Mahadev Narayan

To Potters' Square

To Sidha Pokhri

The square enjoyed one brief, magnificent renaissance during the shooting of Bernardo Bertolucci's **Little Buddha** in 1992, when it was used as the location for many of the ancient flashback scenes. Bertolucci transformed the area beyond recognition: high, simulated brick walls were erected to block modern sightlines, the palace front was extended with false balconies and columns, and the dead space in the middle was taken up with a raised water tank. Residents won't soon forget that Hollywood facelift – nor the handsome fees Bertolucci paid them for the use of their houses and shopfronts.

The Royal Palace

Bhaktapur's **Royal Palace** originally stood further east, near Tachapal Tol, but was shifted westwards (like the city) in the fifteenth century; the present structure, dating from the eighteenth century, was renovated and greatly scaled down after 1934. Its superbly carved eastern wing, known as the **Palace of Fifty-Five Windows**, was raised around 1700 by Bupathindra Malla, Bhaktapur's great builder-king, whose *namaste*-ing figure kneels on a stone **pillar** opposite.

While the **Golden Gate** (Sun Dhoka) probably wouldn't be so famous if it were made of wood or stone – it is, in fact, made of brass – its detail and sheer exuberance raise it to the level of a masterpiece. The *torana* above the door features a squat Garud and a ten-armed, four-headed Taleju, the Mallas' guardian deity, but to locals the most powerful figures are those of Bhairab and Kali, situated chest-high on either side of the gate. Upon entry, you follow an outdoor passage around to another impressive doorway, depicting Taleju and her heavenly host in wood, beyond which lies the ornate and sacrosanct **Taleju Chowk**. A sentry bars the way to non-Hindus, and guards the store of gold treasures contained within; sacrifices take place here during festivals. Another old doorway nearby leads to **Sundari Chowk**, Bupathindra Malla's regal bathing tank fed by an ornate stone spout and protected by two gilded *nag* figures, once the centrepiece of a now-obliterated palace section.

The palace's western wing houses the excellent **National Art Gallery** (daily except Sat 10am–5pm, in winter closes at 4pm; Rs5), displaying an extensive permanent exhibit of tantric *paubha* and *thangka*, plus a small collection of oblong book covers and illuminated pages of religious texts. There are some terrifically old paintings here (some date to the fifteenth century), including such paradigms of tantric art as the "Sata Chakra Darsan", a medical chart showing the location of the seven power points (*chakra*) of the human body. In the furthest corridor, semi-restored frescoes depict courtly scenes and, in awesome detail, an image of Shiva and Parvati in their "universal", many-limbed forms. Stone friezes at the entrance portray Vishnu Varahi and Narasimha, Vishnu's boar and man-lion *avatar*.

The square

The square itself won't detain you for long. Near the main gate at the west end you can admire a pair of multiple-armed statues of **Bhairab** and **Ugrachandi**, whose sculptor reportedly had his hands cut off by order of the Bhaktapur king to ensure that he wouldn't reproduce the images in Kathmandu or Patan. Among the clutch of minor temples opposite, a Shiva *shikra* showcases the often overlooked Newar art of brickwork.

In the entire square, only the fifteenth-century **Pashupati Mandir** at the busier, more touristy eastern end receives much in the way of reverence. The oldest structure extant here, the temple houses a copy of the exalted Pashupatinath *linga*, and its roof struts sport some wildly deviant erotic carvings.

Next door stands the stone *shikra* of **Batsala Durga** and the obligatory **Taleju Bell** (nicknamed "the Bell of Barking Dogs", its toll evidently inflicts ultrasonic agony on local curs), both from the mid-eighteenth century.

Behind the bell rises the **Chyasilin Mandap**, the Pavilion of the Eight Corners, erected in 1990 as an exact replica of an eighteenth-century structure destroyed in the 1934 earthquake. The restorers have done a bang-up job of relocating original pillars and lintels and integrating them into a sturdy new structure – the steel reinforcing may clash a bit, but this pavilion is going to stay standing when the next quake hits. The upper floor makes a fine vantage point for observing the square. East of here are the platforms of other demolished and half-heartedly rebuilt temples.

Rare for predominantly Hindu Bhaktapur, the well-preserved **Tadhunchen Bahal**, east of the square, attracts Buddhist as well as Hindu worshippers, and is a gathering place for neighbourhood metalsmiths in the evening; you might also hear languorous music performed on harmonium and tabla.

Taumadhi Tol

One hundred metres southeast of Durbar Square, **Taumadhi Tol** is a livelier place to linger, if only to admire the view from the balcony of *Café Nyatapola*. In mid-April this square serves as the assembly point for the high-spirited **Bisket Jaatra**, Nepal's foremost New Year celebration.

Dominating Taumadhi and all of Bhaktapur, the graceful, five-tiered **Nyatapola** (pronounced *Nyat*-pol) is Nepal's tallest and most classically proportioned pagoda. So obscure is its honoured deity, a tantric goddess named Siddhi Lakshmi, that she apparently has no devotees, and the sanctuary has been barred to all but priests ever since its completion in 1702. The Nyatapola's five pairs of temple guardians – Malla wrestlers, elephants, lions, griffins and two minor goddesses, Baghini (Tigress) and Singhini (Lioness) – are as famous as the temple itself. Each pair is supposed to be ten times as strong as the pair below, with Siddhi Lakshmi herself, presumably, being ten times as strong as Baghini and Singhini. Bisket chariot components, including the solid wooden wheels, are stored in an empty lot behind the temple.

The heavy, thick-set **Bhairabnath Mandir** is as different from the slender Nyatapola as one pagoda could possibly be from another. The funniest thing of all about this hulk of a building, in fact, is the tiny Bhairab idol mounted on a sort of mantel on the front of the temple (several other figures are kept inside, including the one that leads the Bisket parade). A story is told that Bhairab, travelling incognito, once came to Bhaktapur to watch the Bisket festivities. Divining the god's presence and hoping to extract a boon, the priests bound him with tantric spells, and when he tried to escape by sinking into the ground they chopped off his head. Now Bhairab, or at least his head, gets to ride in the Bisket parade every year – inside a locked box on board the chariot.

Hidden behind recent buildings southeast of the square, the seventeenth-century **Til Mahadev Narayan Mandir** displays all the iconography of a Vishnu (Narayan) temple: a gilded *sankha* (conch), *chakra* (wheel) and Garud are all hoisted on pillars out in front, in a manner clearly imitating the great temple of Changu Narayan, 5km north of Bhaktapur. The temple's name, it's said, derives from an incident involving a trader from Thimi who, upon unfolding his wares here, magically discovered the image of Narayan in a consignment of sesame seeds (*til*).

The western city

Like a brick canyon, Bhaktapur's main commercial thoroughfare runs from Taumadhi west to the city gate. Roughly 150m along, you'll reach a kind of playground of sculptures and shrines, and a *shikra* that rejoices in the name of **Jyotirlingeshwar Mahadev**, freely translatable as "Great God of the Resplendent Phallus" – a reference to a myth in which Shiva challenges Brahma and Vishnu to find the end of his organ. Further west, where the street's brick cobbles temporarily give way to flagstones, the **Jaya Barahi Mandir** commemorates the *shakti* (consort) of Vishnu the boar; you have to stand well back from this broad edifice to see its pagoda roofs. Non-Hindus aren't barred from entering the upstairs sanctuary, but this intimate space wasn't designed for spectators.

Dark, damp alleys beckon on either side of the main road – north towards Durbar Square and south to the river. The most promising destination in this area is Kumale Tol, the **potters' square**, a sloping open space southwest of Taumadhi Tol. Although you may be buttonholed by the occasional potter's wife angling for a sale, for the most part this low-key production centre has few retail pretensions. The output here consists mainly of simple water vessels, stove pipes, disposable yoghurt pots and ever-popular piggy banks (called *kutrukke*: a word that imitates the sound of a coin being dropped in). For more decorative items, pay a visit to nearby Thimi, the valley's pottery capital – information on production processes is given in that section.

Tachapal Tol

From Taumadhi, the eastern segment of Bhaktapur's main artery snakes its way to the original and still-beating heart of the city, **Tachapal Tol**. Here again a pair of temples looms over the square, older than those of Taumadhi if not as eye-catching. More notably, though, Tachapal conceals Nepal's most celebrated masterpiece of woodcarving, the Pujari Math's Peacock Window, and a superb woodcarving museum. You'll also find the finest **woodwork studios** in Nepal here, which are well worth a browse, even if you haven't got room in your rucksack for an eight-foot, Rs50,000 peacock-window reproduction. Most pieces are made from *sal*, a rich, dark wood that's being systematically looted from the Tarai, so you'll have to wrestle with your conscience before buying.

Just north of Tachapal, a second open space around Ganesh Pokhri is equally busy with *pasal* (shops) and street vendors. South of the square is even better for exploring, as Bhaktapur's medieval backstreets spill down the steep slope to the river like tributaries.

Dattatreya and Bhimsen

Rearing up behind an angelic pillar-statue of Garud, the **Dattatreya Mandir** (accent on the second syllable) is Bhaktapur's oldest structure. The temple was raised in 1427 during the reign of Yaksha Malla, the last king to rule the valley from Bhaktapur, and like the Kasthamandap of Kathmandu, which it resembles, it was allegedly built from a single tree (the front portico was probably added later). Dattatreya, a sort of one-size-fits-all deity imported from southern India, epitomizes the religious "syncretism" (as anthropologists call it) that Nepal is famous for: to Vaishnavas Dattatreya is an incarnation of Vishnu, while Shaivas hail him as Shiva's guru and Buddhists even fit him into their pantheon as a *bodhisattva*. Christians need not feel left out – decorated with tinsel and ornaments, the idol calls to mind a Christmas tree.

The oblong temple at the opposite end of the square belongs to **Bhimsen**, the patron saint of Newar merchants, whose territory Tachapal is. As usual for a Bhimsen temple, the ground floor is open and the shrine is kept upstairs.

Pujari Math and Bhaktapur's museums

Behind and to the right of the Dattatreya temple stands the sumptuous eighteenth-century **Pujari Math**, one of a dozen priests' quarters (*math*) that once ringed Tachapal Tol. Given the nature of the caste system, perhaps it's not surprising that the grandest houses in the city traditionally belonged to priests. Similar to Buddhist *bahal*, these *math* typically sheltered communities of Hindu devotees loyal to a single leader or sect; and like *bahal*, most have now been converted to other, secular uses. The Pujari Math's awesome windows can be seen on two sides; the often-imitated **Peacock Window**, overlooking a narrow lane on the building's far (east) side, has for two centuries been acclaimed as the zenith of Nepalese window-lattice carving.

At all costs don't miss the small **Woodcarving Museum** (daily except Tues 10am–5pm, in winter closes 4pm; Rs5) inside the Pujari Math. Well displayed and lit, it enables you to inspect exquisite temple carvings that are often too high up to fully appreciate *in situ*. Highlights of the collection are an alluring Nartaki Devi of the fifteenth century, several magnificent steles and *torana*, and various abstractly weathered temple struts. The courtyard itself contains possibly the greatest concentration of woodcarving virtuosity in the country.

Somewhat misleadingly, the **Brass and Bronze Museum** (daily except Tues 10am–5pm; winter 10am–4pm; Rs5) across the square contains none of the flamboyant religious art that one might expect, consisting instead of household vessels and implements; for statues and the like, go to the National Museum in Kathmandu.

Nawa Durga Dyochhen and points east

North of Tachapal, the **Nawa Durga Dyochhen** looks like a haunted house, Nepali-style. A tantric temple only open to initiates, it honours the nine manifestations of Durga, who are especially feared and respected in Bhaktapur. According to legend, the Nawa Durga used to eat solitary travellers, turning the area east of Bhaktapur into a Bermuda triangle until a priest managed to cast a tantric spell on them. The Nawa Durga occupy a special place in Bhaktapur's spiritual landscape: the city is said to be delimited by symbolic Nawa Durga stones (*pitha*), and most *tol* (neighbourhoods) have adopted one of the nine as their protector goddess.

Most famous of all are the **Nawa Durga dancers**, a troupe whose members are drawn from the caste of flower sellers. Each wears a heavy painted clay mask which, empowered by tantric incantations, enables the wearer to become the very embodiment of the deity. Every September a new set of masks is moulded and painted, each with its own iconography – there are actually thirteen in all, the Nawa Durga plus four attendant deities. On Bijaya Dasami, the "victorious tenth day" of Dasain, the dancers and accompanying musicians gather at Brahmayani Pitha, about 1km east of town, and dance all the way to the Golden Gate, where they re-enact the legend of Durga's victory over a buffalo demon. The troupe is available for hire throughout the winter and spring wedding and festival seasons until the month of Bhadra (Aug–Sept), when their masks are formally retired and burned; the ashes are saved and added to clay to form the next year's masks.

East along the main road from Tachapal, the **Wakupati Narayan Mandir**, where local Jyapus worship Vishnu as a harvest god, displays no fewer than five Garuds mounted on pillars in a line.

The ghats and beyond

The Hanumante River is Bhaktapur's humble tributary of the River Ganga, its name deriving from the monkey god Hanuman who, locals like to think, stopped here for a drink on his way back from the Himalaya after gathering medicinal herbs to heal Ram's brother in an episode from the *Ramayan*. Several bathing and cremation ghats flank the river as it curls along the city's southern edge, although unfortunately there's no riverside path connecting them. The most active is **Hanuman Ghat**, located straight downhill from Tachapal Tol: morning *puja*, bathing and tooth-brushing are a daily routine for many, while old-timers come here just to hang out. A peaceful spot, the ghat packs an eyeful of cluttered *linga*, statues and trees into a small area; a priest is usually set up in front of the main Hanuman image to prescribe the Hindu equivalent of Hail Marys.

Downhill from Taumadhi Tol, **Chuping Ghat**'s array of temples and statuary is more of the mouldering-ruins school. The long, sloping area above the ghat is the focal point on New Year's Day (Nawa Barsa) in April, when a 25-metre *linga* pole is ceremonially toppled by the throng. **Ram Ghat**, below the potters' square, has little to offer beyond a run-of-the-mill Ram temple, but **Mangal Ghat**, further downstream, boasts a more atmospheric selection of neglected artefacts, and by following the trail of *linga* across the river you'll end up at a forbidding Kali temple in one of Bhaktapur's satellite villages.

Once south of the Hanumante, a ramble up to the densely forested ridge overlooking Bhaktapur might be in order, and **Surya Binayak** makes a worthy target. This most pleasantly situated of the valley's four main Ganesh shrines – catching the valley's first rays of sun – is reached by a steep, kilometre-long paved road from the trolley bus stop. The temple itself is just an ordinary plaster *shikra*, surrounded by usual Ganesh trappings; smeared with red *sindur* paste, the god's image looks like a warm fire in an ornate Victorian hearth. Ganesh is regarded as a divine trouble-shooter and this particular image specializes in curing children who are slow to walk or speak.

Practicalities

Although Bhaktapur is usually regarded as a day trip from Kathmandu, it has perfectly adequate facilities for an overnight stay – and you really ought to stay overnight to do the place justice.

Accommodation
Bhaktapur's **lodges** all fall into the budget category, and none of them has a compelling advantage over the others. Try to arrive as early as possible in the day. You might also consider staying up at Changu Narayan (see below).

Golden Gate Guest House, between Durbar and Taumadhi squares (☎610534). Bhaktapur's newest and cleanest, but rather cavernous. ③/B④.

Luna Guest House, north of Durbar Square (☎611262). Dumpy, but okay for the price. ②.

Shiva Guest House, overlooking the Pashupati Mandir in Durbar Square (☎610740). Good views and reasonably cheerful. ③.

Traditional Guest House, east of Durbar Square (☎611057). The walls are terribly thin, but the rooms are clean and the atmosphere is laid-back. B③.

Eating
Food is likewise basic, but sufficient. All the guest houses have their own restaurants serving the usual line-up, and there are plenty of cheap *bhojanalaya* and *bhatti* west of Durbar Square and around the bus park. If nothing else, you can always load up on thick, sweet yoghurt (Bhaktapur's "king of curds"), available by the clay pot or glass from local stalls at a fraction of the price charged in tourist restaurants. As for **nightlife**, forget it.

Bhaktapur Gate Restaurant, adjacent to *Golden Gate Guest House*. No atmosphere, but it serves palatable *kothe* and other pasta dishes.

Café de Peacock, in a former *math* overlooking Dattatreya Square. You can't beat the surroundings, but it's overpriced for what amounts to fairly primitive tourist grub.

Café Nyatapola, in a former temple in the middle of Taumadhi Tol. Another place with a great location and middling food.

Marco Polo Restaurant, overlooking Taumadhi Tol. More make-do fare, but a better bet for a main meal.

Rooftop Café, in *Shiva Guest House* overlooking Durbar Square. Unexciting tourist menu. It isn't actually on the roof, although it commands a fine vantage of the square.

Shopping
Bhaktapur's best buys are in **wood**: browse around the workshops along the south side of Dattatreya Square to get a feel for different styles, woods and techniques, then haggle for bargains with the traders along the lane that contains the Peacock Window. See *Basics* for more on what's available. Several shops around Durbar Square and Taumadhi sell quality **thangka**, and artists can often be seen painting them.

Nepalis recognize Bhaktapur for its traditional **textiles**, such as black and red *pataasi* material and black *Bhadgaonle topi*, formal headgear now worn mainly by old bureaucrats and government officials. Foreigners will be more attracted by the locally produced *dhaka* in original designs, as well as block-printed, quilted cotton items, *pashmina* shawls and Rajasthani-style tapestries.

Nawa Durga **puppets** and **masks** are widely sold in Bhaktapur, but they're cheaper in Thimi (see below) where they're made. Thimi is better for **pottery**, too.

Changu Narayan

Art and history buffs will get the most out of **CHANGU NARAYAN**, but this beautiful, tranquil site, reached by a delightful walk, is a must for anyone. Perched at the abrupt end of the ridge north of Bhaktapur, the ancient temple complex commands an extraordinary view of the valley in three directions – especially in late afternoon, when the meandering Manohara River turns into a golden ribbon. A basic guest house offers the prospect of staying overnight here, removed from the valley's noise and smog, and makes a potential stopover in a circuit to or from Nagarkot (see Chapter Three).

The site

"One remembers all the wealth of carving of the rest of the Valley," wrote Percival Landon in 1928, ". . . but when all is recalled it is probably to the shrine of Changu Narayan that one offers the palm. Perhaps one drives back home from Bhatgaon more full of thought than from any other expedition to the many out-lying places of this crowded centre of holiness and history and art." Protected by its remote location, Changu Narayan has changed little since Landon's day, with relatively few travellers, or even worshippers, making the effort to visit it. It is, on the face of it, just another pagoda, yet Changu Narayan's palpable age and its collection of the finest, oldest statues outside the National Museum seem to make it the archetypal Nepalese pagoda. Ideally, you should see it before you've burned out on the others.

The valley's **oldest Vaishnava site**, Changu Narayan's documented history goes back to the fourth century AD, and its sculptures attest to continuous worship here ever since. Some historians suspect an even greater antiquity, postu-lating that Changu Narayan and Swayambhu were built on the foundations of prehistoric animist shrines which originated when the valley floor was still under water. Changu is an ancient word meaning "shaking or swinging hill".

The **main temple**, rebuilt around 1700, stands in a quiet quadrangle of rest houses and pilgrims' shelters. A measure of the temple's importance is the exag-gerated size of the four traditional emblems of Vishnu – the wheel (*chakra*), conch (*sankha*), lotus (*padma*) and mace (*gada*) – mounted on pillars at its four corners. The brass repoussé work on the front (west side) of the building is as intricate as any you'll find in Nepal, as are the carved, painted struts supporting the roofs. The *torana* above the main door depicts Vishnu in his *sridhara* posture (see below), brandishing the four emblems in his four hands. A gold-plated seventh-century image of Vishnu is allegedly kept inside the sanctuary, but only the temple priests are allowed to view it. From time to time, the statue is said to sweat miraculously, indicating that Vishnu is battling with the *nag* spirits, and the cloth used to wipe the god's brow is considered a charm against snake bites. **Smaller temples** in the compound are dedicated to Lakshmi (the goddess of wealth, Vishnu's consort), Kali and Shiva.

The base of the *chakra* pillar bears the **oldest inscription** in the valley. Dated 454 AD and attributed to the Lichhavi king Manadeva, it relates how Manadeva, upon the death of his father, dissuaded his mother from committing sati by promising to conquer his foes to the east

The statues

The courtyard of Changu Narayan is an outdoor museum of priceless works of art, displayed in an almost offhand manner and all the more exciting for it. You'll find the oldest, famous statues grouped around the front of the temple (see map opposite) plus loads of other, more recent (but still centuries-old) pieces in the vicinity. With few exceptions, they all pertain to Vishnu or his faithful carrier, Garud.

Probably dating from the seventh or eighth centuries, Changu Narayan's celebrated statue of **Garud** kneels before the temple, looking human but for a pair of wings and a cobra scarf; he used to be mounted on a pillar, the broken base of which is lying just to his right. Garud's association with snakes is legendary. It's said that when his mother was kidnapped by his stepmother, Garud appealed to his serpentine stepbrothers to free her, which they did on condition that Garud brought them ambrosia from Indra's heaven. Although Indra later flew down and reclaimed his pot of nectar (leaving the snakes to split their tongues as they licked up the few drops spilt on the grass), Vishnu was so impressed that Garud hadn't been tempted to consume the ambrosia that he immediately hired him as his mount. The brass statues inside a screened cage next to Garud commemorate **King Bupathindra Malla** of Bhaktapur and his queen Bubana Lakshmi, who ruled during the late seventeenth and early eighteenth centuries.

Though damaged, the eighth-century image of **Vishnu Vishwarup** (Vishnu of the Universal Form) is an awesome example of Hindu psychedelia. The lower portion of this composite image shows Vishnu reclining on the snake of infinity in the ocean of existence, echoing the sleeping statues of Budhanilkantha and Balaju. Above, the god is portrayed rising from the waters before a heavenly host, his thousand heads and arms symbolizing sheer omnipotence. The latter image is borrowed from an episode in the *Mahabharat* in which the warrior Arjuna lost his nerve and Krishna (an incarnation of Vishnu) appeared in this universal form to dictate the entire *Bhagavad Gita* by way of encouragement.

Two notable statues rest on the platform of the Lakshmi Narayan temple. The eighth-century **Vishnu Trivikranta Murti**, Vishnu of the Three Strides, illustrates a much-loved story in which the god reclaimed the universe from the demon king Bali. Disguised as a dwarf (another of his ten incarnations), Vishnu petitioned Bali for a patch of ground where he could meditate, which need only be as far as the dwarf could cover in three strides; when Bali agreed, Vishnu grew to his full divine height and bounded over the earth, sky and heavens. (An even older version of this statue is held in the National Museum.) The adjacent eleventh- or twelfth-century image depicts Vishnu in yet another of his incarnations, that of the man-lion **Narasimha**.

At the northwest corner of the compound, the twelfth- or thirteenth-century **Vishnu Vaikunthanata** – reproduced on the Nepalese ten-rupee note – shows a purposeful Vishnu riding Garud like some sort of hip space traveller. Nearby stands a **Vishnu Sridhara** of the ninth or tenth century, an early example of what has since become a stereotypical Vishnu representation.

Getting there and back

You can approach the temple complex from Bhaktapur, the Sankhu road or Nagarkot – time permitting, the ideal itinerary is to walk from Nagarkot to Bhaktapur via Changu Narayan.

From Bhaktapur, an asphalted **road** forks off from the Nagarkot road about 200m east of the hilltop Mahakali shrine (see the main Bhaktapur map) and climbs right up to **Changu Gaun**, the village immediately east of the temple. The last 2km or so are too steep for a one-speed bike, though if you push up you can freewheel back down. Two **trails** set off from the north side of Bhaktapur towards Changu Narayan, but they soon converge, passing through rural villages before a steep ascent to reach the temple after 5km; the brick-paved, easternmost trail, which isn't indicated on the map, skirts the Mahakali shrine and a sleeping Vishnu water tank en route.

The **trail from the Sankhu road** is only 2km long, but it's hard to find at its lower end and the bridge over the Manohara River is only seasonal. Descending is no problem, although you'll probably end up walking halfway to Boudha before a minibus comes along to take you back to Kathmandu.

The ten-kilometre **hike from Nagarkot** should take two to three hours, and despite a few road crossings the route along the forested ridge is immensely satisfying, with great views all the way. Stick to the trail nearest the ridgeline; the only tricky part is where it dips down into a gap near the halfway mark and just grazes the Nagarkot road.

Accommodation and eating

Changu Narayan's only **accommodation** at the time of going to press is *Changu Narayan Hill Resort* (③/B④), located about 500m east of Changu Gaun, just above the road from Bhaktapur. Facilities are pretty minimal and arguably over-priced, but you pay for the solitude and the fantastic views of Gauri Shankar. It's like Nagarkot, only better: there aren't any other lodges (yet) and there's a proper temple to look at. Brace yourself for no electricity or hot water, however, and something of a language problem. Book through *Traditional Guest House* in Bhaktapur. **Camping** is also possible.

Even if you don't stay at the "resort", you can **eat** in the dining room – breakfast after a cycle up from Bhaktapur, perhaps, or lunch on the way down from Nagarkot. Snacks and drinks should also be available in or around the temple area.

Thimi

Squalid **THIMI**, the valley's fourth-largest town, lies on a plateau 4km west of Bhaktapur. The name is said to be a corruption of *chhemi*, meaning "capable people", a bit of flattery offered by Bhaktapur to make up for the fact that the town used to get mauled every time Bhaktapur picked a fight with Kathmandu or Patan. Its mainly Newar inhabitants are indeed very capable craftspeople, and Thimi is the place to go for papier mâché masks and pottery.

The Bhaktapur trolley bus will drop you off at the southern end of Thimi, but you'll get a far more favourable introduction by cycling in along the old road to Bhaktapur, which skirts the town to the north. Minibuses from Bhaktapur and Kathmandu's Ratna Park also ply this back route. Several **handicrafts shops** – Thimi's only real attraction – are located along the north road. The **papier mâché masks** seen all over Kathmandu are made in Thimi, and you can count on getting the best deal here. Snarling Bhairab, kindly Kumari and elephant-headed Ganesh are most commonly represented by the masks, which are based on those worn by Bhaktapur's Nawa Durga dancers. Nawa Durga **puppets**, again associated with Bhaktapur, are also made and sold here for a fraction of their usual price. Salt and pepper shakers in the shape of the king and queen are quasi-contraband items, and you have to ask for them specially – though expensive, they make great, offbeat mementoes (don't let customs officers see them).

Pottery is an even older local speciality, and you can watch potters at work in alleys and courtyards at the north end of town; the busiest times are autumn and winter, when it's not so hot and the firing process is safer. The manufacture of traditional vessels and tiles is still strong in Thimi, though many potters now also churn out candlesticks, elephant flower pots and the like. As more producers learn how much money they can make from selling these to tourists, the simpler items for local consumption may well fall by the wayside.

The remainder of Thimi is grotty and unglamorously primitive – it's one of the few places in the valley where poverty isn't offset by quaintness. Thimi's only temple of note is that of **Balkumari**, a sixteenth-century pagoda located near the southern end of the main north–south lane. Couples pray to the "Child Kumari" for babies, presenting her with coconuts as a symbol of fertility. Balkumari's vehicle is a peacock, which stands upon a nearby pillar. The temple is the focus of frenzied Bisket **festivities** in April, when dozens of deities are ferried around on palanquins and red powder (red being the colour of rejoicing) is thrown like confetti.

Throwing pots

THIMI'S POTTERS

Like their counterparts throughout Nepal, the **potters** (*kumal*) of Thimi employ low-tech techniques. The clay comes from flooded paddies, kneaded by hand. The solid wooden wheel – or, increasingly, a concrete-filled truck tyre – is literally hand-powered: spurning even a simple foot treadle, the potter uses a pole to spin the wheel to a dervish pitch, allowing four or five minutes' working time before the wheel gradually winds down to a slow wobble and needs to be cranked up again. The potter's creations – still grey at this stage – are set out in soldierly rows to dry in the sun for a day or two before firing. Kilns are uncommon. The usual procedure is to stack the vessels in an empty square, each layer packed with straw, sawdust or dung, then cover the mound with a coating of mud, and poke holes in the surface to let air in at just the right rate to sustain a slow burn. After being baked for a week or more, the wares will be ready for use – and bright red.

Bode

A small, tight-knit Newar community, **BODE** is built on a bluff overlooking the Manohara River, 1km north of Thimi. The village's main shrine, the **Mahalakshmi Mandir**, stands at the northwest corner of the village, a modest and not particularly well-maintained two-tiered pagoda. The goddess of wealth, Maha ("Great") Lakshmi is feted during a three-day festival beginning on New Year's Day (here called Baisakh Sankranti, meaning the first day of Baisakh – April 13 or 14). The highlight of the proceedings comes on the second day, when a volunteer has his tongue bored with a thin steel spike and, thus impaled and bearing a disc-shaped object with flaming torches mounted on it, accompanies the goddess as she's paraded around the village. Volunteers believe that they won't bleed if they've followed a prescribed three-day fast and have sufficient faith, and that by performing this act they'll go directly to heaven when they die.

festivals

Some of the festivals listed in the Kathmandu chapter are also celebrated in the valley. Again, most are reckoned by the lunar calendar, so check locally for exact dates.

MAGH (Jan–Feb)

Magh Sankranti The first day of *Magh* (Jan 14 or 15), marked by ritual bathing at Patan's Sankhamul Ghat; more bathing takes place at Sankhu on the day of the full moon of *Magh*.

FAAGUN (Feb–March)

Losar Tibetan New Year, celebrated at Boudha with processions, horn-blowing and *tsampa*-throwing on the big third day.

Shiva Raatri The Pashupatinath *mela* (fair) attracts tens of thousands of pilgrims and holy men, while children everywhere collect money for bonfires on "Shiva's Night".

BAISAKH (April–May)

Bisket Jaatra Bhaktapur's celebration of Nepali New Year (April 13 or 14), in which chariots are pulled around the city for several days and a *linga* pole is ceremonially toppled to mark the start of the new year. Thimi and Bode have their own idiosyncratic festivities.

Balaju Jaatra Ritual bathing at the Balaju Water Garden on the day of the full moon in April.

Machhendranath Rath Jaatra An amazing, uniquely Newar extravaganza in which an immense chariot is pulled through old Patan in stages over a period of several weeks.

ASAAR (June–July)

Dalai Lama's Birthday Observed informally at Boudha (July 6).

SAAUN (July–Aug)
Janai Purnima The annual changing of the sacred thread worn by high-caste Hindu men, involving bathing and splashing at Patan's Kumbeshwar Mahadev.

BHADAU (Aug–Sept)
Krishna Jayanti Krishna's birthday, marked by an all-night vigil at Patan's Krishna Mandir.
Gokarna Aunsi Nepali "Father's Day", observed at Gokarneswar with bathing and offerings.
Tij A day of ritual bathing for women, mainly at Pashupatinath.

KARTIK (Oct–Nov)
Haribondhini Ekadashi Bathing and *puja* at the Vishnu sites of Budhanilkantha, Sesh Narayan, Bishanku Narayan and Changu Narayan.

MANGSIR (Nov–Dec)
Bala Chaturdashi All-night vigil at Pashupatinath, involving candles and ritual seed-offerings to dead relatives.
Indriani Jaatra Deities are paraded through Kirtipur on palanquins.

travel details

As of early 1993, valley bus services were using several different departure points in Kathmandu as indicated here, but they may soon be consolidated at the former central bus park, on the east side of the Tudikhel.

BUSES AND MINIBUSES
From Kathmandu
Leaving from **Ratna Park** to Pashupatinath (frequent; 20min); Boudha (frequent; 30min); Sankhu (approximately 4 daily; 1hr); Sundarijal (4 daily; 1hr); Patan (frequent; 20min) and Tribhuwan University/Kirtipur (frequent; 30min).
Leaving from **Rani Pokhri** to Budhanilkantha (frequent; 30min) and Balaju (hourly; 20min).
Leaving from **Martyrs' Gate** to Patan (frequent; 15min) and to Dakshin Kali (approximately every 30min; 1hr).

Leaving from the **main bus park** to Bhaktapur (frequent; 45min) and Thimi (frequent; 30min).
The **trolley bus to Bhaktapur** leaves from Tripureswar (about every 15min; 45min).

From Patan
Leaving from **Lagankhel** to Thecho/Chapagaun (hourly; 20min); Godavari (hourly; 45min) and Bhaktapur (hourly; 45min).
Leaving from **Jaulakhel** to Bungamati/Khokana (2–3 daily; 20min).

From Bhaktapur
Leaving from **Sidha Pokhri** to Nagarkot (3 daily; 1hr).
Buses stop at the trolley bus terminal on their way to Banepa (24 daily; 45min); Dhulikhel (24 daily; 1hr 30min); Panauti (4 daily; 1hr) and Bharabise (6 daily; 4hr).

CHAPTER THREE

THE CENTRAL HILLS

Beyond the Kathmandu Valley, major roads meander in three directions, making the **central hills** the most accessible – though not necessarily the most travelled – section of Nepal's jumbled, 700-kilometre band of foothills. To the northeast, the **Arniko Rajmarg** (Arniko Highway) follows the old Kathmandu–Lhasa trade route through broad valleys and misty gorges to the Tibet border; northwestwards, the **Trisuli Road** snakes its way down into a subtropical valley nearly 1000m lower than Kathmandu; and south, the **Tribhuwan Rajpath**, Nepal's first highway, cuts a tortuous cross-section through the hills on its way to the Tarai. If the scenery here is a shade less dramatic than what you'll encounter further west, the land is nonetheless varied and rugged, tamed only in pockets by defiant terraces. It's only when you leave the Kathmandu Valley that you appreciate how atypical it is of this hilly region.

The majority of places described here can be treated as easy overnights from Kathmandu. The most popular are those that involve mountain views and hill-walking: **Nagarkot** and **Dhulikhel**, with well-developed budget accommodation, are acknowledged classics; **Kakani** is equally scenic, though lacking in cheap lodgings, and **Daman** is splendidly off the beaten track. These vantage points can't compare with what you'll see on a serious trek, but they come into their own in winter, when trekking can be a chilly business. Although cultural attractions are relatively few outside the Kathmandu Valley, **Panauti** and **Nuwakot** are among Nepal's most intriguing villages – all the more because they're so seldom visited – and whether or not the most alluring destination of all, Tibet, is open to independent travellers entering from this direction, the **border** still beckons.

To an extent, the boundaries of this chapter are dictated by travel formalities: towns and **day hikes** are described here, while backcountry areas requiring a trekking permit are saved for Chapter Seven. Despite a relative abundance of roads, **buses** in the central hills are slow and infrequent, and indeed few travellers brave them except to get to the start of the Langtang/Helambu and Everest treks. On the other hand, the region contains Nepal's most popular and rewarding **mountain-biking** destinations; an overview of the possibilities is given at the end of the chapter.

Nagarkot

Like many of Nepal's best highways, the road to **NAGARKOT** serves mainly strategic, not scenic, purposes: Nagarkot was originally developed as an army post, and tourist facilities came later, with government encouragement. Set on a ridge northeast of Bhaktapur at about 2000m, it commands a classic panorama of the Himalaya from Langtang Himal to Gauri Shankar, and on a good day you can see from Annapurna South to Everest. The best thing about Nagarkot is that you don't have to stay in an expensive hotel to get a view right out of your window. Hiking and mountain-biking routes up and back down are particularly worthwhile, although it has to be said that there's not much to do once you're here.

Nagarkot is often mentioned in the same breath as Dhulikhel, but chances are you'll only have time to visit one or the other. Be sure to read the Dhulikhel section later in this chapter before deciding.

Getting there – and back down again

The only public **buses** to Nagarkot depart from Bhaktapur's Sidha Pokhri (3 daily); if you're coming from Kathmandu, don't expect an instant connection. The *Galaxy* and *Viewpoint* run a direct **tourist minibus** from Kathmandu to Nagarkot each afternoon, departing from in front of Central Immigration and returning the next morning. Book through any ticket agent (the fare should be around Rs150 return).

Considerably more fun, however, is to walk up – or better yet, take a bus up and **walk back** the next morning. The main trail **to Changu Narayan** (see p.162), a two- or three-hour hike, descends from the *Tara Gaon Hill Resort*, recrossing the Nagarkot road after about 600m. If you're starting from the north end of the ridge, a more convenient trail leaves from the big hairpin turn below the lower bus stop and joins up with the main trail 1km later. From there you keep descending, paralleling the road and for a while walking right beside it, until the trail starts dropping into a notch – at which point you take a trail to the right and follow it along the wooded ridgeline to Changu Narayan. From there it's another hour down to Bhaktapur, or less to the Sankhu road.

If you're **cycling**, the logical itinerary is to ride up the main road to Nagarkot from Bhaktapur and return the back way to Sankhu; this allows you to take in Bhaktapur, Nagarkot, Sankhu and Boudha in a simple two-day ride. The ascent is

NAGARKOT

Sankhu

Green
Peace
Horizon

Niva Home

N

0   500 m

Bamboo Village
Peaceful
Cottage

New Pheasant
Lodge

Hotel Galaxy   Mahakal
Shrine

Pilgrim's
Lodge

Hotel Viewpoint

Hotel Mountain
Sunrise View

Cheese
Project

The Tea House

Changu Narayan

Sunrise
Moonbeam

Army Barrier

Nagarkot
Cottage

Hotel
Floral Hill

Bhaktapur

Tara Gaon

Lookout Tower
(no access)

consistently steep for the last 12km – the vertical gain is 650m – but paved all the way and agreeably devoid of traffic. The dirt road to Sankhu, which isn't marked on the *Schneider* map, is simply a continuation of the road past Nagarkot's northern lodges. It's very steep, rutted and good fun – vehicles can't use the track in its present state, although there are signs it might eventually be upgraded. Pedalling up it would be more challenging.

Orientation and accommodation

Erase from your mind any picture of a quaint hilltop village. There's no such town as Nagarkot – it's only a loose affiliation of lodges stretching for 2km along a cultivated ridgetop. The lodges at the plunging north end of the ridge – the ones with the best views – are reached along a dirt road that forks off to the left at the bus stop. Two landmarks in this vicinity are a tiny **Mahakal shrine** and a small-scale **cheese-making project**. The paved road continues south for another couple of kilometres to a lookout tower, which the army has lately closed off to the public, but ask locally whether it's been reopened, since it makes a great sunrise destination.

BUDGET LODGES
At the time of writing, electricity and hot water were available only at the places indicated, but by the time you read this electricity should have arrived in Nagarkot, and facilities (and prices) no doubt will have changed overnight. Unless you hear otherwise, though, bring a torch (flashlight), and in winter a sleeping bag. Views also are apt to change as new places are built in front of older ones, though it's not actually such a bad thing to have to hike a little bit to a viewpoint.

Bamboo Village. Robinson Crusoe-ish bamboo bungalows and a pleasant enough dining area; hike to views. ⑤.

Green Peace Horizon. Secluded bamboo huts in real *pukka* safari style, with great views. ⑤.

Hotel Galaxy. Slightly classier place with a less complete view. ⑤, with hot water ⑥.

Hotel Viewpoint (☎290870). Tidy brick bungalows and a smart glassed-in dining room; the view is marred by a godawful new skyscraper to one side, but still good. Electricity, hot water. ⑤.

New Pheasant Lodge. Bamboo huts, a bank of other rooms and the welcome "Restaurant at the End of the Universe" at the high point of the ridge. ④.

Niva Home. Unobstructed views, rather dingy facilities. Hot water. ③.

Peaceful Cottage (☎290877). Killer views, new glassed-in dining area. ④.

Sunrise Moonbeam. Rather forlorn and basic. ②.

MODERATELY PRICED PLACES
All the following have electricity, hot water and room heaters (or warm bedding), but except for *Nagarkot Farmhouse* they're short on views. Most will arrange transport from Kathmandu for you.

Club Himalaya Nagarkot Resort. Deluxe 50-room relative of the *Kathmandu Guest House*, planned for the present site of the *Tea House*.

Hotel Floral Hill (☎290863). Lifeless, overpriced and a 15-minute hike to views. B⑧.

Nagarkot Cottage (book through *Natraj Tours*: ☎222532). Rustic bungalows, but again it's a long walk to views. B⑥.

Nagarkot Farmhouse (book through *Hotel Vajra*: ☎272719), located a good 2km down from *Green Peace Horizon* (and off the map). Run by the same folks who brought you the excellent *Hotel Vajra* in Kathmandu. Emphasis on yoga and meditation. ⑦/B⑧.

Tara Gaon Hill Resort (☎211008). Nagarkot's original government-run outfit is a fair deal, despite befuddled service. Note that you have to walk from the army barrier or up the trail from below. B⑦, with discounts for longer stays.

Eating
Food at guest house dining rooms takes a long time to prepare and usually doesn't live up to expectations. But as in trekking lodges, mealtimes are lively social occasions with an intimate, we're-all-in-this-together energy. One reason for eating out might be the *Tea House*, which serves Nepali and Indian food and Western breakfasts in an upmarket atmosphere.

Banepa, Nala and Panauti

Leaving the Kathmandu Valley through a gap at its eastern edge, Nepal's only road to the Tibet border is officially known as the **Arniko Rajmarg** (Arniko Highway), appropriately named after the thirteenth-century Nepali architect who led a delegation to Beijing and taught the Chinese how to build pagodas. Three ancient Newar towns, which once comprised a short-lived independent kingdom, lie just east of the valley rim.

Loads of **buses** and minibuses ply the Arniko Highway as far as Banepa. However, it's much prettier and less stressful to ride a **mountain bike** from Bhaktapur, entering Nala from the east along a dirt road – see the *Schneider* map or similar. Another possibility would be to **walk** down from the summit of Phulchoki – again, you'll need a map (and the whole day).

Banepa

BANEPA, 26km east of Kathmandu, was for centuries an important staging post to Tibet, and now – such is progress – it's an obligatory pitstop for buses heading up the Arniko Highway. The roadside buildup is pretty unattractive, and unfortunately there's not much left of the old bazaar: a fire burned most of it down in the 1960s, and earthquakes have sorely weakened the rest. Cheap cotton cloth, woven here on semi-mechanized looms, is an important local industry. *Banepa Guest House*, near the main roundabout on the highway, is the only place to get a **room** (①) or a **full meal** in these three towns.

One kilometre northeast of town (take a right at the first roundabout), the three-tiered **Chandeshwari Mandir** overlooks a set of cremation ghats at the bottom of a wooded ravine, and is best known for the psychedelic fresco of Bhairab decorating its exterior. The temple commemorates Bhagwati, who according to one of the *purana* (Hindu scriptures) slew a giant called Chandashur here, earning her the title Chandeshwari ("Lord of Chand"). Her image is the object of a three-day **festival** here starting on the full moon of Baisakh (April–May).

Nala

It's a three-kilometre walk northwestwards along a gravel road from Banepa to **NALA**, a quiet, parochial village near the head of the meandering Punyamata Valley. Fanning out at the base of a hill, the classically Newar houses look like a landslide of bricks, frozen in mid-tumble. Nala's main temple, a seventeenth-century pagoda dedicated to Bhagwati, is unusual for having four tiers – even numbers are usually avoided as they're considered unlucky. The weathered image of eighteen-armed Bhagwati is ferried around on a chariot on the third day of Indra Jaatra.

From Nala you can continue west along a wide dirt track, passing a Lokeshwar temple on the outskirts of town, and reach Bhaktapur in 10km.

Panauti

More charming still, **PANAUTI** leads a sleepy, self-sufficient existence in its own small valley 7km south of Banepa. The most pleasant way to get there is by bike – the paved road from Banepa follows the lovely Punyamata Khola – or on foot from Dhulikhel, but there are also minibus services from Kathmandu, Bhaktapur and Banepa.

AROUND DHULIKHEL

To Nagarkot
To Bhaktapur
Nala
(1867 m)
Punyamata Khola
Chandeshwari Mandir
Banepa
To Bhaktapur
ARNIKO HIGHWAY
Himalayan Horizon Hotel
To the Tibet border
Hotel Gauri Shankar Mountain View
New Dhulikhel Lodge
Woodlands Mountain Tower Resort
Dhulikhel
Punyamata Khola
(1859 m)
Nawaranga Guest House
(1715 m)
Kali Temple
Shrikandapur
Kavre
Batase
(1751 m)
Panauti
Khware
Roshi Khola
Punyamata Khola
Sufhi Khola
Shanku
Namobuddha
0   1km

Wedged between the Punyamata and Roshi streams, Panauti forms the shape of a triangle, with a serpent (*nag*) idol standing at each of its three corners to protect against floods. Buses pull up at the newish northwest corner, but the oldest and most interesting sights are concentrated at the streams' confluence at the east end of town. Pride of place goes to the massive, three-tiered **Indreshwar Mahadev**, dedicated to Shiva, the "Lord of Indra" in several myths. Some authori-

Carving from the Indreshwar Mahadev

ties believe this to be the original temple (albeit restored) that was raised here in 1294, which would make it the oldest surviving pagoda in Nepal; the graceful and sensuous roof struts have been dated to the fourteenth century, although they may have been recycled. Unhappily, the building is showing its age, especially since the 1988 Dharan earthquake – which caused minor damage up to the edge of the Kathmandu Valley – shivered its timbers.

The shrine area at the sacred confluence, called the **Khware**, is one of those tranquil spots that can waylay a dreamer for hours. The large *sattal* (pilgrims' house) here, a favourite hangout for local pensioners, sports an eclectic range of frescoes depicting scenes from Hindu (and some Buddhist) mythology: Vishnu in cosmic sleep, Ram killing the ten-headed demon king Ravana, and even Krishna being chased up a tree by a pack of naked *gopi* (milkmaids). Krishna is the featured deity of the temple next door, too, where he's shown serenading his *gopi* groupies with a flute. Beside the river, the tombstone-shaped ramps laid into the ghats are where dying people are laid out, allowing their feet to be immersed in the water at the moment of death; on the opposite bank stands the recently restored seventeenth-century **Brahmayani Mandir**. The Khware has been regarded as a *tirtha*, a sacred power place, since ancient times, and on the first day of the month of Magh, which usually falls on January 14, it draws hundreds of people for ritual bathing.

Dhulikhel

A well-preserved town as well as a mountain viewpoint, **DHULIKHEL** can keep you occupied for days – especially if you're into walking or biking. It sits in a saddle 5km east of Banepa, just off the Arniko Highway, at the relatively low elevation of 1550m, which makes it warmer than Nagarkot. You get a restricted view of the Himalaya from several places around the town, but for the full vista you have to walk to a small nearby summit. But perhaps more than for its views, Dhulikhel is known as the customary starting point of **walks** to Namobuddha and Panauti.

Dhulikhel requires more effort to reach than Nagarkot, at least until some sort of tourist bus service starts up. Local **buses** (every half-hour from Kathmandu or from Bhaktapur's trolley bus stop) are exasperatingly slow. You can ask to be dropped off at any of the hotels along the highway, but for most of the cheap lodgings you'll want to stay on until the small **bus park**. It's a short walk from there to the main square at the new, east end of town – an unfortunately dismal introduction to Dhulikhel but straightforward for orientation.

Old Dhulikhel starts immediately to the west. A close, traditional Newar settlement of remarkable architectural consistency, it consists almost exclusively of four- and five-storey brick mansions, many with ornate wooden lattices in place

DHULIKHEL

of glass windows, affecting a stern, almost Victorian elegance. These huge houses are extended-family dwellings: some Dhulikhel clans number eighty or more members. The older buildings, which are only held together by mud mortar, show some fairly serious cracks from Kathmandu's infamous earthquake of 1934; Dhulikhel also experienced some damage during the 1988 quake centred near Dharan in the eastern Tarai. Wandering around Dhulikhel is basically a matter of following your nose (and occasionally holding your nose – some alleys are used as public latrines), but highlights include the central square of **Narayanthan**, containing a temple to Narayan and a smaller one to Harisiddhi (both emanations of Vishnu), and the **Bhagwati Mandir**, set at the high point of the village for a fine view of the mountains.

Be advised that the schoolchildren in Dhulikhel take a malevolent delight in taunting foreigners, and will sometimes even spit or throw stones. It's a game you cannot win – just don't betray any exasperation, and if you know any Nepali, tease them back.

Practicalities

In busy times you'd be wise to book ahead for a room, or at least arrive early in the day, as Dhulikhel's accommodation market is volatile. Facilities in the budget range are modest, but a handful of fancy new hotels are leading a general move upmarket. There's a **bank** just off the highway at the east end of town (Mon–Thurs & Sun 10.30am–2pm, Fri 10am–noon).

BUDGET LODGES

In 1990 Dhulikhel had just one budget lodge; in 1993 it had six (only four of which are worth mentioning). More may be in the offing, as the trusty *Dhulikhel Lodge* goes upmarket, but none of the new ones has quite got its act together yet. Time will tell how many of them survive.

BAHUNS, CHHETRIS AND OTHER HINDU CASTES

Nepal's human geography gets hideously confusing once you leave the Kathmandu Valley: over the course of millennia, waves of immigrants from Tibet and India have produced a complex overlay of cultures. Nearly half of all Nepalis are members of ethnic minorities and maintain distinct languages, customs and dress. The rest – the majority – are relative newcomers, descendants of Hindus who fled the Muslim conquest of northern India beginning in the twelfth century, or their converts. They are collectively referred to as **Parbatiyas** ("Hill-Dwellers") or, more generically, **Hindu castes**. In India, Hindus are divided into four primary castes, but nearly all the Hindu migrants to Nepal were of the two highest orders, Brahmans and Kshatriyas, who had the most to lose from the advance of Islam. These are sometimes called the "twice-born" castes, because males are symbolically "reborn" through an initiation rite at the age of thirteen and thereafter wear a sacred thread (*janai*), changed annually during the festival of Janai Purnima. Though originally only a small minority themselves, the refugee Hindus' high birth fuelled them with the ambition necessary to subjugate the rest, and in the process provide the country with much of its cultural framework, including its *lingua franca*, Nepali.

Although **Bahuns** (Brahmans) belong to the highest, priestly caste, they're not necessarily the wealthiest members of society, nor are they all priests. Most are farmers. Some are landlords and moneylenders, earning a reputation (by all accounts deserved) for subjecting their borrowers to crippling interest rates and swift foreclosures. Priests, who generally follow their fathers into the vocation, make a living administering rites for fixed fees. Most Brahmans observe a range of rules to maintain the purity of their caste (certain foods and alcohol are prohibited),

Dhulikhel Lodge, just off the main square (☎011/61114). The original and still the best – but slated to be replaced in 1994 by a pricier new facility (see below). Run by a large and likeable Shrestha family, it boasts peaceful garden seating, a retro-1960s dining room (cushions on the floor, leave your shoes at the door), passable food, hot running water and a phone (international calls possible) – but no view. ②.

Gauri Shankar Tara Bhanchha Ghar, on the main highway 2km east of Dhulikhel (Kathmandu office ☎224809). Nice view and flowery grounds, but rather isolated, and way overpriced for the primitive facilities. ④.

Hotel Gauri Shankar Mountain View, on the main highway – see the "Around Dhulikhel" map (Kathmandu office ☎220645). Excellent views from from the patio and the upstairs dining room, but overall the place lacks charisma. ④/B⑤, dorm beds ②.

Nawaranga Guest House, about 500m east of the main square – see the "Around Dhulikhel" map. Tolerable food, but uninviting rooms, and only one bathroom in the whole place (hot water by the bucket). Partial view from the roof. ②.

MODERATE AND EXPENSIVE HOTELS

Dhulikhel's more expensive lodgings keep their distance: three of the four listed here are built off the highway north and west of town, to take advantage of the views (refer to the "Around Dhulikhel" map). All can arrange transport from Kathmandu for a fee.

Dhulikhel Lodge (☎011/61114). Set for completion in 1994, it promises to be the *Kathmandu Guest House* of Dhulikhel. Expected to be ⑤/B⑦.

Dhulikhel Mountain Resort (☎011/61466; Kathmandu office ☎226799). Very scenic, private grounds with individual cottages, but nowhere near Dhulikhel – it's 4km beyond the town along the Arniko Highway. B⑧.

and orthodox Brahmans won't eat with lower castes or permit them to enter the house; orthodox women have it especially hard, as they have to keep strict seclusion during menstruation and for ten days after childbirth, when they're considered polluted.

The majority of Nepali Hindus are **Chhetris**, who correspond to Indian Kshatriyas, the caste of warriors and kings. While Nepali Brahmans usually claim pure bloodlines and exhibit the classic Aryan features of their caste, Chhetris are a more racially mixed lot and easily mistaken for members of other ethnic groups. Most of them are in fact the offspring of Hindus and the hill tribes they conquered, or of compliant hill dwellers who converted to Hinduism and were made honorary Chhetris: in the early days, Brahmans were willing to bend the rules to gain allies. Those of pure Kshatriya blood – notably the aristocratic Thakuri subcaste of the far west, who are related to the king – can be as twitchy about caste regulations as Brahmans. Significantly, it was a Chhetri who unified Nepal and gave the country its abiding martial character, and the old warrior-caste mentality remains a key in understanding the politics of modern Nepal, for Chhetris occupy the palace and command the army to this day.

India's two lower castes, Vaisyas (traders and farmers) and Sudras (menials) aren't really acknowledged in hill Nepal: indigenous Nepalis who would have fallen into these categories saw no advantage in becoming part of the caste system, and simply retained their ethnic affiliation. Those whose professions would have branded them as untouchables – leather-workers, blacksmiths, tailors and so on – obviously did the same. To orthodox Hindus these **occupational castes** still carry the threat of ritual pollution, but untouchability of the kind seen in India isn't observed in Nepal's more open social order.

Himalayan Horizon Hotel (☎011/61296; Kathmandu office: ☎225092). Attractive Newar-style buildings, spectacular back terrace. B⑧.
Woodlands Mountain Tower Resort (Kathmandu office ☎220123). Under construction in early 1993. Will be five-star, with a revolving tower restaurant.

EATING
Dhulikhel has no tourist **restaurants**, other than those attached to guest houses and hotels. Of the cheapies, *Dhulikhel Guest House* does the best food, though the *Nawaranga* has convenience going for it if you're looking for breakfast or lunch after a hard morning's mountain-viewing. Any of the hotel restaurants would be worth a splurge. For simple Nepali fast food, try the places around the bus park, or in the bazaar area east of the *Nawaranga*.

The sunrise walk
The done thing in Dhulikhel is to hike to the high point southeast of town in time for sunrise over the peaks. To get to the top, take the road leading east from the *Dhulikhel Lodge* until the pavement ends, then bear right and follow a gullied path straight up the hill; you'll need to allow about 45 minutes altogether. The peaks from Annapurna to (supposedly) Everest are visible from the summit (1715m), which is marked by a small **Kali Shrine**, and the sight of Dhulikhel's brick houses, salmon in the dawn light and perhaps wreathed in mist, is pretty special, too. If you're running behind schedule or otherwise flagging, the view from the playing field near the end of the paved road might suffice.

On the way back down you can call in at a small, mossy temple complex, hidden down a flagstone path where the paved road gives out. The main **Shiva temple** contains a large bronze *linga*; the adjacent **Ram temple**'s marble statues have been lopped off at the ankles by temple-robbers – a persistent problem in Nepal, and one that's not helped by demand for such treasures from foreign collectors.

To Namobuddha

Dhulikhel Lodge has elevated the so-called **Namobuddha circuit** into something of an institution, and almost everyone who stays there ends up doing it. The walk has perhaps been overhyped, although it remains a fine introduction to the byways of rural hill Nepal. With the rapid construction of roads and grading of paths in the area, it's actually much more exciting for **mountain biking** than walking.

The full circuit takes five or six hours to complete, and tea is available at villages along the way, but you should bring food. There's no point in describing the route here – just ask at *Dhulikhel Lodge* and they'll give you a sketch **map**, complete with landmarks and walking times. It's worth trying to combine Namobuddha with a sunrise walk to the Kali shrine, since the latter is on the way, although this requires a degree of organization that most people won't be able to manage first thing in the morning.

NAMOBUDDHA (or **NAMRO**) itself won't detain you for long, although to Tibetans* it ranks right up there in the hierarchy of holy sites in Nepal. About two and a half hours south of Dhulikhel on foot, the stupa rests on a red-earth ledge near the top of a jungly ridge. It's like a hick version of Swayambhu – smaller and pretty uneventful, except during the February–March pilgrimage season, when Tibetans and Bhotiyas arrive by the vanload to circumambulate it. Among the houses surrounding the stupa is a dinky Tamang *gompa*, which you can enter. A trail leads up to a bigger Tibetan *gompa* on top of the prayer-flag-festooned ridge behind, and in one of the outbuildings is preserved a famous stone relief **sculpture** depicting the legend of Namobuddha. According to the fable, the Buddha, in one of his previous lives as a hunter, encountered a starving tigress and her cubs here, and moved by compassion, offered his own flesh to her, a sacrifice that helped pave the way for his eventual rebirth as the historical Buddha. The stupa is supposed to contain the hunter's bones and hair.

To Panauti

Although the *Dhulikhel Lodge*'s map recommends returning to Dhulikhel by a different route, carrying on **to Panauti** from Namobuddha is equally enjoyable. The Panauti trail veers off to the left at Shanku – a sign points the way in English – and enters Panauti from the east after about an hour and a half. From there you can catch a minibus to Kathmandu or back to Dhulikhel (with a change at Banepa).

A more direct route leaves from just behind the statue in Dhulikhel's main square, passing through terraced fields and the village of Chaukot before joining the paved Banepa–Panauti road after about an hour. It's then another hour's walk along the road to Panauti.

---

*Foreign pilgrims are getting in on the act, too. A retreat centre for overseas groups has been built on a nearby hill, and *Insight Guides* supremo Hans Hoefer is building himself a Third World palace in the area.

To Jiri and the Tibet border

Traffic along the **Arniko Highway** (Arniko Rajmarg) drops off drastically beyond Dhulikhel. Built by the Chinese in the mid-1960s – to India's great distress – the road was once a busy conduit for lorry loads of Chinese goods by way of Lhasa, but landslides north of the border have slowed trade to a trickle. Tour groups enter Tibet this way, and indications are that the border will soon be opened to individual travellers as well.

However, the vast majority of travellers passing this way are bound for Jiri, the starting point of treks in the Everest region, located on a tortuous side road off the Arniko Highway. Public transport along the highway north of the Jiri turning is unreliable on account of the poor state of the road. There are no views of the high peaks along the Arniko Highway past Dhulikhel, and only fleeting ones from the Jiri road.

After Dhulikhel, the road drops 600m into the broad Panchkhal Valley, a lush, irrigated plain cultivated with rice paddy, sugar cane and tropical fruits. The village of Panchkhal is a springboard for treks in the Helambu region. The highway reaches its lowest (and hottest) point 29km beyond Dhulikhel at **DOLALGHAT** (634m), a small market town clumped at either end of the bridge across the impressively vast and braided Indrawati River. Rafting parties put in here for the ten-day trip on the Sun Kosi, which joins the Indrawati just around the corner, and a new *Sun Koshi River Resort* is due to open here in late 1993. **Chautara**, high on the ridge to the north, is the headquarters of a big Australian reforestation project.

The scenery changes abruptly after Dolalghat, as the highway bends northeast-wards up the deep, terraced **Sun Kosi Valley**. Nepal's terraces, while they're marvellous feats of engineering, are a sign of agricultural desperation: with so little flat land available and a growing number of mouths to feed, hill people have no choice but to farm ever steeper and less productive slopes. Terraces make good farming and environmental sense – they stabilize the topsoil and form a stopgap against erosion on deforested slopes – but maintaining them is a tremendously labour-intensive chore that detracts from the actual business of growing food, and building more terraces inevitably brings about further deforestation.

The Jiri road

Kathmandu to Jiri is a wretched bus journey, taking anything up to thirteen hours to cover just 190km. Be wary if stowing luggage on the roof, as there have been reports of thefts along this route.

The **Jiri road** breaks off from the Arniko Highway at the 78-kilometre mark, passing close to a hydroelectric station built by the Chinese. The road climbs a merciless 1800m out of the Sun Kosi Valley, reaching an elevation of 2540m, then contours around two more small basins to the Newar pitstop of Charikot, from which it's a long descent to the Tamba Kosi (800m), a steep climb to a forested ridge (2500m) and finally a dip into the Jiri Valley at 1900m. Completed in 1985, the road was financed by the Swiss government to provide easier access to their long-term development works at Jiri. The presence of these Australian, Chinese

---

TAMANGS

Tamangs dominate Nepal's central hills between about 1500m and 2000m and constitute, numerically, the country's largest ethnic group: about one in every five Nepalis is a Tamang. The tribe is thought to have originated in Tibet and migrated south in prehistoric times, which accounts for their Mongoloid features but leaves the significance of their name, which means "horse trader" in Tibetan, intriguingly unexplained. Tamangs follow a form of Buddhism virtually indistinguishable from Lamaism – religious texts are even written in Tibetan script – but they also worship clan deities, employ *jhankri* (shamans) and observe major Hindu festivals.

Despite their numbers, Tamangs are Nepal's most **exploited** people, and have been ever since the Gorkhali conquest of the late eighteenth century. Geography has been the Tamangs' downfall. The new rulers of Nepal, requiring land to grant to their victorious soldiers, arbitrarily appropriated much of the vast Tamang homeland surrounding the Kathmandu Valley. Wrested from their lands, Tamangs became tenant farmers or bonded labourers for their new masters, or freelanced as porters or woodcutters. Many drifted down to the Kathmandu Valley, to fetch and carry for the new aristocracy. So efficiently did the Tamangs carry out these menial functions that the government came to view them as a strategic asset and prohibited them from serving in the Gurkha regiments. More recently, Tamangs are being deprived of another source of income – woodcutting – due to deforestation and the closing off of the Shivpuri Watershed.

Lacking land and opportunities, the Tamangs remain at the bottom rung of the economic ladder. They are the porters, the riksha drivers, the *thela gada* (cart pullers) of Kathmandu. They comprise an estimated 75 percent of the carpet industry's work force, and create many of the *thangka* and other "Tibetan" crafts sold in Nepal – for contract wages, of course. Tamang boys are lured to the capital to work as *kanchha* (tea boys), and Tamang girls are prime targets for brokers in the flesh trade. Surveys show a disproportionate number of prison inmates in Nepal are Tamangs. A silent underclass in their own homeland, Tamangs often compare themselves to another displaced group, the Tibetans – only nowadays even the Tibetans are the Tamangs' bosses.

and Swiss projects isn't unusual in the Nepalese hills, although as you approach the Everest region you'll be struck by how the most beautiful places often seem to attract the greatest number of aid workers.

Jiri

Once an insignificant hamlet, **JIRI** has somehow been singled out by fate and politicians to receive a booster shot of Western charity. Charlie Pye-Smith, in his book *Travels in Nepal*, has called Jiri "the half-caste offspring of an impoverished Nepalese mother and a wealthy Swiss father". In 1958 the Swiss established the Jiri Multi-Purpose Development Project, a ground-breaking scheme based on the now widely accepted view that development needs – health, agriculture, education and so on – are interrelated and can't be tackled separately. The programme established a hospital, technical school, experimental farm and other facilities; some have since been handed over to HMG, and their subsequent deterioration raises troubling questions about development in Nepal (see *Contexts*). The road, in turn, has transformed Jiri into a busy little boomtown, where lorries constantly drop off supply shipments and porters assemble to carry them on to hill villages (it has all but put nearby **Those**, once the area's main bazaar and an important iron-smithing centre, out of business). Trekkers obviously add a few pennies to the local economy, although most are too eager to hit the trail or get back to Kathmandu to spend more than a night here.

At least a dozen **lodges** jostle on either side of the main street – *Cherdung Lodge and Valley Restaurant* (①) is comfortable enough, with a reasonable choice of food. Shops in the bazaar flog some trekker-oriented food and even rent clothing, although prices are naturally higher than in Kathmandu. Book **return bus tickets** from the hut halfway down the main street on the same side as the *Cherdung* – tickets go on sale at 6pm for the following day, and you need to queue up early.

To the border

Back on the Arniko Highway, 2km past the Jiri turning, Lamosangu (740m) is distinguished by a magnesite processing plant and a wasteland of castings. **BARHABISE**, 8km north, is as far as most buses from Kathmandu go. The highway and electricity have turned Barhabise, like Jiri, into an uncharismatic clutter of tall, slapdash buildings and shops selling cassette tapes and readymade clothes. Several lodges let cheap rooms and serve noodles and *daal bhaat*. North of town you can visit a small mill producing traditional Nepali paper, which is often confused with rice paper but is actually made from the bark of the native *daphne* bush. The pavement ends north of Barhabise and the steep gradient to the border begins a few kilometres later. As dirt roads go, this one is pretty well engineered, but it does its best to self-destruct with each monsoon. Afternoon rain is common up here, even in the dry season, and despite a general scarcity of trees near the river (here called the **Bhote Kosi**), everything is intensely green, with waterfalls splashing down cliff faces at every turn. The gorge is much deeper than it looks from the road.

Buses and minibuses make sporadic runs from Barhabise to Tatopani, 23km further on. Most passengers are bound for Khasa, the first town in Tibet, which is as far as Nepalis can go without travel documents, to do a little innocent **smuggling**. They return the same day, after dark, laden with milk powder, Chinese training shoes and bolts of linen – all of which are considerably cheaper on the

Tibetan side – and attempt to sneak them past the customs checkpost just south of Tatopani. If someone asks you to stow a bag of white powder in your rucksack "for a few minutes", it's probably only milk.

Tatopani
Ten years ago, **TATOPANI** (1530m) enjoyed a small following among Westerners, who came to gaze into Tibet and soak in the village's hot springs (*taato paani* means "hot water"), but has fallen out of fashion now that Tibet is occupied and the Arniko Highway has gone to hell. It remains a quiet, relaxing place – probably too dull for most, but a real find if you're into offbeat locales.

The village stretches along the highway for at least a kilometre, in two parts. Tamangs are in the majority at this altitude, and they maintain a small **gompa** five minutes' walk above the southern bazaar. The building is modest, but it looks out on a fine view of the valley and, up at the head of it, a smidgen of Tibet. The **hot springs** are at the northern end of the village, behind a wooden entrance and down steps towards the river. A hot tub it's not: the water splashes out of pipes into a concrete pool and is used strictly for washing. If you take the waters, remember that nudity offends in Nepal.

Western menus have all disappeared, but a few **lodges** limp on from the good old days. *Kesang Lodge* (①), near the north end, is friendly. Hints of China's near-ness are everywhere: you'll see chopsticks and Thermos flasks in every kitchen, and some places even sell Tsingtao beer.

Kodari and the border
Disabuse yourself of any visions of high, snowy passes into Tibet. The border village of **KODARI** (1640m), 3km on from Tatopani, is just another bedraggled roadside bazaar at the bottom of a deep valley, with nary a yak in sight. The lowest point along the Nepal–Tibet border, Kodari has always been the preferred crossing for traders between Kathmandu and Lhasa. Its balmy elevation isn't so extraordinary as it might seem, though: the main Himalayan chain, which the border generally follows, is breached in several places by rivers that are older than the mountains themselves (the watershed, in fact, runs not along the highest peaks but as much as 100km to the north). In the case of Kodari, the border was actually shifted further south after an ill-advised war with Tibet in 1792.

Shared **taxis** ply between Tatopani and Kodari, and some buses occasionally make it up here. Another long, drawn-out bazaar, Kodari is the Nepali equivalent of a service strip along a highway bypass, while old Kodari, a scattered village with a small *gompa*, perches on the ridge above. Bunk **accommodation** is available at a few lodges along the road. Tatopani is the better bet, but if you're cross-ing into Tibet you'll want to stay here to get an early start.

The border is marked by the so-called **Friendship Bridge**, which spans the Bhote Kosi at the top end of town, guarded at either end by lackadaisical Nepali and Chinese soldiers. Up at the head of the valley, 600m higher than Kodari, the Chinese buildings of **Khasa** (or Dzongmu) cling to the side of a mountain – that's the extent of the view of Tibet from here.

Should you be **crossing the border**, the 9km between the Kodari and Khasa immigration posts is a no-man's-land which when the road isn't washed out will be traversed by some sort of shuttle vehicle. When the road is closed, you'll have to walk; you can hire a porter to carry your pack for about Rs100. If you were wondering how all that pink Chinese toilet paper gets to Kathmandu, here's your answer. Remember that Tibet is two hours and fifteen minutes ahead of Nepal, so you have to set off early to catch the bank in Khasa before it closes. If you're entering Nepal from Khasa, set off as early as possible – it's a very full day's journey to Kathmandu.

The Trisuli road

One of Nepal's earliest forays into road-building, the **Trisuli Road** was constructed in the mid-1960s as part of a hydroelectric scheme on the Trisuli River, northwest of Kathmandu. That's the official story, anyway, although the road probably owes its existence as much to historical nostalgia as progress: the route retraces the triumphal approach of Prithvi Narayan Shah, founding father of Nepal, from his fortress of Nuwakot to the Kathmandu Valley two centuries ago. It's since been extended north to a mining area in the Ganesh Himal. The majority of travellers passing this way are only concerned about getting to Dhunche, the usual starting point for treks to Langtang and Gosainkund, yet Nuwakot is sorely underrated as a stopover, and Kakani makes a serviceable destination in itself.

Some **buses** from Kathmandu go all the way to Dhunche, but you might have to change at Trisuli Bazaar. (Foreigners need a trekking permit to travel to Dhunche, which is why it's covered in the trekking chapter.)

Kakani
KAKANI (*Kaa*-kuh-nee), the closest mountain viewpoint to Kathmandu, straddles the Kathmandu Valley's northwest rim at an elevation of 2070m. Like Nagarkot, Kakani is essentially a tourist invention, as opposed to a town, with a view but not much else. Unlike Nagarkot, it has only one hotel, and it's not cheap – but you don't necessarily have to spend the night.

Weaving a *doko*

Trisuli-bound **buses** drop you off at the pass west of Kakani. From there, follow a side road signposted "Telecom Repeater Station" for 3km (there are shortcuts), passing a large army barracks en route. In the days of Prithvi Narayan Shah, the Kakani pass was the Kathmandu Valley's Achilles' heel – by controlling it, he was able to besiege the valley for two years – but this hilltop post, like the one at Nagarkot, now seems a quaint throwback to the days of hand-to-hand combat. If you get to Kakani early enough, you can **walk back** to Balaju in three or four hours. Follow the dirt road east from Kakani past an agricultural station, then contour beneath the ridge through thick oak and rhododendron forest before bending south and down along a spur (great views); after passing a set of stupas, look for a fork to the left leading to Dharamthali and Balaju. **By mountain bike**, you can cycle up via Budhanilkantha (see Chapter Two) and back down along the Trisuli Road or vice versa.

Kakani's only **accommodation** is the *Kakani Tara Gaon Resort* (☎228222; B⑦, discounts for stays of more than one night), a bit dishevelled but featuring a marvellous back lawn where you can lounge like a sahib, with the Ganesh and Langtang Himals splashed across the horizon and the Likhu Khola coursing through the valley 1000m below. Even if you're not staying, they serve palatable lunches at a fair price. The yellow building next door is the former British Ambassador's bungalow, whose grounds once boasted a miniature golf course.

Trisuli Bazaar

TRISULI BAZAAR (540m) is 17km from Kathmandu as the crow flies, or 70km – and at least four hours – as the bus crawls. Curled at the bottom of a deep, subtropical (and once malarial) valley, it was put on the map by the construction of the Trisuli River hydroelectric project and flourished for a time as the trailhead for Langtang treks. The development bandwagon has moved on, and nowadays most trekkers don't stop in Trisuli for longer than it takes to swill a bottle of Coke and board the bus to Dhunche. Indeed, there's little to see in this ramshackle township, with the possible exception of the old, stair-stepped **bazaar** (reached through a passage at the west end of the bridge) and a small **stupa** perched above the opposite bank. That said, staying overnight at Trisuli permits a visit to nearby Nuwakot, which, if you find yourself with an extra day at the end of a trek, is a good deal more enjoyable than killing time in Dhunche or returning to Kathmandu early. The trek to Gorkha and Pokhara begins here, following the lovely Samri Khola to the west.

For **accommodation**, several lodges on the west side of the river offer ① rooms – their names change often and there's little to distinguish one from another. To return to Kathmandu, **ticket offices** for both private and *Sajha* buses are located across the street from the lodges (*Sajha* buses are faster).

Nuwakot

One of Nepal's proudest historical monuments, Prithvi Narayan Shah's abandoned fortress looms like a forgotten shipwreck on a ridge above Trisuli, casting a poignant, almost romantic spell over the tiny village of NUWAKOT. The **walk** from Trisuli takes less than an hour, although the trail is a tad tricky to find: climb a flight of steps from the water tap near the east side of the Trisuli Bazaar bridge to the Dhunche Road, walk up the road for about two minutes and make a right at the first group of houses. The path becomes wide and eroded as it climbs through a spindly forest of *sal* trees – their leaves are gathered to make traditional biodegradable leaf plates – and reaches Nuwakot on the crest of a ridge about 300m above the valley floor. To **cycle**, take the dirt road that leaves the main road about 1km south of Trisuli.

The **fortress** stands to the right as you enter the village, consisting of three brick towers rising like Monopoly hotels within a walled compound: the tallest one is open to the public, though you may have to track down the caretaker to unlock it for you. The views from the top-floor windows are stupendous, looking out on Ganesh Himal and the pastoral Trisuli and Tadi valleys.

It was from this command centre that **Prithvi Narayan Shah**, the unifier of Nepal, directed his dogged campaign on the Kathmandu Valley from 1744 to 1769, and gazing out through these windows you can gain some insight into the mind of this obsessive but brilliant military tactician. In his determination to conquer the valley, Prithvi Narayan had **three other towers** built in the name of the three valley capitals, perhaps hoping to bring about their downfall by a kind of voodoo; the Kathmandu and Patan towers share the main compound, while the crumbling Bhaktapur tower stands on a rise just outside. After Kathmandu's fall, Nuwakot had just one more moment in the limelight. In 1792, attempting to extend Nepal's territory into Tibet, Prithvi Narayan's successor pushed his luck too far and was driven all the way back to Betrawati, the next village north of Trisuli. In the resulting **peace treaty**, signed at Nuwakot, Nepal ceded to Tibet the lucrative trading posts of Kyirong (north of Trisuli) and Khasa (north of Kodari), accounting for two southward lunges in the border that remain to this day.

Nuwakot's old main street runs south from the fortress along the spine of the ridge and suddenly dead-ends, the land falling away to reveal a vast **panorama** of the Tadi and Trisuli valleys. In the late eighteenth century, when Nuwakot enjoyed a brief flowering as the winter residence of the Kathmandu court, the houses along this boulevard must have looked considerably posher. The only building of note now is a two-tiered **Bhairabi Mandir**, which hosts a festival in honour of Bagh Bhairab in April.

The Tribhuwan Rajpath

Nepal's most magnificent and hair-raising highway, the **Tribhuwan Rajpath** (usually just called the Rajpath) heads west out of the Kathmandu Valley and then hurls itself, through an astounding series of switchbacks, straight over the Mahabharat Lekh to the Tarai. En route it passes through lush stands of rhododendron and takes in superb views of the Himalaya. Mountain bikers regard the road, culminating at the incredible Daman view tower, as something of a holy pilgrimage.

THE TRIBHUWAN
RAJPATH

0   5 km

N

Pokhara

Mahesh Khola

PRITHVI HIGHWAY

Naubise
(945m)

Kathmandu

Aagara Khola

Tistung
(2030m)

TRIBHUWAN RAJPATH

Palung
(1745m)

Daman
(2322m)

(2596m)

(2244m)

Mahabharat

Sim Bhanjyang
(2488m)

Lekh

Khulekani Khola

Mahabir

Manahari Khola

Lamidanda
(1400m)

Bhimphedi

Chuniya

Kaliktar

(2505m)

Narayanghat

MAHENDRA HIGHWAY

TRIBHUWAN RAJPATH

Suparitar

Rapti River

MAHENDRA HIGHWAY

Hetauda
(420m)

Samari Khola

Birganj

Built by Indian engineers in the mid-1950s, the Rajpath was the first highway to link Kathmandu to the outside world – before that, VIPs were carried to the capital by palanquin, and the prime ministers' automobiles had to be portered from India, fully assembled, by 200-strong teams of coolies. Since the construction of the Narayanghat–Mugling road, however, most drivers prefer to miss out the harrowing Rajpath and go the long way around.

The few travellers who come this way generally do it by **mountain bike**, and generally from the Kathmandu side. It's a magnificent, exhilarating but (make no mistake about it) shattering all-day ride to Daman. You'll save yourself a lot of agony by taking a bus as far as Naubise, cutting out the busiest and least interesting stretch – any bus heading to Pokhara or the Tarai will stop there. Pedalling back up from the Tarai involves a really hard-core climb. Keep an eye out for approaching trucks, as the road is narrow and many corners are blind. Only one **bus** a day (*Sajha*) travels along the Rajpath in each direction, taking about eight hours to cover 133km (several night buses also make the journey, but you'd have to have a real death wish to take one). Failing that, a slower alternative is to hitch a ride with one of the many **trucks** ferrying wood and fuel to the capital; they take on passengers for the return journey at Kalimati in south Kathmandu.

Kathmandu to Daman

For its first 26km, the Rajpath follows the upgraded (and heavily used) Prithvi Highway towards Pokhara. Leaving the Kathmandu Valley through its most industrial corridor, it slips through a low point in the rim and descends to **NAUBISE** (945m), near the bottom of the deep, wrinkled Mahesh Khola Valley. Nepali restaurants are plentiful in Naubise; few places have rooms, but you should be able to find something in the ①–② range.

At Naubise the Rajpath leaves the Prithvi Highway and forks off to the left, climbing 34km to Tistung (2030m) before descending to **PALUNG** at 1745m, a Newar village spread out amid tidy terraces (potatoes and spinach – *paalung* – are a local speciality). Very basic food and lodging can be arranged here, but unless you're desperate it's worth toiling up the final, tough 11km to spend the night in Daman. A hardy cyclist could avoid some backtracking by heading south along the dirt road from Palung to Bhimphedi, which rejoins the Rajpath 10km north of Hetauda, and returning to Kathmandu via Daman.

Daman

With fantastic views and a ramshackle viewtower-cum-lodge, **DAMAN** (2322m) has had a cult following among the fat-tyre fraternity for years. Sitting just below the Rajpath's highest point, the hamlet – it's just a cluster of houses and a couple of agricultural research stations – overlooks the peaceful Palung Valley to a magnificent spread of peaks, notably Himalchuli, Ganesh Himal and Langtang.

Technical difficulties

MOUNTAIN-BIKING: HOW, WHAT, WHERE AND WHEN

Nepal was made for **mountain bikes**: the roads are uncrowded and spectacular, the cycling is challenging, and the alternative – buses – is unpleasant. On a bike you can stop where you like, enjoy the scenery, make detours, amaze the locals, and reach your destination in as little as twice the time it takes by bus. A degree of fitness is required, but if you can handle a *Hero* you'll have no trouble with a mountain bike. Tips on renting a bike and bringing your own are given in the "Getting Around" and "Outdoor Pursuits" sections of *Basics*.

The table opposite should help you find a **route** that's about your speed. Bear in mind that you don't have to pedal all the way back to where you started – a lot of people ride down to the Tarai and take a bus back, avoiding a busy stretch of road and a lot of uphill. Don't bike the Prithvi Highway: there's just too much traffic. If you're more adventurous, the possibilities for exploring off the beaten track, especially in the Tarai, are almost unlimited. **Cycle trekking** is yet another option, though one likely to appeal only to the most hard-core gear-wallahs: riding a mountain bike on trekking trails requires great technical skill, and entails carrying the bike a good deal of the time (cycle trekkers rate trails according to the percentage of carrying they require). If you do it, be sure to give other people and livestock priority on the trail. Likely spots for cycle trekking include Helambu and the Trisuli–Gorkha–Pokhara trail; mountain bikes aren't allowed in Langtang and Sagarmatha (Everest) national parks, and the Annapurna region is considered only marginally cyclable.

If you can't be bothered with logistics, join a **cycle tour**. Prices are comparable to organized treks, as are the pros and cons – you can count on good food, reliable equipment, companionship whether you want it or not, and a certain loss of freedom. See p.103 for a list of tour companies in Kathmandu.

However you get here, the mountains will probably be in clouds when you arrive: an overnight stay is obligatory to see them in their best morning light, and you may well want to stay a second night. Continuing along the Rajpath, the daily *Sajha* **buses** to Kathmandu and Hetauda stop at Daman at around 10 or 11am, but they're apt to be full and might not even stop (that's when you might have to flag down a truck).

Certainly one of Nepal's more unusual **lodgings**, the *Everest View Tower and Lodge* looks like a flying saucer on a pillar, with 360-degree windows, an observation deck and coin-operated telescopes (usually out of focus). The futuristic facilities don't, however, extend to such comforts as intact windows, running water or even a toilet; quilts are provided, but bring a sleeping bag in winter. There has been talk of the government privatizing the lodge, however, and if that ever happens the place will no doubt be more diligently maintained. Indeed, there are rumours of other private consortia buying up land in the area for development purposes, so who knows, Daman might someday get on the map after all. The tower has only one room and four beds (① each), but if it's full the truck-drivers' haunts beside the road should be able to put you up in rustic style. These places are also the only source of **food** in Daman, needless to say very basic.

The **gompa** above Daman makes a pleasant excursion. It's reached by walking about twenty minutes up the road to the sixth hairpin turn, marked by a small sign in Nepali, where a trail winds through oak and rhododendron forest to the shrine in another twenty minutes. Run by a Bhutanese lama, the *gompa* is small and unembellished, but the view from its meditation perch is awesome.

MOUNTAIN BIKING ROUTES IN NEPAL

	Distance: return (km)	Cycling days	Elevations (m)	Best time to go	Comments (Refer to map on the next page)
Circuits ex-Kathmandu					
Nagarkot/Sankhu	60	1–2	1300–2000	Oct–Dec, Feb–April	Brisk ascent takes the better part of an afternoon; stay overnight for views; bumpy dirt road back via Sankhu.
Dhulikhel/Namobuddha/Panauti	75	1–2	1300–1700	Oct–May	Main road is easy and unspectacular, but Namobuddha–Panauti is first-class fat-tyre country.
Kakani/Trisuli	150	2–3	540–2070	Nov–Mar	Can take back roads to Kakani via Budhanilkantha, followed by 1500-metre descent; numerous dirt roads east of Trisuli.
Daman	155	2–3	900–2320	Oct–Dec, Feb–April	A classic, tough overnight – you might want to rest a day before returning. Traffic is light, scenery is magnificent.
Kodari (Tibet border)	230	3–4	630–1640	Nov–April	Pretty tough: two or three days up and two days back for most people, with nights spent at Dhulikhel (reserve ahead).
Daman/Hetauda/Chitwan	380	4–5	180–2490	Nov–Mar	A varied, strenuous trip with wildlife viewing at the end. Bus back to Kathmandu.
Pokhara/Butwal/Chitwan/Hetauda/Daman	600+	10+	180–2490	Nov–Dec, Feb–Mar	A grand tour with many variations, which could also include side trips to Gorkha, Tansen and Lumbini. You might want to put your bike on the bus on the Prithvi Highway.
Circuits ex-Pokhara					
Birethanti	70	2	700–1600	Nov–April	Pleasant pedal to village beside the Kali Gandaki.
Tansen	240	2–4	350–1400	Nov–Mar	Winding road with little traffic and challenging terrain, including a 1000-metre climb at the end. As an option, carry on to Chitwan.
Routes to/from India	**one way (km)**				
Kathmandu–Birganj	185	2	90–2490	Nov–Dec, Feb–Mar	A tremendous introduction to Nepal if you're coming from India; shame about Birganj, though.
Kathmandu–Sunauli	380	4	90–1500	Nov–Mar	Superb route offering stopovers in Lumbini, Chitwan and Daman.
Kathmandu–Kakarbitta	540	5–6	80–2490	Nov–Mar	Adventurous tour through little-visited country towards Darjeeling. Possible side trips to Janakpur, Hile, and Ilam.
Kathmandu (or Pokhara)–Mahendranagar	750	8+	80–1500	Nov–Mar	A long but wonderfully virgin route on a newly paved road – the most rural way to or from Delhi.
Pokhara–Sunauli	185	2	90–1300	Nov–Mar	Possible side trips to Tansen and Lumbini.

Beyond Daman

Crossing the pass of **Sim Bhanjyang** (2488m), 3km beyond Daman, the Rajpath enters a landscape of plunging hill country and begins a relentless, 2200-metre descent to the valley below. The higher, south-facing slopes of the Mahabharat Lekh are dramatically greener and wilder than those on the other side – they wring much of the moisture out of the prevailing winds, and are frequently wreathed in fog by afternoon.

The road passes through successive zones of mossy jungle, pine forest and finally terraced farmland until reaching the Bhimphedi turning, 40km from Sim Bhanjyang. The electric transformers seen near here relay power from the Khulekani hydroelectric dam north of Bhimphedi, an important source of power for the region, and, indeed, the whole of Nepal. (See "Development Issues" in *Contexts* for a discussion of the problems surrounding hydroelectric development schemes.)

The devices that look like ski lifts are ropeways, one bringing rocks down to the big cement plant in Hetauda and the other taking finished cement and other raw materials up to Kathmandu. Hetauda, described in Chapter Six, is 10km further on.

festivals

The festivals of Dasain, Tihaar and Holi are celebrated everywhere in the central hills, while Dhulikhel and other Newar bazaars join in many of the Kathmandu Valley's holidays. In addition, look for these local events:

MAGH (Jan–Feb)
Magh Sankranti The first day of the month of Magh, traditionally observed with ritual bathing in the Punyamata Khola at Panauti (Jan 14 or 15).

FAAGUN (Feb–Mar)
Losar Tibetan New Year, celebrated at Namobuddha; Tibetans make pilgrimages to the stupa during the month that follows.

CHAITRA (Mar-April)
Bagh Bhairab Jaatra The festival of Bhairab in his tiger form, held at Nuwakot.

travel details

BUSES

Most of the buses to destinations in this region either begin or end their journeys in **Kathmandu**:

Sajha buses from Kathmandu's Bhimsen Tower to Daman (1 daily; 5hr) and Trisuli (1 daily; 4hr).

Express and local buses from Kathmandu's main bus station to Banepa (frequent; 1hr 30min); Barhabise (3 daily; 7hr); Dhulikhel (frequent; 2hr); Jiri (2 daily, at least 12hr) and Trisuli (4 daily; 4hr).

Night buses from Kathmandu's Bhimsen Tower to Daman (4 nightly; 4hr).

From Bhaktapur Sidha Pokhri bus park to Nagarkot (3 daily; 1hr).

From Barhabise to Tatopani (infrequent; 1hr).

From Trisuli to Dhunche (2 daily; 4hr).

CHAPTER FOUR

THE WESTERN HILLS

he **western hills** are Nepal at its most outstandingly typical: roaring gorges, precariously perched villages and terraced fields reaching to unsupportable heights, with some of the most graceful and accessible peaks of the Himalaya for a backdrop.

In this, Nepal's most populous hill region, people are the dominant feature of the landscape. Magars and Gurungs, the most visible ethnic groups, live in their own villages or side by side with Tamangs, Hindu castes and the usual smattering of Newar merchants. Life is traditional and close to the earth, but relatively prosperous: the oval houses are tidy and spacious, and hill women are festooned with the family gold. The prosperity comes, indirectly, from an unlikely quarter, as the western hills were the original – and still are the most important – recruiting area for **Gurkha soldiers**. It's an often-quoted statistic that Gurkha salaries and pensions were, up until the mid-1970s, Nepal's biggest foreign-exchange earner; in many villages here they still are, and they're arguably the major source of development financing as well. Ex-Gurkhas command the highest respect within their communities, and young men look up to them as role models. They also speak English, happily, and wherever you go there will probably be an ex-Gurkha to help you over the language barrier.

History, too, figures prominently here: the foundations of modern Nepal were laid in the western hills. While the kings of the Kathmandu Valley were building temples, the princes of the hills built forts – many of which still stand – and it's the hillmen who rule Nepal today.

The chief destination here – by far – is **Pokhara**, a restful lakeside retreat as well as Nepal's major trekking hub. On the way there, you can detour northwards to the magnificent hilltop fortress of **Gorkha**, seat of the tiny kingdom that brought down Kathmandu and unified Nepal. Beyond Pokhara, on the road to the Indian border, lies the even less publicized backwater of **Tansen**. All three are excellent bases for **day hikes** – which can be almost as rewarding as trekking, without the commitment and red tape (treks are described in Chapter Seven). Since **rafting** in the Trisuli River also brings many travellers to the western hills, a special section on rivers and preparations is given early in the chapter.

Two main roads cut a swathe through the hills: the **Prithvi Highway** (Prithvi Rajmarg), running west from Kathmandu to Pokhara, and the **Siddhartha Highway** (Siddhartha Rajmarg), which carries on from Pokhara to the Indian border. They're in poor condition these days, but they support frequent **buses**, which is more than can be said for the region's few other roads. Elsewhere, most journeys are made on foot – and you don't have to go far in this area to appreciate how blurred the distinction between travelling and trekking can be.

HEADING WEST: THE PRITHVI HIGHWAY AND GORKHA

If you take one of the **tourist buses** between Kathmandu and Pokhara you might think there's nothing worth stopping for en route, for there are few towns of any consequence along the 200-kilometre Prithvi Highway. Travelling by **local bus**, however, you get a healthy dose of roadside villages. **Cycling** can't really be recommended, on account of all the traffic, though having your own wheels would allow you to explore a few offbeat sights along the way. Certainly the side trip to Gorkha makes a strong case for breaking the journey, even though it will mean giving up your seat on the bus.

Other activities might bring you in contact with the Prithvi Highway: **rafting** trips on the Trisuli River follow the road for about 50km, and **treks** around the Annapurna Circuit start on a side road from Dumre.

Along the Prithvi Highway

Bobbing and weaving through the heart of the hills, the **Prithvi Highway** (Prithvi Rajmarg) is most visitors' initiation into the pain and pleasure of Nepalese bus travel. You may find yourself on it several times, in fact, since besides linking Kathmandu and Pokhara it's also the first leg between either city and the Tarai. Mountain views are only intermittent, though, since the road careers along the bottom of deep valleys most of the way. Nepal's second trunk road when it was built by the Chinese in 1973, the Prithvi Highway has played a crucial role in modernizing the country, opening up the western hills and enabling Pokhara to develop into Nepal's second tourist city. More recently, the government and its foreign-aid bankers seem to have rediscovered the highway's significance for industry as a link between Kathmandu and the Tarai, and have set about upgrading and widening it, at least as far as Mugling. Progress is slow, though: much of the work is done by hand (you'll see crews of women and even

HILL CULTURE: GURUNGS AND MAGARS

Leavened with nothing but the water of God
Comes from Rumjatar the flour of millet pounded,
Gurungs have mastered the knowledge of God
And Brahmans are left astounded.

Nepali poet Jnandil (c.1821–83)

Hardy, self-sufficient peasant farmers, Gurungs and Magars are the "aboriginals" of the western hills. Both groups exhibit Mongoloid features and speak Tibeto-Burman dialects – signs that their ancestors probably migrated here from Tibet, though nobody's sure when. Together, they form the backbone of the Gurkha regiments (see p.213), and also account for a fair proportion of the Nepalese army.

Although **Gurungs** are a common sight around Pokhara, where many have invested their Gurkha pensions in guest houses and retirement homes, their homeland remains the middle elevations from Gorkha to the southern slopes of the Annapurna Himal (those living in the Gorkha area call themselves Ghale). The majority who don't serve in the military herd sheep for their wool, driving them to pastures high on the flanks of the Himalaya, and raise wheat, maize, millet and potatoes. Gurungs were once active trans-Himalayan traders, but the Chinese occupation of Tibet has put a damper on that, while other traditional pursuits such as hunting and honey-gathering are being encroached upon by overpopulation. Their unique form of **shamanism** is coming under pressure, too, as Hinduism advances from the south and Buddhism trickles down with Tibetan settlers from the north. Gurungs employ shamans to propitiate ghosts, reclaim possessed souls from the underworld, and guide dead souls to the land of their ancestors – rituals that contain clear echoes of "classic" Siberian shamanism and are believed to resemble those of the ancient Bon priests of pre-Buddhist Tibet. Some authorities see the ongoing power struggle between Tibetan lamas and Gurung shamans as a modern re-enactment of Buddhism's battle with Bon in seventh-century Tibet; in that instance, Buddhism won.

A somewhat less cohesive group, **Magars** are scattered throughout the lower elevations of the western hills (recently they've colonized parts of the eastern hills as well). A network of Magar kingdoms once controlled the entire region, but the arrival of Hindus in the fifteenth century brought swift political decline and steady cultural assimilation. Nowadays, after centuries of coexistence with Hindu castes, most employ Bahun *pujari* (priests) and worship Hindu gods just like their Chhetri neighbours, differing only in that they're not allowed to wear the sacred thread of the "twice-born" castes. Similarly, with farming practices, housing and dress, Magars are an adaptable lot and not easily distinguished from surrounding groups – the velvet blouses, coin necklaces and *pote* (thin strands of glass beads) worn by many Magar women, for instance, are also common to Gurungs and Chhetris. Even the Magar language varies from place to place, consisting of at least three mutually unintelligible dialects (most Magars speak Nepali). Despite the lack of unifying traits, however, group identity is still strong, and will probably remain so as long as Magars keep marrying only within the clan.

children breaking up rocks for ballast), and every year the monsoon causes setbacks. Whenever you go, expect construction delays somewhere along the way. After parting with the Rajpath at Naubise (see Chapter Three), the highway descends steadily along the south side of the Mahesh Khola, which soon joins the **Trisuli River**. Keep an eye out for magnificent, spidery suspension bridges and precarious ropeways spanning the Trisuli; you might also spot funeral pyres on the sandy banks, and rafting parties running the rapids. The high-water mark on the rocks shows how much the Trisuli, like all Himalayan rivers, swells and rages during the monsoon. The solid, three-storey farmhouses seen here belong to Bahuns and Chhetris, while the humbler mud-and-thatch huts are typical Tamang or Magar dwellings.

Buses often make a mid-morning fuel stop at Malekhu, Charaundi or Fishling, roadside bazaars with teahouses and provisions stores that cater to rafters on the Trisuli. Jogimara, further on, has a grim notoriety as a death spot – most recent rafting accidents seem to have occurred in the vicinity, and in 1992 a bus with more than fifty passengers plunged into the river here and has never been recovered.

Mugling

All buses break for lunch at **MUGLING**, 110km from Kathmandu, whose wide main street and wood-fronted buildings give it the look of a wild-west town. Drivers get free meals for parking in front of certain **restaurants** – you can always check out the dozens of others, but there's little difference between one *daal bhaat* and another here. With buses coming and going twenty-four hours a day, Mugling would be an awful place to spend the night, and in any case only a few "hotels" have **rooms**. Names change often, but try *Hotel Pokhara & Lodge* (③) or *Darjeeling Guest House* (②), or splash out on *Motel du Mugling* (Kathmandu ☎01/225242; B⑦), located across the bridge and commanding a grandstand view of Mugling's latrines. At 280m, Mugling is the lowest point along the Prithvi Highway. Sugar cane is cultivated on a small scale around here, and you'll also see *simal*, a tall, angular Tarai tree that produces red flowers in February and pods of cotton-like seeds in May. Traffic bound for the Tarai turns left (south) at Mugling and continues along the Trisuli River, making the gradual 34-kilometre descent to Narayanghat (see Chapter Five).

The Prithvi Highway crosses the Trisuli just past Mugling and heads upstream along the Marsyangdi River, passing the massive **Marsyangdi Hydroelectric Project** powerhouse 2km later. The dam and reservoir are 12km further on; water is diverted through a tunnel to the powerhouse and then channelled down to the turbines. Completed in 1990, the project is the single most expensive thing ever built in Nepal, costing $210 million of German, Saudi and World Bank money, and it's expected to generate thirty percent of the country's electricity. This diversion is just a puddle compared to some of the others on the World Bank's drawing board: the Arun III project, southeast of Everest, will be several times bigger, and the Karnali project in the far western Tarai, now shelved, would have been the biggest hydroelectric scheme in the world (see "Development Dilemmas" in *Contexts*).

Manakamana, Dumre and Damauli

The spur road to Gorkha (see p.197) leaves the highway at Abu Khaireni, 7km west of Mugling. If you're into really off-the-beaten-track oddities, you can walk from here up to **MANAKAMANA** (Maan-*kaam*-na), a beautiful four-hour hike along a forested trail that begins on the right about 1km up the Gorkha road. Every day scores of pilgrims make the journey to worship at Manakamana's **Bhagwati Mandir**, revered as one of Nepal's five great wish-fulfilling temples – it's especially popular with Newar newlyweds, who come to pray for sons. Animal

RAFTING

Of all the outdoor activities on offer in Nepal, **whitewater rafting** probably tops the list for excitement. Two popular rivers within reach of Kathmandu are well paced for novices, while more distant ones will challenge experienced river-runners.

Unfortunately, rafting is also the single biggest source of disappointment for many travellers, who too often get duped by shady or inexperienced **river operators**. Trip prices and quality vary enormously – as a rule, the only difference between cheap companies and expensive ones is that the latter usually can be relied on to do what they promised. A few of the more reputable operators are listed in the "On from Kathmandu" section of Chapter One; these deal mainly with groups booked from overseas, but they'll take walk-in clients, and if you can muster up a few friends you can arrange your own customized trip. Some of the cut-price outfits in Kathmandu and Pokhara aren't bad, but making recommendations would be misleading – guides come and go, and standards rise and fall from one season to the next. Shop around, and press operators hard on the criteria given below.

Many places advertising rafting trips are merely **agents**, who usually don't know what they're talking about. But if you're having trouble finding an operator who has a trip scheduled for when you want to go, an agent may be able to hook you up with one.

Costs and red tape

Trips cost from $15 to $75 a day, depending on the river, number of people in the party, and standard of service. For trips on the Trisuli, Nepal's most popular river, upmarket companies typically charge $30–40 a day, which should include transportation to and from the river by private van and good, hygienic meals. Budget outfits offer this trip for around $20 a day, but at that price you can expect to travel by local bus and be served pretty unappetizing food; anyone charging less than $20 is likely to make you buy your own bus tickets and meals. These prices assume full rafts, which hold up to seven paying passengers each – smaller group sizes mean a higher price per head. Other rivers cost $10–20 a day extra.

Your rafting company is responsible for arranging the trip **permit**, which costs $5 per person and is normally included in the package (one passport photo required). Fly-by-night operators sometimes collect permit fees and pocket the money – a risky proposition, since as far as the government is concerned, unpermitted trips don't exist and therefore don't need rescuing. In theory, you're supposed to be **insured** in order to get a permit.

Safety and the environment

Lack of **safety** is a perennial complaint. Make sure the company supplies life vests, helmets (not required in "oar" rafts – see below) and a full first-aid kit, and satisfy yourself that the rafts are in good running order and that there will be a safety demonstration before entering the river. The minimum number of rafts is two, in case one capsizes. Most important of all, **guides** must be experienced and speak adequate English – ask what sort of training they've had and how many times they've guided the stretch of river in question (there should be an opportunity to meet guides before departure). The *Nepal Association of Rafting Agents* is supposed to be setting standards for guide training and certification, and may eventually establish minimum prices for trips; companies not belonging to *NARA* are unregulated, so you've got no recourse if things go wrong.

Rafters have the same responsibilities to **the environment** as trekkers, particularly regarding firewood, sanitation and litter – see the tips on p.307.

Equipment

Most companies use "paddle" rafts, in which everyone paddles and the guide steers from the rear; on less exciting "oar" trips, the guide does all the work. Tents, sleeping bags, foam mattresses and kit bags should be provided and each raft should come with a waterproof "ammo" box for storing clothes, cameras and valuables. It's up to you to bring two sets of clothes (one to remain dry) and shoes (trainers are best), a bathing suit, towel, hat, sunglasses, suntan lotion and torch (flashlight).

When to go

Time of year makes an enormous difference to water volumes – if you're a beginner, you do *not* want to raft during the monsoon, and probably not until mid- or late October, when things have calmed down. The rapids are more manageably exciting in November, becoming mellower from December through to April or May, when snowmelt begins to add to flows. March and April are the best months for long, warm days and excellent birdwatching. Winter can be chilly, though not so bad as you might think: most raftable river sections are below 500m elevation.

The rivers *(refer to map on p.196)*

Perhaps ninety percent of all raft trips are done on the **Trisuli River**, west of Kathmandu. The normal itinerary is three days: given that it takes three or four hours to drive each way, two-day trips are a waste of time, and four-day trips often just the three-day in slow motion. The Trisuli contains a good mix of whitewater and scenery, though it's hardly wilderness – a road follows it the entire way. In October and November you'll have to share the river with many other parties and perhaps compete for campsites. Operators' boasts of "road support" mean the overnight gear is kept in a van, which precludes camping on the river's less crowded north side. All the best rapids are above Mugling and many Pokhara-based companies miss these out. Ask where the put-in point is: anything much below Baireni isn't a proper whitewater trip; most companies pull out between Mugling and Narayanghat. Many operators misleadingly advertise trips to Chitwan National Park; though these almost always end at Narayanghat, it's a pleasanter way of getting to the Tarai than by bus.

Next in popularity comes the **Sun Kosi**, an eight- to eleven-day run (depending on the time of year) beginning at Dolalghat, three hours east of Kathmandu, and ending at Chatara, near Dharan in the eastern Tarai. Fewer companies do scheduled trips on the Sun Kosi, so you're less likely to see other parties and the camping is great. Providing a steady diet of increasingly exciting whitewater, the river traverses a remote, roadless part of the country, flowing through a varied landscape of jungle-clad canyons, arid, open valleys and sparse settlements. Some operators also run a gentle, one-day stretch of the **Bhote Kosi**, which joins the Sun Kosi at Dolalghat.

Other rivers are harder to get to – budget operators don't run them, and the few companies that do charge through the nose. The lower **Kali Gandaki** makes a fairly easy three-day float from Ramdi Ghat, south of Pokhara, to Narayanghat; the construction of a new road is expected to open up the more exciting upper section, beginning at Kusma (which also could be combined with a trek in the Annapurna region). Starting at Damauli, east of Pokhara, the **Seti** is a fairly tame but picturesque river, taking one or two days to Narayanghat. Rafting the lower **Karnali** in far western Nepal is a serious expedition, involving an expensive flight and at least a two-day walk-in, but with big whitewater, pristine jungle and wildlife. A tributary of the Karnali, the gentle **Bheri** can be run from the Surkhet road to Bardia National Park. The little-rafted **Arun**, reached by flying to Tumlingtar in the eastern hills and raftable from Tumlingtar to Chatara, offers big whitewater and uspoilt scenery. If you're considering any of these or other off-the-beaten-track trips, you'll definitely want to get yourself a copy of *White Water Nepal* (see "Books" in *Contexts*).

Children swinging during the October Dasain festival

sacrifices are an essential part of the ritual, and locals raise goats and chickens specifically for the sacrificial market. For Nag Panchami, in late July or early August, celebrants construct an entire shrine out of flowers and foliage. Tea and simple food are available in the nearby bazaar. Mountain views from here are good, but they're better from a small *puja* spot another two hours further up the ridge.

The views improve from here on: initially the closest peaks are Boudha and Himalchuli of the Manaslu Himal, while the Annapurna Himal takes over as you get closer to Pokhara. Trekkers tackling the Annapurna Circuit usually stop at **DUMRE** (450m), a drab roadside bazaar 18km past Mugling, but few spend the night here now that they can continue on to Besisahar by truck. If you're cycling from Kathamandu to Pokhara, however, this would be a marginally quieter place to stay than Mugling; *Mustang Lodge* (①) is one of many trekkers' inns left over from Dumre's heyday as a trailhead.

West of Dumre, the hills get gentler and more heavily cultivated. Most Nepalis live in countryside like this, and the **farming** methods seen here are fairly representative of those practised throughout the hills. The land is used intensively but sustainably: trees and bamboo are pruned for fodder; livestock, fed on fodder, pull ploughs and provide milk and manure; and manure, in turn, is dolloped onto the fields as fertilizer (and used as fuel at higher elevations). Goats, chickens and pigs recycle scraps into meat and eggs, and even pariah dogs are tolerated because they eat faeces. Most farmers barter surplus grain for odd essentials such as salt, sugar, pots and pans, and have little to do with the cash economy, though growing numbers near the highway are starting to raise vegetables for cash. Several research stations here are experimenting with improved seeds, but tractors and chemical fertilizers will probably never be appropriate for the vast majority of Nepali farms.

It's 8km uphill and another 8km down from Dumre to **DAMAULI** (350m), a nondescript administrative town overlooking the confluence of the Madi and Seti rivers. A paved road runs south from the highway for 1km to the sadhu hangout of **Vyasa Gupha**, a cave where Vyasa, the sage of the *Mahabharat*, is supposed to have been born and lived. One of the temples contains a life-size statue of Vyasa. After traversing the Madi, the highway rises and then descends gradually to rejoin the broad and featureless Seti Valley, finally reaching Pokhara some 54km from Damauli.

Gorkha

Despite being midway between Kathmandu and Pokhara, **GORKHA** (Gor-*kaa*) remains strangely untouristed, probably because of the longstanding difficulty of getting there. However, the surfacing of the 24-kilometre road up from Abu Khaireni now means it is a relatively painless half-day's ride from Pokhara, Kathmandu or Tadi Bazaar (Chitwan). The government is devoting a large chunk of its tourism budget to sprucing up all of Gorkha's monuments, and there seems to be some vague notion of putting the town on the tourist map; but for the time being, at least, Gorkha is suspended in a happy halfway state, with just enough basic facilities for comfort, though still primitive enough to keep the crowds away.

Cradle of a nation and the ancestral home of the Nepalese royal family, Gorkha occupies a central place in Nepalese history. The village itself is minuscule, but hunched on the hilltop above is its link with that splendid past, the **Gorkha Durbar** – an architectural tour de force worthy of the flamboyant Gorkha kings and the dynasty they founded. Unless you're setting straight off on a trek or just finishing one (the Pokhara–Trisuli trail passes through Gorkha), you'll have to spend the night here. Think about staying two: the Durbar and environs could easily soak up a day, and hikes around the area could keep you busy for a further day or two. The hill climate is agreeable, the pace is easy and, for the moment at least, there's not an apple pie or pizza in sight.

Though there are few direct **buses** to Gorkha, you can get off at Abu Khaireni on the Prithvi Highway and catch any bus or *Tata* lorry chugging up the spur road from there. If you're pedalling, beware that the last 10km is a tough 900-metre climb.

Some history

In a sense, Gorkha's history is not its own. A petty hill state in medieval times, it was occupied and transformed into a sort of Himalayan Sparta by outsiders who used it as a base for a dogged campaign against Kathmandu and then, having won their prize, restored Gorkha to obscurity. Yet during those two centuries of occupation, it raised the nation's most famous son, **Prithvi Narayan Shah**, and somehow bred in him the audacity to conquer all of Nepal.

Prithvi Narayan's ancestors came to Gorkha in the mid-sixteenth century, having been driven into the hills from their native Rajasthan by the Muslim horde, and they soon gained a reputation as a singlemindedly martial lot. His father launched the first unsuccessful raid on the Kathmandu Valley in the early eighteenth century, and when Prithvi Narayan himself ascended the throne in 1743, at the age of twenty, he already had his father's obsession fixed in his

To Ali Bhanjyang & Trisuli

Kaliban

Tallokot (1288 m)

Ram Shah Monument

Kalika Mandir   Palace

Gorkha Durbar (1420 m)

Hanuman Bhanjyang

Upallokot (1522 m)

To Daraundi Khola & Pokhara

Rameshwar Mahadev

TUDIKHEL

Bus Park   Tallo Durbar   Post Office

Hotel Thakali   Bank

Stream

Stream

Stream

0   250 m

Hotel Gorkha Bisauni

To Prithvi Highway

GORKHA

mind*. Within a year, he was leading Gorkha in a war of expansion that was eventually to unify all of present-day Nepal, plus parts of India and Tibet. Looking at the tiny village and meagre terraces of Gorkha today, you can imagine what a drain it must have been to keep a standing army fed and supplied for 27 years of continuous campaigning. The hardy peasants of Gorkha got little more than a handshake for their efforts. After conquering the valley in 1769, Prithvi Narayan moved his capital to the bright lights of Kathmandu, relegating Gorkha to a mere garrison from which the later western campaign was directed. By the early nineteenth century, Gorkha had been all but forgotten, even as an alternative spelling of the name – Gurkha – was becoming a household name around the world.

---

*An odd legend confirms Prithvi Narayan's destiny, but also puts the scale of his accomplishment into perspective. When still a prince he was approached by an old man, who took the boy's hand and spat in it. The spittle turned to yoghurt and the man ordered Prithvi to eat it; the prince, not unreasonably, flung the curd on the ground at his feet. At that, the old man revealed himself to be Gorakhnath, the demigod protector of the Shah kings, and pronounced that Prithvi Narayan would go on to rule wherever he placed his feet – but had he eaten the curd, he could have ruled the world.

The village

Finding **accommodation** in Gorkha is fairly straightforward – the best by a long shot is *Hotel Gorkha Bisauni* (☎064/20107; ②/B③, dormitory beds ①), 400m back down the road from the bus stop, which has the only hot water, international dialling, TV and English-speaking proprietor in town, though rates are on the high side for a budget lodge. The new *Gorkha Hill Resort* (Kathmandu ☎01/271329; B⑦) is more luxurious, but inconveniently located 4km down the road. If money's the only object, there are a half a dozen dives between the *Bisauni* and the bus park; *Hotel Pamper* and *Hotel Thakali* (both ①) offer good views, though it might be worth paying more at *Hotel Sugat* (②), beyond the bus park to the west, for relative quiet. For **food**, the choice is similarly limited. The *Gorkha Bisauni's* little diner does reasonably good Western fare, including seasonal fresh vegetable soups. Plenty of places near the bus park serve up the usual all-you-can-eat *bhaat, momo* or *thukpa*.

Nestled on a shelf beneath a steep ridge, most of the village stretches along a single main path – the layout, with buildings huddled close together to save space for farming, calls to mind a traditional English village. A dirt road from the bus park leads up to the Tudikhel (parade ground) and immediately after that to the temple precinct. The gilded figure kneeling atop a pillar facing the onion-domed **Rameshwar Mahadev Mandir** is Prithvipati Shah; an early Gorkha king, he established most of the temples and shrines still in use around the town, including the Kalika temple in the Durbar. West of here, where the main street opens up to a small plaza, an inconspicuous lane leads to the old **Tallo Durbar** (Lower Palace). Built in around 1750, this imposing Newar-style edifice served as the kingdom's administrative headquarters, while the upper Durbar housed king and court. Seen from above, Tallo Durbar indeed looks like a mini-Pentagon. Its fine brick and woodwork is now getting a facelift – peacock windows and all – and the building is supposed to be opened up as a museum of Gorkha history spanning the generations of Shahs leading up to Prithvi Narayan. You can also get there by a trail climbing up from the driveway of the *Gorkha Bisauni*, which passes through a schoolyard and enters the village the back way.

Gorkha Durbar

It's a brisk, 300-metre ascent to the **Gorkha Durbar** along the main trail from Pokharithok, the junction just east of Tallo Durbar; figure on half an hour. At the top of this route – once the royal approach to the palace – you can marvel at the massive front stairway that's the Durbar's most distinctive feature. Pure ostentation or cheeky bluff, either way it must have cowed visiting vassals into submission – a neat trick for a tinpot realm that could barely muster 150 soldiers at the time of Prithvi Narayan's first campaign.

The climb repays itself with more than history. Set on the ridge crest, the Durbar commands a sweeping **view** of the Himalaya from Dhaulagiri to Ganesh Himal, with Boudha and Himalchuli of Manaslu Himal occupying centre stage. Although the warlike Gorkhalis picked the site for its strategic position, they can't have been unmoved by the scenery.

Conceived as a dwelling for kings and gods, the fortress remains a religious place, and first stop in any visit is the **Kalika Mandir**, probably the most revered shrine this side of Kathmandu. Occupying the left (western) half of the Durbar building, its interior is closed to all but priests and the king of Nepal (others would die upon beholding Kali's terrible image, say the priests), but plenty of

The Gorkha Durbar

action takes place outside: sacrifices are made in the alcove in front of the entrance, and during the twice-monthly observance of Astami – celebrated with special gusto in Gorkha – the paving stones are sticky with blood. Most worshippers arrive cradling a trembling goat or chicken and leave swinging a headless carcass. Chaitra Dasain, Gorkha's biggest annual **festival**, brings processions and more bloodletting in late March, as does the tenth day of Dasain.

The east wing of the Durbar is the historic **durbar**, site of **Prithvi Narayan's birthplace** and, by extension, the ancestral shrine of the Shah kings. This accounts for King Birendra's regular visits (his helipad is just west of the Durbar) and the government's spare-no-expense renovation of the Durbar's exceptional eighteenth-century woodwork. Though predating the Gorkhali conquest of Kathmandu, the palace bears the unmistakeable stamp of Newar craftsmanship: the Gorkhalis, who never pretended to have any art or architecture of their own, imported workmen from Kathmandu. Upstairs are said to be Prithvi Narayan's **throne** and an **eternal flame** that's been burning ever since he unified Nepal. Sentries discourage photography in the courtyard and bar the interior to all foreigners – a vandal could kick out the fire and cast a serious hex on Nepal's monarchy.

The remaining space within the fortress walls is fairly littered with other Hindu shrines. By the main entrance is a small temple built around the holy **cave of Gorakhnath**, the centre for worship of the shadowy Indian guru who gave Gorkha its name and is regarded as a kind of guardian angel by the Shah kings. Sadhus of the Gorakhnath cult are known as *kaanphata* ("split-ears"), after an initiation ceremony in which they insert sticks in their earlobes – which is a walk in the park compared to some of the other things they get up to in the name of their guru.

Upallokot and Tallokot

The notch in the ridge just east of Gorkha Durbar is known as **Hanuman Bhanjyang** (Hanuman Pass), after the valiant monkey king who guards the crossroads from a niche above the popular shady *chautaara* (rest stop). Cross the main trail (a branch of the Pokhara–Trisuli porter route) and follow a steep, stone-paved path up the ridgeline. Just above the crossing is a vantage-point where you can stand in the stone "footsteps" of Ram, hero of the *Ramayan* and Hanuman's best buddy, and snap a postcard picture of the Durbar.

From Hanuman Bhanjyang it's another half-hour hike to **Upallokot** (Upper Fort), a 1520-metre eyrie at the highest, easternmost point of the ridge. Except for the slight intrusion of a microwave relay tower, the panorama here is total. If you can manage it, sunrise is the best time to visit: to the east, the ridge abruptly plunges 500m to misty depths while the sun's first rays play across the peaks. Late afternoon is pretty special, too, as the sun slants behind the Durbar and fills the Daraundi Khola Valley to the west with a golden haze. From this angle, looking down the spine of the ridge, the Durbar looks like Nepal's answer to Mad Ludwig's castle. The one thing lacking is a sense of wilderness: nearly every hill and valley is cultivated and tamed, except for **Kaliban**, the forest covering the northern crest of the ridge. Spookily alive with rhesus monkeys, this sacred grove supplies wood for the Durbar's eternal flame. Upallokot itself is more a hut than a fort, its thatched roof long gone. The small walled pen contains an old grinding wheel and a set of stones laid out in the shape of a reclining human figure – obscure icons of Bhairab and Kali.

At the other end of the ridge stands **Tallokot**, a watch post with more limited views north and west. You can easily stroll there from the Durbar's front entrance, passing a small but active Kali temple and a new monument to Ram Shah, the seventh-generation ancestor of Prithvi Narayan Shah who is reckoned by some to have been the progenitor of the Shah title. A rough track descends directly from Tollokot to Gorkha, tripping down terraces past small clusters of farmhouses and the odd communal spring.

Longer walks

If that circuit whets your appetite for **longer walks**, there are two main options. The high road through Hanuman Bhanjyang descends gently for about an hour and a half to **Ali Bhanjyang** (shops), then ascends along a ridge with fabulous mountain views, reaching **Khanchok Bhanjyang** two and a half hours later. This would be about the limit for a day hike, but given an early start you could continue down to the subtropical banks of the Budhi Gandaki at **Arughat**, a long day's 20km from Gorkha, and find basic lodging there – at this point you'd be a third of the way to Trisuli. Other, less distinct trails from Upallokot and the Ram Shah monument take roundabout routes to Ali Bhanjyang. Alternatively, follow the main trail west out of Gorkha village, which descends to the untrammelled

---

CHAUTAARA

A uniquely Nepali institution, the **chautaara** is more than just a resting place – it serves important social and religious functions as well. Every hill village has its *chautaara*, and you'll find them at appropriate intervals along any reasonably busy trail. The standard design consists of a rectangular flagstoned platform, built at just the right height for porters easily to set down their *doko*, and sometimes a smaller platform atop that. Two trees planted in the earthen centre provide shade for all who gather underneath: passing strangers, old friends, couples, village assemblies.

Chautaara are erected and maintained by individuals as an act of public service, often to earn religious merit or in memory of a deceased parent. Commonly they'll be found on sites associated with animist deities, indicated by sundur-coloured stones. The trees, too, are considered sacred. Invariably, one will be a **pipal**, whose Latin name (*Ficus religiosa*) recalls its role as the bodhi tree under which the Buddha attained enlightenment. Nepalis regard the pipal, with its heart-shaped leaves, as a female symbol, and women will sometimes fast and pray before one for children, or for success for the children they already have. Its male counterpart is the **banyan** (*bar* in Nepali), another member of the fig genus that sends down Tarzan-vine-like aerial roots which, if not pruned, will eventually take root and establish satellite trunks. A *chautaara* is incomplete without the pair; occasionally you'll see one with a single tree, but sooner or later someone will get around to planting the other.

Daraundi Khola Valley (1hr 30min) to join the main Pokhara–Trisuli trail. You could continue on for another three hours to **Khoplang**, a beautiful hill village with lodgings. You could even do a two-day loop: Gorkha to Khanchok Bhanjyang, from there down to the Daraundi at Ulte, head downstream to Chorkate, and then back up to Gorkha. For trekking from here, see Chapter Seven.

POKHARA AND AROUND

The Himalaya form the highest, sheerest rise from subtropical base to icy peaks of any mountain range on earth, and nowhere is the contrast more marked than at **POKHARA** (pronounced *Poke*-rhuh). Sited at just 800m above sea level, it boasts a nearly unobstructed view of the 8000-metre-plus Annapurna and Manaslu Himal, 25km north; completely dominating the skyline, in beauty if not in height, is the double-finned summit of Machhapuchhre – "Fish Tail" – only one of whose peaks is visible from Pokhara. Basking in the view, Nepal's main "resort" area lolls beside the shore of **Phewa Tal** (Phewa Lake), well outside the actual town of Pokhara. This is Nepal's little budget paradise: carefree and culturally undemanding, though highly commercialized, with a steaks-and-cakes scene second only to that of Kathmandu.

If you're spending more than a week in Nepal, chances are you'll touch down in Pokhara at some point – as the main destination served by "tourist" buses, it's usually the first place travellers venture to outside the Kathmandu Valley. For trekkers, Pokhara is the gateway to Nepal's most popular trails; for everyone else, it's the most beautiful place in Nepal that's accessible by public transport. Day trips around the Pokhara Valley beckon, and if the area is short on temples and twisting old alleys, you might find that a relief after Kathmandu's profusion. Despite its shallow hedonism – which definitely gets cloying after a while – Pokhara is an ideal place to recharge your batteries, especially after a trek. By comparison, Kathmandu seems downright claustrophobic.

Because it's 500m lower than the capital, Pokhara is a better place to be in winter, but rather hot from April onwards. With lower foothills to the south, it's also less protected from the prevailing rains, and receives about twice as much precipitation as Kathmandu. Touring the valley, you'll be struck by the active, shaping presence of water everywhere: lakes and rivers are conspicuous features here, and the paddies are traced by canals of roiling mountain water.

Orientation and accommodation

Pokhara's layout requires some explanation if you plan to do any sightseeing (an activity which, admittedly, isn't a top priority for most visitors here). To get your bearings, start with the tourist areas of **Lakeside** and **Damside**, set 1km apart on the eastern and southeastern edges of **Phewa Tal**, where you'll find the vast majority of **budget lodgings** and **restaurants**.

Northeast of the lake, **Pokhara Bazaar** (in Nepal, *bazaar* refers to any commercial centre) is maddeningly diffuse, sprawling a good 5km along two north–south roads and a ladder of cross streets – the map doesn't begin to suggest how interminably far it is to cycle the entire length of it. Roughly 1km east of Damside are Pokhara's **airport**, tourist office and several of the upmarket

To Tashi Palkhel & Phedi
To Mahendra Cave
Kali Khola
Bhalam Khola
To Siklis
Gurkha Training Camp
Seti Khola
KISINGH PUL
Bhim Bazaar
Shining Hospital
BAG BAZAAR
Kahun Danda
Bindyabasini Mandir
Prithvi Narayan Campus
Seti Khola
To Sarangkot
BHIMSEN TOL
District Police
PHULBARI
To Sarangkot
CHIPLEDHUNGA
Army Camp
0   1 km
SIMALCHAUR
POKHARA-BAGLUNG HIGHWAY
Post Office
MAHENDRA PUL
MAYA BAZAAR
Western Regional Hospital
Tibetan Monastery
MANSWARA
Pokhara Museum
LAKESIDE (BAIDAM)
Tibetan Handicrafts Centre
PRITHVI CHOWK
Hungry Eye
Ratna Mandir (Royal Palace)
Bus Park
PRITHVI HIGHWAY
Pokhara Gate
Phewa Tal
Tal Barahi
Central Immigration
Tourist Office & Tara Gaon Resort
New Hotel Crystal
Bank
RNAC
Fish Tail Lodge
DAMSIDE (PARDI)
Hotel Mount Annapurna
To Kathmandu
Pardi Dam
Hotel Dragon
MUSTANG CHOWK
SIDDHARTA HIGHWAY
MAHENDRAPUL
To Tansen & The Tarai
Devin's Fall
Airport
Seti Khola
Tashiling Tibetan Village

POKHARA

hotels, with **Prithvi Chowk**, home of the **bus park**, 1km north of the airport. A further 1.5km northwards, the bustling **Mahendra Pul** (Mahendra Bridge) area forms the heart of the new, southern end of town, while the subdued **old bazaar** occupies the highest ground further north.

Arrival

A half-dozen **tourist buses** (variously billed as "Swiss", "Deluxe" and "2x2 Minibuses") shuttle between Kathmandu and Pokhara daily. Due to a rather sly arrangement between lodge proprietors, taxi drivers and touts*, tourist buses refuse to drive on to Lakeside/Damside, and instead deliver passengers into the clutches of the hotel touts at the **main bus park**, 2–3km away. After the jarring ride, you'll want to spend as little time as possible here – unless you're on a skeletal budget, a taxi is the only sensible way to reach the lake (about Rs40). The touts and drivers really go into a feeding frenzy at the arrival of Westerners, and the only way to escape intact is to state your destination with great certitude and decide on a driver as quickly as possible. (To upset their incentive structure, pick the least aggressive driver.) If you're entering from the south along the Siddhartha Highway, ask to be let off at Pardi (the local name for Damside) and walk a short way west to get to lodgings.

Flying from Kathmandu to Pokhara ($61) cuts out some of the hardships of the journey, but be prepared, as always, for Kafkaesque scenes at the airport. The mountain views from aloft are stupendous; take the earliest flight available, before clouds obscure the peaks, and book early for a seat on the righthand side of the plane. A taxi from the airport to Lakeside/Damside should cost about Rs40.

Getting around

Poor local transport makes getting around Pokhara time-consuming, widening the divide between lake and bazaar and making it that much harder to tear yourself away from the tourist fleshpots. A crosstown journey on one of Pokhara's **local buses** takes the better part of an hour. There are three principal routes (refer to map): Lakeside up to the Prithvi Narayan campus via Mahendra Pul; Damside to the campus via Chipledhunga; and Ram Bazaar (east of the bus park) to Mahendra Cave. Catch buses in Damside near *K.C.'s Restaurant* and in Lakeside near the *Hungry Eye* and the municipal campground.

Taxis are seldom to be found around the Lakeside and Damside guest houses, but innkeepers will book one for you given a couple hours' notice. The nearest taxi hangout is the roundabout at the beginning of the Baidam (Lakeside) road, and taxis can also usually be found near the bus park, the Shining Hospital car park and the airport. Taxis are unmetered and fares are always more expensive for foreigners. You can keep the price down by telling the driver you're willing to share.

A **bicycle** or **mountain bike**, rentable all over Lakeside and Damside for roughly the same prices as in Kathmandu (figure on upwards of Rs100 a day for a good one), multiplies your mobility and flexibility tremendously. A mountain bike is often the most practical way to explore the valley, which has a lot of slopes to it.

---

*Lakeside and Damside lodge owners each argue that they'd be unfairly discriminated against if buses went to the other area first, so the buses stop instead at a point that's equally inconvenient for everybody. Touts and taxi drivers, meanwhile, are guaranteed business.

For speedier zipping around the valley, it may be worth considering a **motorcy-cle**: these cost about Rs500 a day (plus fuel) from a few Lakeside outlets. Pokhara has a few plodding *tonga* (horse-drawn carts), but no tempos, autorikshas or pedal rikshas.

Accommodation

Pokhara is glutted with cheap and moderately priced **accommodation**. Scores of small lodges have been built in recent years by ex-Gurkhas and Thakalis (the enterprising innkeepers of the trekking region north of Pokhara), but things are beginning to get out of hand. At any given time there seem to be a dozen concrete behemoths in the pipeline, and every small lodge owner has a scheme to replace his perfectly nice building with an ugly new one. The result is that the homely establishments that brought travellers here in the first place are being steadily edged out, and the lakeside accommodation districts are going the way of Goa and Ko Samui. But looking on the bright side, you'll never have any trouble finding a room, and given the oversupply, you'll seldom have to pay the published rate, even in high season (in the off-season, expect discounts of fifty percent or more). Indeed, these are the cheapest hot-water lodgings in Nepal, although rooms with baths are generally overpriced.

Just about all independent travellers stay in Lakeside or Damside. Far removed from the din of the bazaar, overlooking the lake and peaks, and awash with Western food and comforts, both areas certainly offer a numbingly easy existence. If you're looking to get away from other tourists, however, consider staying across the lake, or overnighting in one of the outlying destinations described later, such as Sarangkot or Hyangja. Lodgings listed in the first few sections here fall into the cheap or moderately priced categories, with rated hotels listed separately later. By the way, the most expensive unrated guest houses now charge more than the cheapest rated hotels – but in terms of clientele, the classifications still hold up.

Lakeside
With its strip of bamboo restaurants, corrugated-tin curio shacks and breeze-block guest houses, **Lakeside** is like Robinson Crusoe meets Las Vegas. It's Thamel all over again, full of self-conscious idleness and obsessive eating, but it's more laid-back, and it's still – despite a decade-long building boom – essentially rural.

ROOM PRICE SCALES

All guest houses and hotels have been price-graded according to the scale outlined below, which represents the cheapest available double room in high season; codes prefixed by B denote the cost of a room with attached bathroom. See *Basics*, p.21, for a fuller explanation of the system.

① Less than Rs75   ⑤ $8–12
     ($1.50 if quoted in US$)   ⑥ $12–20
② Rs75–150 ($1.50–3)   ⑦ $20–40
③ Rs150–250 ($3–5)   ⑧ $40–70
④ $5–8   ⑨ Over $70

Lakeside covers a large area, and the further north you stay, the further you'll have to walk or pedal to get to most destinations. Also bear in mind that mountain views are better to the south. That said, the area north of Lakeside (off the map) preserves some of the undeveloped ambience of old, with several rough-hewn lodges and unmolested views of the lake. Avoid guest houses overlooking the main strip, as you'll be tormented by early-morning buses revving their engines and honking for passengers.

CHEAP

Blue Heaven Guest House. Simple, tiny, cheap – and an endangered species on this lane, now that it's been paved. ①.

Himalayan Country Lodge. The only place that can be recommended on this busy road, with well-appointed bungalow-style rooms. B④.

Hotel Fewa (☎061/20151). The only budget lodge right on the lake, with boats for rent and a nice lawn – you're hardly aware of the Lakeside bustle here. Primitive but lovely bungalows ②; rooms in the main building are overpriced at B⑥.

Native Lodge. Humble family-run operation located on the northern outskirts of Lakeside. ①.

Nepali Cottage. Funky little place with a traditional Gurung house on the grounds. Facilities are basic, but the central location pushes up the prices. ③.

New Lake View Guest House (☎061/21477). Very shady grounds, good views of mountains (not so good of the lake). B④.

New Star Lodge. A traditional holdout in a relatively uncommercialized area. ②/B④.

Noble House. Unpretentious outfit with an attractive building and grounds. ③.

Sunset View Lodge. The last word in seclusion, set on a hilltop with a magnificent view of the lake – but it's a longish hike to food or drink. ①.

Teacher Krishna Lodge. Farmhouse accommodation in an ochre-painted old house: delightful but spartan, and it probably won't withstand modernization much longer. ①.

Trekkers Retreat Lodge (☎061/21458). A friendly, no-frills place at the quiet southern fringe of Lakeside. ②/B④.

MODERATE

Hotel Barahi (☎061/21880). Surprisingly peaceful and large lawn seating area for such a central location. B⑥.

Full Moon Lodge (☎061/21511). Swish new place with supreme views over the lake and Baidam, located up a steep path. Expected to be B⑦.

Gurkha Lodge. Gardening buffs will love this place, tucked down a long Baidam lane, run by an ex-Gurkha and his English wife. Bungalows B⑤ (single or double occupancy).

Hotel Hungry Eye (☎061/20908). Overpriced but popular: centrally located, it's the nearest thing to a *Kathmandu Guest House* in Pokhara. B⑦.

Hotel Monal (☎061/21459). Good facilities, adequately set back from the strip. ⑤/B⑥.

Damside

If Lakeside is a rural Thamel, **Damside** is a suburban one. The social scene is less affected, its focus shifted from cafés to guest-house compounds, making the streets quieter and the neighbourhood more residential. The mountain views are better here than in Lakeside, but there's a distinct lack of greenery, and the choice of restaurants and handicraft shops is more limited. On the other hand, Damside is more centrally placed for the bank, Central Immigration and sightseeing around the valley.

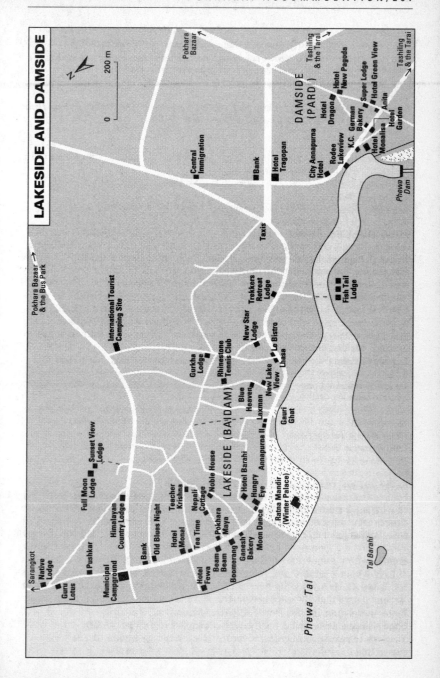

LAKESIDE AND DAMSIDE

CHEAP
Hotel Garden (☎061/20870). Spacious, with a good location and views. ③/B⑤.
Hotel Green View (☎061/21844). Lovely secluded garden restaurant. The new building is kind of a monstrosity, but the cheap rooms are in an older wing. ②/B⑤.
New Hotel Pagoda (☎061/21802). Modest but spotlessly clean, with a small garden seating area. ②/B④.
Super Lodge (☎061/21861). Clean and efficiently managed. The next-door *New Hotel Anzuk*, run by a Gurkha captain, is similarly good value. ①/B③.

MODERATE
City Annapurna Hotel (☎061/21878). Clean, with well-laid-out grounds, lawn seating and a competent restaurant. Breakfast included. B⑥.
Hotel Jharna (☎061/21925). The best location in Damside, overlooking the lake with great mountain views. B⑦.
Hotel Monalisa (☎061/20863). The second-best location in Damside. ⑤/B⑦.

Across the lake: Anadu
Anadu, directly across the lake from Baidam, is not one of Nepal's friendliest or best-kept villages, but there's a certain bohemian attraction to staying in a place that can only be reached by boat. (Actually, you can walk to Anadu from the high-way on the other side of the ridge behind, but let's not spoil the atmosphere.) The nearest of the places listed here, the *Typical*, can be reached in about thirty minutes' rowing from the palace area of Lakeside; *Gurung Cottage* is another ten minutes to the right and around the corner. Negotiate with the boatman for an overnight rate – you should be able to work out a ferry deal with someone in Anadu if you decide you want to stay on.
Gurung Cottage. Electricity and (occasional) hot water, otherwise basic, but friendly. ①.
Hotel Fewa (☎061/20151). A resort-type place right next to the *Typical*, operated by the Lakeside hotel of the same name (book through them). B⑦. The Lakeside *Fewa* can also arrange rooms in private houses in Anadu for ②.
Monal Resort (☎061/21459). A posh new hotel going up high above the lake, expected to be completed in late 1993 with rooms in the B⑦ range. Book through *Hotel Monal* on Lakeside.
Typical Guest House. A slightly more developed version of *Gurung Cottage*, with a better place to pull ashore and more variety in the food department. ①.

In the bazaar: Mahendra Pul and Prithvi Chowk
Pokhara Bazaar has little going for it, and its lodgings, catering mainly to Nepali and Indian businessmen, charge more for less. Realistically, you'd have to be either really stuck or really antisocial to stay here. That said, the **Mahendra Pul** area, Pokhara's main commercial centre, certainly has got spark, and you can get almost anything you need here. A messier, more organic locale, **Prithvi Chowk** seethes with a tumultuous melange of Nepalis, Indians and Tibetans; it happens to have a couple of new and rather posh guest houses, but otherwise it's grotty and takes its cues from the nearby bus park. If need be, you can find plenty of cheaper places than the ones listed here.
Hotel Anand, Prithvi Chowk (☎061/20029). Rooftop garden, TV. ④/B⑥.
Hotel Kailash, Mahendra Pul (☎061/21726). Clean, with roof garden. ②/B④.
New Hotel Sunkoshi, Mahendra Pul (☎061/21569). Drab but adequate. ②/B④.
Palace Hotel, Prithvi Chowk (☎061/20488). An Indian businessman's dream. ②/B④.

Pokhara's rated hotels

Pokhara's older **hotels** are rather unhappily situated near the airport, relics of the days when the only way to get here was by air. Quite a few others have more recently been built in Lakeside and Damside. It's advisable to book hotel rooms in advance, especially during the high season; where hotels have a Kathmandu booking office, the relevant phone numbers are given.

Fish Tail Lodge, Lakeside (Kathmandu ☎01/221711). Set amidst fabulous landscaping, the only hotel on the west side of Phewa Tal enjoys an unrivalled view of the lake and the classic profile of the mountains behind. Access by rope ferry. Two stars. B⑨.

Hotel Dragon, Damside (☎061/20052). Pretty garden with good views. Air-conditioned rooms with Tibetan furnishings. Two stars. B⑦.

Hotel Mount Annapurna, opposite the airport (☎061/20037). Disappointing rooms, though the lawn is worthy of the Raj. Two stars. B⑦.

Hotel Tragopan, Damside (Kathmandu ☎01/225898). New, good value for money. One star. B⑦.

New Hotel Crystal, opposite the airport (Kathmandu ☎01/228561). Pokhara's biggest hotel, with a pool and tennis court. Three stars. B⑦; with air conditioning B⑧.

Tara Gaon Resort, opposite the airport (Kathmandu ☎01/470409). Part of the government-run chain, with tidy bungalows but forlorn grounds. Two stars. B⑥.

Tiger Mountain Lodge (Kathmandu ☎01/222706). Luxurious new resort on a ridgetop east of Pokhara, scheduled to open in 1994.

Camping

There are two developed **campsites** in Lakeside: *International Tourist Camping Site*, a fairly stark affair with cold-water showers and a small shop, charging Rs20 per tent; and the even drearier municipal campground, which has no facilities other than toilets, and charges Rs40 per tent. If you're set on pitching a tent or need a place to park a van, you'd do better to work out a deal with one of the guest houses along the back lanes of Lakeside.

The lake and the bazaar

Visitors to Pokhara typically spend most of their time within arm's reach of apple pie, which means staying close to the lake. This is not fertile territory for cultural interaction, but a growing number of activities on the lake will at least help you to work off the calories. Real life goes on in the bazaar, which, though it pales in any comparison with the lake area, deserves more attention than it usually gets.

Phewa Tal

According to a local legend, **Phewa Tal** covers the area of a once-prosperous valley, whose inhabitants one day scorned a wandering beggar. Finding only one sympathetic woman, the beggar warned her of an impending flood: as the woman and her family fled to higher ground, a torrent roared down from the mountains and submerged the town – the "beggar" having been none other than the goddess Barahi Bhagwati. The woman's descendants settled beside the new lake and erected the island shrine of **Tal Barahi**; for local innkeepers and restauranteurs, who've done rather well out of the lake, a few alms at her shrine still don't go amiss.

The other, geological explanation is that the entire Pokhara Valley, like the Kathmandu Valley, was submerged about 200,000 years ago when the fast-rising Mahabharat Lekh dammed up the Seti River. Over time, the Seti eroded an ever-deeper outlet, lowering the water level and leaving Phewa Tal and several smaller lakes as remnants. However, the legend might contain a grain of truth, as submerged tree stumps at the lake's northern end indicate that the water level rose in the not-too-distant past, perhaps because an earthquake blocked the outlet. Phewa was further enlarged by the installation of Pardi Dam in 1967, which brought electricity and irrigation to the valley, and gave Damside its name. The dam, meanwhile, may be the death of the lake: some experts are predicting that siltation will fill it up in as little as thirty years – if the sewage doesn't kill it first. The local authorities make noises of concern about the lake's health, yet they recently gave serious consideration to a proposal to build a floating hotel in the middle of the lake. Now *that's* going to do wonders for water quality. What's next – Srinagar-style houseboats?

Lakeside (Baidam)

Next to eating, promenading along **Lakeside's** pipal-shaded main drag is the favourite pastime in Pokhara. It's a pleasant enough stroll in parts, but new

---

NAUTICAL PURSUITS

Boating (or just floating) on Phewa Tal is the easiest way to get away from the business of getting away from it all. Oversized **rowing boats** – they'll hold six easily – can be rented all along the eastern shore; after bargaining, the rate should settle at no more than Rs50 per hour, or Rs150 for the day. Wooden **sailboats**, available from *Hotel Fewa* and elsewhere, cost Rs100 per hour or Rs500 per day, double that for fibreglass ones. You can even rent a **fishing rod** from some Lakeside shops, and try to land carp-like *sahar*. Keep an eye on the **weather**, especially if sailing – wind squalls are common in late spring, and it's easy to be becalmed at other times of the year. The shore around the Royal Palace is off-limits, and if you see gesticulating security guards you're too close. **Swimming** is best done from a boat, as the shore is muddy, but the bacteria count doesn't bear thinking about.

An obvious first destination is **Tal Barahi**, the island shrine located a few hundred metres offshore from the palace. While the temple itself is modern and not much to look at, it's a busy spot on Saturdays, when the lake goddess exacts a steady tribute of blood sacrifices. If that doesn't put you off your lunch, the island makes a fine place for a picnic. During the spring wedding months you might find yourself caught up in a flotilla of merrymakers headed for the island, where music, dancing and *raksi*-drinking go on until all hours.

From the island it's about the same distance again to the far shore which, with dense jungle, manic monkeys and few places to put ashore, is most easily observed from the water. If you want to walk around on the other side, make for **ANADU**, the diffuse Gurung village that covers the hillside directly opposite Lakeside, about a half-hour's row from the palace. Food is available at the *Typical Guest House*, a whitish building set just back from a shingle beach, to the left of the main part of the village. Further to the right, trails from various points along the shore climb up through Anadu's scattered houses and terraced fields to eventually reach the ridgetop for great views. For some real exercise, you could row clear to the opposite (northwest) end of the lake and up the meandering Harnan Khola, the main tributary feeding the lake.

construction in this area (known locally as **Baidam**) has largely spoiled the area's former rural character: the concrete hotels and metal-shuttered bunkers sprouting everywhere suggest that their builders have somehow missed the point. Incidentally, many of these architectural monsters are in violation of the local building code, which prohibits structures over seven metres high, but the local council looks the other way because they're owned by influential government supporters. For years politicians have been talking about establishing a green belt between the road and the lake, which accounts for the temporary appearance of most of the buildings there. The idea has never been officially dropped, although at this point it would be political suicide to carry it through.

A pretty spot – it would be prettier if it were kept a little cleaner – is **Gauri Ghat**, just up from the *Hotel Kantipur*. Screened by a leafy *chautaara*, a set of steps leads steeply down to the lake and a *linga* shrine set atop a rocky outcrop. Midway along the Lakeside strip sits Ratna Mandir, the winter **Royal Palace**, a definite no-go area during the king's residence each February. At the palace's western edge, a road leads down to the lake at a shady spot known as **Barahi Tol**, where Nepalis and visiting Indians often go to escape the Western-dominated strip. Numerous other lanes head back away from the lake into lush Baidam: farmers are rapidly selling out to developers here, but a few holdouts still retain their traditional oval thatched cottages, sugar-loaf haystacks, vegetable plots and banana-palm borders. At the northern end of Lakeside, the road becomes a dirt track which can be followed along the less developed **northern shore**; side trails lead up to Sarangkot (p.212) from here.

Damside (Pardi)

In **Damside (Pardi)**, go for mountain views – the classic scene, captured in a ubiquitous Ministry of Tourism poster, can be viewed from a small Vishnu shrine in the triangle of land between the spillway and the lake.

Pardi Dam is of no intrinsic interest, and unfortunately you can't walk across it; but from the footbridge that crosses the Pardi Khola, downstream, trails lead south to Devin's Fall (see below) or up the ridge to the west. The ridge walk takes a good 45 minutes, passing through deep, monkey-populated jungle before reaching a Buddhist shrine at the top. Rumour has it a ropeway is going to be built to this point, to take advantage of the phenomenal views of the lake and mountains.

Pokhara Bazaar

Most of **Pokhara Bazaar** was destroyed in a fire in 1949, leaving little of interest. The active, southern end of town around **Mahendra Pul** is new since the fire, while the remnants of the original Newar quarter begin 1km further northwest, running from Bhimsen Tol up to Bag Bazaar. Perched on a hillock in the middle of this area you'll find the **Bindyabasini Mandir**, Pokhara's main cultural attraction, a quiet temple complex more noteworthy for its sweeping mountain views than its collection of shrines. The featured deity, Bindyabasini, is an incarnation of Kali, the mother goddess in her bloodthirsty aspect; animal sacrifices are common here, particularly on Saturdays and the ninth day of Dasain in October. Bindyabasini has a reputation as a bit of a prima donna: in one celebrated incident, her stone image began to sweat mysteriously, causing such a panic that the late King Tribhuvan had to order special rites to pacify the goddess. The fire that swept the bazaar in 1949 started here, when an offering burned out of control.

The **Pokhara Museum** (daily except Tues 10am–5pm; Rs5), located south of Mahendra Pul, contains a small exhibit of photos and artefacts relating to Nepalese ethnic groups, haphazardly arranged and with minimal English commentary. Tucked away in one corner of the Prithvi Narayan Campus at the northeastern part of town, the **Annapurna Regional Museum** (daily except Sat 10am–5pm; free) offers a similarly slapdash treatment of Nepal's natural history, the prize exhibit being a collection of Himalayan butterflies. An adjacent **information centre**, maintained by the *Annapurna Conservation Area Project*, contains some exhibits not found at the Central Immigration office and the *ACAP* headquarters in Ghandruk, but it's not worth a special trip.

Immediately east of town lies the mossy, almost invisibly narrow **Seti River gorge**, where the abrasive torrent has cut like acid though the valley's soft sediments. It can easily be seen from the bridge east of Mahendra Pul (*pul* means bridge) – there's something remarkable about witnessing natural forces at work so close to the bazaar – but the footbridge east of the airstrip, and K. I. Singh Pul at the northern end of town on the way to Mahendra Cave (see below), provide less rubbish-strewn vantage-points.

Exploring the valley

Day trips around the **Pokhara Valley** make excellent training for a trek, and are an effective antidote to lakeside idleness. Excursions generally entail a healthy amount of cycling or hiking, often both. Start early to make the most of the views before the clouds move in and the heat builds – it can get really sticky here in all but the winter months – and bring lunch and a full water bottle. If you're feeling adventurous (or running behind schedule), you can **stay overnight** at Sarangkot, Tashi Palkhel or Begnas Tal.

Many of the **ethnic groups** that make treks north of Pokhara so popular – Gurungs, Magars, and Bahun and Chhetri Hindu castes – are equally well represented around the valley, and less touched by tourism here. In addition, the three **Tibetan villages** in the area are less commercial, and more instructive about Tibetan culture, than Patan's Jaulakhel settlement.

Sarangkot

For the classic, full-length spectacle of the Himalaya – featuring Dhaulagiri, the Annapurnas, Manaslu and the graceful pyramid of Machhapuchhre – hike up one of the hilltops north and east of Pokhara. **Sarangkot**, a high point (1590m) on the ridge north of Phewa Tal, is the more popular and well developed of the two, with food, refreshments and overnight facilities.

Two principal routes ascend the ridge, one directly from Lakeside, the other from the Bindyabasini temple in the bazaar. The **Lakeside route** bypasses the bazaar, but it's a longer, steeper climb, with no mountain views until the very top – if you're running late you might miss them altogether. Follow the road north from Lakeside until it becomes a trail, where it traverses a large cultivated area and then snakes alternately through jungle and pastures; you'll be doing well to make it to the top in less than two and a half hours. When in doubt, stay on the flagstoned trail and keep heading generally towards the summit. This route is used by an increasing number of trekking parties, but usually on the descent, since it's

THE GURKHAS

As I write these last words, my thoughts return to you who were my comrades: the stubborn and indomitable peasants of Nepal. Once more I hear the laughter with which you greeted every hardship. Once more I see you in your bivouacs or about your fires, on forced march or in the trenches, now shivering with wet and cold, now scorched by a pitiless and burning sun. Uncomplaining, you endure hunger and thirst and wounds; and at the last, your unwavering lines disappear into the smoke and wrath of battle. Bravest of the brave, most generous of the generous, never had a country more faithful friends than you.

Ralph Lilley Turner, *Dictionary of the Nepali Language* (1931)

Comprising an elite Nepalese corps within the British and Indian armies for over 175 years, the **Gurkha regiments** have been rated among the finest fighting units in the world. Ironically, the regiments were born out of the 1814–16 war between Nepal and Britain's East India Company: so impressed were the British by the men of "Goorkha" (Gorkha, the ancestral home of Nepal's rulers) that they began recruiting Nepalis into the Indian Army before the peace was even signed.

In the century that followed, Gurkhas fought in every major British military operation, including the 1857 **Indian Mutiny** and campaigns in Afghanistan, the North-West Frontier and Somaliland. More than 200,000 Gurkhas served in the two world wars, and, despite being earmarked for "high-wastage roles", earned universal respect for their bravery: ten of the one hundred **Victoria Crosses** awarded in World War II went to Gurkhas. Following India's independence after the war, Britain took four of the ten Gurkha regiments and India retained the rest. More recently, Gurkhas have distinguished themselves in Sarawak, Cyprus and the 1982 Falklands War, and are currently stationed in Hong Kong, Brunei, Belize and the UK.

Gurkhas hail mainly from the Magar, Gurung, Rai and Limbu hill tribes (growing up in the Nepal hills is ideal preparation for the army). Most boys from these groups dream of making it into the Gurkhas, not only for the money – the annual salary of £5000 is about fifty times the Nepalese average – but also for a rare chance to see the world and return with prestige and a comfortable pension.

The Gurkhas' long and faithful service to Britain is winding down, however. With Hong Kong (the Gurkhas' headquarters) to be handed over to China in 1997, and the Sultan of Brunei's contract for Gurkha protection due to expire in 1998, Britain's need for military forces in Asia is expected to decline. Army brass have announced plans to amalgamate the four British regiments into two and integrate them in some way with the regular army. Anticipating this, the main Gurkha recruiting and training centre in Dharan was handed over to civilian use at the end of 1989, and all remaining operations are now carried out at the smaller facility in Pokhara. Would-be recruits can still try out for places in the lower-paid Indian regiments – which is what most who failed to make the cut for the British Gurkhas used to do anyway – but the gradual loss of salaries and pensions is apt to take the steam out of many Nepali hill communities.

awfully steep for a first day out. The hike **from the bazaar** follows a road for much of the way, which is a drawback, but it's a gentler ascent, and the scenery – both mountains and lake – just gets better and better as you go. From just south of the Bindyabasini Temple follow the signposted turn-off for about five minutes, then take the right fork and follow that road for about an hour and a half to a set of shops (taxis will drive this far for about Rs600 return); a wide path leads from there to the summit in another half-hour. Soft drinks are sold along both routes.

Annapurna South Annapurna I   Machhapuchhre   Annapurr
(7237 m)   (8091 m)   (6997 m)   (7555 m)

**THE HIMALAYA AS SEEN
FROM POKHARA**

The **village** of Sarangkot, nestled just below the summit, has tea shops, handicrafts sellers and several trekking-standard **lodges** (with electricity, no less) – if you're not planning to trek, at least spend one night here. For the **summit**, continue another ten minutes up to a walled compound, where the local council will hit you for a donation for their water supply. If you've hiked up from Lakeside, the sudden view here will come as a staggering revelation. The peaks seem to levitate above their blue flanks, the gathering clouds add a quality of raw grandeur, while to the south, Phewa Tal shimmers in the hazy arc of the valley. If you hadn't been planning on trekking, this is where you might change your mind.

Kaski, seat of the kingdom that once ruled the Pokhara Valley, lives on as a village (with more basic lodges) about half an hour further west, just below the ridge. From there you can march up a long stone staircase to Kaskikot, where low walls and a small Durga shrine are all that remain of the citadel of the Kaski kings, which fell to the Gorkhalis without a fight in 1781. Continuing west along the ridge for another hour and a half, the trail joins the Pokhara–Baglung Highway at **Naudanda** (or Nagdanda), a busy and rather unappealing bazaar, but the first place from which Machhapuchhre's true fishtail profile can be seen. The road from the Bindyabasini temple is eventually supposed to be extended to here. Though you can't continue any further west without a trekking permit, you can spend the night here (plenty of places to choose from), or catch a ride back to Pokhara via Phedi.

Kahun Danda

If the view from **Kahun Danda**, the hill east of Pokhara, is a shade less magnificent than Sarangkot's, a lookout tower near the top gives you a better crack at it. The trail up the ridge is totally uncommercialized and consequently hard to find (the tourist map's depiction of trails is wildly misleading). Although the furthest from Lakeside/Damside, the easiest and most interesting starting point is the **Tibetan monastery** 2km east of Mahendra Pul. At the top of a breathless couple of hundred steps at the southern base of Kahun Danda, the Karma Dhubgyu Chhokhorling Nyeshang Korti Monastery occupies a breezy spot – always good for keeping the prayer flags flapping – with valley views east and west. Around thirty monks and monklets inhabit the monastery, which is modern and contains all the usual Vajrayana paraphernalia (chanting daily around 4pm).

III   Annapurna IV   Annapurna II   Lamjung Himal
       (7525 m)   (7937 m)   (6986 m)

The trail to the lookout tower starts at the bottom of the steps, hugs the western base of the ridge for about 1km, and then climbs through several lazy settlements collectively known as **Phulbari**. Keep heading towards the blocky tower (1460m), which is visible most of the way, and can be reached in about an hour and a half from the monastery. From the half-finished concrete platform, you can contemplate the tremendous force of the Seti River and its tributaries, which tumble out of the Annapurna Himal clouded with dissolved limestone (*seti* means white) and, merging at the foot of the Kahun Danda, split the valley floor with a bleached chasm.

Descending back to the monastery, paths bearing to the left may suggest a longer circuit via the valley and villages on the east side of the ridge. Also eminently worth exploring is the tidily terraced side valley of the **Bhalam Khola**, immediately north of Kahun Danda, which is an alternate approach for the Siklis trek. To get there directly from the tower involves some nasty bushwacking, so it's better to backtrack towards the monastery until you pick up the first main northbound trail. It's also accessible by a rough (mountain-bikeable) track heading northwards on the east side of the Seti River.

Mahendra Cave

While it just about scrapes a description as a geological wonder, **Mahendra Cave** (Mahendra Gupha) is probably best thought of as a base from which to explore the snug hills and side valleys north of Pokhara, even though it's a long nine-kilometre haul from Lakeside/Damside. To get there, cross K. I. Singh* Pul (Bridge) at the top end of Pokhara and head north past the Gurkha Training Camp, turn right up a paved road 600m beyond the bridge, and follow it for about 3km to the end. The climb is relentless and if you're on a one-speed bike you'll have to push much of the way (the reward comes on the way back). Some city buses come up this way from the bazaar east of the bus park, via Prithvi Chowk.

---

*A cross between Robin Hood and Che Guevara, **K. I. Singh** led the western insurgents in the 1951 overthrow of the Rana regime and restoration of Nepal's monarchy. Although on the winning side, his radical socialism kept him from office and eventually landed him in jail.

A *gaaine*

Water percolating down from the limestone hills above has etched away at the valley's alluvial sediments, creating a honeycomb of caves. Mahendra Cave used to be well known for its limestone stalactites, but these have unfortunately been ransacked by vandals; a few surviving **stalagmites** are daubed with red sindur and revered as Shiva *linga* because of their resemblance to phalluses.

Admission to the caves is Rs5, plus *bakshish* for someone to "watch" your bike and for the local kid who won't leave you alone until you hire him as a guide. Though the cave is neither dangerous nor vast – the accessible part takes about ten to fifteen minutes to tour – a guide is still useful, if only to show you which way to point your torch (a fairly essential item, since the electric generator rarely works and guides make do with feeble candles). They'll probably try to sell you a tour of **another cave** about ten minutes' walk away, promising a bigger chamber and better stalactites. It is, surprisingly, as advertised, but it's a hell of a scramble, and once inside it may strike you that, were it not for Nepalis' innate honesty, you could be rolled for everything you've got. For serious spelunkers only.

Eastwards from Mahendra Cave, a trail beckons up the **Kali Khola**, a minor tributary of the Seti, to the village of Armala. Horseshoe-shaped and stepped with perfect terraces, the valley looks like an immense sprouting Roman amphitheatre. Adventurous types might want to forge on. Scrambling up the cultivated slopes on either side of the valley might make for some interesting encounters, though no mountain views. By traversing the ridge to the south, you should theoretically be able to return to Pokhara the same day via the Bhalam Khola.

About 1km south of Mahendra Cave, the road from Pokhara passes through **BATULECHAUR**, a village locally famous for its **gaaine**. Wandering minstrels of the old school, *gaaine* are still found throughout the hills, earning their crust by singing ballads to the accompaniment of the *sarangi*, a four-stringed, hand-hewn violin: "I have no rice to eat/let the strings of the *sarangi* set to," runs the *gaaine*'s traditional opening couplet. These days, many find they can make better money down at Lakeside serenading tourists, spawning legions of inept imitators.

The Pokhara–Baglung Highway

A second road heading northwest from the bazaar through the valley of the Yamdi Khola – already provisionally christened the **Pokhara–Baglung Highway** – provides the chief access for treks in the Annapurna region (see Chapter Seven). By early 1993 passable as far as the Modi Khola, just south of Birethanti, the highway is being steadily extended and will soon reach Baglung, the zonal headquarters of the intensely populated hill area west of Pokhara, and someday all the way up the Thak Khola to Jomosom. Many trekkers use this road to get to various trailheads, but other than that it sees few foreign faces. It would make a worthy mountain-biking route for one or more days, with a possible stopover at the Tibetan village of Tashi Palkhel (see below), but remember that you need a trekking permit and ACAP receipt to proceed beyond Naudanda; eventually a separate road to Naudanda via Sarangkot will be completed, making a one-day loop possible. **Accommodation** is available at Tashi Palkhel, Naudanda and other towns en route.

As has happened elsewhere, the new highway is introducing enormous changes to the local social order, bringing wealth and prosperity to a few (mostly outside developers) and luring young people away to the cities. Only a decade ago, Shining Hospital was the end of the road, the region beyond accessible only by foot or pack animal. Today, the Yamdi Khola has been transformed, not only by vehicles, but also by a hydroelectric power project and a roadside smattering of modern concrete dwellings emanating like a comet's tail from Pokhara Bazaar. The old walking route is falling into disuse, since trekkers and locals alike seldom walk when they can ride a bus, and villages along the highway are finding they must adapt or die.

The Tibetan villages

If Tibet were free tomorrow, we'd drop our hammers and go. We wouldn't even think about it.

A Tibetan working on a building project at Tashi Palkhel

Twenty-five years ago, Dervla Murphy worked as a volunteer among Tibetan refugees in Pokhara, and called the account she wrote about her experiences *The Waiting Land* (see "Books" in *Contexts*). Pokhara's Tibetans are still waiting: three former refugee camps, now self-governing and largely self-sufficient, have settled into a pattern of permanent transience. Because Pokhara (unlike Kathmandu) has no Buddhist holy places, most Tibetans have remained in the camps, regarding them as havens where they can keep their culture and language alive. Many plainly don't see the point of moving out and setting up permanent homes in Nepal when all they really want is to return to their former homes in Tibet.

Located northwest, southwest and near the centre of Pokhara, the settlements are open to the public, and a wander around one is an experience of workaday reality that contrasts with the otherworldliness of, say, Boudha or Swayambhu. You'll get a lot more out of a visit if you can get someone to show you around – and if the tour inevitably finishes with a sales pitch back at your guide's one-room home, so much the better.

Tashi Palkhel (Hyangja)

With one thousand residents – sixty of them monks – **TASHI PALKHEL** (commonly known as **HYANGJA**, after the village at the top of the hill) is the largest and also the least commercial of the three settlements. The entrance is clearly marked, about 4km northwest of Shining Hospital on the Pokhara–Baglung Highway, at the foot of Sarangkot; get there by bike (preferably mountain bike), taxi or bus from Shining Hospital. If you're doing the Siklis trek you'll hit the trail not far from here.

As soon as you enter the village you'll be adopted by friendly but insistent saleswomen, who'll escort you to the **gompa** and wait to make their pitch as you come out. The *gompa* is of the Kagyu-pa sect, and portraits either side of the Buddha statue inside the hall depict the Dalai Lama and the late Kagyu leader, the sixteenth Karma Lama. A long **weaving hall** is the focal point of Tashi

TIBETANS IN POKHARA

At the time of the Chinese invasion of Tibet in 1950 and the Dalai Lama's flight in 1959, the **Tibetans** now living in Pokhara were mainly peasants and nomads inhabiting the border areas of western Tibet. The political changes in faraway Lhasa left them initially unaffected, but as the Chinese occupation turned genocidal, thousands streamed south through the Himalaya to safety. They gathered first at Jomosom, where the terrain and climate were at least reminiscent of Tibet, but within months the area became overcrowded and conditions desperate. Under the direction of the Swiss Red Cross, three transit camps were established around low-lying Pokhara and about two thousand refugees were moved down. Thirty years on, the subtropical heat still heightens Tibetans' sense of displacement.

The first five years were hard times in the camps, marked by food rationing, chronic sickness and general unemployment. Relief came in the late 1960s, when the construction of Pardi Dam and the Prithvi and Siddhartha highways provided welcome work. Since then, the Tibetans' fortunes have risen with Pokhara's tourism industry, and carpet-weaving and other handicrafts have become the main source of income, especially for women. Many of the men work seasonally as trekking porters or guides, where they can make better money than in the camps. A small but visible minority have become smooth-talking curio salespeople, plying the cafés of Lakeside and Damside, but whereas Tibetans have by now set up substantial businesses in Kathmandu, opportunities are fewer in Pokhara, and prosperity has come more slowly. See *Contexts* for more on the lives of Tibetan exiles.

Palkhel's carpet industry, and forming the other sides of a quadrangle are wool dyeing and drying areas and a cooperative shop. The community also has a school and, the latest project, an old people's home – many of the original refugees are now getting on in years. **Handicrafts** can be purchased at the cooperative shop, whose profits support community projects (they have another outlet in Damside), as well as a couple of private enterprises. If you decide to stay overnight, the camp's cooperative **guest house** can supply rooms (③), hot showers are available, and camping is possible. Get **food** at the guest house or at one of the camp's smoky, buttery holes-in-the-wall.

Tashiling and Devin's Fall

Much easier to reach, **TASHILING** lies about 2km west of Damside beside the main highway to India. On a bicycle you can be there in ten minutes. With some 550 residents, Tashiling is smaller than Tashi Palkhel, but laid out on much the same lines. It's best to make straight for the weaving hall and wool-dyeing shed, a good 400m down the main drive at the far end of the camp. A short walk from here to the camp's southern edge brings you to an abrupt drop and a glorious panorama of the valley of the Phusre Khola, a Seti tributary. On the way back to the entrance are a *gompa*, a primary school, several rows of distinctly Tibetan barracks-style stone houses (the windows trimmed with characteristic orange and white skirts) and, in a separate compound, a "children's village" for Tibetan orphans from all over Nepal. The inescapable souvenir peddlers and **shops** near the entrance sell the usual trinkets. If you're planning to make any purchases while in Pokhara, it's worth coming here first to establish the going rate – and even if things aren't any cheaper here, you'll have the satisfaction of buying them in their natural environment.

On the opposite side of the highway, **Devin's Fall** (entrance Rs5) marks the spot where the Pardi Khola (the stream that drains Phewa Tal) enters a grottoed channel and sinks underground in a sudden rush of foam and fury. Given a good monsoon run-off in the autumn it can be damn impressive, as the green water corkscrews and thunders into the earth, forcing up a continuous plume of mist; in the spring it's a washout.

The spot is perhaps more interesting as a source of pop mythology: known to locals as Patale Chhango (roughly, "Underworld Plunge"), the sinkhole is said to have acquired its Western-sounding nickname when a "female European" was drowned while skinny-dipping with her boyfriend. An alternate spelling, David Fall, suggests it may have been the boyfriend who perished. The sign at the entrance reads "Devi's Fall", illustrating the Nepalese propensity to deify everything that moves (*devi* means goddess). The whole story sounds like a fabrication to warn local youth to shun promiscuous Western ways.

Paljorling (Tibetan Handicrafts Centre)
The smallest of Pokhara's Tibetan settlements, **PALJORLING** (signposted merely as the **Tibetan Handicrafts Centre**) is now not so much a community as a factory with on-site housing; little wonder then that it rarely goes by its original name these days. The emphasis is on retail sales, and its inhabitants work over any foreigners who inadvertently fall into their web from the nearby bus park. To its credit, the camp is much smaller and easier to suss out than the other two, so given its location it can be easily fitted in as a side trip on the way to town.

Begnas Tal and Rupa Tal

With Lakeside and Damside approaching build-out, **Begnas Tal** and **Rupa Tal**, twin lakes lying 10km east of Pokhara, look destined to be the next big tourist discoveries. Begnas Tal, the bigger and better-known of the two, is framed by meticulously engineered paddy terraces marching right down to its shore, while Rupa, on the other side of an intervening ridge, remains pristinely hidden in a bushy, steep-sided valley. Roads and trails open up a wealth of itineraries in the area, which hopefully will resist uglification for at least a little while longer.

Don't let the distance on the map put you off: **getting there** is easier than it looks and an outing needn't take the whole day. Buses, departing every hour or so from New Road just south of Chipledhunga, take 45 minutes and tend to be crowded. Cycling is more scenic, and with a mountain bike you'll be able to probe well into the countryside. After the first (mostly downhill) 10km along the Prithvi Highway, turn left at the

Harvesting rice

Traditional Gurung house

sign onto a straight, paved road, and from there it's 3km to the end of the line at **SISUWA**. You'd never guess it, but Begnas Tal is right around the corner from here. Sisuwa itself is a cipher – typical of so many roadhead towns, it seems to exist only as a conduit for corrugated roofing, bags of cement and other tools of progress for the surrounding hills – but basic **food** and **lodging** are available if needed.

The quick approach to Begnas – not to be confused with the scenic one – is the dirt road to the left immediately before the cul-de-sac where the buses stop in Sisuwa. It's not even five minutes' walk along here to the dam at the south end of the lake, below which the Ministry of Agriculture is building a huge **fish farm**, consisting of concrete holding tanks fed by water from the lake. Fish farming is getting to be big business here, with Chinese carp, *sahar* and *mahseer* being raised for restaurants in Pokhara and Kathmandu. Phewa-style **boats** are rented out beside the lake just beyond the dam; with tent-shaped Annapurna II for a backdrop, the boating here is at least as scenic as at Phewa Tal, and you'll probably have the lake to yourself. This may not be the case for long, however, as big changes are afoot: a "ring road" around Begnas Tal is planned, and rich outsiders have bought up much of the prime shorefront land for future development, while at least one resort hotel is already under construction up on the ridge between Begnas and Rupa lakes.

A better introduction to the lakes, although it involves a fair amount of up and down, is the trail along **Panchbhaiya Danda**. Starting in Sisuwa, follow a graded road north for about twenty minutes, then take the trail to the left, which ascends steadily along the ridge dividing the two lakes (mountain-bikers, stay on the road). Begnas is visible first, on the left, and then Rupa comes into view after the highest point of the ridge is passed, about 45 minutes from Sisuwa. What appear to be fences peeping above the water of both lakes are more fish farms – Rupa Tal is said to be particularly rich in nutrients. In another ten minutes or so the trail rejoins the road near a cluster of shops, and from here on it's follow-your-nose time.

A trail leading off to the right, signposted "Karputar", descends to the north end of Rupa Tal and the village of Talbesi, with the additional possibility of a steep side trip to the hilltop fortress of **Rupakot**. This trail makes an attractive alternative way into the Annapurna Circuit. Further down the road, a trail to the left leads to another village called Begnas and from there down to the lake, and a further trail off that one climbs to the top of a ridge for magnificent views. The road itself swings around to Talbesi, and is eventually supposed to be pushed all the way through to Besisahar. When buses are able to negotiate this route, expect it to vie in popularity with the one from Dumre – but also to kill off the walking route.

Practicalities

Whatever you're looking for, it's a buyer's market in Pokhara. Everything comes so easily, the main challenge is sifting through the growing multitude of possibilities. New businesses pop up like mushrooms after each monsoon, and disappear just as quickly; cheap places have a habit of going upmarket, great views get blocked, and what's hot today may be dead tomorrow. No guidebook can hope to keep up with all the changes, so take the following recommendations with a pinch of salt.

Eating

Restaurants are everywhere in Pokhara, and food is a major preoccupation. Lakeside, in particular, is one long trough of feeding opportunities. Eating also sets the social agenda: there's not much nightlife after around 10pm, but the congenial restaurants and cafés around the lake are easy places to make friends and find trekking partners. Candlelight (often imposed by load-shedding) adds to the romance. Take the implausibly international menus with a pinch of salt, and don't be fooled by the fanciful cake and pie displays – you might not get what you thought you'd ordered, but it'll probably taste pretty good anyway (especially after three weeks on the trail). Prices are generally comparable to Kathmandu's Thamel area – around Rs100–150 for a dinner at most places.

If pseudo-Western food gets you down, many restaurants do set **Nepali meals**. For cheap and cheerful meals, try one of the myriad **momo** shacks, whose chatty proprietors play your choice of music on beat-up ghetto blasters. Watch out for the **juice** sellers, though: they'll charge whatever they think they can get, and dilute the juice with water and sugar if you're not looking.

Lakeside

Annapurna II Beer Garden. Cheap, casual, and it does indeed have a view of said mountain.

Beam Beam. Lively place with bar and back garden.

Boomerang. Great for breakfast or an afternoon snack: seating under umbrellas and thatched pavilions on a vast lawn sloping down to the lake. Many neighbouring outfits have now started to copy the formula, but this is still the best. Also a takeaway counter for bakery goods.

Ganesh Bakery. The best place for bread, croissants and muesli curd. Very cheap (even Nepalis eat here).

Guru Lotus. Modest place with wild culinary ambitions, but it has a delightfully earthy atmosphere, garden seating and an interesting proprietor.

Hungry Eye. Firmly established as the epicentre of Lakeside eating, serving decent pasta, steaks and sometimes inspired desserts – although its prices reflect its reputation.

Laxman. Funky, shoestring decor and a laid-back feel.

Le Bistro. Established outdoor café, good for breakfast; the usual overconfident menu, but fish is a speciality.

Lhasa. Serene atmosphere, though Tibetan food is almost an afterthought.

Moon Dance. An engaging retro-Sixties haunt – sort of a Nepali version of Alice's Restaurant.

Tea Time. Good for daytime people-watching, drinks and snacks.

Damside

Damside's guest houses tend to have their own self-contained restaurants, so there are fewer separate eating places to recommend.

Anita. One of a few small and simple Indian eateries near here, this one specializing in southern dishes.

German Bakery. A candidate for breakfast or lunch ingredients: good views, tolerable croissants and wholegrain bread.

K.C. One of two restaurants in Pokhara directly overlooking the lake; barbecue meats a speciality. No relation to the Kathmandu restaurant of the same name.

Nest Restaurant, in the *Hotel Tragopan*. Decent north Indian food in a more upscale setting; moderately priced.

Rodee Lakeview. The only other restaurant with patio seating beside the lake, and the home of Damside's premier cake display; cheap, and excellent for breakfast.

Pokhara Bazaar

Indian traders have moved in on Pokhara Bazaar, as they have wherever there's commercial potential, and Indian restaurants are a welcome result of their presence. You'll find several serviceable eateries around the northwest corner of Prithvi Chowk (west of the bus park), and a few others in Mahendra Pul and Chipledhunga. For tourist food, try Mahendra Pul.

Nightlife

While nightlife around Pokhara usually just means a second helping of pie, a good way to break the routine is to catch a **culture show**. Of the two held near the lake area, the ninety-minute programme at Damside's *Hotel Dragon* (nightly during the high season, usually at 7pm, but check – times vary) is the more entertainingly amateur. The show at the *Fish Tail Lodge* (nightly at 6 or 6.30pm) only lasts an hour and the musicians are kept offstage for most of the performance. Tickets for both shows cost about Rs75 and are available through agents.

A few Lakeside **nightspots** are now pushing back the usual 10pm bedtime barrier, at least during the high season. Their turnover rate is high, but the following were still raving as we went to press:

Beam Beam. Loud music, mixed drinks and a sociable atmosphere, but a slightly urban edge.

Old Blues Night. Laid-back night club open till late (in season). Occasional live music.

Pokhara Maya. Excellent rooftop bar, lake view, cocktails, happy hour.

Pushkar. The party never seems to stop on the roof of this rowdy guest house. Lake view, good sound system, happy hour.

Tea Time. Popular for after-dinner drinks. Good sound system.

Shopping

Shopping is still a mainly outdoor activity in Lakeside and Damside, where laid-back curio stalls make a welcome change from the hard-driving salesmen of Kathmandu, even if their prices and selection don't quite compare. Specialities include batiks, wooden flasks and fossil-bearing *shaligram* stones from the Kali Gandaki (see p.228). Hand-stitched wall hangings in simple Tibetan designs have been designed for the tourist market, but are attractive nonetheless. Persuasive

Tibetans peddle their wares in Lakeside's cafés, but these aren't produced locally, and carpets are best purchased at the Tibetan villages. Hand-knitted woollen sweaters, socks and such aren't of very good quality here, but may fit the bill for trekking. Other than that, you'll find the usual range of tourist bait, most of it imported from Kathmandu: ritual masks, *thangka*, Kashmiri papier-mâché widgets, embroidered T-shirts (wear that trek!), cloth bags and prison clothes. Stalls along the strip opposite the palace are extremely competitive.

Moving on

Buses link Pokhara with Kathmandu via the Prithvi Highway, and with the Tarai and India via the Siddhartha Highway. All four domestic airlines connect Pokhara with Kathmandu.

Buses and planes

Tourist buses to Kathmandu pick up passengers in front of the major guest houses in Lakeside and Damside. Though roughly twice as expensive (Rs150–200) as local equivalents, they're more comfortable and an hour or two quicker. The so-called express buses **to Sunauli and Tadi Bazaar** (for Chitwan) also start from Lakeside/Damside but then proceed to the bus park, where they fill every remaining cranny with local passengers. All of these services can be booked through a ticket agent and you'll need to shop around, since not every agent deals with every bus, and you'll get the best seat assignment from the main agent (he'll be the one with the seating chart). Agents can also arrange tickets for **other destinations** – the service charge may be more than the price of the ticket, but it's well worth it to avoid an extra encounter with the bus park. If you're heading **to India**, read the section on ticket agents in the Kathmandu chapter first.

For **flights**, go through an agent or contact the airlines directly (phone numbers given below).

Trekking

There are any number of ways to get to the start of a **trek** in the Annapurna region north of Pokhara. At the time of writing most people were taking a taxi from Lakeside/Damside to **Phedi** (about Rs200) and either hitting the trail from there or catching a truck on to **Lumle**. In the coming years the road will be paved to Lumle and beyond (see "The Pokhara–Baglung Highway", p.216), presenting the opportunity of longer and more expensive taxi rides; rickety buses also ply this road, departing hourly from the far end of the Shining Hospital lot, but few would choose this punishment. You can also enter the region by hiking straight in from Lakeside, **via Sarangkot**, or by hiring someone to row you across the lake and upriver to a point below Naudanda. Those trekking the Annapurna Circuit typically start at Besisahar, reached by taking a bus to **Dumre** (on the way to Kathmandu), from where trucks shuttle the rest of the way; an alternative trailhead is **Sisuwa** (Begnas Tal), reached by local bus from Chipledhunga in the bazaar.

Recommending **trekking agencies** in Pokhara is even riskier than in Kathmandu. Anyway, you don't need an agency to trek the Annapurna region unless you're doing something unorthodox, in which case organize it in

Kathmandu. Don't sucker for pony trekking – it's utterly worthless, usually just a very local plod on a malnourished, maltreated creature. **Guides** and **porters** can be hired through almost any guest house or equipment-rental stall. See "Listings" for information on the local Central Immigration office, and Chapter Seven for full details on trekking routes.

Rafting

Several **rafting operators** have offices in Lakeside, but, as in Kathmandu, their personnel change so often that it's not worth mentioning them by name. Most stick to budget specials on the Trisuli, running only the tamer lower section, though this can serve as a satisfying segue into the Tarai. With the completion of the Baglung Highway to Kusma, trips on the Kali Gandaki will soon become feasible and Pokhara will probably attract a better selection of quality operators. See the "Rafting" box earlier in this chapter (p.195) for more information on choosing a trip.

Listings

Airlines *Everest* (☎061/21883), next to the airport, daily 9am–7pm; *Necon* (☎061/20256), Ratna Chowk (near Central Immigration), Mon–Fri & Sun 10am–5pm, Sat 10am–noon; *Nepal Airways* (☎061/21178), opposite the airport, daily 10am–5.50pm; *RNAC* (☎061/21021), at the airport, daily 10am–1.30pm & 2–5pm.

Banks *Nepal Grindlays* in Lakeside handles foreign exchange and Mastercard/Visa cash advances daily except Sat 10am–4pm. *Rastriya Banijya*'s foreign-exchange counter, a short distance north of Damside, is open daily 7am–7pm.

Black market The rate is usually better in Kathmandu. Far from approaching you, Pokhara shopkeepers and hoteliers have to be persuaded to change money unofficially, and few touts work the streets.

Books Though the stalls around the lake are small, collectively they can muster a good selection of new and second-hand books.

Car rental $40–50 a day through travel agents.

Central Immigration A short walk north of the bank, it issues trekking permits (Annapurna and Jumla regions only) and visa extensions. Application hours are daily except Sat 10.30am–1pm (12.30pm in winter); permits and visas are ready later the same day. For most trekking permits, an additional Annapurna Conservation Area fee is payable. Passport photos are available in half an hour from studios near the office (about Rs75).

Dope is available, but sold more discreetly than in Kathmandu. If you're going trekking, you'll find it much cheaper on the trail.

Film and processing Films are available at roughly Kathmandu prices. A couple of places near Mahendra Pul do processing, and shops around the lake can arrange it for a small surcharge.

Health The *Western Regional Hospital* (☎061/20066), with foreign and Nepali staff, handles emergencies and does stool tests. A few pharmas in Lakeside/Damside will send your stool to the lab for a fee (about Rs100), and one or two offer ayurvedic medicine. Contact *Hotel Monal* about Tibetan medicine.

Laundry Most lodges take laundry for a few rupees per item; the places calling themselves "dry cleaners" return your clothes dry, but wash as wet as the others.

Massage Various shacks advertise acupressure and shiatsu; *Hotel Monal* can be recommended. What the barbers call "massage" looks extremely painful and is probably best avoided.

Meditation The Osho (Rajneesh) people have a meditation centre in Mahendra Pul.

Newspapers and magazines *International Herald Tribune, Time* and *Newsweek* are available in bookshops, usually one or two days late.

Post office The main office, in Mahendra Pul, is open Mon–Thurs & Sun 10am–5pm (4pm in winter), Fri 10am–3pm. They've got a poste restante department, but it's something of a black hole – don't have anything of value sent to you here. Some tourist bookshops sell stamps and take letters to the post office for franking.

Provisions Basically, everything you can get in Kathmandu, you can get in Lakeside/Damside: chocolate, dried fruit, tinned food, cheese, muesli, toiletries, batteries, etc. Pokhara can't match Kathmandu for brown bread, but the croissants aren't bad.

Teaching English *Pokhara English Language Institute* (☎061/21756), in Mahendra Pul opposite the GPO, needs native-speaking instructors.

Telephone calls As in Kathmandu, you'll find plenty of ISD/IDD businesses, plus many guest houses have international dialling facilities. International calls are charged at around Rs200 per minute, depending on country (shop around), trunk calls to Kathmandu about Rs60 for three minutes.

Tennis Yes, tennis – the *Rhinestone Tennis Club* in Lakeside charges $10 an hour ($4 if you bring your own racquet and balls). Going into the 1993 monsoon, the clay courts were reasonably flat.

Trekking equipment The selection of gear for rent isn't as good as in Kathmandu, although you'll pay for fewer days by renting locally. Sleeping bags, packs and parkas are no problem.

Tourist information The sleepy office opposite the airstrip can answer simple, specific questions. Open Mon–Thurs & Sun 10am–5pm (10am–4pm in winter) and Fri 10am–3pm.

SOUTH OF POKHARA

Sticking to roads, the only way to continue beyond Pokhara is to go south: a slow, uncomfortable, but occasionally rewarding journey along the **Siddhartha Highway** (Siddhartha Rajmarg) to the Tarai. In 160km the highway traverses four major river drainages, negotiates countless twists and turns, and usually claims a tyre or an axle; eight hours would be a fast run. Although it's the most direct route between Pokhara and the Indian border, give some thought to going via Chitwan if you're travelling by bus. Cyclists, however, will enjoy the variety, light traffic and relatively easy gradients.

From Pokhara, the road labours for an hour and a half to a high point at Naudanda, a little-used alternative starting point for treks into the Kali Gandaki/Annapurna region; minibuses from Chipledhunga in Pokhara shuttle up here every half-hour or so. An old Kaski fortress guards the pass from the hill just to the east. Entering the **Amdhi Khola** watershed, the highway wriggles tortuously across the side of the valley, purposely avoiding the flat, straight valley floor – in a country so reliant on agriculture, you don't put a road through the best farmland. After the dumpy bazaar of Syangja, the valley draws in and the hills rear up spectacularly in places, although you can't help noticing how badly overworked and eroded the land is in settled areas. Lunch is invariably at Waling, a nondescript wayside that owes its existence to busloads of hungry travellers. The road drops down to cross the rugged canyon of the **Kali Gandaki** at Ramdi Ghat, where cremations are sometimes conducted, before climbing almost 1000m to its highest point. A few kilometres beyond is the turning for Tansen, the only town of note in this area, situated some 3km off the highway. From the Tansen turning, it's an hour and a half's descent to Butwal (covered in Chapter Five).

Tansen

TANSEN is thoroughly second-rate, but endearingly so if given half a chance. Once the seat of a powerful kingdom, it's now a lowly district headquarters, slightly seedy and somehow left behind – shopkeepers still display black-and-white portraits of the king and queen. Yet slowly, almost reluctantly, Tansen yields its secrets: clacking *dhaka* cloth looms glimpsed though doorways; the potters of Ghorabanda; the view from Srinagar Hill, and superb hill-walking beyond. As such it's probably chiefly of interest to connoisseurs of the offbeat, although travellers coming up from India might consider breaking the journey here, for Tansen makes a more authentic introduction to Nepal than Pokhara.

Tansen's **history** goes back to the early sixteenth century, when it was known as Palpa, and when the Sen clan of princes, already established at Butwal, chose it as a safer base from which to expand family holdings that soon covered the length of the lower hills, almost to Sikkim. Makunda Sen, Palpa's legendary second king, allegedly raided Kathmandu and carried off two sacred Bhairab masks, only to be cut down by a plague sent by the Pashupatinath *linga*. Chastened by the king's death, his successors settled for forming a strategic alliance with Gorkha, which bought them breathing space when the latter began conquering territory in the mid-eighteenth century. Aided by a friendly Indian rajah, Palpa staved off the inevitable until 1806, when it became the last territory to be annexed to modern Nepal. Tansen remains the headquarters of Palpa District, and many still nostalgically refer to it as Palpa. You might also hear it called Tansing, which was its original Magar name – the hills here are Magar country, although the town is now predominantly Newar.

Arrival and accommodation

Try to get on a bus that's going directly to Tansen: buses bound for Pokhara or the Tarai don't leave the Siddhartha Highway, and instead drop you off at Bartun, the village at the start of the three-kilometre Tansen spur road. If you're lucky you may be able to flag something down to the Tansen bus park, otherwise you'll have to hoof it up the steep one-kilometre short cut that starts immediately north of the intersection (there are no taxis or rikshas in Tansen). The town spills down the flank of Srinagar Hill, with the **bus park** occupying the lowest, newest level, surrounded by a tacky bazaar area.

As you'll soon discover, Tansen prepares a number of frustrations for the traveller, the first being a marked lack of cheerful **budget accommodation**. Most lodges are ranged around the bus park, which is terrifically noisy and a long slog from the centre. Quieter and more central, *Gautam Siddhartha Hotel* is clean and friendly (②). Near the top of the pedestrian shortcut to town, *Hotel Dhaulagiri* (labelled *Janapriya* on the map) is comparable in price, but somewhat scruffier. Power cuts are common and water in constant short supply, as there's not enough electricity to drive the town water pump – the government has been trying for years to coax the town to shift down to the valley where water is plentiful. All this needn't concern you if you're on a bigger budget. *Hotel Srinagar* (☎075/20045; B⑦; there may be some dorm beds), on the ridge above town, has all mod cons, though it's rather pokey for the price.

Don't expect much of the **food** and you won't be disappointed. Loads of nameless diners around the bus park serve *daal bhaat*, road snacks and sweets, and most of the guest-house restaurants can do eggs and a sort of toast in the morn-

TANSEN

To Rani Ghat
To Ridi
Hotel Srinagar
Srinagar Hill
Hospital
To Pokhara
To Ridi
Bhagwati Mandir
SHITALPATI
Amar Narayan Mandir
Gautam Siddhartha Hotel
Durbar
Bank
Post Office
Hotel Janapriya
Tribhuwan Campus
TUDIKHEL
Bus Park
Hotel Siddhartha
SIDDHARTHA HIGHWAY
BARTUN
To Butwal
0   200 m

ing. If you're passing through before or after hill-walking, *Hotel Srinagar* can help break the monotony: breakfast comes with a splendid view, and they also do hearty packed lunches.

The Town

Things improve once you've escaped the bus park and found your way to the **upper town**. The direct footpath past the *Hotel Dhaulagiri* emerges at what English-speakers call Bank Street, home of a modest bazaar (*pote* – beads – and *dhaago* – tassels – are specialities) and a *Nepal Bank* branch; across the street is the prosaic twentieth-century Durbar. Bank Street ends at Shitalpati, where you'll find the only visible reminder of Tansen's grand past – **Baggi Dhoka** (Chariot Gate), tall enough for elephants and their riders to pass through, and reputedly the biggest of its kind in Nepal. West of here are Tansen's oldest neighbourhoods, whose cobbled alleys and brick houses could pass for parts of Kathmandu, minus the crowds. The lane going east from Shitalpati leads down to the nineteenth-century **Amar Narayan Mandir**, a pagoda-style temple that's the stopping place for sadhus on their way to Janai Purnima festivities at Muktinath in late July or early August.

Wherever you wander, keep an eye out for **dhaka weavers**, who work at wooden treadle looms shaped like upright pianos. Woven in many hill areas, *dhaka* fabric is created by shuttling coloured threads back and forth across a constant vertical background to form repeating, geometric patterns. Palpali *dhaka*'s trademark is the use of brightly dyed *pashmina*, a fine goat's wool, against a white cotton background – it's famous throughout Nepal, and many *topi* (Nepali caps) are made from it. The simplicity of *dhaka* designs allows for almost infinite improvisation: each weaver decides without chart or counting threads where to lay the colours to form the patterns; many know a hundred or more basic designs and invent new ones all the time. The process is labour-intensive and the fabric doesn't come cheap: a good-quality Palpali weave will set you back Rs400 a metre.

Out from Tansen: Srinagar Hill and beyond

The best thing about Tansen is getting out of it and exploring the outlying hill country and unaffected Magar villages. People on the trail will likely greet you with delighted smiles and the full palms-together *namaste*. They might also ask for medicine – the few Westerners who frequent these parts are usually doctors from the United Mission Hospital, 1km east of Tansen.

First stop on most excursions is **Srinagar Hill** (Srinagar Danda), north of town. The most direct route, which takes about half an hour, starts from a small Ganesh temple above Shitalpati, but you have to zigzag a bit to get to the temple; from *Hotel Srinagar* it's an easy twenty-minute walk east along the ridge. The top (1525m) is planted with thick pine forest – there's no special place to catch the view, but the soft needles are great for picnicking. To the north, the Dhaulagiri and Annapurna Himal hover on the skyline; at this distance, Machhapuchhre is less dominant than from the perspective of Pokhara. On the other side, beyond Tansen, lies the luxuriant Madi Valley, which in autumn and on winter mornings is filled with a silver fog.

To Ridi Bazaar

For walks beyond Srinagar there are at least two strong options, the first being a thirteen-kilometre hike to **RIDI BAZAAR**. From *Hotel Srinagar*, walk west to a fork at a guard shack, bear right and in half an hour you'll reach Chandi Bhanjyang; turn left here and descend through a handsome canyon before rejoining the unpaved road for the last 7km. Set on the banks of the Kali Gandaki, Ridi is considered sacred because of the wealth of **shaligrams** – fossil-bearing stones associated with Vishnu – found in the river here. It used to be said that if a person were cremated at Ridi and his ashes sprinkled into the river, they would congeal to form a *shaligram*, and if the stone were then made into a likeness of Vishnu, the devotee would be one with his god. The spiral-shaped ammonite fossils found in *shaligram* are 150–200 million years old, dating from a time when the entire Himalayan region was submerged under a shallow sea.

Ridi has declined in importance over the years, but remains an occasional cremation ground and, in October and January, a pilgrimage site for ritual bathing. The colourful commercial end of town lies across a stream that joins the Kali Gandaki here, while the magical eighteenth-century **Rishikesh Mandir** is south of the stream, just above the bus stop. According to legend, the idol inside the squat temple, a form of Vishnu, was fished out of the river and originally bore the likeness of a young boy, but over the course of years has matured into adult form.

Several **buses** a day head back to Tansen, taking two hours. The return journey can be combined with a visit to **Palpa Bhairab**, up a short path off the road 8km before Tansen. The Bhairab image here is supposed to be so scary that not

Terraced fields in the western hills

even the priest is allowed to look at it (a bit of quaint hocus-pocus, given that it's a replica of Kathmandu's easily viewable Kalo Bhairab), and the gilded *trisul* is claimed to be the biggest in Asia. Dakshin Kali-style animal sacrifices are performed on Saturdays and Tuesdays.

Rani Ghat

An equally eventful hike begins 200m east of *Hotel Srinagar* and descends about 14km to **RANI GHAT**, site of a fantastically derelict palace along the Kali Gandaki. Following a stream through a narrow gorge, the trail passes through an immensely satisfying landscape of jungle, terraced fields and trailside hamlets, reaching the river in about three hours. Set in a steep-sided canyon, Rani Ghat hosts regular *puja* and ritual bathing, as well as an annual **festival** during Ram Navami, Ram's birthday (late March or early April). But the main attraction here is the spooky old **palace** about twenty minutes' walk upstream, which was built in the late nineteenth century by a former government minister who, according to the custom of the day, was exiled to Palpa after a failed palace coup. It's now nothing but an overgrown shell, empty but for a small, locked shrine.

Instead of slogging back up to Tansen, follow the heavily trafficked trail downstream through pleasant forest, reaching **RAMDI GHAT** beside the Siddhartha Highway in about two hours. You can get tea here while you wait for a bus or truck to take you back up to the Tansen turn-off.

Ghorabanda

The most fascinating of the villages east of Tansen, **GHORABANDA** is locally famous for its **potters** (*kumal*). It's just off the Siddhartha Highway, 3km north of the Tansen turning, but without your own wheels you'll have to walk. Take the dirt road from the Amar Narayan temple towards the United Mission Hospital, bear right onto a trail after about 500m, descend and then contour through extensive paddy – if you've done it right, you'll drop down to the highway after about 2km, with Ghorabanda another 1km further along the road. Ghorabanda's potters, members of the Kumal caste, throw their almost spherical water jugs on heavy clay flywheels, shaping them and adding a stipple pattern with a wooden paddle, then sun-drying and finally kiln-firing them. The farmhouses and potteries of Ghorabanda spread down the hill from the *Palpa Pottery Industry* shop. The arrival of a Westerner here is a major diplomatic event; it may be a good idea to enlist the help of the shop's proprietor, who speaks English.

festivals

Besides the national holidays of Dasain, Tihaar, Shiva Raatri and Holi, a few other festivals are specially celebrated in the western hills:

MAGH (Jan–Feb)
Magh Sankranti A day of ritual bathing in the Kali Gandaki River at Ridi and elsewhere, held on the first day of the month of Magh (Jan 14 or 15).

FAAGUN (Feb–March)
Losar Tibetan New Year, celebrated at the Tibetan refugee settlements in and around Pokhara.

CHAITRA (March–April)
Chaitra Dasain The "small Dasain", celebrated at Gorkha Kalika with processions and animal sacrifices.

SAAUN (July–Aug)
Janai Purnima The annual changing of the sacred thread worn by high-caste Hindu men is conducted at many river confluences, and brings sadhus to Tansen and Pokhara.

BHADAU (Aug–Sept)
Bhagwati Jaatra Processions in Tansen commemorate the goddess Bhagwati and an 1814 battle in which Nepal routed British troops nearby.

travel details

Buses

From Pokhara tourist buses to Kathmandu (2–7 daily, depending on season; 6–7hr). Departures from Lakeside/Damside. Night buses to Kathmandu also depart from Lakeside/Damside (8 nightly; 10hr). All other long-distance buses leave from the main bus park: to Biratnagar (1 nightly; at least 18hr); Birganj (stopping at Tadi Bazaar for Chitwan, 6 daily; 10hr); Butwal (10 daily; 7hr); Gorkha (2 daily; 6hr); Janakpur (1 nightly; 12hr); Kakarbitta (3 nightly; at least 20hr); Kathmandu (8 daily; 8–9hr); Narayanghat (5 daily; 4hr); Nepalganj (4 nightly; at least 15hr); Sunauli (6 daily, 4 nightly; at least 10hr) and Tansen (2 daily; 6–7hr). Local buses from Shining Hospital to Phedi (hourly; 2hr). Local minibuses from Chipledhunga to Naudanda (infrequent; 1hr) and Sisuwa (hourly; 45min).

From Gorkha to Abu Khaireini (infrequent; 1–2hr); Bhairawa (1 daily; 9hr); Birganj (4 daily; 7hr); Kathmandu (4 daily; 6hr); Narayanghat (4 daily; 3hr) and Pokhara (2 daily; 6hr).

From Tansen to Butwal (7 daily; 1–2hr); Kathmandu (3 daily and 1 nightly; at least 12hr) and Ridi (6 daily; 2hr).

Planes

From Pokhara to Baglung (1 daily; 15min); Jomosom (1–3 daily; 25min); Jumla (0–1 weekly; 1hr); Kathmandu (up to 7 daily; 35min) and Manang (0–3 weekly; 25min).

Connections to India

It's possible to book **bus/train packages to India** through Pokhara ticket agents – but see caveats in the "On from Kathmandu" section in Chapter One.

CHAPTER FIVE

THE WESTERN TARAI

In a country best known for its mountains, the lowland **Tarai** often gets short shrift. A narrow strip of flatland extending along the entire length of Nepal's southern border – including several *dun* (inner Tarai) valleys north of the first range of hills – the Tarai was originally covered in thick, malarial jungle. In the 1950s, however, the government identified the fertile southern plains as a major growth area to relieve population pressure in the hills, and, with the help of liberal quantities of DDT, brought malaria under control. Since then the jungle has been methodically cleared and the Tarai has emerged as Nepal's most productive agricultural and industrial region, representing seventy percent of the country's arable land and accounting for more than half its GDP. The barrier that had once insulated Nepal from Indian influences as effectively as the Himalaya had guarded the north, making possible the development of a uniquely Nepali culture, has been replaced by the geographic and political equivalent of a welcome mat. An unmistakeable quality of Indianness now pervades the Tarai, as evidenced by the avid mercantilism of the border bazaars, the wearing of *lungyi* and the chewing of betel, Muslim mosques and orthodox Brahmanism, the heat and dust, the jute mills and sugar refineries, and the many roads and irrigation projects built with Indian aid.

Fortunately, the government has set aside sizeable chunks of the **western Tarai** in the form of national parks and reserves, which remain as some of the finest **wildlife** and bird havens on the subcontinent. Dense riverine forest provides cover for predators like tigers and leopards, swampy grasslands make the perfect habitat for rhinoceros, and vast, tall stands of *sal*, the Tarai's most common tree, throng with what at times seems to be the entire cast of *Bambi*. You'll probably only have the time to visit one national park. **Chitwan**, the richest in game and the most accessible, is deservedly popular, but if crowds bother you and you're willing to invest some extra effort (or money), check out **Bardia** or **Sukla Phanta**.

The region's other claim to fame is historical: the Buddha was born 2500 years ago at **Lumbini**, and his birthplace – one of the four most important pilgrimage sites for Buddhists – is an appropriately serene place.

Travel to the western Tarai is straightforward, though exhausting as ever. **Bus** connections from Kathmandu and Pokhara are well developed via Narayanghat or Butwal, the two most common destinations are Tadi Bazaar for Chitwan and Sunauli for the **Indian border**. The Tarai itself is traversed by a single main road, the **Mahendra Highway** (Mahendra Rajmarg), now paved all the way to the far western border. At the time of writing the

Water buffalo

Mahendranagar border crossing had recently been reopened, reviving an adventurous backdoor route from Kathmandu to Delhi. However, overland travel in Nepal's far west is not for the faint-hearted – internal **flights**, while not always reliable, can spare you a lot of agony. Early spring is the **best time** for wildlife-viewing in the Tarai: in February and March, after the tall grass has been burned off, animals are at their most visible, temperatures are mild and *palash* ("flame of the forest") trees ignite into tongues of brilliant red. Autumn, for its part, brings unforgettable sunset views of the distant Himalaya. Winter's a good time to come down out of the hills, although even in the Tarai, mornings are misty and cold.

CHITWAN AND AROUND

Whatever your itinerary, **Chitwan National Park** is likely to be your first destination in the Tarai. The park is just a short detour off the Prithvi (Kathmandu–Pokhara) Highway, and if you're travelling to or from India it can be visited on the way to save backtracking.

Chitwan is the name not only of the park but also of the surrounding *dun* valley and administrative district. The name means "heart of the jungle" – a description that, sadly, now holds true only for the lands protected within the park, yet the rest of the **valley**, though it's been reduced to a flat, furrowed plain, still provides fascinating vignettes of a rural lifestyle that's different again from the hill-clinging existence of upland Nepal. Really ugly development is confined to the wayside conurbation of **Narayanghat/Bharatpur** – and even this has left the nearby holy site of **Devghat** unscathed.

Chitwan National Park

The best and worst aspects of **CHITWAN NATIONAL PARK** are that it can be done on the cheap and it's relatively easy to get to. In recent years the park has risen meteorically on the list of Things to Do in Nepal, so that these days, unless you go during the steamy season, you'll have to share your experience with a lot of other people.

You're forgiven if you thought **Sauraha** is where all budget tourists stay in Chitwan. For all intents and purposes, it is. About fifteen years ago some genius had the idea of setting up a little thatched-roof lodge just outside the Sauraha entrance to the park, and the village has basically had a monopoly ever since. But package trips have taken a lot of the spontaneity out of Sauraha, and in autumn, with the inhabitants of forty-odd lodges all converging on the same finite patch of park, the area can get uncomfortably crowded. If you don't mind roughing it a little, try **Jagatpur** or **Meghauli** instead. Or, if you've got the money – usually at least $100 a night, all-in – go for pampered seclusion at any one of half a dozen luxury lodges and tented camps **inside the park**.

CHITWAN NATIONAL PARK

Chitwan has perhaps been oversold in recent years, often with misleading promises of "safari adventure". While its **wildlife** is astoundingly concentrated, remember that the dense vegetation doesn't allow the easy sightings you get in the savannas of Africa. But go with realistic expectations, don't buy into the package-tour mentality, and it's still possible to enjoy yourself. **Elephant rides, jeep tours, canoe trips** and just plain **walks** each give a different slant on the luxuriant, teeming forest.

Park entry permits are valid for two days at a time, which tends to dictate the length of most travellers' stay. Rushed as it is, this can work out quite reasonably, but don't be led into thinking that you can "do" Chitwan in two nights and three days.

About budget packages

Avoid them. The reasons are many, but suffice to say that a three-day "safari" only gives you a day and a half in the park, doesn't save you any hassle, limits your flexibility, and invariably costs more than doing Chitwan under your own steam (up to half the money you pay for a package goes straight into the booking agent's pocket). Often you don't even get to choose what to eat. If you must be bound by an itinerary, at least book it direct through the lodge's own office in Kathmandu or Pokhara, which will be more accountable for arrangements than an agent will be. You can get office addresses and phone numbers by collecting brochures from agencies.

A visit to Chitwan can also be combined with a **raft trip** on the Trisuli River, bookable through rafting operators in Kathmandu and Pokhara. But while this can cut out some of the long drive, no matter what the salesman says, the raft won't take you all the way to the park: Narayanghat is normally the end of the line.

Sauraha

SAURAHA (pronounced *So*-ruh-hah), Chitwan's original budget safari village, is one of those unstoppably successful destinations at which Nepal seems to excel. It is, in fact, the spitting image of Pokhara's Lakeside a decade or so ago: a quiet, unpaved lane with a strip of folksy guest houses; a few provisions stalls, a smattering of bikes for rent; a bookshop, the odd guide or ticketing office, and the first multistorey concrete eyesores beginning to go up (as if in homage, there's even a *Hungry Eye Restaurant*). The village still retains much of its intimacy and its unhurried, almost soporific character, though each year it strays a little further from its rustic roots. Electricity (due to arrive in late 1993) will no doubt bring more sophistication, but hopefully won't change Sauraha's fundamentally rural nature.

Getting there

The nearest **bus** stop is **Tadi Bazaar**, about 15km east of Narayanghat on the Mahendra Highway. In season, two companies – *Baba Tours & Travels* and *Shanti Mini Travels*, at last check – operate daily tourist bus services between Kathmandu and Tadi; the fare is Rs120 and the journey takes about six hours. Public buses take at least an hour longer (*Sajha* buses are preferable). Tadi isn't a final destination for public services, but any bus bound for Birganj or points east will let you off at Tadi, where touts will have prepared the usual ambush for you. (It's also possible to **fly** to Bharatpur – see p.248.)

Sauraha is a dusty 6km south from Tadi, at the park boundary on the banks of the Rapti River. Most people get there by **jeep**, which costs Rs30, assuming full occupancy. Each guest house has its own jeep, so whoever you ride with will probably make every effort to win your business – you don't have to stay at their place, of course, but count on being dropped off there. **Ox carts** (aka "jungle helicopters", "Chitwan taxis") also cost Rs30 but take at least two hours, which is slower than walking: you only do it once. **Bikes** are for rent at Tadi – an option worth considering only if you think you can pedal with a pack on – and all around Sauraha.

As soon as you know when you plan to **move on**, have your lodge book the onward bus ticket for you so that you can be sure of a seat. Several ticket agencies in Sauraha can also do this, and can arrange air tickets from Bharatpur.

Accommodation

Sauraha has a great tradition of "camp"-style **accommodation** – the guest houses here are like rustic little country clubs, with simple mud-and-thatch huts, airy dining pavilions and shady gardens or open lawns. Most now line up shoulder to shoulder along the village's main north–south strip, but other, more

Asian one–horned rhino

secluded guest houses are scattered in the area east of the park entrance. A whole lot of newer outfits are proliferating along the road leading westwards to the elephant breeding project. When deciding where to stay, aim for a place that isn't too far from the park entrance – after a four-hour jungle walk, the last thing you'll feel like doing is trudging an extra fifteen minutes along a road in the midday heat.

Beware new lodges, many of which have lost touch with what foreigners like about Sauraha. The worst of these, with their regimental rows of concrete bunkers and little or no shade, are more like prison camps than jungle camps. The listings given below aren't exhaustive, but the map is: if you don't see a particular guest house on the map, that should be a warning that it's either new or it's changed its name (probably because it acquired a bad reputation under the old one).

BUDGET GUEST HOUSES
Accommodation in Sauraha can be divided into three broad categories. The basic **budget guest houses**, which outnumber the rest by a wide margin, are the ones so relentlessly promoted by the touts at Tadi. They charge a fairly constant rate of Rs75–100 for rooms with common bath, or Rs300–500 for attached bath where available; prices will often drop dramatically when occupancy is low, and discounts for singles can generally be negotiated. Guest houses equipped with generators charge more, so expect across-the-board rate increases when electricity comes to Sauraha. Facilities are virtually interchangeable, and the following are recommended only because they stand out from the rest in some way. But by far the biggest variable is the staff – turnover is high – so heed word-of-mouth referrals.

ROOM PRICE SCALES

All guest houses and hotels have been price-graded according to the scale outlined below, which represents the cheapest available double room in high season; codes prefixed by B denote the cost of a room with attached bathroom. See *Basics*, p.21, for a fuller explanation of the system.

① Less than Rs75 ($1.50 if quoted in US$)	⑤ $8–12
	⑥ $12–20
② Rs75–150 ($1.50–3)	⑦ $20–40
③ Rs150–250 ($3–5)	⑧ $40–70
④ $5–8	⑨ Over $70

MAN VERSUS NATURE

It's an open question whether Chitwan has been blessed or cursed by its own riches. Its big game couldn't escape the notice of trigger-happy maharajas for long: when Jang Bahadur Rana overthrew the Shah dynasty in 1846, one of his first actions was to make Chitwan a private hunting preserve for rulers and visiting dignitaries. The following century saw some truly hideous **hunts** – King George V, during an eleven-day shoot in 1911, killed 39 tigers and 18 rhinos. In those days the technique, if you could call it that, was to send *shikari* (trackers) into the forest to locate a tiger and set out a buffalo calf as bait. The sahibs were then alerted, loaded onto elephants and, joined by other huntsmen, the whole party of as many as 600 elephants and riders would approach the spot from all directions. As the circle closed, helpers would spread white sheets between the advancing elephants to keep the tiger from breaking through. High up in their howdahs, the sahibs could get off shots at point-blank range.

Still, the Ranas' patronage afforded Chitwan a certain degree of protection, as did malaria. That all changed in the early 1950s, when the Ranas were thrown out, the monarchy was restored, and the new government launched its malaria-control programme. Settlers poured in and **poaching** went unpoliced – rhinos, whose horns were (and still are) valued for Chinese medicine and Yemeni knife handles, were especially hard-hit. By 1960, the human population of the valley had trebled to 100,000, and the number of rhinos had been slashed from 1000 to 200. With the Asian one-horned rhino on the verge of extinction, Nepal emerged as an unlikely hero in one of conservation's finest hours. Chitwan was set aside in 1964 as a **rhino sanctuary** (it became Nepal's first national park in 1973) and, despite the endless hype about tigers, rhinos are Chitwan's biggest attraction and its greatest triumph.

Chitwan now boasts 400 one-horned rhinos – a quarter of the species total – and numbers are growing healthily. Poaching isn't nearly the problem here that it is in

Eden Guest House. Friendly, with good music programmes. ②/B⑤.

River View Jungle Camp. Pricier than most, but with nice grounds; mosquito netting provided. ③/B⑥.

Sauraha Jungle Lodge. Has an especially roomy compound. ②.

Tharu Lodge. On the primitive side, but it's secluded and near the river. ②.

Wendy Lodge. One of Sauraha's pioneers: good location, nice grounds. ②.

UPMARKET GUEST HOUSES

In Sauraha, **upmarket guest houses** are really only budget guest houses with delusions of grandeur. They get by mainly on package business, but accept walk-ins, charging somewhere in the region of $8–20 a night for a room with attached bath (only packages can be booked by phone, however). Although Kathmandu booking offices try to pass these outfits off as luxury safari camps, the only tangible extras you'll get for your money are mosquito netting, a bit of felt carpeting and maybe a thicker mattress. The food won't be any different. That said, at least one operation in this category, *Tiger Camp*, can be highly recommended.

Jungle Safari Camp (Kathmandu ☎01/216736). Shady grounds, otherwise standard facilities; run by *Island Jungle Resort*, one of the luxury in-park camps. ④/B⑤.

Osho Camp (Kathmandu ☎01/225392). Rates include food and meditation sessions. B⑦.

Tiger Camp (Kathmandu ☎01/522641; Pokhara ☎061/21435). Overlooking the river right at the park entrance, with a good restaurant. *Machaan*-like huts with common bath are the best deal here (④ – but destined to go up); the regular bungalows (B⑦) are nothing special.

Africa, no doubt thanks to the deployment of an entire army batallion in the park, although a recent rise in the number of killings is an ominous trend. (Many observers believe the culprits are employees inside the park, who know where the animals are and how to poach them without being detected.) About 60 **tigers** have been counted in the park; they, too, are on the rebound, and the establishment in 1984 of Parsa Wildlife Reserve, along Chitwan's western edge, secured a vital secondary habitat for them. Altogether, 51 mammalian species are found in Chitwan, including four kinds of deer, langur, gaur, sloth bear, leopard, the rare gangetic dolphin and an elusive herd of wild elephants that stomp around the southeastern corner. Chitwan is also an important sanctuary for **birds**, with more than 400 species recorded, as well as two varieties of **crocodile**.

But Chitwan's seesaw battle for survival continues. As the population of the valley swells, conservationists wonder how much longer locals will tolerate the setting aside of such fertile land, not to mention the destruction of their crops by the rhinos that are protected there. Tourism has undoubtedly helped make animals and trees worth more alive than dead, but only to those few in the tourist industry. All everyone else gets out of the park is a two-week open season on **gathering thatch** each January, and even this benefit is being devalued year by year as tourist lodges use more thatch for themselves. Many locals feel cheated: the way they see it, the government is managing the park for foreign exchange, not conservation, and while it tells them they have to stay out of the park, it's actually *encouraging* foreigners to enter. Meanwhile, the Rs650 **entrance fee** – an enormous amount of money by Nepali standards – disappears into some black hole in Kathmandu. Diverting even a portion of that fee to local communities would give them a real stake in the park's continued protection; failing that, even an army batallion won't be able to safeguard the park for much longer.

For more detail on Tarai wildlife, see "Natural History" in Contexts.

PACKAGE-ONLY LODGES

Finally, there are Sauraha's **package-only** operations, which normally won't deal with walk-ins. Facilities, service and food should be of a high standard. However, rates for these places aren't significantly lower than those charged by deluxe lodges and camps inside the park – $175 and up for a two-night package including all food and activities. For that price, why share the jungle with all the Sauraha riffraff? If you're still unconvinced, try these:

Hotel Elephant Camp (Kathmandu ☎01/222823). A long-standing favourite, with huge, leafy grounds. $190 for 2 nights.

Jungle Adventure World (Kathmandu ☎01/225393). Good riverside location; snazzy glassed-in dining hall, solar hot water. $225 for 2 nights (camping can be arranged).

Royal Park Hotel. Completion expected late 1993. Should be pretty fancy.

Food and other provisions

Most people just eat what their **guest house** puts in front of them. In the budget category, food varies little from one place to the next, being limited to variations on cutlets, macaroni, chop suey and trusty *daal bhaat* – not very appetizing, by and large, but you get to hobnob with guides and fellow travellers, and dinner often ends with music and dance.

Sauraha's stand-alone **restaurants** are a good example of Nepali supply-side economics: they're on the increase not because of demand, but because to locals they seem like a great way to make money. They may improve with time, but for now – with the possible exception of *Tiger Camp*'s proficient riverside café – the food they serve is usually no better than in the guest houses, and somewhat pricier. They're also architecturally out of keeping with Sauraha; if you want to discourage this kind of development, spend your money elsewhere.

Provisions stalls stock most of the same stuff sold in Kathmandu and Pokhara: chocolate, jam, muesli, biscuits, rum, bottled water, film, batteries, toilet paper, postcards and so on. You can even buy and sell books.

Park practicalities

Park **entry permits** (Rs650 for 2 days) are purchased at the ranger's office (daily 6am–noon & 1–5pm) to the left of the visitor centre. The permit queue can be slow around opening time, so get there early, or pay someone at your lodge to wait for you (Rs100 surcharge). Ask to see the ticket before setting off, as guides sometimes try to sneak tourists into the park with invalid tickets (if caught, you'd have to pay the fine). There's no formal park **entrance**; you enter by canoe or by wading across the river.

The **visitors' centre** (daily 8am–5/6pm) has a modest but informative display on the ecology of the park. The **maps** on the wall are useful for getting your bearings; park maps are only sporadically available in Sauraha, so it's advisable to get one before you leave Kathmandu (see "Information and Maps" in *Basics*).

Guides

Don't enter rhino or tiger habitat, inside or outside the park, without a **guide** (but see "Staying Alive", below). Sauraha's guides are some of the most keen, personable characters you'll meet in Nepal, on and off the job. Their knowledge of species, especially birds, can be encyclopedic (much of it lifted from K.K. Gurung's *Heart of the Jungle* and Flemings' *Birds of Nepal* – see "Books" in *Contexts*). Guides are certified as "senior" or "junior" under a Peace Corps-initiated programme, and should be able to show their credentials. English usually isn't a problem, although bear in mind that if your guide yells *look*, this means "hide" in Nepali! Oh, and women should watch out for those infamous "night walks".

Every lodge has its own **in-house guides**, but you can also hire one through any of the growing number of freelance **guide services**. If you sign up with an in-house guide you may get stuck trailing around with a group of package tourists, with little choice of departure time or itinerary, although this will work out cheaper if you're on your own (for prices, see "Activities"). A freelance guide will let you call the shots, and since he's his own boss he'll also be more willing to negotiate on price – figure on Rs100 (junior) to Rs150 (senior) for three hours. Hire a freelance if you want to do any non-standard walks or explore other parts of the park (or other parks: Dilip at *Chitwan Tiger Guide Service*, near the *hatti-sar*, has experience guiding in Bardia).

Alternative bases

At least two other villages outside the park's northern boundary have guest houses, but not, as yet, guides, elephants or other services. Until they do – and keep your ear to the ground, because this is likely to change – you're better off first going to Sauraha and hiring a guide who's familiar with these other less-trodden parts of the park. Both villages can be reached on foot through the park – see "Jungle Treks", below.

Jagatpur

The government and developers are beginning to eye **JAGATPUR** as a promising alternative to overused Sauraha. About 20km due west of Sauraha, it's within easy range of Kasara park headquarters, the gharial breeding project, Lami Tal and a good patch of jungle. The park starts 1km south of the village, on the other side of Rapti River: cross by dugout canoe and pay your entry fee to one of the soldiers on the other side. The government is talking about establishing an official entrance station and possibly quartering elephants here. Little more than a bus stop with a few newish buildings and electricity, Jagatpur itself offers no attractions.

If you come with a guide, he'll probably bring you here on foot from Sauraha and then back by slow bus via Bharatpur and Tadi; alternatively, you could take a jeep tour to Kasara and walk the final 2km. A very big question mark hangs over the second **international airport** proposed for Sukra Nagar, a few kilometres west of Jagatpur. Nothing's decided yet, and it would take years to construct in any case, but HMG seems to favour this site and in 1992 took the first steps in preparation for compulsory land purchases. Heaven only knows what a major airport here would do to the park, but it would certainly thrust Jagatpur into the limelight.

Guides have been bringing tourists to Jagatpur from Sauraha for years, but as of early 1993 there was still only one **guest house**, the *Tourist Hotel & Lodge*, just west of the signposted side road to the park. It has just a few ① rooms (not huts), but it's clean and hospitable; the owner speaks English and can rustle up basic food. *Narayani Safari Hotel* operates a deluxe lodge east of Jagatpur, just outside the park – for booking details see the Narayanghat section.

Meghauli

MEGHAULI, 15km west of Jagatpur, is home to the **airstrip** used by guests visiting *Tiger Tops*, which all but owns this part of the park (up to 3 flights daily from Kathmandu; $72). Consequently the village sees daily herds of upmarket tourists migrating back and forth on planes and jeeps, but has absolutely nothing to do with them. Few independent travellers make it here either, as it's two days' walk from Sauraha, or about an hour and a half by **bus** from Narayanghat. The bus drops you off at the newest, easternmost end of the village; several separate settlements, all considered part of Meghauli, are dotted along the dirt road that leads westwards past the airstrip (which begins about 1.5km from the bus stop) and on to the Rapti River crossing (another 2km). Dugouts ferry *Tiger Tops* guests across here, but the boatmen are told not to assist independent travellers, so *bakshish* may be necessary. Bhimle **guard post**, where you have to pay the park entrance fee, is another 3km beyond, and the main rhino habitat for this area is beyond that.

Remarkably, Meghauli supports two primitive but unmistakeably Saurahaesque safari **lodges**. *Meghauli Jungle Lodge*, just beyond the western end of the airstrip, is closer to the park; *Chital Lodge* is located down a northbound lane between the bus stop and the airstrip. Both places offer mud-floored huts with no electricity (②), and serve only Nepali food.

Inside the park: luxury lodges and tented camps

Accommodation **inside the park** includes the most expensive lodgings in Nepal, and that's no exaggeration. They pay the government massive fees to stake out exclusive concession areas, with the result that you really feel like you've got the park all to yourself. Some are lavish **lodges** with permanent facilities, others are more remote **tented camps** – camping in the softest sense, with fluffy mattresses, solar-heated showers and fully stocked bars – and some are both. All activities are included in the price. You **book ahead** for these places. They arrange your travel there and back by private vehicle, plane or raft, which in most cases costs extra.

Chitwan Jungle Lodge (Kathmandu ☎01/228918). The biggest operator in the park, with 32 rooms. $260 per person for 2-night, 3-day package (includes transport).

Gaida Wildlife Camp (Kathmandu ☎01/220940). Lodge situated close to Sauraha, $245 for 2 nights; jungle camp 8km south at base of hills, $92 per night.

Island Jungle Resort (Kathmandu ☎01/216736). Tented camp on an island in the middle of the Narayani River. $240 for 2 nights.

Machan Wildlife Resort (Kathmandu ☎01/225001). The lodge has the only swimming pool in the park, $318 for 2 nights; tented camp $180 for 2 nights (all prices include transport).

Temple Tiger Wildlife Camp (Kathmandu ☎01/221585). Tented camp at the west end of the park. $327 for 2 nights.

Tiger Tops (Kathmandu ☎01/222706). The first and still the most fashionable. Perched on stilts, the lodge is pure jungle Gothic, $576 for 2 nights; tented camp is $210 per night; *Tharu Village*, Tiger Tops' culture camp, costs $123 per night.

Activities in the park

Most **activities inside the park** take place in early morning or late afternoon, when wildlife-viewing is best. All of the following can, and in most cases should, be arranged through your lodge or a guide service. It's essential to book the night before, or even earlier during the cut-throat months of October and November. All prices are in addition to the park entry fee.

Guided walks

Walking is the best way to observe the park's prolific **bird** life. The region is an important stopover spot for migratory species in December and March, as well as being home to many year-round residents – bring binoculars and look for parakeets, Indian rollers, paradise flycatchers, kingfishers, hornbills, ospreys and literally hundreds of others. By walking you'll also be able to appreciate the smaller attractions of the jungle at your own pace: orchids, strangler figs, six-foot-high termite mounds, tiger scratchings, rhino droppings piled up like cannon balls. Experienced jungle-walkers say they get their best animal sightings on foot, although that usually doesn't apply when they've got four or five flat-footed neophytes in tow. Throw away that shopping list of animals; you have to be content with what's on offer. You are virtually guaranteed a **rhino** (probably several), and deer and monkeys are easy to spot, but tiger sightings are rare – maybe one or two a week.

The best **season** for walking is spring, when the grass is shorter, though at other times of year you can compensate by spending more time in the forest. The **cost** is Rs60 and up per person for a morning's walk and Rs200 for a full day with lunch, plus a few rupees for the guide's nominal entry fee. An all-day walk doesn't necessarily increase your chances of seeing game – most of the rhinos hang out close to Sauraha – but it gets you further into the park where you aren't running into other parties every two minutes.

One short walk you can probably chance **unguided** is to Isle Machaan, a hide overlooking a rhino wallow. The trail goes southeast from the visitors' centre, follows a creek and then crosses it to reach the *machaan* after half an hour.

Elephant rides

In terms of cost per hour the jeep's a better deal, but how often do you get to ride an **elephant**? The park keeps a dozen rideable animals and sends them out on one-hour trips at around 8am and 4pm; the **cost** is Rs650, plus an extra Rs100 for your lodge to arrange the trip for you. During slack times you can sign yourself up at the ranger's office at 6am for one of that day's rides, but normally the queue starts forming in the wee hours. A word of warning: rides aren't held on major holidays (for instance, the eighth and ninth days of Dasain, and Lakshmi Puja), and the king has been known to spirit Chitwan's elephants away for months at a time for royal hunting expeditions.

A *mahout* and his charge

The elephant's stately gait takes you back to a time, as recently as the early 1950s, when this was the way foreign delegations entered Nepal. The *mahout* (driver) sits astride the animal's neck, giving it commands with his toes and periodically walloping its huge skull, and attentively fending branches out of passengers' way. An elephant is the safest way to get around in the grasslands – especially in summer and autumn, when the grass towers 8m high – and it's the best way to observe **rhinos** and possibly wild boar or sloth bear. Rhinos have terrible eyesight and rely on their keen sense of smell, but since the elephant's scent masks your own it's possible to approach quite close and without fear of attack. From the height of an elephant's back you get a clear view of these prehistoric tanks, with their armour-plated skin, twitching ears and highly coveted horns.

Jeep rides ... and gharial crocodiles

A **jeep ride** is the closest thing to a tour of Chitwan, as it also takes in the park's two permanent sights, the gharial crocodile breeding project and Kasara Durbar, both about 20km west of Sauraha. For big game, however, you're limited to what you can see through the dusty wake of an army surplus vehicle, which pretty much means **deer**. The whole trip takes three or four hours and **costs** Rs650, plus Rs15 to see the gharials. Most lodges have their own jeep; the park only allows four or five in at a time, but as long as you book early enough your lodge will get you a seat on whichever jeep is going. The **best season** is February–April, after the grass has been cut and the new shoots attract the deer. Note that jeeps can't cross the river after the monsoon until mid-November; during that time alternative trips may be run to the elephant breeding project and Bis Hajaar Tal (see below).

The longest of the world's crocodiles – adults can grow to more than 6m from nose to tail – the **gharial** is an awesome fishing machine. Its slender, broom-like snout, which bristles with a fine mesh of teeth, snaps shut on its prey like a

STAYING ALIVE IN CHITWAN

Lodge owners and guides often play down the risks associated with tracking wild-life, so as not to scare off business. In fact, **safety** is a serious issue in Chitwan. Since record-keeping began in Chitwan in 1979, over 100 people have been killed by rhinos and 17 by tigers; sloth bears also present very real dangers. Most of those killed have been locals during the January thatch-gathering, but it's unusual for a year to go by without several tourist maulings as well. There are no emergency medical facilities in or near the park – the closest hospital is in Bharatpur, a mini-mum two-hour evacuation when you add up all the stages, which means if there's major bleeding the patient is essentially out of luck.

The best safety tip is not to go into the jungle without a guide, but even a guide can't guarantee your personal safety. Most guides are young and gung-ho, and in their eagerness to please will sometimes encourage tourists to venture too close to animals. And no matter how competent, a guide can't know where all the animals are, nor can he, in an emergency, assist more than one person at a time – so if you're in a group, consider yourself on your own. A few **tips**: a rhino will lower its head and take a step back if it's about to charge; if it does, try to run in a zigzag path and throw off a piece of clothing (the rhino will stop to smell it), or better yet, climb the nearest big tree. If a bear or tiger charges, climb a *small* tree. Don't get anywhere near a mother with young ones of any of these species.

spring-loaded trap. Unfortunately for the gharial, its eggs are regarded as a deli-cacy, and males are hunted for their bulb-like snouts (*gharial* means bulb), which are believed to have medicinal powers.

In the mid-1970s, the world suddenly realized there were only 1300 gharials left. Chitwan's **breeding project** was set up in 1977 to incubate eggs under controlled conditions, upping the survival rate, which is only one percent in the wild, to 25–30 percent. A few gharials from the first (1978) hatch are kept here for breeding, though there has been no success with this yet. The majority of hatchlings are released back into the wild after three years, when they reach 1.2m in length; more than 500 have been released so far into the Narayani, Kosi, Karnali and Babai rivers. Unfortunately gharials are still rarely sighted in the wild, and without reliable estimates of current numbers (the most recent figure, from 1981, is 1367 individuals) it's hard to gauge the project's success. As if the gharials didn't already have the deck stacked against them, they now face a new threat: in a clas-sic case of one hand of the government not knowing what the other is doing, HMG has allowed the construction of two Chinese-sponsored paper mills on the Narayani upstream of Chitwan – with little or no effluent control. Biologists fear that chemicals released into the river from these mills, which started operating in 1989, will be the final nail in the Narayani gharials' coffin. So see them while you still can.

Kasara Durbar, constructed in 1911 for George V's infamous hunt, has now been rebuilt in concrete and serves as the park's administrative headquarters. Inside is a meagre **museum**, with not much on offer besides animal skulls, a small display of butterflies and various pickled reptiles, all accompanied by signs (in Devanaagari) bearing the collected wisdom of His Majesty. The lovely safari camp opposite the headquarters is kept ready for use by HM and his retinue for a few days each spring. (The king comes to hunt tigers – despite the fact that they're protected as an endangered species by an international agreement, to which Nepal is a signatory.)

Lami Tal ("Long Lake"), a marshy oxbow lake about 1km to the east, is a prime spot for watching **birds** and **mugger crocodiles**. There's a rickety view tower about midway along. This would be a good place to wait for tigers or rhinos very early in the morning, but on a jeep trip you'll blow through here in mid-afternoon.

River trips

Wooden canoes are moored at the end of the lane in front of the visitors' centre. The standard itinerary is to depart after breakfast, float down the **Rapti River** for 45 minutes and then walk back in time for lunch. Every package includes this trip, and since everybody has to walk back along the same trail, it's just a steady stream of tourists all morning – the animals know better than to hang out here. Either take the earliest possible morning trip, or go in the afternoon.

In **winter**, when the water's cool, your chances of seeing **mugger crocodiles** sunning themselves on the gravel banks are better than even; ruddy sheldrakes also winter here in profusion. In hot weather the outing is less rewarding, and the walk's a sticky chore, though you'll be assured of plenty of birds.

The canoe ride only **costs** Rs25, but the guided walk back is Rs60–150, plus you have to pitch in for the guide's boat ticket.

Jungle treks

To get well clear of the Sauraha crowds you need to walk for two or more days, overnighting en route – think of it as a **jungle trek**. Staying with the trekking analogy, there's one "teahouse" route in the park, plus any number of other possibilities for those willing to camp.

The teahouse route follows the forest road from **Sauraha to Kasara** and on to **Meghauli**, or vice versa. The full trek takes two days of roughly equal length, or you could just do one half or the other. There are of course no teahouses inside the park, but you can spend nights at Meghauli and Jagatpur (see earlier sections). The Sauraha–Kasara leg is more commonly trekked, and is also the route taken by jeep tours out of Sauraha. If possible, go with a guide who's done this trek before – many haven't.

Although it involves more logistics, **camping** gives you a much more intimate, exciting and – well, let's be honest – dangerous encounter with the jungle. (The government is considering setting up a network of permanent shelters in the park, which would reduce the risk.) Camping is permitted only in designated sites in the park, and the charge is Rs300 per person per night. Obviously, you'll need a guide who's familiar with these sites, and you'll also have to fork out for a cook and/or porter(s), all of whom will expect hazard pay. Allow a couple of days for your guide to make all the arrangements. Tents, sleeping bags and other equipment are hard to come by here, so you're better off bringing them from Kathmandu.

Activities outside the park

After you've had your two days in the park, you might be reluctant to shell out for another permit. Here are a few admission-free options.

The elephant stables and breeding project

The majority of Chitwan's elephant workforce is housed at the government **hattisar** (elephant stables), on the southeastern edge of Sauraha. The best time to catch them is mid-afternoon, when they're sure to be around for feeding time. In

ASIAN ELEPHANTS

In Nepal and throughout southern Asia, **elephants** have been used as ceremonial transportation and beasts of burden for thousands of years, earning them a cherished place in the culture – witness the popularity of elephant-headed Ganesh, the darling of the Hindu pantheon. Thanks to this symbiosis with man, Asian elephants (unlike their African cousins) aren't seriously endangered, even though their native habitat has all but vanished.

With brains four times the size of humans', elephants are said to be as **intelligent** as dolphins; recent research suggests they may communicate subsonically. What we see as a herd is in fact a complex social structure, consisting of bonded pairs and a fluid hierarchy, usually headed by a female. Though they appear docile, elephants have strongly individual personalities and moods. They can learn dozens of commands, but they won't obey just anyone – as any handler will tell you, you can't make an elephant do what it doesn't want to do. That they submit to such cruel head-thumping by drivers seems to have more to do with thick skulls than obedience.

Asian elephants are smaller than those of the African species, but their statistics are still formidable. A bull can grow up to three metres high and weigh four tons, although larger individuals are known to exist (see "Sukla Phanta Wildlife Reserve", home of the biggest elephant in Asia). An average day's intake is 230 litres of water and 200kg of fodder – and if you think that's impressive, wait till you see it come back out again. The trunk is controlled by an estimated 40,000 muscles. Life expectancy is seventy to eighty years and, much the same as with humans, an elephant's working life can be expected to run from its mid-teens to its mid-fifties; training begins at about age five. If you want to spend some time with these magnificent creatures, visit the government elephant stables or breeding project (see below).

hot weather they're taken down to the river for a bath at midday – immensely photogenic. To the west of here, the former Project Tiger facility now functions as the base of the **Nepal Conservation Research and Training Centre**, established by the King Mahendra Trust for Nature Conservation to promote community forestry in the area; biologists are also tracking sloth bears from the centre, in an effort to learn more about the behaviour of this little-studied mammal.

Sauraha lodges offer jeep tours out to the **elephant breeding project**, 4km west of the village, where baby elephants are the main attraction. You can visit the project independently either on foot or bicycle, though you have to cross a stream just this side of the project; come with a guide, who can explain the goings-on and then take you on to Bis Hajaar Tal (see below). Until a decade or so ago, it was common practice to buy elephants from India, where they were captured in the wild and trained in captivity. But in recent years the price of elephants has skyrocketed – a trained animal now goes for upwards of Rs300,000, despite the fact that it may already be halfway through its working life. Feeling the pinch, the Nepal government began breeding and training its own elephants, first at the old *hattisar* and then, in 1988, establishing this separate facility, where elephants can mate in peace, and mothers and babies can receive special attention. At any given time the project is home to three or four breeding bulls and about as many cows; at the time of writing there were two calves, with two more on the way. Calves need to spend as much time as possible with their mothers to become socialized into elephant society. The best time to see them is in late afternoon, after they've returned from educational trips to the river and the jungle.

Bis Hajaar Tal

Large patches of jungle still exist outside the park, albeit in a less pristine state. The most easily accessible of these starts just west of the elephant breeding project, reaching its climax about 5km to the northwest in the area known as **Bis Hajaar Tal** (Twenty-Thousand Lakes). The name refers to a maze of marshy oxbow lakes, many of them already filled in, well hidden among mature *sal* trees. Although this island of forest has been partially cleared by locals, and you're always conscious of chopping and other human activity around the fringes, it's still favoured by deer, monkeys and even a few rhinos – especially during the January thatch-gathering, when animals in the park are disturbed and flee here.

Jeep tours to the elephant breeding project usually finish up with a toddle through this general area. To explore it more fully, have a guide lead you in **on foot** from the breeding project, and allow a full day. (Some shysters offer bootleg elephant rides here, but most of the time is spent dodging wardens, not seeing animals.) Without a guide, you'd be wise to take the long way round to avoid getting lost: **cycle** to Tadi Bazaar, from there follow the main highway 3km west to just before it crosses a canal (the village here is called Tikauli), then go southwest on a gravel road beside the canal for about 2km until you begin to see the lakes. This road continues along the canal for another 8km or so to Gita Nagar, on the Bharatpur–Jagatpur road.

Tharu villages and bike rides

Guided Tharu village walks out of Sauraha usually mean a loiter through the few houses behind *Hotel Elephant Camp*, or out to Bachhauli, a village just to the east of Sauraha. It's all rather voyeuristic, especially when you consider how many tourists have trooped through here before you, and the way guides point at residents and pick up their tools without asking is not something that should be encouraged. Staged **Tharu stick dances** are equally inauthentic, but much more exciting. The original purpose of the dance, it's said, was simply to make a lot of racket to keep the wild animals away at night. On any given night in the high season, several Sauraha lodges will lay on performances for package groups, which anyone can attend; audience participation is expected, if not enforced. These dances are performed for real during Faagun Purnima, the full moon of February–March.

With or without a guide, you'll learn a lot more about real Tharu (and Bahun) life by hopping on a bike and just getting lost on the back roads to the east and west of Sauraha. In November, when the **rice** is harvested, you'll be able to watch villagers cutting the stems, tying them into sheaves and threshing them – or, since it's such a busy time of year, piling them in big stacks to await threshing. January is **thatch-gathering** time, when you'll see people bringing huge bundles out of the park, to be put by until a slack time before the monsoon when they can repair their roofs. In early March, the **mustard** or **wheat** that was planted after the rice crop is ready; **corn** is then planted, to be harvested in July for animal fodder, flour and meal. During each of these harvest seasons you'll hear the rhythmic toot-toot of local mills, hulling or polishing grain, or pressing oil.

From Sauraha, the most fertile country for exploration lies to the east: heading towards Tadi along the eastern side of the village, make a right after about 500m and you can follow that road all the way to **Parsa**, 8km away on the Mahendra Highway, with many side roads to villages en route. Given a full day and a good (mountain) bike, you could continue eastwards fom Parsa along the highway for another 10km, and just before Bhandara make a left onto a track leading to **Baireni**, a particularly well-preserved Tharu village. Another 10km east of Bhandara lies **Lothar**, where by following a trail upstream you'll reach the waterfalls on the Lothar Khola, a contemplative spot with a healthy measure of birdlife.

To reach the country west of Sauraha you need to pedal to Tadi and west along the Mahendra Highway to Tikauli. From there the canal road (see "Bis Hajaar Tal") leads about 10km through beautiful forest to Gita Nagar, where you join the Bharatpur–Jagatpur road, with almost unlimited possibilities from there.

Narayanghat, Bharatpur and Devghat

It's hard to travel very far in Nepal without at least passing through **NARAYANGHAT**: the construction of the Mugling–Narayanghat highway has made it the gateway to the Tarai and the busiest crossroads in the country. What was, a decade ago, a far-flung intersection is now a 500-metre strip of diesel and *daal bhaat*, and it's said that real estate changes hands here for almost as high stakes as in Kathmandu. **BHARATPUR**, its sister city to the east and the headquarters of Chitwan District, can muster a large regional college, the *Tuborg* and *San Miguel* breweries, and an airstrip (in danger of being replaced by a proposed international airport to the south). Unflattering as all that may sound, you may have occasion to stay, or at least eat, in the area; the side trip to Devghat should provide an incentive.

Buses to Pokhara and Devghat have their own bus park, at the north end of Narayanghat on the road to Mugling. All others stop at the fast-food parade just east of Pulchowk (the intersection of the Mugling and Mahendra highways), except for minibuses to Tadi Bazaar, Meghauli and other local destinations, which start from Sanghamchowk (the next major intersection to the east). **Rikshas** should take you anywhere within the two towns for Rs10 or less.

For **lodging**, the most palatable budget option is *Hotel River View*, behind the Pokhara bus park, which really does have a river view (②/B③). *Eagle Rest House* (②/B③) is the largest of several in Pulchowk; near Sanghamchowk there's the *New Bisauni Guest House* (B③). Higher-class accommodation is available in Bharatpur at *Hotel Narayani Safari* (☎056/20130; in Kathmandu ☎01/525015), which has air conditioning, a pool and tennis courts (B⑧). **Food**, plentiful but not wildly exciting, can be found around Pulchowk. Standing out slightly from the greasy spoons and whisky shacks are *Rooftop Restaurant* and, across the street, *Fishtail Lodge and Restaurant*, with English menus and Indian/Chinese/ "Continental" (ie, everything with chips) food. *Hotel Narayani Safari*'s dining room does astonishingly good meals that run to about Rs250 a head.

Devghat

DEVGHAT (or Deoghat), 5km northwest of Narayanghat, is a lot of people's idea of a great place to die. An astonishingly tranquil spot, it stands where the wooded hills meet the shimmering plains, and the blue-green Trisuli and the black Kali Gandaki merge to form the Narayani, one of the major tributaries of the Ganga (Ganges). The ashes of King Mahendra, the present king's father, were sprinkled at this sacred *tribeni* (a confluence of three rivers: wherever two rivers meet, a third, spiritual one is believed to join them), and scores of *sunyasan*, those who have renounced the world, patiently live out their last days here hoping to

TARAI CULTURE: THARUS AND NEWCOMERS

Two mysteries still surround Nepal's second-biggest ethnic minority, the Tarai-dwelling **Tharus**: where they came from, and how they came to be resistant to malaria. The Rana Tharus of the far west claim to be descended from high-caste Rajput women who were sent north by their husbands during the Muslim invasions and, when the men never returned for them, married their servants. There's some circumstantial evidence to support this, as traces of a matriarchy are still in evidence among Rana Tharus; the Tharu name could derive from the Thar Desert of Rajasthan in India, and Tharu women's preference for carrying objects on their heads is characteristically Rajasthani. However, anthropologists dismiss this theory – it doesn't account for Tharus' Hindu-animist beliefs and somewhat Mongoloid features, nor does it explain the wide variety of Tharu dialects and customs – and speculate that the tribe migrated from India's eastern hills, filtering across the Tarai over the course of millennia. Firm evidence is lacking either way.

As to the matter of **malaria resistance**, red blood cells seem to play a role – the fact that Tharus are prone to sickle-cell anemia might be significant – but very little research has been done. At least as important, Tharus boost their natural resistance with a few common-sense precautions, such as building houses with tiny windows to keep smoke in and mosquitoes (and ghosts) out.

Tharus are **farmers** and livestock raisers, clearing patches in the forest and warding off wild animals from flimsy watchtowers called *machaan*. Their whirling stick dance evokes their uneasy but respectful relationship with the spirits of the forest, as do the raised animal emblems that decorate their doorways. **Fishing** is an important activity – given the Tarai's high water table, it's easy enough to scoop out a pond and stock it – and you're likely to see fisherwomen wielding hand-held nets between crossed poles, or carrying their catch home in wicker boxes.

Tharu **houses** are made of mud and dung plastered over wood-and-reed frames, giving them a distinctive ribbed effect. Traditionally, western Tharus built communal **longhouses**, big enough for a half a dozen families or more and partitioned by huge vial-shaped grain urns, but most have now moved up to detached models. While **clothing** varies tremendously by area, Tharu women often wear thick silver bracelets above the elbow; tattooing of the forearms and lower legs is common among older women but is falling out of fashion with the younger generation.

The Tarai has long been viewed as Nepal's frontier and the Tharus dismissed as primitive aboriginals, and since the turn of the century – when, as a preliminary step to abolishing slavery, the government encouraged **slaves** to homestead in the Tarai – it's been seen as a place where a settler can clear the land and start a new life. The government's malaria-control programme accelerated the process, and several million gung-ho **immigrants** from the hills and India (the border is highly porous) have now cleared, tamed and transformed the Tarai into the breadbasket of Nepal, felling much of the valuable timber in the process. The migration is far from over – the Tarai's population is doubling every seventeen years (urban areas are doubling every ten years). Prosperity has probably peaked, however, and since productivity isn't keeping up with population, the Tarai's agricultural surplus is steadily declining.

In one generation, the Tharus have been outflanked, outfarmed and in many cases bought out and reduced to sharecropping. Traditional culture is still strong in the far west, particularly among the Dangauria and Rana groups, but in other areas it's been all but drowned by a tide of hill, Indian and Western tendencies. Like indigenous peoples the world over, Tharus know more about their own environment than anyone, but they're not being listened to.

achieve an equally auspicious death and rebirth. Many have retired to Devghat because they have no children to look after them in their old age and to perform the necessary rites when they die. *Pujari* (priests) also practise here – their professional signs are the only advertising you'll see – and often take in young candidates for the priesthood as resident students.

Occasional **buses** shuttle between Narayanghat and Devghat, taking about half an hour, but the one-hour **walk** along the **footpath** that parallels the river through the woods is much more pleasant. In either case, you come to the Trisuli and cross it by a footbridge (recently immortalized in the Nepali film *Kanchhi*, in which a heartbroken lover attempts suicide here), then bear left to the village. You can also cross the river further downsteam by **dugout canoe** – for the return to Narayanghat, the ferryman, if he thinks he can be spared from his duties, might consent to take you back for Rs40 or so.

Though dozens of small shrines lie dotted around the village, none is big or particularly interesting: you come here more for the atmosphere than the sights. Devghat is home of a well-known guru, the one-armed **Ashori Baba**, who gives audiences to serious seekers; a statue of his late predecessor, Jaleshwar Baba, is usually surrounded by a congregation of devotees. Rafting guides are fond of telling stories about the "Crazy Baba", another recently deceased guru who was famed for his penile performances. A huge **pilgrimage**, the Tribeni Mela, is held here on the new-moon day of January–February, and Shiva Raatri, one lunar month later, brings many Indian devotees. At other times, sadhus and pilgrims do *puja* at the point where the rivers meet – cremations are also held here – and old-timers meditate outside their huts in the sun. Be sensitive to the residents, and don't disturb them or touch anything that might be holy: many are orthodox Bahuns and your touch would be polluting. There's **no lodging** at Devghat, but it wouldn't be appropriate to stay overnight anyway.

LUMBINI TARAI

Hordes of travellers hurry through this ancient part of the Tarai, west of Chitwan; few take the time to look around. It's best known, unfairly, for **Sunauli**, the main tourist border crossing between Nepal and India. Yet only 20km away, seldom visited and utterly unhyped, is **Lumbini**, birthplace of the Buddha and the site of ruins going back almost three thousand years.

Getting there isn't too difficult: two main highways – the Siddhartha and the Mahendra – connect the region with Pokhara and the rest of the Tarai, and buses to Sunauli are frequent. The journey to Lumbini is a bit taxing, but well worth the extra effort. Accommodation and food here, as in most other parts of the Tarai, are readily available but usually very basic.

Butwal

Westwards from Narayanghat the Mahendra Highway runs across a washboard of cultivated fields, skirts the occasional cemetery of charred stumps and briefly climbs over a jungle-cloaked spur of the Chure Hills. The road is good and it's a relatively painless, if dull, three hours to BUTWAL. Crouching uninvitingly at the mouth of a canyon, Butwal is the hub of the Lumbini administrative zone: north lies Pokhara; south is Sunauli and the Indian border; and to the west, the Mahendra Highway zooms along towards Nepalganj and Nepal's western border.

Placed at the start of both an important trade route to Tibet, and the pilgrim trail to Muktinath, the **tax post** at Butwal was for centuries a tidy little earner for Palpa (Tansen) and then Kathmandu. Much later, it came to be an important staging post for Nepal's most lucrative export: Gurkha soldiers, bound for the recruiting office at Gorakhpur in India. In the early nineteenth century, Nepal and the East India Company fell into a dispute over the territory around Butwal, and the murder of some British police here touched off a two-year **war with Britain**. Nepal scored several improbable early victories here and elsewhere but, outnumbered four to one, was eventually forced to surrender. Under the terms of the resulting treaty, the Tarai territories from Butwal west had to be ceded to the British (Nepal struck a deal to get the disputed land around Butwal back the same year). Any reminders of the past are, however, conspicuously absent in modern Butwal.

Practicalities

Express **buses** stop at "Traphik Chowk", a bazaar area on the Siddhartha Highway as it skirts the east side of town. Local buses use the bus park at the west end of town, a few hundred metres south of the bridge over the Tinau River. If you need a cheap **room**, walk past *Hotel Sandeep* (where rooms are airless and overpriced) and make for *Butwal Guest House* (①/B③) at the big roundabout two blocks south of Traphik Chowk, or, across the street, *Hotel Shayapatri* (②/B②). Failing that, try *Santosh Guest House* (①/B②), two blocks west of Traphik Chowk. Butwal has a **posh hotel**, the *Sindoor* (☎073/20189; B②), which, though stranded in an industrial wasteland just south of the bus park, has river views and a decent restaurant serving food at Kathmandu prices.

Bhairawa, Sunauli and the border

Half an hour south by bus, **BHAIRAWA** (officially, the name has been changed to **SIDDHARTHANAGAR**, but it's not catching on) is a virtual rerun of Butwal. The bazaar, located west of the main roundabout on the Siddhartha Highway, supports a sizeable minority of Muslim traders and, like so many border towns, exists primarily to peddle mundane Western goods to acquisitive Indians. As a base camp for Lumbini, though, it does the job, especially if the where's-the-party atmosphere of Sunauli isn't your style.

For orientation purposes, Bhairawa's three main streets form a triangle: the eastern side is the border highway, the other two comprise the bazaar. Buses stop on the border highway near the *Hotel Yeti* (a handy landmark), which stands at the southeastern apex of the triangle; rikshas and tempos bound for Sunauli wait here, and the bazaar lies to the west. The road to Lumbini leaves the border highway about 1km north of the *Hotel Yeti*, just north of the triangle's northern apex.

For **lodging**, try – in descending order of price and hygiene – *Hotel Yeti* (☎071/20551; B⑥, or B⑦ with air conditioning); *Hotel Himalayan Inn* (☎071/20347; B⑤), on the border road about 500m north of the *Yeti*, towards Butwal; or *City Guest House*, in the bazaar west of the *Yeti* (B②). *Hotel Himalayan Inn*'s dining room does competent Indian and Chinese meals. For **onward bus tickets** there are agents near *Hotel Yeti*; all long-distance buses originate at Sunauli, but getting a seat from Bhairawa is no problem as long as you book it the day before.

Sunauli and the border

Four kilometres south of Bhairawa – Rs3 by tempo or jeep – SUNAULI (Soo-*no*-li) is the most convenient **border crossing** between Nepal and most parts of India. Bus and train package deals to or from India usually involve an overnight here (see the "On from Kathmandu" section in Chapter One for more on these). It's a good place to glean information from travellers coming the other way or meet up with people going the same way, but when the bus leaves the next morning you'll want to be on it.

Only budget **accommodation** is available in Sunauli, and it tends to be noisy, dirty and redolent of toilets. The half-dozen guest houses are all fairly similar, but close enough together so you can shop around (if you're not already committed) to see which one's been remodelled most recently. Currently the best deal is *Nepal Guest House*, a big place with a sociable atmosphere and a vegetarian roof-top restaurant (②/B②). Another contender is the *New Cottage Lodge* (B②). Better accommodation is available in Bhairawa and on the India side of the border, if you're willing to spend more. The **food** in Sunauli's guest houses isn't bad – whichever way you're heading, the menus give a taste of what's in store further on (if you're coming from India, you might welcome the sight of Coca-Cola). Note that all guest houses and hotels listed in the book have been price graded according to a scale detailed in *Basics* (see p.21).

As a funnel for traffic from India, Sunauli is well served by **buses**, but be sure to book ahead, since an empty seat in Sunauli might be spoken for in Bhairawa. For onward tickets or general advice, *Hotel Mamta* has a branch of *Student Travels*.

The **bank** on the Nepal side is open daily from 7.30am to 6pm, but the one on the Indian side doesn't open till 10am, after most buses have left. The **money-changers** in Sunauli don't give a speck over the official rate, so if you're entering Nepal wait till Kathmandu to do any serious changing (see *Basics* for advice on money-changing and the black market); Indian rupees are readily accepted in Sunauli but not beyond. Figure on half an hour to get through Nepalese and Indian **border formalities**, and remember that Nepal **time** is fifteen minutes ahead of India. The offers of riksha rides across the border aren't to be taken seriously, since from start to finish it's only a distance of about 200m.

Lumbini

> *After I am no more, Ananda! Men of belief will visit with faithful curiosity and devotion to the four places – where I was born . . . attained enlightenment . . . gave the first sermons . . . and passed into Nirvana.*
>
> The Buddha (c.543–463 BC)

For the world's 300 million Buddhists, **LUMBINI**, 22km west of Bhairawa, is where it all began. **The Buddha's birthplace** is arguably the single most important historical site in Nepal, and not only the source of one of the world's great religions but also the centre of Nepal's most significant **archeological finds**, dating from the third century BC. Little-visited and positively oozing with serenity, it's the kind of place you could whizz round in two hours or soak up for days.

The Buddha has long been a prophet without much honour in his own country: the area around Lumbini is now predominantly Muslim, while the main local **festival** is a Hindu one, commemorating the Buddha as the ninth incarnation of Vishnu – it's held on the full moon of the Nepali month of Baisakh (April–May). Celebrations of **Buddha Jayanti** (the Buddha's birthday) are comparatively meagre because, as the local monks will tell you with visible disgust, Buddhists from the hills think Lumbini is too hot in May.

But big changes may be in store. The government has set aside land and devised a hugely ambitious **master plan** for a eight-square-kilometre religious **park** consisting of monasteries, cultural facilities, gardens, fountains and a tourist village. Far-fetched as it sounds, the project has the backing of the United Nations and has raised piles of cash from Japan, Korea and other Buddhist countries. Several buildings and acres of landscaping have already been completed, and since the construction of a deluxe hotel here, Japanese tour groups have begun to add Lumbini to their whirlwind tours of the Buddhist holy sites. If the remaining plans come off, Lumbini could be a radically different place in a few years' time. Should we be sceptical? With Nepal, you never know . . .

The Sacred Garden

The **"Sacred Garden"**, where the Buddha reputedly was born, contains all of Lumbini's ancient treasures in an area no bigger than a football pitch. By all accounts a well-tended grove in the Buddha's day, the spot was consecrated soon after his death, and at least one monastery was attached to it by the third century BC when Ashoka, the great north Indian emperor and Buddhist evangelist, made a well-documented pilgrimage to the spot. Ashoka's patronage established a thriving religious community, but by the time the intrepid Chinese traveller Hiuen Tsang visited in the seventh century it was limping, and must have died out after the ninth century.

The garden was lost for six hundred years and its **rediscovery**, in 1895, was one of the greatest (and luckiest) finds of the century. Armed with archaic and often

LUMBINI

N

Pilgrims' Accommodation

Lumbini Hokke Hotel

0   500 m

← Taulihawa   Bhairawa →

Museum
Library

Bridge

WEST MONASTIC ZONE

EAST MONASTIC ZONE

Eternal Flame

Lumbini Village Lodge

Maya Devi Mandir

Tibetan Monastery

Dharmsala

SACRED GARDEN

Theravada Monastery

Pool

Information Booth

Telar Khola

Lumbini Gardens Guest House

↓ Indian Border

↳ Pararia

contradictory accounts, the German archeologist R. A. Führer had managed in the previous year to unearth some separate but related relics near Taulihawa. Believing he was on the Buddha's trail, he arranged to return to the same spot, but at the last minute his Nepali escort requested a more convenient meeting place about 25km to the east. By sheer coincidence, the party made camp practically on top of the garden; while Führer slept, a porter – no doubt answering the call of nature – stumbled upon the ruins, which had been obscured by thick jungle.

The centrepiece of the site is the **Maya Devi Mandir**, whose boxy appearance belies great antiquity: the ornate brickwork on the west side dates the building to the Indian Gupta period (fourth to seventh centuries), and it's likely that it was built on the site of an even earlier structure. The gigantic *pipal* (bodhi) tree arching over the entrance has for several years been marked for removal because its roots are interfering with the monuments, but has so far been spared. Inside is a bas-relief sculpture of the Buddha's birth that may be as old as the third century BC – so worn are the features, from centuries of *puja*, that Führer at first dismissed the temple as Hindu because locals were worshipping the image as Tathagata, a fertility goddess. A recent replica reconstructs the tableau: Maya Devi, the Buddha's mother, grasping a tree branch for support, a tiny Buddha standing fully formed at her feet, and (ecumenical, this) the Hindu gods Indra and Brahma looking on. The sculpture illustrates an elaborate Buddhist nativity story, according to which the baby Buddha leapt out of the womb, took seven steps and proclaimed his world-saving destiny. The square, brick-sided **pool** beside the temple is supposed to be where Maya Devi bathed after the delivery.

West of the temple, the **Ashokan Pillar** is the oldest monument in Nepal. Again, it's not much to look at – fenced in and capped with concrete, it looks like smokestack – but the inscription (also Nepal's oldest), recording Ashoka's visit in 249 BC, is the best evidence available that the Buddha was born here. Site guides, who ought to know, insist that the pillar is original, even though the original cap that rests at its base is of a different stone. The metal bands around it are to keep it from splitting if hit by lightning. Pillars were a sort of trademark of Ashoka, serving the dual purpose of spreading the faith and marking the boundaries of his empire: this one announces that Ashoka granted Lumbini tax-free status in honour of the Buddha's birth. The heavily restored **brick foundations** of buildings and stupas around the site, dating from the second century BC to the ninth century AD, chart the rise and fall of Lumbini's early monastic community. The two mounds north and south of the garden aren't ancient – they're merely piles of earth and bricks removed during excavations.

Buddha's birth

BUDDHA: A LIFE

The year of the Buddha's **birth** is disputed – it was probably 543 BC – but it's generally agreed that it happened at Lumbini while his mother, Maya Devi, was on her way to her maternal home for the delivery. He was born Gautama Siddhartha ("he who has accomplished his aim"), the son of a king and a member of the Shakya clan, who ruled the central Tarai from their capital at Kapilvastu (see "Tilaurakot", below). Brought up in his father's palace, Gautama lived a sheltered life until, at the age of 29, he made a fateful trip into town where, according to legend, he encountered an old man, a sick man, a corpse and a hermit: old age, sickness and death were the end of life, he realized, and contemplation seemed the only way to understand the nature of suffering.

Gautama fled the palace and spent five years as an ascetic before concluding that self-denial brought him no closer to the truth than self-indulgence. Under the famous *bodhi* tree of Bodh Gaya in India, he vowed to keep meditating until he attained **enlightenment**. This he did after 49 days, at which time Gautama became the Buddha, released from the cycle of birth and death. He made his way to Sarnath (near modern Varanasi in India) and preached his **first sermon**, setting in motion, Buddhists believe, *dharma*, the wheel of the truth. Although he's said to have returned to Kapilvastu to convert his family, and according to some stories he even put in an appearance in the Kathmandu Valley, the Buddha spent most of the rest of his life preaching in northern India. He **died** at the age of 80 in Kasia (Kushinagar), about 100km southeast of Lumbini. For a full explanation of Buddhism, see "Religion" in *Contexts*.

Two active monasteries face the Sacred Garden and are open to the public; neither is tremendously old, and like all the modern buildings in the area they're slated for demolition to make way for the master plan (their monks are promised bigger and better premises in the new Lumbini). The soaring **Tibetan monastery** displays a typical array of prematurely aged frescoes and gilded Buddhas and *bodhisattva* in glass cabinets. It provides a winter residence for up to fifty monks from an affiliated monastery in Boudha, who can be heard chanting in the early morning and mid-afternoon; there's only a skeleton crew staying on during the hot months. The more austere **Theravada** establishment offers less to look at, but its solitary gold-robed monk speaks good English. Built by the government of Nepal, the monastery has the feel of something designed by a civil servant, with an eclectic mix of Newar woodwork, Burmese and Thai images and Tibetan-style paintings.

A walk northwards from the Maya Devi temple, pleasant for its own sake, hits the highlights of the slowly unfurling master plan. The elevated path passes through what will be a reflecting pool encircling the Sacred Garden, and beyond burns an **eternal flame**, a fitting remembrance of the "Light of Asia". From here you can follow the kilometre-long central canal past the future locations of the East and West Monastic Centres, to be designed and built by the governments of Japan, Thailand, China and Sri Lanka: no sign of any monasteries yet, but the canal is alive with birdlife – around sunset, flocks of parakeets whistle past with a sound like boomerangs. Work is further advanced on **"Lumbini Village"** at the north end of the canal; at the time of writing, the Korean-built museum and library were in place (but forlornly vacant), while the auditorium, restaurants and shops remained stubbornly on paper.

Practicalities

Dust off your Buddhist tolerance, because connections to Lumbini are slow. Decrepit **minibuses** from Bhairawa (approximately every 30min) take an interminable hour to hour and a half, depending on stops. Most are bound for **Pararia**, the village immediately south of the master plan area, which means you'll want to hop off earlier, near the monasteries; to be sure of a seat for the return trip you may have to board at Pararia (last bus back is at 5.30pm). You can speed the journey from Bhairawa by renting a **jeep** with driver at *Hotel Yeti*, which should cost Rs300 return, but you'll have to make separate arrangements if you want to stay at Lumbini more than an hour or two. If possible – and if it's not too hot – go by **bike**: head west out of Bhairawa, bear left at a fork after 20km (there should be a sign for *Lumbini Hokke Hotel* pointing straight ahead here), and turn right onto a dirt track about 2km later. An **information** booth has been temporarily erected about 1km down this road, just south of the Sacred Garden, but it's due to be shifted to the north end of the park, and it's not very helpful anyway.

Accommodation is spread thinly over a wide area. At the **budget** end, *Lumbini Village Lodge*, located in the hamlet immediately east of the master plan area, serves basic food and can provide hot water by the bucket (④). More and possibly better options are bound to arise near here in the next few years – it might be a good idea to check these out before entering the park, where lodgings are controlled by the government and unlikely to improve. Inside the park, you ideally want to stay as close as possible to the Sacred Garden, but the only options here are the monasteries, which shelter pilgrims informally but are sorely lacking in things like bedding or hot water. The Theravada monastery has a *dharmsala* tranquilly set in a mango garden, while the Tibetan monastery can put visitors up in its monks' quarters outside of the busy winter months (donation expected). A new pilgrims' accommodation building, located 3km north of the Sacred Garden and operated by the government of Sri Lanka, was due to open sometime in 1993 – no word on price, but it should be reasonable. The future of the more **upmarket** *Lumbini Gardens Guest House* is uncertain, as it was closed indefinitely in 1992, but if it reopens (probably under a new name) it should offer rooms in the B⑦ range. Finally, the four-star *Lumbini Hokke Hotel* (Kathmandu ☎01/521348), a crypt-like fortress in the northern sector of the park, is patronized almost exclusively by Japanese tour groups (B⑨).

Other than guest houses, the only sources of **food** are the two grass-shack eateries which are to be found in the courtyards of each of the monasteries, and the fry stalls of Pararia.

Tilaurakot (Kapilvastu)

A dusty 24km west of Lumbini, **TILAURAKOT** is believed to have been the capital of ancient **KAPILVASTU**, and the Buddha's childhood home. Although it's yielded up far more ruins and relics than Lumbini, due to its back-of-beyond location it's recommended only for diehard archeology buffs.

The Tilaurakot **excavations** have unearthed the remains of a palace, consisting of thick fortress walls, four gates, a moat and a couple of giant stupa bases. At least thirteen layers of human habitation have been found, going back to the eighth century BC. The area surrounding Tilaurakot has also yielded up two

Ashokan pillars, erected to commemorate the birthplaces of mythical Buddhas of previous ages. Admission to the palace excavation site is free, and the lonely guards will probably be happy to give you a sign-language tour around the shaded grounds. Notable relics include the reconstructed western gate and the ruined **eastern gate** – the latter of great metaphorical significance to Buddhists, as it was the start of his journey in search of enlightenment. A small temple near the centre, its bricks lashed together by the roots of a pipal tree, contains a trove of terracotta elephants, donated by local people whose prayers have been answered.

A small **museum**, located opposite the start of the side road to the excavation, displays some of the three thousand coins found in the area (including one bearing the Shakya name), together with Lumbini and Kapilvastu pottery spanning three distinct periods and a thousand years. Even older pottery discovered in caves near Jomosom, high in the Himalaya, is for some reason also displayed here. The contents of this museum may soon be transferred to Lumbini's new museum.

Practicalities

If you're planning on getting to Tilaurakot by public transport, you're stuck with the two morning **minibuses** which make their way from Bhairawa to **Taulihawa**, 22km beyond Lumbini on the same road; you could try flagging these down from Lumbini at the intersection near the *Lumbini Hokke Hotel*, but don't expect to get a seat. (Buses to Taulihawa from the Mahendra Highway are more frequent, but it's just too impractical to get to where they pass.) From the centre of Taulihawa, walk 3km along the main (paved) northbound road until the pavement gives out, where a short track to the right leads to Tilaurakot. If you've got a bicycle you could pedal from Lumbini to Tilaurakot in about two hours, but the road is very bumpy.

Basic **food** is available at Taulihawa – if you get stuck and need a place to **stay**, try *Lumbini Hotel* (①), a short distance north of the town centre along the road to Tilaurakot.

THE FAR WEST

Until recently, the sheer misery of travelling the Mahendra Highway was enough to deter all but the most dedicated from entering Nepal's remote **far west**. Now, with the highway paved and the bridge over the Karnali River slated for completion as this book goes to press, this once-neglected quarter of the country looks poised to open its doors to travellers. It's still a hell of a haul to get here, and not for the faint of heart, but the new highway makes this an up-and-coming route to or from Delhi (which is just ten hours by bus from the far western border crossing).

As the word gets out, expect the sights described in this section to grow in popularity and sophistication. Two in particular, **Bardia National Park** and **Sukla Phanta Wildlife Reserve**, may some day become serious rivals to Chitwan National Park – so far they've only been developed by a couple of Chitwan-style luxury safari operators, but with proper preparation they can be done independently.

Nepalganj and Birendranagar

The Mahendra Highway makes good time to Nepalganj, 190km west of Butwal, crossing a spur of the Chure Hills and following the pleasingly rural Rapti Valley (no relation to the river of the same name in Chitwan). North of here lies Dang, home of the white-clad Dangaura Tharus and, by the look of it, fine cycling country. Nearing Nepalganj on the main highway, the hills to the south peter out and the bleached vastness of the Indian plains flattens the spirit.

Nepalganj

Trade and transport hub of the far west – for what little trade and transport there is in the far west – **NEPALGANJ** is, more interestingly, Nepal's most Muslim city. The presence of Muslims in the Tarai is hardly surprising, of course, since the border with India, where Muslims comprise a significant minority, was only determined in the nineteenth century. Until just prior to the 1814–16 war with the British, this part of the Tarai belonged to the Nawab of Oudh, one of India's biggest landowners; after Nepal's defeat it was ceded to the East India Company and only returned to Nepal as a goodwill gesture for services rendered during the Indian Mutiny of 1857. A fair few Muslims fled to Nepalganj during the mutiny – Lucknow, where the most violent incidents occurred, is due south of here – and others filtered in during the Rana years, seeing chances for cross-border trade. The result is a permanent Muslim community, self-contained but maintaining business and family links with India. Indeed, the entire city feels overwhelmingly Indian, with its cheap neo-Mughal architecture and frenetically mundane bazaar. Imperious warnings against trade in Indian rupees ("by order of the Nepal Rastra Bank") are a further reminder that India is just a betel-spit down the road.

Nepalganj sprawls more than a city of 50,000 should; lately its numbers have been swollen by labourers and project managers working on the Mahendra Highway. Its heart is **Tribhuwan Chowk**, the lively but dilapidated intersection of the city's two main shopping thoroughfares, south of which rikshas wait beneath an Indian-style Hindu temple that sits in the middle of the road like a toll booth. The **Muslim quarter** lies northeast of Tribhuwan Chowk – "picturesque" is probably too strong a word, but one canopy-shaded section is almost like a souk, with bearded traders done up in crocheted caps and pyjama-like clothes, and transactions conducted on wooden benches in the street. The mosques in this area are disappointingly modern, and at any rate out of bounds to nonbelievers. Hindu worship and trade is centred around the nondescript **Bageshwari Mandir**; behind the temple is a large pool with a jaunty statue of Mahadev (Shiva) in the middle – marvellously kitsch.

Practicalities

Hardly anybody sets out to see Nepalganj, but a few people heading further west end up spending an unintended night here. If you're flying to any of the far-western airstrips there'll be a change in Nepalganj and, all too often, some problem or other with the onward flight. Nepalganj's **airport** (see below for details), the country's second busiest, is a six-kilometre plod north of town by *tonga* (horse-drawn cart) or riksha. The **bus park** has been inconveniently banished to the extreme north end of the city, and it might be a good idea to buy an onward ticket when you arrive to avoid the extra trip later on. The **border**, which is open to tourists, is 6km south of town.

Nepalganj has a surprisingly good selection of **accommodation**, though there's nothing fancy. Top of the line is *Hotel Sneha* (☎081/20119; B⑥, camping possible), a favourite with Western project workers. *New Hotel Bheri* runs a distant second, but is priced more reasonably (②/B⑤). Closer to town but correspondingly noisier, several cold-water lodges are grouped between the Bageshwari temple and Birendra Chowk. Best of these are *Shital Guest House* (①), *Punjabi Hotel* (②/B②) and *Narayani Guest House*, now renamed *Hotel Orient* (②/B③); the proprietor at the last may be able to fix you up with a bicycle.

If you don't speak Nepali, **eating** in Nepalganj is pretty much a smile-and-point operation at roadside carts or *bhojanalaya*. North of the Bageshwari temple, a couple of holes in the wall run by displaced Sherpas and Humla Bhotiyas do terrific *momo*, but that's all they do. Out towards the bus park, the popular and efficient *Punjabi Hotel* specializes in "daal-fried-roti" and fish curry. The *Sneha*'s restaurant serves decent Western food, but it's not worth a special trip if you're not staying there.

Onwards: flights

If you're moving any further west, consider **flying**: western Nepal is where domestic services really come into their own, and Nepalganj is the hub for all flights in the region. *RNAC*'s Mahendranagar flight ($77) will cut out at least six hours in a bus, and if you're planning to trek around Jumla ($44), Simikot ($88) or Dunai ($77), flying from Nepalganj saves a good deal of money over flying from Kathmandu. (All domestic airlines cover the Kathmandu–Nepalganj route, which costs $99.) *Everest* also has a Jumla flight, and other carriers might eventually follow suit. *RNAC*'s office (☎081/20239) is out on the highway that bypasses town, west of Tribhuwan Chowk. The queue for tickets starts forming early.and there's a mad dash when the doors open, but foreigners paying dollar fares can get "preferred" service upstairs. Other airlines with offices in Nepalganj are *Everest* (☎081/20035) and *Nepal Airways* (☎081/20119).

Birendranagar (Surkhet)

Ninety kilometres northwest of Nepalganj – too far off the beaten track for most – **BIRENDRANAGAR** (as often as not called by its old name, **SURKHET**) comes as a pleasant surprise. Placed in the middle of an undulating *dun* valley, it's neither as hot, flat nor Indian as towns closer to the border. It's also managed to escape the usual shabby fate of Tarai boomtowns, thanks, surprisingly, to government planning: HMG is in the process of transferring the western regional headquarters from Nepalganj to here, a move that's creating plenty of jobs and trade. A good deal of development effort is going into the valley, too, led by a big Canadian IRDP (integrated rural development project) and a gaggle of Peace Corps, VSO and other volunteers.

You might find yourself in Birendranagar for the start of a trek – from here it's a week to Rara Lake – or to raft in the Bheri River, which is half an hour south of town. By **bus**, it's a rugged six-hour trip from Nepalganj, but the road is being improved all the time. No one seems to have tried it yet, but this route would make an excellent ride on a **mountain bike** – and once here, the bike would come in handy for getting around the valley. A trekking permit is required for travel north of the valley.

The must-see of the area is 2km out of town on a wooded knoll in the middle of the valley: **Karki Bihar** houses the remains of an ancient Buddhist temple, and the surrounding forest contains deer and (supposedly) leopards. In town, the only real attraction is **Bulbule Tal**, a new but agreeably cool and shady park that's good for bird-watching. **Food** and **lodging** in Birendranagar is of the most basic sort, with only one hotel, the *Rada* (①). For help, the best tactic might be to latch onto one of the many Western aid workers.

Bardia National Park

With Chitwan becoming increasingly mass-market, **BARDIA NATIONAL PARK**, northwest of Nepalganj, beckons as an unspoiled alternative. In many ways, it's what Chitwan used to be: hard to get to and still barely developed, it's the largest area of undisturbed wilderness left in the Tarai. Budget lodging is available and camping is allowed, but there's nothing like Sauraha here – if you're planning to do Bardia independently, you're strongly advised to come with a guide hired in Sauraha. In addition, a luxury lodge and two tented camps operate inside or just outside the park.

A wildlife reserve since the 1970s, Bardia was upgraded in 1988 to a national park. Ecologically, it spans the same subtropical habitats as Chitwan, from dry hills and *sal* stands to thick riverine

A typical Tarai shop

forest and grassland. Nepal's biggest river, the awesome **Karnali**, forms the park's western boundary and major watering hole, and the density of wildlife and birds along this western edge is second only to Chitwan.

Bardia's star species is the **blackbuck**, an uncommonly graceful antelope with corkscrew horns, found in greater numbers here than anywhere else. Langurs, wild boar and deer are seen everywhere, and about forty **tigers** inhabit the park – as in Chitwan, the chances of seeing one are slim – along with leopards, sloth bears and assorted other nocturnal creatures. **Rhinos**, hunted to extinction in Bardia this century, have been reintroduced since 1986 and appear to be flourishing; a small herd of **wild elephants** often crashes around the western side of the park. The Karnali River is probably the best place in Nepal to get a peep at rare **gangetic dolphins**, which favour the river's deep channels, and **mahseer**, a form of carp that can weigh up to 40kg; mugger (and with a lot of luck, gharial) crocodiles might also be spotted in winter. The commonest sight of all around Bardia are **termite mounds**, looking like sand-coloured volcanoes, which reach their greatest height – up to eight feet – here.

Bardia straddles the Mahendra Highway, which is new and admirably smooth in this section. The **park headquarters** is at **THAKURDWARA**, located off the highway in a game-rich corner of the park near the Karnali River.

Bardia on a budget

Doing Bardia independently is still a challenge, but it's steadily getting easier. A daily morning **bus** now connects Nepalganj directly with Thakurdwara, following the Mahendra Highway to Motipur (sometimes called Ambassa) and then a dirt access road for another 8km to the headquarters. Other buses will let you off at Motipur, and you'll have to hoof it from there.

Thakurdwara was due to get a Sauraha-style **guest house** in time for the start of the autumn 1993 season, which should really break the ice for budget travel here. Prices are supposed to be in the ② category, though if the place is as nice as they say it's going to be you should expect to pay quite a bit more. Alternatively, it's possible to stay in **tea shops** here and in other villages adjoining the park, but you'll definitely need a guide to help you find them. **Camping** is permitted in a designated site near the employees' canteen, for a fee of Rs300 per person per night – a high price to pay for zero facilities, but it probably reflects the true environmental cost of using the park more accurately than the room charges at Sauraha.

Park **entry permits** cost Rs650 and are valid for two days. Park **guides** can be hired through the warden's office for about Rs100 per day, if you haven't already got one, and although none speaks English they can at least lead you to wildlife and keep you out of harm's way. Ask about **elephant rides** which, when available, cost Rs650 per person for an hour; the *hattisar* (elephant stable) is a 45-minute walk south of Thakurdwara. See the Chitwan section (p.244) for hints on safety.

Bardia in luxury

Two companies offer **luxury packages** in the park. The newer and cheaper of the two, *Karnali Safari Lodge*, situated not far from the HQ, charges $166 for a two-night package, which includes transport from Nepalganj. Bardia's other operator is *Tiger Mountain* (of *Tiger Tops* fame), which runs both *Karnali Tented Camp* and *Karnali Lodge* (Kathmandu ☎01/222706). The tented camp, overlooking the mighty Karnali and serving as the base for jeep rides, bird walks and raft trips, costs $316 for a two-night stay, plus $50 for transport to and from Nepalganj. Just outside the park's southern boundary, the lodge does elephant rides and Tharu village walks, charging $346 (plus transport) for two nights.

The wild west: Chisapani, Dhangadhi and Mahendranagar

The completion of the Mahendra Highway from Nepalganj to the far western border post of Mahendranagar is, for Nepal, something of an engineering marvel. Laying down 240km of asphalt was easy; building bridges over the countless streams that dice the route (not to mention spanning the Karnali) has been the real challenge. At the time of writing, the bus ride from Nepalganj to Mahendranagar still took twelve hours – down from twenty just two years earlier – but when all the bridges are passable that time will drop to about eight hours. This fast link with the rest of the country promises to introduce big changes to the far west – mostly positive ones, it appears, though it's too early to say whether it will have been worth the vast cost.

Chisapani and the Karnali crossing

The halfway stop is the boomtown of **CHISAPANI**, where the road veers north to cross the Karnali River, surging out of a gap in the rugged foothills, at its narrowest point. Overlooking the forested west bank of the river, Chisapani's polyglot little bazaar does a steady trade with shoppers from the hills, some of whom walk a week or more to buy basic provisions here. If you're stuck, there are a few makeshift bunkhouses at the west end of the bazaar.

The state-of-the-art **Karnali Bridge**, the longest single-span suspension bridge in the world, has been built here with World Bank money, and should be officially open by the time you read this. (If it's not, you'll have to take the cable ferry, which makes the crossing, two vehicles at a time, between 10am and 6pm.) The World Bank also has had its hand in another, even bigger project 1km upstream: the **Karnali Dam**, surveyed in detail but for the moment shelved, would (if fully configured) be the biggest hydroelectric dam in the world. Environmentalists argue that the project would destroy one of the last remaining habitats of the gharial crocodile – if you take a walk north of town you stand a good chance of seeing one (for more on gharials, see "Chitwan" above).

Dhangadhi

Another 100km west and back out of the trees, **DHANGADHI** is a flatter, duller and altogether more conventional border town sitting 12km south of the highway, off a paved spur road to India; unless you're catching a bus to Dipayal or one of the other hill towns to the north (see "Travel Details"), there's little reason to be here. The **bus park** is about 400m east of the main roundabout on the India road, and the breezeblock bazaar about 1km east of that. The **airstrip** ($149 to Kathmandu) lies 10km north of town on the way back to the highway – rikshas are plentiful – and the **RNAC office** (☎091/21205; Mon–Fri & Sun 8am–4pm, Sat 8am–noon) is by the main roundabout. **Lodgings** are pretty grim, the most palatable being *Sangan Lodge* and *Hotel Taruan & Lodge* in the bazaar (just opposite the *Jesus Bookstore*! both ①). Best bet for **food** is *Motimahal Restaurant*, which is also a good place to hook up with development workers.

Mahendrandagar and the border

The end of the line is **MAHENDRANAGAR**, another border town but with a good deal of spark, thanks to daytripping shoppers from India. The town is laid out in an

unusually logical grid south of the highway; the **bus park** is at the northwest end and the **airstrip** a long, clattering riksha ride southwest, almost at the entrance to Sukla Phanta Wildlife Reserve (see below). **Lodging** is clustered along the street one block east of the road into town: *Samjhana Hotel & Lodge* is the finest (②), while *Gauri Hotel* and *Mahakali Hotel & Lodge* (both ①) are less clean but tolerable. You'll find the **RNAC office** (☎21196; erratic hours) on the same street. **Eateries** around the hotels and along the main east–west drag do a fair range of Nepali meals, snacks and Indian sweets.

The **border** is 8km west of Mahendranagar, at the Mahankali River, and Banbasa, the Indian immigration post, is just beyond that. The **bank**, opposite the *RNAC* office, is apparently not always able to exchange foreign currencies except Indian rupees.

A Rana Tharu girl

Mahendranagar's bustle is only a border aberration, and the outlying region is one of the more traditional parts of the Tarai. Tharu sharecroppers work the fields, maintaining an apparently happy symbiosis with their old-money landlords, and their **villages**, scattered along dirt tracks north of the Mahendra Highway, still consist of traditional communal longhouses. Villagers go completely over the top for visitors and positively preen for the camera – a Polaroid would be a *big* hit – but it's bad manners to breeze in without at least enough Nepali to repay them with thanks and a little conversation.

Sukla Phanta Wildlife Reserve

In Nepal's extreme southwest, a different feature appears on the land: *phanta*, great swathes of natural grassland that could almost be mistaken, albeit on a smaller scale, for the savannas of East Africa. **SUKLA PHANTA WILDLIFE RESERVE**, south of Mahendranagar, is dotted with them, and touring it is, for once, really like being on safari. The reserve is home to the world's largest population of swamp deer – sightings of 1000 at a time are common – and a herd of wild elephants. Doing Sukla Phanta independently is next to impossible, but a lone in-park operator offers luxury safaris.

Several four-wheel drive tracks crisscross the reserve, making itineraries flexible, but first stop is bound to be *the* **Sukla Phanta** at the southwestern end, a rippling sea of grass which turns silvery-white in October (*sukila* means white in the local Tharu dialect). You're guaranteed **swamp deer** here, and in quantity – make for the view tower in the middle and scan for them with binoculars. As *barasingha* ("twelve points"), the swamp deer was one of Kipling's beloved *Jungle Book* animals – "that big deer which is like our red deer, but stronger" – and common throughout the plains and hills; today it's an endangered species, finding safety in numbers in the *phanta* and particularly the boggy parts where seasonal fires don't burn off the grasses. **Tigers** make occasional kills, but **poachers** present the greatest threat: the reserve has a chronic poaching problem, and the sound of gunshots coming from the southern (Indian) end is distressingly frequent. Although guards have orders to shoot poachers on sight, they haven't got much clout without a vehicle.

Having seen your obligatory *phanta*, make a beeline for **Rani Tal** (Queen's Lake), near the centre of the reserve. Surrounded by riotous, screeching forest, the lake – a lagoon, really – is like a prehistoric time capsule, with trees leaning out over the shore, deer wading shoulder-deep around the edges and crocodiles occasionally peering out of the lotus-littered water. The **birdlife** is like nothing you've ever seen, a dazzling display of cranes, cormorants, eagles and scores of others. You can watch all the comings and goings from a tower by the western shore. Nearby is an overgrown **brick circle**, 1500m in circumference, which locals say was the fort of Singpal, an ancient Tharu king (Rani Tal is said to have been his queen's favourite spot); the fact that the remains have never been excavated shows how little historical research has been done in western Nepal.

Though you'd think they'd be hard to miss, chances are Sukla Phanta's **elephant herd** will give you the slip – they spend winters south of the border, feasting on sugar cane. Evidence of their passage is abundant, however, especially along the road south from the entrance, where in places the forest looks like it's been hit by a tornado. The dominant male, dubbed **Thulo Hatti** (Big

INDIA

Chure Hills

(1528 m)▲

0   5 km

To Delhi

MAHENDRA HIGHWAY

Mahendranagar

Airstrip ✈

Mahakali River

Reserve HQ

MAHENDRA HIGHWAY

To Dhangadhi

Sukla Phanta
Wildlife Reserve

Silent Safari
Tented Camp △

Tower ■ ▲ *Rani Tal*

Tower ■

Sukla Phanta

INDIA

**SUKLA PHANTA
WILDLIFE RESERVE**

Elephant), leaves footprints nearly two feet in diameter; based on what few sightings have been made, he's estimated to stand eleven feet tall at the shoulder, weigh over five tons, and have tusks a metre long, making him the biggest Asian elephant alive.

Practicalities

The reserve **entrance** is within a kilometre of Mahendranagar's airstrip; *RNAC* **flies** there once a week from Kathmandu ($160) and up to three times a week from Nepalganj ($77). Alternatively, fly to Dhangadhi (twice a week from Kathmandu; $149) and take the bus the rest of the way. From Mahendranagar, the reserve entrance is reached by riksha.

As with Bardia, there's an easy way and a hard way to visit Sukla Phanta, and the easy way involves more money – still, even if you hate the idea of a **luxury safari**, this might be the place to do one. An unpretentious family outfit, *Silent Safari* (☎099/21230; Kathmandu ☎01/227236; PO Box 1, Mahendranagar, Kanchanpur District) runs customized trips in the park for about $140 per person per night, and can also arrange Tharu village treks. *Silent Safari* is a man – Col. Hikmat Bisht, former hunter, retired military attaché, patrician landowner and self-styled man of the forest – and a trip with him is one of the most delightfully idiosyncratic experiences in Nepal. His **tented camp** is pitched next to a water-hole in deep jungle – real Tarzan country – and there's also the unique opportu-nity to spend a night or two in a *machaan* (tree-top blind) for nocturnal sights and sounds.

Doing Sukla Phanta **on the cheap** isn't impossible, but you'd have to be pretty resourceful. The stumbling block is **transport** within the reserve, since pedestri-ans and cyclists aren't allowed (the guards don't want a mauling on their hands). Elephants, which are theoretically for rent, would in any case only be good for short forays. You really need a vehicle, preferably a jeep – which is the only feasi-ble way to track game across the *phanta* – but there aren't even any taxis in Mahendranagar, and your chances of hitching a ride are as slim as the visitor's book. You could try offering money around town, or you might be lucky and meet up with an expat worker going for a weekend break; if you manage to crack it, the **entry fee** is Rs650 and **camping** is Rs300 per person per night. Sleeping in the open isn't recommended, but the towers at Rani Tal and Sukla Phanta would make superb shelters. The nearest **food** is in Mahendranagar.

festivals

In addition to the following local festivals, Dasain (known as Dashera near India), Tihaar (Diwali), Shiva Raatri and Holi are celebrated in most Tarai areas.

MAGH (Jan–Feb)
Tribeni Mela Pilgrimage to Devghat on the day of the first new moon in Magh.

BAISAKH (April–May)
Vishnu Jaatra Celebration of the Buddha as an incarnation of Vishnu at Lumbini on the full moon of Baisakh.

Buddha Jayanti Anniversary of the Buddha's birth, enlightenment and death, held at Lumbini.

KARTIK (Oct–Nov)
Jithiya Similar to Tij (see *Basics*), a festival for women celebrated in Tharu villages on the full moon during Kartik.

travel details

BUSES
From Tadi Bazaar tourist buses to Kathmandu (0–2 daily; 6hr); local buses to Narayanghat (frequent; 45min). Other buses stop here, but orig-inate elsewhere.

From Narayanghat/Bharatpur to Bhairawa (1 daily; 4hr); Devghat (4–6 daily; 30min); Gorkha (4 daily; 4hr); Jagatpur (4 daily; 2hr); Meghauli (4 daily; 1hr 30min); Pokhara (5 daily; 4hr) and Tadi Bazaar (frequent; 45min). These buses all origi-nate in Narayanghat, though countless others stop on their way through.

From Butwal to Kathmandu (4 daily; 9hr); Nepalganj (9 daily; 6hr); Pokhara (10 daily; 7hr); Sunauli (frequent; 1hr) and Tansen (7 daily; 2hr).

From Bhairawa to Kathmandu (*Sajha*: 1 daily; 9hr); Lumbini (every 30min; 1hr 30min) and Taulihawa (2 daily; 3hr).

From Sunauli to Kathmandu (8 daily, 4 nightly; at least 10hr) and Pokhara (6 daily, 4 nightly; at least 10hr).

From Nepalganj to Birendranagar (8 daily; 6hr); Birganj (3 daily; 14hr); Dhangadhi (1–2 daily; 6hr); Kathmandu (6 daily; 15hr); Pokhara (4 nightly; at least 15hr) and Thakurdwara (1 daily; 3hr).

From Dhangadhi to Baitadi (1 daily; at least 16hr); Dadeldhura (1 daily; at least 8hr); Dipayal (1 daily; at least 14hr) and Mahendranagar (10 daily; 3hr).

PLANES

From Nepalganj to Dipayal (2–4 weekly; 40min); Jumla (1–2 daily; 45min); Kathmandu (1– 2 daily; 1hr 30min); Mahendranagar (1 weekly; 1hr 35min); Sanfebagar (6 weekly; 35min) and Simikot (seasonal; 1hr).

From Dhangadhi to Dipayal (4 weekly; 25min); Kathmandu (1–2 weekly; 2hr) and Sanfebagar (4 weekly; 25min).

From Mahendranagar to Kathmandu (1 weekly; 2hr 30min) and Sanfebagar (3 weekly; 25min).

CONNECTIONS TO INDIA

Buses from Sunauli (India side) to Gorakhpur (hourly; 3hr); Varanasi (3 daily; 8hr) and Delhi (5 daily; 22hr). From Gorakhpur you can make broad-gauge **train** connections throughout India.

CHAPTER SIX

THE EASTERN TARAI AND HILLS

A s with the west, the **eastern Tarai** – the portion east of Chitwan – is where Nepal dovetails with India, and in many ways it offers the best of both worlds. Overwhelmingly rural, the plains have a timeless, almost genteel quality: thatched houses perch on stilts, clumps of bamboo and palms erupt in green explosions, and the foothills, if not the Himalaya, are always within sight. Most travellers only flit through here on their way to the border crossings of **Birganj** (for Patna) and **Kakarbitta** (for Darjeeling), and outside these places you won't find a speck of commercialism. The cities are admittedly awful, but with one outstanding exception: **Janakpur**, a pilgrimage centre that's immensely famous among Hindus but seldom visited by Westerners, which provides all the exoticism of India without the attendant hassles. Although large tracts of jungle are less common east of Chitwan, birdwatchers can check out **Koshi Tappu Wildlife Reserve**, straddling the alluvial plain of the mighty Sapt Koshi River.

What few visitors the **eastern hills** get tend to be trekkers bound for the Everest or Kanchenjunga massifs, which rear up like goalposts on the northern horizon – but while the prospect of travelling twenty-plus hours by bus from Kathmandu puts most people off, this isn't a problem if you're already in the eastern Tarai. By turns riotously forested and fastidiously terraced, the hills are great for day-hiking, even if you've vowed not to trek (but get a permit anyway, just in case you change your mind). At least two towns here are worth visiting in their own right: **Hile**, a rowdy frontier bazaar with a Tibetan ambience, and **Ilam**, Nepal's tea-growing capital.

Both the eastern Tarai and hills are noticeably better off than the non-touristed parts of the west; **travel connections** are (by Nepali standards) comprehensive, and even in remote places you should be able to **eat** well, if not Western. A phenomenon specific to eastern Nepal is the **haat bazaar**, or weekly market, and it's worth trying to coincide with one or two of these pan-cultural extravaganzas.

THE EASTERN TARAI

For travellers coming by road from other parts of Nepal, Hetauda is the gateway to the eastern Tarai: from Tadi Bazaar (Chitwan) it's an easy two-hour bus ride to Hetauda along the **Mahendra Highway**, hugging the hills as it follows the attractive *dun* (inner Tarai valley) of the Rapti River; the **Tribhuwan Rajpath** (see "The Central Hills") enters the town from the north and continues south to the Indian border at Birganj.

Both west and east of Hetauda, **buses** along the Mahendra Highway are frequent and relatively fast. If you're **cycling**, many of the small bazaars en route can provide basic food and, at a pinch, lodging.

The Rajpath: Hetauda to the border

> *There is something peculiarly sinister and ominous about the jungle of the Tarai. You have that feeling that danger in one form or another lurks around every corner . . . Over everything a strange, oppressive silence broods . . . A big gray ape chatters at us maliciously from his perch on an overhanging rock. A leopard, camouflaged almost to invisibility by his spotted hide, steals on stealthy feet across the road. There is a sudden crash of underbrush behind the jungle wall – an elephant or a tiger perhaps.*

E. Alexander Powell, *The Last Home of Mystery* (1929)

For centuries the only developed corridor through the Tarai, this route was, before air travel, every foreigner's introduction to Nepal. A narrow-gauge railway used to run from Raxaul, the last Indian station, as far as Amlekhganj; dignitaries were transported from there by elephant over the first band of hills to Hetauda

Phaplu

Arun River

0   50 km

Tumlingtar

Taplejung

Bhojpur

Basantapur

Phidim

Hile

Dhankuta

Tamur Kosi River

Ilam

Pashupati

To Darjeeling

Dharan

Sapt Koshi River

Koshi Tappu Wildlife Reserve

Beldangi

Itahari

MAHENDRA HIGHWAY

Damak

Birtamod

Kakarbitta

To Darjeeling

Rajbiraj

Biratnagar

Jogbani

INDIA

before being carried the rest of the way to Kathmandu by donkey or sedan chair. Those few who made the journey during Nepal's isolation years before 1951, such as our Mr Powell, did so only by invitation of the prime minister or king. The construction of the **Rajpath** in the 1950s eliminated the need for elephants and sedan chairs, but the railway wasn't decommissioned until the 1970s (the tracks are still in place). If you're driving your own vehicle in from India, the Rajpath makes a great introduction to Nepal, overnighting in Daman (see p.185).

Hetauda

Clumped around the junction of the Mahendra Highway and the Rajpath, **HETAUDA** is still a staging-post on the India–Kathmandu route, but whatever romance it may once have had has long gone. Dilapidated Indian trucks rumble through with fuel and bulk goods for Kathmandu, while buses stop here at all hours: it's a restless, transient place. Among Nepalis, Hetauda is probably most famous for its cement plant, whose output is transported to the Kathmandu Valley by ropeway (visible from the Rajpath). The smoke from its chimneys may be the shape of things to come. The government is making noises about encouraging the carpet industry to move to Hetauda from the Kathmandu Valley, where effluents from the washing process are polluting the water. And where would the effluents go if the factories moved to Hetauda? Down the Rapti River into Chitwan

National Park. It might sound preposterous, but the Department of Roads has even gone so far as to propose a new highway from Kathmandu to Hetauda via a tunnel through the Mahabharat Lekh – any donors?

Practicalities

Hetauda's **bus park** is located southwest of the main intersection. If you're trying to get from here to Daman or Kathmandu, **trucks** take on passengers at the north end of town, where you'll also find a number of tea stalls and a couple of serviceable *sekuwa* restaurants.

Cyclists will probably **spend the night** here, as there are no other worthwhile places to stay between Daman and the border or Chitwan. Fortunately, *Motel Avocado* (☎057/20429; ③/B④) more than compensates for Hetauda's shortcomings: located in a quiet compound well north of the bazaar, the grounds are shaded by a small grove of avocado trees (planted by displaced Californians when this was the USAID guest house), and in late autumn practically everything on the menu has avocado in it. Running a distant second is *Hotel Rapti* (☎057/20882; B③), at the south end of town; cheaper lodges in the bazaar are apt to be very noisy.

South to Birganj

Heading south over the low **Chure Hills**, the Rajpath enters a strange landscape of stunted trees, wide gravel washes and steeply eroded pinnacles. These hills are the newest wrinkle in the Himalayan chain, heaved up as the 30-million-year-long collision between the Indian and Asian continental plates ripples southwards – less than half a million years old, they're so young that the surface sediments haven't yet been eroded to expose bedrock.

Leaving the hills once and for all, the road passes Amlekhganj, the former rail terminus (now Nepal's main fuel depot), and 4km further on, the entrance to **Parsa Wildlife Reserve**. An annex of Chitwan National Park, providing secondary habitats for its wild elephant herd and many of its sub-adult tigers, the reserve isn't developed for tourism; no food or lodgings are available, and visitors aren't allowed in on foot without a guide (who may also be unavailable). However, camping is supposed to be allowed (Rs300 per person per night, plus the Rs650 entry fee), so a self-sufficient traveller would theoretically stand to have the run of the whole place.

The Mahendra Highway branches off to the east at Phatlaya, 3km south of the Parsa entrance, and Simara, another 3km south, heralds a dreary succession of factories and fields that continues all the way to Birganj. For obscure reasons of national security, Nepal passed a law in the mid-1980s requiring that all new factories must be built at least 10km from the Indian border, which is causing the major border cities to flare northwards.

Birganj and the border

Nepal's busiest port of entry, **BIRGANJ** is a thoroughly disagreeable place – an unflattering introduction to Nepal if you're just arriving and a rude send-off if you're leaving. The latest census (1991) puts Birganj's population at 69,000, but like most of the Tarai's urban centres it must be growing at an annual clip of at least five percent. A new highway bypass has made the main street south of the prominent clocktower vastly more liveable, but all traffic to and from the border still converges on the city's northern approach, reducing it to an uncrossable torrent of lurching trucks, buses and bullock carts.

Nevertheless, some travellers may have to pass this way, and if you're touring India and Nepal by bicycle you might want to cross here once to avoid backtracking. **The border** is 4km south of the city centre, and Raxaul, the first Indian town, sprawls for another 2km south of the border. Horrendous traffic jams are a regular occurrence here – if you're driving it can take hours to get through physically, leaving aside the paperwork. If you don't have your own transport, rikshas charge about Rs40 from Birganj to Raxaul (make sure the price quoted is in Nepalese rupees); *tonga* (horse-drawn carts) are cheaper, but they won't wait while you go through customs and immigration.

If you're stranded in Birganj, you could probably kill a few hours in the old-ish market area around **Maisthan**, a mother-goddess temple just off the main drag. Beyond that, though, the city has little to offer: **Adarsh Nagar** is a fairly humdrum market area that's unlikely to appeal to anyone except daytripping Indian shoppers, and the new (and as yet unfinished) west side of town is devoid of interest.

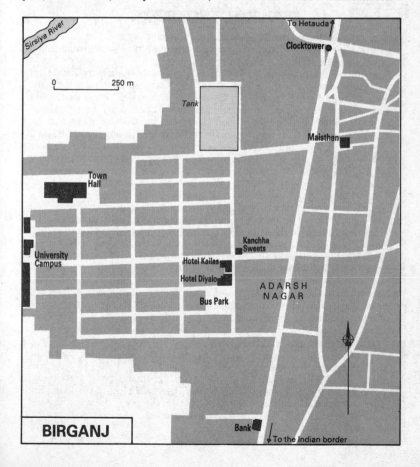

Practicalities

Buses connect Birganj with Kathmandu, Pokhara and most Tarai cities. Express and *Sajha* buses use the efficient new bus park, located almost 1km east of the clocktower beyond the bypass (and off the map); the old bus park near Adarsh Nagar now serves only night and local buses.

You can manage quite comfortably for **food** and **lodging** in Birganj, but there are no facilities at the border. The best bets are the rather Indian *Hotel Kailas* (②/ B③) and the more Nepali *Hotel Diyalo* (B④), side by side near the night bus park. Cheaper guest houses can be found west of the night bus park, but the mosquitoes are vicious in this part of town. Both the *Kailas* and *Diyalo* have fine, if seedy, Indian restaurants, while *Kanchha Sweets*, nearby, serves up a miraculous assortment of Indian goodies. You'll also find *sekuwa*, fried fish and other street food in stalls around the night bus park. Note that we've price graded all guest houses and hotels in the book, according to a scale detailed in *Basics* (see p.21).

THE ETHNIC SCENE

There seems to be an unwritten rule in Nepal that all migrations have to be from west to east, with the result that contingents of almost every Nepalese ethnic group now jostle together in the eastern quarter of the country.

The original inhabitants of the eastern hills were the **Kirantis** (or Kiratas), a warlike tribe mentioned in the *Mahabharat* who may well have been the same Kiratas who ruled the Kathmandu Valley in semi-mythological times. The Kiranti nation long ago fragmented into several tribes, the most important ones being the **Rais** and **Limbus**. Like the Magars and Gurungs of the west, members of these dauntless hill groups make up a significant portion of the Gurkha regiments; similarly, they follow their own form of shamanism, but increasingly embrace Hindu or Buddhist practices, depending on their location. Unusually, the Kiranti clans bury their dead (as opposed to cremating, which is the usual practice throughout the subcontinent) and Limbus erect distinctive rectangular, whitewashed grave markers: three tiers high for women, four for men. Rais, who have a reputation as a staunchly independent people, traditionally occupy the middle-elevation hills west of the Arun River, while Limbuwan, as the Limbu homeland is sometimes still called, is centred around the lower slopes of the Tamur Kosi Valley, further east.

Rais and Limbus had the hills virtually to themselves until a spate of migrations, beginning in the late eighteenth century, completely transformed the ethnic map of eastern Nepal. The Gorkhali army marched in and annexed the region in 1776; in their wake, **Bahuns** and **Chhetris** began infiltrating the Arun basin and **Newars** took over the trading crossroads. At about the same time, **Sherpas** and **Tamangs** were steadily elbowing the Rais out of Solu, and more recently, **Magars** and **Gurungs** have hopped across from their traditional homelands in the west. Little wonder, then, that when the Rais and Limbus were recruited by the British in the last century to pluck tea in Darjeeling, they, too, headed east.

Even more than in western Nepal, the clearing of the eastern Tarai during the past three decades has spurred a feverish new land rush, as hill people in turn displace native **Tharus** and the Maithili-speaking Hindus who predominate between Janakpur and Biratnagar. Meanwhile, **Biharis** and **Bengalis** keep arriving in droves from India. Bouncing along the Mahendra Highway, where housing and dress styles change from one village to the next, you almost feel as if you're watching the migration in motion.

Birganj's **bank** (Mon–Thurs & Sun 10am–3pm, Fri 10am–noon) isn't very efficient, so if you're staying in one of the hotels you might as well change money there; there's also a small bank at the border on the Nepal side (unreliable hours). Birganj has no black market.

Janakpur

JANAKPUR, 165km east of Birganj, is indisputably the Tarai's most fascinating city. Often called **Janakpurdham** (*dham* denoting a sacred place), it's a holy site of the first order, and its central temple, the ornate **Janaki Mandir**, is an obligatory stop on the Hindu pilgrimage circuit. Although Indian in every respect except politically, the city is, by Indian standards, small and manageable: motorized traffic is all but banned from the centre, tourist hustle is largely absent, the poverty isn't oppressive and the surrounding countryside is delightful. To top it all, Janakpur's **steam railway**, the only railway still operating in Nepal, makes an entertaining excursion in itself.

Hindu mythology identifies Janakpur as the capital of the ancient kingdom of **Mithila**, which probably controlled a large part of north India between the tenth and third centuries BC, and the city features prominently in the *Ramayan*: it was in Janakpur that **Ram** – the god Vishnu in mortal form – strung a magic bow to win the hand of **Sita**, daughter of the Mithila King Janak. Recounting the divine couple's separation and heroic reunion, the *Ramayan* holds Ram and Sita up as models of the virtuous husband and chaste wife; in Janakpur, where the two command almost cult status, the chant of "Sita Ram, Sita Ram" is repeated like a Hindu Hail Mary, and sadhus commonly wear the tuning-fork-shaped *tika* of Vishnu.

Despite the absence of ancient monuments to confirm its mythic past – no building is much more than a century old – Janakpur remains a strangely attractive city. Religious fervour seems to lend an aura to everything; the skyline leaves a lasting impression of palm trees and the onion domes and pyramid roofs of local shrines. Most of these distinctively shaped shrines are associated with **kuti** – self-contained pilgrimage centres and hostels for sadhus – some 500 of which are scattered throughout the Janakpur area. Janakpur's other distinguishing feature is its dozens of **sacred ponds** (*sagar*), which here take the place of river ghats for ritual bathing and *dhobi*-ing. Clearly man-made, the roughly rectangular tanks might, as locals claim, go back to Ram's day, although it's more likely that they've been dredged over the centuries by wealthy merit-seekers.

Janakpur runs a full and varied **festival** calendar, the highlight being Biwaha Panchami, the re-enactment of Ram's and Sita's wedding, which draws at least 100,000 pilgrims in late November or early December. Ram Navami (Ram's birthday), celebrated in March or April, attracts nearly as many, while some 10,000 people join the annual one-day *parikrama* (circumambulation) of the city in the first week of March, many performing prostrations along the entire eight-kilometre route. And finally on Chath, which normally follows a few days after Tihaar in October–November, women line Janakpur's ponds with elaborate offerings to the sun god Dinanath. But at any time of the year, Janakpur's atmosphere is charged with an intense devotional zeal. New shrines are forever being inaugurated and idols installed, while *kuti* loudspeakers broadcast religious discourses and the mesmerizing drone of *bhajan*.

The City

A palatial confection of a building in the Mughal style, the **Janaki Mandir** (pronounced *Jaa*-nuh-ki) is supposed to mark the spot where a golden image of Sita was discovered in 1657 and, presumably, where the virtuous princess actually lived. The present marble structure, erected in 1911 by an Indian queen, is already looking a little worse for wear. The outer building encloses a courtyard and inner sanctum, where at least twice a day (generally 8am and 4pm) priests draw back a curtain to reveal an intricate silver shrine and perform various rituals for attending worshippers; non-Hindus are allowed to watch, and the priests even seem willing to bestow blessings on unbelievers – upon payment of the appropriate fee, of course. It's an enchanting place at night and early in the morning, when the devout gather in lamplit huddles and murmur haunting hymns. The temple is also a traditional place for boys to get their first haircuts, and male dancers in drag (*natuwa* in

Nepali), who are often hired to perform at the hair-cutting ceremony, can sometimes be seen here.

Climb the stairs to the roof of the outer building for a view of the central courtyard and the dense, brick-laned **Muslim village** butting right up against the temple's rear wall: one of Janakpur's most extraordinary aspects is the way rural life can be seen almost in the heart of the city. North of the temple, the new and rather sterile **Ram Janaki Biwaha Mandap** (Ram Sita Wedding Pavilion) houses a turgid tableau of the celebrated event.

The city's oldest, closest quarter lies to the south and east of the Janaki Mandir – making your way

The Janaki Mandir

through this area, with its sweet shops, *puja* stalls and quick-photo studios, you begin to appreciate that Janakpur is as geared up for Indian tourists as Kathmandu is for Western ones. The main landmark here, the pagoda-style **Ram Mandir**, isn't wildly exciting except when it serves as the venue for Ram Navami festivities. Immediately to the east, **Dhanush Sagar** and **Ganga Sagar** are considered the holiest of Janakpur's ponds. The sight of Hindus performing ritual ablutions in the fog at sunrise here is profoundly moving, and during festivals the scene is on a par with Varanasi's famed ghats in India.

Walk westwards from the Janaki Mandir to the highway and you reach **Ramanand Chowk**, the nucleus of many of Janakpur's *kuti* and a major sadhu gathering place during festivals. In an alcove at the southwest corner of the intersection, devotees have been chanting the names of Ram and Sita continuously since 1986 (the vigil, sponsored by wealthy individuals, is to last a total of twelve years). Two well-known establishments, Ramanand Ashram and Ratnasagar Kuti – the latter, rising grandly in the midst of farmland, looking uncannily like a Russian Orthodox church – are located in this area, but are closed to the public.

If by this time you're tiring of the serious side of Hinduism, head to **Hanuman Durbar**, a small *kuti* 100m south of Ramanand Chowk on the west side, to see the **world's biggest rhesus monkey**. Bauwa Hanuman weighs 55kg, and he's been certified as the world's biggest by the Triflorous Explorers Association, whatever that is – a certificate is on display near the cage. It's a gross sight if ever there was one. By the way, *bauwa* is a pet term for a baby monkey.

The steam railway

If you've already had dealings with Indian trains, Janakpur's **steam railway** will be less of a thrill, but it's still an excellent way to get out into the countryside. This part of the Tarai features some of the most meticulously kept farmland you'll see anywhere, and on a misty winter's morning the ride past sleepy villages and minor temples is nothing short of magical. Built in the 1940s to transport timber to India from the now-depleted forest west of Janakpur, the narrow-gauge line these days operates primarily as a passenger service. The dilapidated locomotives and carriages are undoubtedly original, and may well be even older than the railway, since Nepal tends to acquire much of its machinery as hand-me-downs from India.

Janakpur is the terminus for two separate lines, each about 30km long: one eastbound to Jaynagar, just over the border in India, and the other westbound to Bijalpur. **Trains for Jaynagar** depart at 7.30am and 3.30pm, and trains coming the opposite way are supposed to leave Jaynagar at the same time (but check: times may vary). You'll doubtless be stopped by Nepalese customs at Khajuri, about two hours from Janakpur (if not, you could have trouble re-entering Nepal). For a shorter trip, get off at Baidehi, about an hour from Janakpur, and catch the train coming the other way about half an hour later – or you could walk the 12km back. The **Bijalpur service** runs only once a day each way, departing at 2.45pm at either end, so you'll have to alight at Khunta or Loharpati in order to return to Janakpur the same day; alternatively, you can walk the 8km or so to Khunta by way of Ramanand Chowk and return by train.

The **fare** to Jaynagar is Rs9 in second class or Rs24 in first, the latter being far from luxurious but perhaps a shade less crowded. Arrive early for a seat; on the way back you'll probably end up sitting astride a consignment of mustard-oil tins or suchlike on the roof.

Practicalities

Getting to Janakpur – and leaving – can be a headache. The city lies 30km off the Mahendra Highway, so it's not on the way to anywhere else, and most day **buses** come from Birganj; only a couple come from Kakarbitta each day, and only one (*Sajha*) from Kathmandu. The rest are night buses. Try for *Sajha* first, but if you can't get a ticket you'll have to do penance on a night bus or take your chances with Birganj. The bus park is an easy riksha ride from the city centre. When

---

MITHILA PAINTING

For three thousand years, Brahman women of the region once known as Mithila have maintained an unbroken tradition of **painting**, using techniques and ritual motifs passed down from mother to daughter. The colourful, almost psychedelic images can be viewed as fertility charms, meditation aids or a form of storytelling, but on a deeper level they represent, in the words of one critic, "the manifestation of a collective mind, embodying millennia of traditional knowledge".

From an early age girls practise drawing complex symbols derived from Hindu myths and folk tales, which over the course of generations have been reduced to *mandala*-like abstractions. By the time she is in her teens, a girl will be presenting simple paintings to her arranged fiancé, perhaps using them to wrap gifts; more complicated papier mâché versions may follow, and the courtship culminates with the painting of a **kohbar**, a sort of marriage proposal in the form of an elaborate fresco on the wall of the couple's future bedroom. Based on the *linga* and *yoni* symbols, the *kohbar* is a powerful celebration of life, creation and everything; other motifs include footprints and fishes (both representing Vishnu), the *swastika* (an auspicious symbol in Hinduism), Ram and Sita, and Surabhi, "the Cow of Plenty, who inflames the desire of those who milk her".

The usual technique is first to outline the intended design in black, embellishing it with fantastic detail until it fills the entire surface, and finally illuminating it with brilleaving Janakpur, note that the *Sajha* bus originates at Ramanand Chowk, not the bus park. You could conceivably **fly** here from Kathmandu ($55), in which case you'll land at the airstrip 2km south of town. *RNAC*'s office (☎041/20185), located at the northeast end of town, is open daily from 10am to 4pm. There is a small-time **border crossing** about 20km south of town at Jaleswar, and another at Jaynagar (reached by steam railway), but neither of these is officially open to foreigners.

Though the city is easy enough to **get around** on foot, rikshas are a terrific deal – they wait in efficient ranks all over town and are supposed to stick to a fixed-price structure, though it's hard for a foreigner to get them to abide by it. You might be able to rent a bicycle informally through your hotel.

While Janakpur's scarcity of **accommodation** normally doesn't present a problem, you need to book well ahead during the big festival times. *Hotel Welcome* (☎041/20224; ②/B③), though nothing fancy, is fairly central and is at least used to dealing with foreigners. *Hotel Rama* (☎041/20059) is a quieter but more out-of-the-way alternative (B②), while *Shree Janak Lodge* – along with a few other nearby places without English signs – offers cheaper, dingier rooms (①). If you're prepared to **camp**, you could probably pitch a tent in one of the pilgrims' groves just north of the bank or south of Ratnasagar Kuti.

Food is plentiful, and if you like Indian sweets or *chiura dahi* (beaten rice and curd) you can take your pick from a host of nameless places around the Janaki and Ram temples. *Hotel Welcome* does beautiful Mughlai food (if you can decipher the menu), or for vegetarian curries hit the *Sagar* (labelled *Amber* on the map) or any of the nearby no-frills canteens. To sample the local brew, ask for *sophi* or *dudhiya*, aniseed-flavoured spirits that are just about drinkable when mixed with Sprite.

The typically uninformative **tourist office** (Mon–Thurs & Sun 10am–4pm, Fri 10am–3pm) is in Station Road, east of Bhanu Chowk (named after a much-loved Nepali poet, whose statue graces the intersection). There's a **bank** at the southern end of town (Mon–Thurs & Sun 10am–2pm, Fri 10am–noon).

---

liant primary **colours** (though garish, the dyes used somehow reflect the intensity of the local landscape). Perhaps the most striking aspect of Mithila art is that, almost by definition, it's ephemeral: paintings are intended to be thrown away like wrapping paper, and even the most amazing mural will be washed off within a week or two. Painting is seen as a form of prayer or meditation; once completed, the work has achieved its end.

Although Mithila paintings are much more common across the border in India's Bihar state, murals can occasionally be seen in village temples outside Janakpur, and items made in an income-generation project here are sold in Kathmandu non-profit shops. For caste reasons, you're unlikely to be invited into a Brahman home, but if you're interested in arranging a private **tour** of artists' houses contact Swami Dharmajyoti at the *Hotel Vajra* in Kathmandu.

Detail frrom a Mithila painting

Koshi Tappu Wildlife Reserve

East of the Janakpur turnoff, the Mahendra Highway rolls along uneventfully all the way to the Sapt Koshi River. The latter half of this section barrels across long stretches of farmland punctuated by bamboo thickets and idyllic little villages – the kind of places you can't imagine anyone would ever leave – which probably explains why cyclists passing though here sometimes complain of being stared at by locals.

The landscape changes markedly at the Sapt Koshi, eastern Nepal's biggest river. Crossing the **Koshi Barrage** – not a dam, but a series of flood-control gates – you can look in amazement at the immense body of water that squeezes through here before fanning out again into the shimmering haze of India. Reaching the far side, the highway bends north and runs parallel to a disused railway: keep an eye out for the rusty old steam engines which, until the railway tracks were severed in the 1988 Dharan earthquake, hauled rubble to build up the ten-metre embankments that keep the Sapt Koshi in check during the monsoon.

Straddling a vast floodplain of shifting grassland and sandbanks north of the barrage, **KOSHI TAPPU WILDLIFE RESERVE** is the most low-key of the Tarai's parks. It's not bound to appeal to most travellers – there are no tigers or rhinos, nor even any jungle – but birdwatchers can have a field day here, for Koshi Tappu is one of Asia's most important stopping places for migratory **birds**; though Chitwan boasts more species, the number of individuals here is greater, and you're certain to tick off several varieties you haven't seen anywhere else. The reserve was established to protect one of the subcontinent's last surviving herds of **wild buffalo** (*arnaa*), now 160 strong and recovering healthily after a devastating 1985 flood. However, wildlife experts are concerned about the number of domestic buffalo getting into the reserve and mating with the wild ones: if this is allowed to continue, the result could be a semi-domestic herd whose continued protection would be hard to justify.

Also resident in the reserve are blue bull (*nilgai*), wild boar, langur, spotted deer (*chital*), and a semi-wild bull elephant dubbed Ganesh Maharaj by locals, who consider him sacred and set out food for him; passengers on the Kathmandu–Kakarbitta night bus have reported seeing the patriarchal pachyderm lumbering across the Mahendra Highway around dawn. In addition, gharial crocodiles from the Chitwan hatchery have been introduced here – it's too early to say if they'll survive – and a small number of gangetic dolphins are reportedly trapped upstream of the barrage.

Visiting Koshi Tappu

The reserve is marked by a yellow sign beside the Mahendra Highway about 12km east of the barrage – or if you're coming from the other direction, 3km west of Laukhi – and from here an access road leads 3km north to the reserve head-quarters (generally known as the *warden ophis*). The warden maintains a mud-walled **"lodge"** that sleeps eight (①) and a hand pump for washing, and you can get *daal bhaat* and tea at the minuscule hamlet of Kusaha, just to the east of the office. The daily **entry permit** (Rs650) is extendable for as long as you stay at the warden's lodge. **Elephants** are allegedly for rent (Rs650 per hour), but they're kept clear on the other side of the river at Phattepur (theoretically reachable by

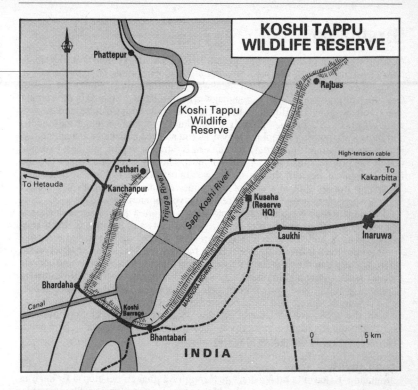

local bus from Kanchanpur). Vehicles aren't allowed in the park, although you could cycle for miles along the eastern embankment. The reserve has no guides, English-speaking or otherwise.

With no rhinos or large carnivores, Koshi Tappu is comparatively safe for wandering around **on your own**. Generally speaking, the area east of the Sapt Koshi is boring and you're better off making for the opposite shore, where the game- and birdwatching is best. From the reserve headquarters, follow the dirt road onto the embankment, turn left and then make a right at the second man-made breakwater (just after the 13km marker). At last check, dugout canoes were ferrying passengers across the Sapt Koshi from a point about 1km west of here, but enquire locally about the current situation, as the river changes course every monsoon.

Once across the river you're on *the* Koshi Tappu, an isthmus between the Sapt Koshi and Trijuga rivers (*tappu* in Nepali means "island", which is what this is during the wet months), and the scrub forest here is the main stomping ground of buffalo and *nilgai* ("blue bull"; actually an antelope). Stalking the wild cousins of common water buffalo is sometimes hard to take seriously – especially when they moo – yet these are big animals that can make a thunderous noise when frightened; and while they normally run away at the first scent of humans, you have to make sure not to block their escape route.

Biratnagar

About 200km east of the Janakpur turnoff, **BIRATNAGAR** (population 130,000) is Nepal's second-biggest city, and growing at a galloping rate. Though the city is prospering as a magnet for industry and trade – it's on a direct line to the port of Calcutta – foreign observers foresee major growth-related problems in the coming years. Jute is in decline, Birganj is muscling in on trade with Calcutta, and government offices have been shifted north to Dhankuta – yet immigrants from the hills and India keep pouring in looking for work. You still see bullock carts hauling raw jute to the mills near the border, but modern Biratnagar is probably best exemplified by the prosaic zipper factory north of town. The city's one other claim to fame is as a political hotbed: thanks to its proximity to India's West Bengal state, Biratnagar has long been a sort of safe house for many of Nepal's communist parties, which were banned until the restoration of democracy in 1990.

More Indian than Nepali, Biratnagar's streets are lined with a depressing array of concrete buildings and border-bazaar shops. That said, the city centre is relatively laid-back and traffic-free. There are few sights, but if you're here on a Wednesday don't miss Biratnagar's **haat bazaar**, held in a field east of town, where you can count on a colourful assembly of Tharus, Rais, Limbus and various Indian castes. In the countryside surrounding Biratnagar, Tharus and Danuwars (a related group, whose women wear their homespun saris like togas) are indigenous: to sample **village life**, head out on the road towards Rangali, east of town, or visit the area around Duhubi, off the main road about halfway between Biratnagar and the Mahendra Highway. The Jogbani border crossing, 5km south of town, is closed to foreigners (officially, anyway).

Practicalities

Kathmandu–Kakarbitta **buses** don't go through Biratnagar, but stop at **Itahari**, an unpleasant crossroads bazaar on the Mahendra Highway (basic lodgings available); Biratnagar is 23km south, and Dharan (covered later in this chapter) lies to the north. Direct buses to Biratnagar let you off at the dismal bus park southwest of the city centre. Travelling to or from the eastern hills, **flights** from here to Kathmandu ($77), Tumlingtar ($44) and Taplejung ($50) might prove useful. The airport is 4km north of town (Rs20 by riksha); the offices of *RNAC* (☎021/22576), *Everest* (☎021/22227) and *Nepal Airways* (☎021/26160) are all at or near Mahendra Chowk.

Biratnagar's newest and best **accommodation**, *Hotel Anand* (☎021/23712; B③, B④ with hot water), sits well south of town – the rooms are pricey but the place has a pleasant lawn and serviceable restaurant. Closer to the city centre, *Hotel Namaskaar* (B②, B④ with hot water) is popular with businessmen, despite being noisy and overpriced. Of the cheap lodges out on the main road, *Hotel Geetanjali* (②) is the brightest and least smelly. Be sure to request mosquito netting.

For **food**, make for the affable *Byanjan* or one of the other rough-and-ready eateries north of Mahendra Chowk, which do tasty *sekuwa* and *maachhaa masaala* (local carp fried in a spicy tomato sauce); try also *chiura badhmas* (a snack of beaten rice, toasted soyabeans, spring onions, ginger and oil) and *dudhiya*, the local aniseed-flavoured *raksi*. For breakfast there's always the *Namaskaar*. The main shopping street running north from the *Namaskaar* contains a few unexceptional sweet shops (*mitho pasal*). The **bank** changes money Sunday through Thursday from 10am to 4pm, Friday 10am to 3pm.

To the Airport &
Mahendra Highway

Singyahi River

Post
Office

Stadium

Bank

To Rangali

Haat
Bazaar

Daily
Market

Byanjan

MAHENDRA
CHOWK

Hotel
Namaskaar

Milan
Hotel

RNAC

Hotel
Geetanjali

Bus Park

Dhankuta
Lodge

0   500 m

Mahendra
Campus

To Hotel
Anand   To the Indian border

BIRATNAGAR

East to the border

From Itahari, the Mahendra Highway's final 100-kilometre leg crosses the frontier districts of **Morang** and **Jhapa**. Once renowned for its virulent malaria, Morang remains untamed in parts, but hill settlers, encouraged by the government, are steadily moving in, and logging companies are whittling away at the

BHUTANESE REFUGEES

The plight of **Bhutanese refugees** in Jhapa and Morang – who numbered at least 85,000 as of mid-1993 – has scarcely been acknowledged outside of Nepal. The remoteness of the refugee camps only partly explains how such a large-scale tragedy could go unreported. A greater factor has been the international community's fuzzy romanticism about tiny Bhutan, a kingdom of misty mountain monasteries and dashing archers, whose leader says all the right things about sustainable development and the "gross national happiness" of his subjects. It's hard to believe that the torture, rape and forcible expulsion of ethnic Nepalis could be happening in such an idyllic land.

Members of Nepali hill groups began migrating into Bhutan in significant numbers as long ago as the mid-nineteenth century, eventually accounting for at least a third of Bhutan's population and earning the designation **Lhotshampas** (southerners), after the southern hill areas where they came to predominate. Right up to the early 1980s, multicultural government policies encouraged their integration with Bhutan's ruling **Drukpas**. However, during the mid-1980s, the continued influx of ethnic Nepalis and a rise in Nepali militancy in neighbouring Darjeeling and Sikkim gave rise to a wave of Drukpa nationalism. The Drukpas, believing their language and unique Kagyu Buddhist tradition to be under threat, were quick to make scapegoats of the Lhotshampas – who, not coincidentally, controlled lands that were emerging as the economic powerhouse of Bhutan.

In 1986, King Jingme, apparently under pressure from the family of his four wives, instituted the **Drig Lam Namzha** code of cultural correctness, which among other things required all residents of Bhutan to wear the traditional *gho* (for males) or *kira* (for females), heavy wool garments that were neither natural nor practical for the southerners. In 1988, after a national **census** was taken, the government began a process of systematic discrimination against anyone who couldn't provide written proof of residency in Bhutan in 1958. A campaign of **ethnic cleansing** gathered momentum, culminating in 1992 when "illegal" families were forced to sign "voluntary leaving certificates" and evicted from their lands with little or no compensation, while those identified as "anti-nationals" (and their families) were harassed, imprisoned, tortured and violated.

Receiving little encouragement from India, most refugees continued on to their ethnic homeland, Nepal. During the height of the exodus, as many as 25 trucks a day arrived at the Kakarbitta border post, overburdened with refugees and the few possessions they had managed to flee with. The first wave was settled at Maidhai, an encampment between Birtamod and Damak on the Mahendra Highway, but as their numbers swelled, the Nepalese government, wanting to keep the problem out of sight, established new **refugee camps** at Timai and Goldhap (south of Birtamod), Pathari (southeast of Itahari) and, biggest by far, Beldangi I, II and II (north of Damak). The UN High Commission on Refugees (UNHCR) has put the Lutheran World Service in charge of running the camps; the UN World Food Program distributes food rations, while Save the Children and other organizations are trying to address health problems stemming from malnutrition, poor sanitation and disease.

The Nepalese government feels a reluctant responsibility to the refugees, but has no intention of harbouring them indefinitely. India, which has its own fears of pan-Nepali resurgence, is disinclined to take them. All parties agree that **repatriation** to Bhutan is the only permanent solution to the problem, but most refugees refuse to budge until they're assured of their democratic rights in Bhutan. UNHCR observers note that even if Bhutan reversed its policies tomorrow, it would take several years to repatriate 100,000 refugees; realistically, they say, the Lhotshampas won't be going home before the turn of the century.

jungle. Jhapa, further east, is already largely cultivated and dotted with monoto-
nously similar villages, each containing a wide, dusty bazaar full of people selling
delicious oranges and cheap bangles; the half-timbered houses on stilts are the
work of transplanted Limbus. The latest and most numerous immigrants in these
parts are refugees from Bhutan – the majority live in three big refugee camps,
Beldangi I, II and III, located up a side road north of the Mahendra Highway at
Damak. Jhapa's tea plantations, though flat and not much to look at, are a reminder that Darjeeling is barely 50km away as the crow flies, and Ilam, Nepal's prize
tea-growing region, sits in the hills just north of here.

Kakarbitta and the border

A border crossing with a real backwoods flavour, **KAKARBITTA** feels like one of
those all-night shantytowns that Indian buses always seem to stop at, where you
wake up to men selling peanuts and *bidis* by candlelight and ask "where the hell
are we?" Unlike other border towns, it's too far out in the sticks to be much of a
trading centre, and the only apparent link with the rest of the world is the fleet of
night buses that roars in from Kathmandu every morning and roars out again
every afternoon. You don't want to stay here any longer than necessary.

If you need to **spend the night**, *ABC Lodge* is Kakarbitta's finest (②), with
Apsara Lodge running a slightly more rustic second place (①). Places around the
bus park serve snacks and *daal bhaat*, but *Hotel Shere Punjab*, which does a few
passable Indian dishes, is the only one that could properly be called a **restaurant**
– it's also something of a nightspot, although the electricity never seems to stay
on long enough to make the drinks cold. There's no black market in Kakarbitta:
lodges and restaurants will swap Nepalese and Indian rupees at the market rate,
but to change hard currency you'll have to use the **bank** (*Nepal Rastra Bank*, a
pink building signposted only in Nepali; daily 7am–5pm). The tourist office is
useless.

The wide Mechi River forms **the border**, about 500m east of town, and as it's a
fifteen-minute walk between Kakarbitta and Raniganj, the first Indian village, you
might as well take a riksha (not that you'll be able to fend them off anyway).
Foreigners driving their own vehicles are allowed through this crossing, which is
pleasantly low-key for border formalities. Jeeps and buses to Siliguri, the train

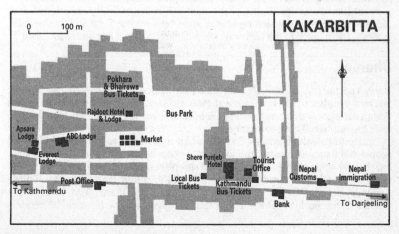

station for Darjeeling and Calcutta, depart from the junction just east of Raniganj; touts offer to "guide" travellers to Darjeeling for Rs100 or so, but you can easily do it yourself for half that. If you're coming from India and planning to catch one of the night buses to Kathmandu, they tend to leave Kakarbitta in staggered intervals between 3 and 5pm, but try to arrive a couple of hours early to be sure of a good seat; most other routes are plied by day buses.

THE EASTERN HILLS

Two roads link the Tarai with the hills east of the Sapt Koshi – the **Dhankuta road**, leaving the Mahendra Highway at Itahari, and the **Ilam road**, beginning at Charali. Bus services are more fickle here than along the Mahendra Highway, so it's always wise to make an early start. Either road would make a superb jaunt on a mountain bike. While this section describes short hikes in the area, remember that you're officially supposed to have a trekking permit to go more than a day's walk off a road.

The Dhankuta road

Call it development or call it colonialism by another name, but the big donor nations have staked out distinct spheres of influence in Nepal, and nowhere is this more apparent than in the British bailiwick around Dhankuta. Britain's interest in this area has not been without ulterior motives: roughly half the recruits for the Gurkha regiments have traditionally come from the eastern hills, and the biggest Gurkha training camp was, until recently, in Dharan. In the 1970s, no doubt pricked by a sense of obligation to the people of the area, Britain initiated a series of projects based in Dhankuta under the banner of the **Koshi Hills Development Programme**. Agriculture, forestry, health and cottage industries have all been funded by British aid through this programme (Princess Di lent royal support to these projects with a visit in 1993), but the biggest and most obvious undertaking has been the road to Dharan, Dhankuta, Hile and Basantapur.

From the Mahendra Highway, the road winds languidly through forest as it ascends the Bhabar, the sloping alluvial zone between the Tarai and the foothills. Dharan, 16km north of the highway, sits a slightly cooler 300m above the plain.

Dharan

Noisy and tawdry, **DHARAN** isn't much of a place to linger – unless, that is, you're a member of the development elite and staying out at the former Gurkha Camp, the closest thing in Nepal to Club Med. If you're heading for Dhankuta or Hile, though, you'll have to stop here.

Dharan hit world headlines in 1988 when a powerful **earthquake** killed 700 people and flattened most of the town – the main bazaar has been hastily rebuilt, but bricks and rubble are still piled in places and things look decidedly ramshackle. Disaster struck a second time at the end of 1989 when the **British Army**, foreseeing forces reductions, pulled out of Dharan and handed the Gurkha Camp back to HMG. The withdrawal dealt a blow to would-be recruits here, who must now travel all the way to Pokhara to compete for even fewer places in the regiments (for more on the Gurkhas, see p.213); most of Dharan's *khukuri* smiths disappeared overnight, and shopkeepers still bemoan the loss of Gurkha trade.

Yet the **bazaar** continues to do a bustling business, since for people throughout the eastern hills Dharan is the proverbial Bright Lights where they come to sell oranges by the sackload and spend their profits on kitchen utensils, provisions and bottles of *Urvashi* from the bazaar's well-stocked spirits stalls. In the area northeast of the central Bhanu Chowk you'll see hill women investing the family fortune in gold ornaments – the age-old safe haven – and shops selling fantastic Raj-era silver coins to be strung into necklaces. If you happen to be in the market for a cauldron, check out the brass-workers' quarter further east.

The most amazing thing about Dharan is the sheer contrast between the bazaar and the **Gurkha Camp** (as it's still called), a Rs15 riksha ride west of the bus stand. You can wander freely around the grounds now, which you wouldn't have been allowed to do when the Gurkhas occupied it, and although there's not much to see, the long, tree-lined lanes are blessedly quiet – it's like a university campus during summer break. The camp has been handed over to the Ministry of Health, which now runs the hospital but doesn't seem to have a clue what to do with the rest of the facilities. Rather than watch the best golf course in Nepal go to seed, the British transition team has leased it from the government and renamed it the **Dharan Club**: for about Rs200 you can rent clubs, hire a caddy and play eighteen holes, and the swimming pool and tennis and squash courts can be used for Rs100 per day.

Fifteen kilometres west of Dharan is **Chatara**, the finishing point for rafting trips on the Sun Kosi; Land Rovers make the trip starting from west of Chatta Chowk (Rs20). Walk an hour north of Chatara and you reach the sacred confluence of **Barahakshetra**, site of a temple to Vishnu incarnated as a boar (Barahi) and an annual pilgrimage on the day of the full moon of October–November.

Practicalities

All **buses** terminate in Dharan. Services from here to Biratnagar are fairly frequent, and up to six (night) buses ply between Dharan and Kathmandu – to reach other Tarai destinations, change at Itahari or Biratnagar. Buses to Dhankuta and points north are always chronically overcrowded, and it can be a real ordeal getting a seat; enquire about road conditions, as landslides sometimes turn the journey into two separate rides.

The *Dharan Club*'s tourist bungalow is without a doubt the quietest and cleanest **accommodation** here (B④), and serves Western breakfasts. In the bazaar, *Hotel Ever Green* seems to be the best bet if you can get in (B③); failing that, you'll have to settle for *Yug Hotel* (①/B③) or *Hotel Step-In* (①), both grotty and noisy. Service at the *Yug*'s and *Ever Green*'s **restaurants** is neither swift nor enthusiastic, but the food isn't bad, whereas the *Yeti* and *Makalu* restaurants are maddeningly inept; street vendors around Bhanu Chowk sell some weird and wonderful fried morsels.

North to Dhankuta

From Dharan the road switchbacks abruptly over a 1400-metre saddle with dramatic views, then descends to cross the Tamur Kosi at Mulghat (280m) before climbing once again to **DHANKUTA**, stretched out on a ridge at 1150m. Some buses carry on to Hile and Basantapur, but you might have to change here.

Though you'd never guess it by looking at it, Dhankuta is the administrative headquarters for eastern Nepal; the logic of this choice is unclear, but it perhaps stems from Kathmandu's mistrust of leftist Biratnagar and Dharan. Unfortunately, the road that was supposed to consolidate Dhankuta's position has, if anything, undermined it by siphoning off trade to Dharan and Hile, and the only thing that seems to be holding the place together is British aid: the Koshi Hills project is based here (you see their shiny Land Rovers everywhere), as are Save the Children, Britain Nepal Medical Trust and assorted VSO and Peace Corps volunteers. But for travellers who make it this far, it's an easygoing, predominantly Newar town, with pedestrian-only streets, smartly whitewashed houses and shady *chautaara*. The outlying area is populated by Rais, Magars and Hindu castes, who make Dhankuta's **haat bazaar**, on Thursday, a tremendously vivid affair.

Although you can't see the Himalaya from here, the area makes fine **walking** country, and you're bound to run into chatty aid workers or ex-Gurkhas on the trail. In **Santang**, a Rai village about 45 minutes southeast of town, women can be seen embroidering beautiful shawls and weaving *dhaka*, which is as much a speciality of the eastern hills as it is in the west (see p.227). You can walk to Hile in about two hours by taking short cuts off the main road: stick to the ridge and within sight of the electric power line.

Dhankuta practicalities

Project workers get first priority at the *Koshi Hills Development Programme Rest House*, Dhankuta's most salubrious **place to stay**, but it doesn't hurt to ask at the *KHDP* office (☎353), at the north end of the bazaar just off the road to Hile; the spanking-clean rest house, located south of the bus park, features a garden, solar hot water and dining room (B④). Cheapies in the bazaar are cold-water, trekking-standard outfits – *Hotel Parichaya* is the friendliest and quietest (①). Try the nameless Sherpa **restaurant** 100m downhill from the *Parichaya* for excellent *momo* and *tongba*, *Lodge Sangalo* for snacks, or the *Rest House* for stodgy Western fare.

Hile

HILE (pronounced *Hee*-lay) is one of the most exciting places a traveller can visit in Nepal without a trekking permit. That's a deliberately barbed compliment: if you're here to start (or finish) a trek – and you'd be crazy to come all this way and *not* trek – Hile might seem anticlimactic, yet this spirited little pioneer settlement would merit a stay even if it weren't a trailhead.

Seemingly teetering over the deep, often fog-shrouded Arun Valley, Hile huddles along the main road, 10km beyond Dhankuta and 750m higher up along the same ridge, and buses make the trip fairly regularly on the newly paved surface. A straggling strip of temporary-looking shops, a few hotels and a couple of one-room *gompa* just about sums up the **bazaar**; you can walk the length of it in five minutes. The shops bristle with commodities like plastic containers, readymade clothes, metal pots and salt, all bound for the hinterland: **porters** gather in Hile by the hundreds, and the trail to Tumlingtar, three days up the Arun Valley, is like a *doko* highway.

Local Rais, Newar merchants and Indian entrepreneurs are all dicing for a piece of Hile's action, but its most visible minority are Bhotiyas (see "The Himalayan Trekking Regions"), who have relocated en masse from the highlands near Kanchenjunga. Undoubtedly one of the most exotic things you can do in Nepal is to spend an evening in a flickering Bhotiya kitchen sipping hot millet grog from an authentic **tongba**: unique to this area, these miniature wooden casks with brass hoops and fitted tops look like they were designed for Genghis Khan. Hile's **haat bazaar**, on Thursday, is lively, but not as big as Dhankuta's.

A jhankri (shaman) of the hills

Magnificent **views** (even by trekking standards) can be had just a half-hour's hike from Hile. Walk to the north end of the bazaar, bear left up a dirt lane and after 150m go right up a set of steps to join the Hattikharka trail, which contours around the hill, skirts an army base and finally reaches a grassy plateau. The panorama spreads out before you like a trekking map: to the northwest, Cho Oyu and Makalu float above the awesome canyon of the Arun (though Everest is hidden behind the crest, you can see its characteristic plume); the ridges of the Milke Danda zigzag to the north; and part of the Kanchenjunga massif pokes up in the northeast. It's heaven – pity about the army base, though*. A quicker, truncated view can be had from the top of the ridge south of Hile. The trail to Tumlingtar angles to the left near the north end of the bazaar, passing the British-funded agricultural research station at Pakhribas en route.

Practicalities

Hile's Bhotiya **lodges** are pretty savvy about catering to foreigners, though innkeepers don't speak much English. *Hotel Gajur*'s rooms are clean (①) and its kitchen is legendary for *momo*, *sokuti* (fried meat) and *tongba*. The rooms are somewhat bigger at *Hotel Himali* (①), but the walls are thinner and the dining area isn't so cosy. Lodges and shops are surprisingly well stocked with tinned food, chocolate, instant coffee and other trekking **provisions**.

To return to Kathmandu from here, hourly **buses** go as far as Dharan, where you can try for a seat on the nightly bus to the capital or continue on to Itahari and intercept one of the night buses coming from Biratnagar.

Basantapur and beyond

About six buses a day rumble on to the end of the road – which for the moment is **BASANTAPUR**, a dusty hour and a half from Hile – but this is the kind of country where you just hitch a ride with any vehicle that's going. You get tremendous views of the Makalu massif for most of the way, and Everest manages to pop into view near the end.

Very much a rerun of Hile, Basantapur's lively, muddy bazaar sits in a saddle at 2400m. Besides being the main supply line for the entire northeast corner of Nepal, Basantapur has begun to play host to trekking groups bound for Kanchenjunga, and several **lodges** have sprung up, the most aggressive being *Hotel Yak* (①), which even sports a "Today's Menu" board. The hills around here are a delight for **walking**: mixed pasture and dense mossy forest, rhododendrons, orchids, jasmine, and very friendly villages. Likely targets are Chauki, a pleasant village a couple of hours north of Basantapur, and Kopha Pokhri, a lake with great views two or three hours further on. Anything beyond that is a trek.

During the next few years the road is supposed to be extended from Basantapur to Num, 30km from the Tibet border beside the Arun River, where the controversial **Arun III** hydroelectric diversion is planned to go. Opponents fear the road will cause more environmental disruption than the diversion itself. Fortunately the World Bank, which has backed more than its share of Third World white elephants in the past, apparently sees Arun III as an opportunity to

---

*The military presence here suggests that, as is so often the case, the Dhankuta–Hile road has been built more for reasons of security than development; and given the base's location, one suspects its purpose is to deter domestic unrest, not foreign invasions.

demonstrate a new environmental sensitivity, and has tied the project's $870 million financing to an ambitious conservation programme upstream in the Makalu-Barun area. Work on the project is supposed to begin after the 1994 monsoon and take ten years.

The Ilam road

Like the Dhankuta road, the Ilam road keeps getting longer: originally engineered by the Koreans to connect the tea estates of Kanyam and Ilam with the Tarai, it now reaches Phidim and is in the process of being extended to Taplejung.

Buses to Ilam start at Birtamod, located on the Mahendra Highway 8km west of the actual start of the road at Charali – they tend to be very crowded, and the last one leaves at 10am or 11am. The journey takes about six hours by bus; by bike it would probably be a two-day trip. After traversing lush lowlands, the road begins a laborious 1600-metre ascent to Kanyam and its undulating monoculture of tea. At Phikal, a few kilometres further on, a side road heads east to the obscure border crossing of Pashupati, which according to unconfirmed reports has been reopened to travellers, raising the possibility of an intriguing short cut to Darjeeling. Beyond Phikal the road descends 1000m in a series of tight switchbacks – where it hasn't been cleared, the forest here is magnificent – to cross the Mai Khola before climbing another 500m to Ilam (1200m).

Ilam

To Nepalis, **ILAM** (Ee-*laam*) means tea: cool and moist for much of the year, the hills of Ilam district (like those of Darjeeling, just across the border) are perfect for it. Ilam town, headquarters of the district, is a tidy little bazaar whose colourfully painted wooden houses, featuring prim balconies and decorated eaves, give it an unmistakeably alpine air. It looks a lot like Darjeeling, in fact, without all the hype and new construction, and if it only had better food and mountain views Ilam would make a terrific alternative hill resort.

Settled by Newars, Rais and Marwaris (a business-minded Indian group with interests in tea), Ilam was at one time eastern Nepal's main centre of commerce. While hill towns like Ilam have lost much of their trading importance to the Tarai in recent years, its exuberant **haat bazaar** (held on Thursdays) still draws shoppers from a wide radius, and of course tea cultivation provides an anchor for the local economy. Unaccustomed to dealing with foreign travellers, **accommodation** here is on the spartan side, but the proprietor of *Deurali Lodge* (①) at least speaks some English. Simple **meals** are available at the *Deurali* and in several nameless eateries along the main drag – mostly it's just *daal bhaat* and packaged noodles, but you can get tasty *thukpa* at a place opposite the bank near the top of the bazaar.

The tea gardens and factory
The most pleasant thing to do in Ilam is stroll around the **tea gardens**, which carpet the ridge above town and tumble down its steep far side; between April and December you can watch the pluckers at work, and at other times it's just a relaxing place to be. Nepal's first tea estate, it was established in 1864 by a relative of the prime minister after a visit to Darjeeling, where tea cultivation was just

becoming big business. Marwaris, who had already cornered the cardamom trade here, soon assumed control of the plantation on a contract basis, an arrangement that lasted until the 1960s, when the government nationalized this and six other hill estates under the direction of the Nepal Tea Development Corporation. In 1992 the new Congress government announced its intention to re-privatize the estates, a move that's expected to open the door to Indian ownership but also to introduce a much more professional approach to production. If Nepali teas such as Ilam and Kanyam could be properly marketed, industry observers say, they'd soon rank in international reputation alongside Darjeeling.

You can visit the **tea factory** to see how the world's most popular beverage is produced. The process begins with the plucked leaves being loaded into "withering chutes" upstairs, where fans remove about half their moisture content. They're then transferred to big rolling machines to break the cell walls and release their juices, and placed on fermentation beds to bring out their characteristic flavour and colour. Finally, most of the remaining moisture is removed in a wood-fired drying machine and the leaves are sorted into grades ranging from the coveted TGFOP (Tippy Golden Flower Orange Pekoe, "tippy" referring to the tenderest new leaves) to the lowly PD (Pekoe Dust). Ilam's TGFOP compares favourably with the best of Darjeeling, and indeed most of it is exported to Germany to be blended into "Darjeeling" teas. A 500g bag costs about Rs150 here – much less than the comparable grade in Darjeeling. Tarai tea, incidentally, is processed by the more mechanized CTC (Curling, Tearing and Crushing) method, which produces the cheaper drink served just about everywhere in Nepal.

Beyond Ilam: walks and the road to Phidim

The Ilam area is noted for its greenness – higher up, the jungle is profuse and exuberant, and even the terraced slopes are teemingly fertile. Keep an eye out for **cardamom**, which grows in moist ravines and has become an important cash crop here. This black cardamom (*sukumel*), which is an inferior form of the tropical green variety (*elaichi*) grown in Kerala, is shipped through India to Singapore where it's sold on the world market. Another common cash crop cultivated in this area is broom grass (*umsilo*), which is used to make traditional Nepali whisks. Rais make up the majority of villagers, followed by Bahuns, Chhetris and Limbus.

Rewarding **walks** set off in at least three directions. From the tea gardens, you can contour westwards and cross the Puwamai Khola, ascending the other side to Mangalbare, site of a Wednesday **haat bazaar** even bigger than Ilam's (there are supposed to be views of Kanchenjunga from further south along this ridge). A trail heading east from Ilam descends to cross the Mai Khola, where the annual **Beni Mela** attracts thousands of Hindus on Magh Sankranti (January 14 or 15), and continues on to Naya Bazaar. A sacred pond atop a wooded ridge north of Ilam, **Mai Pokhri** can be reached by walking or hitching along the road towards Phidim and making a right at Bibliarti, from where it's another two or three hours' ascent; **Sandakpur**, a superb viewpoint on the Indian border, is a day's walk further, which suggests an illicit trek from here to Darjeeling. Finally, if you're looking for a quick leg-stretch, check out the small but attractively sited **Bhagwati Mandir**, about 1km down the main road from *Deurali Lodge*.

Buses ply the road north of Ilam as far as **PHIDIM**, a run-of-the-mill district headquarters deep in Limbu territory, six hours further on. Although there's no checkpost, you're supposed to have a trekking permit to travel here, and the local authorities are sensitive about having foreigners in the area ever since an awkward incident in 1989 in which an American and a Canadian were arrested for distributing Christian tracts (they got off on a technicality).

festivals

Major holidays such as Holi, Dasain (known as Dashera in the Tarai) and Tihaar (Diwali) are celebrated everywhere, and Shiva Raatri is popular in Hindu areas. In addition, look for these local festivals:

MAGH (Jan–Feb)
Beni Mela A celebration of the first day of Magh (Jan 14 or 15) with ritual bathing in the Mai Khola, near Ilam.

FAAGUN (Feb–March)
Losar Tibetan New Year, which is observed at Hile, Basantapur and other Buddhist places in the hills.

CHAITRA (March–April)
Ram Navami Ram's birthday, celebrated at Janakpur's Ram Mandir.

KARTIK (Oct–Nov)
Barahakshetra Mela A pilgrimage to the Sapt Koshi River at Barahakshetra, near Dharan.

Chath The Janakpur women perform ritual bathing and make fertility offerings to a local deity.

MANGSIR (Nov–Dec)
Biwaha Panchami Janakpur's biggest festival, lasting five days and attracting 100,000 pilgrims to watch the wedding of Ram and Sita re-enacted at the Janaki Mandir.

travel details

BUSES

From Hetauda to Kathmandu (1 *Sajha* daily, 4 night buses; 8–9hr); many other buses pass through.

From Birganj to Janakpur (7 daily; 5 hr); Kathmandu (6 daily, including 2 *Sajha*, plus 2 nightly; 10hr) and Pokhara (6 daily; 10hr); for Tadi Bazaar (Chitwan), take any Kathmandu or Pokhara bus.

From Janakpur to Biratnagar (3 nightly; 8hr); Birganj (7 daily; 5hr); Kakarbitta (2 daily; 9hr); Kathmandu (6 night buses, 1 *Sajha*; 10–12hr) and Pokhara (1 night bus; 12hr).

From Biratnagar to Dharan (frequent; 2hr); Janakpur (3 nightly; 8hr); Kakarbitta (hourly; 4hr) and Kathmandu (7 nightly; 16hr).

From Kakarbitta to Biratnagar (hourly; 4hr); Birtamod (frequent; 30min); Dharan (6 daily; 4hr); Janakpur (2 daily, 9hr); Kathmandu (8 nightly; at least 20hr) and Pokhara (3 nightly; at least 20hr).

From Dharan to Basantapur (6 daily; 5hr); Biratnagar (frequent; 1–2hr); Dhankuta (12 daily; 3hr); Hile (12 daily; 4hr); Kakarbitta (6 daily; 4hr) and Kathmandu (6 nightly; 18hr).

From Dhankuta to Hile (12 daily; 30min) and Basantapur (6 daily; 2hr).

From Birtamod to Ilam (5 daily; 6hr) and Phidim (2 daily; 12hr).

PLANES

From Janakpur to Kathmandu (3 weekly; 40min).

From Biratnagar to Kathmandu (3–4 daily; 1hr); Phaplu (2 weekly; 40min); Taplejung (3 weekly; 30min) and Tumlingtar (4 weekly; 25min).

CONNECTIONS TO INDIA

From Raxaul (Birganj), buses run frequently to Patna (4hr), where you can catch broad-gauge trains to most parts of northern India.

From Raniganj (Kakarbitta), buses run approximately hourly to Siliguri and New Jalpaiguri (2hr), termini for Calcutta and the "toy train" to Darjeeling.

CHAPTER SEVEN

THE HIMALAYAN TREKKING REGIONS

A hundred divine epochs would not suffice to describe all the marvels of the Himalaya.

Hindu proverb

Rearing up over the subcontinent like an immense, whitecapped tidal wave, the **Himalaya** (Hi-*maal*-aya) are, to many travellers' minds, the whole reason for visiting Nepal. Containing eight of the world's ten highest peaks – including, of course, Everest – Nepal's 800-kilometre link in the Himalayan chain puts all other attractions in the shade. More than just majestic scenery, though, the "Abode of Snow" is also the home of Sherpas, yaks, yetis and snow leopards, and has always exerted a powerful spiritual pull: in Hindu mythology the mountains are where gods meditate and make sacrifices, while the Sherpas hold certain peaks to be the very embodiment of deities; mountaineers are often hardly less mystical.

Nepal's **trekking regions**, as defined by the government, take in all parts of the country more than about a day's walk from a main road – a huge area covering nearly the entire northern half of Nepal, and including not only the Himalaya but also large sections of the hills. These regions span an incredible diversity of terrain and cultures, but one thing they all have in common is that you need a **trekking permit** to travel in them.

Trekking needn't be expensive nor agonizingly difficult. Most treks follow established routes where you can eat and sleep in simple inns for less money than you'd spend in Kathmandu; trails are often steep, to be sure, but you walk at your own pace, and no trek goes higher than about 5500m (the *starting* elevation for most climbing expeditions). That said, trekking is not for everybody – it's demanding, sometimes uncomfortable, and it does involve an element of risk. This chapter is organized to help you decide if you want to trek, and if so, how and where you might like to do it. The first section covers things you need to know about trekking in general, and the second gives overviews of the most popular, and a few of the more notable out-of-the-way, treks.

Where you go will depend to a great extent on the **time of year**. In general, October and November are good for all mid- and high-elevation treks; December to February is a time to stay low; in spring you want to go high to get above the haze, especially from April on; and the monsoon (mid-June to late September or early October) is a difficult time to trek, of course, though not out of the question. More specific tips are given in the relevant trek descriptions.

TREKKING BASICS

This section runs through the different **styles** of trekking, **preparations** you'll have to make before setting off, **health** matters to be mindful of, and other factors of **life on the trail**. It's designed to complement the information given in standard trekking guides (see "Books" in *Contexts*), with particular emphasis on the nuts and bolts of independent trekking.

Trekking styles

How you choose to trek will depend on your budget, your time frame, and what sort of experience you're after. Trekking independently saves money and gives you a more individualized experience, but involves more preparation. Joining an agency trek minimizes hassles and enables you to reach remote backcountry areas, but you pay dearly for it.

Trekking independently

Trekking independently means making all your own arrangements instead of going through a trekking agency – most budget travellers trek this way simply because it's cheaper. By carrying your own pack and staying in teahouses, a trek should **cost** no more than Rs350 ($7) a day – often as little as Rs100 ($2) a day –

not including trekking permit and national park fees. Hiring a porter to carry your stuff will add about Rs250 ($5) a day, a guide Rs500 ($10) a day (somewhat more if you do it through an agency).

Doing it yourself gives you more **control** over many aspects of the trek: you can go at your own pace, stop when and where you like, choose your travelling companions and take rest days or side trips as you please. The downside is that you have to spend two or three days lining up trekking permits and bus tickets, renting equipment, buying supplies and perhaps tracking down a porter or guide. A further drawback is that you're effectively confined to **teahouse routes**; trekking to remote areas is difficult unless you speak Nepali or you're prepared to deal with considerable porter logistics.

Life on the trail is described later, but suffice to say that an independent trek is **less comfortable** than one arranged through an agency. Lodges can be noisy and lacking in privacy, while the food is often fairly uninteresting. The active teahouse **social scene** goes some way to compensating for this, however – even if you start out alone, you'll quickly meet up with potential trekking companions.

By not being part of a group, you're better placed to learn from Nepali ways rather than forcing Nepalis to adapt to yours. Equally important, a high proportion of the money you spend goes directly to the local economy (whereas most of the money paid to trekking agencies goes no further than Kathmandu, and often finds its way overseas). However, independent trekking contributes to **deforestation** – there's no way around it. If you stay in teahouses and order meals cooked over wood fires you encourage innkeepers to cut down more trees, and if you bring along a guide or porter, so do they. The hideous streamers of toilet paper

Anything can
fit in a *doko*

seen on popular trails are by and large the work of teahouse trekkers, since groups usually dig toilet pits and bury their waste. There are, however, ways to minimize your environmental impact – see the conservation tips on p.307.

Hiring porters and guides

Porters are an important part of the Himalayan economy and there's no shame in hiring one. With a porter taking most of your gear, you only have to carry a small pack containing the things you need during the day; this can be a great relief at high elevations, and it's essential when trekking off established routes, where tents, food and cooking equipment have to be brought in. As porters rarely speak much English, you might want to pay more for a **guide** who does. An increasing number of them are willing to carry gear as well, but this isn't always the case: ask. Guides are really only necessary on esoteric routes, but any trek will be enlivened by the company and local knowledge of a guide, who may well take you on unusual side trips to visit the homes of family and friends.

Hiring a porter or guide is simple enough – just ask your innkeeper, or try any trekking agency or equipment-rental shop. If you're not sure you need a porter, or you think you'll only need one for a few tough days of a trek, you can usually hire someone on the spot at Namche, Jomosom and a few of the other mountain airstrips. The business is very informal and not always reputable, so shop around and interview more than one candidate if necessary. Make sure the agreed wage includes food – a porter can run up a huge bill if you're paying – and don't pay too much of it up front. Expect also to pay a Rs300–500 tip at the end of the trek, assuming the work was well done, and perhaps one or two articles of clothing (but clean them first!).

However, the **responsibilities** of employing a porter or guide cannot be overstated. Several porters die needlessly each year, typically because their sahib (pronounced "sahb") thought they were superhuman and didn't mind sleeping outside in a blizzard. You *must* make sure your employees are adequately clothed for the journey – on high-altitude treks, this will mean buying or renting them good shoes, a parka, sunglasses, mittens and a sleeping bag; establish beforehand if something is a loan. If they get sick, it's up to you to look after them, and since most porters hired in Kathmandu and Pokhara are clueless about altitude-related problems, it's your responsibility to educate them. Don't let a porter carry a double load, even if he volunteers, and don't hire anyone who looks underage.

If you've never trekked before, don't try to organize a trek off the teahouse routes. Finding a guide familiar with a particular area will be hard, and transporting him with a crew of porters and supplies to the trailhead a major (and expensive) logistical exercise. Getting a trekking agency to do it might not cost much more.

Trekking with an agency

Treks organized through an **agency** are for people who haven't got the time or inclination to make their own arrangements, or who want to tackle ambitious routes that can't be done independently. They **cost** from $15 to $150 a day, depending on the standard of service, size of the group, remoteness of the route and whether you book the trip in your home country or in Kathmandu. The price should always include a guide, porters, food and shelter, although cheap outfits often charge extra for trekking permits, national park fees and transport, and may cut other corners as well. The cheaper the price, the more wary you need to be.

A trek is hard work however you do it, but a good agency will help you along with a few **creature comforts**: you can expect good food, "bed tea" and hot "washing water" on cold mornings, camp chairs and a latrine tent with toilet paper. Depending on the size of your party, a guide, *sirdar* (guide foreman) or "Western trek leader" (native-English-speaking guide) will be able to answer questions and cope with problems. Trekking groups usually sleep in **tents**, which, while quieter than teahouses, may be colder and are certainly more cramped. The daily routine of eating as a group can get monotonous, and gives you **less contact** with local people. There's something to be said for safety in numbers, but trekking with a group imposes a somewhat **inflexible itinerary** on you, and if you don't like the people in your group, you're stuck.

In theory, agency treks are more **environmentally sound**, at least in the Everest and Annapurna areas, where trekkers' meals are required to be cooked with kerosene. In practice, however, cooks use wood whenever possible so they can sell the kerosene at the end of the trek – and, worse still, for each trekker eating a kerosene-cooked meal, two or three porters and other staff are cooking their *bhaat* over a wood fire.

The main advantage in trekking with an agency is it enables you to get **off the beaten track**: there's little point in using an agency to do a teahouse trek.

Budget agencies

Small "walk-in" outfits in Kathmandu and Pokhara, charging $15–25 a day (or rupee equivalent), are notoriously hard to recommend: most are fly-by-night operations offering mainly customized treks, but be advised that they're rarely

---

QUESTIONS TO ASK TREKKING AGENCIES

Trekking agencies in Nepal speak the green lingo as fluently as anyone, but in many cases their walk doesn't match their talk. Here are some specific questions to put to agencies to find out what they're actually doing to mitigate their impact. You probably won't find an agency able answer every question satisfactorily, but the exercise should help establish which outfits are genuinely concerned about the environment.
• Do they carry enough kerosene to cook all meals for all members of the party, including porters?
• What equipment do they provide to porters – tents, proper clothing, shoes, UV sunglasses?
• Do they separate trash and carry out all non-burnable/non-biodegradeable waste?
• Have staff attended the annual Ecotrek workshop on responsible trekking? (Attendees will be able to show a certificate.)
• Do staff have wilderness first-aid training?

competent to handle anything off the mass-market routes. Names change and standards rise and fall – if you hear of a good one by word of mouth, try it. A few of the more established agencies run scheduled treks, but again, usually only to the most popular areas; one exception is *Mountain Adventure Trekking* (☎01/414910; PO Box 3440, Kathmandu), located in front of the *Kathmandu Guest House*, which does a few unorthodox trips for $30 a day.

Bigger agencies
Kathmandu's **big operators** mainly package treks on behalf of overseas companies, but some offer scheduled or customized treks for the local market at a lower price (typically $30–60 a day). Write for brochures to make sure your schedule coincides with theirs; for customized treks to exotic areas, write several months in advance, or be prepared to wait up to a week in Kathmandu while arrangements are being made. If you pay in foreign currency, be sure to get an official exchange receipt. The following list should get you started:

Asian Trekking, Keshar Mahal (off Tridevi Marg), Kathmandu (☎01/412821; PO Box 3022).

Journeys Mountaineering & Trekking, Kantipath, Kathmandu (☎01/225969; PO Box 2034).

Rover Treks & Expeditions, Naksal, Kathmandu (☎01/414373; PO Box 1081).

Sherpa Co-operative Trekking, Durbar Marg, Kathmandu (☎01/224068; PO Box 1338).

Yangrima Trekking & Mountaineering, Kantipath, Kathmandu (☎01/225608; PO Box 2951).

Overseas agencies
Booking through an **overseas agency** lets you arrange everything before you leave home, but expect to pay £50–100/$75–150 per day. Some agencies have their own subsidiaries in Kathmandu, others use independent outfitters like those listed above. The overseas operator will look after all your arrangements up till the time you leave your home country, and will also play a part in maintaining quality control in Nepal. Some may allow you to join up in Kathmandu at a reduced price. See "Getting There" in *Basics* for names and addresses.

Preparations

Arranging a trek is like anything else in Nepal: complications arise, things inevitably take longer than planned, but it's unquestionably worth it in the end. How you trek will have a bearing on this, since trekking independently involves more preparation than joining an organized group. The remainder of this chapter is geared specifically to independent trekkers, although most of the information will apply to groups as well.

Trekking permits
A **trekking permit** is required for entry into any of the areas described in this chapter. Apply at the Central Immigration offices in Kathmandu or Pokhara (details on p.106 and p.224). Pokhara is generally easier to deal with than Kathmandu, but both are frantic during October – especially just before and after the week-long Dasain holiday. Note that Pokhara issues permits for the Annapurna region only. For all standard trekking areas, permits cost $5 per week

(payable in rupee equivalent) during the first thirty days of your stay in Nepal, $10 per week thereafter. Permits for the Dolpo and Kanchenjunga areas cost double, for Manaslu they're $75 per week, and for Mustang they're $500 per week. Be sure to fill in the correct form: blue for Helambu/Langtang, yellow for Annapurna, pink for Everest and white for all other regions or treks in more than one region. Permits should be ready later the same day.

A trekking permit still doesn't give you free run of the country – most border areas are closed, and peaks are restricted. Two dozen designated **trekking peaks**, ranging in elevation from 5587m to 6654m, can be attempted with an additional permit ($150–300 per party) obtainable from the *Nepal Mountaineering Association*, Ram Shah Path, Kathmandu.

Before setting off, **register with your embassy** in Kathmandu, as this will speed things up should you need rescuing. You can have the *Himalayan Rescue Association* (see below) forward the details to your embassy. It's also advisable to be **insured** for trekking – note that most travel-insurance companies add 25 percent or more to their rates to cover "hazardous sports" such as trekking.

Information, maps and books

The best sources of current trekking **information** are the *Kathmandu Environmental Education Project* and *Himalayan Rescue Association* (☎01/418755), which share offices in Tridevi Marg just west of the Kathmandu Central Immigration office. *KEEP* keeps a logbook full of comments from returning trekkers – invaluable for tips on routes and trekking agencies – and can advise on trail conditions and equipment. The organization doesn't take a position on independent versus agency trekking, but encourages trekkers to use their clout as consumers to effect changes in the trekking industry; exhibits in the office give a primer on trekkers' impact on the environment and culture. *HRA* provides information on altitude sickness and health posts, and can register you with your embassy. A noticeboard in the hall outside the office is good for finding **trekking partners**.

Nepal's trekking regions are fairly well **mapped**, although the rule, as always, is you get what you pay for. The locally produced *Mandala* series includes colour maps of the most popular routes and dyeline versions of many more obscure areas. Better, though pricier, are the *Schneider* maps of the Everest and Langtang/Helambu areas and the *ACAP* map of Annapurna, all of which are available in the bigger Kathmandu bookshops. Specific titles are recommended in the area descriptions given later in this chapter.

Trekking **guidebooks** and general books on the Himalaya are detailed in *Contexts* (p.382); all can easily be bought in Kathmandu.

What to bring

Having the right **equipment** on a trek is obviously important, but when you see how little porters get by with you'll realize that high-tech gear isn't essential – bring what you need to be comfortable, but keep weight to a minimum. The equipment list given here is intended mainly for independent trekkers staying in teahouses; if you're planning to camp, you'll need quite a few more things, and if you're trekking with an agency you won't need so much.

By **renting** bulky or specialized items in Nepal, you'll avoid having to lug them around during the rest of your travels. Kathmandu has dozens of rental shops, and Pokhara a somewhat more limited selection; if you're trekking in the Everest region, you can rent high-altitude gear in Namche. However, you might have trouble finding good gear during the busy autumn trekking season. You'll be expected to leave a hefty deposit, typically $50-plus or an international air ticket. Inspect sleeping bags and parkas carefully for fleas (or worse) – if there's time before setting off, have them cleaned – and make sure zippers are in working order. Don't rent boots, as you're unlikely to get a good fit. You can often buy equipment from travellers leaving Nepal: check the restaurant noticeboards in Kathmandu and at *KEEP/HRA*.

Clothes must be lightweight and versatile, especially on long treks where conditions vary from subtropical to arctic. Many first-time trekkers underestimate the potential for extremes in temperature. What you bring will depend on the trek and time of year, but in most cases you should be prepared for sun, rain, snow and chilly mornings; dress in layers for maximum flexibility. As explained in "Cultural Hints" in *Basics*, Nepalis have innately conservative attitudes about dress: in warm areas, women should wear calf-length dresses or skirts with demure tops; men should wear a shirt and long pants wherever possible, and both sexes should wear at least a swimsuit when bathing.

For **footwear**, running shoes will suffice for most trekking situations, and serve as a good backup for evenings. However, lightweight (corduroy/suede)

EQUIPMENT CHECKLIST

Items marked (*) can be purchased in Nepal and those marked (**) can also be rented, but if you want to be absolutely sure of having it, bring it with you.

Essentials
Backpack** – one with an internal frame and hip belt is best.
Sleeping bag** – a three-season bag is adequate for hill treks; above 4000m, or in winter, you'll need a four-season bag and possibly a liner.
Foam mat** – but optional for teahouse treks in the Annapurna and Everest regions.
Medical kit – see "Health".
Water bottle*
Toiletries*
Toilet paper* – see "Conservation Tips".
Towel*
Torch (flashlight)* – remember that batteries run down faster in the cold.
Pocket knife*
Sunglasses* – a good UV-protective pair, ideally with side shields.
Sunscreen/lip balm – at altitude you'll need a high protection factor or zinc oxide.

Footwear
Hiking boots** – lightweight boots are best; leather stompers are usually only necessary for treks over 4000m.
Trainers – okay for most trails, handy for evenings.
Flipflops* – may be useful for evenings at low elevations.

Clothes
Shirts/T-shirts*
Trousers* – baggy (to leave room for thermal underwear) and with plenty of pockets; separate lightweight pair for warm days.

hiking boots, by providing better traction, ankle support and protection, will take you through a greater range of the sort of conditions you're likely to encounter. Leather boots are heavier but, being sturdier and more easily waterproofed, might be worth bringing for treks at high elevations or during the winter or monsoon. Bring plenty of socks, because you'll be changing them often.

Bringing **camera** equipment involves a trade-off between weight and performance – a pocket 35mm model may be a good compromise. An SLR body with long and short zoom lenses will produce much better results, especially with a tripod and polarizing filters, but it's heavy and obtrusive. You'll find more general tips on photography in *Basics*.

Health and emergencies

Guidebook writers tend to go overboard about the **health** hazards of trekking, particularly altitude sickness. Don't be put off – the vast majority of trekkers never experience anything worse than a mild headache. That said, health is of paramount concern when doing any strenuous physical activity, and all the more so when trekking, which routinely takes you a week or more from the nearest

---

Skirt/dress* – mid-calf length is best.
Shorts – not recommended, for cultural reasons.
Sweat pants – can be worn over shorts in morning; also good for evenings.
Socks – several thin cotton/blend and thick woollen* pairs.
Underwear – thermal underwear essential for high-altitude or winter treks.
Sun hat – helpful at low elevations.
Wool sweater* – or a synthetic pile jacket.
Bandana – to use as a handkerchief, sweatband or scarf.
Parka** – preferably filled with down or lightweight fibre.
Wool hat* – one that covers the ears is best.
Wool mittens* – ski gloves are warmer, but bulkier.
Rain shell/poncho – breathable waterproof material (such as Gore-Tex) is best. An umbrella* will suffice at lower elevations, and can also function as a parasol.

High-altitude gear – optional
Gaiters** – worth having for passes where snow is likely.
Down pants** and booties – welcome luxuries on cold evenings.
Ski poles** – may be useful for keeping your balance in snow.
Ice axe** – rarely needed on teahouse treks.
Crampons** – ditto.

Other useful items
Day pack
Camera equipment
Sewing kit
Stuff sacks – handy for separating things in your pack and for creating a pillow when filled with clothes.
Plastic bag* – to put over your pack in the rain.
Candles*
Emergency snack food*
Entertainment* – book, cards, musical instrument, etc.

medical facilities. Stomach troubles can spoil a trek, while injuries or altitude sickness, if untreated, could prove fatal. It's best to err on the side of caution.

Children, seniors and people with disabilities have all trekked successfully, but a minimum **fitness** level is required. Needless to say, the better prepared you are physically, the more you'll enjoy the trek. If you're in any doubt about your ability to cope with strenuous walking, see your doctor; it's also worth seeking advice if you have any allergies, especially to antibiotics.

Stomach troubles
The risk of **stomach troubles** is particularly high while trekking, and water is the usual culprit: you need to drink lots of fluids on the trail. Innkeepers normally boil water and tea, but not always for the statutory ten minutes, and at high altitudes the boiling point of water is so low that germs might not be killed. All running water should be assumed to be contaminated – wherever you go, there will be people, or at least animals, upstream.

Treating the water is not only the best line of defence against illness, it also reduces your reliance on boiled water. Iodine is the safest method, either in tablet form or, more commonly, as a two-percent liquid solution: use two to five drops per litre, depending on the cloudiness of the water, and wait at least twenty minutes before drinking; you might want to cover up the taste with powdered fruit drink. Chlorine-based tablets may not be effective against amebas and giardia. Ceramic filter pumps produce pure water without the aftertaste, although they're expensive and take up space.

See "Health and insurance" in *Basics* for tips on treating stomach upsets.

Minor injuries
Most minor injuries occur while walking downhill; **knee strains** are common, especially among trekkers carrying their own packs. If you know your knees are weak, bind them up with crepe (ace) bandages as a preventative measure, and hire a porter. Good, supportive boots reduce the risk of **ankle sprains** or twists. It's hard to avoid getting **blisters**, but make sure your boots are well broken in and always wear two pairs of socks, changing them regularly (especially if they get wet). Apply moleskin to hotspots as soon as they develop, making sure to clean and cover blisters so they can heal as quickly as possible.

Coping with altitude
Barraged by medical advice and horror stories, trekkers all too often develop altitude paranoia. The fact is that just about everyone who treks over 4000m experiences some mild symptoms of **acute mountain sickness (AMS)**, but serious cases are very rare, and the simple cure – descent – almost always brings immediate recovery.

CAUSES
At high elevations there is not only less oxygen but also lower atmospheric pressure, which can have all sorts of weird effects on the body: it can cause the brain to swell, cause the lungs to fill with fluid, and even bring on uncontrollable farting. The syndrome varies from one person to the next, and strikes without regard for fitness – in fact, young people seem to be more susceptible, possibly because they're more hung up about admitting they feel rotten. Most people are capable of acclimatizing to very high elevations, but the process takes time and must be

FIRST-AID CHECKLIST

Most of the following items can be purchased in Kathmandu or Pokhara for much less then they cost back home. This is a minimum first-aid kit – trekking guide-books usually give much longer lists. See "Health and Insurance" in *Basics* for tips on self-diagnosis, and use antibiotics advisedly.

FOR INJURIES
Band-Aids – large and small sizes.
Gauze pads
Sterile dressing
Surgical tape
Moleskin – synthetic adhesive padding for blisters.
Elastic support bandages – for knee strains, ankle sprains.
Antiseptic cream – for scrapes, blisters, insect bites.
Tweezers
Scissors
Thermometer – one that also reads low temperatures, in case of hypothermia.

FOR ILLNESSES
Aspirin/Paracetamol

Cold medicine
Throat lozenges – sore throats are common at high elevations.
Diarrhoea tablets
Jeevan Jal – a Nepali brand of oral rehydration formula for diarrhoea.
Tinidazole – an anti-protozoan, for giardia.
Antibiotic – Ciprofloxacin, Norfloxacin or Cephalosporin for intestinal bacteria, Erythromycin for throat/bronchial infections. Other drugs may also be used – consult a doctor or trekking guidebook.
Diamox – for treatment of mild AMS symptoms (optional).
Mycostatin – vaginal tablets for yeast infections.

done in stages. The golden rule is **don't go too high too fast**. Above 3000m, the daily net elevation gain should be no more than 500m; take mandatory acclimatization days at around 3500m and 4500m – more if you're feeling unwell – and try to spend these days day-hiking higher. These are only guidelines, and you'll have to regulate your ascent according to how you feel. Trekkers who fly directly to high airstrips have to be especially careful to acclimatize.

SYMPTOMS
AMS usually gives plenty of warning before it becomes life-threatening. Mild **symptoms** include headaches, dizziness, insomnia, nausea, loss of appetite, shortness of breath and swelling of the hands and feet; one or two of these shouldn't be cause for panic, but they're a sign that your body hasn't yet adjusted to the elevation. You shouldn't ascend further until you start feeling better, or, if you do keep going, you should be prepared to beat a hasty retreat if the condition gets worse. Serious symptoms – persistent vomiting, delirium, loss of co-ordination, bubbly breathing and bloody sputum, rapid heart rate or breathlessness at rest, blueness of face and lips – can develop within hours, and if ignored can result in death.

CURE
The only effective cure for advanced AMS is **descent**. Anyone showing serious symptoms should be taken downhill immediately, regardless of the time of day or night – hire a porter or pack animal to carry the sufferer if necessary. Recovery is usually dramatic, often after a descent of only a few hundred vertical metres.

Drink plenty of liquids at altitude – the body tends to retain water, and the air is incredibly dry. The usual adage is that you're not drinking enough unless you pee clear. Keeping warm, eating well, getting plenty of sleep and avoiding alcohol will also help reduce the chances of developing AMS. Some doctors recommend acetazolamide (a diuretic better known under the brand name **Diamox**) to relieve mild AMS symptoms, although it has to be stressed that this does nothing to treat the underlying cause of AMS; the dose is 250mg twice a day. For further advice on AMS, visit the *Himalayan Rescue Association*'s aid posts at Manang (on the Annapurna Circuit) and Pheriche (on the Everest trek).

OTHER DANGERS
Other altitude-related dangers such as **hypothermia** and **frostbite** are encountered less often by trekkers, but can pose real threats on high, exposed passes and in bad weather. Common-sense precautions bear repeating: wear or carry adequate clothing; keep dry; cover exposed extremities in severe weather; eat lots and carry emergency snacks; and make for shelter if conditions get bad. **Snowblindness** isn't a worry as long as you're equipped with a good pair of sunglasses.

Emergencies
Ninety-nine percent of the time, trekking in Nepal is a piece of cake and it's hard to imagine something going wrong. But while few trekkers ever have to deal with **emergencies** – illness, AMS, storms, missteps, landslides and avalanches are the main causes – they can happen to anyone.

Bezruchka's *A Guide to Trekking in Nepal* (see "Books" in *Contexts*) gives full advice on emergency **procedures** and a rundown of hospitals, aid posts, airstrips and radio transmitters found near the main trekking routes. In non-urgent cases, your best bet is to be carried by porter or pack animal to the nearest **airstrip** or **hospital**, although bear in mind that medical facilities outside Kathmandu and a few other major cities are very rudimentary. Where the situation is more serious, send word to the nearest village equipped with a radio to request a **helicopter rescue**. A typical rescue costs $1200–2000, and they won't come for you until they're satisfied you'll be able to pay; being registered with your embassy will speed the process of contacting relatives who can vouch for you.

Trekking life

A trek, it's often said, is not a wilderness experience. Unlike other mountain ranges, the Himalaya are comparatively well settled, farmed and grazed – much of their beauty, in fact, is man-made – and the trails support a steady stream of local traffic. If you're trekking independently, you'll be sleeping and eating in teahouses and making equal contact with locals and other foreigners. You'll need a good deal of adaptability to different living situations, but the payback comes in cultural insights, unforgettable encounters, and of course breathtaking scenery.

The trailhead is typically reached at the end of a long, bumpy bus ride, and **getting there** is an integral part of the experience. This is also a big factor in deciding where to trek, as the going and returning can eat up two days (or more) and, in the case of far-flung treks reached by plane, can represent the single biggest expense. See *Basics* for general information on bus and air travel.

CONSERVATION TIPS

The main environmental problem in the Himalaya is **deforestation**, and trekking puts an additional strain on local wood supplies – it's been estimated that one trekker consumes, directly and indirectly, between five and ten times more wood per day than a Nepali. In addition, trekkers leave litter, strain local sanitation systems and contribute to water pollution. The following are suggestions on how to minimize your impact on the fragile Himalayan environment.

- Where the choice exists, eat at teahouses that cook with kerosene or electricity instead of wood.
- Bring plenty of warm clothes so you (and your porter) are less reliant on wood fires to keep warm.
- Try to time your meals and co-ordinate your orders with other trekkers; cooking food in big batches is a more efficient use of fuel.
- If trekking with an agency, see that all meals are cooked with kerosene, and complain if they aren't.
- Use latrines wherever possible. Where there's no facility, encourage the innkeeper to build one; go well away from water sources, and bury your feces.

- Try not to take hot showers, except in inns where the water is heated by electricity, solar panels or fuel-efficient "back boilers".
- Treat water with iodine instead of asking innkeepers to fill your canteen with boiled water.
- Burn your toilet paper – there's nothing worse than the sight of pink toilet paper littering a beautiful mountain scene, and it can also spread disease. Better yet, don't use toilet paper at all – use water, as Nepalis do.
- Use biodegradable soap and shampoo, and don't rinse directly in streams.
- Carry all non-burnable litter back out – that includes tins and especially batteries.

Trails

The **walking** slays everyone at first, but you find your own rhythm after a few days. Most people take it in easy stages, from one glass of *chiya* to the next – there's no race to the top. It's best to set off early each morning to make the most of the clear weather, as clouds usually roll in around midday. Pad your schedule for rest days, weather and contingencies, and make time for at least one unusual side trip – that's when things get really interesting.

Trails are often steep and rough, and bridges precarious, but getting lost is seldom a worry. Stopping to chat and ask directions is part of the fun, and a good opportunity to learn some Nepali. **Trekking alone** is safe, but try to stay within sight of other people, as there have been a few mysterious disappearances over the years. Nepalis think all lone travellers are a bit odd, so you might find it worthwhile teaming up with others just to avoid the constant question, *Eklai?* ("Alone?"). Be sure to read "Cultural Hints" in *Basics*; again, *don't* give pens or rupees to children, whether they ask or not – if you do, every trekker that comes after you will be hounded for handouts.

Teahouses

Teahouses along the major trekking routes are efficient little operations, with English signs, menus and usually an English-speaking manager. Although they cater exclusively to trekkers and their porters, these tourist teahouses follow the Nepali tradition of providing practically free lodging – usually Rs20 or less a night – to dinner customers. Separate rooms are available at the most popular stopping places, but elsewhere dormitory accommodation is the rule. The beds may or may not come with padding; a sleeping bag is obligatory and a foam mat comes in handy. Many places have wood stoves and a growing number have electricity.

You'll find fewer comforts on **less-trekked trails**, however, where lodgings are likely to have private kitchens and meals are eaten by the fire amid eye-watering smoke. Such places rarely advertise themselves, but once you've spent a little time off the beaten track you'll start realizing that almost every trailside house with an open front is potential shelter.

Food and drink

Trekking cuisine is a world unto itself. Although teahouses' plastic-coated cardboard menus promise tempting international delicacies, items often turn out to be permanently *paindaina* (unavailable), and you'll notice that the "spring roll" wrappings, "enchilada" tortillas, "pizza" crusts and "pancakes" all bear more than a passing resemblance to chapatis. But at any rate, eggs, porridge, custard and even (sometimes) apple pie are all reassuringly familiar, and goodies like chocolate and muesli are available on the main trails.

However, many trekkers order "Western" food simply because it's there, not because it's good, and indeed it costs much more than **local food**. In highland areas you'll be able to eat such Tibetan dishes as *momo, thukpa* and *riki kur*, and instead of porridge you might be served *tsampa* (see "Eating and drinking" in *Basics*); at lower elevations, *daal bhaat* and packet noodles are the standard offerings. A further advantage of eating local fare is that it's almost always quicker: there are usually unlimited quantities of *daal bhaat* steaming away on the back burner, whereas foreign food has to be made specially. On less-travelled routes, where *daal bhaat* and potatoes are often the only food available, you'll have to force yourself to eat large amounts to get enough calories and protein (you might also want to bring vitamin tablets).

When **ordering**, bear in mind that the cook can only make one or two things at a time, and there may be many others ahead of you: simplify the process by co-ordinating your order with other trekkers. Most innkeepers expect dinner orders to be placed several hours in advance, and there's usually a dog-eared notepad floating around on which you're meant to keep a tally of everything you've eaten. Pay when you leave, and be sure to bring plenty of small money on the trek, since innkeepers often have trouble changing anything over Rs100.

Tea and "hot lemon" are the main **drinks** on the trail. Bottled soft drinks, water and even beer are common along the popular routes, but the price of each bottle rises by about Rs10 for each extra day it has to be portered from the nearest road. Don't miss trying *chhang, raksi* and *tongba* – again, see *Basics* for fuller explanations of these alcoholic specialities.

Sanitation

Washing and toilet facilities, where they exist, are primitive. You'll generally have to bathe and do laundry under makeshift outdoor taps in freezing cold water, which explains why hot springs are such major attractions. Teahouses in the Annapurna and Everest regions generally provide hot water for washing, and some even rig up primitive shower cubicles, but this is an environmentally dubious practice. An increasing number of teahouses are installing outdoor latrines (*chaarpi*), but don't be surprised if you're pointed to a half-covered privy hanging over a stream, or simply to a paddock.

THE TREKS

Nepal's mountains can be divided into five regions, the first three being most suitable for first-time trekkers. On a limited budget and schedule, you'll be restricted to the **Annapurna** and **Helambu–Langtang** regions, north of Pokhara and Kathmandu respectively. Given more time or money, you'll be able to tackle **Everest** or some of the longer Annapurna routes. With experience, or a sense of adventure, you should consider treks in the more remote regions of **eastern** and **far western Nepal**.

The sections below give overviews of the areas and describe the major trekking possibilities within them, but if you want a step-by-step route description you'll need a full-blown trekking guidebook (see *Contexts*). The box on the next page summarizes the major teahouse treks.

North of Pokhara: Annapurna

About sixty percent of all trekking permits are issued for the **Annapurna** region north of Pokhara. The popularity is well deserved, since nowhere else do you get such a rich feast of spectacular scenery and varied hill culture. Compared to most other regions, **logistics** are simple: treks all start or finish close to Pokhara, and transportation to trailheads is well developed; with great views just three days up the trail, short treks are particularly feasible. Pokhara is the only place outside Kathmandu with a Central Immigration office that issues **trekking permits**, and the Pokhara office is, if anything, saner than Kathmandu's. If your trek starts and ends in Pokhara, you'll be able to store excess luggage and **rent equipment** there as well.

That said, the popular treks in the Annapurna region have become **highly commercialized** and culturally rather tame – this is the Costa del Trekking. To be fair, most trekkers regard familiar food, mattresses, English signs and Western company as pluses, but if you're looking to get away from it all, look elsewhere.

Annapurna Himal faces Pokhara like an enormous settee, 40km across and numbering nine peaks over 7000m, with Annapurna I above all at 8091m. It's an area of stunning diversity, ranging from the sodden bamboo forests of the southern slopes (Lumle, northwest of Pokhara, is the wettest village in Nepal) to windswept desert (Jomosom, in the northern rain shadow, is the driest). The *himal* and adjacent hill areas are protected within the **Annapurna Conservation Area Project** (ACAP), for which you have to pay a Rs200 **entry fee** (expect this to increase substantially) when applying for your trekking permit. The money goes to a good cause. A quasi-park administered by a non-governmental trust, ACAP has won high praise for its holistic approach to tourist management. Its twofold aims are to protect the area's natural and cultural heritage, while at the same time ensuring sustainable economic and social benefit for local people. The project has set up kerosene depots to wean innkeepers away from wood fuel, while latrines and rubbish pits are being constructed to cope with the strain trekkers put on local sanitation. Meanwhile, ACAP is training lodge owners in the basics of hygiene and hotel management; to their credit, lodges with ACAP certificates are usually run to high standards.

TREKS AT A GLANCE

Trek	Days*	Best Months	Elevation (m)	Difficulty	Comments
Helambu	3–10	Oct–April	800–3600	Moderate	Easy access, uncrowded, varied; only modest views.
Gosainkund	5–7	Oct–Dec, Feb–May	1950–4380	Strenuous	Sacred lakes; festival in July–August.
Poon Hill	5–8	Oct–April	1100–3200	Moderate	Easy access, excellent views; very commercial.
Siklis	4–7	Oct–April	1100–2200	Moderate	Easy access; need 2 days' supplies.
Rara	6–8	Oct–Nov, April–June	2400–3500	Moderate	Fly in; must be prepared to camp; pristine lake and forest.
Pokhara – Trisuli	7–10	Nov–March	400–1450	Easy	Pleasant hill walk, snow-free in winter; basic teahouses.
Dolpa	7–14	April–Sept	2100–5110	Strenuous	Fly in; remote and rugged, must be self-sufficient.
Langtang	8–12	Oct–May	1700–3750	Moderate	Beautiful alpine valley close to Kathmandu.
Lower Kali Gandaki	8–12	Nov–March	900–3200	Moderate	Longer version of Poon Hill, returning a less commercial way.
Annapurna Sanctuary	9–12	Oct–Dec, Feb–April	1100–4130	Moderate/ Strenuous	Spectacular scenery, easy access; acclimatization necessary.
Dhorpatan circuit	10–14	Oct–April	470–3400	Moderate	May need guide, shelter and food.
Jomosom/ Muktinath	12–16	Oct–April	1100–3800	Moderate	Spectacular, varied; very commercial.
Everest (Lukla fly-in)	14–18	Oct–Nov, March–May	2800–5550	Strenuous	Superb scenery; flights a problem; acclimatization necessary.
Annapurna circuit	16–21	Oct–Dec, March–April	450–5380	Strenuous	Incredible diversity and scenery; high pass requires care and acclimatization.
Everest (Jiri walk-in)	26+	Oct–Nov, March–April	1500–5550	Very strenuous	Wonderful mix of hill and high-elevation walking, but with a lot of up and down.
Everest (E. approach)	30+	Nov, March	300–5550	Very strenuous	Similar, but with an even greater net vertical gain.

* Not including transport to and from trailhead.

THE ANNAPURNA REGION

Weather-wise, autumn is the **best season** for treks around Annapurna, but winter is fine for the shorter, lower treks, and much less crowded; spring can be disappointingly hazy, and quite hot at the lower elevations from mid-April on. The region is covered by ACAP's reasonably accurate "Annapurna" (1:125,000) **map**; cheaper, but less reliable, is the *Mandala* "Round Annapurna" (1:125,000).

The Jomosom trek

The **JOMOSOM TREK** is an acknowledged classic: an ideal sampler of Himalayan scenery and culture, and, not surprisingly, the most commercialized stretch of trail in Nepal. A guide definitely isn't necessary. **Food and lodging** are of a relatively high standard, and many lodges have electricity and hot showers; all have English menus and outdo each other with the Westernness of their cuisine. For this they charge **higher prices** than on any other trek: for basic food, drink and lodging you need to budget about Rs300–400 ($6–8) per day.

The full Jomosom trek takes about two weeks, but the trail network is extensive, so shorter and longer variations are possible; the first half of the trek, which can be done on its own, is described first. The usual **starting point** is moving

A lead donkey heading
up the Thak Khola

slowly uphill: at the time of writing, the procedure was to take a taxi from Pokhara to Phedi, but the road has been extended to the Kali Gandaki, just south of Birethanti, and is bound eventually for Baglung, Beni and Jomosom (see p.216). By 1994 the road should be paved to the Kali Gandaki, which will chop two or three days off treks in this area. Less conventional types might want to start the trek by boat from Lakeside (see p.223) or by trail via Sarangkot (p.212).

To Poon Hill

If you haven't time to do the full Jomosom trek, you can get a taster of it by turning the first half into a circuit of four to six days. The route ambles through steep, lush hill country, taking in some lovely Gurung villages and, weather permitting, rewarding you with outstanding views of the Annapurnas and Machhapuchhre. The **trails** are wide and well maintained, though steep in places. The highest point reached is 3200m, which shouldn't present any altitude problems, but it's high enough that you'll need **warm clothes** at night; rain gear is also advisable.

Several trails make for Poon Hill, all generally heading west of Pokhara. Most people start up the more southerly route, calling at **Naudanda** (or Nagdanda), **Kaare** and the picturesque stream-side village of **Birethanti**. A day and a half northwest of Birethanti, and 2000m higher, is **Poon Hill**: watching the mountains at sunrise from here is probably the single most done thing in the trekking universe. If clouds block your view, as they often do, it's well worth hanging on for an extra day. From Poon Hill, you can return through magnificent stands of giant **rhododendrons** dripping with **orchids** to the pretty Gurung town of **Ghandruk** (headquarters of ACAP), where the Annapurna Sanctuary trail heads north, and on back to Pokhara.

The Thak Khola

North of Poon Hill, the trail drops into the valley of the Kali Gandaki (locally called the **Thak Khola**) and the fun really begins: as you follow the course of the world's deepest gorge – the 8000-metre hulks of Dhaulagiri and Annapurna tower on either side – the scenery changes by the mile; the valley is also famous for its ethnic diversity, Thakalis being the dominant group.

The walking actually gets easier after Poon Hill (and by this time you should be in better shape), and the trail stays below 3000m until the last day's climb to Muktinath at 3800m – make way for the jingling donkey trains that feature so prominently in this area. There's essentially only one route through the Thak Khola, so unless you fly, **backtracking** is unavoidable; but by the same token, you can walk as far as you like and head back when you need to. The round trip

BHOTIYAS AND THAKALIS

Bhotiya is the Nepali term for all northern border peoples of Tibetan descent. Unfortunately, Bhotiyas themselves have tended to resent the label ever since an 1854 government edict, intended to find places for all minority groups in the Hindu caste system, placed them in the lowly category of "enslavable alcohol-drinkers" because they ate yak meat (which Hindus regarded as being almost as bad as eating beef). Most prefer to identify with a specific regional group, of which there are at least a dozen in Nepal; Sherpas, the best-known Bhotiya group, are highlighted in the Everest section later in this chapter.

In most ways, Bhotiyas are indistinguishable from Tibetans. Except in certain areas in the far west, where some have been influenced by Hinduism, they are exclusively **Buddhist**, and their *chorten* (stupa-like cremation monuments), *mani* walls (consisting of slates inscribed with the mantra *Om mani padme hum*), *gompa* (monasteries) and prayer flags (*lung ta*: literally, "wind horse") are the most memorable man-made features of the Himalaya. Farmers, herders and trans-Himalayan traders, they always settle higher and further north than other ethnic groups. The climate there is harsh, and life is a constant struggle to eke out a living. Bhotiya villages vary in appearance, but those in the Annapurna region are strongly Tibetan, with houses stacked up slopes so that the flat roof of one serves as the grain-drying terrace of the next. Like Tibetans, they like their tea flavoured with salt and yak butter, and married women wear trademark rainbow aprons (*pangden*) and wrap-around dresses (*chuba*).

Unencumbered by caste, Bhotiyas are noticeably less tradition-bound than Hindus, and **women** are better off for it: they play a more nearly equal role in household affairs, speak their minds openly, are able to tease and mingle with men publicly, and can divorce without stigma. Having said that, even Bhotiyas tend to consider a female birth to be the result of bad karma, and during death rites lamas customarily urge the deceased to be reincarnated as a male.

A hill group with influence far beyond their small numbers, the **Thakalis** are the ingenious traders, innkeepers and pony-handlers of the Thak Khola, the valley followed by the Jomosom trek. Their entrepreneurial flair goes back at least to the mid-nineteenth century, when the government awarded them a regional monopoly in the salt trade; since then, many have branched out into more exotic forms of commerce – importing electronics from Singapore and Hong Kong is a popular wheeze – while others have set up efficient inns in many parts of the western hills.

from Pokhara to Muktinath takes about two weeks. If you **fly** from Pokhara to Jomosom, or vice versa, you cut the time in half; there are three or four scheduled flights a day in the high season ($50), but they're often delayed or cancelled due to poor weather or visibility.

The towns of the Thak Khola are worthy destinations in their own right. **Tatopani** is renowned for its Western food, videos (cringe) and **hot springs** (*taato paani* means "hot water"). Further up, the trail passes through thick, monkey-infested forest to Tukche, once the main Thakali trading centre, and **Marpha**, a tidy, stone-clad village surrounded by apple and apricot orchards. **Day hikes** and overnight trips up from the valley floor are the best way to appreciate the incredible dimensions of the Thak Khola and the peaks around it: little-trekked trails lead to North Annapurna Base Camp, the Dhaulagiri Icefall and Dhampus Pass. Above Tukche, the vegetation dies out as you begin to enter the Himalayan rain shadow, and a savage, sand-blasting wind from the south makes it unpleasant to trek after midday. **Jomosom**, though it gives its name to the trek, is no place to linger unless you've got business at the airstrip – far more romantic is the fortress town of **Kagbeni**, only a couple of hours further on, with its medieval ruins and terracotta Buddhist figures. Geographically speaking, you're on the edge of the Tibetan plateau here, with the main Himalaya chain looming magnificently to the south.

Finally, it's a 1000-metre climb up a side valley – out of the wind, thankfully – to poplar-lined **Muktinath**, one of the most important religious sites in the Nepal Himalaya. The *Mahabharat* mentions Muktinath as the source of mystic *shaligram* fossils (see p.228); a priest will show you around the Newar-style temple and its wall of 108 water spouts, while further down the trail you'll find a Buddhist shrine that shelters two miraculous perpetual flames. Yartung, a madly exotic **festival** of horse-riding, is held at Muktinath around the full moon of August–September.

The lower Kali Gandaki

On the return journey, if you don't feel like slogging back up to Poon Hill, you can keep following the Kali Gandaki River south from Tatopani, a low-key **valley walk** with occasionally impressive views; since there's little up and down, it's possible to make good time. This route sees far fewer trekkers than the main Jomosom trail, so **accommodation** and **food** are cheap but rudimentary. At this low elevation the weather is balmy in winter, but in spring and early autumn the heat and mosquitoes are unpleasant. The trail passes through cultivated land and villages, where Magars and Gurungs are the dominant **ethnic groups**, as well as the big Newar bazaars of Beni, Baglung and Kusma. When the road from Pokhara is finished, this is bound to become a more popular escape route from the Jomosom area, but for the time being, starting and finishing points are Birethanti, Naudanda (on the Siddhartha Highway) or Tansen (see *The Western Hills*).

The Annapurna Sanctuary

The aptly named **ANNAPURNA SANCTUARY** is the most intensely scenic short trek in Nepal. From Ghandruk on the Jomosom route, the trail bears single-mindedly north into the very heart of the Annapurna range: following the short, steep Modi Khola, it soon leaves all permanent settlements behind, climbs through dense bamboo jungle and finally, rising above the vegetation line, makes for a narrow notch between the sheer lower flanks of Machhapuchhre and Hiunchuli. Once past this sanctuary "gate", it stumbles across moraines to a cluster of huts (sometimes still called "Machhapuchhre Base Camp") and, further on, to the so-called **Annapurna Base Camp**. Wherever you stand in the sanctuary, the 360-degree views are unspeakably beautiful, and although clouds roll in early, the curtain often parts at sunset to reveal radiant, molten peaks. The altitude is 4100m: bring warm gear.

The sanctuary can be treated as a week-long side trip from the Jomosom trek, or a ten- to twelve-day round trip from Pokhara, accessed from Phedi. The actual distance covered isn't great, but **altitude**, **weather** and **trail conditions** all tend to slow you down – the trail gains more than 2000m from Ghandruk to the sanctuary, so unless you're already well acclimatized you'd be wise to spread the climb over four days. Frequent precipitation makes the trail extremely slippery at the best of times, and in winter it can be impassable due to snow or avalanche danger. The many **lodges** above Chhomrong are seasonal, but getting more comfortable all the time, though **food** hasn't been one of their strong points ever since ACAP instituted a standard menu and removed all creative competition.

The Annapurna Circuit

The **ANNAPURNA CIRCUIT** is a challenging but rewarding three-week trek with excellent views, plenty of cultural contact and the greatest net vertical gain of all the popular routes. Starting in subtropical paddy at about 500m, the trail ascends steadily to the 5415-metre **Thorung La** (Thorung Pass) before returning along the previously described Jomosom route. A minimum of sixteen days is required, but a few extra days should be set aside for digressions, acclimatization and other contingencies. The trek is strenuous, and you'll need boots, gloves and very warm clothes for the pass, and a good four-season bag for a night spent at 4400m.

Although the eastern half of the circuit is much less developed for trekkers than the Jomosom side, **food and lodging** are always available, and somewhat cheaper (Rs250/$5 per day should be plenty). A guide isn't necessary. The full circuit is best done between mid-October and mid-December – crossing the Thorung La is risky from January till March, though not out of the question, while the lower parts of the trek are uncomfortably warm from April on. Snow can block the pass at any time of year, so be prepared to wait it out or go back down the way you came. You can **fly** in or out of Manang ($88 from Kathmandu, $50 from Pokhara), saving a week of walking, but *RNAC* runs only a limited and seasonal schedule.

Nearly everyone goes around the circuit anticlockwise, the only reason being that the Thorung La makes a longer climb from the Jomosom side, requiring an extra acclimatization day above Muktinath: the upshot of this is that if you go anticlockwise you'll be in step with the same people for the entire trek, whereas if you go clockwise you'll be constantly passing people coming the other way. The usual **starting point** is Dumre. In dry weather, surplus Russian army trucks shuttle from there along a primitive track to Besisahar (4hr, Rs75), cutting out the first day and a half of the trek – if all goes well, you can leave Kathmandu in the morning and be in Besisahar that night – but the truck ride is so ghastly that you may prefer to walk. If you're coming from Pokhara, you can avoid Dumre and instead follow the Pokhara–Trisuli trek (see below) to Besisahar in two days.

In the upper Marsyangdi Valley

The route follows the Marsyangdi Valley north and then west all the way to the pass. The first few days are a long preamble through terraced farmland and frequent villages, with only fleeting views to whet your appetite, but then, in the course of two days, the valley constricts and the trail climbs steeply, leaving the paddy behind and passing through successive climatic zones: temperate forest, coniferous forest, alpine meadows and finally the arid steppes of the rain shadow. The walk from Chame to **Manang** is spectacular and shouldn't be rushed. The sight of the huge, glacier-dolloped Annapurnas towering almost 5000m above the valley will stay with you forever. Manang is the largest town of the Manang-pa, the Bhotiya clan that has settled the upper Marsyangdi, and its architecture, like that of all the older villages here, is strongly Tibetan; *gompa* at Manang and Braga are well worth visiting. Manang also has an airstrip and a **Himalayan Rescue Association post**, where they give a daily talk on AMS. If you're going for the Thorung La, the next night will probably be spent at **Phedi**, a grotty place where you'll be woken up at 4am by trekkers who've been told (wrongly) that they have to clear the pass by 8am. The climb up the pass, and the knee-killing 1600-metre descent down the other side to Muktinath, is a tough but exhilarating day. The remainder of the circuit follows the Jomosom trek (see above).

Other Annapurna treks

Aside from the fact that they share some of the same trails, the following treks have nothing in common with the razzle-dazzle teahouse trails in the Annapurna area. You'll only find Nepali food and lodging along these trails, and except for the Pokhara–Trisuli route, you'll need to be equipped to spend nights out and cook for yourself. If you're not trekking with an agency, you'll need a **guide**.

Pokhara–Trisuli
The old **POKHARA–TRISULI** trail is little trekked now that it's been superseded by the Prithvi Highway, and that's its chief recommendation. A gentle, low-altitude trek, it wanders though typical hill country and dozens of laid-back ethnic villages, with Annapurna, Manaslu and Ganesh Himal popping up often enough to keep things ticking over scenically. This is the only serious trek that's snow-free all year, making it a good choice for winter.

The trek can be done in six days, but allow eight or ten; many trekkers start or finish at Gorkha, the midway point, for an easy outing of four to five days. There are any number of ways to get started from Pokhara, but to bypass a lot of road-walking, take a bus to Sisuwa (Begnas Tal) and take any trail heading east and north towards Besisahar on the Annapurna Circuit – try to go by way of **Ghanpokhara**, a lovely Gurung village – finally reaching Gorkha in a minimum of three days (more like five via Ghanpokhara). From there it's another four days or so of undulating between subtropical valleys and scenic ridges to Trisuli, which is linked by road with Kathmandu.

The Siklis trek
An uncrowded but scenic alternative to other short treks in the Annapurna region, the **SIKLIS TREK** is becoming increasingly popular with groups; independently, you'd have to travel with enough supplies to camp for two nights. The most satisfying of several possible itineraries takes a week, starting at Begnas Tal and heading north to the Madi Khola, then following the river's west bank up to well-preserved

Siklis (1980m), Nepal's biggest Gurung village, which looks across to the Lamjung Himal and Annapurnas II and IV. From here you strike westwards over the thickly forested ridge that separates the Madi and Seti drainages and then descend via Ghachok, another Gurung settlement, to reach the Birethanti road. Variations on this route are often touted as the "Royal Trek", after a rally-the-troops swing Prince Charles took through the area in 1980 to visit the villages of Gurkha recruits. ACAP is planning to develop this into a model ecotrekking route, so more facilities may be in the offing.

The Dhorpatan circuit

The **DHORPATAN CIRCUIT** breaks away from the Jomosom trek at Beni (see above) and wanders westwards up into high, open hill country with commanding views of Dhaulagiri Himal. The trail climbs steadily up a tributary of the Kali Gandaki, crossing a tough but beautiful 3400-metre pass and reaching the broad Dhorpatan Valley in about four days, where the attraction isn't the valley itself but the opportunities for exploring the huge **Dhorpatan Hunting Reserve** to its north. In a day, you can get up onto the 4100-metre summit immediately north of the valley for dynamite views; if you're prepared for a few nights out you can continue into the rugged Dhaulagiri area, check out mountaineering base camps and maybe even see some **blue sheep**.

Leaving Dhorpatan, two lower, less dramatic routes complete the circuit, one returning to Pokhara via Baglung and the other finishing at Tansen. Really ambitious, self-sufficient trekkers could take a high route north of Dhaulagiri (8167m) via the Mayangdi Khola and French and Dhampus passes, joining the Jomosom trek at Marpha.

Two weeks would be a realistic time frame for Dhorpatan. The circuit is fairly demanding, taking you a long way from conventional tourist places. Lodging is available throughout, but you'll have greater flexibility if you **bring your own equipment**. Anytime between October and April is fine for Dhorpatan, although in winter the high route may be blocked by snow.

Around Manaslu

It takes three weeks to trek **AROUND MANASLU**, a challenging circuit east of the Annapurna area that ventures into extremely remote country and over a 5200-metre pass. Government restrictions on travel in this area mean you need a special ($75 per week; $90 in Sept–Nov) trekking permit and a government liaison officer accompanying your group, plus you must be self-sufficient for a full week of the trip. The trek usually starts in Gorkha, first heading east and then north up the valley of the Budhi Gandaki, finally rounding behind Manaslu (8163m) over the Larkya La (5213m). From there it's two days down to Bagarchap on the Marsyangi River, the rest of the trek follows the Annapurna Circuit in reverse to Besisahar.

Mustang

Since 1991 trekkers have been allowed in limited numbers into **MUSTANG**, the high desert region north of Jomosom that still has its own nominal king. ACAP has taken over the management of the area for tourism purposes, but it's expensive to visit: $500 a week for the permit, plus the liaison officer's fee and agency expenses, since you can't come here independently. The starting point is Jomosom – groups usually fly in and out – and the trip takes a minimum of nine days, following the Thak Khola north to two walled cities before doubling back on the same trail.

North of Kathmandu: Helambu, Langtang and Gosainkund

Trekking **north of Kathmandu** is curiously underrated and uncrowded. The most accessible of all the trekking regions, it's well suited to one- or two-week itineraries, which is handy if you're trying to cram a trek into a short stay in Nepal or you don't want to stray far from Kathmandu. What it lacks in superlatives – there are no 8000-metre peaks in the vicinity (unless you count Shisha Pangma, across the border in Tibet) – it makes up for in base-to-peak rises that are as dramatic as anywhere. Langtang, in particular, delivers more amazing views in a short time than any other walk-in trek in Nepal, with the possible exception of the Annapurna Sanctuary.

Two distinct basins and an intervening *lekh* (ridge) lend their names to the major treks here; each stands on its own, but given enough time and good weather you can mix and match them. **Helambu** is closest to Kathmandu, comprising the rugged north–south valleys and ridges that lie just beyond the northeast rim of the Kathmandu Valley. North of Helambu, running east–west and tantalizingly close to the Tibet border, lies the high, alpine **Langtang Valley**, which in its upper reaches burrows spectacularly between Langtang and Jugal Himals. Northwest of Helambu, **Gosainkund** comprises a series of sacred lakes set on a high, treeless plateau. One practical inconvenience is that the connections between these three treks aren't reliable – snow often blocks the passes between Helambu and the other two – and done on their own, the Langtang and Gosainkund treks require you to retrace your steps for most of the return journey.

Food and lodging here is patchy, but never a problem on the usual routes, and isn't expensive – Rs200 ($4) a day should suffice, perhaps slightly more in Langtang. The area is covered by the *Mandala* and *Schneider* **maps**, both on the scale 1:100,000.

Helambu

HELAMBU (or Helmu) is great for short treks: access from Kathmandu is easy, and an extensive trail network enables you to tailor a circuit to your schedule. The area spans a wide elevation range – there's a lot of up and down – but you need not go higher than about 2700m, so acclimatization is rarely a consideration. Winter treks are particularly feasible. The peaks of Langtang Himal are often visible, but the views aren't as dramatic as those in other areas. Helambu was once considered a hidden, sacred domain, and its misty ridges and fertile valleys are still comparatively isolated; relatively few people trek here, and with so many trails to choose from, they tend to spread themselves out. The food is generally limited to *daal bhaat*. Helambu's Bhotiyas call themselves **Sherpa**, although they're only distant cousins of the Solu-Khumbu stock (see below): their ancestors probably migrated from Kyirong, the area just north of the Kodari border crossing. Tamangs are also numerous, while the valley bottoms are farmed mainly by Hindu castes.

Sundarijal, a local bus or taxi ride from Kathmandu, is the most common **starting point**, but alternative trailheads include Budhanilkantha, Sankhu, Kakani, Nagarkot and Panchkhal. However you go, first impressions are somewhat dispir-

HELAMBU, LANGTANG AND GOSAINKUND

iting – the Kathmandu Valley approaches are heavily populated, and the route from Panchkhal follows a road for several hours (buses ply at least to Sipa Ghat) – but things get progressively better as you move northwards. Most trekkers make a loop around two main ridges and the valley of the Malemchi Khola, trying to stay as high as possible and taking in the villages of **Malemchigaun**, **Tarke Ghyang** and **Shermathang**. The walk between the second two is especially rewarding, passing picturesque monasteries and contouring through forests of oak, rhododendron and daphne, whose bark is used to make paper. Birdlife is also abundant here.

Other variations on Helambu are more challenging. Gosainkund can be reached by a long day's walk from Malemchigaun, via a 4600-metre pass, but an overnight stop at Gopte (3430m) to acclimatize is advisable. The route to Langtang heads north from Tarke Ghyang over the 5122-metre **Ganja La**, a very tough three-day hike for which you'll need a tent, food, crampons and ice axe (it's usually impassable Jan–March). From Tarke Ghyang, obscure trails lead to **Panch Pokhri** (3800m), a set of lakes two or three days to the east, and from there you could continue east or south to the Arniko Highway. All these routes take you into Langtang National Park (entry fee Rs650).

Langtang and Gosainkund

In contrast with Helambu, the Langtang and Gosainkund treks make straight for specific destinations, gaining elevation quickly and then leaving you to explore at your own pace; to return, a certain amount of backtracking is unavoidable, unless you cross into Helambu. Culture is not a big part of either, except during Janai Purnima, a massive Hindu **pilgrimage** held at Gosainkund during the full moon of July–August.

Both treks **start** at Dhunche, about eight hours by bus from Kathmandu. Above Trisuli the road is unpaved and agonizingly slow, even though it's only 20km as the crow flies. The road has replaced what used to be the first two days of these treks, and Dhunche, an unmemorable administrative centre, has boomed since its completion.

Both treks fall within **Langtang National Park**; the **entry fee** of Rs650 is collected at Ramche, about halfway between Trisuli and Dhunche.

Langtang

The **LANGTANG TREK** can be done in as little as a week, but day hikes in the upper valley are sure to detain you for another two or three days. It takes about a day to get interesting, first following the continuation of the Dhunche road (a spectacularly destructive feat of engineering, built to reach a lead and zinc mine in the Ganesh Himal) up the unpromising valley of the Trisuli River before leaving the road and rounding a bend to Syabru in the Langtang Valley. The next two days are spent climbing briskly up the gorge-like lower valley, where oaks and rhododendron give way to peaceful hemlock and larch forest; after ascending an old moraine, snowy peaks suddenly loom ahead and the gorge opens into a U-shaped glacial valley. Springtime is excellent for flowers here, and in autumn the berberis bushes turn a deep rust colour.

Two Bhotiya villages occupy the upper valley: **Langtang** (3300m), the bigger of the two, makes a good place to spend a night and acclimatize, while **Kyangjin** (3750m) boasts a small *gompa*, a cheese "factory" (fabulous yoghurt) and an attractive chalet-lodge. The Langtang Glacier is a full day's walk further up the valley. You'll want to spend at least a couple of nights in the upper valley to explore the glaciers and ascend the 5033-metre **Yala Peak** (Tsergo Ri), from which you can view an awesome white wilderness of peaks, including 8013-metre Shisha Pangma.

You can **return** by crossing into Helambu over the Ganja La (see above), but most people go back down the valley, varying the trip by going via Khangjung, high up on the grassy northern side, and Syabrubensi, site of a Tibetan resettlement project. To link up with Gosainkund, you have to backtrack to Syabru.

Pilgrims walking to Gosainkund

Gosainkund

GOSAINKUND can be trekked on its own in as little as five days, but because of its high elevation – 4380m – it's perhaps best done after acclimatizing in Langtang or Helambu. Combined with either of these, it adds three or four days; a grand tour of all three areas takes sixteen or more days.

From either Dhunche or Syabru, trails lead up through rhododendron forest to the monastery and cheese factory of **Sing Gompa** (3250m). Above here, the trail climbs through more forest before emerging above the tree line for great views of Manaslu and Ganesh, and finally reaching a high, barren plateau. At least two rough-and-ready lodges sit by the shore of Gosainkund, the most sacred of the half-dozen **lakes** here that Hindus associate with various gods. A famous legend recounts how Shiva, having saved the world by drinking a dangerous poison, struck this mountainside with his *trisul* to create the lake and cool his burning throat. In good weather you can climb a nearby summit (5144m) for superb views.

Everest (Solu-Khumbu)

Everest – or to give it its proper Nepali name, **Sagarmatha** ("Brow of the Ocean"), or its even more proper Sherpa name, **Chomolungma** ("Mother Goddess of the World") – seems to be more of a pilgrimage than a trek. As with all pilgrimages, it is a tough personal challenge with a clear goal at the end. Lasting images, however, are of the revelations along the way: remote monasteries, irrepressible Sherpas, and peaks with almost human moods and personalities. Prior experience isn't strictly necessary, but treks in this region require extra effort.

The Everest region is the main trekking destination east of Kathmandu, and in terms of popularity it runs a rather distant second to Annapurna. It divides into two distinct areas, the lower, greener and more populous country to the south being **Solu** – if you're not flying in, you'll probably begin at Jiri and spend the first week of your trek walking eastwards across Solu's deep canyons and tall ridges. **Khumbu**, wedged between Solu and the Tibetan border, comprises the spectacular, harsh landscape of Everest and the surrounding peaks and glaciated valleys.

The dilemma of **getting there** puts many people off. The choice is between **flying** into Lukla, at 2800m on the doorstep of Khumbu ($83 from Kathmandu; note the wrecked planes beside the runway), and taking the **bus** to Jiri in Solu (which adds 5–7 days' walking each way). In an ideal world, you would walk in from Jiri to get acclimatized, and fly out of Lukla to avoid backtracking, but it seldom works out that way: high-season flights are often booked up by organized trekking parties or grounded due to bad weather. Largely for this reason, more than half the people who trek Everest go with a group.

The walking in Solu is very strenuous, while in Khumbu, **altitude** is the overriding factor – to get a good look at Everest, you'll have to spend at least four nights above 4000m and at least one at around 5000m. There is a risk of developing acute mountain sickness (AMS) and you must know the signs. Not only is this the highest of the standard treks, it's also the **coldest**, so you'll need a good four-season bag, several layers of warm clothes, and sturdy boots that will keep

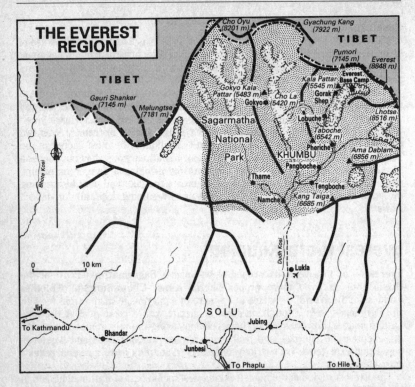

THE EVEREST REGION

TIBET

Cho Oyu (8201 m)

Gyachung Kang (7922 m)

TIBET

Pumori (7145 m)

Everest (8848 m)

Everest Base Camp

Gauri Shanker (7145 m)

Melungtse (7181 m)

Kala Pattar (5545 m)

Gokyo Kala Pattar (5483 m)

Cho La (5420 m)

Gorak Shep

Gokyo

Lhotse (8516 m)

Sagarmatha

Lobuche

National

Taboche (6542 m)

Pheriche

Park

KHUMBU

Ama Dablam (6856 m)

Pangboche

Thame

Tengboche

Namche

Kang Taiga (6685 m)

Bhote Kosi

Dudh Kosi

0   10 km

Lukla

SOLU

Jubing

Jiri

To Kathmandu

Bhandar

Junbesi

To Phaplu

To Hile

out mud and snow. A great help on this front are the well-stocked rental shops of Namche, in Khumbu, where you can stock up on high-altitude gear and return it on the way back down. Because of weather, the **trekking "window"** is especially short in Khumbu – early October to mid-November, and late March to late April – and this, in turn, creates a seasonal stampede on the trails and at the Lukla airstrip. Winter isn't out of the question, but it's just that much colder.

While Everest isn't nearly as heavily trekked as Annapurna, its high-altitude **environment** is even more fragile. Khumbu, with only 4000 inhabitants, receives more than 9000 trekkers a year (plus probably twice as many porters); locals spend three times longer collecting firewood than they did a decade ago, and the demand for wood is now estimated to be three times the regeneration capacity of the area. Even some trek leaders privately admit that the best thing for Khumbu would be to give it a rest from trekking for a few years. Most of Khumbu is protected within **Sagarmatha National Park**, which is helping to preserve the remaining forest, but it can't be said often enough: have as little to do with wood-burning as possible.

The popular trails through Solu-Khumbu are all equipped with **teahouses**. The main Jiri–Lukla–Namche–Base Camp route is very straightforward, but a **guide** is advisable if you're planning to do anything unusual. Solu-Khumbu is the easiest area in Nepal to hire a **woman porter** – a Sherpani – although few speak enough English to serve as guides.

Solu: the Jiri walk-in

The **JIRI WALK-IN** is the most popular Everest approach, as Jiri is connected by bus to Kathmandu, and innkeepers along the trail are reasonably accustomed to serving Westerners (other approaches are described later in the "Eastern Nepal" section). The **bus** is no picnic, though, taking anywhere from nine to thirteen hours – experienced climbers often joke that they'd scale Everest tomorrow but they'll never take the bus to Jiri again. It's also possible to catch one of the three **flights** a week to Phaplu, four days east of Jiri, though it's not much cheaper ($77) than flying all the way to Lukla, three days further on.

Cutting across the lay of the land, the trail bobs between valleys as low as 1500m and passes as high as 3500m: the ups and downs can be disheartening, but the fitness and acclimatization gained come in handy later on. A few glimpses of peaks – notably Gauri Shankar (7145m) – urge you along during the first five or six days, although Solu's lasting images are of tumbling gorges, rhododendron forests and terraced fields hewn out of steep hillsides. In the past thirty years Solu has benefited from several projects funded by **Edmund Hillary's Himalayan Trust**; groups of children may accompany you on their way to one of the "Hillary" schools in the area.

The route passes through some important Sherpa villages, notably Bhandar and Junbesi, the latter with an active monastery. Most trekkers are

---

THE SHERPAS

Nepal's most famous ethnic group, the **Sherpas** probably migrated to Solu-Khumbu four or five centuries ago from eastern Tibet; their name means "People from the East". They were originally nomads, driving their yaks to pasture in Tibet and wintering in Nepal, until change came from an unlikely quarter: the introduction of the potato in the 1830s is believed to have been the catalyst that caused Sherpas to settle in villages, and the extra wealth brought by this simple innovation financed the building of most monasteries visible today.

Sherpas maintain the highest permanent settlements in the world – up to 4700m – which accounts for their legendary hardiness at altitude. Their mountaineering talents were discovered as early as 1907, and by the 1920s hundreds of Sherpas were signing on as **porters** with expeditions to Everest and other Himalayan peaks – from the Tibet side, ironically, as Nepal was closed at the time. When mountaineering expeditions were finally allowed into Nepal in 1949, Sherpas took over the lion's share of the portering work, and four years later **Tenzing Norgay** reached the top of Everest, clinching Sherpas' worldwide fame. The break couldn't have come at a better time, for trans-Himalayan trade, once an important source of income, was cut short by the Chinese occupation of Tibet in 1959. Since then, Sherpas have deftly diversified into tourism, starting their own trekking and mountaineering agencies, opening lodges and selling souvenirs; conveniently, the trekking season doesn't conflict with summer farming duties.

Like Tibetans and other Bhotiya groups, Sherpas are devout Buddhists – most villages of note support a *gompa* and a few monks (or nuns) – but in a throwback to animism that's perfectly permissible in Lamaist Buddhism, they revere **Khumbila**, a sacred peak just north of Namche, as a sort of tribal totem, and regard fire as a deity (it's disrespectful to throw rubbish into a Sherpa hearth). Sherpas eat meat, of course, but in deference to *dharma* they draw the line at slaughtering it – they hire Tibetans to do that.

understandably impatient to get up to Everest or back to Kathmandu, but **side trips** to the cheese "factory" at Thodung and the Thubten Chholing *gompa* north of Junbesi are fascinating. From **Jubing**, a Rai (see *The Eastern Tarai*) village five days in, the trail finally bends north towards Everest, following the valley of the Dudh Kosi. Two days later, it sidesteps **Lukla** and joins the well-trodden route to Khumbu.

The bulk of traffic through Solu consists of porters humping in gear for trekking groups and expeditions flying into Lukla, and this is reflected in the no-frills **food and lodging** available. You'll have a hard time spending more than Rs250 ($5) a day here. Solu is covered by the *Mandala* "Lamosangu to Mount Everest" **map** (1:110,000), though *Schneider's* "Tamba Kosi" and "Shorong/Hinku" (both 1:50,000) show the route in greater detail.

Khumbu: the Everest trek

The trail north from Lukla is the trunk route of the **EVEREST TREK**: everyone walks it at least once, and all but a few backtrack along it as well. Most trekkers follow it to the end at Kala Pattar (the classic viewpoint of Everest) and Everest Base Camp, both about eight days northeast of Lukla; quite a few combine this with a trip to the beautiful Gokyo Lakes, about the same distance north of Lukla.

Khumbu **lodges** are heavily geared for trekkers, and you should have no trouble getting a bunk and a good meal wherever you go along the busier trails (in Lukla and Namche you can even get hot showers and cinnamon rolls). **Prices** aren't unreasonable, considering the distance supplies have to be carried, and daily expenses should come to around Rs300 ($6) a day, rising to Rs400 ($8) a day higher up – that's if you don't drink too many Cokes, which cost as much as Rs100. An additional expense is the Rs650 **entry fee** for Sagarmatha National Park.

Khumbu is well **mapped**. By far the best for the area north from Namche is *Schneider's* "Khumbu Himal" (1:50,000), while *Mandala's* "Khumbu Himal" (1:50,000) covers the route from Lukla north. An even more detailed map of the immediate Everest area, originally created for *National Geographic* and now reprinted, is available in some Kathmandu bookshops.

Lukla to Everest Base Camp and Kala Pattar

From Lukla the trail meanders north along the Dudh Kosi before bounding up to **Namche** (3450m), where Khumbu and the serious scenery start. Nestled handsomely in a horseshoe bowl, the Sherpa "capital" has done very well out of mountaineering and trekking over the years. Besides trekking equipment, Namche's shops sell absolutely anything a trekker could desire – film, maps, batteries, Mars bars from around the world, a dozen styles of Swiss Army knife, albeit all at inflated prices – and there's also a bank and post office. Most lodges have electricity (one even has a microwave oven). Try to make your trip coincide with the pan-cultural **Saturday market**, or visit the national park **visitors' centre**, perched on the ridge east of town, which contains an informative museum. About an hour north of Namche stands the recently reopened *Everest View Hotel*, the only luxury hotel anywhere in the Nepal Himalaya ($310 for a double – oxygen in every room!).

Beyond Namche, the trail veers northeast into a tributary valley and climbs to **Tengboche**, surrounded by protected juniper forest and commanding a show-stealing view of everybody's favourite peak, Ama Dablam. Tengboche's much-photographed monastery burned down in January 1989 when its newly installed electrical wiring malfunctioned (is there a lesson in this?). The monastery, rebuilt at a cost of $220,000, should be operational by the time you read this, although the painting of interior frescoes won't be completed for several more years. Mani Rimdu, the Sherpa dance-drama **festival**, is held here on the full moon of November–December. The trail continues to **Pangboche**, containing Khumbu's oldest *gompa*, where for a donation the lama will show you some yeti relics, and on to **Pheriche** (4250m), site of a **Himalayan Rescue Association post** (AMS talks every afternoon during the trekking season). From here up, settlements are strictly seasonal, and their stone enclosures and slate-roofed huts are reminiscent of Scottish crofts.

From Pheriche the route bends north again, ascending the moraine of the Khumbu Glacier and passing a series of monuments to Sherpas killed on Everest, to reach **Lobuche** (4930m). Another day's march along the glacier's lateral moraine brings you to **Gorak Shep** (5180m), the last huddle of teahouses – and a cold, probably sleepless night. The payoff comes when you climb up the grassy mound of **Kala Pattar** (5545m): the extra height provides an unbelievable panorama, not only of **Everest** (8848m) but also of its neighbours Lhotse (Nepal's third-highest peak, at 8516m) and Nuptse (7861m), as well as the sugarloaf of Pumori (7165m). A separate day trip can be made across the amazing Khumbu Glacier to **Everest Base Camp**. You may encounter a half-dozen or more expedition parties here, constantly ferrying supplies up the dangerous Khumbu Icefall to higher camps; the climbers may be happy to have well-wishers, but if they seem wary of trekkers you can't blame them.

Gokyo Lakes

The scenery is every bit as good at **Gokyo Lakes**, in the next valley to the west, and other trekkers are noticeably fewer. If you're equipped to spend a night out in a yak-herder's hut and are good at route-finding (the *Schneider* map will help), you can be there in two days from Gorak Shep, crossing the strenuous 5420-metre **Cho La** (Pass) west of Lobuche and descending a treacherous scree slope. Otherwise, you'll have to backtrack almost to Tengboche, and then follow the Dudh Kosi north for two days to Gokyo, set beside the immense Ngozumba Glacier (the biggest in Nepal). Several brilliant blue lakes, dammed up by the glacier's lateral moraine, dot the west side of the valley above and below Gokyo. The

Namche bazaar

EVEREST

In 1849, while taking routine measurements from the plains, members of the Survey of India logged a previously unnoted summit which they labelled simply Peak XV. Three years later, computations revealed it to be the world's highest mountain, and the British subsequently named it after **Sir George Everest**, head of the Survey of India from 1823 to 1843. Politically off-limits until the early twentieth century, the climb to the summit was first attempted from the Tibetan side in 1922 by a British party that included **George Mallory**, who coined the famous "because it is there" phrase. Two years later, Mallory and Andrew Irvine reached at least 8500m – without oxygen – before disappearing into a cloud; their bodies were never found, but some believe that they reached the summit. Several more attempts were made until World War II suspended activities, and climbs were further hampered by the Chinese invasion of Tibet in 1950, which closed the northern approach to mountaineers.

With the opening of Nepal in 1951, however, attention turned to southern approaches and a race between the Swiss and the British was on. The mountain was finally scaled, using a route via the South Col, by New Zealander **Edmund Hillary** and Sherpa **Tenzing Norgay** in a British-led expedition in 1953. On the morning of May 29, Hillary planted the Union Jack, the Nepalese and United Nations flags on the summit; Tenzing left an offering of sweets and biscuits to the mountain's gods.

Throughout the next two decades, increasingly big expeditions put men and women on the top by various routes, and sometimes got carried away in their bids for lucrative sponsorship – in 1970 a Japanese, Yuiichi Miura, skied most of the way down the mountain, breaking a number of bones in the process. Since the mid-1970s the trend has been away from large-scale assaults in favour of small, quick "alpine-style" ascents. Dominating the field for more than a decade, Austrian **Reinhold Messner** was one of two climbers to reach the summit without oxygen in 1978, and in 1980 he made the first successful solo ascent of Everest. The mountain continues to attract as many as thirty expeditions a year, mainly from the Nepal side – thirty people reached the summit on a single day in May 1992.

high point of Gokyo is an overlook called, again, **Kala Pattar**, surveying a clutter of blue teeth – Cho Oyu, Everest and Lhotse are just the ones over 8000m – and the long grey tongue of the Ngozumba Glacier. You can also scramble north beside the glacier as far as Cho Oyu Base Camp.

Eastern Nepal

Treks in **eastern Nepal** are hampered by a fundamental problem of access: Hile, the usual trailhead, is two days from Kathmandu by bus. However, it's possible to enter (or leave) this region by way of Everest, which cuts out the long ride in one direction. Flights are also good value for money here – the one from Kathmandu to Tumlingtar costs only $44. **Food and lodging** is patchy, though, and seldom geared for trekkers.

You're supposed to have a white "mixed-area" **permit** to trek in this region, but no one is going to hassle you if you've got an Everest permit and you're just passing through on your way down. The only trekking **map** of the area is the *Mandala* "Dhankuta to Kanchenjunga, Mt Everest, Makalu & Arun Valley" (1:192,500).

Ethnically, eastern Nepal is even more diverse than the Annapurna region: Rais and Limbus are dominant in the hills, Gurungs and Magars are found in smaller numbers, while Sherpas, Tamangs and other Bhotiyas inhabit the high country and Hindu castes the valleys. Everest, Makalu and Kanchenjunga provide stunning **views** from most high points. Flora and fauna are also of great interest to specialists, especially the **butterflies** and other insects of the upper Arun Valley, and the **rhododendrons** of the Milke Danda, a long ridge east of the Arun.

The Everest eastern approach

While still not nearly as developed as the Jiri walk-in, the **EASTERN APPROACH** to Everest is becoming more popular and facilities along it are expanding yearly. It's usually treated as an "escape route" from Everest by trekkers who want to avoid the long backtrack to Jiri; there's no reason why the itinerary can't be done in reverse, except perhaps that it's better to gain some confidence on the more developed Everest trails before tackling this less-trekked region. Another factor to consider is the **season**: try to do the lower section of the trek when it's cooler.

The **route** leaves the Jiri walk-in at **Kharte**, about a day south of Lukla, and heads southeastwards to reach Tumlingtar five to seven days later. Part of this stretch traverses the planned Makalu-Barun Conservation Area (see below), and an entrance fee may soon be required. The first half of the route passes through tangled hills inhabited mainly by Rais; after reaching a high point at the lush and wild Salpa Bhanjyang (3350m), it descends steadily to the deep, hot and predominantly Hindu Arun Valley. **Tumlingtar** is a busy bazaar overlooking the Arun; *RNAC* flies from there to Kathmandu about four times a week ($44), although the flights are often booked up for some time in advance. If you're returning to Kathmandu by bus, carry on to Hile (see *The Eastern Tarai*), two days south and 1400m higher; alternatively, you could walk another week from Tumlingtar **to Ilam** (see *The Eastern Tarai*) by way of Chainpur, a tidy village renowned for its brassware. Both routes are eqipped with **teahouses** and a guide isn't needed, but don't expect English signs or any fancy food – you'd be wise to bring a few days' worth of provisions just in case.

At least one **other route** aims roughly due south from the Everest region to the Lamindanda airstrip (twice a week to Kathmandu; $66). If you can't get on a flight there, trails continue south to the Tarai or east to Hile via Bhojpur, Nepal's most famous *khukuri*-making centre.

Other treks in eastern Nepal

Many hill treks north of Hile and Ilam are probably feasible without supplies. Development workers in the area rave about a circuit from Phidim to Basantapur via Taplejung. Bhojpur, Chainpur and Khadbari, quintessential Newar hill towns within two or three days' walk of Hile, also make great targets. The construction of an access road from Basantapur north to Num, as part of the massive Arun III hydroelectric project, will no doubt open the region up further. This is great country for adventurous trekkers who like exploring places that aren't written up in guidebooks, and this book isn't going to spoil that pleasure by writing about them.

However, here are three more conventional treks which, though they can't be done independently, are finding their way into agency brochures.

The Milke Danda and Jaljale Himal

A long north–south ridge famed for its rhododendrons, the **MILKE DANDA** can be linked up with a visit to Chainpur for a ten-day trek that combines spectacular flora with one of Nepal's best bazaars. The route goes no higher than 3000m, but takes in plenty of mountain views. You can fly back to Kathmandu from Tumlingtar or carry on back up the hill to Hile. A high-altitude extension of the Milke Danda north into the **JALJALE HIMAL**, returning to Taplejung or Phidim, takes at least two weeks and requires group support. The village near the high point is Topke Gola.

Makalu Base Camp

MAKALU BASE CAMP, a three-week trek from Hile up the Arun Valley and over the Shipton La (4127m), requires a tent and food for ten days; the last teahouse is at Tashi Gaun, less than a day from the Arun. Much of this trek passes through the vast new **Makalu-Barun National Park** and the contiguous **Makalu-Barun Conservation Area**, which forms a protective buffer zone in the inhabited area to the south and east. The park is intended to stem the growing human pressure around the base-camp area and preserve what is regarded as one of the most biologically diverse areas in the Himalaya. The conservation area, meanwhile, will be modelled on the Annapurna Conservation Area Project and operate on similar principles of involving locals in conservation.

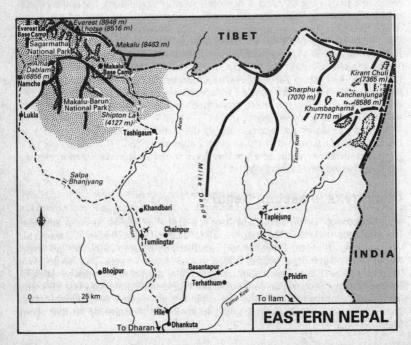

THE YETI

The **yeti** ("man of the rocky places") has been a staple of Sherpa and Tibetan folk-lore for centuries, but stories of hairy, ape-like creatures roaming the snowy heights first came to the attention of the outside world during the early days of British rule in India. British explorers in Tibet reported seeing mysterious moving figures and large, unidentified footprints in the snow – captivated by the reports, an imaginative Fleet Street hack coined the term "abominable snowman" – but it wasn't until 1951, during the first British Everest expedition from the Nepal side, that climber Eric Shipton took clear photographs of yeti tracks. Since then, several highly publicized yeti-hunts, including one led by Sir Edmund Hillary in 1960, have brought back a wealth of circumstantial evidence but not one authenticated sighting.

Sceptics dismiss the yeti as a straightforward myth, of course, arguing that the hairy creatures in question are more likely bears, and that the oversized footprints could be any animal's tracks, melted and enlarged by the sun. Meanwhile, relics kept at the *gompa* of Pangboche and Khumjung have failed to provide scientific proof of the yeti's existence – the "skulls" have been examined by experts and deemed to be made of serow (Himalayan wild goat) skins, while the skeletal hand at Pangboche is presumed to be human. Yet yaks continue to be mauled, and Sherpas insist the yeti isn't a hoax. Perhaps the most significant aspect of the yeti is humans' reaction to it: we want it to exist, like the Loch Ness Monstér – some secret part of the world that mankind hasn't yet discovered and explained – yet in our endless curiosity we want to find and dissect it. Thankfully, it has eluded us so far.

Kanchejunga

Reputedly the most incredible trek in this part of Nepal is to the foot of **KANCHENJUNGA**, at 8586m the third-highest peak in the world. Because of its remote location in the extreme northeastern corner of the country, Kanchenjunga is an expensive trek; most groups fly in and out of Taplejung (weekly from Kathmandu; $110). Two separate routes head northeastwards from there, one to the so-called North Base Camp and Pang Pema, the other to the South Base Camp and the Yalung Glacier; these routes can be combined into a circuit.

Far western Nepal

West of Dhaulagiri, the Himalaya subside somewhat and retreat north into Tibet, and the band of foothills flares out to become an almost impenetrable jumble. The northern third of the region, left in the rain shadow of the foothills, receives little monsoon moisture – in every way but politically, this highland strip is part of Tibet. Jagged Himalayan grandeur isn't so much in evidence, but there's a wildness and a vastness here, and the feeling of isolation is thrilling. The **far west** is the deep end of trekking in Nepal, and the treks here are well off the beaten track: they're a chore to get to, they require a lot of preparation and, with the exception of Rara Lake, you'll find that very few Westerners have gone before you. All that might appeal if you're an experienced trekker looking for new challenges, but if you're a first-timer, forget it.

Logistics make or break a trek in the far west. Given the distances involved, you'll need to fly to the starting point, but **flights** from Kathmandu are few and often delayed; connections from Nepalganj are more frequent and considerably cheaper, though no more reliable, and Nepalganj isn't a great place to be stuck waiting for a plane. **Food and lodging** are in uncomfortably short supply, so you'll need to bring a tent, cooking utensils and at least some provisions. You should be prepared to carry it all yourself, because **porters** here are a fickle lot and often can't be spared from their farmwork. **Guides** are also scarce, so you shouldn't venture out without a reasonable command of Nepali. If you go on an **organized trek** you may not be entirely insulated from these inconveniences, and for this reason agencies will probably try to steer you towards more easterly destinations.

As roads gradually penetrate into the far west, trekking might become easier. In the meantime, the four treks described below are the most realistic possibilities. Three require a white "mixed area" **permit**; the fourth, Dolpa, requires a special permit. For **maps**, see the *Mandala* "Jumla to Api & Saipal Himal" and "Jomosom to Jumla & Surkhet" (both 1:250,000).

Rara National Park

RARA NATIONAL PARK is the best known – and for the non-specialist, probably the least daunting – of the far western treks. The usual itinerary is a loop that starts and ends at Jumla, 150km north of Nepalganj, and takes about a week. The country is wild but unspectacular: a sea of choppy, mostly forested hills, offering only glimpses of modest Himalayan peaks, but the highlight is pristine **Rara Lake**, Nepal's largest, surrounded by a wilderness area of meadows, forest and abundant wildlife.

In terms of practicalities, the Rara trek has always been a challenge. You want to **fly in and out**. *RNAC* and *Everest* fly to Jumla from Nepalganj ($44) and less frequently from Kathmandu ($127), but delays and cancellations are the rule and you can't get a confirmed booking for the return flight in advance – try to arrange this as soon as you arrive, but be prepared to walk out to Birendranagar (Surkhet), a week's hike away. **Food** can be bought in Jumla, at inflated prices, but beyond the bazaar is often unavailable at any price. There are **lodges** in Jumla and a bunkhouse at the lake; in between, there are a few teahouses where you might be able to stay, but camping is more pleasant and certainly more reliable. The orthodox Hindus of the area aren't keen on having outcaste Westerners in their homes, but may let you sleep on the roof. The **park fee**, payable at the lakeside hut, is Rs650.

Technical difficulties aside, Rara makes a fair compromise between the popular treks and the really obscure ones, and in a way combines the best of both worlds: like the popular treks, Rara is given detailed route descriptions in the trekking books so you can do it without an organized group or even a guide, yet it's remote enough to ensure that you'll see few if any other foreigners. Starting at Jumla (2400m), the route crosses two 3500-metre ridges before reaching the lake at 3000m. The park is one of the best places in Nepal to see mountain **wildlife**, including Himalayan black bear, thar, goral, musk deer and the rare red (lesser) panda. Autumn and spring are the **best seasons**, and Rara is particularly worth considering in May and June, when the weather elsewhere is getting too hot or unpredictable. Winter flights are unreliable – a pity, since the far northwest offers the best potential skiing in the country. A day and a half south of the lake is **Sinja**, where the ruins of the capital of the twelfth- to fourteenth-century Khasa dynasty (see "The Historical Framework" in *Contexts*) can be viewed across the river.

Dolpa (She-Phoksundo National Park)

DOLPA (often written Dolpo) is an enormous, isolated district northwest of Dhaulagiri and bordering Tibet, the western half of which has been set aside as **SHE-PHOKSUNDO NATIONAL PARK**, Nepal's biggest. The park, established in 1984, protects an awe-inspiring region of deep valleys, unclimbed peaks, remote monasteries and rare fauna. Dolpa was the setting of Peter Matthiessen's *The Snow Leopard* (see "Books" in *Contexts*), and until recently the book was as close as most foreigners were allowed to get to it. Southern ("Inner") Dolpa is now open to trekkers, including individuals, but it's a food-deficit area, so independent trekkers will need to be self-sufficient. A guide/porter is essential – hire in Dunai. The climate here is continental and only slightly affected by the monsoon, so the **best time to go** is May to September.

Dolpa lies between Dhorpatan and Rara, and two of these treks, or even all three, could be combined into a single tour from Pokhara to Jumla – but this would take a minimum of four weeks. Dolpa on its own takes one to two weeks, assuming that you **fly in and out** of Juphal ($77 each way from Nepalganj), the airstrip for the district headquarters of **Dunai**. Everyone heads north from Dunai, entering the park after about a day (Rs650 **entry fee**) and reaching Ringmo and the stunningly blue **Phoksundo Tal** after another two days. There are plenty of dayhiking opportunities around the lake. From here you can retrace your route to Dunai or, given an extra week, take a much longer, harder route westwards over the Kagmara La (5114m), returning eastwards over the Balangra La (3837m).

Other treks in far western Nepal

These last two treks are so out of the way that even trekking agencies don't touch them, and they haven't yet been described in any trekking guidebook. They're only recommended for experienced trekkers, though either one can be done independently with only a couple of days' worth of supplies.

Humla

Tucked away in the extreme northwest corner of Nepal, **HUMLA** is high, dry and strongly Tibetan. Rounded, snowcapped peaks hem the district in on three sides and shut out most outside influences, including the monsoon. Trekking facilities are nonexistent, but the Buddhist highlanders are more accommodating to strangers than the caste-conscious Hindus further south.

RNAC **flies** from Nepalganj to **Simikot** (Humla's district headquarters) up to three times a week (seasonal; $88). From there it's seven to nine days to Jumla, stopping at Rara Lake along the way. Doing it vice versa – going towards the mountains – would seem more natural, but bear in mind that Jumla is easier to get out of than Simikot. The trail involves a good deal of up and down, but goes no higher than 3600m. In May–June, which is the **best time** to go, the wildflowers are out of this world. Most of the country north and east of the route is out of bounds to foreigners, which knocks out a few tempting side trips, but one allowable exception is **Raling Gompa**, the most sacred of Humla's many Buddhist monasteries, a tough, full-day's climb north of Simikot.

Khaptad National Park

Set on a plateau in the middle of the foothills, **KHAPTAD NATIONAL PARK** is, for lack of a better term, a spiritual park. A five-square-kilometre core area has been set aside for "meditation and tranquillity", comprising a pilgrimage spot of Hindu shrines and sacred streams. The centrepiece of the park, literally, is the Khaptad Baba, a famous holy man in the grand old mountaintop-guru tradition.

Two year-round **airstrips** – at Dipayal ($66 from Nepalganj, $138 from Kathmandu) and Sanfebagar ($61 from Nepalganj) – are within one or two days' walk of the park, making it possible to do this trek in as little as a week. **Food and lodging** are available at the airstrip towns, the southern park entrance and the park HQ. The food is poor and you'll want to bring as much of your own as possible, but you should be able to get by without a porter. The park **entry fee** is Rs650.

Hovering at about 3000m, the **central plateau** consists of rolling, open grassland and forest, with views of Saipal (7031m) and Api (7132m), the far west's tallest peaks. The attractions of the plateau are a sacred confluence, site of the

A chorten

Ganga Deshara **festival** in May–June, and the Baba's hut. Numerous tales surround the **Khaptad Baba**, all impossible to substantiate because he declines to answer questions about himself. His followers swear he's over 100 years old (he doesn't look it) and that he used to be a doctor in Kashmir before moving up to Khaptad forty years ago to meditate. He speaks excellent English and, hardest to explain, always seems mysteriously well informed about any subject, however esoteric. A surprising cross-section of the Nepalese intelligentsia follows the Baba, and even the king has been known to fly in for consultation; no doubt thanks to his pull with HM, the Baba won a long campaign to establish Khaptad as a national park in 1985.

festivals

The festivals listed below are mainly high-altitude affairs; at mid- and lower elevations you'll also encounter the popular celebrations of Holi, Dasain, Tihaar, Magh Sankranti and Shiva Raatri.

FAAGUN (Feb–March)
Losar Tibetan New Year, celebrated at *gompa* throughout the high country.

JETH (May–June)
Ganga Deshara Thousands of pilgrims gather at Khaptad five days before the full moon of Jeth.

ASAAR (June–July)
Dalai Lama's birthday Observed in Tibetan areas with parades and prayers (July 6).

SAAUN (July–Aug)
Janai Purnima The annual changing of the sacred thread worn by high-caste Hindu men draws pilgrims to Gosainkund and Muktinath.

BHADAU (Aug–Sept)
Yartung A fair with horse-racing, dancing, drinking and gambling, held at Muktinath.

MANGSIR (Nov–Dec)
Mani Rimdu A traditional Sherpa dance-drama, held at Tengboche (also at Thami in May).

travel details

BUSES
From Kathmandu to Dhunche (2 daily; 8hr); Gorkha (4 daily; 6hr); Jiri (2 daily; at least 12hr); Sundarijal (4 daily; 1hr) and Trisuli (5 daily; 4hr).
From Pokhara to Gorkha (2 daily; 6hr); Naudanda (infrequent; 1hr); Phedi (hourly; 2hr); Sisuwa (hourly; 45min) and Tansen (2 daily; 6–7hr).
From Hile to Dhankuta (12 daily; 30min) and Dharan (12 daily; 4hr).

PLANES
From Kathmandu to Baglung (2 weekly; 50min); Baitadi (1 weekly; 2hr 40min); Dipayal (1 weekly; 2hr 30min); Jomosom (0–3 weekly; 45min); Jumla (1–3 weekly; 1hr 20min); Lamidanda (1–2 weekly; 35min); Lukla (0–6 daily; 40min); Phaplu (0–3 weekly; 35min); Taplejung (1 weekly; 1hr 15min) and Tumlingtar (2–5 weekly; 1hr).
From Pokhara to Baglung (1 daily; 15min); Jomosom (1–3 daily; 25min); Jumla (0–1 weekly; 1hr) and Manang (0–3 weekly; 25min).
From Biratnagar to Phaplu (2 weekly; 40min); Taplejung (3 weekly; 30min) and Tumlingtar (4 weekly; 25min).
From Nepalganj to Baitadi (1 weekly; 50min); Dipayal (2–4 weekly; 40min); Jumla (1–2 daily; 45min); Sanfebagar (6 weekly; 35min) and Simikot (seasonal; 1hr).
From Dhangadhi to Dipayal (4 weekly; 25min) and Sanfebagar (3 weekly; 25min).
From Mahendranagar to Sanfebagar (3 weekly; 25min).

PART THREE

THE

CONTEXTS

THE
HISTORICAL
FRAMEWORK

For a tiny Himalayan backwater, Nepal has played a surprisingly pivotal role in Asian history. In its early days it reared the Buddha and hosted the great Indian emperor Ashoka; much later, its remarkable conquests led it into wars with Tibet and Britain, and during the past three decades it has come to be regarded as a vital buffer state by both India and China. Its name and recorded history go back nearly 3000 years, although it has existed as a nation for barely 200: before 1769, "Nepal" referred only to a kingdom based in the Kathmandu Valley.

BEGINNINGS

Neolithic tools found in the Kathmandu Valley indicate that humans have inhabited parts of Nepal for tens of thousands of years – and the fact that the shrines of Swayambhu and Changu Narayan are located on hill tops suggests that ancient animists may have lived and worshipped there as much as 200,000 years ago, while the valley floor was submerged under a primordial lake. The Newar creation myth, which tells of the *bodhisattva* Manjushri releasing the waters and establishing Swayambhu, perhaps preserves a dim racial memory of that prehistoric era.

Nepal's early semi-mythological geneologies aren't borne out by any archeological evidence, but at some points they tally with other sources. The **Kirata** (or Kiranti) tribe pops up in several Hindu texts – and even in Ptolemy – although the term might well have applied to all hill people in the first millennium BC; significantly, the Kirata were often described as a warlike people known for carrying deadly knives. Whoever they were, by the sixth or seventh century BC the Kirata appear to have divided into two distinct groups, one controlling the eastern hills and the other the Kathmandu Valley.

Hindus were by this time encroaching on the less malarial parts of the Tarai and founding the city-states of **Mithila** (modern Janakpur), the scene of many of the events in the *Ramayan* epic, and **Kapilvastu** (now Tilaurakot), where the Buddha spent his pre-enlightenment years during the sixth or seventh century BC. North India was unified under the **Mauryan empire** (321–184 BC), whose most famous ruler, Ashoka, was responsible for spreading Buddhism throughout the subcontinent, including Nepal. Following the fall of Maurya, north India was again divided among a number of states and Hinduism began a slow but inexorable comeback in the Tarai.

EARLY DYNASTIES

Nepal's history comes into sharper focus with the arrival of the **Lichhavis**, a north Indian clan who overthrew the Kiratas around 200 AD and established their capital at Deopatan, near modern Pashupatinath. Exploiting Nepal's position as a trading entrepôt between India and Tibet, the Lichhavis founded a strong, stable and culturally sophisticated dynasty. No buildings from the period survive, but contemporary accounts by Chinese travellers describe "multi-storeyed temples so tall one would take them for a crown of clouds" – perhaps a reference to the pagoda style that was to become a Nepali trademark. Under Lichhavi sponsorship, artisans ushered in a classical age of stone sculpture and produced Nepal's most acclaimed pieces, many of which still casually litter the Kathmandu Valley. Although Hindus, the Lichhavis endowed both Hindu and Buddhist temples – Pashupatinath and Swayambhu were built, or at least expanded, during their rule – and established a policy of religious tolerance that has been maintained to the present day.

Much of what we know about the Lichhavis comes from a handful of stone inscriptions whose authors were probably more intent on self-praise than historical accuracy. The earliest inscription, dated 454 AD and still on view at Changu Narayan, extols **Manadeva**, the legendary builder of the Boudha stupa. The greatest of the Lichhavi line, **Amsuvarman** (c. 600–620) is said to have composed the first Sanskrit grammar and struck the first Nepalese coins. "Down to the reign of this monarch the gods showed themselves plainly in bodily shape," intone the Nepalese chronicles, "but after this they became invisible." By this time Nepal had become a vassal of Tibet, and Amsuvarman's daughter Bhrikuti, who was carried off by the Tibetan king, is popularly credited with introducing Buddhism to Tibet.

The Lichhavi era came to a close in 879, and the three centuries that followed are sometimes referred to as Nepal's "Dark Ages". The Nepalese chronicles record a long list of **Thakuri kings**, although the title was probably a Hindu honorific and not the name of an hereditary dynasty; these kings may well have been puppets installed by one or more of the powers controlling the Tarai at the time. Nonetheless, learning and the arts continued to thrive, and from the eleventh century onwards the valley became an important centre of tantric studies (see "Religion", p.347).

THE KHASAS AND MALLAS

While the Thakuris were ruling central Nepal, yet another Hindu clan, the **Khasas**, were migrating up from the plains and carving out a small fiefdom in western Tibet. In the early twelfth century a Khasa king, Nagaraja, moved his capital down to Sinja in the Karnali basin and established a powerful dynasty which at its height controlled a broad sector of the Himalaya from Kashmir to present-day Pokhara. The history of the Khasas is little understood, for they left few written records and only minor ruins at Sinja (now Hatsinja) and Dullu, south of Jumla.

Nepal entered a new and much better documented period of its history when the Thakuri king of Bhaktapur, Arideva, took the title **Malla**, probably in the year 1200. Malla was, in fact, a popular form of royal address in India at the time – the Khasa kings also called themselves Mallas – but the name has come to be associated with at least three separate dynasties, lasting more than five centuries, that presided over the renaissance of Nepali culture during which most of the temples and palaces still on display in the Kathmandu Valley were built.

The early Malla era was marked by great instability: the Khasas mounted several raids on the valley, although they were never able to gain a ruling foothold, and in 1349 Muslims swept up from Bengal and pillaged both Hindu and Buddhist holy sites in a brief spree of destruction and violence. Despite these disruptions, trade flourished, many of the valley's smaller cities were founded, and Arniko, the great Nepali architect, was dispatched to the Ming court to instruct the Chinese in the art of building pagodas. In 1382 **Jayasthiti Malla** (1295–1382) inaugurated a period of strong central rule from Bhaktapur, but his most lasting contribution was to dragoon his Buddhist subjects into the Hindu hierarchy by dividing them into 64 occupational castes – a system which remained enshrined in Nepali law until 1964. Malla power reached its zenith under **Yaksha Malla** (1428–82), who extended his domain westwards to Gorkha and eastwards as far as present-day Biratnagar. Upon his death, the kingdom was divided among three sons, and for nearly three centuries the independent city-states of Kathmandu, Patan and Bhaktapur (and occasionally others) feuded over lucrative trade arrangements with Tibet. Judging by the opulent durbars built during this period, there must have been enough to go around, and the intense rivalry seems to have been good for both art and business.

The Khasa kings didn't fare so well, and by the late fourteenth century their empire had fragmented into a collection of petty provinces. The Muslim conquest of north India during the early part of the century figured indirectly in Khasa's downfall: a steady stream of princes from Rajasthan, which had borne the brunt of the invasion, limped into the Khasa hills in search of consolation prizes, and rapidly wheedled their way into positions of power. Those who took the reins of the Khasa provinces came to be known as the **Baaisi Raja** (Twenty-two Princes), while others who subjugated Magar and Gurung states to the east became the **Chaubisi** (Twenty-four).

UNIFICATION

For three centuries the Chaubisi and Baaisi confederacies were able to maintain an uneasy status quo, forming numerous defensive alliances to ensure that no one state could gain control over the rest. Divided, they were small, weak and culturally backward. **Gorkha**, the most easterly territory, was no different from the rest, except that it was that much closer to the Kathmandu Valley and that much more jealous of the Mallas' wealth. Under the inspired, obsessive leadership of **Prithvi Narayan Shah** (1722–75), Gorkha launched a campaign that was to take 27 years to conquer the valley, and as long again to unite all of modern Nepal.

At the time of Prithvi Narayan's rise to the throne, in 1743, rivalry between the three Malla kings had reached an all-time high. Still, Gorkha wasn't nearly strong enough to invade Nepal outright; Prithvi Narayan first captured Nuwakot, a day's march northwest of Kathmandu, and from there directed a ruthless twenty-year **war of attrition**. By 1764 he was able to enforce a total blockade, starving the valley and at the same time replenishing Gorkha's coffers with Tibetan trade. Kirtipur was targeted for the first major battle, and surrendered after a six-month siege. Answering a plea from the Kathmandu king, Jaya Prakash Malla, the East India Company sent in 2400 soldiers against the Gorkhalis, who proceeded to cut them to shreds; only 800 returned. On the eve of Indra Jaatra in 1768, Jaya Prakash, by now rumoured to be insane, let down the city's defences and **Kathmandu fell** to the Gorkhalis without a fight. They took Patan two days later, and Bhaktapur the following year, and by 1774 had marched eastwards all the way to Sikkim.

Suspicious of Britain's growing influence in India, Prithvi Narayan adopted a closed-door policy that was to remain in force until the 1950s. Missionaries were thrown out forthwith: "First the bible, then the trading station, then the cannon," he warned. The bloody **battle for succession** that followed Prithvi Narayan's death set the pattern for Nepali politics well into the twentieth century. Yet when they weren't stabbing each other in the back, his successors managed to subdue Gorkha's old Chaubisi and Baaisi rivals in the west, so that by 1790 Nepal stretched far beyond its present eastern and western borders. Lured on by promises of land grants – every hillman's dream – the Nepali army became a seemingly unstoppable fighting machine, with Kashmir in its sights.

Westward progress was interrupted, however, by a brief but chastening **war with Tibet**. Troubles had been brewing for some time over trade relations, and the Tibetans were growing alarmed by Nepal's encroachments on their ally, Sikkim. In 1788 and again in 1791, Nepal invaded, plundered a few monasteries and exacted tribute from Tibet, but in 1792 the Tibetans launched a counterattack, penetrating as far as Nuwakot and forcing Nepal to accept harsh terms.

Nepal's further adventures in the west brought it into increasing **conflict with Britain**'s East India Company, which by now controlled India, and open hostilities broke out in 1814 when Nepal annexed the Butwal sector of the Tarai. For the British, the dispute provided a perfect pretext to "open up" Nepal, which had been so tantalizingly closed to them, and thus to muscle in on trade with Tibet. Britain attacked with a force of 50,000 men against Nepal's 12,000, expecting an easy victory; in the event it took two years and heavy losses before Nepal was finally brought to heel. The **Treaty of Segauli** forced Nepal to accept its present eastern and western boundaries and surrender much of the Tarai, and worst of all, to admit an official British "resident" in Kathmandu. Yet so impressed were the British by "our valiant opponent" – as a plaque at an Indian battle site still proclaims – that they began recruiting Nepalis into the Indian Army before the treaty had even been signed. These companies formed the basis for the famed **Gurkha regiments** (see p.213). Britain restored Nepal's Tarai lands in return for its help in quelling the Indian Mutiny of 1857.

THE RANA YEARS

The Kathmandu court was practically paralyzed by intrigue and assassinations during the first half of the nineteenth century, culminating in the ghastly **Kot massacre** of 1846, in which more than fifty courtiers were butchered in a courtyard off Kathmandu's Durbar Square. In the ensuing upheaval, a shrewd young general, **Jang Bahadur**, seized power, took the title

Rana and proclaimed himself prime minister* for life, an office which he later made hereditary by establishing a complicated roll of succession. For the next century, the kings of Nepal were nothing more than puppets, while Ranas ruled like shoguns and packed the palace with their ever-increasing offspring. Authoritarian and blatantly exploitative, they built grandiose palaces while putting virtually no money into public works, suppressed education for fear it would awaken opposition, and remained firmly isolationist to avoid losing control to the British. (Ironically, an impoverished Nepal suited Britain, since it assured a steady supply of willing Gurkha cannon fodder.) Only a handful of foreign dignitaries were allowed to enter – usually only as far as Chitwan – and even the British resident wasn't allowed to venture beyond the Kathmandu Valley. To survey Nepal and Tibet, Britain had to send in Indian spies disguised as Buddhist monks.

Yet Jang Bahadur knew the value of staying on good terms with the British Raj, now at its zenith; in 1850 he broke with tradition and travelled to England, where he met Queen Victoria and by all accounts cut a dashing figure. He returned with several Western affectations, including a fondness for neoclassical architecture and epaulettes; soon after, to his credit, he abolished the practice of *sati*.

Other Ranas continued in the same vein. **Chandra Shamsher Rana**, who came to power in 1901 by deposing his brother, is best known for building the thousand-roomed Singha Durbar and (belatedly) abolishing slavery; he also made some feeble attempts at modernization, including the construction of Nepal's first college, railway, hydroelectric plant and paved roads. By 1940, underground resistance against the regime was developing, and **Juddha Shamsher Rana** had four plotters executed; after the fall of the Ranas these men were declared martyrs and a monument near the Kathmandu GPO was erected in their honour.

---

*Though the "Rana" title has generally been equated with that of a prime minister, technically it conferred a grade of kingship. The holder's full title was Shri Tin Maharaja (short for Shri Shri Shri Maharaj, "Shri" being an honorific prefix); the king's was, and still is, Shri Paanch (Five Shri) Maharajdhiraj.

THE MONARCHY RESTORED

The Ranas' anachronistic regime wasn't able to survive long after World War II, from which over 200,000 soldiers returned with dangerous ideas of freedom and justice. In 1948 the British withdrew from India, and with them went the Ranas' chief support; the new Indian government mistrusted the Ranas, and became genuinely worried about Nepal's weakness as a buffer state after the Communist takeover of China in 1949. Seeking stability, India signed a far-reaching **"peace and friendship" treaty** with Nepal in 1950 which, despite the upheavals that were to follow, remains the basis for all relations between the two countries.

Later the same year the strategic balance shifted again, as a result of the Chinese invasion of Tibet and the **Nepali Congress Party**, recently formed in Calcutta, called for an armed struggle against the Ranas. Within a month, King Tribhuwan had requested asylum at the Indian embassy and was smuggled away to Delhi; the next morning, the Nepali Congress Party launched simultaneous assaults on Birganj and Biratnagar. Sporadic fighting continued for two months until the Ranas, internationally discredited, reluctantly agreed to enter into negotiations. Brokered by India, the so-called **Delhi Compromise** arranged for Ranas and the Congress Party to share power under the king's rule, with Nepalis given the right to vote in the parliamentary-style democracy.

The compromise was short-lived. **Tribhuwan**, a previously retiring figure, emerged somehow as a "hero of the revolution" and an adroit politician, and before the end of 1951 he had dismissed the Rana prime minister. This was an end to the Rana regime, but not Rana influence: by an agreement that has never been made public, the Shah royal family continues to appoint Ranas to most key military posts, and the families are inseparably tied by marriage (the queen is a Rana, and two of her sisters are married to two of the king's brothers). In his four years as king, however, Tribhuwan neither consolidated his power nor delivered the elections he promised. Unaccountable to the voters, the party bosses who controlled the interim government were hardly an improvement over the Ranas.

PANCHAAYAT POLITICS

Crowned in 1955, **King Mahendra** lost no time in offsetting the parties' power by developing his own grassroots network of village leaders, forcing the parties to do likewise. They demanded elections; the king stalled, but finally agreed to a vote in 1959. Amazingly, the Nepali Congress Party swept 70 percent of the seats, and under Prime Minister **B. P. Koirala** began bypassing palace control and creating a party machine very much like India's. Mahendra was none too pleased with this "**experiment with democracy**", as it came to be called – the following year he sacked the cabinet, banned political parties and threw the leaders in jail; for the rest of his reign he relied on heavy police measures to quell dissent.

In place of democracy, Mahendra offered the "**partyless**" **panchaayat system**, a uniquely Nepali form of government that grew out of the king's old-boy village network. Village councils (*panchaayat*) were established to look after local affairs; these were to send one representative on to a district council, which in turn elected members to a national assembly. The king chose the prime minister and cabinet and appointed one fifth of the national assembly, which served as a rubber stamp for his policies. "Partylessness" meant, of course, one party – the king's. The *panchaayat* system conveniently preserved an illusion of democracy while silencing opposition and ensuring loyalty to the king: in other words, it was a new and improved version of absolute monarchy. Corruption was the same as before, only now more decentralized, as every village *panchaayat* wallah had a tiny piece of the pie.

India was unhappy with the changes, but Mahendra, unlike his father, didn't owe his crown to India, and sought wider international support. He threw open Nepal's doors to **foreign aid**, which endeared him to the major powers, enriched the state's coffers and swelled the bureaucracy (see "Development dilemmas"). After the 1962 Sino-Indian border war, Mahendra was able to exploit Nepal's buffer position with particular skill, alternately playing off the two powers against each other to obtain economic and military aid; no sooner had India completed the Rajpath, Nepal's first highway from the plains to Kathmandu, for example, than Mahendra persuaded the

Chinese to extend the road to Tibet, much to India's horror. The "**China card**" became an important unofficial strand of foreign policy, but ultimately it was to help bring about the downfall of the *panchaayat* system.

The present king, **Birendra**, assumed power after Mahendra's death in 1972, although for astrological reasons wasn't crowned until 1975. Educated at Eton and Harvard, the young king set out as an enlightened reformer, taking steps to curb the bureaucracy and cronyism that had flourished under his father. Reacting to Mahendra's laissez-faire policies on tourism – which had become Nepal's major industry – he cracked down on the growing hippy population by tightening visa restrictions. In 1975 he made the shrewdest and most popular move of his career when he proposed designating Nepal a **Zone of Peace**, a Swiss-style neutrality pledge that would at first glance appear to be completely unassailable. India, however, has consistently opposed the measure as a violation of the 1950 "peace and friendship" treaty, which provides for mutual defence, while cynics like to point out the irony of Nepal – home of the Gurkhas, the world's most formidable mercenary soldiers – declaring itself a peace zone.

Birendra's domestic reforms soon ran out of steam, and discontent grew over corruption and the slow pace of development. Widespread uprisings broke out in 1979, forcing the king to promise a national **referendum** in which voters could choose between the *panchaayat* system and multiparty democracy. Democracy lost by a margin of 55 to 45 – many say the vote was rigged – and the *panchaayat* system was retained.

During the 1980s Birendra proved himself to be an earnest but weak leader, easily manipulated by advisers and the queen – forever chaperoned by minders with walkie-talkies, he simply fell out of touch with the people. Despite token tinkerings with the system, the gravy train got more crowded throughout the decade, and insiders, sensing that the regime's days were numbered, tried to grab everything they could in the time remaining. In 1988 the king's brother, Dhirendra, was forced to relinquish his title as prince to avoid wide-ranging corruption charges. The king himself was rumoured to have Swiss bank accounts and an island in the Maldives (or Greece). Political opponents were imprisoned, while freedom of speech and the press were nonexistent. Diplomats insist Birendra was uninvolved with any shady dealings, but he would have had to be incredibly naive not to have known what was going on in his name.

DEMOCRACY RESTORED

The chickens started coming home to roost in March 1989, when India, outraged by (among other things) Nepal's purchase of anti-aircraft guns from China, retaliated with a crippling **trade embargo**. Indian Prime Minister Rajiv Gandhi – who had long professed a deep distaste for Birendra's antiquated monarchy – apparently believed shortages of fuel and medicines would touch off a popular uprising and topple the regime in a matter of weeks. Only his timing was off. The government rode out the immediate crisis by closing the universities, rationing fuel and whipping up traditional anti-Indian sentiment, until the Indian elections in December, when Gandhi's more conciliatory successor, V. P. Singh, eased the embargo.

But after eight months of hardship, inflation and police action, Nepalis were fed up, and India could no longer be cast as the villain. The previous year had witnessed China's failed pro-democracy movement at Tiananmen Square and the spectacularly successful revolutions in Eastern Europe: Nepalis were enormously stirred by these examples. Seeing their chance, the banned opposition parties united in the so-called **Movement to Restore Democracy**, demanding an end to the *panchayaat* system and the creation of a constitutional monarchy. They called for a national day of protest on February 18, 1990 – a date already designated by the government, with unintended irony, as Democracy Day. Hundreds of opposition members, including leaders Ganesh Man Singh and Krishna Prasad Bhattarai, were duly placed under house arrest, and the planned revolt got off to a shaky start. Yet Faagun 7 (the Nepali date of Democracy Day) marked the true launch of the **Jana Andolan** ("People's Movement"), which in subsequent weeks gathered strength, resulting in violent clashes and deaths in Bhaktapur, Narayanghat and Hetauda. Even while under detention, opposition leaders were able to call strikes and blackouts at will. The king, counselled by hardliners, kept silence.

On April 3, protesters overran Patan, and three days later an estimated 200,000 people marched up Kathmandu's Durbar Marg towards the Royal Palace. The army fired into the crowd, killing at least 45 people, and an ominous shoot-on-sight curfew was imposed. Finally moved to action by the **massacre**, the king dissolved his cabinet, legalized political parties and invited the opposition to form an interim government with Bhattarai as prime minister. The *panchaayat* system was dead.

After a few hiccups – when an impatient people suspected the king of playing for time to avoid making real reforms – the changeover to democracy proceeded in an orderly, if leisurely, fashion. The interim government was given two primary responsibilities: drafting a new constitution and holding Nepal's first free elections in more than thirty years. By November 1990 the **new constitution** was ratified, guaranteeing free speech, human rights and a constitutional monarchy. Under its provisions, the king remains the commander-in-chief of the armed forces, but cannot make any executive decisions without consulting the prime minister and cabinet; the old Rastriya Panchaayat was replaced by a Parliament consisting of a directly elected House of Representatives and a smaller National Assembly.

Parliamentary **elections** were set for May 1991, giving the news of democracy a chance to percolate out into Nepal's remoter regions. It was a uniquely Nepali race. Competing for 205 seats were more than 45 parties, many of them mere splinter groups formed around a single candidate, and each with its own identifying symbol (tree, cow, sun, hand, etc): in a nation with few televisions and a literacy rate of just forty percent, elections are largely fought with such iconography. The **Nepal Congress Party**, which had paid its dues in exile for three decades and could claim much of the credit for bringing down the *panchaayat* system, had the backing of many international donors, who regarded it as a safe, middle-of-the-road bet. But while the rest of the world was backpedalling from communism as fast as it could, Nepal's several Communist parties were gaining ground, particularly the **United Marxist-Leninist (UML)** wing with its populist, Nepal-for-Nepalis platform of foreign-aid reduction and radical land redistribution. Most observers expected the Communists to deprive the

Congress Party of an outright majority, which in Nepal's parliamentary system would have forced Congress into a volatile coalition with either the Communists or the hardline, *pancha*-packed National Democratic Party.

In the end, the outcome defied all predictions: Congress won a slim majority, but Bhattarai, the interim prime minister, lost his seat; the Communists maintained their traditional strongholds in the east and, incredibly, swept the comfortable Kathmandu Valley; and the National Democrats went down in a ball of flames. It was a clear referendum against the old guard, but a less than enthusiastic vote of confidence for the Congress Party.

CONGRESS IN POWER

Any government inheriting such immense challenges with so slender a mandate was probably doomed to disappoint; in the aftermath of the *andolan*, with Nepalis impatient for change and many clinging to unrealistic expectations for democracy, the Congress Party faced a seemingly impossible task. By mid-1993, unemployment, unrest, Indianization and festering internal disputes within the party were producing widespread disillusion, and severely undermining the government's ability to manage the country's affairs. Nepal's fledgling democracy was still finding its feet: political parties had yet to develop a consensus on constitutional matters, the old bureaucracy remained resistant to change, and many Nepalis were becoming nostalgic for the paternalistic security of the *panchaayat* days.

The multiparty system had already undergone several potentially destabilizing tests in its short existence, beginning with the formation of the first Congress government. With Bhattarai losing his seat and party patriarch Ganesh Man Singh not participating in the 1991 poll, the mantle of prime minister fell to **Girija Prasad Koirala**, brother of the late B.P. Koirala, Nepal's first democratically elected prime minister. Koirala lost little time not only in attracting the enmity of the opposition Communists but also alienating many in his own party, including Bhattarai and Singh (who wielded the titles of party president and "supreme leader" respectively). The fragmentation of party power made for weak government and left the prime minister vulnerable to numerous political distractions.

The UML and other Communist parties set up a steady drumbeat of criticism, and early on began calling for Koirala's resignation. Given their strength in the increasingly important urban areas, the Communists adopted a style of taking their political gripes to the streets through black-flag marches, general strikes and other actions. One such uprising on the second anniversary of the *andolan*, later euphemistically referred to as the **April 6 "incidents"**, resulted in a mini-revolution in Kathmandu and Patan in which government security forces again fired into the crowds without warning, killing 23 people.

The antagonism between the Indian-sponsored Congress Party and the Communists, who look to China as their only remaining ideological mentor, has produced strong political polarities on almost every issue. For example, Congress has supported the cause of Tibetan refugees in a way that the *panchaayat* regime never did, which the Communists view as provocative to China. Yet the Communists certainly speak for many Nepalis when they accuse Congress leaders of selling out Nepal's interests to India. In 1992 this frustration coalesced into what was to become a long-running squabble over the **Tanakpur project**, a $65 million hydroelectric diversion built by India on the Mahakali River, which forms the western border between the two countries. The government is accused of signing away most of Nepal's rights to the water and power generated from the river; the issue has become a referendum on Koirala's leadership, and his party appears willing to let him take the fall for it.

Beset by such turmoil, the present government has become almost universally disliked and is unlikely to hold onto the reins of power for long. A Congress-led coalition seems inevitable, but whether this will end Nepal's political gridlock is anyone's guess. A shared-power arrangement between Congress and one or more of the Communist parties sounds like a recipe for chaos – yet any government that excludes the Communists can expect obstruction every step of the way. Few expect the king to step in and call a halt to this democratic experiment the way his father did, but Congress leaders, ever mindful of that threat, continue to call for consensus and to portray themselves as the only alternative to the return of *panchaayat*-style repression.

RELIGION: HINDUISM, BUDDHISM, SHAMANISM

To say that religion is an important part of Nepali life is a considerable understatement: it _is_ life. In the Nepali world view, just about every act has spiritual implications; the gods are assumed to have a hand in every success or misfortune and must be appeased continuously. Belief and ritual form the basis of the whole social order, governing the way husbands relate to wives, parents to children and even the king to his subjects.

Three religious strands intertwine in Nepal: Hinduism, Buddhism and shamanism. In theory, these faiths are philosophically incompatible, but Nepalis, being an exceptionally tolerant lot, tend to overlook the differences. As practised by the masses, each employs superstition and rites of passage to get followers through the present life, and codes of behaviour to prepare them for the next; Hindu priests, Buddhist lamas and tribal shamans play similar roles in their respective communities. Indeed, it's really only outside observers who bother to distinguish between the religions and dwell on their outward differences – most Nepalis find such distinctions needlessly academic.

Hinduism is the state religion of Nepal, and the government claims that 90 percent of the population is Hindu. However, there are social advantages to professing Hinduism in Nepal, and official statistics don't reflect the extent to which many Nepalis blithely combine Hinduism with Buddhist or shamanist beliefs. In general, Hinduism prevails at the lower elevations and Buddhism in the Himalaya, while shamanism is strongest among the ethnic minorities of the hills.

HINDUISM

Hinduism doesn't conform to Western notions of what a religion should be, and indeed the word "religion" is totally inadequate to describe it. Hindus call it _dharma_, a much more sweeping term that conveys faith, duty, a way of life and the entire social order. Having no common church or institution, its many sects and cults preach different dogmas and emphasize different scriptures. On social matters, Hinduism can be tragically rigid – witness the caste system – and when it comes to rituals, rather petty. Yet it's a highly individualistic system, offering worshippers an almost limitless choice of deities and admitting many paths to enlightenment. By absorbing and neutralising opposing doctrines, rather than condemning them as heresies, it has flourished longer than any other major religion.

Hinduism has been evolving since approximately 1600 BC, when **Aryan** invaders swept down from central Asia and subjugated the native Dravidian peoples of the Indus and Ganges plains. They brought with them a pantheon of nature gods and goddesses, some of whom are still in circulation: Indra (sky and rain) is popular in Kathmandu, while Surya (sun), Agni (fire), Vayu (wind) and Yama (death) retain bit parts in contemporary mythology. These so-called Vedic gods were first immortalized in the _**Vedas**_ ("Books of Wisdom"), which were probably written between the twelfth and eighth centuries BC, and it was during this period that most of the principles now identified with Hinduism were thrashed out.

To make sure they stayed on top of the conquered Dravidians, the Aryans banned intermarriage and codified the apartheid-like **caste system**; _varna_, the Sanskrit word for caste, means "colour", and to this day members of the higher castes generally have lighter skin. Initially, four castes were established: Brahmans (priests), Kshatriyas (warriors and rulers), Vaisyas (traders and farmers) and Sudras (artisans and menials); over time, the lower two divisions spawned innumerable occupational subcastes. The _Rig Veda_, Hinduism's oldest text, put a divine seal of approval on the arrangements by proclaiming that Brahmans had issued from the mouth of the supreme creator, Kshatriyas from his arms, Vaishyas from his thighs and Sudras from his feet.

Brahmans (called Bahuns in Nepal), entrusted with the brain work, proceeded to exploit their position by inventing preposterously complex rituals and sacrifices, and making themselves the indispensible guardians of these mysteries (cow-worship probably dates from this period). Despite this stagnation, the philosophical foundations of Hinduism were laid during the late Vedic period and recorded in a series of discourses known as the **Upanishads**. Ever since, Hinduism has run along two radically different tracks: the Brahmans' hocus-pocus popular religion, with its comic-book deities and bloody sacrifices, and the profound, intuitive insights of gurus and *rishi* (teachers).

The essence of Hinduism, unchanged since the *Upanishads* were written, is that the soul (*atman*) of each living thing is like a lost fragment of the universal soul – **brahman**, the ultimate reality – while everything in the physical universe is mere illusion (*maya*). To reunite with *brahman*, the individual soul must go through a **cycle of rebirths** (*samsara*), ideally moving up the scale with each reincarnation. Determining the soul's progress is its **karma** – its accumulated "just desserts" – which is reckoned by the degree to which the soul conformed to **dharma**, or correct Hindu behaviour, in its previous lives. Thus a low-caste Hindu must accept his or her lot to atone for past sins, and follow *dharma* in the hopes of achieving a higher rebirth. The theoretical goal of every Hindu is to cast off all illusion, achieve release (*moksha*) from the cycle of rebirths, and dissolve into *brahman*.

Hinduism has assembled a vast and rich body of mythology over the past three millennia, largely in an effort to personalize *brahman* for the masses. Early on, a few of the Vedic gods were renamed, relieved of their old nature associations and given personalities to illustrate divine attributes. The concept of the **Hindu "trinity"** – Brahma the creator, Vishnu the preserver and Shiva the destroyer – was developed, and the process of god-creation was speeded by the invention of numerous **avatar**, or manifestations of gods. Hinduism's best-loved epics, the *Mahabharata* (pronounced *Mahabharat* in Nepal) and the *Ramayana* (*Ramayan*), portray two of Vishnu's *avatar*, Krishna and Ram, as models of human conduct (although as often as not Hindu gods, like their Greek counterparts, are made out to be vain and foolish).

AUM

"AUM" is a word that represents to our ears that sound of the energy of the universe of which all things are manifestations. You start in the back of the mouth, "ahh," then "oo," you fill the mouth, and "mm" closes the mouth. When you pronounce this properly, all vowel sounds are included in the pronunciation. AUM. Consonants are here regarded simply as interruptions of the essential vowel sound.

All words are thus fragments of AUM, just as all images are fragments of the Form of forms. AUM is a symbolic sound that puts you in touch with that resounding being that is the universe. If you heard some of the recordings of Tibetan monks chanting AUM, you would know what the word means, all right. That's the AUM of being in the world. To be in touch with that and to get the sense of that is the peak experience of all.

A-U-M. The birth, the coming into being, and the dissolution that cycles back. AUM is called the "four-element syllable." A-U-M – and what is the fourth element? The silence out of which AUM arises, and back into which it goes, and which underlies it. My life is the A-U-M, but there is a silence underlying it, too. That is what we would call the immortal. This is the mortal and that's the immortal, and there wouldn't be the mortal if there weren't the immortal. One must discriminate between the mortal aspect and the immortal aspect of one's own existence . . . that's why it is a peak experience to break past all that, every now and then, and to realize, "Oh . . . ah . . ."

From "The Power of Myth", by Joseph Campbell, reproduced by permission of Bantam Doubleday Dell.

The explosion of deities has given rise to a succession of **devotional cults** over the centuries, the most important of which nowadays are Vaishnava (followers of Vishnu), Shaiva (Shiva) and Mahadevi (the mother goddess); the last often goes by the name Shakti, a tantric term explained below. Brahma is rarely iconographically depicted and consequently not widely worshipped.

THE HINDU PANTHEON

If you're daunted by Hinduism's technicolour array of gods and goddesses, don't worry: your average Hindu would be hard pressed to name most of them. While Hinduism is said to boast of 300 million deities, they can all be thought of as representations of the one supreme god – a paradox which isn't hard to deal with if you've been trained that everything is illusion anyway. The most important gods, described below, can easily be identified by certain trademark implements, postures and "vehicles" (animal carriers). As for gods' multiple arms and heads, these aren't meant to be taken literally: they symbolize the deity's "universal" (omnipotent) form, while severed heads and trampled corpses signify ignorance and evil.

VISHNU

Vishnu (often known as Narayan in Nepal) is the face of dignity and equanimity, typically shown standing erect holding a wheel (*chakra*), mace (*gada*), lotus (*padma*) and conch (*sankha*) in his four hands, or, as at Budhanilkantha, reclining on a serpent's coil. A statue of **Garuda** (**Garud** in Nepal), Vishnu's bird-man vehicle, is always close by. Vishnu is also sometimes depicted in one or more of his ten incarnations (*das avatar*), which follow an evolutionary progression from fish, turtle and boar to man-lion, dwarf, axe-wielding Brahman and the legendary heroes **Ram** and **Krishna**.

Ram is associated with **Hanuman**, his loyal monkey-king ally in the *Ramayan*, while Krishna is most commonly seen on calendars as a chubby blue baby, flute-player or charioteer. Interestingly, Vishnu's ninth *avatar* is the Buddha – this was a sixth-century attempt by Vaishnavas to bring Buddhists into their fold – and the tenth is Kalki, a messiah figure invented in the twelfth century when Hindus were being persecuted at the hands of Muslim invaders.

Vishnu's consort is **Lakshmi**, the goddess of wealth, to whom lamps are lit during the festival of Tihaar. Like Vishnu, she assumed mortal form in two great Hindu myths, playing opposite Ram as the chaste princess Sita, and opposite Krishna as the passionate Radha.

SHIVA

Shiva's incarnations are countless, ranging from the hideous Bhairab, who alone is said to take 64 different forms, to the benign Pashupati ("Lord of the Animals") and Nataraj ("King of the Dance"). To many devotees he is simply Mahadev: Great God. The earliest and still the most widespread icon of Shiva is the *linga*, a phallic stone fertility symbol* commonly housed in a boxy stone *shivalaya* ("Shiva home"). Shiva temples can be identified by the presence of a *trisul* (trident) and the bull **Nandi**, Shiva's mount, who is himself something of a fertility symbol.

Many sadhus worship Shiva the *yogin* (one who practises yoga), the Hindu ascetic supreme, who is often depicted sitting in meditative repose on a Himalayan mountaintop, perhaps holding a *chillam* of *ganja*. Pashupatinath is the national shrine to Shiva as **Pashupati**, and is patronized by Pashupata, Kaplika and other Shaiva sects, who take it to be Shiva's winter home. Another popular image of Shiva is as the loving husband with his consort, Parvati: the two can be seen leaning from an upper window of a temple in Kathmandu's Durbar Square. Nearby stand two famous statues of **Bhairab**, the tantric (see below) interpretation of Shiva in his role as destroyer: according to Hindu philosophy, everything – not only evil – must be destroyed in its turn to make way for new things.

MAHADEVI

The mother goddess is similarly worshipped in many forms, both peaceful and wrathful, and many of these are reckoned to be the consorts

---

* The phallic aspect of the *linga* is perhaps overplayed by non-Hindus. Gandhi wrote: "It has remained for our Western visitors to acquaint us with the obscenity of many practices which we have hitherto innocently indulged in. It was in a missionary book that I first learned that the Shiva *linga* had any obscene significance at all." Then again, Gandhi denied most things to do with sex.

of corresponding Shiva forms. As **Kali** ("Black") she is the female counterpart of Bhairab, wearing a necklace of skulls and sticking out her tongue with bloodthirsty intent; as **Durga** she is the demon-slayer honoured in the great Dasain festival. In Nepal she is widely worshipped as **Bhagwati**, the embodiment of female creative power. In all these forms, the mother goddess is appeased by sacrifices of uncastrated male animals. On a more peaceful level, she is also Parvati ("Hill", daughter of Himalaya), Gauri ("Golden") or just **Mahadevi** ("Great Goddess").

GANESH AND OTHERS

Several legends tell how **Ganesh**, Shiva's and Parvati's son, came to have an elephant's head: one states that Shiva accidentally chopped the boy's head off, and owing to an obscure restriction on the god's restorative powers, was forced to replace it with that of the first creature he saw. The god of wisdom and remover of obstacles, Ganesh must be worshipped first to ensure offerings to other gods will be effective, which is why a Ganesh shrine or stone will invariably be found near other temples. Underscoring Hinduism's great sense of the mystical absurd, Ganesh's vehicle is a rat.

Of the other Hindu deities, only **Annapurna**, the goddess of grain and abundance (her name means "Full of Grain"), and **Saraswati**, the goddess of learning and culture, receive much attention in Nepal. Saraswati is normally depicted holding a *vina*, a musical instrument something like a sitar.

BUDDHISM

The Buddha was born Siddhartha Gautama in what is now Nepal (see "Lumbini" in Chapter Five) in the fifth or sixth century BC, and his teachings were in many ways a protest against the ritualism to which popular Hinduism had by then been reduced. The Buddha rejected the Hindu caste system and the belief in a creator God, while adapting its doctrines of reincarnation and *karma*, along with many yogic practices; the result was a non-theistic, pragmatic philosophy that placed a greater emphasis on the active pursuit of enlightenment.

Whereas the Hindu ideal is to reunite with the Creator, the Buddhist goal is *nirvana*, a state of being where wisdom and compassion have completely uprooted the "three poisons" of greed, hatred and delusion. The essence of the Buddha's teaching is encapsulated in the **four noble truths**: existence is suffering; suffering is caused by desire; the taming of desire ends suffering; and desire can be tamed by following the **eightfold path**, a set of deceptively simple guidelines for achieving *dharma*. He called the whole prescription the **Middle Way** because it avoided the extremes of sensual indulgence and asceticism, both of which were popularly believed to lead to enlightenment if pursued with sufficient vigour (and the Buddha had tried them both pretty vigorously before rejecting them).

As it developed, Buddhism became for many followers a full-time monastic pursuit. But for most lay people, the lonely quest for enlightenment was too hard-core and impersonal; to restore emotional elements that had been lost in the monastic movement, Buddhism evolved a populist strand known as **Mahayana** ("Great Vehicle"). Reintroducing elements of worship and prayer, Mahayana Buddhism developed its own pantheon of *bodhisattva* – enlightened intermediaries, something akin to Catholic saints, who have forgone *nirvana* until all humanity has been saved. Many of these were a repackaging of older Hindu deities, who were now given new names and roles as protectors of the *dharma*.

Followers of the original teachings called their school **Theravada** ("Way of the Elders"), but to Mahayana Buddhists it came to be known, somewhat disparagingly, as **Hinayana** ("Lesser Vehicle"). This tradition remains active in Sri Lanka and much of southeast Asia. It was the Mahayana doctrine that came to Nepal, around the fifth century, and also spread to China, Korea and Japan, adapting differently to each. Buddhism in India was dealt a death blow in the seventh century by Muslim invasions, which destroyed the great monastic universities and the thousands of monks who lived in them; what was left of Buddhism was effectively absorbed into the ocean of Hinduism.

TANTRA AND VAJRAYANA

Even as Hinduism was on the wane in India, a new religious movement was developing in Bengal and Bihar that would give a radically new bent to both Buddhism and Hinduism. *Tantra* erupted like the punk rock of religion,

proclaiming that *everything* in life can be used to reach enlightenment: the five things normally shunned in orthodox Hinduism and Buddhism as poisons – meat, fish, parched grains, alcohol and sex – are embraced wholeheartedly on the tantric path. Sex, in particular, is regarded as the central metaphor for spiritual enlightenment, and it is this inversion of the sacred and profane that has given *tantra* its somewhat risqué reputation. *Tantra* abounds in esoteric imagery, *mantra* (verbal formulas) and *mandala* (diagrams used to aid in meditation), which together make up a sort of mystic code intended only for initiates.

According to **Hindu *tantra***, the female principle (***shakti***) possesses the creative energy which is capable of activating the male force. The gods are powerless until joined with their female counterparts – in tantric art, Bhairab is often shown locked in a fierce sexual embrace – and in many of her guises the mother goddess has become Shakti, one half of a tantric union of sexual opposites. The human psyche, too, is held to consist of male and female forces that must be harnessed: followers of Hindu *tantra* are trained to visualize the body's female energy rising like a snake from the level of the sexual organs, ascending the seven psychic centres (*chakra*) of the spinal column to reach the male principle at the top of the head, resulting in realization.

Buddhist *tantra*, known as **Vajrayana** ("Thunderbolt Way"), reverses the symbolism of these two forces and makes the male principle of "skill in means" or compassion the active force, and the female principle of "wisdom" passive. In tantric rituals, these forces are symbolized by the the hand-held "lightning-bolt sceptre" (*vajra*; *dorje* in Tibetan), which represents the male principle, and the bell (*ghanti*), representing the female. Expanding on Mahayana's all-male pantheon, Vajrayana introduces female counterparts to the main Buddha figures and some of the *bodhisattva*, and sometimes depicts them in sexual positions.

LAMAISM (TIBETAN BUDDHISM)

Vajrayana Buddhism found its greatest expression in Tibet, which it reached (by way of Nepal) in the eighth century. At the time, Tibet was under the sway of a native shamanic religion (see below) known as **Bön**; Vajrayana eventually overcame Bön*, but only by taking on board many of its symbols and rituals, thus creating the spectacularly distinct branch of Buddhism that outsiders call **Lamaism**.

Lamaism turned Bön's demons into fierce guardian deities (*dharmapala*) – these can usually be seen flanking monastery (*gompa*) entrances – and incorporated elements of Bön magic into its meditational practices. Since blood sacrifices were out of the question, they were adapted into "vegetarian" offerings in the form of conical dough cakes called *torma*. The *Bardo Thödol* ("Tibetan Book of the Dead") is basically a shamanic guide to the after-death experience that probably owes much to Bön.

While its underlying principles aren't much different from that of Mahayana Buddhism, Lamaism has a tendency to express them in incredibly esoteric symbolism. The **Wheel of Life**, often depicted in *thangka* and frescoes at monastery entrances, is an intricate exposition of the different levels of rebirth and the limitations of the unenlightened state. The **stupa** (*chorten* in Tibetan), an ancient abstract representation of the Buddha, is developed into a complex statement of Buddhist cosmology, and Buddhahood is refracted into five aspects, symbolized by the five transcendent or *dhyani* (meditating) Buddhas, which can be seen in niches surrounding the Swayambhu stupa. **Prayer wheels**, usually bearing the *mantra*, *Om mani padme hum* ("Hail to the jewel in the lotus"), are Tibetan innovations that aid meditative concentration, and **prayer flags** also bear *mantra* and wishes for compassion which are meant to be picked up and spread by the wind.

By far the most important feature of Tibetan Buddhism are its ***bodhisattva***, which are often mistaken for deities. Held to be emanations of the *dhyani* Buddhas, they are used in meditation and rituals to help develop the qualities they symbolize, and also serve as objects of devotion. The most popular figures are **Avalokiteshwara** (**Chenrezig** in Tibetan), a white male figure with four arms (or, sometimes, a thousand), who represents

* Unrepentant Bön priests were banished to the Himalayan periphery, and even today vestiges of the Bön tradition may be encountered while trekking in Nepal: for example, a follower of Bön will circle a religious monument anticlockwise, the opposite direction to a Buddhist.

compassion; **Tara**, a white or green female figure, also representing compassion; and **Manjushri**, an orange-yellow male youth gracefully holding a sword above his head, who represents wisdom. Though these figures are peaceful and benign, there are also wrathful ones with bulging eyes, often wearing human skins and drinking blood, who symbolize the energy and potency of the enlightened state and the sublimation of our crudest energies.

From the beginning, Tibetan Buddhism placed great emphasis on close contact with a **lama**, or spiritual guide, who can steer the student through the complex meditations and rituals. Teachings were passed on orally from lama to disciple, so the divergence of various sects over the centuries has had more to do with different lineages than with major doctrinal differences. The leader of each sect, and indeed of each monastery, is venerated as the reincarnation (*tulku*) of his or her predecessor, and is expected to carry on the same spiritual tradition. Of the **four main sects**, the oldest is the Nyingma-pa ("Red Hats"), founded in the eighth century by Guru Padma Sambhava, who, if all the stories told about him were true, meditated in every cave in Nepal. The Sakya-pa broke away in the eleventh century, tracing their line from the second-century Indian philosopher Nagarjuna. The Kagyu-pa order emerged in the eleventh and twelfth centuries, inspired by the Tibetan mystic Marpa and his enlightened disciple Milarepa, who also meditated his way around Nepal. The Gelug-pa ("Yellow Hats") sect, led by the Dalai Lama, is the only one that takes a significantly different theological line; born out of a fifteenth-century reform movement to purge Lamaism of its questionable religious practices, it places greater emphasis on study and intellectual debate.

THE NEWAR SYNTHESIS

Ask a Newar whether he's Hindu or Buddhist, the saying goes, and he'll answer "yes": after fifteen centuries of continuous exposure to both faiths, the Newars of the Kathmandu Valley have concocted a unique **synthesis** of the two. To religious scholars, the Newar religion is as exciting as a biologist's missing link, for some believe that it provides a picture of the way Mahayana and Vajrayana Buddhism functioned historically in India.

Until only the past two centuries, the Newars held fast to the original monastic form of tantric Buddhism – as the *bahal* of Kathmandu and Patan still bear witness – while their rulers pursued the Hindu tantric path. However, the Kathmandu Valley has become progressively "Hinduized" since the unification of Nepal in the eighteenth century: the monasteries have largely disappeared, their monks have married, and the title of **Vajracharya** (Buddhist priest) has become a hereditary caste like that of the Bahun (Brahman) priests. Today, Newar Buddhists are perhaps the only Buddhist culture that no longer maintains active communities of monks or nuns. Although the acceptance of caste and the decline of monasticism have shifted the balance in favour of Hinduism, at the popular level the synthesis remains as well bonded as ever.

When Newars refer to themselves as *Buddha margi* (Buddhist) or *Shiva margi* (Hindu), they often do so only to indicate that they employ a Vajracharya or Bahun priest; even this doesn't always hold true, though, as many *jyapu* (farmers) call themselves "Hindu" and attend Hindu festivals, yet still use Vajracharyas. In any case, Newar rituals vary little from Hindu to Buddhist.

Puja (an act of worship) is performed to gain the favour of deities for material requests as often as for "spiritual" reasons. It is a profound and very personal ritual. An integral part of all Newar rituals is the "*puja* of five offerings", consisting of flowers (usually marigolds), incense, light (in the form of butter lamps), *sindur* (coloured powder) and various kinds of purified food (usually rice, dairy products, sometimes sweets). Before *darshan* (audience with a deity), the devotee or the priest uses consecrated water to wash him or herself and to bathe the deity. After the deity has symbolically accepted and eaten some food, the remainder is taken back by the devotee as *prasad* (consecrated food). This, along with a *tika* made with the coloured powder, confers the deity's blessing and protection.

Priests are ordinarily engaged for the more important **life-cycle rites** (birth, marriage, death) or for larger seasonal festivals; wealthier Newars may also seek private consultations at times of illness or important decisions. Bahun priests don't perform animal **sacrifices**, but they do preside over the rituals that precede them. This brings up one of the rare differences between Hindu and Buddhist Newars: while Hindu Newars are enthusiastic sacrificers – they call the bloody ninth day of the Dasain festival *Syako Tyako* (roughly, "the more you kill, the more you gain") – Buddhists seldom participate. During Dasain, Tibetan monasteries in Nepal hold special services to pray for good rebirths of the sacrificed animals.

THE NEWAR PANTHEON

All the Hindu and Buddhist deities already discussed are fair game for Newars, along with a few additional characters of local invention. Some deities specialize in curing diseases, others bring good harvests – as far as Newars are concerned, it doesn't matter whether they're Hindu or Buddhist so long as they do

the job. The following are some of the figures uniquely adapted by the Newars.

Machhendranath, honoured as a rainmaker par excellence, typifies the layering of religious motifs that so frequently takes place among the Newars. To be accurate, only Hindus call the god Machhendranath; Buddhist Newars know him as **Karunamaya** or any of a number of local names. He is commonly associated with Avalokiteshwara, the *bodhisattva* of compassion, who is invoked by the mantra *Om mani padme hum*. Depending on his incarnation (he is said to have 108), he may be depicted as having anything up to a thousand arms and eleven heads. While it's unclear how Avalokiteshwara came to be associated with the historical figures of Machhendranath and Gorakhnath – who are considered saints by Hindus – it was certainly in part the result of a conscious attempt by Hindu rulers to establish religious and social

A VISIT TO THE ASTROLOGER

His name is Joshi – in Newar society, all members of the astrologer subcaste are called Joshi – and to get to his office I have to duck through a low doorway off a courtyard in the old part of Patan and feel my way up two flights of wooden steps in the dark, climbing towards a glimmer of light and the sounds of low murmuring. At the landing I take off my shoes and enter the sanctum. Joshi-ji doesn't even look up. He's sitting cross-legged on the floor behind a low desk, glasses perched on the end of his nose, scowling over a sheaf of papers and, except for his Nepali-style clothes, looking exactly the way I'd always pictured Professor Godbole in *A Passage to India*. Shelves of books and scrolls are heaped behind him, and over in one corner a small shrine is illuminated by a low-watt bulb and a smouldering stick of incense. An older couple is seated in front of Joshi-ji's desk, nervously asking a question of the great man; he pushes his glasses up on his forehead, scribbles something, then pulls himself up to answer in melodic, nasal tones. I settle down on the floor next to two other waiting couples and together we keep a respectful silence.

To Newars, the **astrologer** is a counsellor, confessor, general practitioner and guide through the maze of life. With the priest and the doctor, he acts as mediator between the self and the universe (which are one); and since astrology is but one branch of Hindu knowledge, his

prognostications on important occasions are considered as important as a priest's blessings, and he is often called upon to provide a second opinion on a doctor's diagnosis. He knows most of his clients from birth. For new parents, the astrologer will prepare complex planetary charts based on the baby's precise time and place of **birth**, together with a lengthy interpretation detailing personality traits, health hazards, vocational aptitude, characteristics of the ideal marriage partner, and a general assessment of the newborn's prospects. When a **marriage** is contemplated, he will study the horoscopes of the prospective couple to make sure the match is suitable, and if so, he'll perform further calculations to determine the most auspicious wedding date. During an **illness**, he may prescribe a protective amulet, gemstone or herbal remedy corresponding to the planets influencing the patient. He may also be consulted on the advisability of a business decision or a major purchase.

While Western astrology is well suited to an independent, egocentric culture, **Hindu astrology** is much more at ease with the insignificance of the individual in the midst of the vast cosmos. And unlike the Western system, which is regarded more as a tool for personal fulfilment, the Hindu tradition emphasizes external events and how – and when – to deal with them. The **horoscope** represents a snapshot of the subject's *karma*: at bonds by grafting two Hindu saints on to a local Buddhist cult.

Kumari, the "Living Goddess", is another often-cited example of Newar syncretism (religious fusing): although acknowledged to be an incarnation of the Hindu goddess Durga, she is picked from a Buddhist-caste family. **Bhimsen**, a mortal hero in the Hindu *Mahabharat*, who is rarely worshipped in India, has somehow been elevated to be the patron deity of Newar shopkeepers, both Hindu and Buddhist.

Manjushri, the *bodhisattva* of wisdom, has been pinched from the Buddhist pantheon to play the lead part in the Kathmandu Valley's creation myth (although he is often confused with Saraswati, the Hindu goddess of knowledge). He is always depicted with a sword, with which he cuts away ignorance and attachment, and sometimes also with a book, bow, bell and *vajra*. Likewise **Tara**, the

embodiment of the female principle in Vajrayana Buddhism, assumes special meaning for Newars, who consider her the deification of an eighth-century Nepali princess.

Quintessentially tantric, the **Bajra Joginis** (or Vajra Yoginis) command their own cult centred at four temples around the Kathmandu Valley. They are regarded as the female aspect of the Buddha and are the subjects of esoteric cults and closely guarded secrets. Harati, the Buddhist protector of children, is zealously worshipped by Newars under the name **Ajima**, the grandmother goddess.

Throughout Nepal, stones and trees marked with *sindur* may be seen: vestiges of older animist practices, these may mark the place where a nature goddess (generically known as **Mai**), local spirit or serpent (*nag*) is supposed to live. There are many types of these lesser spirit beings who require offerings to safeguard passage through their respective domains.

---

the precise moment of reincarnation, the planets display the tally, and although it's misleading to speak in terms of planetary "influences", the *karma* that they reveal strongly implies the future course of one's life. The astrologer's role, then, is to suggest the best way to play the hand one was dealt.

For those who are really into astrology, here's a bit more background. The Hindu method of generating horoscopes follows the same essential principles as in the Western tradition, although technical differences between the two will produce somewhat different results. Hindu astrology recognizes the same twelve **signs of the zodiac**, albeit under different (Sanskrit) names, and assigns many of the same attributes to the planets and houses. The basic **birth chart** indicates the **sun sign** (the sign corresponding to the sun's position at the time of birth), the ascendant or **"rising" sign** (the sign rising above the eastern horizon at the time of birth) and the positions of the moon and the five planets known to the ancients, plus a couple of other non-Western points of reference. The positions of all of these are also noted in relation to the twelve **houses**, each of which governs key aspects of the subject's life (health, relationships and so on). The chief technical difference between Western and Hindu horoscopy is in how they line up the signs of the zodiac with respect to the earth. Western astrologers use the **tropical zodiac**, in which Aries is always assumed to start on the spring equinox

(March 21, give or take a day), even though a wobble in the earth's axis causes the actual constellations to drift out of sync by about 30° (one sign) every 2000 years or so – that's why it's now Pisces that the sun enters on March 21, and pretty soon, New Agers say, we'll be into the age of Aquarius. Hindu astrologers, on the other hand, go by the **sidereal zodiac**, which takes all its measurements from the *actual* positions of the constellations. (Technically speaking, this is a pretty profound difference, but since the Western and Hindu methods of interpretation are different, it all comes out in the wash.) If you have a horoscope done in Nepal, you'll probably be presented with a beautifully calligraphic scroll detailing all these measurements in chart and tabular form, using both tropical and sidereal measurements.

If charting a horoscope is largely a matter of mathematical donkey work, **interpretation** is an intuitive art requiring great eloquence and finesse. The astrologer can draw on numerous texts describing every conceivable conjunction of planets, and the positive and negative effects of every planet on every house; but at the end of the day, the usefulness of the reading must come down to the astrologer's own skill and experience. As I found on my visit to Joshi-ji, the specifics aren't everything. The astrologer isn't peddling facts; he's offering insight, hope, reassurance, and a dash of theatre.

David Reed

SHAMANISM

More ancient than Hinduism or Buddhism, **shamanism** is followed in diverse ways throughout the world by peoples fortunate enough to have been overlooked by the institutional religions. Variously described as medicine men, witch doctors or oracles, shamans perform mystical rituals to mediate between the physical and spiritual realms on behalf of their flock. (Western society has its "shamans", too – faith healers and mediums, for example.)

Shamanism is the traditional religion of most of Nepal's native ethnic groups, and while many have adopted at least outward forms of Hinduism or Buddhism (depending on their location), it is still widely practised in the eastern and western hills. In Nepali, the generic words for shaman are *jhankri* and *dhami*, although each ethnic group has its own term as well. Forms and practices vary from one tribe to another, but a *jhankri* – usually carrying a double-sided drum and often wearing a headdress of peacock feathers – is always unmistakeable.

The *jhankri*'s main job is to maintain spiritual and physical balance, and to restore it when it has been upset. As a healer, he may examine the entrails of animals for signs, gather medicinal plants from the forest, perform sacrifices, exorcize demons, chant magical incantations to invoke helper deities, or conduct any number of other rituals. As an oracle, he may fall into a trance and act as a mouthpiece of the gods, advising, admonishing and consoling listeners. As the spiritual sentry of his community, he must ward off ghosts, evil spirits and angry ancestors – sometimes by superior strength, often by trickery. All this, plus his duties as funeral director, dispenser of amulets, teller of myths and consecrator of holy ground and so on, put the *jhankri* at the very heart of religious and social life in the hills. Little wonder that Hinduism and Buddhism have been so shaped in Nepal by these shamanistic traditions, producing a unique melting pot of religions.

Charles Leech and David Reed

MUSIC AND DANCE

Nepali music hasn't exactly swept the world-music charts. Nepal's recording artists have a hard enough time holding their own against imports from India, let alone exporting their product overseas. Complicating matters is the fact that there are as many styles of Nepali music and dance as there are ethnic groups, and at any rate most of them can only be appreciated live – but all of this puts you in a position to appreciate some wonderfully rare sounds and sights while you're travelling around the country.

CLASSICAL AND RELIGIOUS

Little attempt has been made to chart the history of Nepali music. However, one of the earliest influences surely must have been **Indian classical music**, which goes back to a time when there was no distinction between India and Nepal, and to a region that extended well beyond the present borders of India. Classical music of the north Indian style flourished at the courts of the Malla kings and reached its zenith in Nepal under the Rana prime ministers, who patronized Indian musicians in their court to the exclusion of Nepali folk performers. Though it was always primarily an aristocratic genre, there is still a lively classical music network in Kathmandu, with tourist culture shows supplementing public performances and private recitals (for example, bimonthly at the royal palace).

Newar Buddhist priests still sing esoteric **tantric hymns** which, when accompanied by **mystical dances** and hand postures, have immense occult power. The secrets of these are closely guarded by initiated priests, but a rare public performance is held on Buddha Jayanti, when five *vajracharya* costumed as the Pancha Buddha dance at Swayambhu.

The contemporary layman's form of sacred music is **bhajan** – devotional hymn-singing, usually performed in front of temples and in rest houses. *Bhajan* groups gather on auspicious evenings to chant praises to Ram, Krishna or other Hindu deities; during festivals they may carry on through the night, and round-the-clock vigils are sometimes sponsored by wealthy patrons. Like a musical *puja*, the haunting verses are repeated over and over to the mesmeric beat of the tabla and the drone of the harmonium.

Sherpas and other Bhotiyas have their own ritualistic music rooted in **Tibetan Buddhist** traditions. Rhythm is more important than melody in this crashing, banging music, which is the exclusive preserve of monks. There's a hierarchy of instruments in the lamaist orchestra, from the *ghanti* (bell), *sankha* (conch shell) and *jhyaamta* (small cymbals), through the *bugcham* (large cymbals), *kangling* (small trumpet, made from a human thigh bone) and *dhyangro* (base drum), to the *gyaling* (jewel-encrusted shawm, or oboe) and *radung* (a ten-foot-long telescopic trumpet, which looks like a Swiss alpenhorn and produces a sound like a subsonic fart). The human voice forms a separate instrument in the mix, as monks recite prayers in deep, dirge-like, "self-harmonizing" chanting – a unique practice lately introduced to the West by touring Tibetan ensembles.

FOLK

For Nepalis where electricity and videos haven't yet reached, **folk music** and dancing is still just about the only form of entertainment available. On holidays and festival days, the men of a village or neighbourhood will typically gather in a circle for an evening session of singing and socializing; as a rule only the men perform on these occasions, while the women look on.

The musical backing always consists of a **maadal** (horizontally held two-sided drum), and often also includes other drums, harmonium and *murali* (bamboo flute). After some preliminary tapping on the *maadal*, a member of the group will strike up a familiar verse, and all join in on the chorus; the first singer runs through as many verses as he can remember, at which point someone else takes over, often making up comical verses to suit the occasion. Members of the group dance to the music one at a time, each entertaining onlookers with his interpretation of the song in swirling body movements, facial expressions and hand gestures.

Young men and women sing and dance together (though again, not at the same time) at **rodi ghar**, the Nepali equivalent of a sock hop. Originally a Gurung institution*, *rodi* has been embraced by many other hill groups as an informal, musical means of courtship. Young men and women of the hill tribes also sing improvised, flirtatious duets; the woman may even take the lead in these, forcing the man to come up with rejoinders to her jesting verses. In addition, women also sing in the fields, where singing lightens the burden of manual work – especially during *ropai* (rice transplant-ing), which has its own traditional songs.

Folk musical traditions vary among Nepal's many ethnic groups, but the true sound of Nepal may be said to be the soft and melodic music of the hills. Of several hill styles, **jhya-ure**, the *maadal*-based music of the western hills, has emerged as the most popular. **Selo**, the musical style of the Tamangs that's performed to the accompaniment of the *damphu* (a one-sided, flat, round drum), has also been adopted by other ethnic communi-ties. The music of the **Jyapu** farming caste has a lively rhythm, provided by the *dhime* (big two-sided drum) and a host of other drums, percus-sion instruments and woodwinds, though the singing has an extremely nasal quality that's hard for outsiders to appreciate.

Although folk music is, by definition, a pursuit of amateurs, two traditional castes of professional musicians exist in Nepal. **Gaaine** – wandering minstrels – have always served as an important unifying force in the hills, relaying not only news but also songs and musical styles from village to village. Accompanying them-

selves on *sarangi* (four-stringed fiddle), *gaaine* once thrived under patronage from local chief-tains, whose deeds were the main topics of their songs. They're on the decline nowadays, but a few still ply their trade in the villages north of Pokhara, in the far west, and in Kirtipur in the Kathmandu Valley (needless to say, the so-called *gaaine* in Thamel and Lakeside aren't worthy of the title). Their repertoire includes sacred songs in praise of Hindu deities, bitter-sweet ballads of toil and triumph, great moments in Nepali history and, increasingly, political commentary and even government propaganda.

Much more numerous are the **damai**, members of the tailor caste, who for genera-tions have served as the exclusive guardians of the *paanchai baajaa* (see below), and may also be employed at shrines to play during daily offerings and blood sacrifices. The tailor-musician combination isn't as strange as it might sound: Nepalis traditionally used to have just one set of clothes made each year, for the autumn Dasain festival, so tailors needed an occupation to tide them over during the winter and spring. Handily, that's the wedding season, when musicians are much in demand.

WEDDINGS AND FESTIVALS

No wedding would be complete without the **paanchai baajaa** (five instruments), a tradi-tional Nepali ensemble of *sahanai* (shawm), *damaha* (large kettledrum), *narsinga* (C-shaped horn), *jhyaali* (cymbals) and *dholaki* (two-sided drum). ("They got married without *paanchai baajaa*" is a euphemism for living together.) Despite the name, bands ideally number nine members – eleven is the legal maximum, set to keep wedding costs down (similarly, the number of wedding guests is limited to 51). In the Kathmandu Valley, *paanchai baajaa* musi-cians have largely traded in their traditional instruments for Western brass horns and their ceremonial dress for fanciful, military-style uniforms, but the music remains distinctly Nepali.

Raucous and jubilant, *paanchai baajaa* music is considered an auspicious accompani-ment to processions, Hindu rituals and life-cycle rites. During a **wedding**, the band accompanies the groom to the home of the bride, plays during the wedding ceremony, and again during the return procession. Apart from

---

*Hro dhim means "entertainment house" in Gurung; Nepali-speakers have unnecessarily added *ghar*, which also means "house".

playing popular folk songs and film favourites, the musicians have a traditional repertoire of numbers for specific occasions – for example, the "bride-requesting tune", in which the shawm player mimics the bride's wailing as she departs from her family home, and the music of the rice-transplanting season, which imitates the body rhythm of the workers.

Festivals bring their own interwoven forms of music and dance, especially in the Kathmandu Valley. The Newars of the valley are renowned for their spectacular **masked dances**, in which the dancers enter a trance-like state to become the embodiments of the gods they portray, gesturing and gyrating behind elaborately painted papier mâché masks. Best known of these are Bhaktapur's Nawa Durga dancers and their supporting musicians: their vigorous dance-drama, held on the tenth day of Dasain, recounts the victory of the goddess Durga over a buffalo demon. In Kathmandu, several different troupes take the stage during Indra Jaatra, performing the famous dance of the demon Lakhe, the sword-spinning Sawo Bhaku dance, and tableaux of the Das Avatar (ten incarnations) of Vishnu. The dancing is in a more humorous vein during Gaai Jaatra, when boys and young men play female roles in drag, since women aren't normally supposed to dance in public.

Virtuoso **drummers**, the Jyapus (Newar farmers) of the valley provide the rolling beat for processions on festival days: generally they beat enormous cyclindrical drums (*dhime baajaa*) in groups with two sizes of cymbal. At some shrines, in addition to a singing group, there is a complement of nine drums (*nawa daaphaa*), which are played in sequence during festivals with various accompanying instruments. Another type of popular processional band (*bansuri baajaa*) combines flutes and barrel drums.

Tibetans and Bhotiyas have their own form of dance-drama, *cham*. Tengboche hosts the most famous of such performances, Mani Rimdu, on the day after the full moon of October–November (another performance is held at Thami in May), when monks wearing masks and costumes represent various good and bad guys in the story of Buddhism's victory over the ancient Bön religion in Tibet. Monasteries at Boudha also present *cham* dances around Losar (Tibetan New Year).

MODERN MUSIC

Pre-1951, Nepal had no radio and no recording industry, and those few artists who travelled to Calcutta to record their songs on 78rpm were known only to a handful of aristocrats with record players. The dawn of modern Nepali music came in 1952, the year after the fall of the Ranas, when **Radio Nepal** was established; only a year later, Dharma Raj Thapa made recording history, selling 3000 copies of a novelty song about the conquest of Everest by Hillary and Tenzing Norgay.

A homegrown **recording industry** took root under King Mahendra (1955–72), himself something of a patron of the arts, and with it came Nepal's first wave of **recording stars**. Still the best loved of these, though he died in 1991, is Narayan Gopal, whose songs are praised for their poignant *sukha-dukha* (happiness-sadness). Aruna Lama remains popular for her renditions of sad and sentimental songs, and Kumar Basnet for his folk songs, while Meera Rana is still in her prime, belting out classical, folk and even pop tunes. Several of Nepal's foremost composers also came out of this era, including Amber Gurung (now music director at the Royal Nepal Academy), Nati Kazi and Gopal Yonjan.

More recently, the growth of the Nepali **film industry** has opened up new horizons for composers and singers; television, introduced in the mid-1980s, has provided a further boost. These have in turn contributed to the establishment of new recording studios and cassette-reproduction concerns. That said, cinema and TV have also done their share of harm. By copying third-rate Indian productions, Nepali films have mainly enlarged the market for lowest-common-denominator music, turning audiences and musicians away from traditional styles and opening the floodgates to slick Indian-produced *masaala* ("spicy": a little of this . . . a little of that).

Other recent developments have cut both ways, too. Tourist culture shows have inevitably led to the commercialization of Nepali culture and music, yet they've also helped preserve folk arts by providing a source of income for musicians and dancers. Ghazal, another Indian import (see "Nightlife", p.94), has done nothing for Nepali music, but it too pays the rent for Nepali musicians. Even Radio Nepal gives with one hand and takes away with the other, by providing an important outlet for musicians but at the same time blurring regional differences; its playlist, meanwhile, is increasingly given over to Indian tunes.

Pop music is of course a growing proposition with young urban Nepalis. Locally produced material is pretty unlistenable, and with MTV now available in Nepal via satellite dish, we can only expect quantity (if not quality) to increase. Receiving the most notoriety these days are Deep Shrestha, Prakash Shrestha, Sukmeet Gurung and the group Crossroads.

Gopal Yonjan, Carol Tingey and David Reed

DISCOGRAPHY

Stefano Castelli *Folk Songs of Nepal* (Albatros). *Jhyaure*, Tamang and shaman songs; sleeve notes in Italian.

John Melville Bishop *Music of a Sherpa Village* (Folkways). Introduction to folk music from Helambu.

Caspar Cronk *Songs and Dances of Nepal* (Folkways). A varied collection of short samples of Bhotiya, Thakali, Newar and Sherpa songs; excellent sleeve notes.

Amber Gurung *Kahiry Lahar Kahiry Tarang*. Good lyrics and music, although Gurung is a better composer than singer.

Gopal Yonjan *Kanchi* and *Sindoor*. Nepali film music.

B. Karki & P. Raja Mahat *Dohari*. Folk songs, including everybody's favourite, *Paan ko Paat* (Betel Leaf).

Prakash Gurung *Jhooma*. Nepali film music.

Ranjit Gazmer *Chino* and *Lahuray*. Nepali film music.

Prem Avatari – *Flute Recital*.

Tarabir Tuladher – *Sitar Recital*.

Narayan Gopal *Jeevan Yatra, vols 1, 2 and 3*. Songs expressing life's sentiments by Nepal's number-one vocalist.

Laurent Aubert & M. Lobsiger-Dellenbach *Musique de Fête chez les Newars* (Archives Internationales de Musique Populaire). Varied collection of 1950s and contemporary recordings.

TIBETAN EXILES IN NEPAL

On October 7, 1950, the People's Republic of China, which had concluded its own communist revolution only a year earlier, invaded – or, as Beijing still insists, "liberated" – Tibet. The Tibetan Army was easily overpowered, and by May 1951 Tibet was forced to sign a treaty accepting Chinese rule, on the understanding that China would not interfere with Tibetan government or culture.

During the following eight years, however, Chinese troops gathered in increasing numbers in Lhasa, the Tibetan capital; Tibetan monks were tortured, women raped and children taken from their homes for "re-education" in China. The Chinese imposed disastrous new agricultural methods on Tibetans, causing widespread famine. Tension mounted, fighting flared up in the east, and in March 1959 a full-scale **uprising** erupted in Lhasa. It was brutally crushed by the Chinese and thousands of Tibetans were executed or imprisoned, while Tibet was formally annexed to China. The **Dalai Lama**, Tibet's spiritual and political leader, fled to India; he still resides in Dharmsala, where the Tibetan government-in-exile is based. Tens of thousands of Tibetans followed, making their way into Nepal and India by various routes through the Himalaya.

For three decades, Tibet has endured outright **genocide** at the hands of the Chinese: the Dalai Lama's Bureau of Information calculates that 1.2 million Tibetans have been executed, tortured, killed in battle, starved or died in Chinese labour camps; during the 1966–76 Cultural Revolution, virtually every monastery was deliberately destroyed. An organized **guerrilla movement**, supported by the CIA, fought the Chinese along the Nepalese border until the early 1970s, when the US–China thaw led to its dissolution. Until a few years ago, Tibet's plight was largely ignored by the major powers, but China's Tiananmen Square massacre and the Dalai Lama's receipt of the 1989 Nobel Peace Prize put discussion of Tibetan independence back on the agenda.

Today, 15,000 out of a total of 110,000 **Tibetan exiles** live in Nepal, predominantly in the Kathmandu and Pokhara valleys. A large number of these industrious immigrants have by now achieved success in the carpet and handicrafts businesses, to the point where they can no longer be regarded as an underprivileged group. Many are playing an active role in establishing Boudha as a centre of Buddhist study, thus sustaining Tibetan religion and culture until the Chinese occupation of Tibet is ended.

Given Nepal's reliance on Chinese aid, the Tibetans are a source of discomfort for the government. China regards the exile communities as potential counter-revolutionary hotbeds, and exerts pressure on Nepal to supress any political activities there. While the "Free Tibet" movement is much bigger in India, where the Dalai Lama and the Tibetan government-in-exile are based, a **Tibetan underground** does exist in Nepal, chiefly among the disaffected youth of the former refugee camps. Don't expect anyone to discuss it openly, however, since Tibetan leaders have been warned that any "political" remarks could be grounds for prompt eviction. Recent political changes don't appear to have benefited the Tibetans, either. Nepal's powerful Communist Party has links with Beijing and is therefore keen to help keep Tibetan nationalism in check – in 1991 it managed to block the issuing of a visa to the Dalai Lama to attend a conference on Buddhism in Kathmandu.

The following profiles contrast the experiences of two Tibetans now living in Nepal.

CHOKYI NYIMA RINPOCHE: A LAMA

Chokyi Nyima Rinpoche ("Sun Lotus of the Precious One") was born in Runying, a village about 150 miles north of Lhasa, in the year of the Iron-Hare, 1951, the son of a recognized *tulku* (reincarnate lama) and an aristocratic mother. At the age of one and a half, after successfully completing numerous tests prescribed by Tibetan Buddhist tradition, he was identified as the seventh incarnation of Gar Druchen, a spiritual emanation of Nagarjuna, the second-century Indian Buddhist philosopher. Soon after, the young *rinpoche* ("precious one", a title given to revered Tibetan Buddhist teachers) was enthroned at his predecessor's monastery, Drong Gon Thubten Dargyeling, in central Tibet.

Chokyi Nyima recalls how 35 of the monastery's 500 monks were involved in lifelong retreats, as opposed to the more common three- to nine-year retreats, living in caves with "no door, only a window to pass food through, and they would never come out for the rest of their life" – a testament to the extreme faith with which some 200,000 monks and nuns devoted their lives in over 6000 monasteries and nunneries prior to China's occupation of Tibet.

Following the failed Tibetan uprising and subsequent upheavals of 1959, Chokyi Nyima and his family were whisked into exile in Gangtok, Sikkim, where, along with 53 other young *rinpoche*, he studied briefly in an English boarding school. He soon resumed his traditional monastic education, however, and for the next fifteen years studied under a series of famous Buddhist teachers.

Chokyi Nyima relates how one day, when he was nineteen or twenty, he and another young *tulku* approached their tutor, Gyalwa Karmapa, head of the Kagyu-pa sect of Tibetan Buddhism, with the intention of entering a three-year retreat. "He scolded us, saying, 'You are foolish, you just want to go in a cave to sleep. You are *tulku*, you need to save and help the sentient beings . . . why do you think you are being educated like this? Even though I am very happy that you have a willingness to go on a retreat at such a young age – on the one hand it is a good quality, but on the other hand it is not good *enough*!'" Finally sealing Chokyi Nyima's future, Gyalwa Karmapa said, "I think it is your *karma* to teach, especially to foreigners. You will go to Nepal and help your father (Urgyen Rinpoche) build a monastery." Chokyi Nyima still fondly recalls the wisdom of his teacher: "His mind was like the ocean, whereas our minds were but a drop in that ocean."

In 1974, Chokyi Nyima came to Boudha to help his father build the Ka Nying Shedrupling Monastery, and soon after, on the instructions of Gyalwa Karmapa, was made its abbot. Ka Nying Shedrupling today houses some 120 monks and lay people, who are dedicated to preserving and spreading Tibetan Buddhism through traditional wood-block printing of *pechha* (Tibetan liturgical texts), translating and publishing Buddhist books in English, and maintaining a large library of books on Buddhist topics.

Following the wish of his tutor, Chokyi Nyima began teaching not only the local community but also a growing number of foreigners. "I like to find out what kind of people they are, why they came here and what they are searching for," he says. In fact, one of his first Western *dharma* students is now undertaking a three-year retreat at a Buddhist centre in Scotland. Tibetan Buddhists aren't surprised by the spread of Buddhism in the West, for they regard it as the fulfilment of an eighth-century prophecy attributed to Guru Padma Sambhava, the legendary founder of Buddhism in Tibet: "When the iron bird flies and horses run on wheels, the Tibetan people will be scattered across the face of the earth, and the *dharma* will come to the land of the red men."

One morning, during one of his daily public audiences, where there are invariably two or three Westerners, Chokyi Nyima explains his thoughts on the increasing number of Westerners interested in Tibetan Buddhism. Thoughout the informal talk he is occasionally interrupted by pilgrims and the faithful coming to receive his blessings and exchange *kata*, the white scarves Tibetans give as an offering of good luck. "I've found that the teachings are touching more and more people from different countries, because they ring true," he says. "Many Westerners, especially the younger generation, are putting more faith in Western science only to discover that there are still many unexplained things. But because they have grown up with the idea of always searching for new answers to old phenomena, they usually have a very open mind. This is very much like what the Buddha said: 'Don't take my word for it, but find out the truth for yourself.'"

To this end, one of the aims of Ka Nying Shedrupling, as well as of many other monasteries, is to make Mahayana Buddhism readily available in the West. In Chokyi Nyima's words, "If peace comes to every individual, then there will be no conflicts, no problems, because nowadays too many people think often only of themselves. That's why we train more monks to be sent all over the world to help others to share their knowledge of the peace and caring message of the Buddha."

The often serious tone that Chokyi Nyima uses to make a point is never overshadowed by his humble and good-natured personality. As we leave the morning teaching, he gives us a mischievous look and says, "You must meditate! Don't be lazy and forget what I've said," throwing three oranges at us from a pile given as offerings.

Andy Balestracci

GEN TASHI: A KHAMPA

A boyishly trim man with a chiselled jaw is making the last stitches on a brown *chuba* (Tibetan wrap-around dress). "There! In time for Losar (Tibetan New Year)," he says to a Manang woman, who is wearing several raw-looking chunks of turquoise and coral strung around her neck.

"Please, won't you –"

"No, I said *no*. Your aunt will just have to wear something else. It's two days to Losar, and you want me to stitch another *chuba*? It's Losar, woman; we Tibetans drop all work. You go home and get the altars prepared, and leave me to my preparations."

Gen Tashi takes off his thick glasses, revealing curiously brown-bluish eyes. He bought the round-cut glasses in Lhasa on his way back from his hometown a few years ago; folding them, he puts them away with great care.

In the same room sits a younger man, Karma, shaking out black snuff onto his thumb from an aspirin bottle. He inhales with gusto, then digs out a square piece of woollen cloth from under the rug on his bed to blow his nose. "Drop everything, do your *puja*, and enjoy yourself at Losar – it's only once a year," he tells the woman.

"All right, all right. Losar is Losar I know," she says, laughing. "I won't bother you anymore. *Tashi delek* (Good day) to you – but please, after Losar . . ." And with her new *chuba* wrapped in newspaper under her arm, she leaves Gen's workroom.

For a man of 70, Gen Tashi cuts a trim figure. He sits cross-legged, ramrod straight. When people comment about his lithe figure, he says he is light because of his daily *kora* (circumambulations) around the Swayambhu hill. "The *kora* make you feel you can walk on and on," he says.

Considering his present occupation and boyish good nature, it's hard to believe that Gen spent more than a decade as a guerrilla fighter just south of the Tibetan border. He was born to a peasant family in the valley of Gyelthang, at the southeastern edge of the Tibetan plateau (the district is today part of the so-called Tibetan Autonomous Prefecture of Dechen). At the age of 14 he became a monk at Gyelthang's Sumtseling Monastery, which at the time supported 2000 monks, and for the next 18 years spent at least part of each year at the monastery observing special prayers and liturgies. For the rest of the year, when he was old enough, Gen went on family trading trips east to Dali and Lijiang in Yunnan (China), and west to Lhasa and southwest Kalimpong in Sikkim, where Chinese tea and Indian cotton and manufactured goods were traded. The trade helped finance Gen's monastic exams and initiations.

Chinese troops marched into Gen's district in 1954 and began imposing exorbitant taxes on traders, though they held back from enforcing immediate political changes. At the time of the 1959 uprising, Gen – who had just turned 36, an age considered inauspicious by Tibetans – and his family were on a butter-buying trip near Lhasa, attempting to raise money for their lama's examinations. Joining other Khampas (people of Kham, a province in eastern Tibet) caught away from home by the uprising, Gen rushed to help guard the Norbu Lingka, the Dalai Lama's summer palace in Lhasa, until the Dalai Lama could escape. Anticipating reprisals from the Chinese after the uprising, Gen fled south to Gangtok, Sikkim, where he and many compatriots found work building mountain roads.

Later the same year, the news of a reformed guerrilla movement known as the "Four Rivers and Six Ranges" reached Sikkim. Gen and a dozen fellow Gyelthangbas quickly joined up and were deployed to Mustang, the arid, rugged area north of Pokhara, where he participated in a variety of sabotage activities against the Chinese garrisoned across the border in Tibet. "I became good at hiding arms and ammunition underground," he says, not with bravado but with a sigh at being engaged in martial activities anathema to his vows as a Buddhist monk. (Several years have passed since he relinquished his vows.)

But lacking in international support, the guerrilla operations in Nepal gradually petered out, and the military camps became semi-permanent settlements. Gen dropped out of the movement and took up tailoring, earning a living by sewing *chuba* for the camp. Finally, after twelve years in Mustang, he and Karma, a fellow Khampa, together with Karma's wife, decided to move down to Kathmandu: their lives and the struggle didn't seem to be leading anywhere.

What had it all been for? "Well, we carried the hope that we could return to our fatherland," says Gen, for the first time showing emotion.

For their new lives in the capital, they found themselves hopelessly handicapped. By then, the efforts of other Tibetans to turn the folk art of carpet-weaving into a commercially viable venture was paying off; most of them were no longer refugees. In contrast, Gen, Karma and his wife had to adjust to a new environment, learn a new language and start from scratch. The only livelihood they could turn to was stitching *chuba*.

For years they were barely able to make ends meet, but recently Karma has started earning large commissions selling antique carpets. Now only Gen needs to stitch *chuba*, while Karma's wife manages the household. She and Karma have a twelve-year-old son, Dhendup, who attends a Tibetan school in the valley. Unlike Gen and his parents, Dhendup can write and speak in English, Tibetan and Nepali. He calls Gen grandfather.

Among the shrinking number of first-generation Tibetan exiles in Nepal, especially those of Kham, Gen's story is a common one. Many spent a large part of their adult lives fighting for their country. Now, with just as much hope, though perhaps with less urgency, they still look to the day when they can return to their homeland. Until then, they continue to circumambulate and pray and work for their younger ones.

K.T.G.

To get involved in the Tibetan cause, contact:
International Campaign For Tibet, 1518 K St NW #410, Washington DC 20005 (☎202/628-4123).

Office of Tibet, 241 E 32nd St, New York, NY 10016 (☎212/213-5010).
Tibet Support Group UK, 43 New Oxford St, London WC1A 1BH (☎071/240 2493).

DEVELOPMENT DILEMMAS

This is How a Nation Pretends to Survive

This is Machhapuchhre, Your Excellency!
And that's Annapurna.
And, beyond that are
The ranges of Dhaulagiri.
You can see them with your naked eyes.
I don't think you'll need any binocular, sir.
We want to open a three-star hotel, Your
* Excellency!*
Will you give us some loan?

Your Excellency!
This is Koshi, that's Gandaki
And, that one, yes, that blue one, is Karnali.
You might have read in some newspapers
That rivers in Nepal are on sale.
But that's not true, sir.
In fact, we have named our zones
In the name of these rivers.
It's our plan to generate electricity from them.
Will you give us some loan?

This is Kathmandu Valley, Your Excellency!
I mean country's capital,
Which contains three cities –
Kathmandu, Lalitpur and Bhaktapur.
Please mind the smell!
You may use your handkerchief, if you like.
It's true we have not been able to build
Either the sewer or public lavatories.
But in the next five-year plan
We are definitely going to introduce
"Keep the City Clean" programme.
Will you give us some loan, Your Excellency!

Min Bahadur Bista (1989)

With a per-capita income of just $170, Nepal is one of the world's poorest nations. Its population of 19 million is rising at an annual rate of 2.1 percent, and is expected to triple by the middle of the next century. With agriculture unable to keep pace with population, Nepal's "food deficit" is widening yearly and the country has little hope of ever feeding three times as many people – indeed, because of erosion due to overuse and deforestation, productivity is actually declining.

However, there are silver linings to all these dark clouds.

Nepali schoolchildren are frequently asked to write essays on "What I Would Do if I Were King". There are, of course, no right answers. Nepal is sloshing with foreign experts, all clamouring to offer their suggestions – and money – yet despite the efforts of the past four decades the country remains economically poor. Some say Nepal's underlying problems, and the inefficacy of foreign aid, will keep it forever backward. Others point to tangible improvements that have been made, such as increases in life expectancy and literacy. Still others claim that Nepal's problems have been vastly overstated by the government (to ensure continued aid) and development agencies (to justify their payrolls).

"Development" is a word like "progress": it means different things to different people, and all too often is assumed uncritically to be a desirable end in itself. Throughout the world – not only in Nepal – no one has yet worked out whether development is in fact a Good Thing, and if so what form it should take. But after spending time in the field, many aid workers conclude that Nepalis – who lead rich and elegantly simple lives, nearly self-sufficient and unencumbered by modern problems – have more to teach the "developed" (some would say overdeveloped) world than it has to teach them.

Pragmatists usually argue that development is going to come anyway, and communities should at least be given a fair choice as to what kind of development they want, rather than being forced to choose between development and non-development. But while no one advocates withholding aid or denying Nepalis' aspirations to certain material improvements, many in the development world reckon that Nepali schoolchildren are probably better able to solve their own problems than foreign experts, and that Nepalis ought to be the ones who decide what is appropriate development for Nepal.

Most people agree that Nepal's overarching problem ("challenge", in development parlance) is **poverty**, which can be traced to a number of factors: steep terrain, which makes farming inefficient and communications difficult; landlocked borders; few natural resources; a rigid social structure that entrenches the rich against the poor; and a comparatively late start (the Nepalese government did essentially nothing for its people before 1951). Unable to do anything about these causes, most development organizations have devoted themselves to alleviating symptoms.

All too often, foreigners (and, it has to be said, some Nepalis) have tended to view Nepal's situation as a set of problems that could be identified, measured and solved in isolation. Trouble is, life isn't like that: tackling one problem often only succeeds in shifting it to another area. For example, better health and sanitation are obvious requirements, but providing them increases the rate of population growth, at least in the short term. Curbing population is no simple task, for it is rooted in poverty and the low status of women. In the meantime, agriculture has to be improved to feed the growing population, deforestation reversed to stop the fuelwood crisis, and industry developed to provide jobs. Irrigation projects, roads, hydroelectric diversions are needed . . . you get the idea. Even if you resolve that development should be left to Nepalis, education, or at least "awareness-raising" programmes, will be required to get the ball rolling, and that means not so much building schools as addressing the poverty that keeps children from attending classes.

To take a more holistic approach, the big donor countries have come up with the idea of **integrated rural development projects (IRDPs)**, in which various sub-projects are coordinated to complement each other. The Swiss IRDP at Jiri and the British one in Dhankuta are prominent examples. Unfortunately, projects like these run counter to the "small is beautiful" maxim: they're terribly expensive (and therefore unlikely ever to be successfully passed on to Nepali management), prone to corruption and, in the end, limited to tiny geographic areas. Again, there are no easy, pat answers – only dilemmas.

The following sections only scratch the surface of complex issues. Many simplifications have been made. Some dilemmas are unique to Nepal, but many – if not most – are common to the entire "developing" world. The vast majority of people in the "developed" world are dangerously ignorant of the terrible pressures building in the poorer nations; travelling in Nepal affords a chance to witness the

inequities first hand and grapple with some of the dilemmas, which cannot help but make you re-examine your own lifestyle.

HEALTH

People rarely starve to death – usually **malnutrition** weakens their systems to a point where simple infections prove fatal. It may seem hard to believe, but 80 percent of Nepal's cute little children are undernourished, and up to 15 percent are clinically malnourished. As a result, **child mortality** (ages 0–5) is estimated at 165 per 1000, although this is an improvement over 1960, when the figure was 300 per 1000 – almost one in three. The introduction of cheap oral rehydration packets, together with simple immunization programmes, are largely responsible for saving these lives.

Nepal is one of the few countries in the world where men live longer than women: **life expectancy** is 54 for males, 51 for females. Females are the last in the family to eat (one study found that Nepali girls under the age of 5 suffer 50 percent higher malnutrution than boys) and are expected to work harder (another study estimated women do 57 percent of all farm work in Nepal).

Poor sanitation and crowded, smoky conditions contribute to Nepal's high incidence of **disease**. Up to 80 percent of the population are reckoned to be suffering from parasitic infections at any one time, and 15 percent have TB. On the bright side, mosquito spraying in the Tarai has reduced malaria cases to about 25,000 annually, compared with 2 million a year during the 1950s (but even this is on the way back up). Improved public **sanitation** is gradually being introduced, but in the booming Tarai cities covered sewers are barely keeping pace with growth, while village latrines are still rarely found off the popular trekking routes. Communal taps have been built in most of the more accessible hill villages to provide safe **drinking water**.

Although the government, aided by United Mission to Nepal, has constructed over 110 hospitals to date, Western-style facilities are neither affordable nor appropriate for most villages. A better measure of progress on this front has been the creation of some 800 primary healthcare posts, where health assistants (often local people) are trained in traditional ayurvedic practices.

THE DEVELOPMENT INDUSTRY

Everyone loves to give aid to Nepal. Although carpet manufacture is officially listed as the country's top source of foreign exchange, the development industry is far, far bigger. Aid to Nepal has increased ten-fold in the past fifteen years, and now brings in at least $500 million annually.

Foreign development projects in Nepal fall roughly into three categories. **Bilateral** (and multilateral) aid – that is, money given by foreign governments directly to Nepal – has built most of the infrastructure (roads, dams, airports), as well as the biggest IRDPs. Many smaller projects are carried out by some 200 international **non-governmental organizations (NGOs)**; some of these are well known, such as Oxfam, CARE and Save the Children, while others are just one person doing fieldwork and raising sponsorship money in his or her home country. Voluntary NGOs, such as Britain's Voluntary Service Overseas (VSO) and the US Peace Corps, don't run any of their own projects, but instead slot volunteers into existing HMG programmes. Finally, **international lending bodies** like the World Bank and Asian Development Bank act as brokers to arrange loans for big projects with commercial potential – usually irrigation and hydroelectric schemes.

Many of these organizations do excellent work; almost all are motivated by the best possible intentions. However, money cannot automatically solve Nepal's problems, as some of the biggest projects have learned to their cost. By paying their imported experts ten or twenty times more than Nepalis to do the same job, the big bilateral missions cause resentment or, worse, encourage Nepalis to gather round the aid trough instead of doing useful work. To the extent that they import experts and materials, they undermine Nepalis' ability to do things for themselves, fostering a crippling **aid dependency** that now permeates almost every level of society. In 1973, foreign handouts made up 40 percent of Nepal's development budget; now it's 70 percent, or 15.5 percent of the gross national product – the highest ratio in South Asia. Some wags joke that the country can't *afford* to develop, lest it jeopardize development funding.

At their worst, many argue, bilateral aid and international loans are often little more than pious fronts for **neocolonialism**. Organizations like the World Bank measure Nepal by narrow economic indices and invariably prescribe Western-style technological fixes. Per-capita income, for example, is meaningless in a country where most people are self-sufficient farmers. In Nepal, self-sufficiency is a considerable virtue – encouraging farmers to irrigate and buy fertilizers to grow cash crops may raise their income, but not necessarily their quality of life. It will, however, give Western banks a capital project to finance, Western contractors an irrigation system to build, Western chemical companies a new market for fertilizers, and Western consumer-goods companies new consumers. Meanwhile, Nepalese cash crops will be exported (probably to India), even as Nepalis suffer malnutrition.

For bilateral donors – especially India and China – foreign aid is a handy way of buying **political influence**, and it's also a means of stimulating the donor country's own domestic economy: more than half of British aid to Nepal (which amounts to £10 million annually) is paid directly to British **contractors**. Some of these companies spend tens of thousands of pounds to prepare their bids for advertised contracts – it's a very lucrative business, aid.

Even when foreign governments and agencies try to step back and do the right thing, their charity often still has a corrupting influence. The latest fashionable philosophy is that the best way to get things done is to finance **local NGOs**, which, it's assumed, have a better handle on local problems and solutions than foreign experts. Sounds great in theory, but what's the result? An explosion in local NGOs for every conceivable cause, all sounding just as right-on as could be: "small-scale" this, "women's development" that, "environmental" whatever. (There are now so many local NGOs in Nepal that at least one exists simply to co-ordinate them all.) Unfortunately, many of these organizations aren't doing much besides writing grant proposals, and the only development they're assisting is their director's bank balance.

POPULATION

Slowing **population growth** isn't just a matter of passing out a few condoms. In Nepal, as in other countries, children are considered to be an investment for old age, since there's no state pension to draw on; moreover, Nepalis tend to have large families because they can't be sure all their children will survive. Hindus, especially, keep trying until they've produced at least one son, who alone can perform the prescribed rites (*shradha*) for his parents after they've died.

While it's not the place of aid workers to contradict Hindu beliefs, population-control efforts can have little impact unless the **status of women** (see p.366) is raised, which is a long and difficult matter of education – not so much of women, who already know they're repressed, but of the men who do the repressing. Many "women's programmes" have failed because they've assumed that women only need to be provided with the awareness and skills to improve their situation; in fact they can do little if their husbands still hold the power.

The other reasons for **high fertility** can be removed by reducing the current high levels of poverty and child mortality. This, at least, is what has happened in many other countries and it should work in Nepal, but unfortunately it involves a period of rapid population growth until the birth rate settles down to match the lower death rate.

At the moment, Nepal is still very much in the growth mode. Currently doubling every 33 years, the population has a biological momentum that is unlikely to be checked in the present generation, simply because of the number of girls already approaching child-bearing age. Meanwhile, the government's **family planning** efforts are still woefully inadequate: only 15 percent of Nepalis practice any form of contraception at all. The remoteness of villages makes it all the more difficult to get the message out.

If Nepal's population doubles or triples, where will all the extra people live? As it happens, this is not a brand-new situation, for large parts of the middle hills have probably been overpopulated for the past century. **Emigration** – to the Tarai, India and, more recently, to Kathmandu and overseas* – has always regulated the people pressure. Significantly, the latest census (1991) shows a dramatic decline in the annual rate of population growth – to 2.1 percent, down from 2.6 percent a decade ago – most of which is probably due to emigration. Even so, it's estimated that the country's urban population will double during the 1990s, and most of this increase will be taken up by the Kathmandu Valley and a half-dozen Tarai cities.

*How's this for trivia: in 1992, Nepalis made up 12 percent of South Korea's illegal aliens.

AGRICULTURE

If Nepal's population doubles, **food production** must theoretically double – a seemingly unattainable goal, given that in the past decade the country has gone from being a net exporter of food to a net importer. Indeed, the drought years of 1991 and 1992 saw an alarming widening in Nepal's food deficit, and an increasing reliance on emergency relief from donor nations.

Nepal's farmland is already among the most intensely cultivated in the world. A mere 20 percent of the country's land area is arable; if anything, this figure is decreasing, due to erosion, while cash-cropping is taking other land out of production of basic staples for domestic consumption. Clearing new land for cultivation only adds to deforestation, so it's preferable to find ways of increasing the **productivity** per acre. Various methods have been tried in Nepal, as in other countries. Agriculture experiment stations, such as the British-funded facility at Pakhribas in the eastern hills, have achieved mixed results in showcasing high-yielding seeds and animal breeds; where these have been appropriate, local farmers have readily embraced them, but often they have proved to be impractically expensive. The official **Agriculture Development Bank**, which was created to provide credit for poor farmers to make simple improvements, has unfortunately grown so bureaucratic that only wealthier farmers can avail themselves of it.

Irrigation is a high priority, since it permits an extra crop to be grown during the dry season. Small-scale community projects are now being built with generally good results, but the government's inefficient and poorly maintained programme has resulted in benefit to relatively few farmers (again, usually the best-off ones). It's been estimated that a big government-built system costs at least eight times more per acre than a community-built one. The government has also tried to promote the use of **chemical fertilizers** through subsidies, but this has led to black-marketeering, with much of the fertilizer being resold to India. Sometimes the best technique is the simplest one: in some remote areas, the introduction of a few common garden vegetables is improving local diets and even extending growing seasons.

Stark inequities prevail in Nepal's agriculturally based economy. Controlled by vested interests, the government has done a poor job of enforcing **land reform**, with the result that 63 percent of cultivable land is still owned by 16 percent of the population. Despite a 1964 law prohibiting landlords from charging tenant farmers annual rents of more than 50 percent of their crop, many farmers are locked in a hopeless cycle of debt and victimized by unscrupulous lenders. Most people agree that agriculture must receive the main thrust of development efforts in Nepal. With over 80 percent of Nepalis still making their living from the land, it's unrealistic to look for miracles elsewhere.

DEFORESTATION AND EROSION

In the Nepal hills, population, agriculture and environmental damage combine in a worrying vicious cycle: the need for more food leads to more intensive use of the land, which degrades the environment and lowers productivity, which further increases pressure on the land. An expanding population needs not only more **firewood**, but also more **fodder** for animals, which provide manure to maintain soil fertility. Overuse of firewood and fodder results in **deforestation**, as does any expansion of farmland, and as a result Nepal's forest area is shrinking by an estimated 0.4 percent per year. Trees help anchor the fragile Himalayan topsoil – removing them causes **erosion** and landslides, which not only reduce the productivity of the land but also send silt down to the Bay of Bengal, contributing to disastrous **floods** in Bangladesh.

Or so goes the theory. In practice, emigration seems to stabilize the cycle, and studies give wildly differing estimates for the rate of deforestation. The most that can be said is that the situation is definitely bad in some areas, but not so bad in others. Experts still don't know to what extent deforestation contributes to erosion, but most agree that the prime cause is simply the natural sloughing and shifting of very young mountains.

Even the government now admits it got it wrong in the 1950s when it **nationalized the forests** to protect them. Before that, the forests had been competently managed by local communities; but when the trees were taken away from them, locals felt they had no stake in their preservation, and because government enforcement was weak they easily plundered them. HMG's current policy of **community forestry** is supposed to give the forests back to the people, recognizing that villagers are in fact very ecologically minded and will manage their forests responsibly and sustainably so long as they don't fear re-nationalization. While foreign development projects have concentrated mainly on **reforestation**, newly planted areas account for only about one percent of Nepal's forest cover.

Deforestation is a separate issue **in the Tarai**, where the trees have been felled as a matter of policy, to make way for settlers and to earn money for the government through state-sanctioned timber sales (mostly to India). Although the vast majority of the Tarai's magnificent native forest has gone in the past four decades, the clearing continues. Ironically, the state-owned Nepal Timber Corporation is so inefficient at meeting orders that it's probably helping delay the pace of deforestation – it is, however, ripe for privatization. Nepal has won praise abroad for setting aside large chunks of the Tarai's forests as **national parks** and wildlife reserves, but the government can expect mounting resistance from its own people, who question why such valuable land should be set aside for tourists and crop-destroying animals (see p.238).

TECHNOLOGY: APPROPRIATE AND OTHERWISE

Nepal's **electricity** use, which was tiny only a few years ago, is now soaring. As of early 1993, demand was outstripping supply by 15 percent – and growing at an annual clip of 15 percent. Burgeoning industries, rural electrification and a growing ownership of appliances are all contributing to the increase. Until new sources of power come on line, load shedding (scheduled power cuts) will continue to be a fact of life in Nepal.

Yet many see electricity – specifically **hydroelectricity** – as the logical solution to Nepal's fuelwood crisis. The country's steep, mountain-fed rivers are estimated to have hydroelectric potential to the tune of 83 million megawatts – enough to power the British Isles. **Large-scale** diversions have been built on the Khulekani (south of Kathmandu) and the Marsyangdi (along the Prithvi Highway), and another on the Arun River is scheduled to be built during the next decade. This last, known as Arun III, will cost $700 million and be by far the most expensive project undertaken in Nepal, but it could in turn be dwarfed by a $4.7 billion project being studied for the Karnali River, which would be the largest hydro diversion in the world. No one claims that these dams can directly substitute electricity for firewood in the average Nepali home, but supporters argue that the power generated could stimulate industry and be sold to India for a profit. Opponents counter that large-scale diversions are environmentally disruptive and ludicrously expensive to build in Nepal's inaccessible terrain, requiring vast inputs of foreign aid. They also reject the assumption that a switch from "non-commercial" (ie, free) fuel to electricity would constitute economic growth.

There is more support for **microhydro** projects, dozens of which have already been installed (both with foreign and private Nepalese funding) to supply electricity for a few hundred households each. Yet no matter how it's produced, electricity is no use to the majority of Nepalis who can't afford it, and it can only play a limited role in offsetting deforestation: as far as most rural Nepalis are concerned, wood is free, whereas electricity costs rupees – and electric appliances cost dollars. Some observers reckon that providing electric lights encourages people to stay up later and burn more wood to keep warm. In trekking villages like Namche and Tatopani, however, where innkeepers cook with electricity, the net wood savings is probably worthwhile.

Roads, like hydroelectric and irrigation projects, don't come out well in cost-benefit analyses in Nepal, though planners insist that they're necessary for development. They cost far more than Nepal could ever afford without aid, and are almost as expensive to maintain; many are hastily built for royal visits to remote district headquarters, only to wash away with the next monsoon. The wealthy – bus owners, truckers, merchants, building contractors – benefit from road-building, while porters and shopkeepers along the former walking route lose out. By contrast, **footbridges** put villages within easier reach of jobs and health facilities, and enable villagers to get their produce to market more efficiently, making them perhaps the most useful and popular type of public-works project.

At the household level, appropriate technology has to be something the average Nepali peasant can afford, which isn't much. Several groups have worked hard to introduce "**smokeless**" *chulo* (stoves), which burn wood more efficiently and reduce unhealthy kitchen smoke. Yet even this simple innovation illustrates the dilemmas of tampering with traditional ways: Nepalis complain that the new stoves aren't as easy to regulate and don't emit enough light, while the lack of smoke allows insects to infest their thatched roofs; thus many Nepalis are converting from thatch to corrugated metal.

WOMEN AND CHILDREN

Outside the relative sophistication of Kathmandu, Hindu **women** are a long, long way from liberation. In remote rural areas, they're considered their husband's or father's chattel, given or taken in marriage for the price of a buffalo – a status reinforced by law. Orthodox Bahuns, while in the minority, reveal the extent of female subjugation. They believe a woman is ritually unclean during menstruation and for ten days after giving birth, and that she must remain apart during that period and drink cow's urine to cleanse herself. Polygamy, though officially outlawed, is widely practised in the hills, and if a woman doesn't produce a son she's liable to be replaced. Sherpanis and other Buddhist women are treated much more equally, and high-caste Hindu women may easily flout conventions, but the average Nepali woman does the work of ten men.

Several development problems already touched on – inequities between the sexes in health care and education, and the failure of population-control efforts – proceed directly from the low status of women in Nepal. Another tragic consequence is the **trafficking** of Nepali girls for Indian brothels. It's estimated that 200,000 Nepalis have been sold into sexual slavery in India – a third of them in Bombay alone – where patrons prize them for their beauty and supposed lack of inhibitions. To poor Hindu families in Nepal, daughters are often regarded as burdens, costing money to be married off and then becoming another family's asset; when a middleman comes offering, say, Rs15,000 for a pubescent daughter, many readily agree. A prostitute may eventually buy her freedom, but ordinarily she won't be released until she's been "damaged" – which these

THE END OF THE ROAD

Anna Robinson worked for three years as a VSO volunteer in Doti District, in the far western hills, and is now field officer for VSO Nepal.

Gazing down from the hill, over terraces of paddy fields, we could see the first truck making its hesitant journey up the spiralling new dust road. Local people ran down the main street of the bazaar to meet the first iron monster to complete the ascent.

For them it was the excitement of seeing a machine that moved along the ground. For me it was the feeling that here, at last, was a link with the outside world. There was the weekly plane to Kathmandu, of course. But with only eighteen seats – and $30 a seat at that – it was hardly significant to most people.

Excitement about the road lasted quite a while. Then people became less frightened and awestruck, and the verges were no longer dotted with rapt, admiring observers. Those who could afford the fare became seasoned travellers and were no longer to be seen vomiting out of the windows as the truck lurched along. In fact it became an accepted part of daily life – rather like the plane, it came and went, affecting few people.

Goodies
But down by the airstrip, a shantytown of temporary shacks sprang up overnight with the coming of the road. Here was where all the goodies that came by truck from India were to be found: plastic snakes that wriggled, gilt hair-slides, iron buckets, saucepans and – best of all – fresh fruit and vegetables.

For us foreigners, and the paid office workers, accustomed to going for weeks with nothing but potatoes and rice in the shops, it seemed like paradise. Every day more and more apples, oranges, onions, cabbages and tomatoes would make their way up the hill. There was even a rumour that ten bottles of Coca-Cola had been sighted in the bazaar.

One morning, as I was eyeing a big plastic bucket full of huge Indian tomatoes in a local shop, a woman pulled my arm. "Don't you want to buy mine?" she asked. And there, in her *doko*, were a few handfuls of the small green local tomatoes.

Just a fortnight earlier I would have followed her eagerly, begging to be allowed to buy some. Now the shopkeeper laughed at her: who would want to buy little sour green tomatoes when there were big sweet red ones to be had?

For women like her, trudging in for miles from one of the surrounding villages to sell her few vegetables, there was no longer a market. The influential bazaar shopkeepers negotiated deals with the Indian traders with their truckloads of vegetables. The new road meant new money for the shopkeepers – but less for the poor, whose livelihood was undermined and who had no way of buying the wonderful new merchandise.

Casualties
There were other casualties, too. Gaggles of poor women, who had made a living out of carrying people's baggage from the airstrip to the bazaar, were once a common sight, haggling in angry, spirited voices over the price of their services. But with the coming of the new road, people simply boarded one of the trucks – baggage and all. Ragged and downtrodden at the best of times, these women were reduced to silently and gratefully accepting any rate people were prepared to pay for their help.

I began to wonder about the road. But I needn't have worried. Soon the monsoon rains arrived and the swelling river took charge of things. Within days the bridge was completely washed away, leaving several trucks stranded on the wrong side of the river, never to return to India.

After the monsoon
The original truck continued to creak up and down the winding road between the airstrip and the bazaar, its fuel being hoisted across the river by rope-pulley, but became so overcrowded that one day it broke down halfway up the hill. As the road had been almost completely washed away by the rain, it was simply left there in the middle of the road.

When the monsoon ended, it was overgrown with creepers and made a very pleasant home for a local family.

By then the grand new road was little more than a memory. The women porters went back to climbing regularly up and down the hill; the shantytown vanished as quickly as it had appeared; and everyone went back to eating rice and potatoes as before.

Last I heard, a foreign-aid agency had decided to rebuild the road, with a proper bridge this time: in the interests of development.

Anna Robinson

Reproduced by permission of New Internationalist Publications.

days means she has AIDS (although Nepal claims it has fewer than 100 AIDS victims, in 1992 the World Health Organization put the number at 6000). So far the Nepal government has shown little inclination to act on the growing problem, and concerned NGOs have been left to set up homes for former prostitutes, who would otherwise be shunned by family and friends if they returned to their villages.

The **women's movement** is embryonic in Nepal. Women weren't granted the vote until 1948, and though the All Nepal Women's Organization was formed in 1951, women working for social change were forced to operate underground until the 1990 restoration of democracy. Aid projects and agencies have been chiefly concerned with setting up cottage-industry employment for women, so they can earn spare cash as a first step to some sort of self-determination. A few local NGOs have been set up to disseminate information and raise consciousness on women's issues.

Children, like women, are often victims of poverty in Nepal. However much their parents love them, in poor families they are counted as an economic resource from an early age. **Child labour** has always been essential in agriculture, and in the past it was common for children to work as unpaid servants for village landowners simply so there would be one less mouth to feed. In the growing cash economy, however, children are increasingly being relied on to earn wages as porters, *kanchha* ("boys"), carpet-weavers or tea-pluckers. One survey suggests that two-thirds of the carpet industry's labour force is made up of children under the age of 16. Not only are these youngsters forced to work long hours in unhealthy conditions, and are frequently abused, they are deprived of their childhood – the right to play, be loved and be educated. The government has passed laws against child labour, but this is yet another problem that can only be effectively addressed by attacking its root cause: poverty.

EDUCATION

Nepal's education system has come a long way in a short time. There were few state **schools** before 1951, and they were open only to the children of elites – now there are primary schools within walking distance of most villages, and legions of private schools in the Kathmandu Valley. However, primary-school enrolment is probably well below the official figure of 82 percent, and actual attendance may be less than 25 percent. Only 13 percent of boys – and just 3 percent of girls – finish secondary school. **Literacy** has also made great strides, though the gulf between males (55 percent) and females (25 percent) is telling.

Thus far government policy has stressed quantity over quality, budgeting plenty of money for buildings and leaving little for salaries, but this has probably been a necessary first step in starting an education system from scratch. Since the proportion of qualified **teachers** is very low, most aid programmes have focused on teacher training. Western workers believe education could be a powerful catalyst for change in Nepal, but many complain that the current curriculum is geared for churning out bureaucrats and should be made more vocational and relevant to a peasant population.

Those who do finish high school and go on to one of Nepal's many **colleges** or **universities** often find that there's no work for them when they graduate – a common problem in most countries, but all the more acute in Nepal, whose non-agricultural sectors are particularly poorly developed. A further cultural complication is the prevalent attitude towards education in Nepal: equated with high status, it is all too often pursued merely to avoid physical labour, which carries low status. This, ironically, has the effect of removing many of Nepal's most highly trained people from the productive workforce. Frustrated by a lack of opportunities or bored by their own privileged idleness, educated youth of the Kathmandu Valley make up a growing class of angry young men given to revolutionary talk and *goonda* antics.

INDUSTRY AND TRADE

The government needs to create jobs – agriculture simply cannot absorb all of Nepal's growing workforce. Moreover, a developing nation like Nepal has to produce things, not only for domestic consumption but also for export, so that it can earn foreign exchange to pay for the imported technology and materials it needs for development. That means boosting **industry**, which in Nepal's case accounts for a relatively low 15 percent of gross national product.

Carpets are Nepal's great rags-to-riches story, having now exploded into a $100 million industry employing (directly and indirectly) 300,000 people – and still growing exponentially. Some analysts believe carpet manufacture has the potential to be Nepal's economic salvation: highly labour-intensive, it generates plenty of employment and adds lots of value to relatively cheap materials; it's also helping to diversify the economy away from an overreliance on tourism. But all this comes at a very high price in terms of exploitation, social disruption and pollution – see p.140.

Similarly, **tourism** has its drawbacks. The industry creates tens of thousands of much-needed jobs, plus indirect employment in related industries, but this work tends to be menial and seasonal. Moreover, the economic benefits of tourism are highly localized, and an estimated 80 percent of the foreign exchange earned from tourism goes right back out of the country to pay for imported materials. True, tourism can claim some credit for shaping HMG's mostly progressive environmental record – but it's an open question whether the revenue earned really offsets the ecological and cultural costs. The fruits of tourism, so arbitrarily awarded, have turned legions of Nepalis into panhandlers, in much the same way that aid has done to politicians and institutions.

In many other industries, Nepal finds itself in a classic Third World bind. It can't profitably produce things like vehicles and computers because its domestic market is so small (and poor), and importing even modest amounts of these items quickly runs up a nasty **trade deficit**. The government has therefore put much of its energy into stimulating the production of run-of-the-mill goods for domestic consumption, achieving dubious successes in some sectors. Beer production, to take one example, has increased 400 percent in the past decade. In development economics, this is known as **import substitution**: for a country short on foreign exchange, a penny saved is a penny earned. Soft drinks, cigarettes, biscuits and packet noodles have seen similarly dramatic increases in output. Many of these factories have been set up as licensed **monopolies**, which give the government more control over the pace of development, but tend to concentrate wealth in the hands of a few Kathmandu fat cats (the law requires that all businesses have a majority Nepali ownership, which

makes for some very well-off silent partners). A few essential industries are still run as state-owned enterprises, but the Congress government is gradually privatizing these poorly managed and typically loss-making concerns.

The presence of **India** as Nepal's neighbour to the south inevitably complicates matters. Nepal's main trading partner, India has traditionally levied high import duties to protect its own industries, thus benefiting Nepali border traders (who can sell Western goods for less than their Indian competitors) but crippling Nepali exporters (whose goods become uncompetitive with duty added on). Fortunately, the Congress government's ties with India's leadership have recently resulted in more favourable **terms of trade**, and the decision of both countries to make their currencies fully convertible promises to make their goods more competitive in the world market. Critics, however, warn that Congress politicians are turning a blind eye while Indian entrepreneurs are buying up Nepal's choicest businesses.

KATHMANDU VALLEY PROBLEMS

Solutions often create their own problems. For 40 years, people have been trying to get Nepal to develop – now that it has, in the **Kathmandu Valley**, many are nervously fumbling for the "off" button.

Kathmandu appears to be following in the footsteps of other Asian capitals like Bangkok, Taipei and Seoul, albeit on a smaller scale. Overpopulation is driving a growing **rural exodus**; new roads and bus services are carrying the landless poor away from their villages, while jobs in the carpet and tourism industries attract them to the Kathmandu Valley. Many immigrants land jobs and begin the difficult process of finding a place for themselves in the **big city**, and a few even find their fortune there. But there's no safety net for those who don't. They may end up squatting in the most primitive conditions imaginable – in unhealthy shacks by the river, in empty buildings, in the streets – and scrounging a living from the rubbish heaps or prostitution.

While poverty is a perennial problem in the valley, it's prosperity that's creating the brand-new headaches, starting with **traffic** and **pollution**. Industrial workers get to their factories by tempo or bus. The more affluent drive their own motorbikes or cars. Goods must be moved by truck. Tourists take taxis. The result is ever-growing gridlock and an increasing smog problem from a fleet of vehicles that is doubling every two to three years. In addition, carpet-washing factories release toxic chemicals into the environment, and the tide of raw sewage being dumped into streams rises ever higher with the population. Those who can afford to are moving out to the suburbs, and their commuting only worsens the problem.

Meanwhile, sheer numbers of people are taxing the valley's other infrastructure. In Kathmandu, demand for **drinking water** is about three times higher than supply, with the result that residents in most neighbourhoods have pressure only on alternate mornings or evenings – most pump what water they can get up to rooftop storage tanks, and supplement it with deliveries by tanker. Similarly, the valley accounts for a disproportionate amount of Nepal's energy demand, thanks to personal affluence (videos and refrigerators) as well as industrial growth – which, as already discussed, means rationing in the form of **load shedding**.

The damage that has been done to the valley's **culture** in the name of progress is much less easy to quantify, but is arguably more profound. The traditional architecture is no longer valued. Members of the younger generation are drifting away from the religion of their parents. The *Guthi* (charitable organizations) are in decline and have been forced to leave the upkeep of many temples to foreign preservationists. Tourism has robbed crafts of their proper use, and many performance arts of their meaning. Work outside the home has disrupted family life, and the influx of strangers has introduced social tensions and crime.

But perhaps we shouldn't be unduly pessimistic. The government and aid agencies are working to address all of these problems, or at least the more tangible ones. And what may seem horrendous to an outsider may well be cheerfully accepted by Kathmandu residents as the price of progress – indeed, a little pollution or crime will seem a small price to pay for improvements that are able to keep children from dying and give people greater control over their lives.

BUREAUCRACY, CORRUPTION AND FATALISM

Nepal's slow development as "institutional problems", a euphemism that covers a multitude of sins. They speak of management bottlenecks, where **bureaucrats** hoard power to such an extent that project managers have to spend most of their time in Kathmandu queueing for signatures instead of getting things done in the field. They complain that Nepali managers are overly fond of desk jobs in the capital, regarding remote hill postings as punishment and making no secret of their disdain for the local people they're supposed to be helping. (The most coveted position in Nepal is a job that involves no work and produces a regular paycheck.) Managers frequently leave the important work to untrained underlings, preferring instead to pass their time in seminars. Slogans and planning targets are more in evidence than action, while planners tend to favour rigid, "top-down" approaches without consulting experts in the field. These traits aren't unique to Nepal, of course, and indeed many aid organizations are even more centralized and top-down-oriented.

Unfortunately, though, there is little tradition of public service in Nepalese government, and the free-for-all of **corruption** was particularly bad during the 1980s. Development agencies routinely had to pad their budgets by as much as 30 percent to allow for **"leakage"** – it's been estimated that $1 billion went missing during the decade. The graft has been perpetuated by artificially low salaries and, no doubt, by the sight of apparently limitless piles of development loot. Government regulations seem to have been devised to streamline the process – most bilateral aid, for instance, is required to be disbursed by HMG "line agencies".

These institutional problems are themselves only projections of Nepal's culture, elements of which seem almost designed to thwart Western-style development. One of Nepal's foremost anthropologists, Dor Bahadur Bista, argues compellingly that Nepal's greatest handicap is the **fatalism** peddled by its Bahun (Brahman) elite. According to Bista, along with Nepalis' admirable *ke garne* attitude comes an exasperating apathy, and an obstructive suspicion that development efforts are merely futile attempts to resist fate. Responsibility for actions and decisions is often passed on to higher-ups (whether a boss, an astrologer or a deity), and the relationship between present work and future goals (at least in this life) is glossed over, resulting in haphazard planning and follow-through. Moreover, Nepali society places a great emphasis on connections and old-boy networks (called *aafno maanche* in Nepali: "one's own people"), which make it hard for members of ethnic minorities to advance, and on patronage, in which dependents are rewarded for loyalty rather than skill or innovation. Invaluable as these traits may be in a traditional village society, in a modern nation they tend to produce inept government, and foster a grovelling dependency on foreign patrons.

PROSPECTS

The foregoing isn't intended to make it sound as if Nepal's situation is hopeless, nor that there is no way for outsiders to help. Newcomers to the field tend to be the gloomi-

est ones, while people with a longer perspective are able to cite many major improvements. The country probably lost some ground during the greedy 1980s, and the restoration of democracy in 1990 hasn't proved the great watershed many had hoped – yet Nepal seems more in control of its own development than at any other time in its history, which has to be a change for the better. And given the more open political climate, responsible aid agencies stand a much better chance of achieving the work they've set out to do.

As a traveller, you too are playing a part in Nepal's development. With the right mixture of know-how and humility, you can be an agent of social change just by being yourself. Spent wisely, your money can bring tangible improvements to villages and families. In addition, there are plenty of good causes you may feel inclined to donate money to when you get home: with a little effort you should be able to see a few in action during your travels, and judge them by their fruits.

NATURAL HISTORY

The Himalaya are not only the world's tallest mountains, they're also the youngest — and still growing. Because of them, most of Tibet and parts of northern Nepal are high-altitude deserts, hidden in the Himalayan rain shadow, while many southern slopes, which bear the full brunt of the monsoon, are rainforest: nowhere in the world is there a transition of flora and fauna so abrupt as the one between the Tarai and the Himalayan crest, a distance of as little as 60km. As a result, Nepal can boast an astounding diversity of life, from rhinos to snow leopards.

GEOLOGY

The Himalaya provide graphic evidence for the **plate tectonics** (formerly known as continental drift) theory of mountain-building. According to this theory, the earth's crust is divided into a dozen or so massive plates which collide, separate and grind against each other with unimaginable force. The Himalaya are the result of the Indian subcontinental plate ramming northwards with particular force into the Asian plate — something like a car smashing into the side of a truck. It has been estimated that a 2000-kilometre cross-section of land along the collision zone has been compressed into 1000km, doubling the thickness of the crust and producing not only the Himalaya but also the vast Tibetan Plateau.

The shallow **Tethys Sea**, which once covered the entire region, was the main casualty in the process; its sedimentary deposits, now contorted and metamorphosed, can be seen at all elevations of the Himalaya. The first phase of mountain-building began around 45 million years ago, as the edge of the Asian plate, buckling under pressure from the advancing Indian plate, rose out of the sea to a height of about 2000m. Although it has since been lifted much higher, this **Tibetan Marginal Range**, which parallels the main Himalayan chain to the north, still stands as the divide between the Ganges and Tsangpo/Brahmaputra rivers. Unique among the world's major mountain ranges, the Himalaya don't form a watershed: rivers like the Kali Gandaki, Bhote Kosi (there are several by that name) and Arun cut right through the Himalaya because their courses were established by this earlier Tibetan Marginal Range.

The next major uplift occurred between 10 and 25 million years ago, when great chunks of the Asian plate were thrust southwards on top of the Indian plate, creating a low-altitude forerunner of the Himalayan range. Things appear to have remained more or less unchanged until just 600,000 years ago — practically yesterday, in geological time — when what is now the **Tibetan Plateau** was suddenly jacked up to an average elevation of 5000m, and the Tibetan Marginal Range to about 7000m. From this point on, monsoonal rains became an important erosive force on the south (Nepalese) side of the mountains, while the north, left in the rain shadow, turned into a high desert. Southward-flowing rivers, fuelled by phenomenal gradients of up to 6000m in 100km, further eroded the landscape.

Most of Nepal's present features were created at the geological last minute. Beginning around 500,000 years ago, the Tibetan rim lunged forward along numerous separate fronts to form the modern **Himalaya**. Averaging 8000m, Nepal's *himal* (massifs) show a freeze-frame of the current state of play; geologists calculate that parts of the range are still rising at a phenomenal rate of up to 1cm a year.

But mountain-building produces downs as well as ups: around 200,000 years ago, a broad belt of foothills subsided, creating Nepal's **midland valleys**, while the southern edge of this zone curled up to form the **Mahabharat Lekh** and, still further south, the **Chure Hills** (called the Siwaliks in India). These ridges rose so rapidly that they forced many southbound rivers to make lengthy east–west detours and permitted only three principal outlets to the Tarai; the Bagmati and Seti rivers were initially dammed up by the Mahabharat Lekh, flooding the Kathmandu and Pokhara valleys respectively.

The Himalaya are believed to be rising still, albeit at a slower rate than previously. Periodic and severe **earthquakes** demonstrate that the earth continues to rearrange itself – one in eastern Nepal in 1988 killed 700 people – while **hot springs**, sometimes found near streams along trekking trails, are indicators of tectonic faultlines. **Erosion** is a particular problem in the Himalaya, where the mountains are continually sloughing off their skins, and landslides occur regularly during the monsoon. While **glaciers** play a part in shaping the terrain above about 5000m, the Himalaya aren't highly glaciated due to their sheer slopes (which can't support glacier-breeding snowfields) and relatively low precipitation at high elevations. On the whole, Himalayan glaciers are in a retreating phase, as they are in most parts of the world, and old moraines (piles of rubble left behind by melting glaciers) are commonly seen above 4000m.

Nepal's valleys are like vast cutaway diagrams of geological history, and trekking or rafting in them you'll be able to imagine the forces that have shaped the Himalaya. Igneous intrusions (usually granite) are common, but most outcrops consist of metamorphic rocks (schist, gneiss, limestone and dolomite), deposited as underwater sediments and later mashed and contorted under tremendous pressure; the wavy light and dark bands of the Lhotse-Nuptse Wall, in the Everest region, illustrate this. **Fossils** found in many of these layers have helped geologists date the phases of Himalayan mountain-building. The famous *shaligram* stones of Muktinath in the Annapurna region contain fossilized ammonites (spiral-shaped molluscs) dating from 150–200 million years ago. Of a much more recent origin, the bones of Peking Man and primitive stone tools have been found in the Chure Hills – proving that the Himalaya are so young that early humans were present during their creation.

Nepal's **vegetation** is largely determined by altitude and can be conveniently grouped into three main divisions. The lowlands include the Tarai, Chure Hills and valleys up to about 1000m; the midlands extend roughly from 1000m to 3000m; and the Himalaya from 3000m to the upper limit of vegetation (typically about 5000m). Conditions vary tremendously within these zones, however: south-facing slopes usually receive more moisture, but also more sun in their lower reaches, while certain areas that are less protected from the summer monsoon – notably around Pokhara – are especially wet. In general, rainfall is higher in the east, and a greater diversity of plants can be found there.

THE LOWLANDS

Most of the Tarai's remaining forest consists of *sal*, a tall, straight tree much valued for its wood – a factor which is hastening its steady removal. *Sal* prefers well-drained soils and is most often found in pure stands along the Bhabar, the sloping alluvial plain at the base of the foothills; in the lower foothills, stunted specimens are frequently lopped for fodder. In spring, its cream-coloured flowers give off a heady jasmine scent. Other species sometimes associated with *sal* include *saj*, a large tree with crocodile-skin bark; *haldu*, a tree used for making dugout canoes; and *bauhinia*, a strangling vine that corkscrews around its victims.

The wetter **riverine forest** supports a larger number of species, but life here is more precarious, as rivers regularly flood and change course during the monsoon. *Sisu*, related to rosewood, and *khair*, an acacia, are the first trees to colonize newly formed sandbanks. *Simal*, towering on mangrove-like buttresses, follows close behind; also known as the silk-cotton tree, it produces bulbous red flowers in February, and in May its seed pods explode with a cottony material that is used for stuffing mattresses. *Palash* – the "flame of the forest tree" – puts on an even more brilliant show of red flowers in February. All of these trees are deciduous, shedding their leaves during the dry spring. Many other species are evergreen, including *bilar*, *jamun* and *curry*, an understorey tree with thin, pointed leaves that smell just like their name.

Grasses dominate less stable wetlands. Of the more than fifty species native to the Tarai, several routinely grow to a height of 8m. Even experts tend to pass off any tall, dense stand as "elephant grass", because the only way to get through it is on an elephant; the most common genera are *Phragmites*, *Saccharum*, *Arundo* and *Themeda*. Most grasses reach their greatest height just after the monsoon and flower during the dry autumn months. Locals cut *khar*, a medium-sized variety, for thatch in winter and early spring; the official thatch-gathering season in the Tarai parks (two weeks in January) is a colourful occasion, although the activity tends to drive wildlife into hiding. Fires are set in March and April to burn off the old growth and encourage tender new shoots, which provide food for game as well as livestock.

THE MIDLANDS

The decline in precipitation from east to west is more marked at the middle elevations – so much so that the dry west shares few species in common with the moist eastern hills. Central Nepal is an overlap zone where western species tend to be found on south-facing slopes and eastern ones on the cooler northern aspects.

A common tree in dry western and central areas is **chir pine** (needles in bunches of three), which typically grows in park-like stands up to about 2000m. Various **oak** species often take over above 1500m, especially on dry ridges, and here you'll also find *ainsilo*, a cousin of the raspberry, which produces a sweet, if rather dry, golden fruit in May.

Although much of the wet midland forest has been lost to cultivation, you can see fine remnants of it above Godavari in the Kathmandu Valley and around the lakes in the Pokhara Valley. Lower elevations are dominated by a zone of **chestnut** and *chilaune*, the latter being a member of the tea family with oblong concave leaves and, in May, small white flowers. In eastern parts, several species of **laurel** form a third major component to this forest, while alder, cardamom and tree ferns grow in shady gullies.

The magical, mossy oak-rhododendron forest is still mostly intact above about 2000m, thanks to the prevalent fog that makes farming unviable at this level. *Khasru*, the predominant oak found here, has prickly leaves and is often laden with lichen, **orchids** and other epiphytes, which grow on other plants and get their moisture directly from the air. It's estimated that more than 300 orchid varieties grow in Nepal, and although not all are showy or scented, the odds are you'll be able to find one flowering at almost any time of year. **Tree rhododendron** (*lali guraas*), Nepal's national flower, grows over 20m high and blooms with gorgeous red or pink flowers in March–April. Nearly thirty other species occur in Nepal, mainly in the east – the Milke Danda, a long ridge east of the Arun River, is the best place to view rhododendron, although impressive stands can also be seen between Ghodapani and Ghandrung in the Annapurna region. Most of Nepal's 300 species of **fern** are found in this forest type, as are many medicinal plants whose curative properties are known to ayurvedic practitioners but have yet to be studied in the West. Also occurring here are *daphne*, a small bush with fragrant white flowers in spring, whose bark is pulped to make paper, and **nettles**, whose stems are used by eastern hill-dwellers to make a hard-wearing fabric.

Holly, magnolia and maple may replace oak and rhododendron in some sites. **Dwarf bamboo**, the red panda's favourite food, grows in particularly damp places, such as northern Helambu and along the trail to the Annapurna Sanctuary. Cannabis thrives in disturbed sites throughout the midlands.

THE HIMALAYA

Conifers form the dominant tree cover in the Himalaya. Particularly striking are the forests around Rara Lake in western Nepal, where **Himalayan spruce** and **blue pine** (needles grouped in fives) are interspersed with meadows. Elsewhere in the dry west you'll find magnificent **Himalayan cedar** (deodar) trees, which are protected by villagers, and a species of cypress. Two types of **juniper** are present in Nepal: the more common tree-sized variety grows south of the main Himalayan crest (notably around Tengboche in the Everest region), while a dwarf scrub juniper is confined to northern rain-shadow areas. Both provide incense for Buddhist rites. In wetter areas, hemlock, fir (distinguished from spruce by its upward-pointing cones) and even the deciduous larch may be encountered.

One of the most common (and graceful) broadleafed species is **white birch**, usually found in thickets near the tree line, especially on shaded slopes where the snow lies late. **Poplars** stick close to watercourses high up into the inner valleys – Muktinath is full of them – while **berberis**, a shrub whose leaves turn scarlet in autumn, grows widely on exposed sites. Trekking up the Langtang or Marsyangdi valleys you pass through many of these forest types in rapid succession, but the most dramatic transition of all is found in the valley of the Thak Khola (upper Kali Gandaki): the monsoon jungle below Ghasa gives way to blue pine, hemlock, rhododendron and horse-chestnut; then to birch, fir and cypress around Tukche; then the apricot orchards of Marpha; and finally the blasted steppes of Jomosom.

Alpine vegetation predominates on the forest floor and in moist meadows above the treeline, and – apart from the **dwarf rhodo-dendron** (some species of which give off a strong cinnamon scent and are locally used as incense) – many **flowers** found here will be familiar to European and North American walkers. There are too many to do justice to them here, but primula, buttercup, poppy, iris, larkspur, gentian, edelweiss, buddleia, columbine and sage are all common. Most bloom during the monsoon, but rhododendrons and primulas can be seen flowering in the spring and gentians and larkspurs in the autumn.

MAMMALS

Most of Nepal's rich **animal life** inhabits the Tarai and, despite dense vegetation, is most easily observed there. In the hill regions, wildlife is much harder to spot due to population pressure – along trekking trails, at least – while very few mammals live above tree line. The following overview progresses generally from Tarai to Himalayan species.

The **Asian one-horned rhino** (gaida) is one of five species found in Asia and Africa, all endangered. In Nepal, about 400 rhinos – a fifth of the species total – live in Chitwan, and about a dozen have been introduced to Bardia; they graze singly or in small groups in the marshy elephant grass, where they can remain surprisingly well hidden.

Although trained **elephants** (hatti) are a lingering part of Nepali culture (see "Chitwan National Park"), their wild relatives are seen only rarely in Nepal. Since they require vast territory for their seasonal migrations, the settling of the Tarai is putting them in increasing conflict with man, and the few that survive tend to spend most of their time in India.

Koshi Tappu is the only remaining habitat in Nepal for another species better known as a domestic breed, **wild buffalo** (arnaa), which graze the wet grasslands in small herds. Majestic and powerful, the **gaur** (gauri gaai), or Indian bison, spends most of its time in the dry lower foothills, but descends to the Tarai in spring for water.

Perhaps the Tarai's most unlikely mammals, **gangetic dolphins** – one of four freshwater species in the world – are present in small numbers in the Karnali, Narayani and Sapt Koshi rivers. Curious and gregarious, dolphins tend to congregate in deep channels where they feed on fish and crustaceans; they may betray their presence with a puffing sound which they make through their blow-holes when surfacing. They're considered sacrosanct by Nepali Tharus, but are cruelly hunted in India.

The most abundant mammals of the Tarai, chital, or **spotted deer**, are often seen in herds around the boundary between riverine forest and grassland. Hog deer – so called because of their porky little bodies and head-down trot – take shelter in wet grassland, while the aptly named barking deer, measuring less than two feet high at the shoulder, are found throughout lowland and midland forests. Swamp deer gather in vast herds in Sukla Phanta, and males of the species carry impressive sets of antlers (their Nepali name, barasingha, means "twelve points"). Sambar, heavy-set animals standing five feet at the shoulder, are more widely distributed, but elusive. Two species of antelope, the graceful, corkscrew-horned **blackbuck** and the ungainly **nilgai** (blue bull), may be seen at Bardia and Koshi Tappu respectively; the latter was once assumed to be a form of cattle, and thus spared by Hindu hunters, but no longer.

Areas of greatest deer and antelope concentrations are usually prime territory for **tiger** (bagh), their main predator. However, your chances of spotting one of Nepal's endangered Bengal tigers are slim: they're mainly nocturnal, never very numerous, and incredibly stealthy. In the deep shade and mottled sunlight of dense riverine forest, a tiger's orange- and black-striped coat provides almost total camouflage. A male may weigh 250kg and measure 3m from nose to tail. Tigers are solitary hunters; some have been known to consume up to 20 percent of their body weight after a kill, but they may go several days between feeds. Males and females maintain separate but overlapping territories, regularly patrolling them, marking the boundaries with scent and driving off interlopers. Some Nepalis believe tigers to be the unquiet souls of the deceased.

Leopards are equally elusive, but much more widely distributed: they may be found in any deep forest from the Tarai to the timber line. As a consequence, leopards account for many more maulings than tigers in Nepal, and are more feared. A smaller animal (males weigh about 45kg), they prey on monkeys, dogs and livestock. **Other cats** – such as the fishing cat, leopard cat and the splendid clouded leopard – are known to exist in the more remote lowlands and midlands, but are very rarely sighted. Hyenas and wild dogs are scavengers of the Tarai, and **jackals**, though seldom seen (they're nocturnal), produce an eerie howling that is one of the most common night sounds in the Tarai and hills.

While it isn't carniverous, the dangerously unpredictable **sloth bear**, a Tarai species, is liable to round on you and should be approached with extreme caution. Its powerful front claws are designed for unearthing termite nests, and its long snout for extracting the insects. The **Himalayan black bear** roams midland forests up to tree line and is, if anything, more dangerous. **Wild boars** can be seen rooting and scurrying through forest anywhere in Nepal.

Monkeys, a common sight in the Tarai and hills, come in two varieties in Nepal. Comical **langurs** have silver fur, black faces and long, ropelike tails; you'll sometimes see them sitting on stumps like Rodin's *Thinker*. Brown **rhesus macaques** are more shy in the wild, but around temples are tame to the point of being nuisances. Many other small mammals may be spotted in the hills, among them porcupines, flying squirrels, foxes, civets, mongooses and martens. The **red panda**, with its rust coat and bushy, ringed tail, almost resembles a tree-dwelling fox; like its Chinese relative, it's partial

to bamboo, and is very occasionally glimpsed in the cloud forest of northern Helambu.

Elusive animals of the rhododendron and birch forests, **musk deer** are readily identified by their tusk-like canine teeth; males are hunted for their musk pod, which can fetch $200 an ounce on the international market. Though by no means common, **Himalayan tahr** is the most frequently observed large mammal of the high country; a goat-like animal with long, wiry fur and short horns, it browses along steep cliffs below the tree line. **Serow**, another goat relative, inhabits remote canyons and forested areas, while **goral**, sometimes likened to chamois, occurs from middle elevations up to the tree line.

The Himalaya's highest residents are **blue sheep**, who graze the barren grasslands above the tree line year-round. Normally tan, males go a slaty colour in winter, accounting for their name. Herds have been sighted around the Thorung La in the Annapurna region, but they occur in greater numbers north of Dhorpatan and in She-Phoksundo National Park. Their chief predator is the **snow leopard**, a secretive cat whose habits are still little understood.

AMPHIBIANS AND REPTILES

Native to the Tarai's wetlands, crocodiles are most easily seen in winter, when they sun themselves on muddy banks to warm up their cold-blooded bodies. The endangered **mugger crocodile** favours marshes and oxbow lakes, where it may lie motionless for hours on end until its prey comes within snapping distance. Muggers mainly pursue fish, but will eat just about anything they can get their jaws around – including human corpses thrown into the river by relatives unable to afford wood for a cremation. The even more endangered **gharial crocodile** lives exclusively in rivers and feeds on fish; for more on its precarious state, see "Chitwan National Park" in Chapter Six.

Nepal has many kinds of **snakes**, but they are rarely encountered: most hibernate in winter, even in the Tarai, and shy away from humans at other times of year. Common cobras – snake charmers' favourites – inhabit low elevations near villages; they aren't found in the Kathmandu Valley, despite their abundance in religious imagery there. Kraits and pit vipers, both highly poisonous, have been reported, as have pythons up to twenty feet long. However, the commonest species aren't poisonous and are typically less than two feet long.

Chances are you'll run into a **gecko** or two, probably clinging to a guest house wall. Helpful insect-eaters, these lizard-like creatures are able to climb almost any surface with the aid of amazing suction pads on their feet. About fifty species of **fish** have been recorded in Nepal, but only *mahseer*, a sporty relative of carp that attains its greatest size in the lower Karnali River, is of much interest; most ponds are stocked with carp and catfish.

BIRDS

Over 800 **bird species** – one tenth of the earth's total – have been sighted in Nepal. The country receives a high number of birds migrating between India and central Asia in spring and autumn and, because it spans so many ecosystems, provides habitats for a wide range of year-round residents. The greatest diversity of species is found in the Tarai wildlife parks, but even the Kathmandu Valley is remarkably rich in birdlife. The following is only a listing of the major categories – for the complete picture, get hold of *Birds of Nepal* (see "Books").

In the **Tarai** and lower hills, raptors (birds of prey) such as ospreys, cormorants, darters, gulls and kingfishers patrol streams and rivers for food; herons and storks can also be seen fishing, while cranes, ducks and moorhens wade in or float on the water. Many of these migratory species are particularly well represented at Koshi Tappu, which is located along the important Arun Valley corridor to Tibet. Peafowl make their meowing mating call – and peacocks occasionally deign to unfurl their plumage – while many species of woodpeckers can be heard, if not seen, high up in the *sal* canopy. Cuckoos and "brain fever" birds repeat their idiotic two- or four-note songs in an almost demented fashion. Parakeets swoop in formation; bee-eaters, swifts, drongos, swallows and rollers flit and dive for insects, while jungle fowl look like chickens as Monet might have painted them. Other oddities of the Tarai include the paradise flycatcher, with its lavish white tailfeathers and dragonfly-like flight; the lanky great adjutant stork, resembling a prehistoric reptile in flight; and the giant hornbill, whose beak supports an appendage that looks like an upturned welder's mask.

Many of the above birds are found in **the midlands** as well as the Tarai – as are mynas, egrets, crows and magpies, which tend to scavenge near areas of human habitation. Birds of prey – falcons, kestrels, harriers, eagles, kites, hawks and vultures – may also be seen at almost any elevation. Owls are common, but not much liked by Nepalis. Babblers and laughing thrushes (genus name *Garrulax!*) populate the oak-rhododendron forest and are as noisy as their names suggest. Over twenty species of flycatchers are present in the Kathmandu Valley alone.

Nepal's national bird, the iridescent, multicoloured *danphe* (impeyan pheasant), can often be spotted scuttling through the undergrowth in the Everest region; a range of house paints has been named after it. *Kalij* and *monal*, two other native pheasants, also inhabit the higher hills and lower **Himalaya**. Migrating waterfowl often stop over at high-altitude lakes – Brahminy ducks are a trekking-season attraction at Gokyo – and snow pigeons, grebes, finches and choughs may all be seen at or above the tree line. Mountaineers have reported seeing choughs at up to 8200m on Everest.

INVERTEBRATES AND INSECTS

No other creature in Nepal arouses such trepidation and squeamishness as the **leech** (*jukha*). Fortunately, these segmented, caterpillar-sized annelids remain dormant underground during the trekking seasons; during the monsoon, however, they come out in force everywhere in the Tarai and hills, making any hike a bloody business. Leeches are attracted to body heat, and will inch up legs or drop from branches to reach their victims. The bite is completely painless – the bloodsucker injects a local anesthetic and anticoagulant – and often goes unnoticed until the leech drops off of its own accord. To dislodge one, apply salt or burn it with a cigarette; don't pull it off or the wound could get infected.

Over 600 species of **butterflies** have been recorded in Nepal, with more being discovered all the time. Although the monsoon is the best time to view butterflies, many varieties can be seen before and especially just after the rains – look beside moist, sandy banks or atop ridges; Phulchoki is an excellent place to start in the Kathmandu Valley. Notable hill varieties include the intriguing orange oakleaf, whose markings enable it to vanish into forest litter, and the golden birdwing, a large, angular species with a loping wingbeat. **Moths** are even more numerous – around 5000 species are believed to exist in Nepal, including the world's largest, the giant atlas, which has a wingspan of almost a foot.

Termites are Nepal's most conspicuous social insects, constructing towering, fluted mounds up to eight feet tall in the western Tarai. Organized in colonies much the same as ants and bees, legions of termite workers and "reproductives" serve a single king and queen. The mounds function as cooling towers for the busy nest below; monuments to insect industry, they're made from tailings excavated from the colony's galleries and bonded with saliva for a wood-hard finish. **Honey bees** create huge, drooping nests in the Tarai and especially in the lush cliff country north of Pokhara. **Spiders** aren't very numerous in Nepal, although one notable species grows to be six inches across and nets birds (it's not poisonous to humans). **Fireflies**, with orange and black bodies, give off a greenish glow at dusk in the Tarai. For many travellers, however, the extent of their involvement with the insect kingdom will be in swatting **mosquitoes**: two varieties are prevalent in the lowlands, one of them *Anopheles*, the infamous vector of malaria.

BOOKS

Most of these books are a lot easier to come by in Kathmandu, and some will be available only in Nepal. Where the UK and US publishers are different, the UK publisher is given first – books published in other countries are indicated accordingly.

GENERAL

Lynn Andrews *Windhorse Woman* (Warner, US). One woman's spiritual quest in Nepal; very new age.

Jeff Greenwald *Mister Raja's Neighborhood: Letters from Nepal* (John Daniel, US). The author went to Kathmandu to write the Great Asian Novel and ended up writing a series of letters – though perhaps contemplating his navel a bit too much in the process. *Shopping for Buddhas* (Harper & Row, US) is a sequel.

Harka Gurung *Vignettes of Nepal* (Sajha Prakashan, Nepal). Probably the best book written by a Nepali in English about his country, a vivid travelogue illuminated by a native's insights.

Pico Iyer *Video Night in Kathmandu* (Black Swan/Random House). A collection of essays on popular traveller hangouts in Asia that are stronger on style than substance.

Peter Matthiessen *The Snow Leopard* (Collins Harvill/Viking Penguin). Matthiessen joins biologist George Schaller in a pilgrimage to Dolpa to track one of the world's most elusive cats, and comes up with characteristically Zen insights. A magnificent piece of writing, filled with beautiful descriptions of the

landscape – and ever-perceptive observations of how Matthiessen's quest for the snow leopard became one of self-discovery.

Dervla Murphy *The Waiting Land* (Overlook Press, US). A personal account of working with Pokhara's Tibetan refugees in 1965, written in the author's usual entertaining and politically on-the-ball style.

COFFEE-TABLE BOOKS

Lisa Choegyal and Wendy Brewer Fleming (eds) *Sagarmatha* (Insight Topics, Hong Kong). A pretty picture book conceived by Edmund Hillary in aid of the rebuilding of Tengboche Monastery.

Thomas Kelly and Patricia Roberts *Kathmandu: City at the Edge of the World* (Weidenfeld & Nicolson/Abbeville Press). Stunning photography and extensive essays on culture and religion.

R. Ian Lloyd and Wendy Moore *Kathmandu: The Forbidden Valley* (St Martin's Press, UK, o/p). The photos will make your eyes water, but the text will make you barf.

Eric Valli and Diane Summers *Honey Hunters of Nepal* (Thames & Hudson, UK, o/p). Amazing photos of Gurung men clinging to rope ladders while raiding beehives. The best of the photos were reprinted in the November 1988 *National Geographic*, still sometimes sold in Kathmandu.

HISTORY

Byron Farwell *The Gurkhas* (Norton). One of many books lionizing Nepal's famous Gurkha soldiers.

Percival Landon *Nepal* (Ratna Pustak Bhandar, Nepal). In two volumes, this was the most comprehensive study of the country at the time (1928) and is regarded as a classic – but having been commissioned by the Maharaja, it has a distinct political bias.

Padma Shrestha *Nepal Rediscovered* (Serindia, Nepal). A collection of rare photographs, this presents a fascinating, if elitist, view of Rana-era Nepal.

Ludwig Stiller *The Rise of the House of Gorkha* (Ratna Pustak Bhandar, Nepal). An academic but readable account of Nepal's unification and war with Britain, written by a Jesuit priest turned Nepalese citizen.

CULTURE AND ANTHROPOLOGY

Mary M. Anderson *The Festivals of Nepal* (Rupa, Nepal). Despite the title, this only covers the Kathmandu Valley's festivals, but it's still the most readable and informative account.

Dor Bahadur Bista *Peopies of Nepal* (Ratna Pustak Bhandar, Nepal). The standard overview of Nepal's ethnic groups, though much of the information is now superseded by more recent work.

BHOTIYAS

Christoph von Fürer-Haimendorf *Himalayan Traders* (John Murray, US). An anthropological study of the impact of China's occupation of Tibet on Bhotiya and Sherpa traders.

David L. Snellgrove *Himalayan Pilgrimage* (Shambhala). An insightful travelogue/ anthropological account of a trip through north-western Nepal in the 1950s.

CHHETRIS

Monica Connell *Against a Peacock Sky* (Penguin/Viking Penguin). Beautiful, impressionistic rendering of life among the *matawaali* (alcohol-drinking) Chhetris of Jumla District, capturing the subtleties of village life in Nepal.

GURUNGS

Broughton Coburn *Nepali Aama: Portrait of a Nepalese Hill Woman* (Moon Publications, US). Delightful study of a Gurung woman in a village south of Pokhara, in her own words, with photos.

Stan Royal Mumford *Himalayan Dialogue: Tibetan Lamas and Gurung Shamans in Nepal* (University of Wisconsin Press). An account of myths and rituals practised in a village along the Annapurna Circuit – fascinating, once you get past the anthropological jargon.

MAGARS

Gary Shepherd *Life Among the Magars* (Sahayogi, Nepal). A personal account, with plenty of pertinent insights.

SHERPAS

Hugh R. Downs *Rhythms of a Himalayan Village* (Harper & Row, US). An extraordinarily sensitive synthesis of black-and-white photos,

text and quotes, describing rituals and religion in a Solu village.

James F. Fisher, *Sherpas: Reflections on Change in Himalayan Nepal* (University of California Press, US). A before-and-after account, written by a member of Edmund Hillary's 1964 school-building team, who concludes that Sherpas are more resilient than we give them credit for.

RELIGION

HINDUISM

K. M. Sen *Hinduism* (Penguin/Viking Penguin). An accessible survey, explanatory without being too obscure.

P. Lal (trans) *The Ramayana of Valmiki* (Tarang, Nepal). A condensed version of the classic epic.

Shri Purohit Swami (trans) *The Geeta* (Faber & Faber, UK). A portable, robust translation of the *Bhagavad Gita.*

BUDDHISM

Tenzin Gyatso (the Dalai Lama) *Freedom in Exile* (Abacus/HarperCollins). His Holiness's life story, in his own words. Published in 1990, shortly after he won the Nobel Peace Prize.

Vicki Mackenzie *Reincarnation: The Boy Lama* (Bloomsbury, UK). An intriguing book, recounting the lives of Lama Yeshe, the abbot of Kopan Monastery, who died in 1984, and Osel Hita Torres, who was born in 1985 and enthroned as Yeshe's reincarnation at the age of two.

Chögyam Trungpa *The Myth of Freedom* (Shambhala, Nepal). A useful primer on the metaphysics of Buddhist meditation, one of a welter of books by a master who was instrumental in packaging Buddhism for the West.

ART AND ARCHITECTURE

Lydia Aran *The Art of Nepal* (Sahayogi, Nepal). Surprisingly good overview of Nepalese religion as well as stone, metal and wood sculpture and *thangka* paintings.

Hallvard Kare Kuloy *Tibetan Rugs* (White Orchid, Thailand). A thorough and well-illustrated survey, though, as the title suggests, it doesn't have much to say about modern carpets made in Nepal.

Yves Vequand *The Art of Mithila: Ceremonial Paintings from an Ancient Kingdom* (Thames & Hudson, UK, o/p). Still the only non-scholarly book to be had on Mithila art, with vivid illustrations.

FICTION AND POETRY

Diamond Shumshere Rana *Wake of the White Tiger* (Rana, Nepal). An acclaimed novel set in the early Rana era; the poor translation and confusing geneologies, however, can be offputting.

Kim Stanley Robinson *Escape From Kathmandu* (Unwin/Tor). Pure potboiler, but it might be fun for the real-life *mise en scène* (action starts at the Hotel Star in Thamel).

David Rubin *Nepali Visions, Nepali Dreams* (Columbia University Press, US). Translations of work by Laxmi Prasad Devkota, Nepal's best-loved poet.

Tara Nath Sharma *Blackout* (Nirala, Nepal). A dark novel of life in the Nepal hills, by an author who has served time in jail for his views.

Shailendra Kumar Singh (ed) *Contemporary Nepali Poetry* (Singh, Nepal). A slender pamphlet, but one that succeeds in capturing some of the moods that prevailed during the period just prior to the restoration of democracy.

NATURAL HISTORY

Robert Fleming Jr *The General Ecology, Flora and Fauna of Midland Nepal* (Tribhuwan University, Nepal). A simple ecology text drawing on examples mainly from around the Kathmandu Valley.

Robert Fleming Sr, Robert Fleming Jr and Lain Singh Bangdel *Birds of Nepal* (Nature Himalayas, Nepal). The authoritative field guide.

K. K. Gurung *Heart of the Jungle* (André Deutsch, US). The essential guide to Chitwan's flora and fauna, written by the former manager of Tiger Tops Jungle Lodge.

Dorothy Mierow and Tirtha Shrestha *Himalayan Flowers and Trees* (Sahayogi, Nepal). A pocket-sized guide with colour plates and some useful information at the back.

George Schaller *Stones of Silence: Journeys in the Himalaya* (University of Chicago Press, US). Written by the wildlife biologist who

accompanied Peter Matthiessen on his quest for the snow leopard, this book provides a detailed view of ecosystems of the high Himalaya.

Colin Smith *Illustrated Checklist of Nepal's Butterflies* (Rohit Kumar, Nepal). Beautiful colour plates showing nearly 600 species, by the curator of the Annapurna Regional Museum.

DEVELOPMENT AND POLITICS

When you're in Nepal, look out for *Himal*, a bimonthly magazine devoted to development and environmental issues. It's published in Kathmandu and available in many bookshops there.

Lynn Bennett *Dangerous Wives and Sacred Sisters* (Columbia University Press, US). Good insight into the life and position of Hindu women in Nepal.

Dor Bahadur Bista *Fatalism and Development* (Orient Longman, India). An insightful analysis of the cultural factors that stand in the way of Nepal's development, by the country's best-known anthropologist.

Indra Majpuria *Nepalese Women* (M. Devi, Nepal). Though it wanders quite a bit, this forcibly gets across the hardships and problems facing women in Nepal.

Charlie Pye-Smith *Travels in Nepal* (Penguin/ Viking Penguin). A cross between a travelogue and a progress report on aid projects, this succeeds in giving plenty of facts and analysis without getting bogged down in institutional fudge.

Leo Rose and John Scholz *Nepal: Profile of a Himalayan Kingdom* (Westview, UK, o/p). A political study of Nepal published in 1980, concentrating on the post-1951 period.

David Seddon *Nepal: a State of Poverty* (Vikas, Nepal). A hard look at the issues by one of the longest-serving foreign critics of Nepal's development efforts.

Ludmilla Tüting and Kunda Dixit *Bikas-Binas, Development-Destruction* (Ratna Pustak Bhandar, Nepal). Excellent collection of articles which covers the whole gamut of dilemmas arising out of development, environmental degradation and tourism. It's supposed to speak for the entire Himalayan region, but it really focuses on Nepal.

MOUNTAINS AND MOUNTAINEERING

Mark Anderson *On the Big Hill* (Faber & Faber, UK, o/p). Companion to the Granada TV programme of the same name following the progress of an Everest expedition.

Chris Bonington *Everest South West Face* (Hodder & Stoughton, UK, o/p). An exhaustive tome covering every aspect of a major Himalayan assault – in this case, an unsuccessful one. Also look out for Bonington's *The Everest Years* (Hodder, UK) and his recently published retrospective, *Mountaineer* (The Mountaineers, o/p).

W. E. Bowman *The Ascent of Rum Doodle* (Pimlico, UK). Reprint of the classic 1956 parody of the mountaineering-account genre.

Maurice Herzog *Annapurna* (Paladin, US). Reprint of one of the earliest accounts of mountaineering in the Himalayas, describing the first successful ascent of an 8000-metre peak.

Reinhold Messner *The Crystal Horizon* (Crowood Press/The Mountaineers). Not very well written (or maybe it's the translation), but a nonetheless compelling account of Messner's 1980 solo ascent of Everest. Messner's *All 14 Eight-Thousanders* (Crowood Press, UK) has awesome photos and an interesting appendix of Himalayan mountaineering statistics.

H. W. Tilman *Nepal Himalaya* (Cambridge University Press, UK, o/p). A chatty account of the first mountaineering reconnaissance of Nepal in 1949–51, recently reprinted as part of *The Seven Mountain-Travel Books* (Diadem/The Mountaineers). Though crusty, and at times racist, Tilman was one of the century's great adventurers and his writing remains fresh and witty.

Walt Unsworth *Everest* (Grafton/Cloudcap). Exhaustive history of mountaineering on the world's highest peak.

TREKKING GUIDES

Stan Armington *Trekking in the Nepal Himalaya* (Lonely Planet). A less perceptive, but more portable, alternative. Some people prefer its "Day 1–Day 2" route descriptions.

Stephen Bezruchka *A Guide to Trekking in Nepal*, 6th Ed. (Cordee/The Mountaineers). The most thorough, even-handed and sensitive book on trekking, containing background pieces on Nepali culture and natural history.

Alton C. Byers III *Treks on the Kathmandu Valley Rim* (Sahayogi, Nepal). Mainly day hikes and overnights.

John L. Hayes *Trekking North of Pokhara* (Roger Lascelles, UK). Short on context, but a lightweight option if you only intend to trek in this region.

Steve Martin *Kathmandu and the Everest Trek* (Roger Lascelles, UK). A similar treatment of a single region.

Hugh Swift *Trekking in Nepal, West Tibet and Bhutan* (Hodder/Sierra Club). Gives vivid area accounts instead of hour-by-hour route descriptions; good for obscure treks.

Bill O'Connor *The Trekking Peaks of Nepal* (Crowood Press, UK). Describes climbing routes and trek approaches for eighteen trekking peaks.

Wendy Brewer Lama *Trekking Gently in the Himalaya* (Sagarmatha Pollution Control Project, Nepal). An excellent, concise pamphlet on trekkers' environmental and cultural responsibilities.

OTHER GUIDES

Lisa Choegyal (ed) *The Insight Guide to Nepal* (APA). Great pictures and informative cultural essays, but somewhat short on practical information.

Peter Knowles and Dave Allardice *White Water Nepal* (Rivers Publishing, UK). An indispensable companion for all river-runners, written with great wit and no nonsense; useful maps, stream profiles and hydrographs.

John Sanday *Illustrated Guide to the Kathmandu Valley* (Collins, UK, o/p). The author is the leading authority on restoration of the valley's monuments.

LANGUAGE

Nepali is surprisingly easy to learn, and local people are always thrilled when travellers make the effort to pick up a few phrases. Knowing a little bit of the language certainly comes in handy, too, since while nearly all Nepalis who deal with tourists speak English, few people do off the beaten track.

Nepali (sometimes called *Gurkhali*) is closely related to Hindi and other Sanskrit-based languages, so Nepali-speakers and Indians can usually catch the gist of what each other is saying. However, nearly half of all Nepalis speak Tibetan, Sherpa or one of several dozen other Tibeto-Burman dialects, which are completely unrelated to Nepali – almost all speak Nepali as a second language, but sometimes with difficult to understand regional accents.

Nepali is written in a script known as **Devanaagari**: there's fortunately no need for travellers to learn it since signs, bus destinations and so on are usually written in Roman script. This transliteration, though, often leads to problems of inconsistency – see the note in "Information and Maps" in *Basics* for more on this. For a **glossary of food terms**, see "Eating and Drinking" in *Basics*.

The most useful **phrasebook** on the market is Lonely Planet's *Nepal Phrasebook*, *A Simple Nepali for Trekkers* (Rupa, Nepal), available only in Nepal, goes a little deeper into grammar, but isn't as good for quick reference. For a full-blown **teach-yourself book**, try David Matthews' *A Course in Nepali* (School of Oriental and African Studies, UK).

PRONUNCIATION

Even when Nepali is transliterated from the Devanaagari script into the Roman alphabet using phonetic spellings, there are a number of peculiarities in pronunciation:

A as in *a*lone
AA as in f*a*ther
B sounds like a cross between "b" and "v"
E as in caf*é*
I as in pol*i*ce
J as in *j*ust
O as in n*o*te
R sounds like a cross between "r" and "d"
S sounds almost like "sh"
U as in b*oo*t
W sounds like a cross between "w" and "v"
Z sounds like "dj" or "dz"

The "a" and "aa" distinction is crucial. *Maa* (in) is pronounced as it looks, with the vowel stretched out, but *ma* (I) sounds like "muh" and *mandir* (temple) like "mundeer". The accent almost always goes on the syllable with "aa" in it, or if there's no "aa", on the first syllable.

Some Nepali vowels are nasalized – to get the right effect, you have to block off your nasal passage, producing a slightly honking sound like a French "n". Nasalized vowels aren't indicated in this book, but they're something to be aware of. To hear how they should sound, listen to a Nepali say *tapaai* (you) or *yahaa* (here).

ASPIRATED CONSONANTS

The combinations "ch" and "sh" are pronounced as in English, but in all other cases where an "h" follows a consonant the sound is meant to be aspirated – in other words, give it an extra puff of air. Thus *bholi* (tomorrow) sounds like b'*h*oli and Thamel sounds like T'*h*amel. Note these combinations:

CHH sounds like a very breathy "ch", as in pi*tch h*ere
PH makes an "f" sound, as in *ph*one
TH is pronounced as in pu*t h*ere, not as in think

RETROFLEX CONSONANTS

Finally, the sounds "d", "r" and "t" also occur in retroflex forms – ie, they're pronounced by rolling the tip of the tongue back towards the roof of the mouth. Again, it's not worth going into too much detail about this here, but it's a safe bet that whenever these letters are followed by an "h" they'll be retroflex – an obvious example is *Kathmandu*, which sounds a little like "Kardmandu". Sometimes retroflexion results in a difference in meaning: *saathi* means friend, but with a retroflex "th" it means sixty.

A BRIEF GUIDE TO SPEAKING NEPALI

GREETINGS AND BASIC PHRASES

Hello, Goodbye	*Namaste* (said with palms together as if praying)	My name is . . .	*Mero naam . . . ho*
		My country is . . .	*Mero desh . . . ho*
		I don't know	*Malaai thaahaa chhaina*
Hello (more formal)	*Namaskar*		
Yes/No (It is/isn't)	*Ho/Hoina*	I didn't understand that	*Maile bhujina*
Yes/No (There is/isn't)	*Chha/Chhaina*		
Thank you (formal)	*Dhanyabaad*	Please speak more slowly	*Bistaarai bolnus*
How are things?(informal);	*Kasto chha?*	Pardon?	*Hajur?*
(polite)	*Sanchai hunuhunchha*	No thanks	*Nai; Pardaina* (I don't want it)
Okay, Fine	*Thik chha*		
What's your name? (to an adult);	*Tapaaiko naam ke ho?*	I'm sorry	*Maph garnus*
		Let's go	*Jaun*
(to a child)	*Timro naam ke ho?*	See you again	*Pheri betaunla*

FORMS OF ADDRESS

One of the many delightful aspects of Nepali culture is the familiar forms of address that Nepalis use when speaking to each other, even to strangers: use them to get anyone's attention.

Excuse me . . .	*O . . .*	Mother (women old enough to be your mother)	*Aama*
Elder brother (said to men your age or older)	*Daai; Daaju* (more respectful)		
Elder sister (women your age or older)	*Didi*	Grandfather (old men)	*Bhaje*
Younger sister (women or girls younger than you)	*Bahini*	Grandmother (old women)	*Aamai*
Younger brother (men or boys younger than you)	*Bhaai*	Shopkeeper, Innkeeper (male)	*Saahuji*
Father (a man old enough to be your father)	*Bua*	Shopkeeper, Innkeeper (female)	*Saahuni*

DIRECTIONS

Where is the . . . ?	*. . . kahaa chha?*	Where are you coming from?	*Tapaai kahaabaata aayeko?*
Where is this (bus) going?	*Yo (bas) kahaa jaanchha?*	Here	*Yahaa*
Which is the way to . . . ?	*. . . -jaane baato kun ho?*	There/Yonder	*Tyahaa/Utyahaa*
		(To the) right	*Daayaa (tira)*
Which is the best way?	*Kun baato sabhanda raamro chha?*	(To the) left	*Baayaa (tira)*
How far is it?	*Kati taadhaa chha?*	Straight	*Sidhaa*
Where are you going?	*Tapaai kahaa jaanuhunchha?*	North	*Uttaar*
		South	*Dakshin*
I'm going to . . .	*Ma . . . jaanchu*	East	*Purba*
		West	*Pashchim*
		Near/Far	*Najik/Taadhaa*

TIME

What time is it?	*Kati bajyo?*	Week	*Haptaa*
What time does the bus leave?	*Yo bas kati baaje jaanchha?*	Month	*Maina*
		Year	*Barsa*
When does it arrive?	*Kati baaje pugchha?*	Today	*Aaja*
		Tomorrow	*Bholi*
How many hours does it take?	*Kati ghanta laagchha?*	Yesterday	*Hijo*
		Now	*Ahile*
(Two) o'clock	*(Dui) bajyo*	Later	*Pachhi*
(Nine)-thirty	*Saadhe (nau) bajyo*	Ago, Before	*Pahile*
(Five) past (six)	*(Chha) bajera (paanch) minet gayo*	Next week	*Aarko haptaa*
		Last month	*Gayeko maina*
(Ten) to (eight)	*(Aath) bajana (das) minet bakichha*	(Two) years ago	*(Dui) barsa agi*
Minute	*Minet*	Morning	*Bihaana*
Hour	*Ghanta*	Afternoon	*Diuso*
Day	*Din*	Evening	*Belukaa*
Day (of week)	*Bar*	Night	*Raati*

NEGOTIATIONS

How much does this cost?	*Esko kati parchha?*	I don't have any change	*Masanga khudra chhaina*
How much for a room?	*Rum ko kati parchha?*	I don't need it	*Malaai chahindaina*
How many people?	*Kati jana?*	Please use the meter	*Malaai meter-maa laijaanus*
For (two) people	*(Dui) jana ko laagi*	Just a moment	*Ek chin* (literally, "One
Only one person	*Ek jana maatrai*		blink")
Can I see it?	*Herna sakchhu?*	I'll come back	*Ma aunechuu*
It's very/too expensive	*Dherai mahango bhayo*	Good job, Well done	*Kyaraamro*
Is there a cheaper one?	*Kunai sasto chha?*	Don't worry	*Chinta nagarnus*
		The bill, please	*Bil dinus*

DEALING WITH KIDS

There's no foolproof way to silence pesky kids, but the following phrases might help you parry the taunts. Be sure to use an appropriately teasing or indulgent tone of voice – anger won't work.

Begging is bad	*Magnu raamro hoina*	Don't you have any manners?	*Bhudi chhaina?*
I don't give to beggars	*Maagnelai dinna*		
So loud!	*Kasto karaieko!*	Don't you have anything better to do?	*Aru kaam chhaina?*
Am I deaf?	*Ma bahiro chhura?*		
Be quiet	*Chup laaga*	Don't do that	*Teso nagara*
Go back/Go away	*Pharka/Jau*	Don't touch that	*Tyo nachalau*

OTHER HANDY WORDS

Most of the following words are what we would call prepositions. However, those marked with an asterisk (*) are actually postpositions in Nepali, meaning they come *after* the thing they're describing (eg, "with me" comes out *masanga*).

Above, Over, Up	*Maathi**	But	*Tara*	Or	*Ki*
And	*Ra*	From	*Baata**	Out,	*Bahira**
Below, Under, Down	*Talla**	In, Inside,	*Bhitra**	Outside	*Tira**
Because	*Kinabhane*	In front of	*Agaadi**	To,	*Sanga**
Behind	*Pachhadi**	If	*Yedi*	Towards	*Chuttai**

BASIC QUESTIONS AND REQUESTS

Whether you're making a statement or asking a question, the word order is the same in Nepali – to indicate that you're asking, not telling, make sure you raise your voice at the end.

Do you speak English?	*Tapaai Angreji bolnuhunchha?*	I like ... (very much)	*Malaai ... (dherai) manparchha*
Is there someone who speaks English?	*Angreji bolne kohi chha?*	What's this for?	*Ke ko laagi?*
I don't speak Nepali	*Ma Nepali boldina*	What's the matter?	*Ke bhayo?*
Is/Isn't there a ...?	*... chha/chhaina?* ... *painchha?*	What's this called in Nepali?	*Nepali maa ke bhanchha?*
Is ... available?	*... hunchha?*	What does .. mean?	*... ko mane ke ho?*
Is ... okay?	*Malaai madhat garnus ... dinus*	Really?	*Saachinai?* or *Hora?*
Please help me	*Malaai (bhok) laagyo*	How	*Kasari*
Please give me ...	*Malaai (bhok) laageko chhaina*	What	*Ke*
I'm (hungry)	*Ma ... chaahanchhu/ chaahunna*	When	*Kahile*
I'm not (hungry)		Where	*Kahaa*
		Who	*Ko*
		Why	*Kina*

NOUNS

Bag, Baggage	*Jolaa*	Head	*Tauko*	Restaurant	*Restarant, Bhojanalaya*
Bed	*Bistaara*	Hotel/Lodge	*Hotel/Laj*		
Blanket	*Sirak*	House	*Ghar*	Road	*Rod, Baato*
Boy	*Keta*	Husband	*Srimaan*	Room	*Rum, Kothaa*
Bus	*Bas*	Job, Work	*Kaam*	School	*Skul*
Candle	*Mainbatti*	Lamp	*Batti*	Seat	*Sit*
Children	*Bachha*	Mattress	*Dunlop*	Shoe	*Jutta*
Clothes	*Luga*	Medicine	*Aushadi*	Shop	*Pasal*
Ear	*Kan*	Mistake	*Galti*	Stomach	*Pet*
Eye	*Ankha*	Money	*Paisa*	Success	*Safal*
Family	*Pariwaar*	Mother	*Aama*	Teahouse	*Chiya pasal, Chiya dukan*
Father	*Buwa*	Mouth	*Mukh*		
Fever	*Joro*	Nose	*Naak*	Ticket	*Tiket*
Foot, Leg	*Khutta*	Pain	*Dukhyo*	Toilet	*Chaarpi, Toilet*
Friend	*Saathi*	Paper	*Kaagat*	Town, Village	*Gaun*
Food	*Khaanaa*	Person	*Maanchhe*	Trail/Main trail	*Baato/Mul baato*
Girl	*Keti*	Place	*Thau*	Water	*Paani*
Hand	*Haat*	Problem	*Samasya*	Wife	*Srimati*

DAYS AND MONTHS

It's unlikely you'll ever have to use these. Nepali months start around the middle of our months,
and vary from 27 to 32 days.

Sunday	*Aitabar*	April–May	*Baisakh*
Monday	*Sombar*	May–June	*Jeth*
Tuesday	*Mangalbar*	June–July	*Asaar*
Wednesday	*Budhabar*	July–August	*Saaun*
Thursday	*Bihibar*	August–September	*Bhadau*
Friday	*Sukrabar*	September–October	*Ashoj*
Saturday	*Sanibar*	October–November	*Kartik*
January–February	*Magh*	November–December	*Mangsir*
February–March	*Faagun*	December–January	*Puus*
March–April	*Chaitra*		

ADJECTIVES AND ADVERBS

One tricky thing about Nepali adjectives: the ones that describe feelings are actually nouns. Thus to express the notion "I'm thirsty", you have to say *Malaai thirkaa laagyo* ("To me thirst has struck").

A little	Alikati	Dishonest	Bemaani	Only	Maatrai
Already	Pahile	Dry	Sukeko	Open	Khulaa
After	Pachhi	Early	Chaarai	Often	Kahilekahi
Again	Pheri	Easy	Sajilo	Quickly	Chitto
All	Sabai	Empty	Khali	Right (Correct)	Thik
Alone	Eklai	Enough	Prasasta	Sad	Dukhi
A lot	Dherai	Expensive	Mahango	Same	Eutai
Always	Sadai	Far	Taadhaa	Similar	Ustai
Another	Aarko	Full (thing)	Bari	Slowly	Bistaarai
Bad	Kharaab, Naraamro	Full (person)	Agaayo	Small	Saano
		Fun	Majaa	Soon	Chadai, Chittai
Beautiful	Raamro	Good	Raamro	Steep	Ukaalo
Best	Sabhanda raamro	Happy	Kushi	Stolen	Choreko
		Heavy	Garungo	Strong	Baliyo
Better	Ajai raamro	Hot (person or weather)	Garam	Stupid	Murkha
Big	Thulo			Tall	Aglo
Cheap	Sasto	Hot (liquid)	Taato	Tasty	Mitho
Clean	Safaa	Hungry	Bhok	Terrible	Jhur
Clever	Chalakh	Interesting	Majaa	Thirsty	Thirkaa
Closed	Bhanda	Late	Dhilo	Tired	Thakai
Cold (person or weather)	Jaado	Less	Thorai	Too much	Asadei
		Lost	Haraayeko	Very	Dherai
Cold (liquid)	Chiso	More	Ajai, Ekdum	Wet	Bhijyo
Crazy	Paagal	Near(er)	Najik(ai)	Worse	Khattam
Dark	Adhyero	Never	Kahilei	Worst	Sabhanda naraamro
Different	Pharak	New	Naya		
Difficult	Gaaro	Noisy	Halla	Wrong	Galti
Dirty	Pohor	Old	Purano		

NUMBERS

Unlike the English counting system, which starts using compound numbers above 20 (twenty-one, twenty-two, etc), Nepali numbers are irregular all the way up to 100 – the following are the ones you're most likely to use.

A slight further complication is the use of "counters" when quantifying nouns. In English, we sometimes use counters – for example, two pieces of paper, five plates of rice – but in Nepali the use is more systematic. Fortunately, you can get by with just two counters: *wotaa* for things, *jana* for people.

Thus "five books" is *paanch wotaa kitaab*, "twelve girls" is *baarha jana keti*. But note these irregular counters: *ek wotaa = euta; dui wotaa = duita; tin wotaa = tintaa.*

half	aada	12	baarha	50	pachaas
1	ek	13	terha	60	saathi
2	dui	14	chaudha	70	sattari
3	tin	15	pandra	80	asi
4	chaar	16	sorha	90	nabbe
5	paanch	17	satra	100	ek sae
6	chha	18	athaara	1000	ek hajaa
7	saat	19	unnais	first (time)	pahilo (palta)
8	aath	20	bis	second	dosro
9	nau	25	pachhis	third	tesro
10	das	30	tis	fourth	chautho
11	eghaara	40	chaalis	fifth	paanchau

VERBS

The following verbs are in the infinitive form. To turn a verb into a polite command (eg, "Please sit"), just add -s (Basnus). For an all-purpose tense, drop the -u ending and replace it with -e (eg, Jaane can mean go, going or went, depending on the context). The past participle is formed by replacing the final -nu with -eko

Arrive	Pugnu	Hurry	Hatar garnu	Sell	Bechnu
Ask	Sodnu	Learn	Siknu	Sleep	Sutnu
Believe	Biswas garnu	Leave	Chodnu	Speak	Bolnu
Break	Baanchnu	Lie (speak	Jhutho bolnu	Steal	Chornu
Buy	Kinnu	untruthfully)		Stop	Roknu
Carry	Boknu	Look, See	Hernu	Take	Linu
Come	Aunu	Lose	Haraunu	Think	Bichar garnu
Cook	Pakaaunu	Make	Banaunu	Try	Kosis garnu
Do	Garnu	Need	Chaahinu	Understand	Bhujnu
Eat	Khaanu	Put	Raakhnu	Use	Prayog garnu
Feel	Mahasus garnu	Receive	Paunu	Wait	Parkhinu
Fix	Toknu	Remember	Samjhinu	Walk	Hidnu
Forget	Birsanu	Rent	Badama linu	Want	Chahanu
Get	Linu	Rest	Aaram garnu	Wash	Dhunu (face,
Give	Dinu	Return	Pharkinu		clothes),
Go	Jaanu	Run	Dagurnu		Nuhaaunu
Hear, Listen	Sunnu	Say, Tell	Bhannu		(body)
Help	Madhat garnu	Sit	Basnu	Work	Kaam garnu

SOME NEWARI PHRASES

Newari is still the first language for many in Kathmandu Valley. It's a difficult language to learn, with many local dialects, and knowing it is no more necessary than, say, knowing Welsh in Wales, yet trying out even the tiniest smidgen of it will astound and delight your innkeeper. The following phrases will get you going.

Hello	Namaste	I don't speak	Jing Newa kha	A little	Bhachaa
Yes/No	Ji/Maji	Newari	lhayemasa	Bad	Mabaalaa
Thank you	Dhanyabaad	Please help me	Jitang gwali	Cheap	Dang
How are	Chhitang gaya		yana dishang	Good	Baalaa
things?	chong?	Excuse me	Maph biya	Hungry	Naiya pityaa
Fine	Bala	Can I go in?	Ji wone jilaa?	Thirst	Pyaas
What's your	Chigu naang chhu?	What's this called	Thuyatang chhu	Tired	Thakejula
name?		in Newari?	dhaigu?	1	Chharkaa
My name is . . .	Jigu naang . . . kha	How far is		2	Nirkaa
My country	Jigu chhey . . . kha	it?	Guli taappaa?	3	Sorhkaa
is . . .		How much does	Thukiya guli?	4	Perkaa
I don't	Jing mathu	this cost?		5	Nyarkaa
understand		No thanks	Mha	6	Khurkaa
Can you repeat	Chhaka dhaya	Please give me	Wo chhaka biya	7	Nerkaa
	dishang	that	deshang	8	Chyarkaa
Do you speak	Chhi Englis kha	Begging is	Phonegu jya	9	Gurkaa
English?	lhayadhiya?	bad	baamalaa	10	Jhirkaa

NEPALI NUMERALS

१	२	३	४	५	६	७	८	९	१०
1	2	3	4	5	6	7	8	9	10

A GLOSSARY OF NEPALI, NEWARI AND TIBETAN TERMS

ANNAPURNA goddess of grain and abundance (literally, "Full of Grain"); form of Lakshmi.

ASHTA MANGALA the eight auspicious symbols of Buddhism.

AVALOKITESHWARA the *bodhisattva* of compassion.

AVATAR bodily incarnation of a deity.

BAGH tiger.

BAHAL buildings and quadrangle of a former Buddhist Newar monastery (a few are still active).

BAHUN Brahman, Hindu priest.

BAJRA see "Vajra".

BAJRA JOGINI (or **VAJRA YOGINI**) female tantric counterpart to Bhairab.

BAKSHISH not a bribe, but a tip in advance.

BAN forest.

BARAHI (or **VARAHI**) Vishnu incarnated as a boar.

BAZAAR commercial area of a town – not necessarily a covered market.

BENI confluence of rivers.

BETAL symbol of death, often represented by a pair of skeletons flanking a temple entrance.

BETEL see "Paan".

BHAAT cooked rice; food.

BHAIRAB terrifying tantric form of Shiva.

BHANJYANG a pass (Nepali).

BHARAT India.

BHATTI simple tavern, usually selling food as well as alcohol.

BHIMSEN patron god of Newar merchants.

BHOJANALAYA Nepali restaurant.

BHOT Tibet.

BHOTIYA highland peoples of Tibetan ancestry.

BIDESHI foreigner (but many Nepalis call all foreigners *Aamerikan* – even Japanese).

BIDI cheap rolled-leaf cigarette.

BODHISATTVA in Mahayana Buddhism, one who forgoes *nirvana* until all other beings have attained enlightenment.

BRAHMA the Hindu creator god, one of the Hindu "trinity".

BRAHMAN member of the Hindu priestly caste (*bahun* in Nepali); metaphysical term meaning the universal soul.

CHAARPI latrine.

CHAITYA small Buddhist monument.

CHARAS hashish.

CHAUTAARA resting platform beside a trail.

CHHETRI member of the ruling or warrior caste.

CHHANG (or **CHHYANG**) homemade beer brewed from rice or other grains.

CHILLAM vertical clay pipe for smoking tobacco or *ganja*.

CHOLO traditional half-length woman's blouse.

CHORTEN another name for a *chaitya* in high mountain areas.

CHOWK intersection, square or courtyard (pronounced "choke").

CHUBA Tibetan sheepskin coat; Tibetan dress.

CHULO clay stove.

DAMARU two-sided drum.

DAADA (or **DANDA**) a ridge.

DANPHE Nepal's national bird, a pheasant with brilliant plumage.

DAPHNE shrub used in paper-making.

DAURA SURUWAL traditional dress of hill men: wrap-around shirt and jodhpur-like trousers.

DEWAL stepped temple platform; temple with prominent steps.

DEVI see *mahadevi*.

DHAARA communal water tap or tank.

DHAKA colourful hand-loomed material made in the Nepalese hills.

DHAMI shaman, similar to *jhankri*.

DHARMA religion; correct behaviour (applies to both Hinduism and Buddhism).

DHARMSALA rest house for pilgrims.

DHOKA gate.

DHOTI Indian-style loincloth; Nepali slang for Indian person.

DHYANI BUDDHAS four (sometimes five) meditating figures representing aspects of Buddha nature.

DOKO conical cane basket carried by means of a headstrap.

DORJE Tibetan word for *vajra*.

DUN low-lying valleys just north of the Tarai (sometimes called inner Tarai, or *bhitri madesh* – "inner plains").

DURBAR palace; royal court.

DURGA demon-slaying goddess.

DYOCHHEN tantric temple or meeting hall.

DZOPKIO sturdy yak-cattle crossbreed; the female is called a *dzum.*

GAIDA (or **GAINDA**) rhinoceros.

GAAINE wandering minstrel of the hills.

GAJUR brass or gold finial at the peak of a temple.

GANESH elephant-headed god of wisdom and remover of obstacles.

GANJA cannabis, marijuana.

GARUD Vishnu's man-bird carrier.

GAUN village, town.

GELUG-PA one of four main Lamaist sects.

GHANTA a bell, usually rung at temples as a sort of "amen".

GHAT riverside platform for worship and cremations.

GIDDA vulture; Nepali slang for Israeli.

GOMPA Buddhist monastery.

GOONDA hooligan, thug.

GURKHAS Nepali soldiers who serve in special regiments in the British and Indian armies.

GUTHI Newar benevolent association that handles upkeep of temples, organizes festivals, etc.

HANUMAN valiant monkey king in the *Ramayan.*

HATTI elephant.

HIMAL massif or mountain range with permanent snow.

HITI Newari word for *dhaara.*

HMG His Majesty's Government.

JAAND unstrained *chhang.*

JAATRA festival.

JAL holy water.

JANAI sacred thread worn over left shoulder by high-caste Hindu men.

JHANKRI shaman, or medicine man, of the hills.

JYAPU member of the Newar peasant farming caste.

KAGYU-PA one of four main Lamaist sects.

KALI the mother goddess in her most terrifying form.

KARMA the soul's accumulated merit, determining its next rebirth.

KAROD 10 million (*crore* in India).

KATA white scarf given to lamas by visitors.

KHOLA stream or river; valley.

KHUKURI curved knife carried by most Nepali hill men.

KIRTIMUKHA common temple motif, a gargoyle-like face grappling with a snake.

KOT fort (pronounced "coat").

KRISHNA one of Vishnu's *avatar*, hero of the *Mahabharat.*

KUMARI a girl worshipped by Nepalis as the living incarnation of Durga.

KUNDA pond, water tank.

LA pass (Tibetan).

LALI GURAAS tree rhododendron.

LAKH 100,000.

LAKSHMI consort of Vishnu, goddess of wealth.

LAMA Tibetan Buddhist priest: hence Lamaism.

LEKH mountain range without permanent snow.

LHAKANG interior of a *gompa.*

LINGA (or **LINGAM**) the phallic symbol of Shiva, commonly the centrepiece of temples and sometimes occurring in groups in the open.

LOKESHWAR see Avalokiteshwara.

MACHAAN watchtower used by Tarai farmers to ward off wild animals.

MACHHENDRANATH rain-bringing deity of the Kathmandu Valley; also known as Karunamaya or Bungadeo.

MAHABHARAT (or **MAHABHARATA**) Hindu epic of the battle between two families, featuring Krishna and containing the *Bhagavad Gita*.

MAHABHARAT LEKH highest range of the Himalayan foothills.

MAHADEV "Great God", an epithet for Shiva.

MAHADEVI mother goddess.

MAHAYANA non-monastic form of Buddhism followed in Nepal, Tibet and east Asia.

MAHOUT elephant driver.

MANDALA mystical diagram, meditation tool.

MANDAP pavilion.

MANDIR temple.

MANI STONE slate inscribed with the mantra *Om mani padme hum*.

MANTRA religious incantation.

MASAN riverside cremation platform.

MATH Hindu priest's home.

MELA religious fair or gathering.

NAG snake or snake spirit, believed to have rain-bringing powers.

NAGAR city.

NAK female yak.

NAAMLO tumpline, headstrap for carrying a *doko*.

NANGLO cane tray, used for winnowing.

NANDI Shiva's mount, a bull.

NARAYAN common name for Vishnu.

NATH "Lord".

NIRVANA in Buddhism, enlightenment and release from the cycle of rebirth.

NYINGMA-PA one of four main Lamaist sects.

OM MANI PADME HUM the mantra of Avalokiteshvara, roughly translating as "Hail to the jewel in the lotus".

PAAN mildly addictive mixture of areca nut and lime paste, wrapped in a leaf and chewed, producing blood-red spit.

PADMA SAMBHAVA alias Guru Rinpoche, the eighth-century saint who brought Buddhism to Tibet.

PAHAAD hill.

PANCHAAYAT council or assembly, the basis for Nepal's pre-democratic government.

PARBAT mountain.

PARBATI (or **PARVATI**) Shiva's consort.

PATAKA (or **DHWAJA**) necktie-shaped brass ornament hanging from a temple, to be used by the deity when descending to earth.

PAUBHA Newar scroll painting.

PIPAL common shade tree of the fig genus; also known as *bodhi*, the tree under which Buddha attained enlightenment.

POKHRI pond, usually man-made.

PRASAD food consecrated after being offered to a deity.

PUJA an act of worship.

PUJARI Hindu priest who tends to a particular temple.

PUL bridge.

PURETH Hindu priest who makes housecalls.

RAJPATH, **RAJMARGA** "King's Way", "King's Road".

RAKSI distilled spirit.

RAM mortal *avatar* of Vishnu, hero of the *Ramayan*.

RAMAYAN (or **RAMAYANA**) popular Hindu epic in which Sita, princess of Janakpur, is abducted and eventually rescued by Ram and Hanuman.

RATH chariot used in religious processions.

RINPOCHE "precious jewel": title given to revered lamas.

RUDRAKSHA furrowed brown seeds, prized by *Shaivas*; it's said that the wearer of a *rudraksha* necklace must always tell the truth.

SADHU Hindu ascetic.

SAHIB honorific term given to male foreigners, pronouced "sahb"; women are called *memsahib*.

SAJHA co-operative; the name of a quasi-government bus company.

SAKYA-PA one of four main Lamaist sects.

SAL tall tree of the Tarai and lower hills, valued for its timber.

SARANGI Nepali four-stringed violin.

SARASWATI Hindu goddess of learning and the arts.

SATI (or **SUTTEE**) practice of Hindu widows throwing themselves on their husbands' funeral pyres.

SHAIVA member of the cult of Shiva.

SHAKTI in Hindu *tantra*, the female principle that empowers the male; the mother goddess in this capacity.

SHALIGRAM fossil-bearing stones found near Muktinath, revered by *Vaishnavas*.

SHIKRA Indian-style temple, shaped like a square bullet.

SHIVA "the destroyer", one of the Hindu "trinity" – a god of many guises.

SHIVALAYA one-storey Shiva shrine containing a *linga*.

SHIVA MARGI a Hindu Newar.

SHRI an honorific prefix.

SINDUR red paste used in making *tika* and decorating idols.

SIRDAR Nepali trek leader.

SITA Ram's wife, princess of Janakpur, heroine of the *Ramayan*.

STOL "short takeoff and landing" (read "hair-raising") landing strip.

STUPA large dome-shaped Buddhist monument, usually said to contain holy relics.

SUDRA member of the lowest, menial caste of Hinduism.

TAAL lake.

TANTRA esoteric psycho-sexual path to enlightenment, a major influence on Nepali Hinduism and Buddhism.

TARA Buddhist goddess; female aspect of Buddha nature.

TASHI DELEK Tibetan for welcome, *namaste*.

TEMPO three-wheeled scooter, autoriksha.

THAKURI very orthodox Chhetri subcaste.

THAALI metal platter with compartments for *daal*, *bhaat*, etc.

THANGKA Buddhist scroll painting.

TIKA auspicious mark placed on the forehead during *puja* or festivals or before making a journey.

TOL neighbourhood.

TOLA traditional unit of weight (11.5g); precious metals are sold by the *tola*, as is hashish.

TOPI Nepalese cap; what Indians call Nepalis.

TORANA elaborate wooden carving, or metal shield, above a temple door.

TORMA dough offerings made by Buddhist monks.

TRISUL the trident, a symbol of Shiva.

TSAMPA toasted barley flour, a staple food of Tibetans and Bhotiyas.

TUDIKHEL parade ground.

TULKU lama considered a reincarnation of a late great teacher.

VAISYA (or **BAISYA**) Hindu caste of traders and farmers.

VAJRA sceptre-like symbol of tantric power (pronounced "bajra").

VAJRACHARYA Buddhist Newar priest.

VAJRAYANA "Thunderbolt Way": tantric Buddhism.

VAISHNAVA follower of the cult of Vishnu.

VEDAS oldest Hindu scriptures; hence Vedic gods, which were worshipped at the time.

VISHNU "the preserver", member of the Hindu "trinity", worshipped in ten main incarnations (pronounced "Bishnu").

YONI symbol of the female genitalia, usually carved into the base of a *linga* as a reservoir for offerings.

INDEX

THE ROUGH GUIDES

Title	ISBN	Price
Amsterdam	1858280184	£6.99
Australia	1858280354	£12.99
Barcelona & Catalunya	1858280486	£7.99
Berlin	1858280338	£8.99
Brazil	0747101272	£7.95
Brittany & Normandy	1858280192	£7.99
Bulgaria	1858280478	£8.99
California	1858280575	£9.99
Canada	185828001X	£10.99
Crete	1858280494	£6.99
Cyprus	185828032X	£8.99
Czech & Slovak Republics	185828029X	£8.99
Egypt	1858280753	£10.99
Europe	1858280273	£12.99
Florida	1858280109	£8.99
France	1858280508	£9.99
Germany	1858280257	£11.99
Greece	1858280206	£9.99
Guatemala & Belize	1858280206	£9.99
Holland, Belgium & Luxembourg	1858280036	£8.99
Hong Kong & Macau	1858280664	£8.99
Hungary	1858280214	£7.99
Ireland	1858280516	£8.99
Italy	1858280311	£12.99
Kenya	1858280435	£9.99
Mediterranean Wildlife	0747100993	£7.95
Morocco	1858280400	£9.99
Nepal	185828046X	£8.99
New York	1858280583	£8.99
Nothing Ventured	0747102082	£7.99
Paris	1858280389	£7.99
Peru	0747102546	£7.95
Poland	1858280346	£9.99
Portugal	1858280222	£7.99
Prague	185828015X	£7.99
Provence & the Côte d'Azur	1858280230	£8.99
Pyrenees	1858280524	£7.99
St Petersburg	1858280303	£8.99
San Francisco	0747102589	£5.99
Scandinavia	1858280397	£10.99
Sicily	1858280370	£8.99
Spain	1858280079	£8.99
Thailand	1858280168	£8.99
Tunisia	1858280656	£8.99
Turkey	1858280133	£8.99
Tuscany & Umbria	1858280559	£8.99
USA	1858280281	£12.99
Venice	1858280362	£8.99
West Africa	1858280141	£12.99
Women Travel	1858280710	£7.99
Zimbabwe & Botswana	1858280419	£10.99

You are
A STUDENT

You **travel**
THE WORLD

You **want**
TO SAVE MONEY

Here's
how

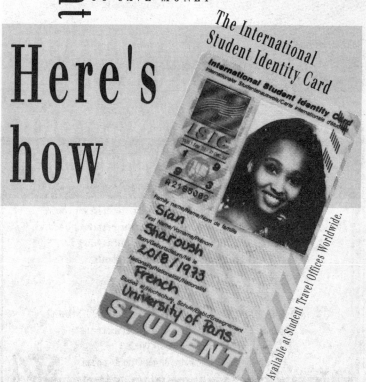

The International
Student Identity Card

Available at Student Travel Offices Worldwide.

Entitles you to discounts and special services worldwide.